176,90
7/96

Computer Networks

Architecture, Protocols, and Software

For a complete listing of the *Artech House Telecommunications Library*,
turn to the back of this book.

Computer Networks

Architecture, Protocols, and Software

John Y. Hsu

Artech House
Boston • London

Library of Congress Cataloging-in-Publication Data
Hsu, John Y.
　Computer networks: architecture, protocols, and software/John Y. Hsu.
　　p.　cm.
　Includes bibliographical references and index.
　ISBN 0-89006-852-6 (alk. paper)
　1. Computer networks　I. Title.
TK5105.5.H78　　　1996
004.6–dc20　　　　　　　　　　　　　　　　　　96-12832
　　　　　　　　　　　　　　　　　　　　　　　　CIP

British Library Cataloguing in Publication Data
Hsu, John Y.
　Computer networks: architecture, protocols, and software
　1. Computer networks　2. Computer networks–Software　3. Data
transmission systems　4. Data transmission systems–Software
I. Title.
004.6'5

ISBN 0-89006-852-6

© 1996 ARTECH HOUSE, INC.
685 Canton Street
Norwood, MA 02062

All rights reserved. Printed and bound in the United States of America. No part of this book may be reproduced or utilized in any form or by any means, electronic or mechanical, including photocopying, recording, or by any information storage and retrieval system, without permission in writing from the publisher.
All terms mentioned in this book that are known to be trademarks or service marks have been appropriately capitalized. Artech House cannot attest to the accuracy of this information. Use of a term in this book should not be regarded as affecting the validity of any trademark or service mark.

International Standard Book Number: 0-89006-852-6
Library of Congress Catalog Card Number: 96-12832

10　9　8　7　6　5　4　3　2　1

To all the computer engineering professionals, past or present, whose work has made a difference to the life of mankind.

Contents

Preface   xvii

Chapter 1   Introduction to Computer Networks   1
- 1.1   Interprocessor Communications   3
  - 1.1.1   Shared Memory   4
  - 1.1.2   Interrupt   4
  - 1.1.3   Channel-to-Channel I/O   5
- 1.2   Computer Network Architecture   5
  - 1.2.1   Multiprocessing Systems   6
  - 1.2.2   Computer Networks   7
  - 1.2.3   Objectives of Computer Networks   7
- 1.3   Classifications of Computer Networks   8
  - 1.3.1   Computer Network Model   8
  - 1.3.2   Distributed System Model   10
  - 1.3.3   Comparisons of Coding Complexity   11
- 1.4   Network Topologies   12
  - 1.4.1   Whip   12
  - 1.4.2   Star   12
  - 1.4.3   Ring   14
  - 1.4.4   Fully Interconnected Network   14
  - 1.4.5   Partially Interconnected Network   15
  - 1.4.6   Mesh   15
  - 1.4.7   Hypercube   16
- 1.5   Computer Network Applications   18
- 1.6   Network Operating Systems   20
  - 1.6.1   Network Access Methods   21
- 1.7   OSI Reference Model   21
  - 1.7.1   Layer Specifications   22
  - 1.7.2   Layer Primitives   27

	1.7.3	Layer Protocol Data Units	31
	1.7.4	Comparisons of the OSI Model, SNA and Internet	33
1.8		Design Considerations of Network System Software	34
	1.8.1	Network I/O Routines on the Communication Processor	35
	1.8.2	Network I/O Routines on the Host	34
	1.8.3	Program Design Language	37
1.9		Network Performance	38
	1.9.1	Performance Analysis	38
	1.9.2	Performance Monitoring	39
1.10		Summary Points	39
Problems			40
References			42

Chapter 2 Physical Layer 45

2.1		Introduction to Data Transmissions	47
	2.1.1	Transmission Media	47
	2.1.2	Digital Waveforms	54
	2.1.3	Transmission Modes	60
2.2		Fourier Theorem	62
2.3		Modulation Techniques	71
	2.3.1	Amplitude Modulation	72
	2.3.2	Frequency Modulation	72
	2.3.3	Phase Modulation	73
	2.3.4	Phase Plus Amplitude Modulation	76
	2.3.5	Pulse Code Modulation	77
2.4		Multiplexing Techniques	79
	2.4.1	Time Division Multiplexing	80
	2.4.2	Frequency Division Multiplexing	82
	2.4.3	Space Division Multiplexing	83
	2.4.4	Baseband Versus Broadband Transmission	83
2.5		Nyquist Theorem	85
2.6		Shannon Theorem	86
2.7		Switching Methods	87
	2.7.1	Circuit Switching	87
	2.7.2	Packet Switching	87
	2.7.3	Cell Switching	88
2.8		Physical Layer Design	88
	2.8.1	Standard Character Set	89
	2.8.2	Communication Controllers	89
	2.8.3	Physical Layer Primitives	92
	2.8.4	Unit Control Block	94
	2.8.5	Physical Layer Software Design	95

2.9	Physical Interfaces		98
	2.9.1	RS-232 Specifications	98
	2.9.2	Null Modem Cable	101
	2.9.3	X.21 Specifications	102
2.10	Summary Points		105
Problems			107
References			112

Chapter 3   Data Link Layer   113
- 3.1 Basic Design Concepts   113
- 3.2 Error-Detecting Codes   115
  - 3.2.1 Vertical Redundancy Check   115
  - 3.2.2 Longitudinal Redundancy Check   116
  - 3.2.3 Cyclic Redundancy Check   118
  - 3.2.4 Hardware Design of CRC Generation/Detection   123
  - 3.2.5 Software Design of CRC Generation/Detection   125
  - 3.2.6 Evaluations of CRC   129
- 3.3 Sliding Window Protocols   130
  - 3.3.1 Stop-And-Wait   132
  - 3.3.2 Go-Back-N   135
  - 3.3.3 Selective-Reject   136
  - 3.3.4 Optimal Window Size   139
- 3.4 Other Design Issues   141
  - 3.4.1 Piggybacking   141
  - 3.4.2 Character-Stuffing Problem   141
  - 3.4.3 Bit-Stuffing Problem   142
- 3.5 Data Link Layer Design   143
  - 3.5.1 Data Link Layer Primitives   143
  - 3.5.2 Data Link Protocol Data Units   147
  - 3.5.3 Data Link Control Block   150
  - 3.5.4 Data Link Software Design   150
- 3.6 Data Link Simulations   154
  - 3.6.1 Simulation of Stop-And-Wait ARQ   154
  - 3.6.2 Simulation of Pipelined Transmission   156
- 3.7 XMODEM   158
- 3.8 Binary Synchronous Communications   159
- 3.9 Synchronous Data Link Control   162
  - 3.9.1 Command and Response   165
  - 3.9.2 Information Frames   165
  - 3.9.3 Supervisory Frames   165
  - 3.9.4 Unnumbered Frames   166
  - 3.9.5 Frame Check Sequence   168

3.10	High-Level Data Link Control	172
	3.10.1 Link Access Procedure	172
	3.10.2 Link Access Procedure, Balanced	173
3.11	Conclusions	174
3.12	Summary Points	174
Problems		175
References		179

Chapter 4 Local Area Networks — 181

- 4.1 Basic Design Concepts — 181
  - 4.1.1 Innovative Technologies — 183
  - 4.1.2 Sublayers — 184
- 4.2 Medium Access Control Sublayer — 185
  - 4.2.1 MAC Sublayer Primitives — 186
  - 4.2.2 MAC Protocol Data Units — 187
- 4.3 Logical Link Control Sublayer — 187
  - 4.3.1 LLC Sublayer Primitives — 188
  - 4.3.2 LLC Protocol Data Units — 189
- 4.4 Ethernet — 192
  - 4.4.1 Ethernet Sublayers — 194
  - 4.4.2 Ethernet Frames — 194
  - 4.4.3 32-Bit Frame Check Sequence — 197
  - 4.4.4 CSMA/CD Access Method — 197
  - 4.4.5 Other Ethernet Primitives — 199
- 4.5 Token Ring — 200
  - 4.5.1 Token-Ring Frames — 202
  - 4.5.2 Token-Ring Access Method — 206
  - 4.5.3 Token-Ring MAC Control Frames — 208
  - 4.5.4 Active Monitor — 209
  - 4.5.5 Other Token-Ring Primitives — 210
- 4.6 Token Bus — 212
  - 4.6.1 Token-Bus Frames — 213
  - 4.6.2 Token-Bus MAC Control Frames — 215
  - 4.6.3 Token-Bus Access Method — 217
- 4.7 Fiber Distributed Data Interface — 219
- 4.8 Distributed Queue Dual Bus — 221
  - 4.8.1 DQDB Architecture — 223
  - 4.8.2 DQDB Frames — 223
  - 4.8.3 DQDB Slots — 225
  - 4.8.4 DQDB Access Method — 227
- 4.9 Conclusions — 232
- 4.10 Summary Points — 232
- Problems — 233
- References — 235

Chapter 5		Network Layer	237
5.1		Basic Design Concepts	238
	5.1.1	Virtual Circuit Model	238
	5.1.2	Datagram Model	239
	5.1.3	Virtual Circuit Plus Datagram Model	241
5.2		Routing Philosophies	241
	5.2.1	Distributed Routing	241
	5.2.2	Source Routing	242
	5.2.3	Centralized Routing	242
	5.2.4	Hierarchical Routing	248
5.3		Roadsigns	249
5.4		Routing Table	253
5.5		Other Design Issues	255
	5.5.1	System Deadlocks	255
	5.5.2	Exchange Buffering	255
	5.5.3	Congestion Control	257
	5.5.4	Concatenation/Separation	260
5.6		Network Layer Design	261
	5.6.1	Network Layer Primitives	261
	5.6.2	Network Protocol Data Units	265
	5.6.3	Network Control Block	267
	5.6.4	Network Software Design	268
5.7		X.25 Packet Layer Protocol	270
5.8		Network Layer Primitives Versus X.25 Packets	276
5.9		Internet Protocol	277
	5.9.1	IP Header	277
	5.9.2	Address Resolution Protocol	283
	5.9.3	Reverse Address Resolution Protocol	284
5.10		Network Management Routines	285
	5.10.1	Internet Control Message Protocol	285
5.11		Network Devices	287
	5.11.1	Packet Assembler/Disassembler	288
	5.11.2	Bridge	288
	5.11.3	Router	288
	5.11.4	Gateway	290
5.12		Conclusions	290
5.13		Summary Points	291
		Problems	292
		References	294
Chapter 6		High-Speed Wide Area Networks	295
6.1		Frame Relay	295
	6.1.1	FR Frames	297
	6.1.2	FR Software Design	299

6.2 Asynchronous Transfer Mode ... 300
    6.2.1 ATM Network Architecture ... 301
    6.2.2 ATM Cells ... 301
    6.2.3 ATM Protocols ... 303
6.3 Comparisons of Frame Relay and ATM ... 307
6.4 Integrated Services Digital Network ... 308
    6.4.1 Evolution ... 309
    6.4.2 Principles ... 309
    6.4.3 Services ... 311
    6.4.4 User Interfaces ... 311
6.5 ISDN Protocols ... 313
    6.5.1 ISDN Frames ... 313
    6.5.2 ISDN Channel Protocols ... 315
    6.5.3 ISDN Messages ... 317
6.6 Broadband ISDN ... 321
    6.6.1 Functional Architecture ... 321
    6.6.2 Services ... 322
    6.6.3 User Interfaces ... 322
6.7 Broadband ISDN Protocols ... 323
6.8 Other Networks ... 323
6.9 Conclusions ... 324
6.10 Summary Points ... 325
Problems ... 325
References ... 326

Chapter 7 Transport Layer ... 329
7.1 Basic Design Concepts ... 330
    7.1.1 Segmentation and Reassembly ... 330
    7.1.2 Upward/Downward Multiplexing ... 331
    7.1.3 Error Control ... 332
    7.1.4 Flow Control ... 332
7.2 Finite State Machine Model ... 333
    7.2.1 Transport Sender ... 333
    7.2.2 Transport Receiver ... 337
    7.2.3 Optimal Window Size ... 342
7.3 Other Design Issues ... 343
    7.3.1 Virtual Circuit Failure ... 343
    7.3.2 Three-Way Handshake ... 343
7.4 Transport Layer Primitives ... 345
7.5 Transport Layer Protocol Data Units ... 349
7.6 Transport Layer Design ... 350
    7.6.1 Transport Control Block ... 351

	7.6.2	Software Design of Transport Layer—VC Model	352
	7.6.3	Software Design of Transport Layer—Datagram Model	354
	7.6.4	Permanent Transports	355
7.7	OSI Transport Protocols		356
	7.7.1	General Design Concepts	356
	7.7.2	Formats of OSI TPDU	356
	7.7.3	Fletcher Checksum	359
	7.7.4	Specifications of OSI TPDU	363
7.8	Transmission Control Protocol		373
	7.8.1	TCP Header Design	373
	7.8.2	User Datagram Protocol	377
7.9	Conclusions		379
7.10	Summary Points		379
Problems			380
References			382

Chapter 8 Session Layer 383

8.1	Basic Design Concepts		383
	8.1.1	Connection/Disconnection	383
	8.1.2	Data Transfer Phase	384
	8.1.3	Synchronization	384
8.2	Session Primitives		385
8.3	Session Software Design		390
	8.3.1	Connect and Rec_connect	390
	8.3.2	Send and Receive	391
	8.3.3	Disconnect and Rec_disconnect	392
	8.3.4	Allocate and Deallocate	392
	8.3.5	Syncpt and Resync	393
8.4	Network Application Software Design		396
	8.4.1	Client-Server Model	396
	8.4.2	File Transfer Server With Multiclients	396
	8.4.3	Group Talk Program	398
8.5	TCP/IP SESSION		399
	8.5.1	TCP Session Services	401
	8.5.2	UNIX Network System Calls	402
	8.5.3	Socket Programming	406
	8.5.4	Multitasking Server/Client Software Design	407
8.6	SNA Session		416
	8.6.1	SNA Session Types	417
	8.6.2	LU 6.2 Session	417
8.7	OSI Session		420

	8.7.1	OSI Session Primitives	421
	8.7.2	OSI Session Protocol Data Units	423
8.8	Conclusions		424
8.9	Summary Points		425
Problems			426
References			427

Chapter 9   Presentation and Application Services   429

- 9.1 Basic Design Concepts — 429
- 9.2 Presentation Services — 430
    - 9.2.1 Data Compression and Decompression — 431
    - 9.2.2 Encryption and Decryption — 434
    - 9.2.3 Code Conversion — 435
- 9.3 Presentation Layer - OSI Model — 435
    - 9.3.1 Abstract Syntax Notation 1 — 442
    - 9.3.2 Presentation Layer Primitives — 443
    - 9.3.3 Presentation Protocol Data Units — 443
- 9.4 Network Applications — 444
- 9.5 Application Services - TCP/IP — 444
    - 9.5.1 File Transfer Protocol — 445
    - 9.5.2 E-mail — 445
    - 9.5.3 World Wide Web — 446
    - 9.5.4 Remote Procedure Call — 446
- 9.6 Application Layer - OSI Model — 447
    - 9.6.1 Application Layer Primitives — 448
    - 9.6.2 Application Protocol Data Units — 451
    - 9.6.3 File Transfer, Access, and Management — 452
    - 9.6.4 Message Handling System — 454
    - 9.6.5 Directory System — 457
- 9.7 Conclusions — 459
- 9.8 Summary Points — 460
- Problems — 461
- References — 462

Chapter 10   Network Management   463

- 10.1 Network Performance Aanlysis — 463
    - 10.1.1 Line Speed — 463
    - 10.1.2 Response Time — 464
    - 10.1.3 Queuing Delays — 465
    - 10.1.4 Error Rate — 467
    - 10.1.5 Reliability — 467
- 10.2 Network Monitoring — 468
    - 10.2.1 Protocol Analyzers — 468
    - 10.2.2 Loop Tests — 469

10.3	Simple Network Management Protocol		472
	10.3.1	SNMP Architecture	473
	10.3.2	SNMP Messages	475
	10.3.3	Management Information Base	479
	10.3.4	Encoding of SNMP Messages	485
10.4	OSI Network Management Model		487
	10.4.1	Common Network Management Services	487
	10.4.2	Distributed Management Environment	488
10.5	Other Network Management Systems		489
	10.5.1	NetView	489
10.6	Conclusions		490
10.7	Summary Points		491
Problems			492
References			493

Appendix A Operating System Essentials 495
- A.1 Interrupt Mechanisms 495
- A.2 Asynchronous Processing 496
- A.3 Task Management Routines 496
  - A.3.1 Task Definition 497
  - A.3.2 Task Control Block 497
  - A.3.3 I/O Interrupt Service Routines 498
  - A.3.4 Task Creation/Termination 499
  - A.3.5 Dispatcher 499
  - A.3.6 State Transition Diagram 500
- A.4 Reentrant Task 501
- A.5 Intertask Communications 502
- A.6 Semaphore 503
- Reference 505

Appendix B Acronyms and Abbreviations 507

Appendix C Products and Standards 513

Selected Bibliography 517

About the Author 519

Index 521

Preface

Writing a high-tech book is an obligation; it is also a privilege.

Motive for Writing This Book

In 1962, while I was working in Taiwan, most of my classmates from the Electrical Engineering Department of National Taiwan University were in the United States attending graduate schools. One of them, Albert Hung, wrote me, "I came, I saw, and I conquered." He had just received an offer from Ford and was promised a new Fairlane at a huge discount. Several friends of mine sent me money so I, too, could come to America. I paid $350 for a propeller airplane ticket, and it took me two full days to get to this promised land. The plane stopped at Okinawa, Guam, Wake Island, and Hawaii before landing in Oakland, California. My total flying time was 39 hours. Today, not only has the flying time been reduced to one-third of that time, so has the price. And technology has made the difference.

After waiting at the airport for more than five hours, I was quite anxious. Bob Chen finally sent a friend of his to pick me up after midnight. When our car passed by the Bay Bridge, the taillights of other cars twinkled like multiple red streams. I was astonished and impressed. The next day, Bob drove me to town and showed me around the restaurants in San Francisco where, he said, I could get a job. He also said that we should study computers and told me to read the book, *Switching Circuits And Logical Design* by S. H. Caldwell. Bob's vision was right. We have all studied and loved computers ever since. Both Albert and Bob were project managers when they passed away in their early fifties. Their dedication and passion set a standard that I strive to emulate in my work.

By the end of 1990, Bob suggested that I write a book on computer networks so people could understand what networks are about. I didn't start until the summer of 1993. It turned out to be an extraordinary experience for me. As a consultant, other people listen to you. As an author, it is the other way around.

Who Should Read This Book

This book explores fundamental design concepts of computer networking and explains why such designs are important. As a prerequisite, readers should understand the basic concept of programming languages and the internal workings of a modern computer. The intended audience is composed of:

- *The upper division undergraduate and graduate students of computer science or engineering*: The materials in the book can be lectured in 30 to 60 hours.
- *Practitioners*: The book also contains very valuable technical information, so anyone can read this book to gain a better understanding of computer networks.

Although there are many approaches to designing computer networks, the basic system concept remains the same. Adding network access methods to a conventional operating system, we obtain a network operating system. The network access methods are complicated, but over the years we have made progress in designing such software.

Organization of This Book

Technologies come and go, but the basic theories remain. It is vital for us to have the ability to absorb new knowledge. Hence, both fundamental and cutting edge information are included in this book, which is divided into ten chapters. Chapters 1, 2, 3, 5, 7, and 8 cover the fundamentals of computer networking, and Appendix A contains operating system essentials. Chapters 4 and 6 cover the special design features of both local area and wide area networks currently under development. Chapters 9 and 10 provide network information of general interest. A brief description of each chapter is given below.

Chapter 1: The first chapter provides an introduction to interprocessor communications, network architecture, network topologies, applications, network operating systems, network access methods, the OSI model, layer primitives, protocol data units, the communication processor, the host processor, performance issues, and program design language.

Chapter 2: The physical layer chapter discusses topics such as transmission media, transmission modes, waveforms, Fourier analysis, signal attenuation/distortion, modulation, multiplexing, Nyquist theorem, Shannon theorem, switching methods, and the physical layer software.

Chapter 3: The data link layer chapter covers design issues, such as error detecting codes, CRC, FCS, sliding window protocols, error control, character stuffing, bit stuffing, piggybacking, and software simulations. An attempt was made to design a data link operating in full-duplex mode. Protocols, such as XMODEM, BSC, SDLC, and HDLC are also examined.

Chapter 4: Chapter 4 is on local area networks. Because various clever technologies are employed, a medium access control sublayer must be in place to solve the contention problem. Case studies, such as Ethernet, Fast Ethernet, token ring, token bus, fiber distributed data interface, and distributed queue dual bus, are all treated with thoroughness.

Chapter 5: The network layer chapter discusses routing issues. Topics include virtual circuit model, datagram model, routing table design, and road signs. Routing philosophies, buffering techniques, and congestion control are also discussed. An attempt was made to design a packet-based N layer. Case studies include the X.25 packet layer protocol, Internet protocol, and Internet control message protocol. Network or switching devices, such as packet assemblers/disassemblers, bridges, routers, and gateways are also discussed.

Chapter 6: The high-speed wide area networks have growing importance. Fast network services, such as frame relay, asynchronous transfer mode, and switched multimegabit data services, are described. Both narrowband and broadband ISDNs are addressed because of their impact on the future.

Chapter 7: The transport layer includes design issues, such as segmentation/reassembly, multiplexing, connection management, error control, congestion control, finite state machine models, and permanent ports. Case studies include the OSI transport protocols (Classes 0–4), the transmission control protocol, and the user datagram protocol.

Chapter 8: The session layer should be designed as a system interface between the user program and the NOS. Basic issues include session connection/disconnection, security checks, data transfers, and synchronization. Advanced program-to-program communications and socket programming are introduced. File transfer server to support multiclients, the group talk program, and the OSI session layer are also discussed.

Chapter 9: This chapter covers upper layer service routines. Presentation services include data compression/decompression, conversion, encryption/decryption, abstract syntax notation, and so forth. Application services include message handling systems, directory services, file transfer, access, and management.

Chapter 10: The last chapter addresses network management issues such as throughput, transmission speed, response time, queuing delays, error rate, and reliability. Monitoring devices, the simple network management protocol, and the management information base are also discussed.

In addition to reference lists at the end of each chapter and a selected bibliography, products and standards that appear in brackets throughout the book are listed in Appendix C.

Acknowledgments

This book was reviewed by many individuals who have provided criticisms and valuable suggestions. In particular, I wish to thank Jim Gray, who has been a friend since graduate school. Wesley Chu has provided both encouragement and support. My students, including Diller Ryan, Greg Bostrom, Don Erickson, Matt Dukleth, Johnanna Madjedi, Steve Lau, and Zac Kaufman were all helpful. I salute all the reviewers who have made a great contribution in shaping the manuscript to its final form. Some of their names and affiliations are listed below.

Jar-Mo Chen (Lockheed Martin)
Wesley Chu (UCLA)
Mike Fitzpatrick (Cal Poly)
Jim Gray (Microsoft)
Wen-Chi Hou (S. Illinois U.)
Haniph Latchman (U. of Florida)
Ten-Hwang Lai (Ohio State)
Elmo Keller (Cal Poly)
Cornel Pokorny (Cal Poly)
Ron Oliver (Cal Poly)
Larry Owen (Fresno State)
C. Ramamoorthy (U. of California, Berkeley)
Alfred Weaver (U. of Virginia)

The project team at Artech House, including Mark Walsh, Kimberly Collignon, and Kate Feininger, deserves recognition. The artwork for the figures was done by my son, David. Since 1967, I have spent thousands of hours in the libraries of Stanford University, to which I feel very much indebted. Finally, I wish to thank my wife, Sheryl, who has put up with me for 30 years. She is the most precious thing that has happened to me besides studying computers.

John Y. Hsu
San Luis Obispo, CA

Introduction to Computer Networks

1

Day, night after flight,
the flock is nowhere in sight. Keep going.

Physically, a computer network is merely a collection of interconnected computers. Each computer is an autonomous node running its own operating system (OS) (i.e., a set of control programs). The terms OS, control programs, system software, or just system all have the same semantic meaning. The term *system* means system software, system hardware, or system software and hardware combined. Computer network architecture refers to the general design of a computer network, which involves both hardware and software. Needless to say, the system hardware is developed to support system software, and the reverse is also true.

The access methods (AMs) in an OS are the input/output (I/O) system routines grouped together to access data on an external device, such as disk, tape, display, or printer. Simply put, the I/O system or subsystem is part of an operating system. The network access methods (NAMs) are the network I/O system routines designed to transmit and receive data between two computers. In other words, the NAMs are developed so that a program running on one processor can communicate with another program running on a different processor. The entire set of control programs running on the node in a computer network constitutes the network operating system (NOS). Hence, the NOS is comprised of all the control programs in an OS plus the system software for network I/O and management. In other words, the NOS is a superset of OSs in that it supports network communications between two user application programs running on two different computers. The two computers may be situated in one room, or they may be 3,000 miles apart. This chapter will introduce the physical layout, applications, protocols, and software design of computer networks.

To start with, a computer is defined as a hardware computing device or machine that has software executing on it. Inside a computer, there is a central processing unit (CPU), which is the main processor. A *processor* is a hardware processing unit that controls and processes data. A computer network is loosely defined as a system that contains several interconnected processing units. A modern microcomputer system has many processors, usually a main processor and several I/O processors. Because its system communication software is very primitive, it is not considered to be a network, but nonetheless has that flavor. In general, the main processor is much more powerful than an I/O processor, which is just a peripheral processing unit designed to handle a particular I/O function (e.g., drive a communication line). A channel is a logical entity that can be thought of as a simple I/O processor, and an I/O controller is a simple channel that controls an I/O device. The I/O processors, channels, and controllers are all physical devices designed to control and process data. They can be placed on a single chip with a size smaller than the CPU.

A computer network is heterogeneous if some of the computers in it are made of different hardware brands running under different operating systems. On the other hand, a homogeneous network consists of computers made of the same or compatible hardware components running under the same OS.

The earliest motive for designing a two-node computer network was to conduct remote diagnostics. The developer at the headquarters wants to examine the memory content of a remote computer, so he or she may instruct people at the remote site to repair the machine and thus save one trip. Consequently, remote diagnostic programs have been written to run on the remote node to generate a memory dump, namely a memory read-out containing test results. Then, the memory dump is transmitted to the developer's computer via a telephone line for review.

Before studying the software design of a computer network, we need to know the various types of networks and the ways by which computers are interconnected. Accordingly, we will next discuss the network operating system concept in general and the open systems interconnection (OSI) reference model. Since network system software is so complicated, it takes one or more chapters to address the related issues of a particular function.

If a program on one processor wants to communicate with another program on a different processor, it sends a message to the other side. First, a hardware connection must exist between the two processors. In addition, software must be written to drive the communication controller (which is hardware). Even though the hardware connection may be wireless (which is not visible to the eye), the communication software simply would not work without a hardware controller; that is, an interprocessor communication scheme must be installed before software can be written to support intertask communications over the network.

1.1 INTERPROCESSOR COMMUNICATIONS

An interprocessor communication scheme is really a hardware connection between two processors. The processor on one side can communicate with the processor on the other side, so to speak. As far as software is concerned, the basic notion is that one side can send a message to the other side. There are three basic schemes in hardware design that can be used individually or jointly to allow message exchanges between two processors:

- Via shared memory;
- Via interrupt;
- Via channel-to-channel I/O.

These are the fundamental hardware mechanisms required to support the implementation of network system software. There is a subtle difference between interprocessor communication and intertask communication over the network. A task can be thought of as a program running on the node. The interprocessor communication scheme is a hardware mechanism, while the intertask communication over the network is a software design feature. A hardware interprocessor communication scheme must exist before two tasks running on two different processors can communicate with each other.

Three hardware schemes for interprocessor communication are shown in Figure 1.1. Between CPU 1 and CPU 2, there exists a shared memory, an interrupt bus, and a channel-to-channel I/O to provide the hardware connection. A dotted line represents interrupt control signals while a solid line represents the data path. Depending on the design, one or more hardware connection schemes must be supported in a computer network.

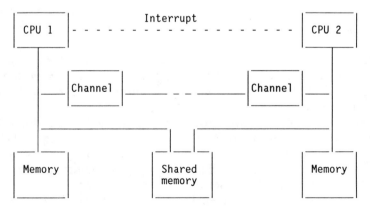

Figure 1.1 Hardware schemes for interprocessor communication.

1.1.1 Shared Memory

The first scheme for interprocessor communication is via shared memory or its derivatives. This is a popular design when two processors are close to each other. In some direct memory access (DMA) chips, each of the hardware registers is either treated as a special I/O register or mapped into a memory word accessible to both processors. One processor writes into the hardware register, which can be read by the other processor. The hardware register in a DMA chip is a shared-memory derivative in concept because both processors can access the same register.

In a multiprocessing system, one approach is to tie all processors together via shared memory. The software on one processor places messages in shared memory for other software routines to fetch, interpret, and execute. Such a design is also considered a tightly coupled computer system.

At each terminal site of a computer network, there is usually a two-processor pair: one host processor and one communication processor. More often than not, the two processors can use shared memory to communicate with each other.

Note that when one processor updates a shared memory block while the other processor is doing the same, we may have a problem. As a simple example, if one processor adds 1 to a variable in memory and the other processor also adds 1 to the same variable, the end result should be adding 2. However, if both processors fetch the same variable in a sequential manner, add 1, and store the result in memory, the end result is adding 1 to this variable instead of 2. Of course, this is wrong. Therefore, we need to set up rules allowing only one processor to update a block in shared memory at one time. A semaphore mechanism, which requires hardware design to support its implementation, is explained in Appendix A.

1.1.2 Interrupt

The second scheme for interprocessor communication is interrupt, a hardware mechanism invented in the late 1950s and later adopted by the famous IBM System/360 in 1964. It is the fourth major programming concept besides looping, indexing, and subroutine.

Interrupt is such a novel feature that one processor may force the other processor to relinquish control of its current program executing on its CPU. The shared memory scheme can be augmented by interrupt if the message is urgent. That is to say, one processor places the message in memory and then executes an instruction to interrupt the other processor. This special instruction is privileged, which means it can only be executed when the CPU is in hardware supervisor state. The main processor can interrupt an I/O processor by executing a start I/O (SIO) instruction [IBM 370]. On the other hand, an I/O processor may also interrupt the main processor by executing an exchange jump (EXN) [CDC 6600]. The special instruction SIO or EXN interrupts the other processor, but not themselves.

1.1.3 Channel-to-Channel I/O

The third scheme is via channel-to-channel I/O. In other words, the message (a piece of data) is transmitted on the line by the channel. Recall that a channel may be an I/O processor, which has its own communication controller. The software on one processor issues a write request to the channel and the software on the other processor issues a read request to receive the same message from its channel. In a computer network, a main processor mostly communicates with other main processors via I/O channels. Such a design requires that its processor communicate with other processors via I/O channels, and therefore is known as a loosely coupled system.

1.2 COMPUTER NETWORK ARCHITECTURE

A computer network consists of many independent processors running simultaneously. It should be mentioned that a mainframe computer contains a main processor and many I/O processors. It is defined as a multistation computer system. The main processor is much more powerful than the I/O processors. Consequently, the main processor and I/O processors are not interchangeable. Each I/O processor runs a particular I/O system routine to drive a printer, disk, tape, display, or communication lines. It is also possible for a mainframe computer or supercomputer to run its OS on an I/O processor in order to relieve the burden of the main processing unit [CDC 6600].

If a mainframe computer has several processors tied together, it has the flavor of a simple computer network. Nowadays, even the microcomputer system has many processors. The keyboard has its own processor, as does the video display; the communication and disk controllers all use direct memory access (DMA) chips, which are smaller processors. In addition, a math processor may be on the side to speed up floating point arithmetic. We conclude that a modern PC or mainframe consists of many processors.

If a mainframe system is connected to a computer network, its CPU is known as the host, which may be augmented by a communication processor serving many communication lines. The interprocessor communication between the host and the communication processor is usually done via shared memory. A host can be interconnected to another host through telephone lines. A typical connection between two hosts in a computer network is shown in Figure 1.2. In the middle of the route, there are many other communication

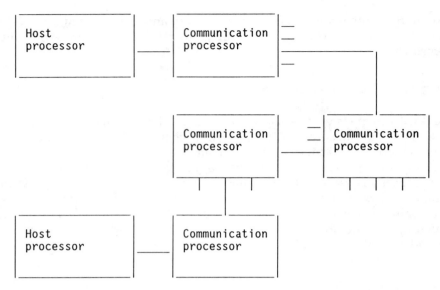

Figure 1.2 Hardware connection between two host processors in a computer network.

processors. Before discussing various types of computer networks, we introduce the multiprocessing systems in the following.

1.2.1 Multiprocessing Systems

The term *multiprocessing* is used to describe a system that has multiple processors. In such a system, the processors are usually identical and interchangeable. A multiprocessing system is a computer network in the sense that all main processors can communicate with each other via shared memory or I/O channels and that it has system software to support intertask communications.

Most multiprocessing systems have their processors located in one room or in one building. The processors either work as a team to achieve a specific common goal or split the workload among themselves.

In a multiprocessing system, there is usually one master processor. The rest are all slaves that take orders from the master and carry out the execution. The master processor dispatches workload to other processors and coordinates and monitors the team effort. If, due to hardware failure, the master processor cannot perform its duty as the monitor, good software design will guarantee that the system won't fail. The OS on the master processor always leaves messages in shared memory to claim that it is the boss. The processor that is second in command checks the message periodically and makes sure that the master processor is in command. At any instant, if there is no message left in memory, the second processor knows that the master processor is down. Therefore, it takes over the duties of the master processor as the new boss. This concept can be applied to the design of an active monitor over a token ring local area network (LAN). It works just like our government, except the third processor in the command chain never rushes to take over the duties before the second processor.

1.2.2 Computer Networks

Many independent computers are interconnected in a computer network. Each computer or node may be located at a different location, made of different hardware running under a different OS. It is essentially the extension of a multiprocessing system in that the main processors may be at different sites and that each node in the network is an autonomous entity as equal as other processors.

Future trends dictate that each corporation will tie all its computing equipment—mainframes, minicomputers, and microcomputers—into a corporate network, which is further connected to a global network. A computer network is supposed to operate 24 hours a day, 365 days a year. Only occasionally may a section of the network be brought down for preventive maintenance.

In a special purpose computer network, there is a specific goal that needs to be accomplished, such as banking or airline reservations. Then, the computer network becomes a distributed system, and each node is designated to perform a specific function.

Can a multiprocessing system be classified as a computer network? Loosely speaking, the answer is yes. If we define that a computer network has several processors tied together, then multiprocessing systems, distributed systems, and general purpose computer networks all belong to the same class. It should be mentioned that the same set of network system software executes on a distributed system as well as on a general purpose computer network.

1.2.3 Objectives of Computer Networks

The main objectives of computer networks are

- Resource sharing;
- Parallel computation;
- Redundancy.

Resource sharing is the primary goal of designing generalized computer networks. Resources include hardware, software, and data. Expensive hardware devices driven by a computer, such as color laser printers, high-performance disks, and special I/O devices making film, can be shared. Software routines implemented as remote procedure calls are also shared by different users at different locations. Data, such as disk files, stock market quotations, and e-mail, are also considered as resources. To share data with another means communication, which plays an important role in our daily life.

Parallel computation is definitely one of the objectives in designing multiprocessing systems. In such a system, all the main processors work as a team to do some common computations. Any computer, in general, has its I/O processors running in parallel with the main processor. Since all I/O processors share the burden of the main processor, we have achieved parallel computation from the system point of view.

Redundancy indicates that the system is fault-tolerant to a certain degree. For instance, a multiprocessing system may be designed for flight control. Each control decision must be voted in by the majority of main processors. Any failed processor will not affect the majority vote. Other systems designed for real-time transactions are also fault-tolerant. In the case where a hardware component fails, it should not bring down the entire system. Since a computer network contains many hardware components, redundancy is always a factor in the overall planning.

1.3 CLASSIFICATIONS OF COMPUTER NETWORKS

Computer networks can be classified into two categories: the computer network model and the distributed system model. Generally speaking, computer networks include LANs, metropolitan area networks (MANs), and wide area networks (WANs), and they also can be interconnected. Even though the basic concepts remain the same, the technologies used in LANs are radically different from those used in WANs and, in turn, change the design of network system software.

1.3.1 Computer Network Model

A computer network is characterized by the following features:

- Autonomous computers interconnected via I/O communication channels;
- Interprocessor communications mostly done via I/O communication channels, but with routing intelligence;
- Distributed processing possible;
- Sharing of resources.

Each node in the network is an autonomous computer running its own OS. A large network may consist of over one million computers. The computers in a network are usually heterogeneous and not compatible. Interprocessor communications are mostly done via channel-to-channel I/O. A task on one CPU may communicate with another task running on a different CPU located several thousand miles away. Between two computers, there may be intermediate nodes in the middle of the route to perform the switching function.

The primary goal of designing a generalized computer network is to achieve the sharing of resources, which includes hardware, software, and data. Since all network I/O system routines are available, it is also possible to write special application software to achieve distributed computing.

Local Area Networks

A LAN consists of all the computers confined within a local area, say a few square miles, such as a corporation or a university. LANs are characterized by the following:

- Fast data rate, up to 100 megabits per second (Mbps) or over;
- Low error rate, 10^{-8} to 10^{-11} errors per bit (Epb);
- Simple routing;
- Moderate distance, within several miles;
- Mostly homogeneous computers;
- Innovative technologies.

Note that ^ is an exponential operator. Several popular LANs exist in the field; some use copper wires while others use fiber optics. Because all the computers are close to each other, high-speed data rates of over 100 Mbps can be achieved. As technology advances so fast, it would not be surprising to see gigabits per second (Gbps) LANs developed in the near future. Because the distance between two nodes is usually less than 2.5 km, its error rate is low. With fiber optics, about one bit flips out of 100 gigabits during transmission. In a single LAN, each computer has one hardware transmitter and one receiver. Taking a token ring for example, when one node transmits, the bits flow on the ring, pass each node, and return to the sender. This means that most of the nodes in a LAN have no routing intelligence.

However, if a LAN is connected to another network, a special switching node (bridge or router) is needed to handle the switching function. In order to ease the maintenance problem, most companies prefer homogeneous computers running the same set of software. However, in a university environment, there may be several LANs of different types, which are further connected to a backbone.

Protocol conversions are necessary to tie different LANs into a single computer network. Summing up, LANs use innovative and intricate technologies in both hardware and software design.

Metropolitan Area Networks

A metropolitan area network is actually a LAN of large size, such as the Community Antenna Television (CATV) network. As far as hardware or software design is concerned, a MAN is not different from a LAN. Taking a token ring LAN for example, the distance between two adjacent nodes can be 2 km. With 360 nodes maximum, the perimeter can be as long as 720 km, or 450 miles. In other words, it is possible to have a LAN that is as large as a city.

Wide Area Networks

WAN technology means that computers can be situated at different locations all over the world. In a WAN, when the data bits arrive at the destination node, transmission stops right there. Two PCs may be interconnected in a room as a WAN. If one PC is moved to New York and the other one stays in San Francisco, the network applications still run on the network and no modifications are needed in either hardware or software. Hence, the WANs and LANs really differ in technologies, but not in size. Well-known WANs are listed below:

- SNA (IBM system network architecture);
- Internet (internetworking);
- DNA (Digital Equipment Corp. network architecture);
- ISDN (integrated services digital network).

SNA is widely used in industry to perform transaction processing or general purpose computing. The Internet (also known as the Net) is the oldest network. It connects all the computers in educational institutions, government, and commercial companies all over the world. In other words, different computer networks are interconnected into a global network. The Internet was evolved from the Advanced Research Project Agency Network (ARPANET) in the early 1970s. ARPANET has changed its name a couple times and is now known as the defense data network (DDN), which is now part of the Internet. DNA is another computer network available commercially.

In the next decade, since telephone voices and video data will be digitized, we will need a computer network to transmit and receive the digital data and ISDN is the proposed solution. As more PCs are available to home users, there will be commercial WANs that provide services of all kinds.

1.3.2 Distributed System Model

A distributed system is a special purpose computer network designed to perform a predefined application. Such a system is characterized by the following features:

- Distributed hardware;
- Distributed control;

- Distributed data;
- Processors designed to achieve a common goal.

Distributed hardware means that some of the processors are located at different geographic locations. The main processors in the system are usually homogenous, made of compatible hardware and running the same software. Each processor may have its own database and is designated to perform a specific function. Each processor may communicate with other processors from time to time. Interprocessor communications are mostly done via channel-to-channel I/O with very little routing intelligence.

If there is a specific goal to accomplish, the basic software design of a multiprocessing system using shared memory is not much different from that of a distributed system. All processors in such systems work as a team to achieve a common goal, and intertask communications over the network must be supported. Suffice to say, distributed systems are used for such applications as banking transactions, airline reservations, process control, mining control, stock market quotations, and battle and game simulations.

1.3.3 Comparisons of Coding Complexity

Usually, a multiprocessing computer system uses shared memory to communicate while a LAN or WAN uses channel-to-channel I/O. It is interesting to compare the relative coding complexity of the three systems. Suppose that we wish to transmit a 100-byte block of data from one task to another task on a different processor; so, we trace the number of instructions executed to accomplish this goal. The relative coding or software complexity of different networks is compared in Table 1.1.

It takes about 50 instructions on a multiprocessing system using shared memory, 500 on a LAN, and 5,000 on a WAN. The difference between each system is about one order of magnitude [1].

Table 1.1
Number of Instructions Executed in a Network

Network Type	Multiprocessing System Using Shared Memory	LAN	WAN
Number of Instructions	50	500	5,000

1.4 NETWORK TOPOLOGIES

A network topology is the geometric shape of the computer network, which also shows interconnections among nodes. There are many different topologies used to connect computers in a network. We will discuss the most popular topologies and the ones of special interest.

1.4.1 Whip

The simplest way to build a computer network is to tie all the computers in a serial manner as shown in Figure 1.3(a). The computer network is called a whip because of its shape. In other words, the first computer is connected to the second computer, the second to the third, and so on in a serial fashion. Each computer in the middle of the whip has two links, and the computer at either end has only one link. Assume that the line length represents cost. If we can find a route to tie all computers serially and the total length of all links is the shortest, we obtain a computer network at the cheapest cost.

A whip topology is used in LAN design, except each node always passes the data to the next node like a bus route. For that reason, a whip is also known as a bus.

1.4.2 Star

A star topology is shown in Figure 1.3(b). One central node is surrounded by many satellite nodes, and it takes two hops to communicate between any two of the satellite nodes. The Ethernet LAN uses a common bus to tie all the nodes together because the distance is short [Ethernet]. A bus can be a coaxial cable or a bundle of wires. Each node on the bus has one transmitter/receiver pair, and there is only one physical connection amongst all the nodes. Usually, one special node on the bus runs the application software (e.g., a file server). Every other node on the bus can transfer data to and from the server. From the software viewpoint, the file server runs on the central node in a virtual star. In the case where the common bus is broken, the Ethernet LAN fails.

In a star WAN, there is a separate physical connection between each satellite node and the central node. If the WAN has five satellite nodes, the central node has five transmitter/receiver pairs and each pair is connected to a satellite node by a telephone line. If one set of telephone lines is broken, the WAN can still be operational but without the node connected to the broken line.

Extending the star concept to multiple levels, we have a cascaded star and each satellite node may be the central node of another star. This is called a hierarchical topology, or tree topology, as shown in Figure 1.3(c). A hierarchical tree has one advantage; that is, its routing strategy is very simple. Depending on the destination address, the message is either sent to the up node or to the down node. This particular feature is attractive in banking network design.

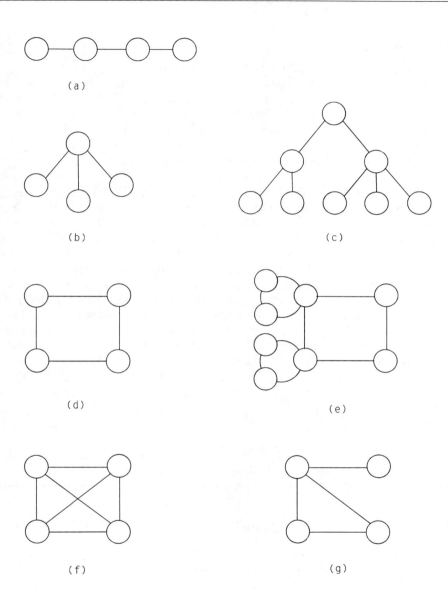

Figure 1.3 Network topologies: (a) whip, (b) star, (c) hierarchical, (d) ring, (e) multilayer ring, (f) fully interconnected, and (g) partially interconnected.

1.4.3 Ring

Several computers can be connected in a ring, as shown in Figure 1.3(d). A ring in a LAN uses a copper or optical-fiber line, and the data bits always flow in one direction just like a circular shift register. The basic idea is to circulate a token of a special bit pattern on the ring; whoever gets the token has the right to transmit. When no one has data to transmit, or the ring is idle, the token circulates continuously on the ring. The token ring LAN also has the drawback that when the optical-fiber or copper line is broken and there is no spare, the entire ring is down.

Each node on the token ring has only one transmitter/receiver pair. The sender transmits a group of bits on the ring, known as a frame, and the frame always flows back to the sender. It is the sender's responsibility to strip the frame off the ring. Another type of ring is the slotted ring. In such a design, each processor has its own time slot assigned to transmit data on the ring and the receiving processor simply receives the slot when the time comes.

A ring in a WAN is different in software design. Nodes are interconnected by telephone lines and each node can transmit in both directions. When a data frame finally reaches the destination node via many intermediate nodes, it stops there. The sender on the origination node never receives a copy of the frame sent. This is strikingly different from the design of a ring LAN. If one line or node is broken, the ring WAN is still operational, but without the failed node.

The token ring LANs may be cascaded to make a multilayer ring as shown in Figure 1.3(e). Each corporation or university may have a token ring LAN backbone. Each computer on the backbone serves as a switching node, which is further connected to one or more sublayers. A ring may also be connected to a star and vice versa.

The combination of stars and rings is widely accepted in LAN design. Like the hierarchical topology, one advantage of using the multilayer token ring is its routing simplicity. In addition, the proven reliability and high speed of a token ring has made it popular in LAN design.

1.4.4 Fully Interconnected Network

Given N nodes, each node has a connection to the other $N - 1$ nodes. Therefore, the total number of links is computed below:

$$(N \cdot (N - 1)) / 2$$

If N equals 4, we have a total of six links between each pair of nodes, which is still acceptable. A fully interconnected network with four nodes is shown in Figure 1.3(f). If the number of nodes is increased to 10, the total number of links becomes 45, as computed below:

$$(10 \cdot 9) / 2 = 45$$

Communication links are costly and it becomes exceptional to have a fully interconnected computer network over 10 nodes. As a compromise, some of the less critical links are removed so the network becomes partially interconnected.

1.4.5 Partially Interconnected Network

Most computer networks in the field are partially interconnected. A partially interconnected network is shown in Figure 1.3(g). The decision whether to have a link between any two nodes should be based on the traffic and the cost between two nodes. There are other topologies of interest because of their uniqueness of routing. Mesh and hypercube are examples given below.

1.4.6 Mesh

If all nodes are arranged in a two-dimensional matrix, say M rows by N columns, we obtain a two-dimensional mesh. If M equals N, then we have a square mesh. A node in the middle of the mesh has four links (left, right, up, and down), and each link is connected to its neighboring node. A four-by-eight, 32-node mesh is shown in Figure 1.4.

Each node in the mesh has a node identification (ID) or address that is partitioned into two parts, (X, Y), where X denotes its horizontal position and Y denotes its vertical position. The interstate highway system in the United States resembles a mesh topology. The routing issue is greatly simplified. Suppose node 1 at $(X1, Y1)$ wants to send a message to node 2 at $(X2, Y2)$. One approach is to compare its horizontal and vertical addresses. If $X2$ is greater than

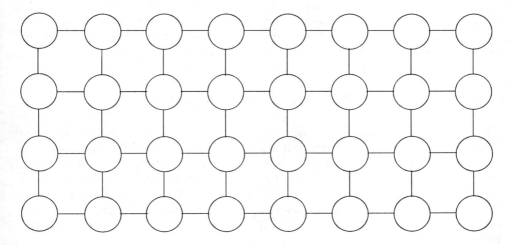

Figure 1.4 A four-by-eight, 32-node mesh network.

$X1$, traverse to the right direction; otherwise, traverse to the left until the intermediate node is reached whose horizontal address is $X2$. Next, compare $Y2$ with $Y1$. If $Y2$ is greater than $Y1$, move up; otherwise, move down until the destination node is reached. Between any two nodes, we conclude that:

- The minimum shortest route is 1.
- The maximum shortest route is $(M + N - 2)$.

A two-dimensional mesh is intuitive and expandable, so it can be used in a multiprocessing system or a WAN backbone [2]. If we add extra links between the two end points of any row or column, we obtain a torus topology, and the maximum shortest route is cut almost to half [3]. In a torus, each row or column is connected as a ring.

1.4.7 Hypercube

Hypercube is interesting in that it has its own uniform way to make connections [4]. Starting with two nodes, the left node has an address 0 and the right node has an address 1. This hypercube is said to be of degree 1. To make a hypercube of degree 2, we duplicate the hypercube of degree 1 twice. We need to append another address bit at the end. The two nodes in the front row have a trailing address bit 0, and the ones in the back row have a trailing address bit 1, as shown in Figure 1.5(a). There are only four nodes in a hypercube of degree 2, and each node is designated by a two-bit address. Each of the two nodes in the front row is connected to its counterpart in the back row.

To make a hypercube of degree 3, we duplicate the hypercube of degree 2 twice and append another address bit at the end. The first set of four nodes has a trailing address bit 0, and the second set has a trailing address bit 1, as shown in Figure 1.5(b). There is a direct connection between any two nodes if their addresses only differ by one bit. To traverse from node (0, 1, 0) to node (1, 0, 1), one approach is to assign the primary route as follows:

$$(0, 1, 0) \rightarrow (1, 1, 0) \rightarrow (1, 0, 0) \rightarrow (1, 0, 1)$$

To derive this primary route, we compare the destination address with the origination address, bit by bit starting from the leftmost bit. There are two possibilities. If the examined bit is different, we traverse to the next node whose address has the different bit but with all other address bits unchanged. This means that we traverse to the node that is closer to the destination by one hop. If the examined bit is the same, we simply skip this bit and compare the next bit. We repeat this process down to the bit at the farthest right or until the destination node is reached.

Examining the addresses of any two nodes, we can determine the distance,

Introduction to Computer Networks 17

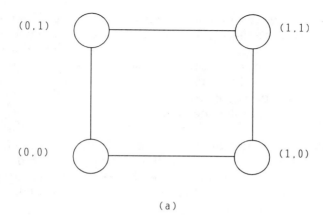

(a)

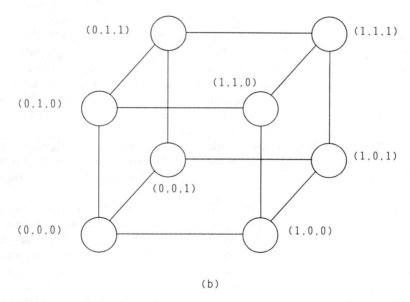

(b)

Figure 1.5 Hypercube networks: (a) a hypercube of degree 2 and (b) a hypercube of degree 3.

which is defined to be the number of hops from one node to the other. The distance is also equal to the number of different bits in the two addresses. In general, a hypercube of degree r contains $2\char`\^r$ nodes, and each node is designated by an r-bit address. Between any two nodes, we have:

- The minimum shortest route is 1,
- The maximum shortest route is r.

Hypercube has its own merits in that its routing is simple and that its maximum shortest route is reasonable. It also provides redundancy. Hence, a hypercube with 64 nodes or less can be used in real-time switching systems or a WAN backbone [5]. Commercial hypercubes of over 1,000 nodes are available to perform parallel computations [nCUBE].

1.5 COMPUTER NETWORK APPLICATIONS

After introducing the basic concept of computer networks, we want to know what computer networks are designed to do. One primary goal of computer networking is to improve efficiency. Assume that we have four PCs connected to a global computer network, as shown in Figure 1.6. The topology of the computer network is immaterial. Each computer may be situated at a different location, or even in a different country. Each user can send electronic mail (e-mail), transfer files, or share information with others. Any user may call a teleconference. Users can even play bridge or mahjongg. If one user is missing, a computer program may be drafted to play instead.

In a WAN or LAN, we may issue a remote procedure call (RPC) in the application program to request a special computation on a remote computer. We can, of course, do a remote login to a computer and execute the same procedure directly.

In a LAN, a color laser printer is considered a valuable resource that is driven by a computer. The notion to transfer a file to a printer really means to transfer a file to a remote computer that drives the printer. From the user's viewpoint, the printer is like a remote file. Any user on the LAN can send a file to the printer to make a hard copy. In reality, the file is first transferred from the user's computer to the remote computer, which then outputs the file on the printer. A hardware connection must exist, and, more importantly, special software must be written to communicate between the two computers. Computer networks can also be used for game simulations, such as tank battle, sea battle, and star war.

This decade, high-speed LANs and WANs will provide a data transfer rate of over 600 Mbps. As a result, multimedia devices consisting of integrated voice, image, and data are becoming common household commodities. With such a

Introduction to Computer Networks 19

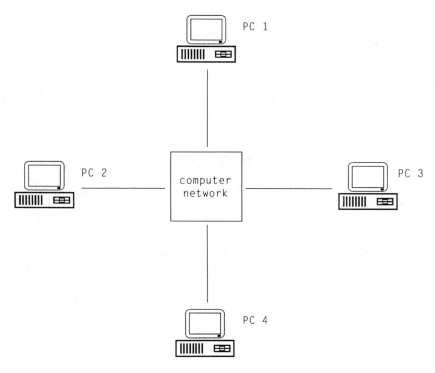

Figure 1.6 Four PCs tied to a global computer network.

device, a person can call a teleconference, watch movies, vote, pay bills, play video games, request information, and more.

Because of the wireless technology under development, mobile computing has become a vital part of our daily life [6]. In other words, all user computers are portable. The police officer can validate a driver's license in a minute. A stockbroker can do trading in an airplane. If its central node is also portable, an entire network can be brought to a classroom so that the teacher and students can have interactions during a lecture.

In the next two decades, there will be global computer networks, each one containing over one billion nodes. Not only will your car be pollution-free, it will also be equipped with a team of powerful PCs functioning as an autopilot. The computers in the car will be interconnected in a LAN. Every day in the morning, after keying in the destination, your garage door will open. Your car will then start, back into the street, and drive to your workplace while you watch the morning news on the road. There will be satellite computers outside the car that constantly monitor and broadcast weather and road conditions. At the intersection of two roads, there will also be computers that direct the traffic. All outside computers will be interconnected in a WAN. The computer in the car will have sensors to read real-time input data and interact with other computers. This is computer networking. It is my belief that a human driver should be able to override the autopilot at any instant on the road. The future is surely promising under your control.

In order to support network applications, NOSs are developed to support intertask communications over the network as introduced in the following.

1.6 NETWORK OPERATING SYSTEMS

In an OS, several I/O system routines can be grouped as an access method (AM). There are various AMs executing on a computer to access I/O data on an external device such as a disk, a tape, a display, or a printer. The network access methods (NAMs), on the other hand, are executed to access I/O data on a network. That is, the NAMs are the network I/O system routines specially designed to enable a task or program running on one computer to send data to, or receive data from, another task running on a different computer. In other words, using the NAMs, two or more programs can communicate in a network, with each program running under its own NOS on its own CPU. The NOS is the collection of a regular OS and many network I/O system routines. Adding NAMs to an OS, we obtain a NOS as shown below:

$$NAMs + OS = NOS$$

Different designs result in different NAMs. Regardless of the approach, a NAM is just as complicated as an OS. Understanding the basic concepts of an OS would help in the learning of NAMs. Appendix A covers operating system essentials, such as interrupts, asynchronous processing, task management, reentrant code, and semaphore. In particular, task management routines are closely related to the design of NAMs, and we will review some of the basic system routines listed below.

1. Interrupt service routine (ISR)—the routine handles the processing of a particular interrupt.
2. Dispatcher—the task scheduler determines which task in the ready queue to execute next.
3. Attach—the routine asks the system to prepare the execution of a descendent task in memory. Passing parameters include task id, starting address, addressing space, and other related information associated with the task.
4. Detach—the routine terminates the task by freeing all the resources allocated to it.

5. Send—the routine sends a message to another task. Passing parameters include task id, message address, status, and so forth.
6. Receive—the routine receives a message from another task. Note that if one task issues a Send, the other task must issue a Receive to accept the message. In other words, each Send issued by one task should find a matching Receive issued by another task as shown below.

Task1:	Task2:
...	...
Send('task2', msg, status);	Receive('task1', msg, status);
...	...
Endtask;	Endtask;

Both the Send and Receive routines can execute on a single computer, but with the support of NAMs they can also execute on two different computers in a network.

1.6.1 Network Access Methods

The NAMs contain all the system routines running on one or two processors to handle the network I/O. If there is no communication processor, all NAMs must run on a single processor (for example, a PC). On the other hand, if a communication processor is available, then we split the workload. The host processor runs routines to handle port connections, segmentation and reassembly of large messages, and synchronization of task executions. The communication processor handles the network I/O routines such as routing, error control, flow control, and physical I/O drivers as well as the network management (NMT) routines. The communication processor and the host processor exchange messages via shared memory or I/O channels.

The development effort for NAMs is as big as that for OSs. Fortunately, after one decade of endeavor, we can divide NAMs into layers. Even though each layer is huge and complicated, it is still manageable. How many layers are needed remains a debatable issue among designers.

1.7 OSI REFERENCE MODEL

The acronym OSI stands for open systems interconnection. Who, around the world, are the players setting standards and making recommendations? There is a group known as the International Telecommunications Union-Telecommunication Standardization Sector (ITU-T), formerly known as the Comite Consultatif International de Telegraphique et Telephonique (CCITT) in French or the International Telegraph and Telephone Consultative Committee in English. The primary goal of ITU-T is to standardize techniques and operations in the telecommunications field to achieve endpoint-to-endpoint compatibility of international telecommunications, regardless of the countries of origin and destination. The State Department represents the United States in ITU-T.

International telecommunications standards are also set by the International Organization for Standardization (ISO), which is itself a member of ITU-T. The ISO members include 89 countries, with the American National Standards Institute (ANSI) representing the United States. Note that ANSI is a nongovernment and nonprofit organization whose members are U.S. manufacturers and other interest groups. Proposals submitted by ANSI are usually approved by ISO as international standards.

In the United States, there is the National Institute of Standards and Technology (NIST), which was called the National Bureau of Standards (NBS) until the Department of Commerce changed its name in 1988, and the Institute of Electrical and Electronics Engineers (IEEE), which is the largest professional society in the world. Both agencies tend to set standards for America and submit them to ISO for approval as international standards. All specification and standard documents are available from the respective agencies or from one common source [Common].

1.7.1 Layer Specifications

Using a layered approach, we can divide and conquer the design of network I/O system software. What is a layer? Designers of the network system can designate a task, a group of subroutines, or a hardware controller as a layer. Some basic design philosophies, however, should be observed:

- Each layer should perform one or more well-defined functions.
- Information flow across the boundary should be minimized.
- Changes made in one layer do not require changes in other layers.
- Each layer usually communicates with the layer above or below except the network management routines.

The OSI reference model first proposed by ISO consists of seven layers in its entire protocol stack [X.200]. As network system specifications are concerned, the seven-layer model is fine. But in regard to NOS design, a five-layer model would be adequate [7–9]. The argument is that no layer is necessary if we can get by without it. To solve this dilemma, major firms such as AT&T, IBM, DEC, and HP, have all created their own application programming interfaces (APIs) for the upper layers. A user may essentially request service from any of the upper layers via its API.

The OSI reference model merely provides a recommendation of ideas. In order to connect computers to a network, it is necessary to obey the standards at both the hardware and software levels. Assume that a layer consists of many software routines that provide one or more well-defined network functions. Between two adjacent layers, the lower layer is a service provider while its immediate upper layer is a service user. For pedagogical reasons, the seven layers of the OSI reference model are listed below:

1. Application (A);
2. Presentation (P);
3. Session (S);
4. Transport (T);
5. Network (N);
6. Data link (DL);
7. Physical (PH).

The A layer is on top while the PH layer is at the bottom. The layer-to-layer connections are shown in Figure 1.7. On the origination node, one application task goes through all seven layers in the protocol stack from top to bottom to transmit a piece of data on the line. On the destination node, another application task receives the same piece of data via all seven layers from bottom to top. The two application tasks are said to be peers, and each task is a peer entity or software routine. Below the application task, each layer communicates with its peer on a remote computer.

At the origination site, there is a physical connection between the node and the computer network. At the destination site, there is also a physical connection between the node and the network. There may be several intermediate nodes in the middle of the route. The upper layers all have direct virtual connections to their peers, as shown by the dotted lines, while the solid lines indicate a physical connection or data path. That is, the bottom three layers on each intermediate node work as a team merely to transmit and receive data. In the seven-layer OSI model, the term *computer network* means a subnet that consists of many communication processors running the bottom three layers.

Physical Layer

The PH layer specifies the physical connection, such as connector shapes, pin assignments, voltage levels, bit positions, data rates, and handshaking procedures at the pin level. The PH layer software mainly consists of I/O drivers, which have access to hardware registers in the communication controller. The group of data bits placed on the line is called a frame. The I/O drivers instruct the hardware controller device to transmit and receive frames. To send a frame, an output driver sets the data bits into the hardware registers of the communication controller, which in turn transmits the bits on the line.

Electronically, a hardware transmitter varies the line voltage as a function of time, and the receiver can detect the voltage change and figure out the bit pattern. If the communication controller is a byte I/O device, the I/O drivers can

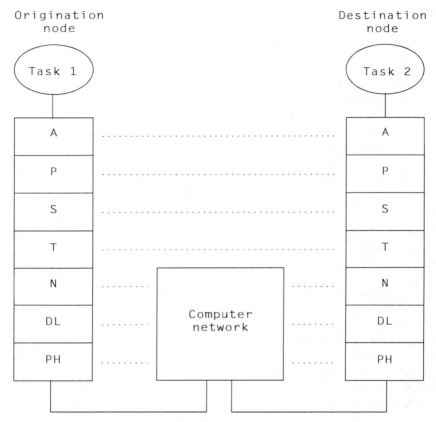

Figure 1.7 Layer-to-layer connections in an OSI reference model.

team up with the interrupt service routines to make the controller look like a block I/O device. That is to say, the PH layer software enables a service user to transmit a 128-byte data block on the line via one driver call.

Data Link Layer

The DL layer software performs two major functions: error control and flow control between two connection points. Each connection point has its own physical link, which is a hardware transmitter and receiver pair. Therefore, a DL can be thought of as a logical entity that contains hardware and software to ensure correct data transmissions on the line [SDLC]. In the case where a PH link is not reliable, a DL may be because of its software design. That is, whenever a frame is not correctly received, the sender is notified to retransmit until the frame is correctly received.

The DLs can be thought of as sections of an information highway and considered to be shared resources. If each DL is well-built, we have a very reliable info highway. To accomplish this goal, an error-detecting code is placed in the frame during data transmission. As far as software is concerned, a DL could be a system task that receives commands from the network layer and then issues a driver call to transmit the frame. When there are two or more nodes in a network, we have a routing problem. That is, the system should know how to deliver a piece of data from one node to the next. As a result of this, the N layer is incorporated in the network software design for routing and congestion control.

Network Layer

The N layer mainly handles such tasks as routing control and congestion avoidance. There are two approaches to designing the N layer: the virtual circuit (VC) model and the datagram model. Each approach has its own merits.

A VC can be thought of as a series of data links. It is like a network pipe between two computers with intermediate nodes in the middle. If a packet is dropped into one end of the pipe, it pops out from the other end. In a VC model, the N layer must establish a VC first. After that, the same route must be followed by all subsequent data transmissions. In a datagram model, the N layer delivers a datagram just like dropping a letter in the mailbox. Each datagram contains its own full destination address. The letters having the same address may not follow a fixed route. They will eventually be delivered to the destination, but sometimes a few letters may be mishandled and lost.

Since the N layer provides either VC or datagram services, the programming entity at either end of a VC or datagram is a network service access point (NSAP). Each node that runs the network layer must be assigned a unique network address. The N layer at the origination node receives a message from its service user, interprets the message, and executes the message. A data request message is equivalent to a VC call or datagram call, depending on the N layer design. The N layer may also receive a data indication message from its DL layer asking for routing control.

If a WAN contains a lot of nodes, the N layer needs a large routing table that contains information on all the routes. Whenever a routing decision needs to be made, it must be made within a reasonable amount of time. The key difference between a VC model and a datagram model is that the VC model follows the same route but the datagram model does not.

When two or more users are running on the host and both need network services, a T layer must be in place. Each service user of the T layer may use a programming port to deliver a large message block to its peer.

Transport Layer

The T layer mainly supports the multiplexing functions in a multiprogramming system on the host. It is capable of maintaining a programming port connection between two programs. A programming port is a private software resource to the service user. Below the port, we have either a VC or a datagram, which may be shared. The T layer also handles segmentation and reassembly. As an example, it may accept a message block as large as 16 MB from its user, chop the message into pieces, and deliver each piece in shared memory for the N layer to fetch, interpret, and execute. At the receiving end, the peer T layer knows how to reassemble the message block and deliver it to its user.

Session Layer

Because the T layer services are not easy to use, it is a good idea to provide a system interface between the user task and the T layer in a five-layer model. Hence, the S interface becomes the fifth layer. In the OSI reference model, all three upper layers exist and the application interface becomes the eighth layer on top of application.

The S layer performs two major functions: connection management and synchronization. During the connection phase, a security check is also performed. In concept, the S layer should be simple and elegant, and it was designed as an API to achieve programming convenience [LU6.2, TCP/IP]. In such a design, the T layer details can be hidden from its service user and the services provided by the session layer are easy to use. Note that the interface is part of a NOS and should provide the same set of system calls to all applications.

Presentation Layer

The P layer contains routines, such as compression, decompression, conversion, encryption, and decryption, for manipulating data. They should be designed just as subroutines. People write presentation service routines as commercial software products. Specifications, however, are needed to convert data from one format to another. In fact, the data encryption and decryption functions can be handled by any layer, or even the hardware.

Application Layer

The A layer consists of all the application routines running on the network. Whether the application routines should be considered as a layer remains a debatable issue. One may argue for breaking a particular network application program into two parts, one written by the system people and the other one written by a user. The part written by the system people may be called the A layer. Consequently, the user needs to interface with the application part in the system, which makes the programming job much easier.

The A layer specifications, however, are necessary. The data format and opcode in a message must be defined for a particular application. For example, in a file transfer protocol, we need to specify subcommands such as get, put, dir, and quit, that are local to this particular application. Each subcommand entered via the keyboard is treated as data to the application service routine, which merely interprets and executes.

By the same token, a banking network must specify the formats of subcommands, such as deposit, withdraw, verify, and report. Because automatic teller machines can only accept one format to transmit data to a bank, it is necessary to standardize the format so that any customer can withdraw cash not only from any automatic teller machine but also from any bank [10]. If a bank uses a different format, then a routine must be employed to do the necessary conversion.

If all the I/O drivers in the PH layer are embedded into the DL layer, then the NAMs merely consist of four layers—namely, DL, N, T, and S—plus the NMT routines. Each layer contains a lot of lines of code, which necessitates an arduous development effort. To communicate between two adjacent layers, the layer primitives are designed for this purpose, as introduced in Section 1.7.2.

1.7.2 Layer Primitives

The layer primitives are issued to exchange information between a service provider and its user in an abstract way. In simple terms, a layer primitive may be a request to the target layer or a Confirm from the target layer. A service user may issue a request to the target layer or service provider. After receiving a request, the target layer starts to take action. When the requested service is completed, the target layer sends a Confirm to its user, which is the upper layer. In a way, the layer primitives are used to describe network I/O operations, and they may be designed as subroutines or just messages between two adjacent layers.

An application task at the origination node may issue a system call to send a data message to its peer application task at the destination node. On the origination node, each layer passes a message down until it reaches the PH layer, which actually does the transmission. On the destination node, each layer passes a message up until it reaches the peer application task.

ITU-T has established a uniform syntax to specify layer primitives [X.210]. Each layer primitive starts with a target layer id followed by an underscore, an action, a period, a basic primitive, and parameters enclosed in parentheses. The underscore, period, left parenthesis, and right parenthesis, are terminal symbols in compiler jargon that show up in the language syntax. The metalanguage used to describe the syntax of a layer primitive is shown in Figure 1.8(a).

```
<layer id>     ==>    'the class of' layer ids.
::=            ==>    'defined to be'
|              ==>    'or'
[...]          ==>    an option, e.g. [, <QOS>] means QOS is
                      optional and the ',' is a terminal symbol.
```

(a)

```
<layer id>_<action>.<basic primitive> (<parameter list>)
```

(b)

```
<layer id>        ::=  PH | DL | N  | T | S | P | A
<action>          ::=  CONNECT | DATA | EXPEDITED_DATA |
                       UNITDATA | DISCONNECT | RESET | ...
<basic primitive> ::=  request | indication | response | confirm
<parameter list>  ::=  <address> [, <sdu>] [, <QOS>]
                       [, <status>] [,<reason>] ...
```

(c)

Figure 1.8 Format specifications of layer primitives: (a) metalanguage to define layer primitives, (b) layer primitive syntax, and (c) class definitions.

The primitive syntax and the classes are listed in Figure 1.8(b) and Figure 1.8(c), respectively. Some of the examples are given below:

T_CONNECT.request(origination_node_id,
          destination_node_id, port_id, QOS, t_sdu);
T_DATA.request(port_id, t_sdu, status);
N_CONNECT.request(origination_node_id,
          destination_node_id, vc_id, QOS);
N_DATA.request(vc_id, n_sdu, status);

A layer id consists of one or two uppercase letters representing the target layer followed by an underscore. An action is coded in uppercase letters indicating a particular command, such as CONNECT, DATA, EXPEDITED_DATA, UNITDATA, RESET, and DISCONNECT. Not all layers support all the actions. For example, we do not need a PH_CONNECT or a PH_EXPEDITED_DATA. The third element is a basic primitive that indicates the progress of a sequence of events.

Basic Primitives

There are four basic primitives in lowercase letters as listed below [X.210]:

1. request;
2. indication;
3. response;
4. confirm.

The logic is described in Figure 1.9. A request or response primitive is sent down to the target layer, while an indication or Confirm primitive is sent up by the target layer to report what has happened. A request informs the target layer to take a specified action. Depending on the type of request, it may take a long time to complete the action. If the request is for data transmission or connection, the target layer needs to send a message to its peer layer at the remote end about the action.

After receiving the incoming request message, the peer layer on the receiving node issues an indication to inform its upper layer about the event. Before doing that, the peer layer takes appropriate action on its part to complete the action of the incoming request. The word *indication* was originated from the telephone industry to indicate an incoming event.

A response is then sent down by the upper layer on the destination node to respond to the indication primitive. Usually during a connection phase, after receiving a response from its upper layer, the destination layer sends an acknowledgment message to its peer as a Confirm to the request.

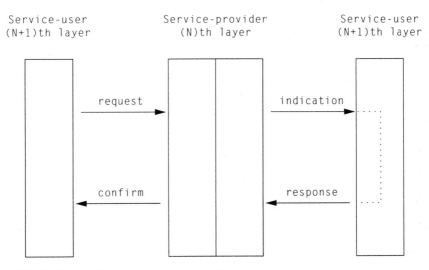

Figure 1.9 Basic primitives.

After receiving the Confirm message, the target layer then issues a Confirm primitive to its user. If the Confirm is positive, its service user on the origination node knows that the request has been successfully carried out.

The parameters passed in a request primitive contain information for the target layer to accomplish its goal. For a CONNECT or DATA request, the address information must be provided, and they vary from layer to layer. A node_id denotes the network address of a node while a port_id or vc_id is a local reference number used by the T and N layers, respectively. A service data unit (SDU) is passed from the service user to the provider. In a T_DATA.request, the parameter t_sdu represents a transport sdu that contains data. In a N_DATA.request, the parameter n_sdu is used instead. Other parameters include quality of service (QOS), status, and reason.

The T layer connect primitives are shown in Figure 1.10, where the dotted

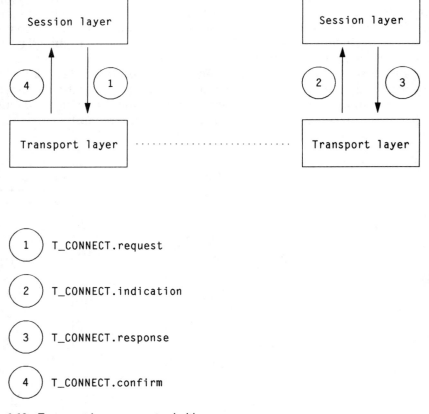

Figure 1.10 Transport layer connect primitives.

line indicates a virtual connection between the two peer T layers. The following events happen in real time as described below.

1. The session layer at the origination node sends a T_CONNECT.request to its T layer. This primitive supplies parameters, such as network addresses of both the origination and destination nodes, senders port_id, QOS, and t_sdu.
2. Assume there is already a VC between two nodes; that is, a pipe is already in place between the two peer T layers.
3. The origination T layer sends a connect request (CR) message via a N_DATA.request or pipe call to its peer T layer at the destination node.
4. After receiving the CR command via an N_DATA.indication, the destination T layer takes appropriate action and sends a T_CONNECT.indication to its session.
5. After receiving the T_CONNECT.indication, the destination session layer sends a T_CONNECT.response to its T layer.
6. The destination T layer then sends, via a N_DATA.request, a Connect Confirm (CC) message to the origination T layer.
7. After receiving the CC message via a N_DATA.indication, the origination T layer issues a T_CONNECT.confirm to its session.
8. At this point, a port connection has been established between two T layers and both service users on top can simultaneously issue a T_DATA.request or port call to their peers.

In practice, the DATA messages only need the request and indication basic primitives but not the response and confirm, so the traffic between two layers can be reduced. The implementation of layer primitives is an internal design issue in that a request primitive can be a message to a task or a subroutine call with passing parameters.

1.7.3 Layer Protocol Data Units

A protocol data unit (PDU) refers to the bits in a message that are transmitted by a sending layer and received by its peer on the remote node. In concept, a layer primitive tells its adjacent layer what to do while a PDU tells its peer on the remote node what to do. Both are closely related and essentially contain the same information to accomplish the job. The bits in a PDU must be clearly defined, and there is no room for ambiguity. That is to say, a layer primitive is a message between two adjacent layers in the same system, and a PDU is a message between two peers on two different computers. Some PDUs are designed for control purposes and they are not passed to the upper layer.

Assume that the $(N + 1)$th layer sends a DATA message to its service provider, the Nth layer. The parameters passed in a DATA request message are an address and an SDU to the Nth layer. The Nth layer adds its own protocol control information (PCI) to the Nth layer sdu to make an Nth layer PDU [X.200].

The information relationship between an SDU and a PDU is shown in Figure 1.11. This relationship is especially true at the DL layer level. The network protocol data unit (NPDU) is also known as the N layer packet. When the N layer at level 3 wants to send a packet to the N layer on the adjacent node, it issues a DL_DATA.request with the packet passed as parameter. The packet becomes a dl_sdu to the level 2 DL layer. The DL layer then adds its PCI, a header, and a trailer to the packet and issues an output driver call to transmit all the bits on the line. The bits are referred to as a data link protocol data unit (DLPDU) or frame. That is, a DLPDU contains a header, a packet, and a trailer.

The DL header mainly contains the operation code (opcode), sequence numbers, and the hardware address of secondary station. The DL trailer contains an error-detecting code. Together they provide the PCI at the DL layer level. At the receiving end, the DL layer interprets the PCI, strips off both header and trailer, and sends only the packet or NPDU via a DL_DATA.indication to its N layer for further routing control.

The protocols at each layer are standards. What are the differences among a protocol, a protocol stack, and a protocol suite? Some explanations are given below.

Protocol, Protocol Stack, and Protocol Suite

A protocol is an individual set of rules that govern the data transmissions between two peer layers. Each layer has its own protocol, which means the entire

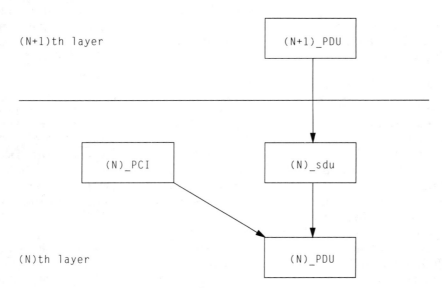

Figure 1.11 Information relationship between an sdu and a PDU.

set of messages or PDUs must be precisely defined and each layer can only understand the PCI field in its PDUs.

A protocol stack means the entire set of protocols required to accomplish the goal of communication between two user tasks on two different computers. The OSI reference model has seven layers. The sending application program must go through all seven layers to transmit a piece of data on the line. Other models may have four or five layers.

A protocol suite, on the other hand, means a family of protocols at a particular layer level. There may be a choice of many different protocols. Depending on the application, the service user can only select one protocol from the family to perform the job. For example, ISO supports a transport protocol family of five classes, and each class provides a level of services based on the user requirements and QOS. Each class in the protocol family serves a particular need, so to speak.

1.7.4 Comparisons of the OSI Model, SNA, and Internet

It is interesting to compare the OSI model with other networks. SNA is the IBM corporate network product, and, Internet is a global network using the transmission control protocol/Internet protocol (TCP/IP). The OSI, the Internet, and SNA are compared in Table 1.2.

In SNA, path control means routing control, which is a major function performed by the N layer. Transmission control and transport control are synonymous. The S layer of SNA provides data flow control, which could be performed by the T layer. The presentation service routines are mainly utilities to perform compression, decompression, data conversion, data encryption, and decryption. The transaction services are the application programs provided by the network system to handle transaction processing. The application software usually uses the services provided by the S layer. Both the presentation and application services are available in the system, but they are not part of the NOS.

Table 1.2
Comparison of the OSI Model, the SNA, and the Internet

Layer	OSI	SNA	Internet
1	Physical	Physical control	Physical
2	Data link	Data link control	—
3	Network	Path control	IP
4	Transport	Transmission control	TCP
5	Session	Data flow control	TCP
6	Presentation	Presentation services	Presentation services
7	Application	Transaction services	Application services

On the Internet, both the S and T layers are combined into the transmission control protocol (TCP) layer. The Internet protocol (IP) is essentially the protocol of the network layer. Its DL layer is empty. However, if the destination IP address in a datagram represents a node in a LAN, the datagram will first be delivered to the server node, which then uses its own DL protocol to deliver the frame to the destination node. The PH layer in TCP/IP mainly contains I/O drivers. The P and A layers are again network application service routines. In DDN, an application task can access the transport services directly without going through the upper three layers. Some telephone systems can provide services at the network layer level.

1.8 DESIGN CONSIDERATIONS OF NETWORK SYSTEM SOFTWARE

In this section, we will discuss the design issues of network system software from the top level. Assuming that we have a five-layer model, the NAMs can be divided into two parts: the upper two layers and the bottom three layers. System throughput and maintenance are our two major concerns. In theory, all five layers can run on the host processor, which usually means a PC. However, if there is a communication processor available on the side, it is wise to implement the bottom three layers plus the NMT routines on the communication processor as introduced below.

1.8.1 Network I/O Routines on the Communication Processor

The communication processor, also known as a front end processor (FEP), interface message processor (IMP), or intermediate system (IS), executes its own OS to provide the basic control functions. In a computer network, there are many independent communication processors interconnected as a subnet. Each processor is a router or switching node whose main function is to route messages. The bottom three layers and the NMT routines should all execute on the communication processor, and this is a very important system concept in computer network architecture.

The NMT routines communicate with other layers, and they can also be used to set and reset control parameters for all three layers. The control parameters in the network layer include entries in the routing table and the parameters in the DL layer include line settings of communication controllers. A simple example to set the line is shown below:

Set   com1, 9600 E71

where set is a command to NMT with passing parameters: com1 for the asynchronous communication controller 1, 9600 for the data rate in bps, and E71 for even parity (7 data bits and 1 stop bit). The NMT routines not only monitor the status of the bottom three layers, but also interact with the NMT routines on other nodes. In addition, they take measurements and record statistics on disk.

1.8.2 Network I/O Routines on the Host

The host computer, known as an end system (ES), is mainly designed for doing computations. In general, it is a mainframe or high-performance computer. The OS on the host computer contains many I/O access methods. Using the basic AMs, the application programmer has more control of the I/O operations to improve system throughput. But the application programmer should understand the internal design of the OS thoroughly and be able to handle certain control functions, such as blocking/deblocking, automatic buffering, and synchronization, without assistance.

The queued access methods (QAMs), on the other hand, handle all the system chores for the application programmer. For example, when a programmer issues an open system call for disk read, the QAMs will go ahead and read disk even though the programmer has not issued a read request yet. This design feature is known as automatic or anticipatory buffering. After a user issues any I/O request, control is not passed to the users program until the I/O operation is completed, which means that the QAMs take care of synchronization. The QAMs also handle blocking and deblocking. As an example, if the physical sector on a disk contains four logical records, the user must issue logical disk write four times to fill up the physical I/O buffer before a QAM issues a physical disk write. Modern microcomputers mainly support QAMs.

The NAMs are designed for telecommunications just like the QAMs. The S and T layers are running on the host. If a connection is established between the two peer S layers, an application task may ask its S layer to deliver a data message to its peer application task running on the destination node. The S layer on the origination node sends down the message to its T layer. The message can be very large, say a 16-MB memory dump of any bit pattern. The origination T layer segments the big message block into pieces and delivers each piece, one at a time, until the entire message is delivered.

The destination T layer receives the small pieces and knows how to put them back into a large message block. It then delivers the big message to its S layer, which in turn delivers the entire message to its application task. The two application tasks running on the host at the two ends are said to be peers.

To further the understanding of network system software design, let us go through a data flow example of intertask communications in a five-layer model as shown in Figure 1.12. If several intermediate nodes reside in the middle of the route, the software design effort will be a challenge. The network application task running on host A sends a piece of data to the application task running on host D. Since there is no direct connection between nodes A and D, the task on

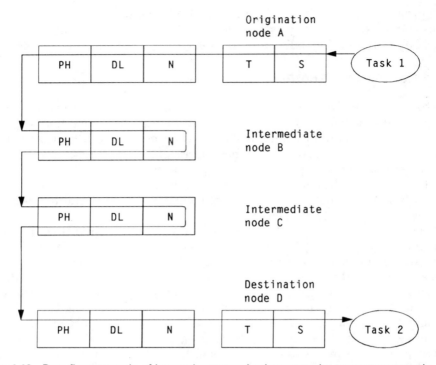

Figure 1.12 Data flow example of intertask communications over the computer network.

node A sends the data via all the layers. It is our intention to trace the data flow from node A to node D.

On host A, the data goes down from the network application task to the S layer and the T layer. It is the T layer that places an N_DATA.request command message in shared memory. The N layer running on its communication processor picks up the data and sends down to its DL layer, then to its PH layer, which finally places the bits on the line. On the intermediate node B, its PH layer receives the data bits, sends the data up to its DL, and then to the N layer for routing control. Then, the N layer running on node B sends the bits down to its DL layer, then to its PH layer, which in turn transmits the bits to intermediate node C.

Node C does the same as node B. Nodes B and C may or may not have a host. They are called the intermediate nodes or systems, which merely provide switching functions in the network. Even if the intermediate node does have a host, the data flow never goes beyond its N layer.

On node D, the data bits are passed to its N layer, which knows from the information in the packet header that its host computer is the final destination.

Accordingly, it places an N_DATA.indication message in the shared memory for its T layer to fetch and interpret. Finally, the T layer on host D sends the data bits to its S layer, which in turn passes the piece of data to the network application task running on node D.

Note that a network for computer communications is different from a network for digital telephone communications. As an example, for telephone communications, a VC is connected after having successfully dialed the phone number and disconnected after hanging up the phone. For computer communications, we may want to keep a permanent VC that may be shared by many users. If a VC crashes in a telephone network, it usually means the end of telephone conversation. However, in a computer network, a powerful T layer can reestablish another VC to recover any errors so that data transmissions may continue. Be that as it may, the basic concept between computer and telephone communications remains the same; that is, to transmit digital data from one computer to another.

1.8.3 Program Design Language

The program design language (PDL) used throughout this book is plain English. The PDL is used to describe the logic flow of a software routine or algorithm. The language comprises structured programming constructs in uppercase letters as listed below:

```
IF — THEN — ENDIF
IF — THEN — ELSE — ENDIF
CASE — ENDCASE
DO — ENDDO
REPEAT — UNTIL
DOWHILE — ENDDO
```

Each construct is used to describe the logic flow, and the keywords in uppercase letters are used to improve the readability of the program. Certain syntactic rules are obeyed and all spaces are suppressed in the language. The name of a system or user routine starts with an uppercase letter followed by lowercase letters, such as Attach, Detach, Send, and Receive. A comment statement is either enclosed in braces or preceded by a semicolon in column 1, as shown below:

    ... { This task may be reentrant.}
    ; This task may be reentrant.

Using the PDL, we can write the pseudocode of a software routine. There are other protocol specification languages [11–13]. There is also a standard notation to describe the bit pattern on the line [ASN.1].

1.9 NETWORK PERFORMANCE

Due to the rapid lowering of cost, computer networking plays an essential role in our daily life. The trend is that each corporation will have its own network that has access to a global WAN. Management is interested in the following:

- Performance improvement to meet future expansions;
- Reduction of cost;
- Reduction of down time.

The ultimate goal is to maximize the performance/cost ratio. If the system operates for a long period of time, the reliability of the network must be taken into account. More importantly, the availability of a network should be good all year around.

1.9.1 Performance Analysis

Network performance depends on the design of computer hardware and software. One obvious goal is to transfer data at a high speed without errors. Given the same set of hardware, a good software design can make a big difference in performance. Network protocols are just part of software design. A good protocol does not guarantee good performance. Even using the same TCP/IP protocol on the same computer, different software products may result in different performance by a factor of 2 to 1 [14]. This illustrates how important software design actually is.

Network throughput can be measured by the number of messages transmitted per unit time. How can we measure throughput? The simplest way is to use a stopwatch and measure the time it takes to transfer a file or to get a response from executing a network command. In that regard, network throughput also implies transmission speed or response time. No doubt a good protocol is important, but the software design of implementing the protocol is even more important. Certain design criteria are listed below:

1. Error control—a good protocol guarantees the correctness of data transmission. What if the real-time entertainment data is not critical? Can we transfer the data faster?
2. Flow control—if a traffic jam is encountered on an intermediate node, the piece of data may be dropped. Consequently, the original sender should reduce its sending rate to avoid serious congestion and long response delays.
3. Buffer management—I/O buffers should be managed wisely and any data movement between layers should be minimized.

4. Innovative technologies—fast and reliable hardware can be used to meet future processing requirements. More importantly, clever software must be written to drive innovative hardware.

Analytic methods, simulation methods, or a combination of both can be used to find the bottlenecks of a network. Knowing the hardware and software characteristics of each component in the system, the chief designer can usually use a pencil and paper to figure out potential bottlenecks. The results can be further verified by a protocol analyzer, which is a computer running special software to monitor the data flows on the network.

Design parameters of the network can be fine-tuned to improve performance. The number one headache experienced by the system administrator occurs when the system crashes for unknown reasons. In that regard, both hardware and software components should be made as reliable as possible.

1.9.2 Performance Monitoring

Many protocol analyzers are developed for network performance monitoring. They can be used to locate bugs, monitor performance, and identify the bottlenecks in the system. The NMT routines are designed to collect performance data, track device status, and change design parameters. They can also interact with a protocol analyzer.

Software monitors are specially designed and hooked into NOSs for performance monitoring. A unified software platform is pushed to gather management data from all components on a network and share the database across a wide range of applications. When trouble hits, a unified view of the corporate infrastructure would solve problems more quickly.

1.10 SUMMARY POINTS

1. In a broad sense, computer networks include multiprocessing systems, distributed systems, LANs, MANs, and WANs.
2. The basic interprocessor communication schemes are via shared memory, interrupt, and channel-to-channel I/O.
3. A binary semaphore is needed to guard a writable memory block shared by many CPUs.
4. A distributed system is a special purpose computer network designed to achieve a predefined goal.
5. The main objectives in designing a computer network are resource sharing, parallel computation, and redundancy.

6. The basic network topologies include whip, star, ring, mesh, and hypercube.
7. The network access methods contain all the network I/O system routines. Adding NAMs to an OS, we obtain a NOS.
8. The OSI model includes seven layers: physical (PH), data link (DL), network (N), transport (T), session (S), presentation (P), and application (A).
9. There are four basic primitives between two adjacent layers: request, indication, response, and confirm.
10. The protocol control information at the DL layer level is usually broken into a header and a trailer. The upper layer passes a PDU to the target layer, which adds PCI to the received PDU and makes a PDU of its own. The bits in a PDU must be precisely specified.
11. If there is a communication processor, the bottom three layers and the NMT routines should run on it.
12. The T and S layers should run on the host. The P and A layers should be just service routines.
13. Analytic methods, simulation methods, and protocol analyzer monitoring can used to identify the bottlenecks of a network.
14. The program design language used in this book is plain English. The language mainly uses structured programming constructs to describe the logic flow of a software routine.

Problems

Problem 1.1

What are the three basic interprocessor communication schemes?

Problem 1.2

What are the main objectives when designing computer networks?

Problem 1.3

What are the basic network topologies?

Problem 1.4

Given five nodes as shown below, can you select a topology using eight links so that the network is partially interconnected but with some redundancy?

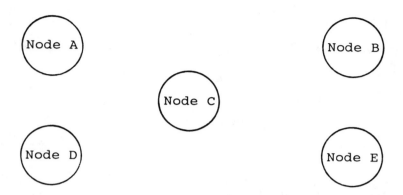

Assume that the central node and four satellite nodes all have heavy traffic among themselves.

Problem 1.5

What is the key difference in software design between a ring topology used in a LAN and a WAN?

Problem 1.6

Name three basic states that a task may be assigned in a computer system. Read Appendix A for help.

Problem 1.7

Describe the functions of a dispatcher in OS.

Problem 1.8

Name the seven layers specified in the OSI reference model.

Problem 1.9

What are the four basic primitives in a primitive between two adjacent layers?

Problem 1.10

Describe the information relationship between an $(N + 1)$th layer PDU and an (N)th layer PDU.

Problem 1.11

If we have a communication processor and a host processor, what are the three layers that should run on the communication processor?

Problem 1.12

What are the structured programming constructs?

Problem 1.13

Form a team of up to three students and tackle the following project. You are requested to think about the design of a network operating system to support a specific application. Discuss the following:

1. What are the NOS application commands that you wish to implement in your system? For example, FTP and mail are network application commands used in an office automation system.
2. What is the NOS interface you wish to implement. The network system interface is what the user task sees. Every network application task uses the same set of network system interfaces designed as system calls. For example, Send is used to transmit data; Receive is used to receive data. Just discuss at the function level; no design is necessary. Read Chapter 8 for more help.
3. Perhaps you should think of an application first and then decide how to implement it. Think hard and be creative. A concise report should be due the end of the fourth week.

References

[1] Gray, J.N., Private Lectures Notes, 1988.
[2] Seitz, C. L., "Mosaic C: An Experimental Fine-Grain Multicomputer," Technical Report, California Institute of Technology, Pasadena, CA, 91125, 1992.
[3] Cypher, R., "Storage-Efficient, Dead-Free Packet Routing Algorithm for Torus Networks," *IEEE Trans. on Computers,* Vol.43, No. 12, Dec. 1994, pp. 1376–1385.
[4] Seitz, C. L., "The Cosmic Cube," *CACM,* Vol. 28, No. 1, Jan. 1985, pp. 22–33.
[5] Chow, E., and E. Upchurch, "Hypercube Project: Hyperswitch and Communication Network Chip Set," Document JPL D-5956, Jet Propulsion Lab, Pasadena, CA, 1989.
[6] Forman, G. H., and J. Zahorjan, "The Challenge of Mobile Computing," *IEEE Computer,* April 1994, pp. 38–47.
[7] Saltzer, J. H., et al., "End-to-End Arguments in System Design," *ACM Trans. Computer Systems,* Vol. 2, Nov. 1984, pp. 277–288.
[8] Gray, J. P., et al., "Advanced Program-to-Program Communication in SNA," *IBM System Journal,* Vol 22, No. 4, 1983, pp. 298–318.
[9] Tanenbaum, A. S., *Computer Networks,* 2nd edition, Prentice-Hall, 1988.
[10] Hsu, J. Y., "On the Design of an Integrated Banking Network," *Proc. of the International Computer Symposium,* Vol. 1, Taiwan, 1980, pp. 501–510.

[11] Rockstrom, A. and R. Saracco, "SDL-CCITT Specification and Description Language," *IEEE Trans. on Communications,* Vol. Com-30, No. 6, June 1982, pp. 1310–1318.

[12] Rekdal, K., "CHILL—The Standard Language for Programming SPC Systems," *IEEE Trans. on Communications,* Vol. Com-30, No.6, June 1982, pp. 1318–1328.

[13] Hornbach, B. H., "MML: CCITT Man-Machine Language," *IEEE Trans. Computers,* Vol. C-30, No. 6, June 1982, pp. 1329–1336.

[14] Tolly, K., "For File Transfers, APPC Leaves TCP/IP in the Dust," *Data Communications,* Feb. 1994.

Physical Layer 2

To stay in tune, we need a physical.

The physical (PH) layer software directly drives the physical link, which consists of a communication (com) controller. In other words, the PH layer software sets the hardware registers, control or data, in the communication controller known as com port. If the data is transmitted out serially, the controller is called a serial port. A com port is a hardware device that communicates with another port or an external device. Since the PH layer software interacts with the controller, which in turn transmits bits on the line, the components are referred to as the physical I/O drivers. It is possible to have a design as depicted in Figure 2.1(a) where two communication controllers communicate via a transmission medium. If data can be transmitted in both directions, then each controller has a hardware transmitter (T) and receiver (R) pair. The transmission medium can be copper conductors, atmosphere, or fiber optics. In practice, there are two types of hardware systems for data communications: data terminal equipment (DTE) and data circuit-terminating equipment (DCE), which may be either a modem (modulator/demodulator) or a switching system. In that regard, DCE also means data communication equipment.

For long-distance digital data communications, a computer is usually connected to a modem, which is further connected to a telephone network. A computer is considered a DTE while a modem is a DCE. Between a DTE and a DCE, there are many parallel wires, as shown in Figure 2.1(b). A DTE is different from a DCE in that each one has its own physical interface defined differently. Some of the wires are for data while others provide status and control. When we define the transmitted data signal, which side is supposed to transmit, DTE or DCE? As DTE is concerned, the transmitted data signal is from DTE to DCE. But, when the same signal gets to the DCE side, it becomes the received data signal of DCE. Furthermore, some operations may require that both DTE and DCE be in ready state before a DTE can transmit data to a DCE. Others may require that

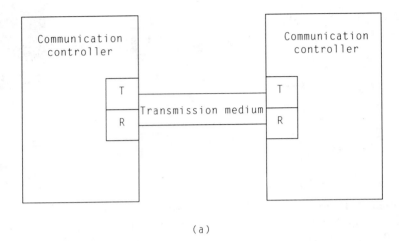

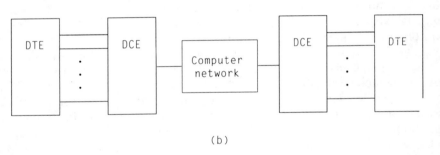

Figure 2.1 Physical connections in a computer network: (a) two communication controllers connected via a transmission medium and (b) DTE-DCE connections.

the DTE send a Request to Send signal to a DCE first and that the DCE respond with a Clear to Send signal to agree. They are the physical level protocols between two communication controllers. The PH layer specifications are important in regard to setting standards as described below.

- Mechanical;
- Electrical;
- Functional;
- Procedural.

Mechanical specifications define the layout of the physical connector. Electrical specifications define the voltage levels on the line. Function specifications define the function of each line including bit positions, data rates, and so forth. Procedure specifications define the handshaking protocol between signal lines. In summary, the PH layer specifications cover both software design and physical interface.

2.1 INTRODUCTION TO DATA TRANSMISSIONS

In this section, we will introduce the basic concept of digital data transmissions. Topics include transmission media, digital signal waveforms, and the way in which they are transmitted.

2.1.1 Transmission Media

One common transmission medium in the past and at the present is the copper wire. Wire, line, and cable are used interchangeably. Both twisted pair and coaxial cables use copper conductors. However, the future trend dictates that more copper wires will be replaced by wireless or optical fibers in data communications, because fibers meet the high-performance requirement and microwaves provide convenience.

Twisted Pair

The most economical transmission medium is the twisted pair as shown in Figure 2.2(a). A twisted pair consists of two copper conductors and each conductor is encased in an insulator made of polyvinyl chloride (PVC). There are about two to twelve twists per foot.

There are two colors interleaved on the outside of each wire. One is the primary color, responsible for a group of five pairs. Each pair in the same group also has a secondary color associated with the primary color. The primary colors are white, red, black, yellow, and violet, and the secondary colors are blue, green, brown, and slate.

The primary reason for twisting the two wires is to reject common mode noise. In other words, if each one of the two wires is connected to the input of a differential amplifier, the common noise on each wire cancels the other out. Consequently, only the difference of the signal is amplified, which is exactly what we want. There are two types of twisted pair in the field: unshielded and shielded. A shielded twisted pair is sometimes used to improve the quality of the line. Most of the telephone lines, however, are using twisted pairs of 24 American wire gauge (AWG), unshielded.

Coaxial Cable

The next transmission medium is the coaxial cable, which is more expensive than the twisted pair. The cross-section of a coaxial cable is shown in

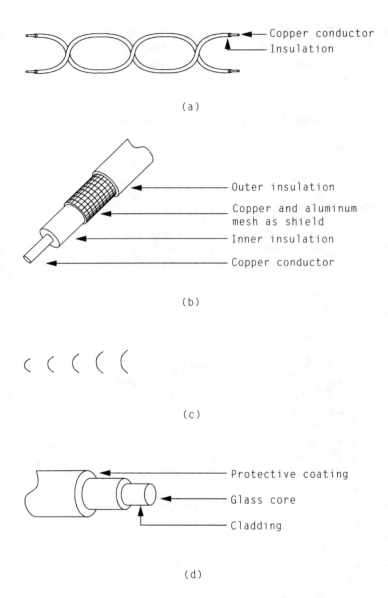

Figure 2.2 Transmission media: (a) twisted pair, (b) coaxial cable, (c) atmosphere, and (d) optical fiber.

Figure 2.2(b). The inside of the coaxial cable is a thick copper wire, close to .1 inch in diameter, surrounded by an inner insulation layer. The next layer of the cable is the mesh made of copper and aluminum metal, which is also the signal ground shield. A good-quality coaxial cable also has an outer insulation layer for protection. One reason for using the coaxial cable is that the noise will not get to the signal line. Coaxial cables are commonly used for long-distance telephone lines, CATV, and LANs.

Atmosphere

Wireless communication means that free space, atmosphere, or vacuum is used as the transmission medium. An electromagnetic wave is the energy propagated through space or media in the form of disturbance due to alternate electric and magnetic fields advancing in space or media. Note that the electromagnetic wave travels in air with a speed almost as fast as light in a vacuum. Radio and TV stations all transmit their signals through atmosphere.

A hertz (Hz) is defined as one cycle per second. The most frequently used electromagnetic wave frequency spectrum is between 300 kilohertz (kHz) and 40 gigahertz (gHz). The term *carrier* means a signal stream transmitted at a constant frequency, and the data signal modifies the carrier first before being transmitted. The composite signal may be voice or video. The trend is that the CATV signals will be digitized, and through satellite transmission a subscriber will be able to select over 100 channels.

With the low end of the frequency spectrum reserved for radio and TV transmissions, the high end (between 1 to 40 gHz) is assigned to microwaves. A communication satellite uses a band between 1 and 10 gHz [1], which has a major impact on computer communications. The most common one is the "C" band at 4 gHz. A satellite transmission between two points on Earth is shown in Figure 2.3. One station transmits microwave signals within a frequency band. The satellite receives the signal at one frequency (called uplink), amplifies the signal, and transmits down at another frequency (called downlink). The other station, several thousand miles away on Earth, receives the signal in that the satellite merely serves as a relay station. In order to provide continuous service, it is necessary for the satellite to rotate with the Earth at the same speed so that it always keeps a stationary position with respect to the two stations on Earth. This particular technique is known as geosynchronization. Two things are worth mentioning. First, the main reason that the uplink and downlink use different frequencies is to avoid interference. In addition, the communication satellite in orbit operates on a number of frequency bands, called transponder channels or just transponders, available for commercial use.

Packet radio hobbyists, cellular phones, and mobile computing networks all use free space to transmit their computer signals. Unfortunately, wireless transmission is deeply affected by the surrounding environment such as noise,

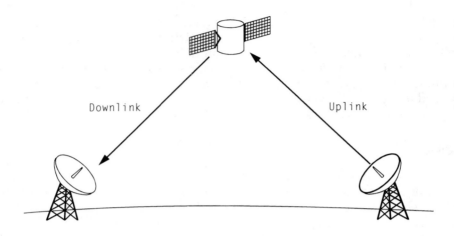

Figure 2.3 Satellite transmission between two points on Earth.

echo, and interference. As a result, wireless technology is characterized by low data rate, high error rate, and spontaneous interruptions. To ensure reliable transmission, it is our challenge to write good software protocols in the network access methods.

Optical Fiber

Fiber-optic technology is the trend of the future and has gained popularity in Europe and the United States as well as the rest of the world. The physical layout of an optical fiber is shown in Figure 2.2(d). The inner core of the cable is made of a solid thin glass or plastic. The diameter of the core ranges from 2 to 100 µm (micron, i.e., 10^{-6}m). A thin fiber is about half the size of a human hair. The next layer is the cladding, which is made of plastic or glass with a different refractive index. If both core and cladding are made of glass, the cladding has a lower refractive index to ensure that the light, while traveling, has a total internal reflection within the core. The diameter of the cladding ranges from 100 to 1,000 mm. The outside of the wire is the protective coating; that is, a sheath made of plastic, PVC, teflon, or steel so the fiber will not break easily. Each fiber wire or line with its cladding is called a strand. A cable may contain a single strand wrapped with a protective coating outside. However, there may be up to 200 strands in a polyethylene conduit filled with gel and encased with a layer of protective coating. Furthermore, many conduits may be bundled into a bigger cable that contains over 1,000 strands as the main trunk of the information superhighway.

A single-mode optical fiber is shown in Figure 2.4(a). There is only one

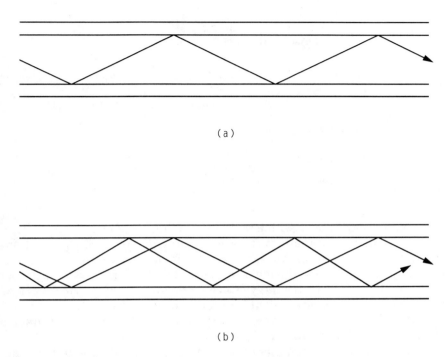

Figure 2.4 (a) Single mode vs. (b) two modes in an optical fiber.

light ray propagating at a fixed angle in the glass. The light ray reflects in the cable many times before it reaches the destination. The light is on or off, representing a 1 or 0. A two-mode optical fiber is shown in Figure 2.4(b). There are two light rays and each of them propagates at a different angle, and usually with a different frequency. The core of a multimode fiber is larger than that of a single-mode fiber.

The light ray can be thought of as an electromagnetic wave at a much higher frequency and the wavelength of the light is computed as

$$\lambda = c / f$$

where λ is the wavelength, c denotes the speed of light in a vacuum (i.e., $3 \cdot 10^{-8}$ m/sec), and f is the frequency of the propagating light ray.

The frequency spectra and wavelengths of different electromagnetic waves are listed in Table 2.1.

The visible light is between red, which has a frequency of $4 \cdot 10^{14}$ Hz and violet, which has a frequency of $7.7 \cdot 10^{14}$ Hz. Beyond the ultraviolet light, we

Table 2.1
Characteristics of Different Waves

Wave Type	Frequency	Wavelength
Broadcast	300 kHz–110 mHz	2.8–1,000m
TV	30–300 mHz	1–10m
Microwave	300 mHz–40 gHz	7,500 μm–1m
Infrared	$2–3.75 \cdot 10^{14}$ Hz	.8–1.5 μm
Red	$4 \cdot 10^{14}$ Hz	.75 μm
Violet	$7.7 \cdot 10^{14}$ Hz	.39 μm
Ultraviolet	$21.4 \cdot 10^{14}$ Hz	.14 μm

have the X and gamma rays, which have even higher frequencies. The light used in the optical fiber is in the infrared range, which is not visible to the human eye. There are two reasons for selecting the frequencies within the infrared range. First, the energy loss during transmission is smaller. Second, it is easy to build the diodes that convert energy from electric to optical, and vice versa. Note that the spectrum frequency of light is different from the frequency of the digital signal, which is actually the envelope of the light. A fiber-optic transmitter and receiver connection is shown in Figure 2.5.

At the transmitting end, there is a light emitting diode (LED) that is made of a semiconductor PN junction. When the voltage is high enough, it excites the diode junction, which then emits a light ray positioned within an angle range. Therefore, the LED is able to convert a digital pulse of electric voltage to a light pulse. The LED can emit a pulse of light at 100 mHz while a laser diode (LD) can emit a light pulse at 11 gHz.

At the receiving end, there may be a photodiode (PD), a PIN diode, or an avalanche photodiode (APD), which converts the light back to an electric pulse of rectangular shape. A PD is a reverse-biased PN junction that has two layers: the P-doped layer and the N-doped layer. A PIN is very similar to a PD except it has an intrinsic layer in the middle that has a high resistivity. When the junction of a PD or a PIN receives the light photon, which represents energy, it becomes excited and generates an electric current that goes through an amplifier. A device that converts the energy from one form to another is called a transducer. It is extremely difficult to design transducers that convert from electrical energy to optical, and vice versa, at a speed over gigabits per second.

A light ray can be emitted from a different angle at a different frequency in an optical fiber, so the total line capacity is greatly increased. Meanwhile, line attenuation is reduced. Per each mode, many channels can be transmitted using time division multiplexing as discussed in Section 2.4. Summing up, multimode fibers can be bundled into a bigger cable.

A special connector (called a splice) is required to connect two optical

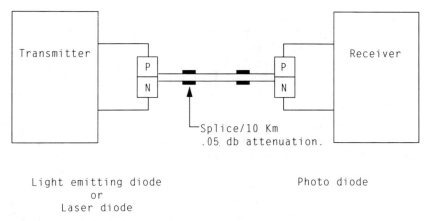

Figure 2.5 Fiber-optic transmitter and receiver.

fibers every 10 km. The two fibers must meet physically with great precision in alignment to ensure a reliable connection without much signal attenuation. In the past, the average loss per mechanical splice was about .1 decibel (dB), or decimal bel. A decibel is used to measure the power ratio of two light rays as defined by

$$\text{Decibel} = 10 \cdot \log_{10} (\text{input power} / \text{output power})$$

A .1-dB power loss means that the output signal power is reduced to only 97.7% of the input signal power. However, recent technology has been developed to pump high current into the fiber to melt the junction of the two fibers, so attenuation is reduced to less than .05 dB. Generally speaking, scientific advances have made it possible to have fiber-optic cables with reasonable cost and superior performance.

If we lay those multistranded fiber cables beside the railroad across the nation, we have the information superhighway for the next century as characterized by the following:

- Low attenuation;
- Low error rate;
- Broad bandwidth;
- Better security.

It is common to have an attenuation of .5 dB/km, which is only one-tenth that of copper wires. A .5-dB/km attenuation means that 89.1% of signal power is retained after transmitting 1 km. New technologies may decrease the number to .1 dB or less. A repeater is a hardware device that strengthens and reshapes the signal. Due to the low attenuation and error rate, the number of repeaters used for optical fibers is about 10% of those used for copper wires. As an example, for twisted pair, a repeater is required every 2 to 10 km; for coaxial cable, every 1 to 10 km; and for optical fiber, every 10 to 100 km. Fewer repeaters also implies lower cost.

The broad bandwidth also implies low distortion and high data rate. Therefore, the total line capacity is increased. A twisted pair can transmit up to 16 Mbps, a coaxial cable up to 500 Mbps, and a fiber-optic cable over 2 Gbps. Line capacity and repeater spacing of twisted pair, coaxial cable, microwave, and optical fiber are compared in Table 2.2. Not only is the data rate higher per channel, but there are more channels per fiber. In addition, more fibers can be bundled into a bigger cable, which further reduces installation cost. We have better security using fibers, and it is almost impossible to eavesdrop.

2.1.2 Digital Waveforms

The term *waveform* also means the shape of a signal pulse. A code is the waveform used to represent a digital signal. To encode a single bit, there are two classes of code: return to zero (RZ) and nonreturn to zero (NRZ).

RZ code means that the voltage level always goes back to 0V. As an example, telephone companies use two types of bipolar code. One alternates 1's while the other alternates 0's. The alternate mark inversion (AMI) code for American Standard Code for Information Interchange (ASCII) "b" is depicted in Figure 2.6(b) with the clock timing shown in Figure 2.6(a). Bit 0 is transmitted first, bit 7 is padded with a 0, and *mark* means 1. A 0 bit is 0V for one full bit time. But the 1 bit alternates either from 0V to a negative voltage for one full bit time or from 0V to a positive voltage for one full bit time, depending on its position. The first 1 goes from 0V to a negative voltage, but the next 1 in the data

Table 2.2
Comparison of Twisted Pair, Coaxial Cable, Microwave, and Optical Fiber

Cable Type	Line Capacity	Repeater Spacing
Twisted pair	16 Mbps	2–20 km
Coaxial cable	500 Mbps	1–10 km
Microwave	100 Mbps	35,000 km
Optical fiber	2 Gbps	10–100 km

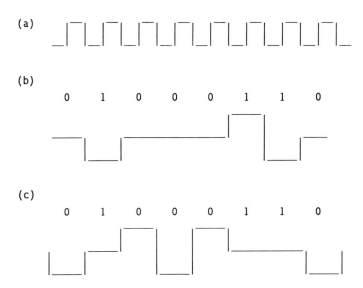

Figure 2.6 Bipolar codes for ASCII b:(a) clock, (b) alternate 1's, and (c) alternate 0's.

signal will switch from 0V to a positive voltage. That is, the 1st, 3rd, 5th, ... 1's go from 0V to a negative voltage, while the 2nd, 4th, 6th, ... 1's go from 0V to a positive voltage. Between two 1's, there may be many 0's.

In ISDN, we alternate the 0's instead as shown in Figure 2.6(c), and the 1 bit is 0V for one full bit time. Bipolar codes are suitable for digital communications, since they are polarity-independent and because they have no direct voltage components to saturate the coil.

NRZ code means that the signal does not return to 0V. There are three popular NRZ codes used in computer design: digital signal, Manchester, and differential Manchester.

Digital Signal

A digital signal uses only two voltage levels. A bit stream is represented by a rectangular waveform. Using positive logic, a 1 has a high voltage and a 0 has a low voltage. There is also a clock signal that controls the timing of all the digital signals. The clock goes up in the middle of the bit and comes down at the end of the bit. In other words, the clock is like a digital signal of alternate 0 and 1 combinations but its frequency is doubled. The waveforms of the clock, the digital signals of alternate 0 and 1 combinations, and a b in ASCII are shown in Figure 2.7.

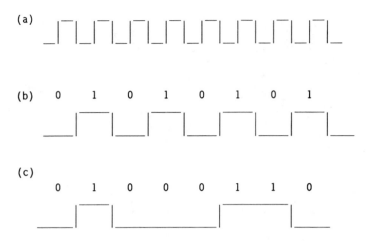

Figure 2.7 Digital signal waveforms: (a) clock, (b) bit string of alternate 0 and 1 combinations, and (c) bit string of ASCII b.

The digital signals are used inside a computer or for short-distance transmission (e.g., between CPU and memory). Telephone companies use the NRZ-inverted (NRZ-I) code between a DTE and a DCE, which is actually the 1's complement of the digital signal. *Inverted* here means complement or negative logic.

Manchester Code

A problem arises when the digital signal is used in a circuit with inductive coupling. If the digital signal contains consecutive 1's or 0's, it acts like a direct current, which would saturate the coil and prevent signals from being induced at the secondary. In order to solve this problem, the Manchester code was first developed in England. Each bit is encoded into a high-low voltage combination. In the middle of a bit, there is always a transition. If the transition goes up, which means a half-bit low followed by a half-bit high, it is 0. If the transition goes down, it is a 1.

Feeding the digital signal and the clock to an exclusive OR gate as inputs, we obtain the Manchester code as depicted in Figure 2.8(a). A bit string of alternate 0 and 1 combinations is shown in Figure 2.8(b), and an ASCII b is shown in Figure 2.8(c). Manchester code is also known as the phase-modulated code and has a frequency in sync with the clock. Note that the clock itself represents a string of 0's, but its inverse or complement represents a string of 1's.

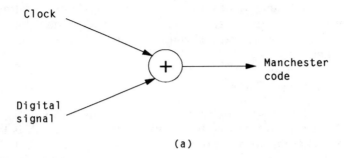

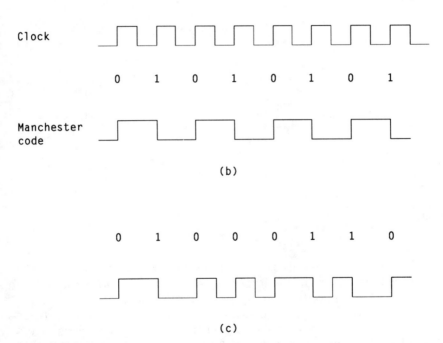

Figure 2.8 Manchester code: (a) exclusive or gate, (b) bit string of alternate 0 and 1, and (c) bit string of ASCII b.

The code is polarity-dependent, and we essentially double its frequency or bandwidth of the signal, so to speak. The Manchester code is used for magnetic recording as well as in Ethernet and some special communication lines [2][Ethernet].

Differential Manchester Code

The differential Manchester code (DMC) is a modified version of Manchester code. Each bit is split into two halves where the second half is the inverse of the first half. There is always a transition in the middle. A bit 0 is represented by a polarity change at the start of the bit time, while a bit 1 is represented by no polarity change at the start of the bit time. Hence, we obtain two sets of waveform to represent a 1 or 0. In other words, the code is polarity-independent.

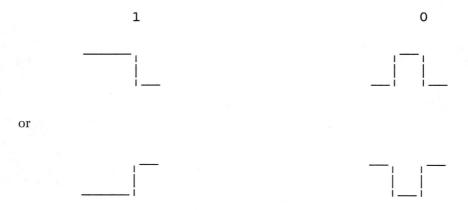

Two different waveforms can used to represent a bit string of alternate 0 and 1 combinations, as shown in Figure 2.9 (a) and the waveforms for ASCII b are shown in (b). A string of 0's is represented by the clock or its inverse.

Looking into the design of DMC, we find out that three time intervals are used to represent a bit. Each time interval can have a high or low voltage, so the total number of combinations is 8 (i.e., 2^3). Four of them are used to represent bits 0 and 1. The other four are called code violations. A code violation does not have a transition in the middle of the bit. Therefore, we have the following definitions.

A violation 1 (V1) code does not have a transition in the middle of the bit, nor does it at the start of the bit. Therefore, it is a straight voltage, high or low. The V1 signal is called the J signal.

A violation 0 (V0) code has a transition at the start of the bit, but no

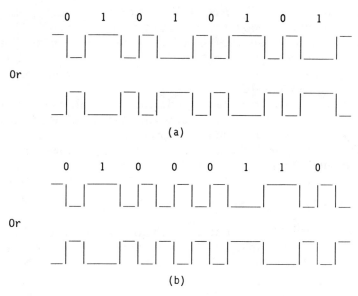

Figure 2.9 Differential Manchester code: (a) bit string of alternate 0 and 1 combinations and (b) bit string of ASCII b.

transition in the middle of the bit. The V0 signal is called the K signal. In the following, we compare the clock signal timing with V1 and V0 code violations.

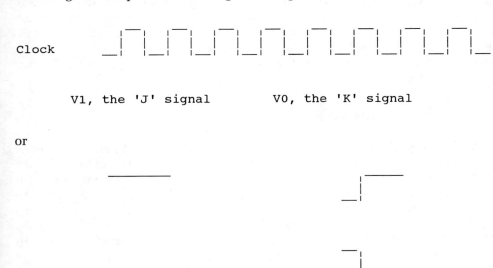

Code violations are actually used in hardware design. They represent some voltage combinations that do not exist in any normal data stream. Therefore, they can be used as frame delimiters. When the synchronous transmission technique is used in a token ring LAN, continuous 1's are transmitted on the line to indicate the quiescent state and a frame delimiter that contains code violations is used to enclose the bit stream [IEEE 802.5].

The digital signal, Manchester code, and DMC all use high-low voltage rectangular waveforms to represent a bit stream. In essence, we change the phase of the clock to obtain the Manchester code. There is no carrier at a higher frequency, and, of course, there is no modulation. All three are classified as baseband transmissions.

2.1.3 Transmission Modes

There are many hardware techniques used in data transmissions. They represent different design concepts that may be used individually or jointly to implement the hardware transmitter or receiver.

Serial Versus Parallel

Serial transmission means that the data stream flows bit by bit in a real-time sequence. For computer-to-computer communications, bits are usually transmitted serially on the line.

If the distance is short, many data lines can be used to transmit data in parallel. A typical design example is the bus between CPU and memory. The number of wires used to transmit data indicates the width of the data bus, which ranges from 8 bits to 64 bits. Another example is the parallel bus between a PC and a printer. Parallel bus obviously increases the speed of transmission. It is possible to design a communication link that transmits data in parallel if cost is of no concern.

Asynchronous Versus Synchronous

Asynchronous character transmission means that the data signal is a series of characters and that each character may start at any time. The quiescent state of the line is usually low voltage, which means 1's. To start transmission, it is necessary to have a start bit that changes voltage from low to high. Because each character is transmitted asynchronously, a time interval is needed to separate two adjacent characters. Therefore, there is always one or two stop bits at the end of each character to restore the line to a quiescent state. Using an oscilloscope, we can display the waveform of a character transmitted at the output pin of a connector. As an example, the waveform of a 7-bit ASCII b or

62 in hex, followed by an even parity bit and one stop bit, is shown in the following:

Note that the start bit is followed by 7-bit data, an even parity bit (which is 1), and one stop bit (which is also 1). Bit 0 (i.e., the lsb) is transmitted first by the universal asynchronous receiver/transmitter (UART) chip.

Synchronous transmission, character or bit, means that there is a continuous data signal flowing on the line in sync with the clock. The data signal contains no start or stop bit. Synchronous character transmission requires that the data signal be preceded by two or more synchronous (SYN) characters and ended by another special character. Synchronous bit transmission, on the other hand, means that the data signal may contain any number of bits and should be enclosed by two Frame flags, one in the front and one in the back. As a simple example, a Frame flag may be eight bits: a 0, followed by 6 1's, and another 0 [SDLC, HDLC]. Using the NRZ-I encoding scheme, the waveform of such a flag is shown below:

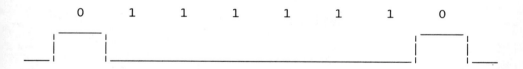

In practice, different encoding schemes may be used and there are many different types of communication controllers: asynchronous, synchronous, or a combination of both.

Simplex, Half-Duplex Versus Full-Duplex

Simplex transmission means that we can only transmit in one direction. It is very much like the one-way street. In our daily life, receiving signals from the radio station or CATV is an example of simplex transmission. The sending station has only one transmitter and the receiving station has only one receiver.

Half-duplex transmission means that either station can transmit but not at the same time. In other words, each side takes turns to transmit and receive. In the old days, our telephone system was set up that way. Nowadays, the CB radio still operates in half-duplex mode. Even though each station has a transmitter and receiver, only one of the two devices can operate at one time.

Full-duplex means that both stations can transmit and receive data at the same time, which is a hardware design feature. If you have two sets of wires, it is not hard to design the transmitter and the receiver. However, if you have only one set of wire, say an unshielded twisted pair (UTP), then each station must use a carrier with a different frequency so the digital signal can be piggybacked on a carrier using a selected modulation technique.

Before we address the transmission techniques, such as modulation and multiplexing, it is important to understand Fourier analysis, which provides the theoretic basis for digital communications.

2.2. FOURIER THEOREM

A sinusoidal wave sf1 is mathematically represented by

$$sf1\ (t) = a1 \cdot \sin(2\pi ft)$$

where t is the instantaneous time, $a1$ is its amplitude, $\cdot$ is the multiply operator, and f is its frequency. The voltage is a sine function of time as shown in Figure 2.10(a).

A cosine function, cf1 is shown as

$$cf1\ (t) = b1 \cdot \cos(2\pi ft)$$
$$= b1 \cdot \sin(2\pi ft + \pi/2)$$

where $b1$ is its amplitude. The cos function has the same waveform but with a leading phase angle of $\pi/2$ as shown in Figure 2.10(b).

Superimposing sf1 and cf1, we obtain a composite sin function that has a different amplitude and a different phase angle as computed below:

$$\begin{aligned}h1\ (t) &= sf1\ (t) + cf1\ (t) \\ &= a1 \cdot \sin(2\pi ft) + b1 \cdot \cos(2\pi ft) \\ &= c1 \cdot ((a1/c1) \cdot \sin(2\pi ft) + (b1/c1) \cdot \cos(2\pi ft)) \\ &= c1 \cdot (\cos \theta1 \cdot \sin(2\pi ft) + \sin \theta1 \cdot \cos(2\pi ft)) \\ &= c1 \cdot \sin(2\pi ft + \theta1)\end{aligned}$$

where

$$c1 = \sqrt{a1^2 + b1^2}$$

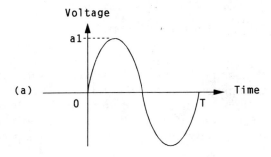

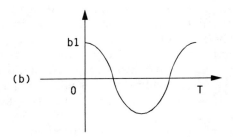

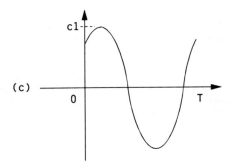

Figure 2.10 Sinusoidal waveforms: (a) sf1 = $a1 \cdot \sin(2\pi ft)$, (b) cf1(t) = $b1 \cdot \cos(2\pi ft)$, and (c) $h1(t) = c1 \cdot \sin(2\pi ft + \theta 1)$.

$$\theta 1 = \arctan\left(\frac{b1}{a1}\right)$$

The function $h1(t)$ is the composite sinusoidal wave; $c1$ is its amplitude; and $\theta 1$ is its phase angle, as depicted in Figure 2.10(c).

All sinusoidal functions, such as sf1 (sin function 1), cf1 (cos function 1), and $h1$ (harmonic 1), can be represented in vector space as shown in Figure 2.11, where the length of the vector is its amplitude and the angle between the vector and the X coordinate is its phase.

Note that the amplitude $a1$ and $b1$ can be negative, but $c1$ is always positive and the phase angle $\theta 1$ can be in any one of the four quadrants.

Writing a program in high-level programming language to compute the phase angle via an arctangent function call, we get either a positive or a negative phase angle. For example, if both $a1$ and $b1$ are negative, we get a positive phase angle via an arctangent function call, which is incorrect. To remedy this discrepancy, we should have a conditional clause in our program to test the value of $a1$. If $a1$ is negative, then we should add π (i.e., 180 degrees) to the phase angle so it is in the right quadrant. However, if we compute the instantaneous voltage point of the $g(t)$ function by superimposing the dc component, sin component, and cos component directly, we get away with this problem.

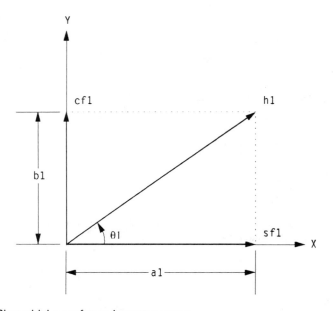

Figure 2.11 Sinusoidal waveforms in vector space.

Fourier Theorem

Any periodic signal g(t) that is a well-defined function of time t can be decomposed into a direct voltage component (dc) and an infinite number of sinusoidal harmonics. The period of this signal is T, which is the inverse of the fundamental frequency (f) of its first harmonic:

$$g(t) = dc + \sum_{n=1}^{\infty} an \sin(2\pi nft) + \sum_{n=1}^{\infty} bn \cos(2\pi nft)$$

$$= dc + \sum_{n=1}^{\infty} cn \sin(2\pi nft + \theta n)$$

where

$f = 1/T$ is the fundamental frequency.
dc is the direct voltage component.
an is the amplitude of the sine component of the nth harmonic.
bn is the amplitude of the cosine component of the nth harmonic.
cn is the amplitude of the nth harmonic and θn is its phase angle.

Integrating g(t) from 0 to T, all an and bn components vanish except the dc, so we obtain the dc term.

Multiplying both sides of g(t) by $\sin(2\pi kft)$ and integrating from 0 to T, we notice that the dc term and all the bn components vanish, as do all the an components except one where $n = k$ as shown below:

$$\int_0^T \sin(2\pi kft) \sin(2\pi nft) \, dt = T/2 \quad \text{for } n = k$$

$$0 \quad \text{for } n \neq k$$

Similarly, multiplying both sides of g(t) by $\cos(2\pi kft)$ and integrating from 0 to T, all components vanish except bk. Therefore, we obtain the generalized equations

$$dc = \frac{1}{T} \int_0^T g(t) \, dt$$

$$an = \frac{2}{T} \int_0^T g(t) \sin(2\pi nft) \, dt$$

$$bn = \frac{2}{T} \int_o^T g(t) \cos(2\pi nft)\, dt$$

$$cn = \sqrt{an^2 + bn^2}$$

$$\theta n = \arctan\left(\frac{bn}{an}\right)$$

Examples of Fourier Analysis

It is interesting to go through the practice with an actual example. Suppose that we have a synchronous communication controller that transmits the ASCII b repeatedly on the line. Therefore, it becomes a periodic signal as shown in Figure 2.12(a). Note that bit 0 is transmitted first and that bit 7 is a padded 0 as it is implemented by most of the controllers.

This periodic signal can be decomposed into a direct voltage component plus an infinite number of sinusoidal harmonics. Since the periodic signal is a rectangular wave, the mathematical derivations are straightforward and left as an exercise. The final results are shown below:

$$dc = \frac{1}{T} \int_o^T g(t)\, dt = \frac{3}{8} = .375$$

$$an = \frac{2}{T} \int_o^T g(t) \sin(2\pi nft)\, dt$$

$$= \frac{2}{T} \left[\int_{T/8}^{2T/8} 1\sin(2\pi nft)\,dt + \int_{5T/8}^{7T/8} 1\sin(2\pi nft)\,dt \right]$$

$$= \frac{2}{T} \left[\frac{-\cos(2\pi nft)}{2\pi nf} \bigg|_{T/8}^{2T/8} - \frac{\cos(2\pi nft)}{2\pi nf} \bigg|_{5T/8}^{7T/8} \right]$$

$$= \frac{1}{\pi n} \left[\cos\left(\frac{\pi n}{4}\right) - \cos\left(\frac{\pi n}{2}\right) + \cos\left(\frac{5\pi n}{4}\right) - \cos\left(\frac{7\pi n}{4}\right) \right]$$

$$bn = \frac{1}{\pi n} \left[\sin\left(\frac{\pi n}{2}\right) - \sin\left(\frac{\pi n}{4}\right) + \sin\left(\frac{7\pi n}{4}\right) - \sin\left(\frac{5\pi n}{4}\right) \right]$$

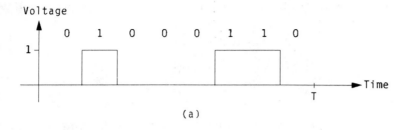

(a)

n	an	bn	cn	θn
dc = 3/8 = .375				
1	-.225079	.093229	.243623	2.74880
2	.159157	-.477465	.503293	-1.24904
3	.075027	-.181128	.196052	-1.17809
4	-.159155	.0	.159155	3.14159
5	.045015	.108680	.117633	1.17811
6	.053049	.159155	.167764	1.24906
7	-.032154	-.013320	.034804	3.53433
8	.0	.0	.0	.0
9	-.025009	.010357	.027069	2.74895
10	.031834	-.095493	.100659	-1.24902

(b)

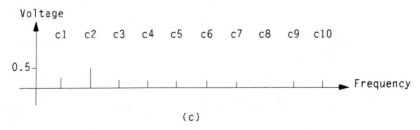

(c)

Figure 2.12 A digital signal and its harmonics: (a) bit string of ASCII b on the line, (b) amplitude and phase angle of the nth harmonic, and (c) amplitudes of the harmonics in the frequency domain.

The amplitude and phase angle of each harmonic are computed as follows,

$$cn = \sqrt{an^2 + bn^2}$$

$$\theta n = \arctan\left(\frac{bn}{an}\right)$$

Writing a computer program in any high-level language to compute the amplitude and phase angle of each of the first 10 harmonics, we obtain the results in Figure 2.12(b).

Note that the first harmonic does not always have the highest amplitude. At the receiving end, if we superimpose the dc component and the infinite number of harmonics, we would get our rectangular wave back in perfect shape. But, reality tells us that at the receiving end, we receive the dc voltage component plus a finite number of harmonics. This finite number is determined by the data rate and the bandwidth of the line. Dividing the period T into 32 divisions, we may write a program to compute all the 32 points by superimposing the dc and the number of harmonics received. The waveforms after receiving 1, 2, 4, and 8 harmonics are shown in Figure 2.13.

In order to gain a better understanding of Fourier analysis, let us examine the same bit string of alternate 1 and 0 but with two different periods. First, we examine two bits at a time and its period T as shown below:

The mathematical part of Fourier analysis is left as an exercise, but the results are shown below.

$$dc = .5$$
$$an = (1 / \pi n) \cdot (1 - \cos(\pi n))$$
$$bn = 0 \quad \text{for } n = 1, 2, 3, 4, \ldots$$

All cos components are 0's. The sin components of even harmonic are also 0's.

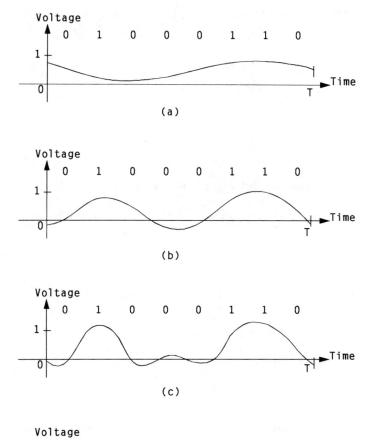

Figure 2.13 Waveforms received: (a) dc + the 1st harmonic, (b) dc + the first two harmonics, (c) dc + the first four harmonics, and (d) dc + the first eight harmonics.

The first harmonic is the major one. After pondering, we agree that the results are truly intuitive. The nonzero amplitudes of the odd sin component are listed below:

dc = 1/2 = .5
$a1$ = .6366
$a3$ = .2122
$a5$ = .1273
$a7$ = .0909
$a9$ = .0707
. . . .

Next, we analyze the same bit string from a different angle. That is, we examine 8 bits instead of 2 bits as the periodic signal. Consequently, the period becomes $4T$ and its fundamental frequency is $1/(4T)$ as shown below:

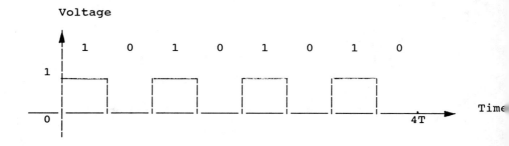

Going over Fourier analysis one more time, we should derive the same algebraic equations as for 2 bits. The mathematical part is omitted as an exercise. Intuitively, the dc component should remain the same, with all cos components 0's. The 1st, 2nd, and 3rd sin harmonics are 0's. In addition, the 5th, 6th, 7th, and 8th sin harmonics are 0's. The 4th harmonic is the major one and has the highest amplitude. All nonzero sin components are listed below:

dc = 1/2 = .5
$a4$ = .6366
$a12$ = .2122
$a20$ = .1273
$a28$ = .0909
. . . .

If 2 bits are used to perform the Fourier analysis, it takes 8 harmonics to construct a pretty good waveform. Now it takes 32 harmonics to obtain the same waveform, provided that 8 bits are treated as the periodic signal. The fundamental frequencies of the two sets of harmonics are different but the algebraic results should be the same.

Conclusions of Fourier Analysis

1. The signal power of the nth harmonic is proportional to its amplitude^2, where ^ denotes an exponential operator.
2. No transmission line can transmit a signal without losing any power. This is called attenuation.
3. The loss of signal power implies harmonic amplitude reduction, namely an, bn, and cn.
4. All harmonics are not equally reduced. This is signal distortion, which causes problems in data transmission.
5. For any transmission line, there is an upper cut-off frequency (fc). Below this frequency, signals are not attenuated much. Above this frequency, signals are strongly attenuated.
6. The bandwidth of a transmission line is the difference between its upper and lower fc. If no capacitive or inductive coupling is used, its lower fc should be 0. Therefore, the upper fc becomes the bandwidth, which in turn determines the maximum data rate of transmission.

A voice-grade telephone line's upper fc is near 3,300 Hz, and its lower fc is near 300 Hz, so its passband is about 3,000 Hz, which is what we call the bandwidth of the line. Suppose we transmit a 2,400 bps digital signal on the line and T is the period to transmit 8 bits. The fundamental frequency of the first harmonic is computed below:

$$2{,}400 \text{ bps} / 8 \text{ bits} = 300 \text{ Hz} = 1 / T$$

The total number of harmonics passed is computed below:

$$3{,}300 \text{ Hz} / 300 \text{ Hz} = 11$$

Harmonics, 12th and above, simply dissipate on the line before they can reach the other end due to the distributed line capacitance. For a modem (modulator/demodulator) to transfer at a much higher rate, we must rely upon modulation techniques to encode more bits per each signal waveform.

2.3 MODULATION TECHNIQUES

Given the bandwidth of a telephone, how to increase the data transfer rate remains a challenge. Can we transmit many carriers at the same time? A carrier is a sinusoidal wave that may be at a much higher frequency than the digital signal. Or, even when we transmit one carrier, can we change the phase and/or the amplitude of the carrier signal to encode bits? To each question, the answer is yes. What we must know is how to piggyback the digital signal on a carrier (i.e., how to modulate a carrier).

There are three basic modulation techniques: amplitude, frequency, and phase. Phase and amplitude modulation techniques can be combined together to modify the carrier. Pulse code modulation (PCM) is different in the sense that an analog signal is digitized into a bit string of 0's and 1's. It doesn't mean that a carrier is modulated by the digital signal at all.

Definition of Baud

The baud rate means the number of signals transmitted per second. A b baud line does not necessarily transmit b bps, because each signal can encode two or more bits. The relationship between baud and bps is shown below:

$$b \text{ baud with } V \text{ signal levels} \rightarrow b \cdot \log2 V \text{ bps}$$

Therefore, b baud with 2 signal levels means exactly b bps while b baud with 16 signal levels means $4 \cdot b$ bps. The basic baud rate is also referred to as the signal bandwidth. In modem design, different modulation techniques are used to encode more bits per signal, so the effective data rate may be 7 or 8 times the signal bandwidth. Some techniques modify amplitude; others modify phase; and some modify both phase and amplitude.

2.3.1 Amplitude Modulation

AM radio stations transmit carriers at different frequencies and the audio signal is used to modify the amplitude of a carrier so it becomes its envelope. Telephone companies also use the amplitude shift key (ASK) modulation technique to transmit digital signals as shown in Figure 2.14(a). When the digital signal is a 1, we have the carrier on the line. If the digital signal is a 0, the carrier just disappears. If we consider light as some sort of electromagnetic wave, we can turn on the light to transmit a 1 and turn off the light to transmit a 0. The envelope of the light ray is the digital signal.

2.3.2 Frequency Modulation

Frequency modulation (FM) can be used to transmit audio signals from radio stations. Depending on the amplitude level of the signal, we change the frequency of the carrier as shown in Figure 2.14(b). FM is also known as frequency

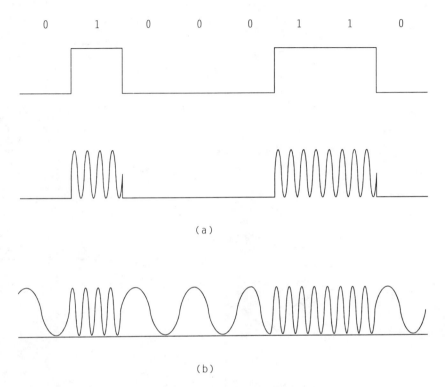

Figure 2.14 (a) Amplitude and (b) frequency modulation techniques.

shift key (FSK). Even though FSK is important in concept, it has been phased out as far as transmitting digital signals is concerned. We use phase modulation instead.

2.3.3 Phase Modulation

Phase modulation techniques are commonly used to design modems. The basic concept is quite intricate, and the carrier is a sinusoidal wave. If we transmit a 1 using one phase of the carrier and transmit a 0 using a different phase of the carrier, we can transmit the digital signal via the phase-modulated carrier as shown in Figure 2.15(a). We essentially piggyback the digital signal on a carrier using the phase shift key (PSK) technique. Phase modulation, a term used by the telephone industry, also means PSK.

Using only two phases, we obtain the mathematical function of the so-called differential phase shift key (DPSK) signal 1 or 0 on the left-hand side and

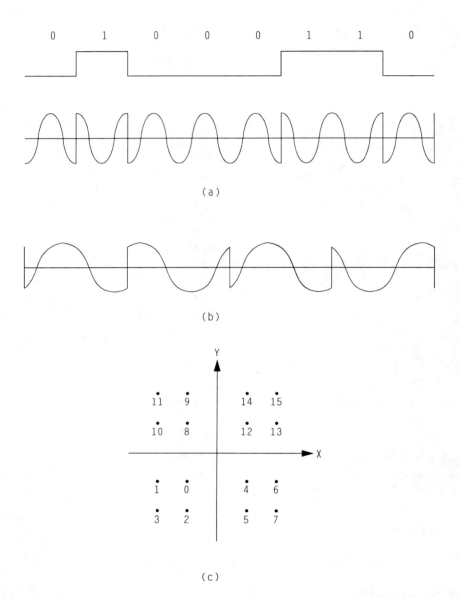

Figure 2.15 Phase modulation techniques: (a) DPSK, (b) QPSK, and (c) 16-signal space diagram.

its vector representation on the right-hand side. Note that the 1 signal has a phase angle of $\pi/2$, instead of 0:

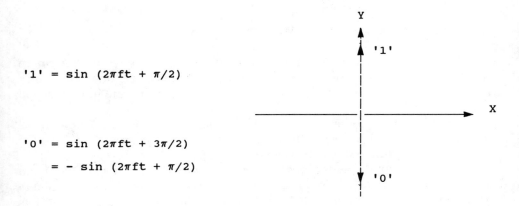

'1' = sin (2πft + $\pi/2$)

'0' = sin (2πft + $3\pi/2$)
    = - sin (2πft + $\pi/2$)

Pushing this concept one step further, we can have four different phases and each signal can encode 2 bits. In the following, we have the mathematical function of each signal on the left and its vector representation on the right. If we only plot the endpoints of the vector, we obtain its signal space diagram:

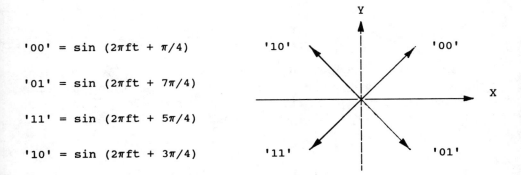

'00' = sin (2πft + $\pi/4$)

'01' = sin (2πft + $7\pi/4$)

'11' = sin (2πft + $5\pi/4$)

'10' = sin (2πft + $3\pi/4$)

Using four different phases, we obtain the quadrature phase shift key (QPSK) signal whose waveform is shown in Figure 2.15(b). If the basic baud rate of the signal is 2,400 Hz on a voice-grade line, using QPSK technique we can transmit data up to 4,800 bps.

2.3.4 Phase Plus Amplitude Modulation

Combining both the phase and amplitude modulation techniques, we have more signal waveforms in encoding. Therefore, the phase plus amplitude modulation (PAM) technique is developed to achieve a much higher bit rate in high-speed modem design.

The 9,600-bps modem uses 16 different signal waveforms. There are 12 different phases, four of which have two different amplitudes. Therefore, the total number of different signal waveforms is 16.

If we only plot the endpoint of each vector, we obtain 16 dots in the signal space diagram as shown in Figure 2.15(c). A decimal number is used to denote a 4-bit binary number, ranging from 0 to 15. Note that each quadrant has 4 dots and the entire space has a total of 16 dots evenly distributed. The intuitive reasoning behind this even distribution concept is to reduce the error rate. Let us examine the signal space diagram carefully. We notice that there are 12 different phases but three different amplitudes. Multiplying 12 by 3, we obtain 36 signal combinations. However, only 16 of the 36 signals are used in the design in order to obtain an even distribution in the signal space.

A modem may support a data rate of 14.4 Kbps. How do they work? If signal synchronization is no problem, we may use 64 different signals, each of which encodes 6 bits, so we obtain a data rate of

$$(2{,}400 \cdot 6) = 14{,}400 \text{ bps}$$

However, the ITU-T actually recommends 128 data signals plus 4 synchronization signals as shown in Figure 2.16 [V.34]. Notice that all dots are evenly distributed in the signal space and that each signal encodes 7 bits. If we transmit 1 sync signal after every 6 data signals, we obtain the 14.4 Kbps effective data rate as computed below:

$$2{,}400 \cdot (6/7) \cdot 7 = 14{,}400 \text{ bps}$$

To push the speed even higher, it is necessary to increase the total number of

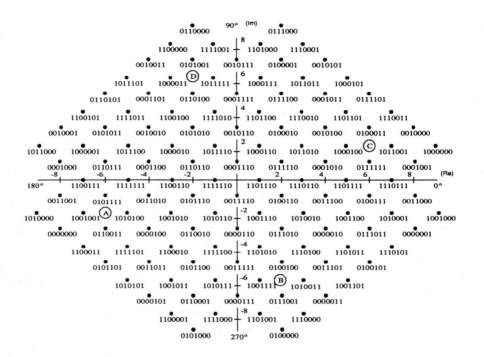

Figure 2.16 Signal space diagram of a 14,400 bps modem, in which each dot encodes a 7-bit integer and A, B, C, and D are synchronization signals. (*Source:* ITU-T recommendation V.34 (September 1994). Reprinted with permission.)

possible signals and/or the basic baud rate. It is possible for a 28.8-Kbps modem to operate at 3,200 baud with each signal encoding 9 bits. Such advanced modems can also handle data compression/decompression.

2.3.5 Pulse Code Modulation

PCM is a technique used to sample an analog signal, audio, or video at fixed time intervals and to convert the amplitude of the analog signal into a digital signal (i.e., bit string). The bit string represents an unsigned integer that may be transmitted later on the line with or without modulation. An analog signal digitized into an 8-bit unsigned integer is shown in Figure 2.17. The amplitude of the signal being sampled at the leftmost instant is 32 in hex, or 0011 0010 in

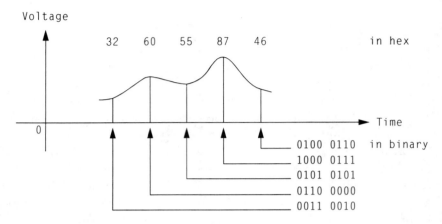

Figure 2.17 Pulse code modulation.

binary. Subsequent amplitudes being sampled are 60, 55, 87, and 46 in hex. The sampling period is usually 125 μs for voice signals.

An analog to digital (A-D) converter box is shown in Figure 2.18(a). The input is the analog signal, and the output provides an 8-bit digital signal representing the amplitude of the input every 125 μs. Using a multiplexer at one end and a demultiplexer at the other end, we can transmit four such bit streams, denoted by S0, S1, S2 and S3, between two endpoints as depicted in Figure 2.18(b). The multiplexer may contain a computer that receives the bit streams and transmits them at a rate at least four times faster than the individual incoming data rate. The demultiplexer at the receiving end is another hardware box that separates and delivers the bit stream to each destination. Through a digital to analog (D-A) converter as shown in Figure 2.18(c), the destination station can reconstruct the analog voice. The accuracy of the restored signal depends on the number of bits representing the amplitude and the fixed time interval of sampling.

Summing up, modulation techniques are used to piggyback a digital signal onto a carrier while multiplexing techniques are used to route different data streams. The two techniques can be used individually or jointly to transmit digital data provided that different bit streams are multiplexed on a line at a much faster rate and that the receiving end can separate the digital signals to different destination lines within a fixed time interval. Various multiplexing techniques for data communications will be discussed in the following sections.

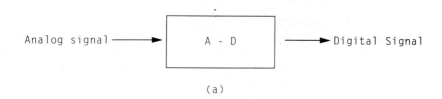

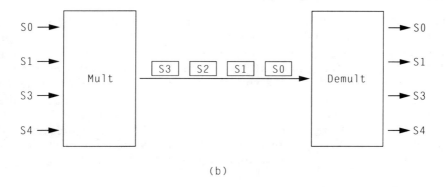

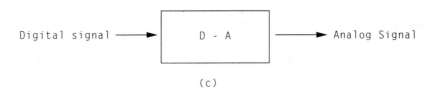

Figure 2.18 (a) A-D converter, (b) multiplexer and demultiplexer, and (c) D-A converter.

2.4 MULTIPLEXING TECHNIQUES

Multiplexing techniques are used to transmit data. At the transmitting end, there is a multiplexer that collects and transmits multiple data streams. At the receiving end, there is a demultiplexer that separates the data streams. Time division multiplexing (TDM) techniques can be used for one transmitter to transmit a single data stream containing multiple channels on the same line during a period of time. In other words, the transmitter sends data from each different channel on the line at different times. Frequency division multiplexing (FDM) techniques, on the other hand, can be used to transmit multiple data streams on the line at the same time using carriers at different frequencies. The purpose is to increase the capacity of the line. A third technique is to share space, namely space division multiplexing (SDM), which uses multiple transmitters to transmit multiple data streams at the same time (with the requirement that each transmitter has its own transmission path).

2.4.1 Time Division Multiplexing

TDM means that we divide time or time share the line. This technique is used in both computer design and digital communications. The time frame is divided into many slots, with each slot representing a channel. This is very much like a slotted ring or shift register, and bits are circulated on the ring accessible to all the processors. Usually, the sending processor is the main CPU and the receiving processor is an I/O processor, or vice versa [CDC 6600]. In digital communications, a sending station can use the time slot to transmit information to the destination station. There are two TDM techniques: synchronous and asynchronous. Intuitively, synchronous TDM ensures that the destination station receives its slot precisely on time, but asynchronous TDM does not.

Synchronous TDM

Each processor has its own assigned time slot in a frame and may receive bits in the slot when its time comes. In other words, the arrival of its time slot is predictable. If there is no information destined for a processor, which means that its slot can not be filled, then it is wasted and no one else can use it. Since the timing of the slot is fixed, it is named synchronous TDM or just TDM. In the telephone industry, most of the circuit-switching systems use TDM.

Asynchronous TDM

Asynchronous TDM, a phrase first coined by W. W. Chu at Bell Lab [3], means that the time slots in a frame are public and that a slot may be used by any processor as long as it is free. Consequently, the arrival of a slot is not predictable to the destination node. How does the destination node find out whether the incoming slot belongs to it or not? First, the slot header must contain an id of the destination node. Second, each station must check the destination id in the slot header when a slot is passing by. One advantage of using asynchronous TDM is that one station can transmit data to another station at a very high speed.

T1 Carrier

In digital communications, the transmission 1 (T1) telephone line uses the synchronous TDM technique to transmit multiple channels. It is called a carrier because the digital signal is transmitted at a constant frequency. A T1 frame is divided into 24 user channel slots, and each slot carries 8 bits data. An extra bit is placed at the end for framing, so the total number of bits is

$$(24 \cdot 8) + 1 = 193$$

All the bits of each channel are not transmitted at the same instant. Instead, the bits of each channel are placed in their own slot via the bipolar encoding scheme. A T1 carrier or line consists of two twisted pairs, one pair for the transmitted data and signal ground and the other pair for the received data and signal ground. Consequently, full-duplex transmission capability is provided. The period of a frame is 125 μs, which implies a sampling rate of 8,000 frames per second. This is based on the fact that a good-grade voice line has a bandwidth of 4,000 Hz, and, according to Nyquist theorem discussed in Section 2.5, it takes at least 2 times of that rate to sample and reconstruct the voice signal. The timing diagram of a T1 carrier is shown below:

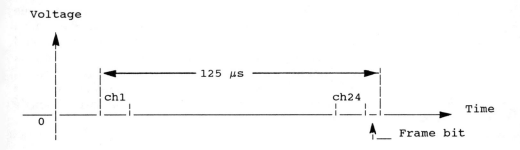

The T1 carrier transmits a 193-bit frame per 125 ms with a data rate of

$$((24 \cdot 8) + 1) \text{ bits} / 125 \text{ μs} = 1.544 \text{ Mbps}$$

The frame (F) bit is the 193rd bit in the frame, used for synchronization. It is interesting to note that the telephone company occasionally borrows the bits in the frame for its own control. Therefore, a technique known as bit robbing or in-band control is used. In other words, the lsbs in some of the user channels are used by the telephone company for control purposes.

T1 is considered as baseband transmission, and each user channel supports a data rate of 64 Kbps as computed below:

$$\frac{8 \text{ bits}}{125 \text{ μs}} = 64 \text{ Kbps}$$

Note that the "k" here is a decimal k, which means 1,000 exactly. T1 carriers are used for long-distance transmission, and repeaters are required to achieve the high bandwidth. A T1 carrier or circuit which can support 24 long-distance phone calls at the same time, may be directly connected to a university or corporate LAN.

T1 has recently been renamed to digital signal 1 (DS1). There are other carriers that can transmit more channels and, therefore, higher data rates. However, the standard used in North America or Japan is different from the one proposed by ITU-T as shown in Table 2.3.

In some of the high-performance carriers, multiple data streams are transmitted at the same time using the FDM technique introduced in Section 2.4.2.

2.4.2 Frequency Division Multiplexing

Do not confuse FDM with FM. FDM means that different transmitters are used to transmit carriers at different frequencies at the same time. The signal, analog or digital, is piggybacked on a carrier using some modulation techniques, and FM is one of them. If two modems operate in full-duplex mode using only one twisted pair as the transmission medium, one side uses one carrier frequency, and the remote side uses a different frequency. Each side can transmit and receive bit streams to and from the other side at the same time. This is full-duplex transmission by hardware definition.

If copper wires are used as the transmission medium, high-speed data are usually modulated. The most popular technique used in modem design is single data stream with phase plus amplitude modulation.

Table 2.3
Data Rates of Different Carriers

Old Name	New Name	(North America Std.)		(ITU-T Recommendation)	
		No. of Channels	Data Rate in Mbps	No. of Channels	Data Rate in Mbps
T1	DS1	24	1.544	30	2.048
—	DS-1C	48	3.152	120	8.448
T2	DS2	96	6.312	480	34.368
T3	DS3	672	44.736	1,920	139.264
T4	DS4	4032	274.176	7,680	565.148

2.4.3 Space Division Multiplexing

SDM means that we divide into space. In a broad sense, a multimode fiber may transmit different light rays, with each ray aimed at a different angle. For short distances, because the emitted angles are different, the light rays may even employ the same frequency. For long distances, if the light rays employ the same frequency, interference may occur toward the end; therefore, each light ray should be emitted at a different angle and with a different frequency. In a narrow sense, SDM is used in both computer design and digital communications. A crossbar switch, which connects M CPUs to N memory modules, is shown in Figure 2.19. Each line represents a memory bus that contains many wires, some of which are used to pass address bits and some to pass data. Any CPU can be connected to any memory module, so long as the memory module is not used by any other CPU. In doing so, the CPU first places address bits on the bus, and certain address bits are used to activate the switch to make a connection provided the memory module is not in use. If the memory module is currently busy, the requesting CPU simply waits until the other CPU releases the memory module.

The old relay-based telephone switching system uses SDM. Each connection requires the establishment of a physical path that is dedicated solely to the transfer of data between two endpoints. Whether the data is digital or analog is irrelevant. In general, SDM means that many transmitters are activated to connect to different lines and that each receiver may receive a data stream from one transmitter.

Because TDM divides into time, it uses only one transmitter to transmit multiple channels, while both FDM and SDM require multiple transmitters.

2.4.4 Baseband Versus Broadband Transmission

Baseband means that the high-low waveform of a digital signal is placed on the line. The entire frequency spectrum of the medium is used to transmit the digital signal. There is no carrier at a higher frequency in a baseband system, and of course there is no modulation. As a result, the design is very simple. Baseband transmission is used in T1 carriers as well as in LANs, such as the Ethernet and token ring.

Broadband means that the frequency spectrum of the medium is divided into channels and that each channel has a different frequency band used to transmit modulated signals. Frequency division multiplexing along with one of the modulation techniques must be used. The voltage response is defined to be the output voltage over the input voltage normalized to 1. A broadband transmission with three channels is shown in Figure 2.20. There are systems that use

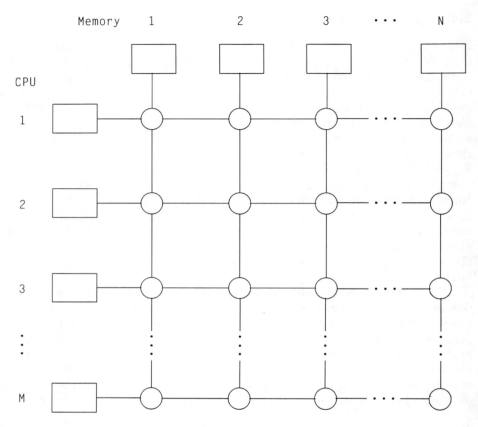

Figure 2.19 Crossbar switch for CPU-to-memory connections.

the broadband transmission technique to support a single channel. In such systems, even though there is only one channel, a carrier at a frequency higher than the data rate is used along with one of the modulation techniques. On the other hand, baseband transmission may also have many channels using TDM. The design of broadband transmission is complicated, but the channel capacity is potentially large. Broadband transmission is used in broadcasting, CATV, and long-distance telephone lines.

In the next decade, more optical fibers will be installed. Even though the light ray is considered to be an electromagnetic wave with a frequency higher than the microwave, a conversion process is required to switch from electric energy to optical energy in its transmitter. The receiver converts from optical energy back to an electric signal. Since the digital signal is a rectangular

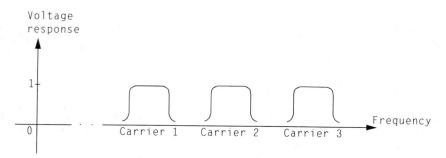

Figure 2.20 Broadband transmission with three channels.

waveform with two voltage levels, a baseband transmission technique is used in the circuit design of both transmitter and receiver.

What is the maximum data rate of transmission on copper wires? Intuitively, the maximum data rate in bps should depend on the noise level of the line as proven by the Nyquist and Shannon theorems.

2.5 NYQUIST THEOREM

Assume that a transmission line has a bandwidth from the lower cut-off frequency 0 Hz to the upper cut-off frequency fc. The Nyquist Theorem states that the minimum sampling rate of data transmission on a noiseless line must not be less than 2 times the bandwidth of the line in order to reconstruct the signal [4]. But if baseband transmission is used with two signal levels, 2 times the bandwidth of the line also becomes the maximum data rate on a noiseless line. Extending this concept one step further, we assume that the rectangular wave signal may have many voltage levels, which means that each signal change may encode more than 1 bit. Thus, we have the following.

Nyquist Theorem

If a noiseless low-pass channel has a bandwidth H with V signal levels, the maximum data rate is computed as

$$C \text{ (channel capacity)} = 2 \cdot H \cdot \log_2 V \text{ bps}$$

If we transmit two-level digital signals on a transmission line with a bandwidth of 3,000 Hz, the maximum data rate is 6,000 bps. If the line is not noiseless, the maximum rate is $k \cdot H$, and k is less than 2 depending on the noise level.

It is interesting to note that on a noiseless line, the number of voltage levels of a rectangular wave signal is denoted by V, which may go up to infinity. Therefore, the theoretical channel capacity of a noiseless line is infinite according to the Nyquist theorem.

Special Case With Two Signal Levels

Intuitively, if the cut-off frequency of the line is 1 Hz, using two signal levels we can transmit up to 2 bps on a noiseless line. However, if we treat 8-bit data as the periodic signal, it would take at least four harmonics to reconstruct the rectangular wave back to shape as computed below:

$$H / (2H / 8) = 4$$

2.6 SHANNON THEOREM

The Shannon Theorem computes the maximum data rate transmitted on a line with noise taken into consideration.

Definitions

$$\text{Signal to noise ratio} = \frac{\text{signal power}}{\text{noise power}} = \frac{S}{N}$$

$$= 10 \log_{10} (S/N) \text{ dB}$$

Shannon Theorem

If a channel has a bandwidth H and a signal-to-noise ratio S/N, we have

$$C \text{ (channel capacity)} = H \cdot \log_2 (1 + S/N) \text{ bps}$$

An actual telephone has a lower fc (300 Hz) and upper fc (3,300 Hz). Therefore, the bandwidth H of the line is 3,000 Hz as computed below:

$$\begin{aligned}\text{Bandwidth of the line} &= \text{upper } fc - \text{lower } fc \\ &= 3{,}300 - 300 \\ &= 3{,}000 \text{ Hz}\end{aligned}$$

For a 30-dB line or $S/N = 1{,}000$ with a bandwidth equal to 3,000 Hz, the channel capacity is

$$C = 3{,}000 \cdot \log_2(1 + 1{,}000) \text{ bps}$$
$$\approx 30{,}000 \text{ bps}$$

The above equation was derived mathematically by Shannon [5]. Note that the base of the logarithm is 2. If the noise power N equals the signal power S, the maximum channel capacity C becomes H, which is really the upper bound. If the noise level N is infinite, C becomes 0, and that means absolutely no transmission. On the other hand, if N is 0, the channel capacity becomes infinite, which is consistent with the Nyquist theorem.

Next, we discuss the three major switching methods used in computer networks. Each method uses a different hardware design supported by specially written software.

2.7 SWITCHING METHODS

Switching methods are used to transmit data from one station to another station. A station may be a computer or any other digital system, such as a memory, a digital switch, or a radar station. From a hardware point of view, switching methods are ways to route data regardless of the transmission medium. Different encoding schemes may be used with or without using a multiplexing technique. The main concern is software. Three major switching methods are used in computer communications: circuit switching, packet switching, and cell switching.

2.7.1 Circuit Switching

Circuit switching implies that there is a connection between two stations. There may be an active element (say, a transistor) in the circuit. A computer may be involved to establish the circuit. But once the circuit is established, the computer is out of the picture and the data streams are transmitted from one station to another station just as they are on copper wires. There are digital switches classified as DCEs using the circuit-switching concept [EQUINOX]. From the software viewpoint, the info bits flowing on the line do not contain any address. Therefore, synchronous TDM is classified as circuit switching in that the end user receives only info bits. On the other hand, packet switching routes packets in the network so each packet always contains a destination address.

2.7.2 Packet Switching

In theory, a transmitter can send a message with no limit in size between two stations. If the message block is too large without synchronization bits, the hardware controller cannot transmit/receive it correctly. Therefore, even when large message blocks are transmitted from a missile to a ground station during a real-time launch, the data block is still broken into smaller frames and each frame is embedded with synchronization bits to ensure that the frames are transmitted and received properly. The sender generally transmits data continuously during the entire mission and the receiver receives whatever is available on the line.

In a computer network, a large message is also broken into smaller pieces (i.e., packets). A packet has its own header and may contain an info field of variable size. The data link software adds its own header and trailer to the packet to make it a frame, which is transmitted on the line. Packet switching requires that each packet header contain an address, which is a reference number to identify the ownership of this packet. Network system software ensures that packets are transmitted and received correctly.

2.7.3 Cell Switching

If the packet size is fixed and short, it is called a cell. A cell of 53 bytes is commonly used in the fast switching device known as asynchronous transfer mode (ATM). In general, cell switching is slightly different from packet switching in that a cell has a fixed boundary. Since each cell still travels on the same line, which is physically shared by other users, cell switching is a variant of packet switching.

Cell switching has some unique features. First, it employs the asynchronous TDM technique. That is, a time slot may be occupied by any user as long as it is free. Secondly, if a synchronous TDM system also uses the same size slot, then both synchronous and asynchronous TDM techniques can be combined. As an example, the double queue double bus LAN uses circuit slots as well as cell slots. A circuit slot is private and reserved for a particular user. If the particular user can not use his or her own time slot, then the slot is left idle and no one else can use it. On the contrary, if a cell slot is public and free, it can be used by any user based on priority or first come, first serve.

To implement a packet- or cell-switching network, the necessary network system software must be written to support the switching function. That is, the bottom three layers need to work as a team to transmit and receive packets or cells between any two computers in the network. Using the bottom-up approach, we first discuss the design of the physical layer software, then the data link layer, and the network layer. Before exploring the I/O driver design, let us discuss the character set used for information interchange, communication controllers, PH layer primitives, and the data structure associated with each controller.

2.8 PHYSICAL LAYER DESIGN

In a modern computer, a byte contains 8 bits (known as an octet). Bit 0 is the least significant bit (LSB) and bit 7 is the most significant bit (MSB), or the sign bit. The ITU-T and IEEE specs use 1's indexing in that the LSB is b1 and b8 becomes the MSB. Furthermore, because b1, the LSB, is transmitted first by most controllers, it is sometimes placed on the left as shown below:

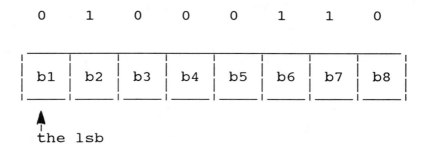

The layout may look different, but the semantics remain the same. Also note that IBM mainframes designate bit 0 as the sign bit or MSB. An octet can be transmitted from one station to another. If the octet contains a 7-bit ASCII, then the sign bit is padded with a 0. The above octet contains the special bit pattern, 0100 0110, which represents an unsigned integer 62 in hex or an ASCII b with a preceding 0.

2.8.1 Standard Character Set

In order for one computer to exchange information externally with another computer in a network, the International Alphabet set No. 5 (IA5) is proposed [T.50]. Each character is an ordered set of 7 bits identical to ASCII. The specifications of IA5 code are shown in Figure 2.21. The bit pattern of each code is specified in a two-dimensional matrix. The upper three bits—b6 b5 b4—constitute a hexadecimal number ranging from 0 to 7, which is the column number and the lower 4 bits—b3 b2 b1 b0—constitute a hex number ranging from 0 to F, which is the row number. The entire set of IA5 is placed in a 16 by 8 matrix with 128 combinations. To obtain the 7-bit code of a particular character in the matrix, locate the symbol first and concatenate its 3-bit column number with its 4-bit row number. For example, looking for b in the matrix, its column number is 6 and its row number is 2, so the code is 62 in hex.

Code 00 to 1F are mainly designed for control purposes as explained in Table 2.4.

The rest of the codes are self explanatory. (Note that SP stands for space and that DEL means delete.)

2.8.2 Communication Controllers

Two types of communication controllers are employed to transmit data serially on the line. The first type is the universal asynchronous receiver/transmitter

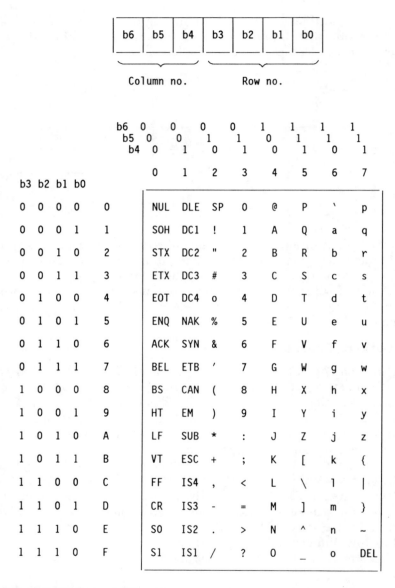

Figure 2.21 Specifications of IA5 code.

Table 2.4
IA5 Code for Control

Code 00 - 0F	Code 10 - 1F
NUL (null)	DLE (data link escape)
SOH (start of header)	DC1 (device control 1)
STX (start of text)	DC2 (device control 2)
ETX (end of text)	DC3 (device control 3)
EOT (end of transmission)	DC4 (device control 4)
ENQ (enquire)	NAK (negative acknowledgment)
ACK (acknowledgment)	SYN (synchronization)
BEL (Bell)	ETB (end of block)
BS (back space)	CAN (cancel)
HT (horizontal tabulation)	EM (end of medium)
LF (line feed)	SUB (substitute)
VT (vertical tabulation)	ESC (escape)
FF (form feed)	IS4 (information separator 4)
CR (carriage return)	IS3 (information separator 3)
SO (shift out)	IS2 (information separator 2)
SI (shift in)	IS1 (information separator 1)

(UART) chip, which is used in PCs to transmit or receive one byte at a time using the asynchronous character transmission technique. In that regard, the UART chip is considered a byte I/O device. The second type is the universal synchronous receiver/transmitter (USRT) chip, which can transmit a block of bytes at one time using the synchronous bit transmission technique [INTEL 8273]. Hence, the USRT chip is a block I/O device. Either type of controller can interrupt the CPU after I/O completion. There are other chips that can do both.

Each UART or USRT chip is used to provide a serial port for digital communications. A modem can be connected to the serial port so that digital data can be transmitted on the telephone line. Between the chip and the physical connector there are buffer gates to provide enough power to drive the modem.

UART CHIP

The characteristics of an UART chip are listed below.

- Asynchronous character transmission.
- User may set control registers and specify:
  - Parity bit—Even, Odd, 1, 0, or None;
  - Code length—5, 6, 7, 8 bits;

- Bit rate—300 bps to 28,800 bps;
- Stop bit—1, 1.5, 2 bits.
- Interrupts and status are provided.

If the receive data register of the UART chip is full, which indicates that an input character has arrived from the line, the controller signals interrupt to the CPU. It should also be mentioned that the UART chip also signals interrupt when its transmit data register is empty, which means it is ready to receive another byte to be transmitted on the line. If the controller operates at 9,600 bps, it takes close to 1.1 ms to transmit an asynchronous character of 11 bits.

USRT Chip

Because the USRT controller can transmit a block of bytes, the PH layer software becomes quite simple and merely contains several lines of code to set the hardware registers in the chip. If we consider the physical I/O drivers as part of the DL layer software, then the DL software becomes the bottom layer in the protocol stack [SNAb]. That is, the USRT controller is a physical I/O device driven by the DL software. But, nonetheless, the physical interface of the controller needs to be specified. Some of the terms, however will not be discussed until the next chapter. As an introduction, the characteristics of a USRT chip are listed below:

- Synchronous bit transmission;
- Data rate up to 64,000 bps;
- Automatic frame check sequence (FCS) generation/detection;
- Compatible with both synchronous data link control (SDLC) and high-level data link control (HDLC) protocols;
- Automatic bit stuffing/stripping;
- Interrupts and status provided.

The USRT chip can be used with a DMA chip to transmit a block of bytes in one system call. Generally speaking, it takes a long time to physically transmit the block, but the main CPU can simultaneously perform other computations.

2.8.3 Physical Layer Primitives

The PH layer mainly receives requests from its service user, which is the DL layer [X.211]. The two data primitives are shown in Figure 2.22. Note that at the PH layer level, no connection or disconnection is necessary. The PH_DATA.request primitive is an output driver call to transmit a frame as follows:

PH_DATA.request(ph_id, ph_sdu, status);

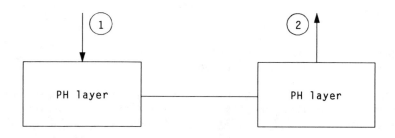

① PH_DATA.request (ph_id, ph_sdu, status);

② PH_DATA.indication (ph_id, ph_sdu, status);

Figure 2.22 Two physical layer data primitives.

where ph_id is used to fetch the unit control block (UCB) of the PH layer, ph_sdu contains the frame, and status indicates what happens after the call. Recall that a layer primitive represents, in an abstract way, the logical exchange of information between the target layer and its service user. The primitive neither specifies nor constrains the implementation of such entities or interfaces.

A PH_DATA.indication is issued by the PH layer to inform its DL layer that a frame has arrived as shown below:

PH_DATA.indication(ph_id, ph_sdu, status);

where ph_id indicates where the frame is from, ph_sdu contains the received frame, and the status flag indicates transmission status. What if the PH layer is a collection of routines instead of an independent task? In that case, the DL layer must issue an input driver call to receive the PH_DATA.indication message from its PH layer and let OS perform the rendezvous.

Other Physical Layer Primitives

The PH layer also handles many control functions. The reset request has the following form:

PH_RESET.request(ph_id, status);

which asks the PH software routine to reset the state of the hardware controller. This call may be issued by the DL layer or the NMT routines. A command entered by the console operator can also have this request initiated. There are other request primitives to change the line settings and so forth.

If the PH link could be popped off the network electronically or manually, we should support two more primitives to deactivate or activate a PH link as follows:

    PH_DEACTIVATE.request(ph_id, status);
    PH_ACTIVATE.request(ph_id, status);

The PH_DEACTIVATE routine sets the special hardware register in the controller to physically disconnect the physical link, including any power supplied to the line, while the PH_ACTIVATE routine connects the physical link back online. Such primitives are used by token ring LANs or ISDNs.

Among all the PH layer primitives, the data primitives are the most important in concept. They are nothing but I/O drivers written as system routines. From the software viewpoint, the I/O drivers merely transmit bits from one station to the other and do not interpret the bits. Therefore, there is no need to have PH layer PDUs. Each physical driver, however, has its own database known as the unit control block (UCB), which contains the characteristics of the I/O device.

2.8.4 Unit Control Block

In a computer system, an I/O unit or device is represented by a UCB, which is a piece of memory containing information pertaining to the I/O device. When a task is running, it has a task control block (TCB) associated with it. There is a pointer in TCB that is the address of a UCB to indicate that this physical I/O device has been allocated to the task. The I/O driver uses the information in the UCB to set the hardware registers in the communication controller. The UCB is global in the system and mainly contains information about the physical I/O device as listed below:

- Characteristics of the I/O device (e.g., a UART chip);
- I/O addresses of the hardware register;
- Pointer to the input request queue;
- Pointer to the output request queue.

The entry of an I/O request queue, called a request queue element (RQE), is private to the service user. The RQE at the head of the request queue contains information about the current I/O operation, such as the following:

- A pointer to the TCB of the issuing task;
- A pointer to the first character of I/O buffer;
- A pointer to the current character position in the I/O buffer;
- A pointer to the next RQE in the I/O request queue.

The I/O request queue is necessary as long as the I/O device supports multiple I/O requests. An RQE is needed to implement the block I/O operations as well as the CTRL-C command, which terminates the application program quickly if there is one. The pointer relationships among the TCB, UCB, RQE, and I/O buffer are depicted in Figure 2.23. From one control block, the addresses of other control blocks can be fetched.

The UART chips are employed in most PCs. Each chip has a UCB associated with it. Each USRT chip as used in a mainframe also needs a UCB to store the device-level information and is usually chained to the DL control block, as discussed in Chapter 3.

2.8.5 Physical Layer Software Design

There are two physical I/O drivers, one to transmit a frame on the line and the other to receive a frame from the line. There may be many different physical links in a system. Some transmit a bit, others transmit a byte, and some even transmit

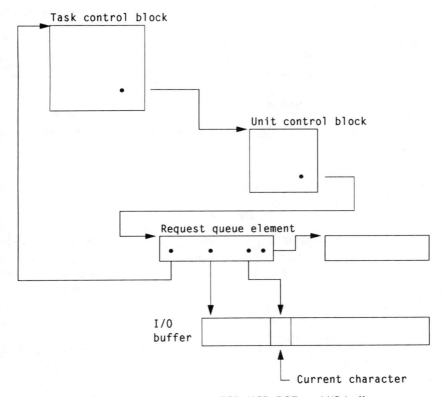

Figure 2.23 Pointer relationships among the TCB, UCB, RQE, and I/O buffer.

a block of bytes. If UART chips are used in a PC, it is desirable to design software drivers that can make a byte I/O device look like a block I/O device so as to support multitasking.

In such a design, the driver must interact with the I/O interrupt service routine (ISR) in order to transmit or receive a block of bytes without the intervention of the DL layer. Suppose that a 132-byte data block is transmitted from one computer to another via the UART chip. The I/O device has a physical record size of one byte, but to the service user the logical record size is 132 bytes. Since the blocking factor is defined to be the ratio of the physical record size and the logical record size, we obtain

$$\text{Blocking factor} = \text{physical record size} / \text{logical record size} = 1 / 132$$

which is a fraction. This is quite in contrast to disk or tape operations whose blocking factors are greater than 1. We can call this reverse blocking, for the blocking factor is less than 1. In other words, for 1 logical write operation, there are 132 physical write operations, and each write must handle its own interrupt completion.

The physical I/O driver calls Sendframe and Receiveframe are issued by the DL layer task. One side of the two computers must issue a Sendframe and the other side must issue a Receiveframe to be in sync.

Software Design of Sendframe

The send frame output driver should be implemented as a system call or subroutine as follows:

    Sendframe(ph_id, ph_sdu, status);
    {In most of the specifications, this
    driver call is also known as:
    PH_DATA.request(ph_id, ph__sdu, status); }

where ph_id is the physical link id, a local reference number through which its associated UCB can be fetched; ph_sdu contains the frame; and status indicates what happened after the call. One important thing is that control is not returned to the next instructions from the call until the entire frame is transmitted. In the UCB, there are I/O addresses that are used by the driver to set the hardware registers in the UART chip. The I/O addresses are either memory addresses or I/O port addresses, depending on the chip design. If memory-mapped I/O is used (i.e., each register in the controller is treated as a memory word), a regular *move* instruction in assembly language can be used to set the hardware register that has an absolute memory address assigned.

The ph_sdu, physical layer service data unit, is the frame to be transmitted.

Whatever bits set in the buffer by the DL layer will be transmitted on the line. Inside the ph_sdu, there is a Count field from which the length of the frame can be derived.

The design of a UART I/O driver is intricate because the chip can only transmit one byte at a time. The transmit ISR examines the output buffer assigned to the controller. If the entire frame has not been transmitted yet, it fetches the next byte in the output buffer, places the byte in the transmit data register, and tells the UART chip to transmit. If the entire frame has been transmitted, the transmitter ISR marks the TCB of the DL layer task as ready so that the task can proceed again. The software design of the Sendframe driver is shown below.

> Sendframe:
> Set up RQE that contains pointers to the TCB of the issuing task and the output buffer;
> Enable transmitter interrupt;
> {Moving data is left to the
> transmitter interrupt service routine.
> }
> Mark the TCB of the issuing task as in wait state;
> Save environment of the issuing task;
> Pass control to dispatcher;
>
> Transmit_ISR:
> Write the current character from the output buffer into the transmit data register in the UART chip;
> IF the entire frame has been transmitted,
> THEN dequeue the RQE;
> Post event by marking the TCB of the issuing task as ready;
> Save environment for the other task being interrupted;
> Pass control to dispatcher;
> ELSE Increment the current pointer to output buffer;
> Exit from interrupt;   {The task being interrupted resumes
> execution.}
> ENDIF;

Software Design of Receiveframe

A receive frame input driver call is issued by the DL layer on the receiving node as shown below.

> Receiveframe(ph_id, ph_sdu, status);
> {This driver call is same as:
> Rec_PH_DATA.indication(ph_id, ph_sdu,
> status);
> }

where ph_id is the physical link id, from which its associated UCB can be fetched; ph_sdu contains the frame; and status reports what happened during transmission. In concept, this routine waits for a Ph_DATA.indication from its PH layer. Control is not returned to the issuing task until the entire frame in ph_sdu has been received. In the receive ISR design, it simply moves the byte from the receive data register in the UART chip into the current position of input buffer. When the input buffer is full, the receive ISR marks the TCB of the data link layer task as ready, which then becomes dispatchable again. The software design of Receiveframe is described in the following.

Receiveframe:
Set up RQE that contains pointers to the TCB of the issuing task and the input buffer;
Enable receiver interrupt;
Mark the TCB of the issuing task as in wait state;
Save environment of the issuing task;
Pass control to dispatcher;

Receive_ISR:
Read character from the receive data register in the UART chip into the current position of input buffer;
IF the entire frame has been received,
THEN dequeue the RQE;
Post event by marking the TCB of the issuing task as ready;
Save environment for the other task being interrupted;
Pass control to dispatcher;
ELSE Increment the current pointer to input buffer;
Exit from interrupt;
ENDIF;

We have illustrated that software can be written to interact between an I/O driver and ISR, and using such a approach we can implement a block I/O request primitive on a byte I/O device in a multitasking environment. Note that the I/O drivers and ISRs are noninterruptible and that identical code sections could be combined into one piece shared by different routines. Goto's may be used in order to make the code compact.

2.9 PHYSICAL INTERFACES

The connector layout and each signal line between a DTE and a DCE should be specified. Two standards, RS-232 and X.21, are discussed in detail.

2.9.1 RS-232 Specifications

If connectors are used to connect a DTE and a DCE, all wires in the cable should be parallel. It is even possible to plug a DTE connector directly into a DCE connector and get rid of the cable in the middle. To describe the function of each signal, we must establish a reference point, which is the DTE. The transmitted data (TxD) signal is transmitted from a DTE to a DCE and the received data (RxD) is from DCE to DTE.

The RS-232-C connector interface was first proposed by the Electronic Industries Association (EIA) in 1969. RS stands for Recommended Standard, 232 is the number, and C is the version. RS-232-C is by far the most popular physical interface used in industry. Both UART and USRT communication controller chips provide an RS-232-C interface. The RS-232-C connector was never pushed by any committee. On the contrary, many committees have tried to push other standards, such as RS-422, IEEE 488, and X.21, to beat the RS-232-C, but none of them seems to have prevailed. RS-232-C is surely the non-standard standard in the computer industry. Some of its characteristics are listed below:

- A 25-pin connector and 15 pins are used. DTE uses the male pin while DCE uses female.
- Interfaced with either an asynchronous or a synchronous controller.
- Full-duplex.
- A 1 means < −3 volts (e.g., −12V).
- A 0 means > +3 volts (e.g., +12V).
- Data rate less than 20 Kbps, but with exceptions.
- Distance less than 15m or possibly longer.

The physical layout, top view of an RS-232-C male connector is shown in Figure 2.24(a). Note that the scale is 1:1.5 and that the real connector is only two-thirds of the drawing size. The outside dimension of the connector is 5.25 cm by 1.2 cm, which is slightly less than 2 in by .5 in. On the top row, the leftmost pin number is 1 and the rightmost pin is 13. On the bottom row, the leftmost pin is 14 and the rightmost pin is 25. Because the shape looks like a letter D with 25 pins, the connector is called a DB-25 connector. There are also other variations of RS-232-C. Some differ in shape, and others differ in pin numbers. The 9-pin, DB-9 connectors are used by PCs.

The signals of an RS-232-C viewed by the DTE are described in Figure 2.24(b). Each signal line is associated with a mnemonic, such as AB, BA, BB, and CA, sorted in alphabetical order, which merely provides another set of ids. Based on pin numbers in sorted order, signal lines are described below:

Pin 1: Chassis Ground (Chassis Gnd), or the protective ground, is connected to the hardware chassis of DTE.
    2: Transmitted Data (TxD) is the transmitted data signal line of DTE.
    3: Received Data (RxD) is the received data of DTE, which should be connected to the TxD of DCE.

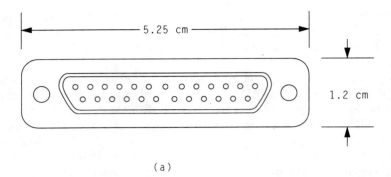

(a)

Pin	Function	Destination	Description
1	Chassis gnd (AA)	DCE	Chassis ground attached to the DTE hardware frame
7	Signal gnd (AB)	DCE	Common signal ground
2	TxD (BA)	DCE	Transmitted data
3	RxD (BB)	DTE	Received data
4	RTS (CA)	DCE	Request to send
5	CTS (CB)	DTE	Clear to send as a positive response to RTS
6	DSR (CC)	DTE	Data set ready or DCE ready (data set is a Bell Lab term for modem)
20	DTR (CD)	DCE	DTE ready
22	RI (CE)	DTE	Ring signal received indicator status line
8	CD (CF)	DTE	Carrier detect status line
21	Signal quality (CG)	DTE	Error signal received status line
23	Data signal rate selector (CH)	DCE	Asserted to select the higher rate of two data rates
24	TxClock (DA)	DCE	Transmitter clock, i.e. signal element timing used by DTE
15	TxClock (DB)	DTE	Transmitter clock, i.e. signal element timing proposed by DCE
17	RxClock (DD)	DTE	Receiver clock, i.e. signal element timing used by DCE

(b)

Figure 2.24 RS-232-C connector: (a) physical layout of a male connector and (b) pin assignments viewed by DTE.

4: Request to Send (RTS) is a level signal, activated high to inform DCE that DTE wants to send.
5: Clear to Send (CTS) is a level signal, activated high by DCE, that informs DTE to go ahead and send.
6: Data Set Ready (DSR) is the same as DCE Ready. Note that Data Set is a Bell Lab term for modem.
7: Signal Ground (Signal Gnd) is the common signal ground used by both DTE and DCE. There are two ground signals altogether, but the signal ground is the one used in the interchange circuit.
8: Carrier Detection (CD) is a level signal from DCE to DTE to indicate that the carrier has arrived.
15: Transmitter Clock (TxClock) is the other clock sent by DCE to DTE so that DTE may use it to shift the data out of its transmitter if it doesn't have its own clock.
17: Receiver Clock (RxClock) is used by DCE but sent to DTE for reference.
20: Data Terminal Ready (DTR) is a level signal, activated high to indicate that DTE is in ready state.
21: Signal Quality is a level signal from DCE to DTE to indicate that an error has been detected.
22: Ring Indicator (RI) is the ring signal received status line from DCE to DTE.
23: Data Signal Rate Selector, when activated high, tells DCE to use the higher data rate of the two possible rates. Therefore, it is possible for two modems, one at each side, to operate in full-duplex mode.
24: Transmitter Clock (TxClock) is the clock used by DTE but sent to DCE for reference.

RS-232-D is a revised version of C with many features added, but it is upward compatible [RS-232]. It has renamed some of the signals (e.g., DCE Ready for Data Set Ready and Shield for the Protective Ground). In addition, a secondary channel is added that needs 8 more signals for data, control and test, as shown in Table 2.5.

The RS-232-D connector is mainly designed to compete for narrowband ISDN applications.

2.9.2 Null Modem Cable

Suppose that we have two PCs situated at two different locations. Either computer is considered to be a DTE. If two modems are used to connect the two PCs via a telephone line, the two computers can communicate with each other. What if they are sitting in one room? No modems are necessary provided that we can develop a cable to simulate the protocols between a DTE and a DCE. Such a cable is referred to as a null modem cable.

Table 2.5
Added Features of an RS-232-D Connector

Pin Number	Purpose
Pin 12	Secondary CD (SCD) is the Carrier Detect signal on the secondary channel
13	Secondary CTS (SCTS) is the Clear to Send signal on the secondary channel
14	Secondary TxD (STxD) is the Transmitted Data signal on the secondary channel
16	Secondary RxD (SRxD) is the Received Data signal on the secondary channel.
18	Local Loopback signal tells the DCE to loop back
19	Secondary RTS (SRTS) is the Request to Send signal on the secondary channel
21	Remote Loopback signal tells the remote DCE to loop back
25	Test Mode signal informs DTE that DCE is in test mode

There are many ways to construct the null modem cable but the simplest way is to use as few as three wires between the two PCs, as shown in Figure 2.25. The wiring should be symmetrical. The Transmitted Data (TxD) of one DTE is tied to the Received Data (RxD) of the other DTE, and vice versa. The Signal Ground is the common ground between two DTEs. The Data Terminal Ready (DTR) on either side is tied to its Data Set Ready (DSR), Ring Indicator (RI), and Carrier Detection (CD). The Request To Send (RTS) is routed back to its Clear To Send (CTS). The Transmitter Clock (TxClock) for output is routed back to the Transmitter Clock (TxClock) for input and the Receiver Clock (RxClock).

2.9.3 X.21 Specifications

According to ITU-T recommendations, X.21 defines the physical level interface between a DTE and a DCE for synchronous operation on a public data network, which may be a circuit-switching network, a packet-switching network, or an ISDN [X.21]. Even though X.25 covers the bottom three layer protocols between a DTE and a DCE in a packet-switching network, its PH layer interface is the same as X.21 [X.25].

The characteristics of the X.21 protocol are listed below:

- Uses a 15-pin connector and 9 pins;
- Synchronous bit transmission;
- Full-duplex;
- Low voltage on the control line means off and high voltage means on.

The X.21 signals are mainly designed to facilitate telephone communications, as shown in Figure 2.26. The Transmit (T) signal means transmitted data and the Receive (R) signal means received data. There are two data lines. The Control (C) and Indication (I) signals are used to indicate the control condition

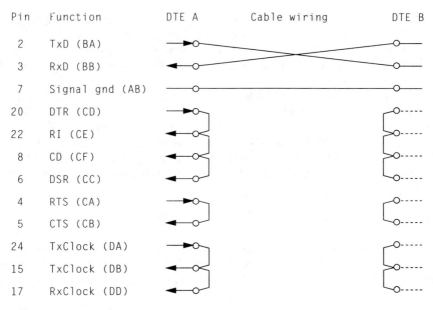

Figure 2.25 Null modem cable.

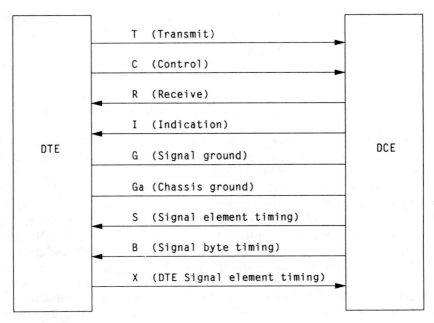

Figure 2.26 X.21 signals.

of DTE and DCE, respectively. The control lines are activated high just like RS-232-C [V.28]. The combination of T and C determines the state of DTE while R and I determine the state of the DCE. Ground (G) is the common signal ground used by both DTE and DCE. Chassis Ground (Ga) is the protective ground of the DTE hardware frame.

Signal element timing (S) (the Transmit Clock at the bit level) and signal byte timing (B) (the Transmit Clock at the byte level) are supplied by DCE. The DTE signal element timing (X) is the Transmit Clock used by DTE.

In an X.25 network, packets are exchanged between two end DTEs, and each DTE communicates with its own DCE. An X.21 protocol example is given in the following to illustrate what happens to a telephone call from beginning to end.

X.21 Protocol Example

There are three basic states of DTE and DCE: ready, controlled not ready, and uncontrolled not ready. The control line is off for all three states. Off means its voltage level is low, less than -3V. On means its voltage level is high, greater than +3V. The bit definition table [V.28] is shown below.

< -3 volts	1	mark	off	stop	condition Z
> +3 volts	0	space	on	start	condition A

A <-3V means a 1, mark, off, stop, or condition Z, while a >+3V means a 0, space, on, start, or condition A.

Ready state requires that the data line signal 1; uncontrolled not ready requires that the data line signal 0; and controlled not ready requires that the data line signal a bit string of alternate 0 and 1 combinations. The DTE and DCE at either site must be in ready state before attempting a telephone call. Controlled not ready means that the device is operational but temporarily unable to render service. Uncontrolled not ready state is due to an abnormal operating condition, such as a call collision. Since telephone calls are real-time events, a call collision means that while a call request is in progress, an incoming call arrives at the same time. The DCE cancels the incoming call by sending a signal to the remote DCE, which in turn changes its state to uncontrolled not ready in order to disconnect.

It is interesting to go through a call example. The quiescent state means that both DTE and DCE are ready; namely, t and r signal 1, while c and i are off. A single lowercase letter is used to denote the signal name, which conforms with the official specifications. On t or r, digital data signals are transmitted in synchronous mode using the NRZ-I code.

First we discuss the calling site and then the called site. The protocol at the calling site is shown in Figure 2.27(a). When a person picks up a phone, the DTE at the calling site changes c from off to on to enter the call request state. DTE and DCE trade bits on t and r to establish a data link connection. If successful, the person hears a line free tone and starts dialing. Then, DTE sends the Call Request signal to DCE. The dialing address is transmitted on t as a bit string. Now, both DTE and DCE are waiting. Then, the calling DTE receives a call progress signal on r, indicating ringing, line busy, or call clear. After the receiving party picks up the phone, the calling DCE receives the Call Accepted signal from the network, sends it to DTE, and changes i from off to on to enter the data transfer state.

Now, both parties can transmit data in full-duplex mode. At the end of the conversation, the calling person hangs up the phone. The calling DTE sends to DCE a Clear Call signal, which is transmitted to the other end. DTE and DCE then trade bits to disconnect the DL connection between them. DTE at the calling side changes c from on to off and the DCE does the same to i to go back to the quiescent state.

The protocol at the called site is shown in Figure 2.27(b). After receiving an incoming call (i.e., Call Arrived signal), the remote DCE changes its Indication (i) signal from off to on, trades bits with its DTE to establish a DL connection, and sends the Incoming Call signal to its DTE. The phone starts ringing; the receiving party picks up the phone. The remote DTE at the called site transmits a bit string on t, which is the Call Accepted signal. Meanwhile, the remote DTE changes its Control (c) signal from off to on and enters the data transfer state.

At the end of conversation, after the caller hangs up the phone, the remote DCE at the called site receives a Clear Call signal and sends it to its DTE. Then, the DCE changes its control signal from On to Off and the DTE does likewise to disconnect the line. Of course, the party being called may also hang up the phone to disconnect. We will understand that the phone connection in a packet-switching network is done by the bottom three layers as we proceed.

2.10 SUMMARY POINTS

1. A physical link consists of a hardware communication controller connected to a transmission medium. The physical layer specifications include mechanical, electrical, functional, and procedural specifications.
2. The transmission media include twisted pair, coaxial cable, free space, and optical fiber.
3. The three popular rectangular waveforms are digital signal, Manchester code, and DMC.

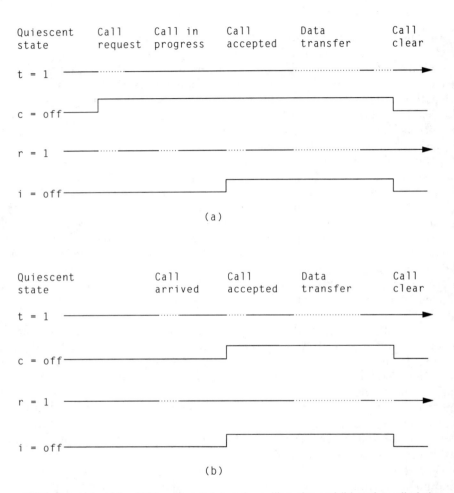

Figure 2.27 Example of the X.21 protocol: (a) at the calling site and (b) at the called site.

4. There are many transmission modes: serial versus parallel, asynchronous versus synchronous, simplex, and half-duplex versus full-duplex.
5. According to Fourier Analysis, any periodic signal that is a well-defined function of time can be decomposed into a dc component and an infinite number of sinusoidal harmonics. No transmission line can transmit a signal without attenuation or distortion. Loss of signal power implies harmonic amplitude reduction. All harmonics are not equally reduced, which means signal distortion. For any transmission line, there is a cut-off frequency (fc). Below this frequency, signals are not attenuated much. Above this frequency, signals are strongly attenuated. The cut-off frequency determines

the bandwidth of the line, which in turn determines the maximum data rate of transmission.
6. There are three popular modulation techniques: amplitude, frequency, and phase. PCM really means that an analog signal is digitized into a bit string.
7. In data communications, the TDM, FDM, and SDM techniques are used to route data or increase line capacity.
8. Baseband transmission means that a digital waveform is placed on the line without going through any modulation technique. Broadband transmission means that many carriers of different frequencies are used to transmit signals. In other words, FDM in conjunction with modulation techniques must be used.
9. If the line is noiseless, the channel capacity should be infinite according to both the Nyquist and Shannon theorems.
10. Communication controllers are designed for asynchronous character transmission, synchronous bit transmission, or both.
11. There are two types of TDM: synchronous versus asynchronous. The two techniques can also be combined.
12. The major switching methods are circuit switching, packet switching, and cell switching. A cell is a 53-byte packet used in ATM.
13. Each physical link is associated with a UCB, which is used by the physical I/O drivers. The UCB contains the private information of the physical link.
14. The RS-232-C connector interface is very popular in computer communications for both asynchronous and synchronous controllers, and RS-232-D is a revision of version C, but upwardly compatible.
15. X.21 defines the physical level interface between a DTE and a DCE for synchronous operations on a public data network.

Problems

Problem 2.1

What are the three popular digital waveforms used in computer design?

Problem 2.2

Plot the Manchester code of a bit string of 0 and 1 combinations.

Problem 2.3

Plot the DMC of a bit string of 1's.

Problem 2.4

Plot the Violation 1 and Violation 0 signals in (DMC).

Problem 2.5

Describe the difference between asynchronous and synchronous transmission.

Problem 2.6

According to Fourier analysis, what does signal distortion mean?

It is recommended that problems 2.7, 2.8, 2.9, and 2.10 be tackled by a project team of up to three students.

Problem 2.7

Derive the mathematical expression of the amplitude of the sin component of the nth harmonic in Fourier analysis.

Hint: Multiply the $g(t)$ function by $\sin(2\pi k f t)$ where k is a positive integer. Then, integrate the product from 0 to T. All terms will vanish except one term, $\sin(2\pi n f t)$ where n equals k, so you obtain the particular coefficient a_k. By generalizing the idea, derive the coefficient a_n.

Problem 2.8

Assume that the synchronous transmitter transmits the ASCII b repeatedly on the line. The LSB in an octet, b_0 is transmitted first, and the period is T. The waveform can be found in Figure 2.7(c).

1. Perform the Fourier analysis and derive the coefficients of the sin and cos components. List the amplitudes of the first 10 harmonics.
2. Plot the waveform after receiving 1, 2, 4, 8, and 10 harmonics by the hardware receiver.

If you have an IBM PC, consider using the Quick Basic programming language to solve this problem. Use the PSET function to plot the curve and the LINE function to plot the coordinates.

Problem 2.9

Repeat the above for a simple bit waveform of 10. The bit 1 is transmitted first and the period is T.

Problem 2.10

Repeat the above for a bit pattern of 10101010. The leftmost bit 1 is transmitted first and the period is $4T$. Note that the fundamental frequency is $1/4T$.

   Intuitively, the harmonics are different, but the algebraic equations derived should be the same as in problem 9. What is the major harmonic in this example and what is its frequency?

Problem 2.11

What are the three modulation techniques used in data communications?

Problem 2.12

Describe the pulse code modulation technique.

Problem 2.13

A good stereo amplifier has a passband between 20 Hz and 20,000 Hz, the lower and upper 3-dB cut-off frequencies. At these frequencies, the power response drops to approximately 50% of the normal output. Plot the response curve. To be precise, what is the exact power response at the 3-dB frequencies? Run Quick Basic on your PC. After seeing the OK prompt, type the following:

   print 10^−.3

and you should get .5011872 as the result.

Problem 2.14

What are the three multiplexing techniques?

Problem 2.15

Describe the difference between baseband and broadband transmissions.

Problem 2.16

What are the major switching methods used in computer networks?

Problem 2.17

What is the Nyquist theorem?

Problem 2.18

What is the Shannon theorem?

Problem 2.19

If you have a UART chip in your PC, design a driver to send a frame on the line that is fully interrupt driven so that software polling should not be used. Coding is optional.

Problem 2.20

Using the same interrupt technique, design a driver to receive a frame.

Problem 2.21

What are the signals used in the X.21 protocol?

Two projects are proposed in the following. Form a team of up to three students, select your own leader, and call meetings to discuss design issues.

Problem 2.22

The first project is to study the Transmitted Data (TxD) signal of the com1 RS-232 port on a PC. Try to understand what asynchronous character transmission is in the PH layer. If you happen to have the Procomm program [PROCOMM], boot PC and run Procomm.exe to emulate the PC as a virtual terminal (VT) 100 terminal. While Procomm is running, parameters may be set. The bottom line on the screen displays the status, as indicated below:

> 'ALT-F10 HELP' means pressing the ALT key and F10 key at the same time, you will see the main menu. Then, press ALT-P to see line settings and ESC to exit.
> 'VT-100' means virtual terminal 100 as set by the service user.
> 'FDX' denotes full-duplex transmission, which is also selected by the user.
> '9600 E71' denotes 9,600 bps, even parity, 7 data bits, and 1 stop bit set by the user.
> 'LOG CLOSED' means no log files are kept and 'PRT OFF' means that the printer is off.
> 'CR' means the input <cr> is translated as a <cr> not followed by a <lf>. The second 'CR' means the output <cr> is translated as a single <cr>.

Actually, you may even write your own routine to read a character from the keyboard and write it on the com1 port. Use an oscilloscope to display the waveforms of asynchronous character transmission. By holding down the b key, the PC will transmit the ASCII b continuously over its RS-232-C port. On the oscilloscope, push the Main Time Base and Auto Sweep buttons and focus the sweep line. Use the position knob to adjust the position of the sweep. Set the amplitude scale to 10V and the time scale to .1 µs.

Note that the quiescent voltage of the line is about −12V. Monitor the voltage between the Transmitted Data (TxD) and Signal Ground (Signal Gnd) on pin 2 and 7.

ASCII b means 1100010 in binary or 62 in hex, and bit 0 is transmitted first as shown below.

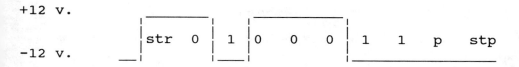

Plot the waveforms for a, b, and c. Note that the even parity bit changes in c. Next, pressing the trig button on the oscilloscope and changing the time scale to 10 μs, find out the time interval between two successive b's transmitted by the system. The answer should be around 90 μs depending on different system software. The reason for this delay is because the OS needs time to process the keyboard interrupt and set data to com1 port.

Problem 2.23

The second project is to perform a local loopback test on a PC without using an oscilloscope. Write a simple I/O driver for com1 port at the byte level in any programming language. Study the Hardware Reference Manual and locate the com1 port on the back of the machine. Find an RS-232-C, DB-9, or 25 female connector and solder wires on the back as shown below:

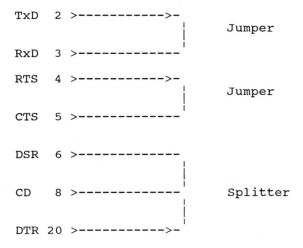

Press the female connector into the com1 port on the back of your PC and run your program to perform a local loopback test on DTE alone. Read a character from the keyboard, output it to com1 port, input the same character from com1 port, and display it on the screen. Have fun.

References

[1] Sharma, R., "A Satellite Network Design Parameters and Trade-Off Analysis," *Telecommunications*, June 1987.
[2] Hsu, J.Y., "A Driver-Receiver Design for Data Communication," *Proc. of the International Computer Symposium*, Taiwan, 1973, pp. 821–832.
[3] Chu, W. W., "A Study of Asynchronous Time Division Multiplexing for Time-Sharing Computer Communications," *Proc. AFIPS*, 35, 1969, pp. 669–678.
[4] Nyquist, H., "Certain Factors Affecting Telegraph Speed," *Bell System Tech. Journal*, Vol. 3, April 1924, pp. 324–346.
[5] Shannon, C. E., "A Mathematical Theory of Communication," *Bell System Tech. Journal*, Vol. 27, July 1948, pp. 399–423.

Data Link Layer 3

*To err is human;
to correct, Selective-Reject . . .*

A data link (DL) is the logical link on top of a physical link [1]. A DL consists of a physical link and the software associated with it [SDLC]. Recall that a physical link is a com port connected to a transmission medium. Sometimes, the DL or link layer implies the software, which includes the physical I/O drivers, either to transmit bits to or receive bits from the line.

Two nodes are connected via a point-to-point connection, as shown in Figure 3.1(a). When one node or station transmits, the other node receives. One of the two stations must be a computer and the other may be a computer or terminal.

If a computer is connected to many other nodes on the same wire, we have a multidrop connection as shown in Figure 3.1(b). Suppose that node A can transmit data to nodes B, C, and D and that node A is called the primary station, which is a computer. Node A may have only one physical link that supports three data links. In other words, a physical link may be shared by many data links, and each data link has its own private data base. On a multidrop line, when one node transmits, every other node on the line receives the frame at the same time. Therefore, an address field is needed in the frame to identify the receiving node. This address may be 1 byte long, or 48 bits long as assigned by some manufacturers as their unique node address in a LAN.

3.1 BASIC DESIGN CONCEPTS

A data link is reliable while a physical link may not be. The basic transmission unit between two DLs is called a frame. A frame may be a DL command or data. The DL layer at the receiving end checks the frame that contains an

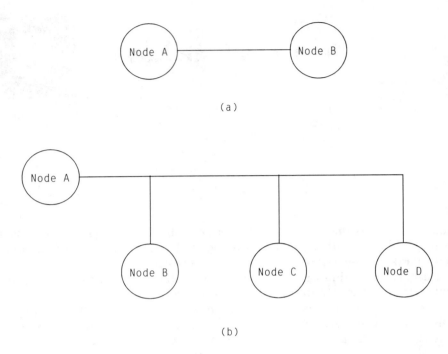

Figure 3.1 Computer connections: (a) point-to-point and (b) multidrop.

error-detecting code. After detecting an error in the frame, the receiver informs the sender to retransmit. In the case where the frame is critical, any errors detected should be corrected as soon as possible. This facilitates debugging, because it is easier to locate the bug in either hardware or software immediately after the error occurs. If we let an error go uncorrected, the same error will ripple through many intermediate nodes to the destination node, which then requests retransmission after generating so much overhead. Thus, it is wise to correct an error sooner than later.

The DL layer is a crucial component in the NAMs if reliable transmission is of concern. Some computers employ hardware communication controllers that can transmit a large block of bits synchronously on the line [INTEL 8273]. In such a system, the PH layer routines are quite simple and merely set the hardware registers in the controller. As a result, the DL layer becomes the bottom layer in the protocol stack.

A frame has a header, followed by optional information and a trailer. To transmit frames between two data links, a good protocol is required to ensure reliable transmission. A good DL protocol should support the following:

1. In the frame, there should be an error-detecting code. The receiver

checks the frame and sends a positive acknowledgment (+ack) if the frame is good; otherwise, a negative acknowledgment (−ack) is sent. Note that −ack is a generic notation because different protocols may use other mnemonics, such as NAK (negative ack) and REJ (reject).
2. The sender should keep a timer. If an ack, + or −, gets lost on the line, the sender times out and retransmits the previous frame. Better yet, the sender should poll the receiver to find out why and take remedial action.
3. If the sender retransmits a data frame, how does the receiver know that this data frame is a duplicate? To cover this, each data frame should contain a sequence number or frame id, and all frames must be transmitted in order.

3.2 ERROR-DETECTING CODES

Even though the error rate of physical links is low, there are cases where errors occur (e.g., wireless transmission has bits flip quite often due to noise or lightening). An error-detecting code is placed in the frame so that the receiver can detect any errors during transmission. A good error-detecting code should catch as many errors as possible. The error-detecting code may be generated by the communication controller or by the DL software, depending on the design. Upper layer protocols can also check the validity of data. For example, in banking applications there are many ways to cross check the financial data.

Error-detecting code is NOT error-correcting code. We rarely use error-correcting code in computer networks. For other applications, Hamming code may be used to detect and correct a single bit error [2]. In such a design, after receiving the frame, the receiver not only detects the single bit error, but also identifies the bit position and corrects the error. This is called forward error correction. In computer networks, when an error is detected, the receiver simply notifies the sender to retransmit. This technique is known as backward error correction or automatic repeat request (ARQ).

3.2.1 Vertical Redundancy Check

The simplest error-detecting code is to add a parity bit on the side of each character being transmitted. A parity bit may be even or odd. An even parity bit means that the total number of 1's in the data, including the parity bit, is an even number, while an odd parity indicates that the total number of 1's is an odd number. When we line up all the transmitted data by characters in a single column, we notice that the parity bits are aligned vertically on one side. Therefore, the parity bit is also called the vertical redundancy check (VRC). The UART controller chip can be programmed to generate an even, odd, or no parity. In some cases, the VRC may also be generated by software. We simply exclusive OR (EOR) all the bits in a character to obtain the even parity bit. EOR means logical sum or modulo-2 sum in that EOR any two bits, the result bit is 1 only if the two bits differ. Therefore, EOR, also means modulo-2 difference as shown below:

```
EOR = Logical sum = Modulo-2 sum = Modulo-2 difference
```

3.2.2 Longitudinal Redundancy Check

At the end of data transmission, the sender may transmit a checksum byte, which is the logical sum of all the bytes in the data block. This particular byte appended at the end of the data block is called the longitudinal redundancy check (LRC), where check really means the checksum code. The size of the data block is usually 128 bytes or 256 bytes long. LRC may be used in conjunction with VRC during data transmissions.

For example, three ASCII characters, a, b, and c, are transmitted using even-parity VRC and LRC as shown in Figure 3.2. The spacing in the code is for clarification. Assume that both the VRC and LRC are used to detect errors during transmission. At the receiving end, EOR all the bits in a character latitudinally including the VRC bit and the result should be a perfect zero if even parity is used with no error. Longitudinally, EOR all the characters including the LRC character and the result should also be zero.

Even though the even-parity VRC and LRC are similar, we have the following two theorems:

Theorem 1:

When even-parity VRC and LRC are used, there is always a consistent lower left corner bit that guards both VRC and LRC correctly.

Proof:

If the entire data block consists of an even number of 1's, then VRC must contain an even number of 1's. LRC must also contain an even number of 1's. Therefore, the lower left corner bit is a 0.

If the entire data block consists of an odd number of 1's, then VRC must contain an odd number of 1's. LRC must also contain an odd number of 1's. Therefore, the lower left corner bit is a 1. The theorem is proved.

Theorem 2:

When odd-parity VRC and LRC are used, we have the two cases stated below:

1. There is always a consistent lower left corner bit that guards both VRC

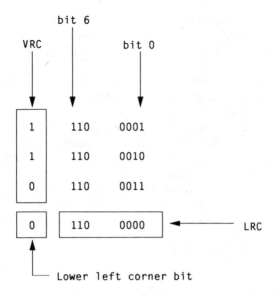

Figure 3.2 Even-parity VRC and LRC.

and LRC correctly only if the number of bits in a character and the number of characters are both even or odd.

2. There is no lower left corner bit that guards both VRC and LRC correctly if the number of bits in a character is even but the number of characters is odd, and vice versa.

The proof is left as an exercise.

Let us try a simple example by transmitting some characters using odd-parity VRC and LRC. Each character contains 4 bits, which is an even number, and the total number of characters transmitted is 3, which is an odd number. The corner bit cannot guard the VRC and the LRC at the same time, as shown in the following:

$$
\begin{array}{cc}
1 & 0011 \\
1 & 0110 \\
1 & 1100 \\
? & 0110
\end{array}
$$

The even-parity scheme has an edge over the odd-parity scheme. However, in practice, the communication controller generates the VRC bit by hardware. The controller at the receiving end strips this parity bit and the programmer does not even see it. If odd-parity LRC is used, the lower left corner bit is the VRC for the character. The generation of LRC is usually done by software that could use even parity, odd parity, or an arithmetic checksum. An arithmetic checksum means that all the characters in the data block are added arithmetically mod 128.

When even-parity VRC and LRC are used, we can even correct a single bit error. That is, if a single bit flips, the VRC detects the row number and the LRC detects the column number. The intersection of the row number and the column number indicates where the error is. But the truth is: whenever error occurs, we don't know how many bits have been flipped. Therefore, in computer networks, the receiver routine does not correct errors. Instead, the receiver informs the sender to retransmit the erroneous frame.

When VRC and LRC are used, if any 4 bits in a rectangular pattern are flipped at the same time, it will not be detected. To improve the efficiency, different codes are developed as follows.

3.2.3 Cyclic Redundancy Check

The cyclic redundancy check (CRC) is considered as a more advanced error-detecting code [3]. First, we define a simple function as

$$G(x) = x^4 + x + 1$$

where $G(x)$ is the generator polynomial of degree 4 and ^ is the exponential operator. When x equals 2, we obtain a positional notation with the value of an unsigned integer as shown below.

This 5-bit polynomial code divisor has its high-order and low-order bits as 1's.

Next, we define logical divide as a series of EOR operations between a dividend and a divisor. Logical divide differs from arithmetic divide in two points. First, modulo-2 difference instead of arithmetic difference is performed during divide. Secondly, during each step, if the leading bit of the remaining dividend is a 1, then the EOR operation is performed; otherwise the remaining dividend is shifted to the left or the end of operation is reached. Note that when

EOR is performed, the leading bits of the remaining dividend may have a value smaller than the divisor.

We attempt to generate the 4-bit CRC for 1 byte of ASCII b, which has a sign bit padded with a 0. If the CRC is computed by software, we can further assume that the sign bit is transmitted first. This assumption is reasonable so long as the bit stream is available in memory and both sides understand the rules. We first append 4-bit 0's to the message so the dividend has 12 bits, then logically divide the polynomial code into the dividend as shown below.

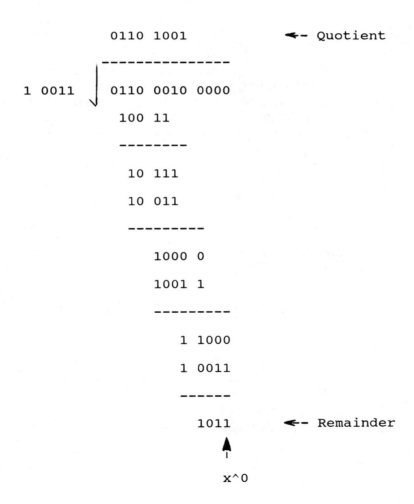

The remainder, 1011, is the 4-bit standard CRC algebraically represented by $(x^3 + x + 1)$. The message transmitted is the original message plus the CRC as shown below.

0110 0010 1011

At the receiving end, the entire message including the CRC should be logically divisible by the same polynomial code if no error has occurred during transmission. In practice, a polynomial of degree 16 or 32 is usually used. The CRC algorithm is generalized in the following.

CRC Generation Algorithm

1. Select a polynomial code $G(x)$ of degree
2. Append r 0's to the original message block of k bits so that we obtain a bit string of $(k + r)$ bits. We call these r 0's the residual remainder.
3. Logically divide the $(r + 1)$ bit string of $G(x)$ into the $(k + r)$ bit string and we obtain a remainder of r bits with possible leading 0's.
4. Append the remainder to the original message and we obtain a $(k + r)$ bit message to be sent.

The well-known ITU-T polynomial

$$G(x) = x^{16} + x^{12} + x^5 + 1$$

is of degree 16 representing a 17-bit divisor as shown below.

$$1\ 0001\ 0000\ 0010\ 0001$$
$$\uparrow$$
$$x^0$$

Interestingly enough, the polynomial code is not a prime whose value is

$$2^{16} + 2^{12} + 2^5 + 1 = 65{,}536 + 4{,}096 + 32 + 1 = 69{,}675$$

which is divisible by 5.

If b is transmitted using the ITU-T polynomial, the logical divide operation is shown below

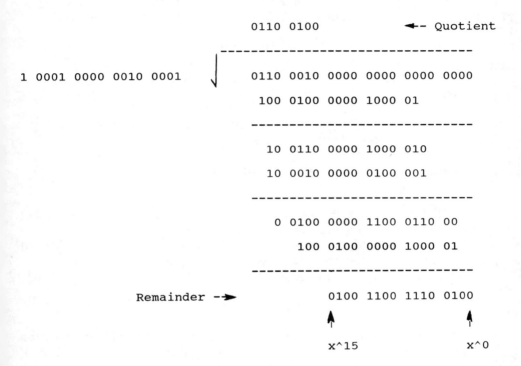

The entire message is transmitted as

0110 0010 0100 1100 1110 0100

or 624ce4 in hex, which is the 8-bit b followed by a 16-bit CRC. Note that x^0, the LSB of CRC, is transmitted last and that the 16-bit CRC may be represented algebraically by

$$x^{14} + x^{11} + x^{10} + x^7 + x^6 + x^5 + x^2$$

where x equals 2, so each term denotes a 1 in CRC. The last bit is a 0, which is the coefficient of the x^0 term. At the receiving end, if the same bit string is received without error, then after the same divide operation we should obtain the residual remainder as a 16-bit 0. The quotient is immaterial in the design and is not even generated by either sender or receiver.

Mathematical Proof of CRC

The mathematical proof of CRC is not only interesting but also essential to understanding its hardware and software implementations. If A and B represent a bit or a bit string and + denotes EOR, we have the following findings.

Operations	Description
$A + A = 0$	0 if A is EORed with itself.
$A + \backslash A = 1$	1 if A is EORed with its complement.
$A + 0 = A$	Same if A is EORed with 0.
$A + 1 = \backslash A$	Complement if A is EORed with 1.
$(A + B) + B = A + (B + B)$ $= A$	Associative law.
$(A + B) + A = B + (A + A)$ $= B$	Commutative law.

Assume that the dividend is the concatenation of the original message M and 16-bit 0's. At the sending end, after the logical divide operation, we obtain two parts: the quotient and the 16-bit remainder. Note that the remainder is of primary concern and the equality shown below implies that each side merely represents the derived remainder:

$$((M \cdot 2^{\wedge}16) + 0) / D = R / D$$

where the integer value of the message is raised to $M \cdot 2^{\wedge}16$, $\cdot$ denotes the arithmetic multiply operator, $^{\wedge}$ is the exponential operator, 0 means a 16-bit 0, D is the 17-bit polynomial divisor, / denotes the logical divide operator, and R is the 16-bit CRC.

At the receiving end, if no error occurs during transmission, the receiver should receive a bit string, $(M \cdot 2^{\wedge}16) + R$. Performing the same divide operation, we obtain a perfect 16-bit 0 as the remainder:

$$((M \cdot 2^{\wedge}16) + R) / D = (M \cdot 2^{\wedge}16) / D + R / D$$

$$= R / D + R / D$$

$$= (R + R) / D$$

$$= 0 / D$$

It is interesting to show that the residual remainder selected before the logical divide operation could be any bit pattern. At the receiving end, if the same divide operation is performed, the same residual remainder should be obtained if no error has occurred. Therefore, we derive another theorem in the following.

Theorem of CRC

Given a polynomial code of degree r, we append an r-bit residual remainder of any bit pattern to the original message and perform the logical divide operation to obtain the r-bit CRC, which may contain leading 0's. The original message and the CRC are transmitted. At the receiving end, logically dividing the same polynomial code into the received message, we should obtain a remainder that is exactly the same as the residual remainder selected.

Proof:

Given the equation
$$((M \cdot 2^r) + S)/D = RS/D$$
where M is the original message;
S is the selected residual remainder;
D is the polynomial code divisor;
RS is the derived CRC using S as the selected residual remainder.

At the receiving end, we obtain

$$((M \cdot 2^r) + RS)/D = (M \cdot 2^r)/D + RS/D + (0/D)$$

$$= (M \cdot 2^r)/D + RS/D + (S/D + S/D)$$

$$= ((M \cdot 2^r) + S)/D + RS/D + S/D$$

$$= RS/D + RS/D + S/D$$

$$= S/D$$

Note that the distributive law holds for the logical divide, the commutative law holds for EOR, and S is derived as the remainder after the logical divide operation. The theorem is proved.

We can also show that,
$$RS = R + S$$
where R is the standard CRC using a 16-bit 0 as the residual remainder. Interestingly enough, if we EOR any two of the three (R, S, or RS), we obtain the third one as the answer.

3.2.4 Hardware Design of CRC Generation/Detection

Before addressing the hardware design of CRC generation/detection, we say that the standard CRC-4 is the logical sum of the following.

1. The remainder of 4 0's followed by k 0's logically divided by the polynomial code where k is the number of bits in the original message;

2. The remainder of the k-bit message followed by 4 0's logically divided by the same polynomial code.

Because remainder 1 (R1) is a 4-bit 0, the logical sum is actually remainder 2 (R2) (i.e., the CRC-4). Furthermore, because the distributive law holds for the logical divide operation and the commutative law holds for EOR, the EOR and divide operations can be combined into one step as

$$R1/D + R2/D = (k+4) - bit\ 0's/D + (M \cdot 2^4 + 0)/D$$

$$= (M \cdot 2^4 + 0)/D$$

$$= R/D$$

where 0 denotes a 4-bit 0 and R is CRC-4.

Figure 3.3 depicts the hardware design of a 4-bit shift register to generate/detect CRC-4 using the 5-bit polynomial code divisor, $x^4 + x + 1$. The signals for timing control are not shown in the schematic. The 4-bit shift register is preset to 0's. The original message is 1 byte, 0110 0010 in binary assuming that the sign bit is transmitted first. At the sending end, after shifting the original message into the register, we obtain CRC-4 in the register and x^0 denotes the lsb last transmitted. The same result can be obtained through the logical divide operation as demonstrated in Section 3.2.3.

At the receiving end, after receiving the 8-bit original message, the shift register should contain 1011 as CRC-4 if no error has occurred. Since the CRC-4 in the incoming message has the identical bit pattern, we continue the logical divide operation until the end, and the shift register should contain a perfect 4-bit 0 as proven below:

$$(R + R)/D = 0/D$$

Note that the proposed design works for any number of bits in the message. In practice, synchronous communication controllers are used to transmit or receive a large block of bits at one time. The hardware controller generates and detects a 16-bit frame check sequence (FCS). However, when a UART chip is used to transfer data, we need to generate the 16-bit CRC or FCS by software. In other words, the CRC or FCS must be computed first and delivered to the UART chip before being transmitted. Understanding the basic circuit in Figure 3.3, we are ready to study the software design of CRC and FCS. To implement FCS-4, we modify the 4-bit shift register with two alterations:

1. Presetting the shift register to all 1's;
2. Shifting out the complement of the shift register content as the error-detecting code.

The mathematical interpretation of FCS-4 is left as an exercise.

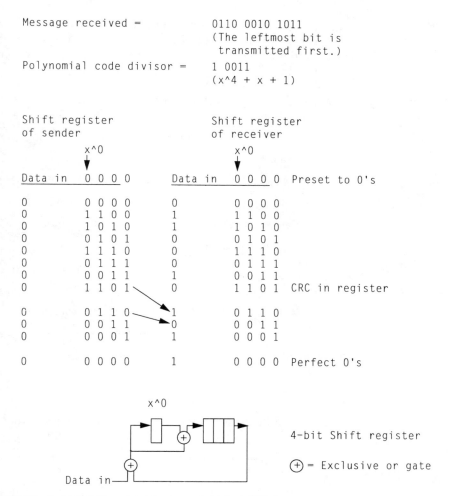

Figure 3.3 A 4-bit shift register to generate/detect CRC-4.

3.2.5 Software Design of CRC Generation/Detection

Most computers can handle 16-bit logical operations easily, but the polynomial code divisor has 17 bits. To solve this problem, it is necessary to exploit some programming tricks. First, a 16-bit register is used to store the lower 16 bits of the divisor. The data block contains the dividend, which is a string of bits. The leading bit of the dividend is tested. If it is a 1, shift the dividend 1 bit to the left and then perform a 16-bit EOR operation between the dividend and the lower 16-bit of divisor. If it is a 0, merely shift the dividend 1 bit to the left. This is equivalent to EOR the 17-bit divisor with the dividend and then shift 1 bit to the left.

Because the commutative law holds for a sequence of EOR operations, we need not shift the entire data block in generating CRC. In the following, the software design to generate/detect CRC can easily be converted to any programming language.

Software Design of CRC-ITU-T Generation/Detection

```
; ---------------------------------------------------------------------------
;   crc:            a 16-bit unsigned integer containing the cyclic
;                   redundancy check.
;   divisor:        a 16-bit unsigned integer containing the lower 16-
;                   bit of the polynomial code. It has a statically
;                   assigned value, 0001 0000 0010 0001 in binary
;                   or 1021 in hex.
;   data_block:     an array of 8-bit characters whose address
;                   is passed as a parameter.
;   n:              the size of the data_block passed as a parameter.
; ---------------------------------------------------------------------------
    Function crc (data_block, n)
    Initialize crc to 0's;
    REPEAT
        Fetch the next character from the data_block into a 16-bit word, logically shift
            8 bits to the left and EOR it into crc;
; ------------------------------------------------------------------ Inner repeat loop
        REPEAT
            IF the leading bit of crc is 1,
            THEN shift crc 1 bit to the left;
                EOR the divisor into crc;
            Else shift crc 1 bit to the left; ENDIF;
        UNTIL 8 times;
; ------------------------------------------------------------------ End repeat
    UNTIL n times;
    Return crc;
```

The software design of CRC detection is the same, and two things should be observed.

1. The message received should include the original data block plus the standard CRC.
2. The CRC returned should be a perfect 0 in the end.

Next, we will discuss a clever programming technique to speed up the CRC computation.

CRC-ITU-T Generation Using Table Lookup

The basic idea is to precalculate the 16-bit CRC for a byte of any bit pattern and place this CRC in a table. Therefore, when we need to generate the CRC for this byte, we simply fetch the result from the table directly. We need to compute the CRC for a byte with a value ranging from 0 to 255 in decimal (i.e., from 00 to ff in hex). Placing the CRCs in a table whose position is determined by the value of the byte, we can use the value of the byte as an index to access the table directly and fetch its CRC.

Any programming language may be used to implement this fast CRC algorithm. A CRC table (crctab) in C is shown in Figure 3.4. Let us try to find the CRC for ASCII b in the table. The value of b is 62 in hex or 98 in decimal. Since the numbering system used in a computer starts with 0, we add 1 to 98 to make 99. Looking for the 99th entry in the table, we find 4ce4 in hex, which is the CRC for b.

In software design, we include this table in the code and replace the inner repeat loop by the following table lookup routine:

> DO; Use the left 8-bit of the crc as an index to fetch the entry in crctab and
> EOR it into the crc after first shifting crc 8 bits to the left; ENDDO;

As an example, we transmit a data block of 2 b's, or 6262 in hex, and trace the steps to obtain the standard CRC as follows.

1. Initialize the CRC variable to 0's.
2. Fetch the first byte 62 from the data block into a 16-bit word, logically shift the word 8 bits to the left, and EOR it into CRC. We obtain 6200.
3. Using the left 8-bit field in CRC, which is 62, as an index to fetch the entry in crctab, which is 4ce4. EOR it into CRC after first shifting CRC 8 bits to the left. We obtain 4ce4.
4. Repeat the loop by fetching the second byte 62 from the data block into

```c
static unsigned short crctab[256] =
{
    0x0000, 0x1021, 0x2042, 0x3063, 0x4084, 0x50a5, 0x60c6, 0x70e7,
    0x8108, 0x9129, 0xa14a, 0xb16b, 0xc18c, 0xd1ad, 0xe1ce, 0xf1ef,
    0x1231, 0x0210, 0x3273, 0x2252, 0x52b5, 0x4294, 0x72f7, 0x62d6,
    0x9339, 0x8318, 0xb37b, 0xa35a, 0xd3bd, 0xc39c, 0xf3ff, 0xe3de,
    0x2462, 0x3443, 0x0420, 0x1401, 0x64e6, 0x74c7, 0x44a4, 0x5485,
    0xa56a, 0xb54b, 0x8528, 0x9509, 0xe5ee, 0xf5cf, 0xc5ac, 0xd58d,
    0x3653, 0x2672, 0x1611, 0x0630, 0x76d7, 0x66f6, 0x5695, 0x46b4,
    0xb75b, 0xa77a, 0x9719, 0x8738, 0xf7df, 0xe7fe, 0xd79d, 0xc7bc,
    0x48c4, 0x58e5, 0x6886, 0x78a7, 0x0840, 0x1861, 0x2802, 0x3823,
    0xc9cc, 0xd9ed, 0xe98e, 0xf9af, 0x8948, 0x9969, 0xa90a, 0xb92b,
    0x5af5, 0x4ad4, 0x7ab7, 0x6a96, 0x1a71, 0x0a50, 0x3a33, 0x2a12,
    0xdbfd, 0xcbdc, 0xfbbf, 0xeb9e, 0x9b79, 0x8b58, 0xbb3b, 0xab1a,
    0x6ca6, 0x7c87, 0x4ce4, 0x5cc5, 0x2c22, 0x3c03, 0x0c60, 0x1c41,
    0xedae, 0xfd8f, 0xcdec, 0xddcd, 0xad2a, 0xbd0b, 0x8d68, 0x9d49,
    0x7e97, 0x6eb6, 0x5ed5, 0x4ef4, 0x3e13, 0x2e32, 0x1e51, 0x0e70,
    0xff9f, 0xefbe, 0xdfdd, 0xcffc, 0xbf1b, 0xaf3a, 0x9f59, 0x8f78,
    0x9188, 0x81a9, 0xb1ca, 0xa1eb, 0xd10c, 0xc12d, 0xf14e, 0xe16f,
    0x1080, 0x00a1, 0x30c2, 0x20e3, 0x5004, 0x4025, 0x7046, 0x6067,
    0x83b9, 0x9398, 0xa3fb, 0xb3da, 0xc33d, 0xd31c, 0xe37f, 0xf35e,
    0x02b1, 0x1290, 0x22f3, 0x32d2, 0x4235, 0x5214, 0x6277, 0x7256,
    0xb5ea, 0xa5cb, 0x95a8, 0x8589, 0xf56e, 0xe54f, 0xd52c, 0xc50d,
    0x34e2, 0x24c3, 0x14a0, 0x0481, 0x7466, 0x6447, 0x5424, 0x4405,
    0xa7db, 0xb7fa, 0x8799, 0x97b8, 0xe75f, 0xf77e, 0xc71d, 0xd73c,
    0x26d3, 0x36f2, 0x0691, 0x16b0, 0x6657, 0x7676, 0x4615, 0x5634,
    0xd94c, 0xc96d, 0xf90e, 0xe92f, 0x99c8, 0x89e9, 0xb98a, 0xa9ab,
    0x5844, 0x4865, 0x7806, 0x6827, 0x18c0, 0x08e1, 0x3882, 0x28a3,
    0xcb7d, 0xdb5c, 0xeb3f, 0xfb1e, 0x8bf9, 0x9bd8, 0xabbb, 0xbb9a,
    0x4a75, 0x5a54, 0x6a37, 0x7a16, 0x0af1, 0x1ad0, 0x2ab3, 0x3a92,
    0xfd2e, 0xed0f, 0xdd6c, 0xcd4d, 0xbdaa, 0xad8b, 0x9de8, 0x8dc9,
    0x7c26, 0x6c07, 0x5c64, 0x4c45, 0x3ca2, 0x2c83, 0x1ce0, 0x0cc1,
    0xef1f, 0xff3e, 0xcf5d, 0xdf7c, 0xaf9b, 0xbfba, 0x8fd9, 0x9ff8,
    0x6e17, 0x7e36, 0x4e55, 0x5e74, 0x2e93, 0x3eb2, 0x0ed1, 0x1ef0,
};
```

Figure 3.4 CRC-ITU-T table in C code.

a 16-bit word. Logically shift the word 8 bits to the left and EOR it into CRC. We obtain 2ee4. The EOR operations are shown below:

```
  4ce4   in hex              0100 1100 1110 0100   in binary
+ 6200                       0110 0010 0000 0000
-----------                  -------------------
  2ee4                        0010 1110 1110 0100
```

5. Using the left 8-bit in CRC, which is 2e, as an index, fetch the entry in crctab, which is c5ac. EOR it into CRC after first shifting CRC 8 bits to

the left. We obtain 21ac, which is the final result in CRC. The EOR operations are shown below:

```
   c5ac              1100 0101 1010 1100
 + e400              1110 0100 0000 0000
 ------              -------------------
   21ac              0010 0001 1010 1100
```

Steps 2 to 5 are performed in the outer loop and the data block may have a variable length. This algorithm is faster than the one without using table lookup. There are two tradeoffs. First, the table must be precalculated. Second, it occupies additional memory space in the code.

Software Design of CRC-32 Generation/Detection

The software design of CRC-32 is similar to CRC-ITU-T, with minor modifications. First, a 33-bit polynomial code divisor (introduced in the next section) is used and the derived CRC is 32-bit. Secondly, after fetching the character from the data block into a 32-bit word, we need to logically shift it 24 bits to the left and EOR it into the 32-bit CRC. The rest of the design remains the same. Similarly, a table lookup routine can also be used to speed up the computation, one byte at a time instead of one bit.

3.2.6 Evaluations Of CRC

VRC and LRC are considered as the first generation of error detecting code while CRC is the second generation. Popular polynomial codes are compared below:

CRC-12	$x^{12} + x^{11} + x^2 + x + 1$
CRC-16	$x^{16} + x^{15} + x^2 + 1$
FCS-ITU-T	$x^{16} + x^{12} + x^5 + 1$
FCS-32	$x^{32} + x^{26} + x^{23} + x^{22} + x^{16} + x^{12} + x^{11} + x^{10}$ $+ x^8 + x^7 + x^5 + x^4 + x^2 + x + 1$

The CRC-12 polynomial is used for the 6-bit transcode, which can represent all the alphabets, digits, and some special characters in an automatic teller machine. The CRC-16 polynomial is used in the binary synchronous communications protocol [BSC]. The FCS-ITU-T polynomial is widely accepted in WANs using the synchronous or high-level data link controls protocol [SDLC, HDLC].

The popular LANs such as Ethernet and token ring, all use the FCS-32 polynomial. The 32-bit error-detecting code is generated and detected by the hardware controller. Consequently, more flip-flops and gates are used in the design, which also implies more cost and less reliability. The improved performance seems negligible, especially when the line is reliable. With a basic understanding of error detection, we will discuss the basic concepts of sliding window protocols (SWPs).

3.3 SLIDING WINDOW PROTOCOLS

An SWP comprises a set of rules governing the transmission of data or information frames between two computers with error/flow control. Recall that a data link comprises a com port and the associated software to drive it. The sender means a collection of software routines, and likewise the receiver.

Basic Definitions

1. The sender transmits information (I) (i.e., data frames) in an ordered sequence and each I frame contains a sending sequence number Ns to identify the frame and an error-detecting code.
2. The receiver returns an ack, + or −, which contains a receiving sequence number Nr that it is expecting. Nr has a special meaning, that up to $Nr - 1$ I frames have been correctly received.
3. The sequence number is either a 3-bit or 7-bit unsigned integer.
4. Each window has two edges—the leading edge and the trailing edge—that are represented by sequence numbers. A window is closed if its leading edge coincides with its trailing edge.
5. The sending window contains all the sequence numbers of those I frames that have been sent but not yet acknowledged. Thus, the sending window is initially closed and can open up to a size as allowed by the software designer. The allowed size also implies the number of buffers allocated to sender. An allowed size of 2 means that the difference between its leading edge and trailing edge cannot exceed 2.
6. The receiving window contains all the sequence numbers of those I frames that the receiver is expecting. Hence, the receiving window is always open, with a size that is usually the same as the allowed size of the sending window.

If the allowed sending window size is greater than 1, we have pipelined transmission. Note that the allowed window size also implies the number of buffers allocated by the OS for sender or receiver. In practice, each data frame contains a 3-bit sequence number that starts from 0 to 7 wrap-around, mod 8. Therefore, it is possible for the leading edge to be smaller than the trailing edge. If the leading edge is 1 while the trailing edge is 7, the window size is 2 as computed below:

$$(1 + 8) - 7 = 2$$

Data Link Layer   131

Two different window diagrams are depicted in Figure 3.5. In Figure 3.5(a), we have a pie-shaped window that contains sequence numbers 7 and 0. The leading edge with an arrow is placed below or to the left of sequence number 1 and the trailing edges are below the sequence numbers 7. In Figure 3.5(b), we have the same window laid out on a plane and the rectangle-shaped window also contains the sequence numbers 7 and 0. Next, we will discuss the basic functions and different error-recovery routines performed by both sender and receiver.

Basic Functions—Sender

1. The sender transmits I frames, one by one, before receiving an ack from receiver.
2. The sender advances the leading edge of its window after sending the next I frame.
3. If the sender receives a +ack with a sequence number Nr in it, the sender advances its trailing edge below Nr.
4. The sender is *blocked* if its window is full because all the assigned buffers are used up. The term *blocked* means that the sender cannot proceed further.

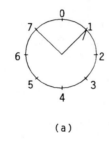

(a)

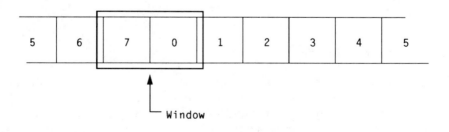

(b)

Figure 3.5 Two different window diagrams: (a) a pie section window and (b) a rectangular window.

Basic Functions—Receiver

If the received I frame is a good one with a sequence number Ns as expected, the receiver returns a +ack with Nr equal to $Ns + 1$ and advances its window below Nr. That is, both of its trailing and leading edges are incremented by 1.

Under the assumption that the window size is 1 for both sender and receiver, the sender's and receiver's window edge movements are depicted in Figure 3.6. Assume that the ack frame does not include a sequence number in it, so an ack frame really means a character in ASCII. At the initial state in Figure 3.6(a), the sending window is closed and the receiver is expecting I0 (I frame 0), which really means a data frame with a sequence number 0 in it. In Figure 3.6(b), the sender sends I0 and advances the leading edge of its window. In Figure 3.6(c), the receiver receives I0 as expected, sends a +ack, and advances both edges of its window. The sender receives a +ack, so it advances the trailing edge of its window. Now the sending window is closed as shown in Figure 3.6(d). In Figure 3.6(e), the sender sends out I1 and advances its leading edge. In Figure 3.6(f), the receiver returns a +ack for the good I1 as expected. After receiving a +ack, the sender advances the trailing edge of its window and now the sending window is closed.

The sliding window protocol runs smoothly if no error occurs. The real problem is how to recover errors. The baseline is that whenever an error is detected, the receiver returns a −ack to request retransmission. Different protocols handle error control differently as discussed in Section 3.3.1.

3.3.1 Stop-and-Wait

The Stop-and-Wait (SAW) ARQ is the simplest kind for error/flow control. Its window size is 1, and the receiver merely returns a +ack or a −ack character without having a sequence number in it. In addition, no error-detecting code is used to guard the ack character. The error-recovery functions of SAW ARQ are described below.

Error Recovery—Sender

1. After receiving a −ack, the sender unwinds its leading edge to coincide with its trailing edge and flushes its window. In other words, the sending window is closed, and whatever is left in the window must be retransmitted.
2. Whenever a time-out error occurs, it is like a −ack, and the sender flushes its window and retransmits. Note that any +ack, −ack, or data frame missing on the line will trigger a time-out error.

Data Link Layer 133

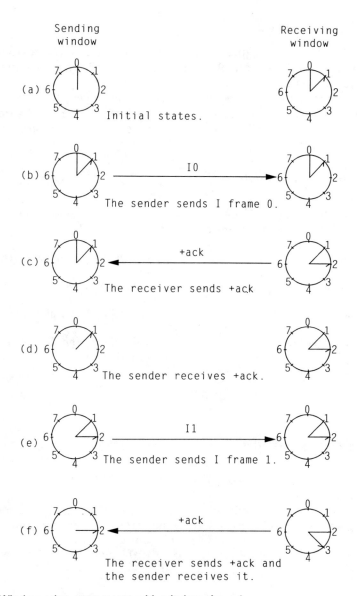

Figure 3.6 Window edge movements with window size = 1.

Error Recovery—Receiver

1. If the data frame is corrupted with a sequence number Ns as expected, the receiver discards the frame and sends a −ack. This response message tells sender to retransmit.
2. If the data frame is a good one but below the trailing edge of the window, the receiver returns a +ack and discards this duplicate under the assumption that a +ack or −ack is not allowed to contain a sequence number. Otherwise, a −ack would put the sender in an infinite loop.

Software Design Of Sender

REPEAT
Send data frames one at a time and wait for a response from receiver. The last frame contains an end of transmission (EOT) control character;
  CASE response of
   +ack: transmit the next frame and advance its window;
   −ack: retransmit the current frame, i.e. flush its window;
   corrupted ack: take no action and wait for time-out error;
   time-out error: retransmit the current frame, i.e. flush its window;
  ENDCASE;

UNTIL all frames are transmitted;
End.

Software Design Of Receiver

REPEAT
Wait to receive a frame from sender;
  CASE frame of
   good data in the window: send +ack and advance its window;
   good data out of the window: send +ack and discard this frame which is a duplicate;
   bad data: send −ack and discard the frame;
   EOT character: exit;
  ENDCASE;

UNTIL forever;
End.

The above protocol is simple, but not perfect. For example, should a −ack become a +ack on the line, the protocol would fail because the ack has no sequence number in it. A more serious drawback is that the sender cannot transmit the next frame on the line before receiving a +ack for the first one. To improve throughput, we tend to transmit two frames on the line before receiving an ack.

Pipelined Transmission

Pipelined transmission means that the sending window size is greater than 1. In other words, the sender may transmit two or more frames on the line before receiving an ack. Normally, the sending and receiving window size should be equal. But it is possible to have a sending window size 2 and a receiving window size 1 provided that the processing speed of the receiver is twice as fast as the sender. In real design, the receiver determines the window size, which is usually honored by the sender. In addition, an ack frame should contain a sequence number Nr that the receiver is expecting. The number Nr in a +ack or a −ack frame has a special meaning that up to $Nr - 1$ frames have been correctly received as explained below:

- A +ack1 means that all the previous frames up to I0 have been correctly received and that no error has been detected by the receiver.
- A −ack1 means that all the previous frames up to I0 have been correctly received but that I1 is corrupted.

Based on this crucial concept, the sender will never receive a +ack with a higher sequence number in it while the previous frame is corrupted. As a consequence, two protocols Go-Back-N (GBN) and Selective-Reject (SRJ) have emerged.

3.3.2 Go-Back-N

The GBN ARQ means that whenever an error occurs during transmission, the sender must go back to the frame with Nr in it and retransmit everything from there. That is to say, after receiving a −ack, the sender flushes its window and retransmits any old frames in the window. The error-recovery functions of both sender and receiver are described below.

Error Recovery—Sender

If the sender receives a −ack with Nr in it to indicate that the receiver is expecting the data frame Nr, then the sender advances its trailing edge below Nr and flushes its window. This means that the sender unwinds its leading edge to coincide with its trailing edge, so the sending window is closed. Whatever was left in the sending window must be retransmitted.

Whenever a time-out error occurs, the sender transmits a command to poll the receiver about its status and the sequence number it is expecting. After receiving a response, +ack or −ack with Nr in it, the sender moves both of its window edges below Nr and starts from there. This is because that all the I frames in the sending window may be corrupted on the line without being detected. Note that a data frame or −ack missing on the line will definitely trigger a time-out error because the receiver must discard any subsequent data frames that are out of sequence.

Error Recovery—Receiver

After detecting that the expected frame is definitely corrupted, the receiver will enter the error state. There are two possible conditions to detect an error. First, the data frame is corrupted, but with a sequence number Ns as expected. Secondly, the receiver detects a good frame, but out of sequence. That is, a missing frame is treated the same way as a corrupted frame. In either case, the receiver discards the received frame and sends a −ack with Nr in it, as expected. This response message tells the sender to go back Nr. The receiver should discard any subsequent data frames that are out of sequence. Until the expected frame arrives, the receiver will not get out the error state.

After being polled, the receiver returns the previous response, a +ack or a −ack.

The window edge movements of GBN ARQ with window size 2 are shown in Figure 3.7. In Figure 3.7(a), the sender transmits I0 and −I1 where a minus sign in the front indicates that the I frame is corrupted. Now, the sender must be blocked because its sending window is full. In Figure 3.7(b), the receiver returns a +ack1 and advances its window. The sender now receives the +ack1 and advances the trailing edge of its window below 1. The Nr 1 indicates that all data frames with sequence numbers up to 0 have been correctly received. In Figure 3.7(c), the sender sends out I2, but alas, the receiver detects −I1, which was sent previously, so it returns a −ack1. The Nr 1 in the −ack frame indicates that I1 was corrupted. The receiver cannot advance its trailing edge without receiving a perfect I1 as expected. After receiving a −ack1, the sender flushes its window in Figure 3.7(d) and retransmits I1 and I2 as shown in Figure 3.7(e). Now, the receiver receives the I2 frame that was sent previously but out of sequence. Therefore, the receiver discards this I2 frame and expects I1 to arrive. In Figure 3.7(f), the receiver receives two good frames, I1 and I2, returns +ack2 and +ack3, and advances its window twice. After receiving the two +ack frames, the sender advances its trailing edge twice and its window is closed.

3.3.3 Selective-Reject

If the receiver has many buffers to store the incoming I frames after the corrupted one, the sender needs to retransmit the particular I frames that are incorrect. This

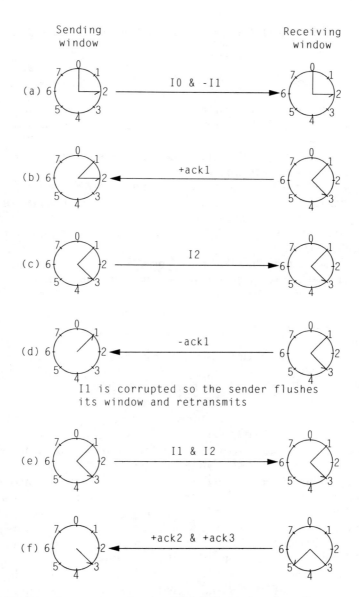

Figure 3.7 Window edge movements using GBN ARQ, window size = 2.

is known as the SRJ ARQ. The recovery functions of sender and receiver are described below.

Error Recovery—Sender

If the sender receives a −ack frame containing a sequence number Nr, it advances its trailing edge below Nr and retransmits the I frame with sequence number Ns equal to Nr.

If no response is received within a specified time interval, the sender times out and polls the receiver to find out why.

After polling, if the response is a −ack with a sequence number Nr in it, then the sender knows that an I frame was corrupted, advances its trailing edge below Nr, and retransmits the previous I frame with sequence number Ns equal to Nr. If the response is a +ack with Nr in it, the sender simply advances its trailing edge below Nr.

Recall that a +ack means that the receiver has not detected any error that but a −ack indicates otherwise and the sender must retransmit the I frame as expected.

Error Recovery—Receiver

If the received I frame is corrupted or missing, the receiver sends a −ack frame with Nr equal to Ns that it is expecting. The receiver then buffers the m good incoming I frames after the bad one and waits for the arrival of the I frame as expected.

Eventually, when the I frame arrives as expected, the receiver acknowledges with a +ack with a sequence number $Nr + 1$, and then +acks $Nr + 2$, $Nr + 3, \ldots, Nr + m + 1$ mod (maximum sequence number +1) for the rest of the I frames received but not yet acknowledged. The receiver must go through the buffered frames one by one and deal with them as they have just arrived. While acknowledging, the receiver advances its window accordingly. If any of the subsequent frames are also corrupted, then when its turn comes, the receiver transmits another −ack with a sequence number to indicate that this particular frame must be retransmitted. In other words, the receiver must withhold all the subsequent −acks to guard the trailing of its window.

Note that the sequence number Nr in an ack frame provides valuable information about the history of transmission. Without this ingenious idea, the SRJ ARQ algorithm can hardly become productive.

The window edge movements of SRJ ARQ with window size 2 are depicted in Figure 3.8. In Figure 3.8(a), the sender sends out I0 and −I1 and its window is full; so, the sender is blocked. In Figure 3.8(b), the receiver detects a good I0, returns a +ack1, and advances its window. The sender receives the +ack1 and advances the trailing edge of its window. In Figure 3.8(c), the sender sends I2 and advances its leading edge. Alas, the receiver now detects the −I1 or the bad I1, returns a −ack1, and meanwhile keeps the incoming I2 in its buffer. At this point, the sender retransmits I1 without flushing its entire window as in Figure 3.8(d). In Figure 3.8(e), after receiving a good I1, the receiver returns a +ack2, then a +ack3, and advances its window accordingly. By the same token, the sender advances its trailing edge twice so its window is closed.

SRJ ARQ works because the receiver always guards its trailing edge carefully. If any error is detected during transmission, the receiver sends a −ack back to the sender because the event is deterministic. However, if a −ack or an I frame is lost on the line, a time-out error will definitely be triggered. Whenever that happens, the sender polls the receiver to find out why and take appropriate action. That is, using a good SWP, the receiver should never receive a duplicate.

A half-duplex SRJ ARQ has been simulated on two PCs and the protocol can stand an error rate up to 90% [4]. Even though the state of the sliding window is continuously changing, it is possible to design sender and receiver tasks as two finite state machines if transmission is half-duplex. An example using a 1-bit sequence number with a window size 2 is described in Chapter 7 on the T layer design. The design of a full-duplex SRJ ARQ remains a challenge.

The pipelined transmission technique is intended to keep the line busy all the time. Will a large window size help system throughput? We will find out in Section 3.3.4.

3.3.4 Optimal Window Size

The window size really means the number of buffers allocated to sender or receiver by the OS. In the DL layer, both sides would like to transmit data frames at the same time. A +ack is usually piggybacked onto an outgoing data frame. The optimal window size is 2 so long as we can keep the line busy. A larger window size would waste resources and not improve throughput.

If the SWP is used by either the N or T layer, the initial window size should be the number of hops between the origination node and the destination node. If a congestion condition is detected in the middle of the route, the window size should be reduced accordingly.

In an SWP, what is the maximum window size allowed? Recall that when the sender is not sure about the receiving status, it polls the receiver to find out why so that no duplicate frames will be transmitted. Based on this notion, if n denotes the number of bits in a sequence number, the window size could be as large as 2^n. However, should all 2^n frames in the window disappear on the line without being detected, the protocol would fail. In that regard, the maximum window size is set to be $(2^n - 1)$ to play it safe. With a 3-bit sequence number, the maximum window size is 7 regardless of which ARQ method is used, GBN or SRJ.

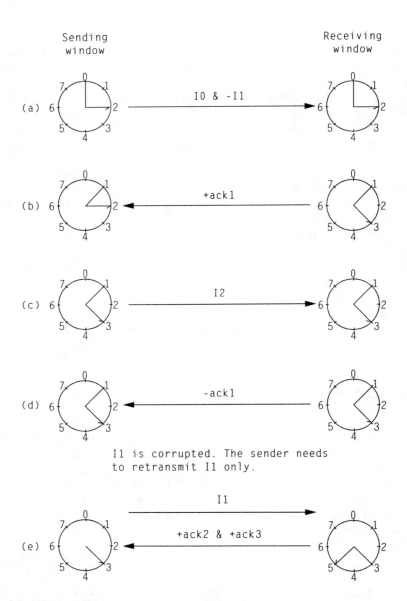

Figure 3.8 Window edge movements using SRJ ARQ, window size = 2.

Between two stations, if both sides can transmit data frames at the same time, we have the full-duplex transmission from the software viewpoint and the programming effort is not trivial. For each data link, there are two I/O tasks running in parallel; one task transmits frames and the other task receives frames. All the I/O operations should be interrupt-driven, and the data frames can be transmitted simultaneously in both directions. In practice, the GBN ARQ with a window size 2 is adequate for DL transmissions [SDLC, LAP, LAPB]. In such a design, the receiver needs only one buffer (i.e., its window size can be 1 if it is fast enough).

Other issues of DL layer design include character stuffing, bit stuffing, and piggybacking. They are popular techniques and therefore worth knowing.

3.4 OTHER DESIGN ISSUES

Character and bit-stuffing techniques are used to solve a particular transmission problem and a new encoding method can eliminate the problems altogether. Piggybacking, on the other hand, is a clever software technique that allows both stations to transmit data frames at the same time.

3.4.1 Piggybacking

With full-duplex transmission, it is possible to combine a +ack of an incoming data frame into the next outgoing data frame. The data frame has a field to place Nr, which implies a +ack. That is, a +ack is piggybacked on an outgoing data frame. In practice, a −ack is not piggybacked on an outgoing data frame. Instead, a −ack is sent back as a separate control frame. This is because a −ack is more serious than a +ack and needs an error-detecting code to fully guard its bits in the frame. The piggybacking concept is vital in DL layer design to increase system throughput.

3.4.2 Character-Stuffing Problem

The character-stuffing technique is used to guarantee that data are delivered correctly from one station to another to achieve so-called data transparency. In a character-oriented protocol, continuous 1's are transmitted on the line as the quiescent state. Special characters are transmitted for the hardware or receiver to interpret and execute [BSC]. For example, a frame is always preceded by two or more SYN characters, used to synchronize the hardware. In other words, at any time the hardware fires after receiving two SYN characters [5]. Control characters may also be transmitted as commands to the receiving station. What if the communication controller operates in transparent text mode and the data block contains any bit pattern including two syncs or any other control characters? The solution is that, when operating in transparent mode, any control character in the data stream (e.g., STX, ETB, ETX, SYN, and ENQ) must be preceded by a special data link escape (DLE) character. The receiving station knows that if the control character has a DLE in the front, it is data; otherwise, it means control. This technique introduces another problem in that there may be a DLE character followed by another control character in the text. To solve this dilemma, any DLE character in the text must also be preceded by another DLE character, a duplicate so to speak. Altogether, three DLEs and a control character are placed in the data stream. The receiver disregards the first DLE character and treats the second DLE as data and the next escape sequence as a control character.

In addition, certain control characters, such as EOT and NAK, are too important to the receiving station. To ensure the correctness of transmission, the EOT or NAK character is followed by a special padded character of all 1's. This padded character serves as an error-detecting code, which ensures that the receiver must receive all 16 bits correctly before taking action. The character-stuffing technique is usually done with software. It is a clever way to change an 8-bit code into a 16-bit code.

3.4.3 Bit-Stuffing Problem

With bit-synchronous transmission, each frame is enclosed by a special bit pattern, 01111110, at each end [SDLC, HDLC]. The special bit pattern is a Frame flag that has a 0 followed by six 1's and by another 0. The special Frame flag fires the hardware to signal the coming of the frame on the line. Consequently, the sender is not allowed to send the bit pattern 01111110 in the text; otherwise, the receiving hardware would interpret this bit pattern as the end delimiter. To solve this problem, a bit 0 is always inserted after five consecutive 1's in the frame regardless of what the next bit is. At the receiving end, the inserted bit 0 is always stripped off the frame by hardware. This bit-stuffing technique is designed to accomplish data transparency in that the receiver routine can receive data of any bit pattern without seeing the stuffed bits. In practice, the USRT controller chip stuffs the 0 bits after generating the FCS and strips the bits before detecting the FCS.

It should be mentioned that newly developed technologies may use different encoding schemes to eliminate the bit-stuffing problem altogether. As an example, the IBM token ring LAN uses the DMC. Certain waveforms, known as code violations, are not allowed in the regular data streams, but they can be embedded in the frame delimiters. As a result, the special code violation waveforms in the Frame flag signal the receiving hardware that the frame is coming.

In Section 3.5, we will discuss DL primitives, PDUs, data structures, and the software design of a data link.

3.5 DATA LINK LAYER DESIGN

In a computer network, a DL could be a resource shared by multiple service users. It is like a section of an information highway shared by many commuters. Therefore, after booting the system, both DLs exchange bits on the line to agree upon which operating mode to follow. As an example, one side may act like the primary station while the other side merely listens and obeys. After setting the operating mode, the DL at each side can accept requests from its service user. If the DL is left on in the system, it becomes a permanent resource. This is especially true in a generalized computer network in that when the network is up, there is always a DL between two stations that are interconnected.

In a telephone network, a DL is connected at the beginning of a telephone call and disconnected afterwards. In such a system, the N layer issues a connect/disconnect. The N layer issues a DL connect request to tell its DL how to set operating mode. That is, the origination DL needs to transmit a set mode frame on the line and wait for acknowledgment. After receiving an ack, the origination DL issues a DL connect confirm to report to its N layer. If the DL connection is successful, the origination N layer can issue a DL_data.request that asks its DL layer to transmit a packet to the receiving node. The dl_sdu in the first data request is usually a network connect packet that contains the dialing address.

A DL may be comprised of two concurrent tasks running in parallel, one to transmit and the other one to receive. Either task is ready to execute as long as there is a message in its message queue.

3.5.1 Data Link Layer Primitives

The ITU-T has proposed a set of DL connect/disconnect primitives [6] [X.212]. If a DL is temporary, then the DL connect and disconnect phases are performed as needed. A DL may also be permanent. In such a system, after system boot the two DLs on each side of a connection exchange bits to agree upon the operating mode to follow. Note that this handshaking procedure is performed only once without the involvement of N layers, so the traffic between a DL and its N layer can be minimized. An efficient DL should handle its own protocol and operate autonomously without getting much involved with its N layer.

Temporary Data Link

To make a DL connection, the service user (which is the N layer) issues the following:

    DL_CONNECT.request(dl_id, operating_mode);

where dl_id is a local reference number on the sending node and operating-

_mode specifies the protocol between two stations. From dl_id, the data structure containing the information of the DL can be fetched. Some other DL primitives are shown in Figure 3.9. After receiving a connect request, the DL transmits a set operating mode command frame to its peer. Note that either side may be a DTE or DCE. After receiving the set mode command, the destination DL issues an indication as follows:

DL_CONNECT.indication(dl_id, operating_mode);

where dl_id is a local reference number on the receiving node. Its N layer then issues a response as follows:

DL_CONNECT.response(dl_id, status);

Figure 3.9 Data link primitives.

After receiving the response, the destination DL transmits a frame on the line to acknowledge. After receiving the ack frame, the origination DL issues a confirm as shown below:

    DL_CONNECT.confirm(dl_id);

If the confirm is positive, we have a DL connection. After that, the N layer at either side of a DL connection can transmit an N layer packet to the N layer on the other side via a DL_DATA.request or a DL call. Note that the two DLs are peers but that their upper N layers may not be. The pair of N layers are just service users running on two adjacent nodes. Each packet is an NPDU that contains either network control information or data.

Whenever a telephone conversation is done, the DL at either side may issue a disconnect request as follows:

    DL_DISCONNECT.request(dl_id, reason);

where reason explains why. After receiving the request, the DL sends a DISC (Disconnect) frame on the line.

After receiving the DISC frame, its peer DL issues an indication as shown below:

    DL_DISCONNECT.indication(dl_id);

The receiving N layer issues a response:

    DL_DISCONNECT.response(dl_id);

After the response, the receiving DL transmits an ack frame on the line. After receiving the ack frame, the DL on the sending node issues a confirm as follows:

    DL_DISCONNECT.confirm(dl_id);

At this point the DL is disconnected to complete the call. To simplify the design, after telephone hang-up the two DLs may just go ahead and disconnect without waiting for acknowledgment.

Permanent Data Link

In a computer network, a DL should stay permanently online until system shutdown. A permanent DL can be thought of as a system resource and can be shared by many service users. The status of a DL is monitored by the system and the NMT routines. A DL connection really means that the DL is online, or activated. After system boot, the DL and its peer should perform the necessary handshaking procedure to set operating mode, and after that the DL should operate on a 24-hour-a-day basis without fail.

After a DL is initialized, the N layer may issue a DL data request to deliver a packet to the N layer on the receiving node as shown below:

DL_DATA.request(dl_id, dl_sdu, status);

where dl_sdu contains a packet and status indicates what happened after the call. The Count field in the packet is used to derive the length of the frame. The dl_id is a local reference number from which its associated data link control block (DLCB) can be fetched.

The DL on the receiving node strips the frame header and trailer and issues an indication as shown below:

DL_DATA.indication(dl_id, dl_sdu, status);

where dl_id is a local reference number on the receiving node, dl_sdu contains the packet, and status indicates what happened after the call. The dl_id identifies the DL and is used for recording statistics. Note that each DL_DATA.indication to the N layer on the receiving node is due to the successful completion of a DL_DATA.request on the sending node. The DL_DATA.response and DL_DATA.confirm messages are not mandatory in design.

There are other types of data requests and each one has a different syntax. Because some control packets may have higher priority, they need to be transmitted first. For this reason, the expedited data request is designed to transmit an urgent packet as follows:

DL_EXPEDITED_DATA.request(dl_id, dl_sdu, status);

and the packet is transmitted on the line as a regular I frame without having to wait in the queue. At the DL level, there is no need to design a special I frame for the expedited data transfer.

A unit data request is designed to transmit real-time data where speed is of utmost importance. Neither SWP nor acks are implemented during transmission. The format of this request is shown below:

DL_UNITDATA.request(dl_id, dl_sdu, status);

which is always mapped into an unnumbered information (UI) frame. Other DL primitives include the following:

DL_INIT.request(dl_id);
DL_RESET.request(dl_id); etc.

The INIT request initializes the DL at the link level and the RESET request resets the hardware control functions of the physical link. In summary, the N layer passes information to its DL via a request. If the request is a data call, then the

DL transmits a frame on the line via its output driver. All the bits on the line constitute a frame or data link protocol data unit (DLPDU).

3.5.2 Data Link Protocol Data Units

A DLPDU is known as the frame on the line. Each DLPDU contains a header and trailer, prepared mostly by DL. The header contains the local address of the receiving DL and the Control field provides information about items such as opcode and sequence numbers. The trailer contains an error-detecting code. A DLPDU is very much like a computer instruction in the sense that the DL at the receiving end receives, interprets, and executes it.

It is interesting to compare a DL primitive and a PDU, as shown in Figure 3.10 [6].

After receiving a DL_CONNECT.request, the origination DL transmits a set asynchronous balanced mode (SABM) frame on the line. The destination DL conveys a DL_CONNECT.indication to its N layer. After receiving a positive DL_CONNECT.response from its N layer, it places an unnumbered ack (UA) frame on the line. After receiving the UA frame, the origination DL reports to its N layer with a DL_CONNECT.confirm. Now, the data transfer or transmission phase may begin in full-duplex. The service users at either side may issue a DL_DATA.request, which is mapped into an I frame with a sending sequence number Ns. If the I frame is good, as expected, the receiver returns a Receiver Ready (RR) frame with a receiving sequence number Nr. In addition, the receiving DL reports a DL_DATA.indication to its N layer. If the packet is a data packet that needs to be routed to another node, its N layer determines the data link id of the next node and passes the same packet back to the DL via another DL_DATA.request with the right dl_id. After receiving the request, the DL sends the same packet out with a new DL header and trailer, and a data flow example at the DL layer level can be found in Figure 3.11.

The implementation of DL primitives depends on the designer. It may be a message from one task to another or just a subroutine call. Examining the bits on the line, we see a packet preceded by a header and followed by a trailer. The header begins with a Frame flag prepared by the communication controller. The DL software prepares the rest of the header, which contains a multidrop address and a Control field. The trailer contains the FCS followed by another Frame flag, all prepared by the hardware controller.

Besides data or information frames, there are control frames, such as initializing, setting operating mode, polling, and exchanging station id. There are also flow control frames like + or −ack. The DL software interprets and executes the opcode in a control frame and passes only the packet in a data frame to its N layer.

In a multidrop line, one computer may be connected to many terminals. There is only one physical link, which may be shared by many data links. Each

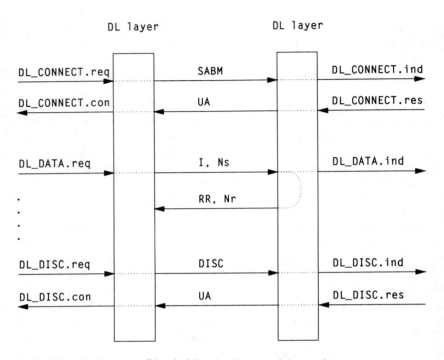

Figure 3.10 Mapping between DL primitives and protocol data units.

terminal has its own DL. Consequently, each DL must have its own private database, known as the DLCB.

3.5.3 Data Link Control Block

The DLCB contains information pertinent to the DL with which it is associated. If the communication controller can only transmit one byte at a time like UART, DLCB should contain a physical link id from which the UCB of the device can be fetched. On the other hand, if the communication controller can transmit a block of bytes on the line without being interrupted, a DLCB should contain the characteristics of the hardware device. Given a data link id (dl_id), its DLCB, a data structure in software design can be fetched that contains the following:

- Characteristics of the DL, such as the I/O addresses of the hardware register in the controller, various command codes, and operating modes.

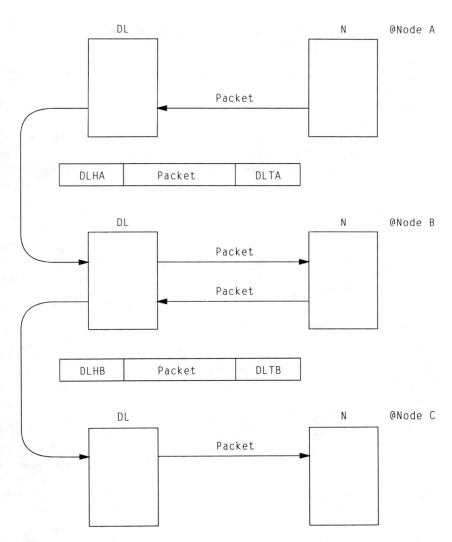

DLHA (Data link header A) ≠ DLHB (Data link header B)
DLTA (Data link trailer A) ≠ DLTB (Data link trailer B)

Figure 3.11 Data flow example at the data link layer level.

- Dl_id, sender's address, and receiver's address. These are the local addresses in a multidrop line. For a point-to-point connection, the addresses should all be 0's.
- Status flags—deactivated or activated. If the DL is activated, it may be in a busy or idle state.
- Pointer to its data packet queue. Each data packet is a data link service data unit (dl_sdu).
- Leading and trailing edges of its sending window. Ns is the leading edge.
- Leading and trailing edges of its receiving window. Nr is the trailing edge.
- Sending and receiving window sizes (i.e., the number of buffers allocated to sender and receiver).
- Pointers to buffers.
- Time stamp of each frame sent.

In theory, one real-time timer should be supported by the system. When this timer expires, it triggers an interrupt. Then, the timer ISR takes over control and wakes up the sender if there is a time-out error. The sender in turn polls the receiver for possible error recovery.

3.5.4 Data Link Software Design

If one station transmits data frames and the other station transmits ack frames at the same time, we have achieved full-duplex transmission by hardware definition. However, in software design it is still half-duplex. If both stations can transmit and receive data frames at the same time, we have truly full-duplex transmissions. In other words, a +ack must be piggybacked on an outgoing data frame and the multitasking capability of the OS must be employed.

All activities happen in real time and the routine to receive a frame must be activated all the time. In some systems, two physical lines are used and each line handles half-duplex transmission. Combined, the two lines provide the full-duplex transmission capability [Call 370]. Our challenge is to use one physical link and to implement full-duplex transmission. Each side has a sender/receiver pair. The sender on one side talks to its peer receiver on the other side. But on each node, both the sender and receiver must share the same hardware to transmit and receive.

We sketch the data link design using GBN ARQ with a window size of 2. An FSM model using SRJ ARQ is described in Chapter 7, which covers transport layer design. Note that at the DL layer level, all popular protocols use GBN ARQ with a window size of 2 [LAP, LAPB, SDLC].

No matter what the physical I/O device is, all I/O operations must be interrupt-driven to keep the line fully utilized. Two tasks are running in parallel on each side, one to transmit and the other one to receive. Therefore, two Attach system calls are issued on each side as shown below:

Data Link Layer 151

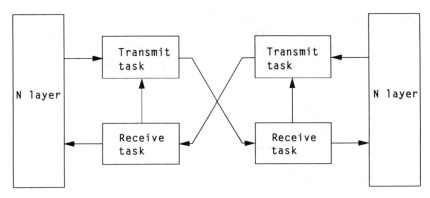

Figure 3.12 Full-duplex data transmission between two data links.

Attach('DLTTASK', Transmit_task, address_space, dl_id, etc);
...   {Modify address_space, dl_id, etc.}
Attach('DLRTASK', Receive_task, address_space, dl_id, etc);

DLTTASK (DL transmit task) is the task id; Transmit_task is its start address; and address_space points to its private addressing space. Transmit_task mainly transmits frames on the line. DLRTASK (DL receive task) is the receive task id and Receive_task is its start address. Receive_task receives frames, interprets, and takes appropriate actions. Each task has its own TCB that contains the running environment of the task. After issuing an I/O driver call, the task must wait until its I/O is completed. Each task is designed as an infinite loop that mainly receives a message, interprets, and executes it. Transmit_task is similar to sender and Receive_task is similar to receiver. The logical functions performed by sender and receiver on one side are embedded into the two I/O tasks as shown in Figure 3.12.

The arrow indicates the direction of message flow. Transmit_task receives messages from its N layer as well as the Receive_task on the same node, and it transmits frames to the Receive_task on the other node. For example, when the receiver wants to return an ack to the remote sender, it must prepare an ack frame first and deliver it to the transmit_task on the same side, which then transmits the ack on the line. On the other hand, after transmitting a Polling command, the sender expects its Receive_task to receive a response from the remote end and act accordingly.

If a permanent DL is established during system boot, the front section of the Transmit_task may perform handshaking, initialization, and so forth. Then, both the sender and receiver enter Normal state. After detecting a transmission error, the receiver enters Error state. The receiver will not switch back to Normal until the error is corrected after retransmission. When data transfer begins, both

Transmit_task and Receive_task on one station work as a team to communicate with the two corresponding tasks on the other station. After transmitting a data frame, the sender expects to receive an ack within a time interval. The delay limit is the sum of the round-trip transmission time plus the processing time of the receiving station. For a typical satellite link, the time-out (TO) delay is estimated about 900 ms [SDLC].

The software design of Transmit_task is sketched below.

```
Transmit_task:
    ...                     {Handshake and initialize.}
Transmit_loop:
Wait for a message in the queue or time-out;
IF at least one frame is ready to be transmitted,
THEN
        CASE frame of
        −ack: Continue;
        Data frame:     IF there is also a +ack frame ready to be transmitted,
                        THEN
                        Prepare a ph_sdu containing the data frame with the
                        +ack piggybacked on it;
                        ENDIF;
                        Advance the leading edge of its sending window;
                        Set the timer;
        +ack:           Continue;
        ENDCASE;
        Sendframe( phl_id, ph_sdu, status);
                        {This is the PH_DATA.request which transmits a
                        frame on the line. Control is not returned until the
                        entire frame is transmitted.
                        }
ELSE
        IF a time-out error occurs,
        THEN pause for a while;
        prepare a Polling command frame in ph_sdu;
        Set the timer and enter the polling state;
        Sendframe( phl_id, ph_sdu, status); ENDIF;      {Find out why.}
        CASE other message from the received task of
        +ack:           IF the sender is in polling state,
                        THEN advance both of its trailing and leading edges
                        of its sending window below Nr and start from there;
                        Go back to normal state;
                        ELSE advance the trailing edge of its sending window
                        below Nr;
                        Free its transmit buffer; ENDIF;
                        Reset the timer;
```

                −ack: Flush the sending window by moving both of its
                                trailing and leading edges below Nr;
                                Prepare retransmission whatever was left in the
                                window;
            ELSE: Interpret and execute;
            ENDCASE;
    ENDIF;
    Goto Transmit_loop;
    Endtask;

The Receive_task routine is sketched in the following:

    Receive_task:
        ...   {Handshake and initialize.}
    Receive_loop:
    Receiveframe(phl_id, ph_sdu, status);
            {This is the same as to receive a PH_DATA.indication.
            In other words, control is not returned until the entire
            frame is received.}
    CASE frame of
    Good data frame as expected:
            Send a message to Transmit_task to transmit the +ack, Nr
            frame;
            Advance its receiving window;
            Issue a DL_DATA.indication (dl_id, dl_sdu, status);
                    {If the N layer is implemented as a task, issue the
                    following system call instead,
                    Send (n_layer_task_id, dl_sdu, status);}
            IF the receiver is in Error state,
            THEN switch its state back to Normal; ENDIF;
    Corrupted or missing data frame:
            IF the receiver is in Normal state,
            THEN enter Error state;
            Send a message to Transmit_task to transmit the −ack, Nr
            frame; ENDIF;
            Discard the frame;
    +ack:
            Send the +ack received message to Transmit_task;
    −ack:
            Send the −ack received message to Transmit_task;
    Polling command:
            IF the receiver is in Normal state,
            THEN prepare a +ack, Nr frame;
            ELSE prepare a −ack, Nr frame; ENDIF;
            Send a message to Transmit_task to transmit the ack frame;

ELSE: Interpret and execute;
ENDCASE;
Goto Receive_loop;
Endtask;
End.

How to test a DL protocol? One simple solution is to simulate the DL software extensively with human-introduced errors using any general purpose programming language. After passing the test of all possible errors, the proposed SWP is placed in the field for beta test.

3.6 DATA LINK SIMULATIONS

The SAW ARQ simulation is quite simple because its transmission is half-duplex. Placing four subroutine calls in a loop, we can prove whether the protocol works correctly or not. Next, we discuss the simulation techniques of pipelined transmission. Simulations can be performed on one or two computers. With two computers, we are able to simulate real-time operations. Even with one computer, we can simulate the asynchronous processing concept with a multitasking design.

3.6.1 Simulation of Stop-and-Wait ARQ

The system block diagram to simulate SAW ARQ is shown in Figure 3.13(a). We introduce the medium task in the middle, which receives frames from the sender, introduces errors, and delivers the frame to the receiver. The medium task also receives ack frames from receiver, generates errors, and delivers the frame to the sender. Error rate can be programmed directly from the keyboard based on a given probability. For example, we may assume that 6 out of 16 times, transmission is perfect; 5 out of 16 times, make the frame disappear; and 5 out 16 times, bits in the frame flip in a random manner as shown in Table 3.1.
    The sum of all probabilities is computed as

$$(6/16 + 5/16 + 5/16) = 16/16 = 1$$

To obtain the error rate with a given probability, we may call a random number generator or just read the lower 4 bits of a real-time clock. Depending on the bits, we take appropriate action. For example, if the value is between 0 and 5 inclusive, we have a perfect transmission; between 6 and 10 make the frame disappear; and between 11 and 15, the bits flip in the frame.

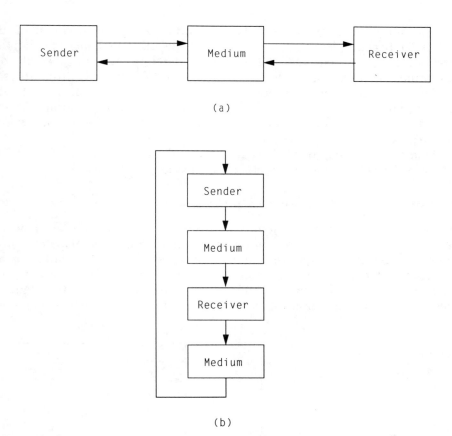

Figure 3.13 SAW ARQ simulations: (a) system block diagram and (b) four subroutine calls in a loop.

Table 3.1
Probability of Events

Event	Probability
Perfect transmission	6/16
Frame disappeared	5/16
Bits flip randomly	5/16

The simplest design is to simulate the half-duplex transmission using the SAW ARQ. Because the window size is 1, the execution sequence is fixed; that is sender, medium, receiver, and medium. Therefore, we can place all four subroutine calls in a loop as shown in Figure 3.13(b). The only difficulty is to simulate time-out errors. One simple solution is to set bits in a particular message to inform the sender that a time-out error has occurred. Frames can be two or three characters long, and after transmission is completed, the receiver may display a graphical pattern or flag on the screen.

It is more challenging to simulate pipelined transmission using either the GBN or SRJ ARQ on one or two PCs as discussed in Section 3.6.2.

3.6.2 Simulation of Pipelined Transmission

First, if the pipelined transmission is simulated on one computer, we have the system block diagram as shown in Figure 3.14(a). We add the dispatcher task, which manages message queues and determines which routine should execute next. Each task receives control from the dispatcher and, after execution, must return control to the dispatcher. If the window size is 2 or more, the sequence of task executions is not predicable. This concept is derived from the OS, except

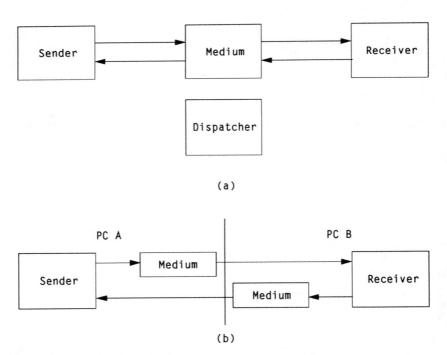

Figure 3.14 Simulations of pipelined transmission: (a) on one PC and (b) on two PCs.

that all routines are still running under one user task. To the OS, there is only one task control block (TCB) representing the user task or program. Even though the dispatcher passes control among different routines, each routine does not have a TCB. As a consequence, if any routine is placed in wait state by the OS, the entire program is in wait state. Our goal is to simulate the asynchronous processing concept with multiple tasks.

Asynchronous Processing Simulations

Assuming that the window size is 2, we assign a count variable for each task. The count of the sender is 2, the medium is 0, and the receiver is 0. The count really means the number of messages in the input queue of the task. A count greater than 0 means that the task is ready to execute; otherwise, the task is blocked. Initially, only the sender can proceed; both the medium and receiver tasks are blocked. After a task is being executed, its count is decremented by 1. Depending on the direction of data flow, the count of the next task is incremented by 1.

The medium task actually has two count variables, one for each direction. The medium task has two input queues. We can use a Direction flag to differentiate the two identical medium tasks, namely the forward medium task and the backward medium task. Initially, the sender has a count of 2, which means that the sender can execute twice in a row. After the sender executes once, its count is decremented by 1, and the count of the forward medium task is incremented by 1. At any instant, the total sum of the count variables of all tasks is equal to the window size, 2. The dispatcher keeps track of all count variables and manages the input/output queues.

To determine which task to execute next, the dispatcher calls a random number generator, mod 4. Action is taken depending on the value of the random number as described in the following:

```
CASE random number of
0:    execute sender;
1:    execute forward medium task;
2:    execute receiver;
3:    execute backward medium;
ENDCASE;
```

If the selected task has a count 0, the dispatcher must call the random number generator again until it hits a ready task. Assuming that four tasks, Sender (S), Forward Medium (FM), Backward Medium (BM), and Receiver (R) are running, verify the conclusions below after executing the given sequence:

1. S − FM − R − BM   {Forward Medium, Backward Medium and Receiver are all blocked. Only Sender can execute.}

2. S – S – FM – FM   {Only Receiver can execute.}
3. S – FM – R – S – FM – R {Only Backward Medium can execute.}

If two PCs are available, we can simulate pipelined transmissions in real time as shown in Figure 3.14(b).

The sender and forward medium tasks run on one PC while the receiver and backward medium tasks run on the other PC. In between, there is a null modem cable. Everything remains the same except that the dispatcher is no longer needed. To simulate activities in real time, we may add one more feature. If both the sender and receiver can execute, generate a random number (mod 2) to determine whether to impose a delay as shown below:

> CASE number of
> 0:   Skip execution and pause;
> 1:   Continue;
> ENDCASE;

There are many DL protocols in the field that can do the job well. There may be some minor differences, but the basic theories remain the same. Some DL protocols may be more reliable with less speed while others may be faster but less reliable.

3.7 XMODEM

The XMODEM protocol was proposed in the early 1980s to handle file transfers between two microcomputers [7]. It is simple and intuitive and the protocol works well, especially when the line is reliable. Since the UART chip is used in the microcomputers, we can transmit a block of ASCII characters asynchronously to the receiving computer. There may be a time delay between two successive characters, but the receiver starts processing only after receiving the entire block of characters. The features of XMODEM are listed below:

- Point-to-point connection;
- Asynchronous character-oriented transmission;
- Half-duplex;
- Fixed-length data;
- LRC;
- SAW ARQ.

The file is divided into logical sectors and each sector is 128 bytes long. Data frames are always 132 bytes long and control frames are all 1 byte in length. The data frame contains a 3-byte header followed by a 128-byte sector of data and a 1-byte LRC error detecting code. The first byte in the header is always the start of header (SOH) character. The second byte is the sector number mod 128 starting with 1. The third byte is the 1's complement of the second byte, the sector number. The sector number is the sending sequence number, which is guarded by its complement in the data frame. The last byte LRC is the arithmetic checksum of the 128-byte data mod 256 (i.e., 2^8). At the end of transmission, the sender transmits the EOT character. The receiver returns a +ack character, 06 in hex, to conclude the transmission.

It should be pointed out that the ack frame does not contain any sequence number that the receiver is expecting. If a +ack gets corrupted on the line, it induces a time-out error so the sender simply retransmits. If the receiver receives a data frame that is good but out of its window and the sending sequence number is 1 less than expected, the receiver knows it is a duplicate, discards the frame, and sends back a +ack. Note that the receiver should not return a −ack since that would put the sender in an infinite loop and the program would have to be aborted. Should a −ack be changed into a +ack on the line, the XMODEM protocol would crash.

Because the protocol requires that its data frame be fixed in length, the last sector in the data frame may be padded with garbage bytes (i.e., random bits). A header packet should be transmitted first to inform the receiver the exact length of the file, the direction of transfer, and so forth. The receiver on the destination node needs to store the valid bytes of the last sector on disk.

There are protective measures built into the protocol. The sender will not retransmit more than five times in a row, and the total number of errors received by the receiver should not exceed 10. In later versions, XMODEM is renamed to YMODEM and ZMODEM and uses a 16-bit CRC-ITU-T instead of LRC. Note that the protocol does not require any handshaking before data transfer. At the end of transmission, the sender sends an EOT character and expects an +ack from receiver to conclude the data transfer session. Note that the XMODEM protocol, even though simple, may be used in any computer network.

3.8 BINARY SYNCHRONOUS COMMUNICATIONS

The binary synchronous communications protocol remains widely used by most computer terminals [BSC]. It is pronounced as bi-sync because continuous 1's are transmitted as the quiescent state, and two or more synchronous (SYN) characters must be transmitted each time before the frame to synchronize the hardware. The characteristics of BSC are listed below:

- Point-to-point or multidrop connection;
- Synchronous character-oriented transmission;
- Half-duplex;
- Block check character (BCC);
- CRC-16 for the 8-bit extended binary coded decimal interchange code (EBCDIC);

- CRC-12 for the 6-bit transcode;
- Odd-parity VRC and LRC for the 7-bit ASCII;
- Variable block size;
- SAW ARQ.

Primary Versus Secondary Station

Handshaking procedures or station dialogues are built in BSC before data can be transmitted. The primary station is the computer and the secondary station may be a terminal or a computer. A primary station is the master, which has total control of the line. A secondary station is the slave, which listens to the primary all the time. A secondary can transmit only with the permission of the primary.

First, the primary station sends three characters:

SYN	SYN	ENQ

Two SYN characters, followed by an enquire (ENQ) character, are transmitted to the secondary station to enquire the line. In a multidrop line configuration, it is necessary to insert an address character in front of the ENQ character, and this optional Address field is used to address the secondary station as shown below:

SYN	SYN	Address	ENQ

The secondary station may send back one of the three responses. Each response contains two SYN characters followed by a control code with no error-detecting code to guard the response frame:

SYN	SYN	ACK0
SYN	SYN	NAK
SYN	SYN	WACK

The response ACK0 means that the receiver is ready to receive the data frame 0, which is considered an even frame. The second possible response is a negative Ack (NAK), which means the receiver is not ready. The third possible response is a wait but Ack (WACK), which means the receiver wants sender to wait for a while and try later with an ENQ frame. This implies some of kind of flow control. If the response is an ACK0, the sender sends a frame containing some header information as shown below:

SYN	SYN	SOH	Header	ETB	BCC

The header contains user-defined information, such as time-stamp and command code at the application level. The Header field is preceded by a SOH character and followed by an end transmission block (ETB) character and then a block check character (BCC) for error detection. If the receiver responds positively, then the sender sends subsequent frames in the following format:

| SYN | SYN | STX | Text | ETB | BCC |

where STX stands for start of text, ETB means end of block, and Text represents the text data block of variable size inside the frame. When the data frame is the last frame and there are no more frames to follow, the sender changes the ETB character to ETX, which means end of text, as shown below:

| SYN | SYN | STX | Text | ETX | BCC |

In BSC, the SAW ARQ is used with the window size equal to 1. This means that we need to include a 1-bit sequence number in the frame. Interestingly enough, the data frame does not contain any sequence number. Instead, the 1-bit sequence number is encoded in the +ack. So, besides ACK0, there is an ACK1 that tells the sender that the receiver is expecting an odd frame. After receiving a data frame, the receiver sends a control frame back containing two SYN characters followed by a control code as follows:

SYN	SYN	ACK0
SYN	SYN	ACK1
SYN	SYN	NAK
SYN	SYN	WACK
SYN	SYN	RVI

The control code of ACK0, ACK1, WACK, or reverse interrupt (RVI) is actually implemented as a two-character sequence, and the preceding character is the data link escape (DLE). The RVI frame informs the sender that the receiver needs the line. If the sender responds with a SYN ACK0, then the receiver may start to transmit. In other words, the secondary station becomes the sender and the primary station is the receiver. In the middle of data transmission, when a (TO) error occurs, the sender may send an ENQ frame to the receiver in order to restore things back to normal. At the end of data transmission, the sender sends the EOT character:

| SYN | SYN | EOT |

and the receiver acknowledges to conclude the session.

In BSC, the SAW ARQ is used for error/flow control. The window size is 1 for both sender and receiver. It supports three kinds of acknowledgments—ACK0, ACK1, and NAK. The data frame does not contain a sequence number. It is embedded in the +ack frame instead. When the sender sends a duplicate data frame, how does the receiver know? We even question whether the protocol is flawless. After thinking and debating, we conclude that BSC is a clever design.

Let us examine the following scenario. Suppose that a NAK is lost on the line; the sender times out and retransmits. There will be no confusion for the receiver because the receiver cannot advance its window until the correct data frame is received. But when a +ack gets lost on the line, the sender times out and retransmits. Now, can the receiver detect a duplicate frame? No, the receiver cannot, but the sender can. Suppose an ACK0 is lost on the line. The sender times out and retransmits the even frame. The receiver doesn't know it is a duplicate, so it sends an ACK1. But the sender is expecting an ACK0 and now receives an ACK1. The sender knows from ACK1 that the receiver has got a duplicate, so it sends a cancel (CAN) command to tell the receiver to cancel the previous data frame as shown below:

SYN   SYN   CAN

In the following, a more elegant solution is proposed to handle the (TO) error. Assuming after the sender sends out the I frame 1, the receiver returns an ACK0, which is lost on the line. Consequently, a (TO) error occurs. This is considered to be an abnormal condition that happens when either a +ack, −ack, or data frame gets lost on the line. The sender sends the ENQ command to poll the status of the receiver. If the receiver responds with an ACK1, the sender knows that an ACK0 got lost on the line and it should advance its window and send the next frame (i.e., I frame 1). On the other hand, if the received response is an ACK0, the sender knows that I frame 0 got lost and that it should retransmit the previous frame (i.e., I frame 0 as expected by the receiver). After things are smoothed out, processing goes back to normal.

We cannot implement pipelined transmission using XMODEM or BSC. Therefore, to develop a more advanced protocol, we implement the following:

1. Both the data frame and ack frames should contain sequence numbers to support a window size of 2 or more (i.e., pipelined transmission).
2. The piggybacking technique must be used so that the line can be fully utilized from the software point of view. In other words, the DL on either side can transmit data frames at the same time.

3.9 SYNCHRONOUS DATA LINK CONTROL

The synchronous data link control (SDLC) protocol was first proposed by IBM and later evolved to comply with the ISO standard [8][SDLC]. The SDLC has many unique features:

- Point-to-point or multidrop connection;
- Synchronous bit-oriented transmission;
- Full-duplex;

- Piggybacking;
- FCS-ITU-T;
- Variable frame size;
- Pipelined transmission using GBN ARQ.

There are three different frame types: the information (I), the supervisory, and the unnumbered. The SDLC frame format is shown in Figure 3.15(a). Each frame is enclosed by two Frame flags and each flag has a bit pattern, 01111110, in binary. The bit-stuffing technique is used to ensure that there is no such bit pattern in the middle of the frame. If a bit pattern of six consecutive 1's is found in the frame, it is considered to be a control signal and transmission is aborted.

The Frame flag is followed by a 1-byte Address field and a 1-byte Control field. In a point-to-point connection, the Address field should contain all 0's. However, in a multidrop connection, the Address field contains an address of the secondary. A secondary may have more than one address (e.g., an individual address and a group address). The broadcast address contains all 1's, which means every secondary on the line receives the transmission. The Control field contains the command code, a flag bit, and sequence numbers depending on the frame type. The I frame contains an Info field of variable length in bytes. All unnumbered frames do not have an Info field except the unnumbered information (UI) frame.

The next field is the 16-bit FCS, the error-detecting code for all the bits in the frame, which includes address, control, and info. Note that the stuffed bits of 0 in the frame are handled by hardware and therefore are not part of the data stream for frame check.

Flag	Address	Control	Information	FCS	Flag

(a)

7-bit	0	7-bit	0	7-bit	1

(b)

Figure 3.15 (a) SDLC frame format and (b) its extended 21-bit address field.

There are two sets of sequence numbers, 3-bit mod 8 or 7-bit mod 128. The mod 128 sequence number is also called an extended sequence number. SDLC handles both sets of sequence numbers.

Some special hardware equipment can also be used to support an extended Address field using the chaining technique. The Address field may have two or more bytes. The LSB in each byte is a chaining indicator. Using negative logic, a bit 0 indicates that more address bits are to follow and a bit 1 indicates the end of address. Since the chaining bit is not part of address, we can only encode an extended address as a multiple of 7 bits. A 3-byte Address field to encode a 21-bit extended address is shown in Figure 3.15(b).

The Control fields of an SDLC frame are shown in Figure 3.16. (Their bit definitions are listed in Figure 3.18.)

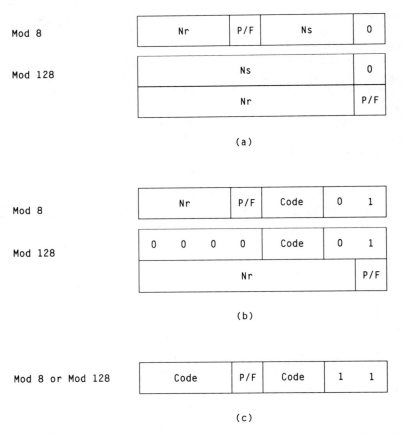

Figure 3.16 Control fields of an SDLC frame: (a) information frame, (b) supervisory frame, and (c) unnumbered frame.

3.9.1 Command and Response

The frame sent by the primary station is called a command that has a poll (P) bit in it. The frame sent by the secondary is called a response that contains a final (F) bit occupying the same bit position as the P bit. However, sometimes the secondary may send a control frame that is still called a response but it is truly a command in a semantic sense. By the same token, when the primary station returns a reject (REJ) frame, it is called a command but it is truly a response.

3.9.2 Information Frames

Bit 0 in the Control field is the main operation code (opcode), which differentiates an I frame from other control frames. In a mod 8 format of an I frame, the next 3 bits denote the Ns, which is the sending sequence number. Bits 5, 6, and 7 denote the Nr, which is the sequence number placed by receiver piggybacked on an outgoing I frame. Otherwise, Nr should be 0. The sequence number Nr indicates that up to $Nr - 1$ data frames have been correctly received. When the sending window size is 1, Nr becomes the sequence number that the receiver is expecting. Bit 4 is the P/F bit. P means poll while F means final. The primary station sets the P bit to poll the secondary as to whether it has any data to send. The secondary can transmit only when the P bit is set in a command. As the secondary sends the data frames one by one, it sets the same bit in the last data frame to indicate that transmission is final with no more data frames to follow. Now, control is passed back to the primary station.

> I (command or response): The I, or data, frame passes data from one station to the other. Since full-duplex transmission is allowed, either station may send I frames at the same time.

3.9.3 Supervisory Frames

Supervisory frames are considered to be control frames. Bits 2 and 3 are used as an extended opcode. Normally, the primary station sends a command to the secondary station and waits for a response from the secondary. Each of the three supervisory frames is a command or a response.

RR (command or response): The Receiver Ready (RR) frame is sent by the
> primary with the P bit set to indicate it is ready to receive. The secondary returns an RR frame with the F bit reset. Now, both stations can transmit I frames in full-duplex mode. When the secondary finishes transmitting all its I frames, it returns an RR frame with the F bit set to indicate final transmission. Therefore, RR really means a separate +ack. Nr is the sequence number placed in the frame by the station, either primary or secondary, to indicate that the station is expecting frame Nr. In other words, up to $Nr - 1$ frames have been correctly received. This idea is a truly

ingenious in that when a (TO) error occurs during transmission, the sender issues an RR frame with the P bit set to 1 polling the receiver. The receiver sends out an RR frame likewise. This scheme would work even if (TO) errors of both stations occur at the same time during full-duplex transmission. It is the Nr coded in the RR frame to inform the other station to take appropriate action.

RNR (command or response):   The Receiver Not Ready (RNR) frame indicates that the receiver is not ready to receive at this moment.

REJ (command or response):   The Reject (REJ) frame indicates a $-$ack to tell the sender to go back Nr. Note that a $-$ack is a more serious response that is implemented as an independent control frame that is not piggybacked. A REJ frame is sent by the receiver, which may be either station.

3.9.4 Unnumbered Frames

The third type includes the unnumbered or nonsequenced frames. They are also control frames between primary and secondary stations. A secondary may operate in one of three modes: initialization mode, normal response mode, or normal disconnected mode. Initialization mode means that the secondary has initialized its sequence numbers to 0's. Normal response mode means that the secondary cannot initiate any unsolicited transmissions unless it is requested to do so. It transmits only in response to a polling command from a primary; namely, a P bit is set in the Control field of a command frame. Normal disconnected mode means that the secondary is disconnected from the system after receiving a Disconnect (DISC) command or right after initialization. The unnumbered frames are described in the following:

BCN (response):   The Beacon (BCN) response from the secondary tells the primary that loss of input has occurred.

CFGR (command or response):   The primary sends the Configure (CFGR) command frame with a 1-byte function descriptor in the Info field. This function descriptor is a subcommand code that tells the secondary to perform various diagnostic tests and return a CFGR response to acknowledge it.

DISC (command):   The Disconnect (DISC) command puts the secondary in normal disconnected mode. The secondary responds with an Unnumbered Acknowledgment (UA). Usually, when hardware failures are suspected in the secondary, the secondary may send a Request Disconnect first. Then, the primary sends back a DISC command so the secondary can be disconnected offline and repaired. Offline means that the DL is no longer part of the system.

DM (response):   The Disconnect Mode (DM) response sent by the secondary tells the primary that the secondary is in Normal Disconnected Mode (NDM) after receiving a command with a P bit set in the frame. If the polling command is an RR frame, it responds with a Request Initiation Mode (RIM) frame instead.

FRMR (response): The Frame Reject (FRMR) is a response to the primary that the secondary has received an invalid command frame.

RD (response): The Request Disconnect (RD) frame asks the primary to send a DISC command to the secondary so it can be disconnected offline. RD and DISC share the same opcode in the Control field.

RIM (response): The Request for Initialization Mode (RIM) frame is sent by the secondary station to ask the primary to send a command to initialize. While the secondary is in Normal Disconnect Mode, it responds with an RIM frame after receiving a RR command frame.

SIM (command): The Set Initialization Mode (SIM) command tells the secondary to initialize and set its Ns and Nr to 0's. Note that SIM and RIM share the same opcode.

SNRM or SNRME (command): The Set Normal Response Mode (SNRM) command tells the secondary to operate in Normal Response Mode, mod 8. The Set Normal Response Mode Extended command (SNRME), however, tells the secondary to operate in Extended Normal Response Mode, mod 128. The primary sends either command after receiving a successful UA to a previous SIM command. The secondary station in Normal Response Mode, either mod 8 or 128, is not allowed to transmit unless requested to do so by the primary.

Test (command or response): The Test command is sent to the secondary in any operation mode to solicit a test response. If an Information field is encoded in the command frame, it will be returned in the Test response frame provided that the secondary station has enough buffering space to store the Information field.

UA (response): The UA is sent by the secondary to indicate a positive ack to an Unnumbered command, such as SIM, SNRM, SNRME, or DISC.

UI (command or response): The Unnumbered or non-sequenced I (UI) frame indicates that the I frame transmitted does not belong to the sequence. This is a special command designed to transmit real-time data frames and no ack is required during transmission. A DL_UNITDATA.request command message sent to the data link layer from the network layer will be translated into a UI frame.

UP (command): The Unnumbered Poll (UP) command with a P bit set polls the addressed secondary, and the secondary must respond. When the P bit in this command is cleared, the secondary sends an optional response only under certain conditions.

XID (command or response): The Exchange Station Identification (XID) frame has an Information field that contains the identification of the sending station. The receiver dittos.

3.9.5 Frame Check Sequence

The FCS field contains a 16-bit error detecting code that is computed as the complement of the logical sum of the following:

1. The remainder of 16-bit 1's followed by k 0's logically divided by the ITU-T polynomial code where k is the number of bits in the frame between, but not including, the final bit of the opening Frame flag and the first bit of the FCS, excluding the 0 bits inserted for transparency;
2. The remainder of the k-bit frame followed by 16-bit 0's logically divided by the same polynomial code.

Hardware Design of FCS-ITU-T Generation/Detection

The hardware shift register to generate/detect FCS is shown in Figure 3.17 [SDLC]. The same design is used for both transmitter and receiver. The preset and clock control signals are not shown in the schematic. The compute signal controls the timing of FCS generation/detection.

Note that in Figure 3.17, bits are laid out from left to right and x^0 denotes the LSB. The shift operations described below are toward x^{15}, the sign bit. Since the commutative law holds for EOR operations and the distributive law holds for logical divide, we can combine the two logical divide operations into one step.

At the sending end, we preset the 16-bit shift register with all 1's. If the x^5 bit in the register is different from the leading bit of the data stream, then logically shift the register 1 bit toward the sign bit and EOR the lower 16-bit of the polynomial code into the shift register; otherwise, just logically shift the register 1 bit toward the sign bit. Repeat this process until the data stream is exhausted. After dividing, the complement of the shift register is shifted out as FCS.

At the receiving end, we perform the same operation for the data stream, including the appended FCS. Before reaching FCS in the data stream, the shift register may contain any random bit pattern but the FCS to follow is the complement of it. Continuing the logical divide operation, we always obtain the same fixed remainder:

```
0001 1101 0000 1111
              ↑
             x^0
```

or 1d0f in hex, which may be represented algebraically by

$$x^{12} + x^{11} + x^{10} + x^8 + x^3 + x^2 + x^1 + x^0$$

Data Link Layer   169

3-bit data	Shift register of sender	Input to receiver	Shift register of receiver
	x^0		x^0
	1111 1111 1111 1111		1111 1111 1111 1111
0	1111 1011 1111 0111	0	1111 1011 1111 0111
1	0111 1101 1111 1011	1	0111 1101 1111 1011
1	0011 1110 1111 1101	1	0011 1110 1111 1101
	0001 1111 0111 1110	0	1001 1011 0111 0110
	0000 1111 1011 1111	1	1100 1001 1011 0011
	0000 0111 1101 1111	0	1110 0000 1101 0001
	0000 0011 1110 1111	0	1111 0100 0110 0000
	0000 0001 1111 0111	0	0111 1010 0011 0000
	0000 0000 1111 1011	0	0011 1101 0001 1000
	0000 0000 0111 1101	0	0001 1110 1000 1100
	0000 0000 0011 1110	0	0000 1111 0100 0110
	0000 0000 0001 1111	1	1000 0011 1010 1011
	0000 0000 0000 1111	0	1100 0101 1101 1101
	0000 0000 0000 0111	0	1110 0110 1110 0110
	0000 0000 0000 0011	0	0111 0011 0111 0011
	0000 0000 0000 0001	0	1011 1101 1011 0001
	0000 0000 0000 0000	0	1101 1010 1101 0000
	0000 0000 0000 0000	1	1110 1001 0110 0000
	0000 0000 0000 0000	1	1111 0000 1011 1000

↑ 3-bit data and 16-bit FCS

Fixed remainder

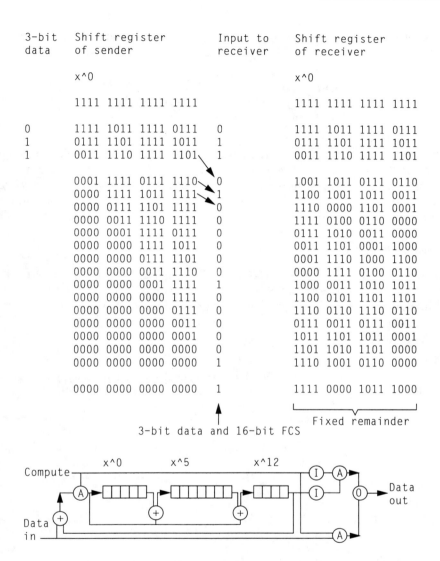

Gates: + = Exclusive or   0 = Or
        I = Invertor   A = And

Figure 3.17 A 16-bit shift register to generate/detect FCS.

It is exactly the same as the remainder of 16-bit 1's followed by 16-bit 0's divided by the polynomial code, as proven below:

$$(P \cdot 2^{\wedge}16) / D + (\backslash P \cdot 2^{\wedge}16) / D = ((P + \backslash P) \cdot 2^{\wedge}16) / D$$
$$= (16\text{-bit 1's} \cdot 2^{\wedge}16) / D$$
$$= 0001\ 1101\ 0000\ 1111$$

where P is any 16-bit pattern in the shift register before reaching FCS in the data stream and $\backslash P$ is its complement. It should be mentioned that this scheme does not cost any additional hardware or time delay. Therefore, its performance should be comparable with the standard CRC. FCS-ITU-T can also be simulated by software, and its design is both elegant and important as explained below.

Software Design of FCS-ITU-T Generation/Detection

The software design of FCS-ITU-T generation is similar to that of CRC-ITU-T with two alterations. First, FCS is initialized to all 1's. Secondly, after all shift and logical operations are completed, the complement of FCS is the answer as shown below:

```
;-------------------------------------------------------------------------
;       fcs:            a 16-bit unsigned integer containing the frame ; check sequence.
;       divisor:        a 16-bit unsigned integer containing the lower 16-
;                       bit of the polynomial code. It has a statically
;                       assigned value, 0001 0000 0010 0001 in binary
;                       or 1021 in hex.
;       data_block:     an array of 8-bit characters whose address ; is passed as a parameter.
;       n:              the size of the data_block passed as a parameter.
;-------------------------------------------------------------------------
;
        Function fcs (data_block, n)
        Initialize fcs to all 1's;
        REPEAT
        Fetch the next character from the data_block into a 16-bit word,
        logically shift 8 bits to the left and EOR it into fcs;
                REPEAT
                IF the leading bit of fcs is 1,
                THEN shift fcs 1 bit to the left;
                EOR the divisor into fcs;
                Else shift fcs 1 bit to the left; ENDIF;
                UNTIL 8 times;
        UNTIL n times;
        Complement fcs;
        Return fcs;
```

This design works as long as the data message contains an integer multiple of bytes. If the message contains 128 ASCII b's and assuming that bit 7 is transmitted first, the computed FCS should be 7692 in hex. The same routine can be used to detect errors. If we feed only the data portion of the message to this routine, the returned FCS should match the FCS received if no errors have occurred during transmission.

It is interesting to find out what happens if we feed the entire message including the received FCS to this routine for error detecting. What should be the returned FCS? Note that the total length of the message should be 2 bytes longer because of the 2-byte FCS appended at the end. Immediately after the logical divide operation, the FCS derived in the routine should contain 1d0f in hex, which is the remainder of 16-bit 1's followed by 16-bit 0's divided by the polynomial code. But the result is complemented before return, so the FCS returned should be e2f0 in hex if no errors have occurred. Just like computing CRC, the same table lookup technique can be used to compute FCS.

Special Case

If the data stream contains exactly 16 bits as a DL command frame, we could apply the standard CRC generation algorithm to obtain the FCS-ITU-T directly. The selected residual remainder appended to the original message before the divide operation should be

$$1110\ 0010\ 1111\ 0000$$
$$\uparrow$$
$$x\hat{}0$$

or e2f0 in hex, which is the complement of the remainder derived by dividing the polynomial code into a dividend of 16 1's followed by 16 0's. The reasoning is intuitive, because if we place 16 1's in the shift register followed by 16 0's, a remainder is derived after the logical divide operation. But, the FCS is the complement of what remains in the shift register. Therefore, the selected residual remainder should be the complement of this derived remainder. From the FCS definition, we have

$$FCS = \backslash(R1 + R) = R + \backslash R1 = R + S$$

where Remainder 1 ($R1$) is the first remainder; R is the second remainder or CRC-ITU-T; and S is the complement of $R1$. Looking at this equation, we find that the FCS is the same as the derived remainder using S as the selected residual remainder in the divide. In other words, if we append e2f0 to any 16-bit data message and perform the logical divide operation, we obtain the derived remainder FCS directly. It should be stressed that this algorithm only works when the data message is exactly 16 bits long.

3.10 HIGH-LEVEL DATA LINK CONTROL

The HDLC protocol is the superset of many protocols [HDLC]. The Control fields of an HDLC frame, mod 8 are specified in Figure 3.18. HDLC was derived from SDLC by adding more features, described below:

1. A SREJ supervisory frame was added to facilitate the SRJ ARQ algorithm.
2. Two more operating modes were added. The first one is the Asynchronous Response Mode (ARM), which means that the secondary may send a response first without being polled by the primary. The secondary may issue a Set Asynchronous Response Mode (SARM) response first to initiate a connection. The second one is the Asynchronous Balanced Mode (ABM), which means that either side is a combined station of a primary and secondary, which can transmit any command or response. Therefore, either station may issue a Set Asynchronous Balanced Mode (SABM) command to initiate a connection.
3. A Reset (RSET) command was added to inform the secondary to reset its hardware control functions.

Note that X.25 defines the interface between a DTE and a DCE for terminals operating in packet mode and connected to a public data network by dedicated lines [X.25]. In other words, X.25 covers the bottom three layer protocols in a packet-switching network. DTE and DCE can be treated as computers. The DL protocol in X.25 is either the link access procedure (LAP) or the link access procedure, balanced (LAPB). Each one is a subset of HDLC. Consequently, X.25 and HDLC are used interchangeably.

3.10.1 Link Access Procedure

LAP operates in ARM. DTE is the primary station, and DCE is the secondary station. For Call Request, DTE simply transmits a SARM command and DCE responds with a UA response to confirm.

When an incoming call arrives, it is the ideal situation to have a three-way handshake as shown below:

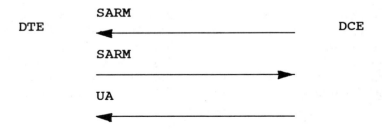

Information	I	r	r	r	P/F	s	s	s	0
Supervisory	RR	r	r	r	P/F	0	0	0	1
	RNR	r	r	r	P/F	0	1	0	1
	REJ	r	r	r	P/F	1	0	0	1
	SREJ	r	r	r	P/F	1	1	0	1
Unnumbered	BCN	1	1	1	P	1	1	1	1
	CFGR	1	1	0	P/F	0	1	1	1
	DM/SARM	0	0	0	P/F	1	1	1	1
	DISC/RD	0	1	0	P/F	0	0	1	1
	FRMR	1	0	0	F	0	1	1	1
	RSET	1	0	0	P	1	1	1	1
	RIM/SIM	0	0	0	P/F	0	1	1	1
	SABM	0	0	1	P	1	1	1	1
	SABME	0	1	1	P	1	1	1	1
	SARME	0	1	0	P/F	1	1	1	1
	SNRM	1	0	0	P/F	0	0	1	1
	SNRME	1	1	0	P/F	1	1	1	1
	TEST	1	1	1	P/F	0	0	1	1
	UA	0	1	1	F	0	0	1	1
	UI	0	0	0	P/F	0	0	1	1
	UP	0	0	1	P	0	0	1	1
	XID	1	0	1	P/F	1	1	1	1

r r r - Receiving sequence no.
s s s - Sending sequence no.

Figure 3.18 Control fields of an HDLC frame, mod 8.

with the following explanations:

1. DCE transmits a SARM response to its DTE to request a DL connection.
2. DTE responds with a SARM command to ask DCE to operate in ARM.
3. DCE responds with a UA response to confirm.

After the phone conversation or any abnormal condition is encountered, DTE may transmit a DISC command to tell DCE to disconnect and DCE responds with a UA response. DCE may also initiate the disconnect process by having the three-way handshake. DCE transmits a Request Disconnect response first, DTE transmits a DISC command next, and DCE returns a UA response to confirm.

3.10.2 Link Access Procedure, Balanced

LAPB is the preferred protocol for all new DTE installations. Either the DTE or the DCE can issue a SABM command and the other side responds with a UA response to establish a DL connection as shown below:

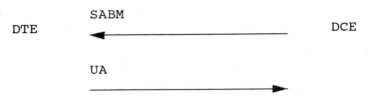

1. DCE transmits a SABM response to its DTE to request a DL connection.
2. DTE responds with a UA response to confirm.

To support both LAP and LAPB, a DCE keeps an internal mode variable. After receiving a SARM/SARME command from its DTE, a DCE sets the mode variable to 0 to indicate LAP mode. On the other hand, after receiving a SABM/SABME from its DTE, the DCE sets the mode variable to 1 to indicate LAPB mode. Both LAP and LAPB protocols use GBN ARQ with window size equal to 2.

When a DTE and a DCE operate in ABM, either side is a combined station of a primary and secondary that may transmit any command or response. After the conversation, either side can initiate a DISC command. The other side responds with a UA response to disconnect.

3.11 CONCLUSIONS

It should be mentioned that a DL exchanges frames with its peer on a computer that has a direct connection. The N layer mainly handles routing. If the routing function is not performed in a network with only two computers, then the N layer need not be implemented. Furthermore, if each computer supports only one single user task that transmits and receives packets, we can get rid of the T layer, which mainly handles multiplexing. Such a simple system may be used in a lab or classroom, and the DL layer becomes the only service provider in the NAMs. But, generally speaking, a computer network supports the upper layers, namely network, transport, and session.

Yet, there are other systems that do not have a DL layer and the error-recovery functions are performed by upper layers. As an example, in a real-time voice or video data transmission system, the error-recovery function may not be required because the data bits are less critical. On the other hand, a system may be designed to support a real-time control mission. That is, a good DL is required in the system to ensure reliable transmissions among ships in a sea battle or between an aircraft and its ground-based control station during landing. This is especially true when wireless technology is used. As a solution to this problem, we can write good DL software for error/flow control.

3.12 SUMMARY POINTS

1. The DL layer software handles flow/error control. It is an essential element in the design of a NAM.

2. The even-parity scheme has a theoretical edge over the odd-parity scheme if both VRC and LRC are used during data transmission.
3. Standard CRC is used as the error-detecting code in the microcomputer industry, and the selected residual remainder can be any bit pattern.
4. If the real-time mission is critical, any error that occurs during transmission in a computer network should be detected and corrected without delay.
5. Whenever the receiver detects an error, it sends a −ack to the sender, which simply retransmits.
6. When a TO error occurs, the sender should poll the status of receiver and ask for the data frame it is expecting, so the sender can restore things back to normal.
7. In an SWP, the sender must guard the trailing edge of its window carefully. The receiver places Nr in an ack frame to indicate that up to $Nr - 1$ data frames have been correctly received.
8. Pipelined transmission means that the size of the sending window is greater than 1.
9. The piggybacking technique is used in full-duplex transmission, which means that a +ack is combined into an outgoing data frame.
10. Character-stuffing and bit-stuffing techniques are used to solve certain protocol design problems.
11. A DL could be a shared resource in a multiprogramming environment. It should handle its own handshaking procedures.
12. A DL should be reliable. It may be the bottom layer in a network access method provided that the hardware communication controller can transmit a block of bytes.
13. Each DL frame has its own header and trailer, which are not passed to its N layer. The header defines the DL PDU and the trailer contains an error-detecting code. 14. The design of the T layer is very similar to the DL layer using the sliding window protocol.

Problems

Problem 3.1

What are the three essential elements in the design of a good DL protocol?

Problem 3.2

If we only transmit 7-bit ASCII characters a and b using even-parity VRC and LRC, what are the bits in the message?

Problem 3.3

If we only transmit 7-bit ASCII characters a and b using odd-parity VRC and LRC, what are the bits in the message?

Problem 3.4

Prove that when odd-parity VRC and LRC are used, there is always a consistent lower left corner bit that guards both the VRC and LRC correctly provided that the number of columns and the number of rows are both even or odd. Hint: Assume two cases: the data block contains an even number of 1's or an odd number of 1's.

Problem 3.5

Prove that when odd-parity VRC and LRC are used, it is not possible to have a lower left corner bit that guards both the VRC and LRC correctly if the number of columns is even but the number of rows is odd, and vice versa.

Problem 3.6

Assuming that we use a polynomial code $x^4 + x + 1$ as the divisor to compute the CRC and ASCII b is in the data block, what is the entire message transmitted? Hint: Assuming that bit 7 is transmitted first, the entire message should be 62b in hex and the CRC is 4 bits long.

Problem 3.7

In the above problem, should the designer decide to send the CRC in its complement form, the entire message would become 624 in hex. At the receiving end, verify that the residual remainder should be four 1's after the same logical divide operation.

Problem 3.8

Write a routine in any high-level language to generate the CRC-ITU-T using the standard CRC algorithm:

1. Verify that the answer is 4ce4 in hex if the data block contains one b or a 2-byte 0062 in hex.
2. If the data block contains 128 bytes of ASCII b's, verify that the answer should be 7967 in hex or yg in ASCII.

Problem 3.9

Repeat the above problem by rewriting the routine in any assembly language.

Problem 3.10

Write a routine in any high-level language to generate the CRC-32 using the standard CRC algorithm. For an ASCII b, the CRC-32 is a527 fdfa and for 128 b's, the CRC-32 is 4fca 8abb.

Problem 3.11

In BSC, there is a 1-bit sequence number embedded in the +ack frame instead of the data frame. Is it adequate to implement a SAW ARQ?

Problem 3.12

In SDLC, the primary station sends out a Disconnect (DISC) command to the secondary. What is the response returned by the secondary if accepted?

Problem 3.13

In SDLC, after the primary sends a Set Initialization Mode (SIM) command to the secondary and receives a UA response. What is the next command to be sent?

Problem 3.14

State the algorithm to generate the FCS-ITU-T in SDLC or HDLC.

Problem 3.15

Assume that the data stream contains, 1000 0000 1100 1110 in binary or 80ce in hex:

1. Compute the FCS-ITU-T. Note that the first byte is a multidrop address, the second byte is a UA response, and bit 0 of each byte is transmitted first. In addition, the hardware controller generates the FCS based on the actual bit string and the entire message should be 80ce c1ea in hex.
2. Verify the answer as the derived remainder if we append a residual remainder e2f0 to the data stream, then logically divide the polynomial code into the dividend.
3. Presetting the shift register in Figure 3.17 to all 0's and going over the same logical divide to the end, we obtain a fixed bit pattern in the register that is the remainder by dividing the polynomial code into the residual remainder, e2f0 in hex followed by 16-bit 0's. The final remainder is also a fixed bit pattern, 99cf in hex.

You deserve extra credit if you try to understand why. After finishing dividing the first 16-bit data, the shift register should contain a CRC that is the remainder by dividing the polynomial code into the 16-bit data message followed by 16-bit 0's.

The next 16-bit stream to follow is the FCS, which is the CRC obtained by dividing the polynomial code into the 16-bit data message followed by the residual remainder, e2f0 in hex. It is interesting to note that there is a fixed relationship among the standard CRC obtained by using a residual remainder, 0; the CRC obtained by using a special residual remainder; and the residual remainder itself. EOR any two of them, and we obtain the third one. Therefore, EOR the CRC that is obtained by using a residual remainder, 0 and the FCS, and we obtain the residual remainder, e2f0. But logical divide operation continues. So, in the end we should obtain a remainder, 99cf in the shift register, which is the remainder by dividing the polynomial code into e2fo followed by 16-bit 0's.

Problem 3.16

The empire of a little guy in the galaxy transmits data in 4-bit nibbles using the FCS-4 as defined below:

1. The polynomial code divisor is $x^4 + x + 1$.
2. FCS-4 is computed as the complement of the logical sum of the following:
   a. The remainder of the 4-bit 1's followed by k-bit 0's divided by the polynomial code where k is the length of the data stream.
   b. The remainder of the k-bit data stream followed by 4-bit 0's divided by the polynomial code.

If the data stream is 1111 in binary, what is the entire message to be sent? The answer should be intuitive. Since the data stream is exactly 4 bits long, the standard CRC algorithm can be applied to this particular case. Dividing the polynomial code into the dividend, which is the 4-bit data followed by a residual remainder, we should obtain the remainder directly as FCS-4. What should be the 4-bit selected residual remainder appended to the data block before divide?

Problem 3.17

This is a project proposal. Form a team of up to three students, select your own leader and programming language, conduct design meetings, and implement one of the two projects described below:

1. If you have access to a PC or any computer, write a routine to simulate a particular protocol, such as XMODEM, BSC, or SDLC.
2. If you have two PCs, build a null modem cable to connect the two machines. Then, write the DL software to implement a SWP specified by you.

No matter which project you choose, simulate the sliding window protocol using SAW, GBN, or SRJ ARQ. Have fun.

References

[1] Field, J., "Logical Link Control," *Proc. IEEE INFOCOM*, Apr. 1986, pp. 331–336.
[2] Hamming, R. W., "Error Detecting and Error Correcting Codes," *Bell System Tech. Journal*, Vol. 29, April 1950, pp. 147–160.
[3] Peterson, W., and D. Brown, "Cyclic Codes for Error Detection," *Proc. of the IRE*, Jan. 1961, pp. 228–235.
[4] Yao, G., A Study of Selective-Repeat ARQ and Sliding Window Protocol in Data Link Control, Master Thesis, Dept. of Computer Science, Cal Poly, San Luis Obispo, CA, 93407, 1992.
[5] Hsu, J. Y., "A Driver-Receiver Design for Data Communication," *Proc. of the International Computer Symposium*, Taiwan, 1973, pp. 821–832.
[6] Conard, J. W., "Services and Protocols of the Data Link Layer," *Proc. of the IEEE*, Vol. 71, No. 12, Dec. 1983, pp. 1378–1383.
[7] Clark, D. D., "Lmodem: A Small Remote-Communication Program," *Byte Journal*, Nov. 1983, pp. 410–428.
[8] McNamara, J.E., *Technical Aspects of Data Communication*, 2nd edition, Digital Press, 1982.

Local Area Networks 4

The Lord grants us two ends, one for thinking and one for sitting. Your success depends on which end you use. Heads you win.

In a WAN, a typical terminal site is usually connected to a cluster of computers grouped into one or more LANs, as shown in Figure 4.1. Router A is a switching node connected to three different LANs at one site and router B is connected to other LANs at a different site. Each LAN has its own design features. Routers A and B are interconnected through telephone lines.

LANs are so named because the distance between two adjacent nodes rarely exceeds 2.5 km. In addition, all nodes are normally confined within a few square miles. A node means a computer or station. Each LAN uses an ingenious hardware design driven by a special software access method. Because the distance between any two nodes is short, special hardware transmitters and receivers are designed without using modems. All communication circuits, including the processor, are placed on a single board, sitting side by side with the main processor.

Since future LAN design dearly affects our daily life, we devote one whole chapter to the discussion of LAN-related design issues before proceeding to the next chapter on routing.

4.1 BASIC DESIGN CONCEPTS

One common feature of LAN design is that when a node transmits, all other nodes receive the data frame either at the same time or after a short period of delay. As far as hardware design is concerned, there are two major approaches:

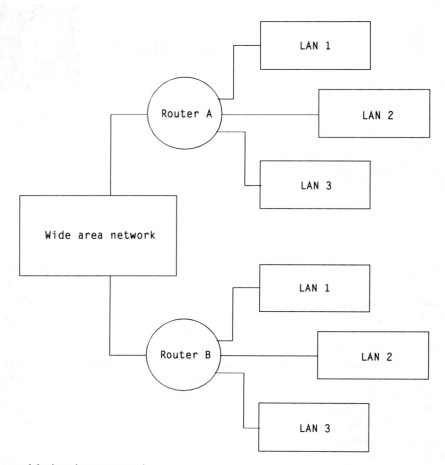

Figure 4.1 Local area networks.

one uses a common bus and the other uses point-to-point links. On a common bus, each node is connected to the transmission medium via a tap, which is a passive port as shown in Figure 4.2(a). A passive port contains a transmitter and receiver pair that is directly coupled with the medium. The signal remains the same on the line, with very little attenuation. There is no bit delay introduced because the node does not retransmit the signal. A point-to-point link, however, is an active port that intercepts the signal and retransmits it on the line with or without modifying the bits in the frame, as shown in Figure 4.2(b). An active port always introduces some bit delays.

Even with the same hardware, different software can be written to support a special access method. Therefore, from the viewpoint of software, there are

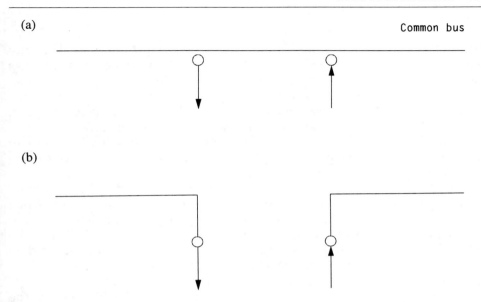

Figure 4.2 (a) Passive vs. (b) active port.

four major approaches: the common bus, token ring, token bus, and dual bus. Other variations include the dual ring and slotted rings.

4.1.1 Innovative Technologies

Each of the above mentioned approaches uses innovative technologies in hardware and software, or combinations of both.

The first approach is to use one common bus to tie all computers together. At the end of the bus, there is a terminal impedance required to damp the reflections of standing waves. One special computer on the bus runs the server program, which connects the LAN to an outside WAN. Each node can transmit data to and receive data from the server. In that regard, the common-bus technology becomes a star in software design. Because of the hardware connection, it is also possible to write an application server on each node so that all the nodes on the bus can communicate with each other. Collisions occur when two or more nodes try to transmit their frames at the same time. One simple solution is to ask all nodes involved in a collision to retransmit after waiting for a random period of time.

The second approach is to tie all the computers in a ring using point-to-point links. The ring is like one big circular shift register. After initialization, a token is flowing on the ring. The token is just a special bit pattern representing the right to transmit. Each node on the ring must compete for the token with access based on an assigned priority. Whichever node grabs the token, becomes the next sending node. The data flows from the sending node, passes all other nodes on the ring, and returns to the sending node. It is the responsibility of the sending node to strip its own data off the ring and retransmit the token. Thus, collisions are avoided. Such a design is known as the token ring.

The third approach is to use a common bus but write special software to support the token-passing concept. The fourth approach uses dual rings; one goes clockwise and the other one goes counterclockwise to provide redundancy. A fifth approach, widely used in the CATV industry, is called dual unidirectional buses. On each bus, all the nodes are connected together in a whip using point-to-point links. Traffic flows in one direction on bus 1 and flows the other way on bus 2. There is no common bus, no token passing, and no collision. The head of each bus passes free slots from one end to the other at fixed time intervals. Whenever a node has data to transmit, it finds a free slot on the bus, places data in it, and transmits the slot to the destination node.

The DL layer in a LAN is divided into two sublayers. The PH layer may be one single layer or divided into two sublayers, as introduced in Section 4.1.2.

4.1.2 Sublayers

Different software is designed to support different hardware. Even with the same hardware, different software techniques may be written to support different access methods. Except for the server node, which is connected to the outside world, all other nodes on a LAN do not support routing functions. To put it bluntly, there is usually no N layer on a LAN if it is isolated.

A standard LAN model is shown in Figure 4.3(a). The DL layer is divided into two sublayers: the logical link control (LLC) and the medium access control (MAC). The combination of MAC and LLC in a LAN provides the equivalent functions of the DL layer in a WAN. Note that every LAN has a MAC sublayer that resides between the LLC sublayer and the PH layer. In regard to software design, the PH layer is hardware-dependent, and the LLC sublayer provides error/flow control just like the DL layer in a WAN.

Because the physical level I/O routines interact with the hardware registers of the controller and the transmission medium may be different, the routines can be grouped as one single PH layer or divided into two sublayers: the physical signal (PLS) and the physical medium dependent (PMD), as shown in Figure 4.3(b). The PLS sublayer provides the physical level services to its MAC sublayer while the PMD sublayer simply drives a special hardware controller, which in turn transmits signals to the medium. Note that the software services provided by PLS or PH to the MAC sublayer are pretty much the same.

There are also NMT routines that interact with the four sublayers running on the station. The station management (SMT) routines in a LAN are just the same as the NMT routines in a WAN.

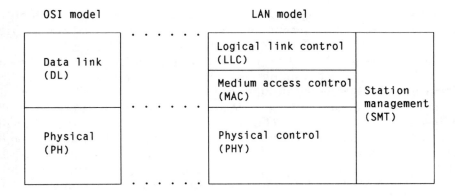

Figure 4.3 Comparisons of the OSI and LAN models: (a) one physical layer in a LAN and (b) two physical sublayers in a LAN.

4.2 MEDIUM ACCESS CONTROL SUBLAYER

The MAC sublayer is unique to a particular LAN. In other words, each LAN has its own MAC.

In Ethernet, the sending node listens to the line first before transmitting a data frame. If no one is transmitting on the line, then the sending node transmits. It is still possible that two or more nodes transmit at the same time; this effect is known as a collision. When a sending node transmits, it also receives. If the received bits do not match with those transmitted, the node realizes there is a collision. When that happens, the sending node transmits a jam signal on the line to inform all other nodes that a collision has been detected. Each of the collided senders must retransmit their frames after waiting for a random period of time in order to avoid a subsequent collision.

In a token ring LAN, a token or frame is always flowing on the ring. A token is actually a string of bits. A simple design is to grant the token based on the first in first out (FIFO) queuing discipline. Whoever is first gets the token and transmits. This indicates that everyone on the ring has equal priority, just like a university environment. In practice, each node is assigned a priority. Any node on the ring must request a token first based on its assigned priority. If no one on the ring has a token request with higher priority, when the token flows back to the requesting node, it can grab the token and become the sending node.

All intermediate nodes receive and retransmit the data on the ring. The receiving node does the same except it copies the data into its own receive buffer. It also sets bits in the frame trailer to indicate acknowledgment. The frame trailer contains an error-detecting code and status bits. Any node on the ring can validate the correctness of the data frame as it receives the frame. When the data frame flows back to the sending node, the sending node knows from the status bits in the trailer whether the data transmission is perfect or not. If the status bits indicate errors, the sending node retransmits the data. Therefore, in a token ring, the sliding window protocol is not implemented in LLC.

The token may be lost on the ring due to exceptional conditions, such as lightening. When that happens, the active monitor simply places another token on the ring. In the middle of data transfer, a node can also be inserted into or removed from the ring manually or electronically. The active monitor manages the transitions smoothly without major disruptions.

Token bus uses a common bus, but its software is a token ring. Yet another way is to modify two slotted rings to a dual bus. Even though the software access methods are different because of different MAC control primitives, all MAC data primitives are simple and uniform. MAC sublayers are connectionless, and each one tries to solve the contention problems in a special way.

4.2.1 MAC Sublayer Primitives

The service user of a MAC sublayer is the LLC sublayer, which can send a protocol data unit (PDU) to its peer logical link via a MAC sublayer data request as shown below:

>   MA_DATA.request(destination_address, m_sdu, service_class);

where destination_address is the unique hardware address of the receiving node, m_sdu is the MAC service data unit, and service_class denotes the proposed priority of data transfer. All the bits placed on the bus constitute a MAC data frame.

The receiving MAC sublayer issues a data indication primitive to its LLC sublayer as follows:

MA_DATA.indication(destination_address, source_address, m_sdu, service_class, status);

where source_address is the hardware address of the sending node, status reports what has happened to this data transfer, and the rest of parameters are the same as in a MA_DATA.request.

The MAC sublayer can be designed as an independent task. After issuing a data request, the LLC is free to do something else and the MAC issues a data confirm primitive as follows:

MA_DATA.confirm(service_class, status);

where service_class is the provided service class and status indicates success or failure after the request. Retransmission too many times is considered a failure.

4.2.2 MAC Protocol Data Units

An LLC protocol data unit (LPDU) is passed from the LLC sublayer to its MAC sublayer in a request primitive and the same unit becomes an m_sdu. The LPDU (i.e., m_sdu in a MA_DATA.request or indication) contains either control or data information that the sending LLC wants the receiving LLC to see. The two LLCs are peers. The MAC sublayer adds its own header and trailer to encapsulate the m_sdu and make it a MAC protocol data unit (MAPDU). It then asks its PH layer to transmit the MAC data frame on the line. The bits in the header are used to define the types of MAPDUs, which may be different from LAN to LAN as discussed later.

The MAC sublayer at the receiving end strips the header and trailer and delivers the LPDU to its LLC sublayer via a data indication. The LLC primitives are internal software routines, but the LLC protocol data units are standards.

4.3 LOGICAL LINK CONTROL SUBLAYER

The LLC sublayer in a LAN is quite similar to the DL layer in a WAN, but there are some minor differences. The LLC sublayer supports three types of frames—information, supervisory, and unnumbered—just like SDLC and HDLC. Because the MAC sublayer has a unique design feature in a particular LAN, it also affects the design of its LLC sublayer. As an example, the LLC sublayer of Ethernet can use SWP to transmit info frames between a client node and a server node. But in a token ring or token bus LAN, sliding window protocol is not necessary because the sending node also receives the frame from the ring and it can detect errors and retransmit if necessary. The receiver routine changes its philosophy accordingly. Needless to say, the software routine on the destination node always uses the latest copy of a data frame to replace any old copy that contains the same sending sequence number.

4.3.1 LLC Sublayer Primitives

Two types of LLC sublayer services are provided, connection-oriented and connectionless. For connection-oriented services, a logical link connection is established before data transfer can begin, as shown in Figure 4.4. The upper layer issues a LLC connect primitive as shown below:

L_CONNECT.request(local_address, remote_address, service_class);

where local_address is a global LLC service access point (LSAP) of the origination node, the remote_address is the LSAP of the destination LLC, and service_class denotes a proposed priority of data transfer in the MAC sublayer. An LSAP is the concatenation of a local reference number and its global hardware address of the node. In the MAC sublayer header, both the origination and destination LSAPs are unique to the LAN.

The destination LLC sublayer sends a connect indication to its upper layer as shown below:

L_CONNECT.indication(local_address, remote_address, service_class);

The upper layer at the destination node sends down a connect response as follows:

L_CONNECT.response(local_address,remote_address,service_class,status);

where service_class is the approved priority of data transfer and status indicates whether the connection is successful or not. Finally, the origination LLC sublayer sends a connect confirm as shown below:

L_CONNECT.confirm(local_address, remote_address, service_class, status);

There are two types of data primitives: one needs a connection and the other does not. The connection-oriented data primitive request is shown in the following:

L_DATA.request(local_address, remote_address, l_sdu);

where l_sdu is the link service data unit. The LLC sublayer will pass sufficient information to its MAC sublayer, which in turn transmits an information frame on the line. The receiving LLC delivers the frame to its upper layer via an L_DATA.indication primitive as shown below:

L_DATA.indication(local_address, remote_address, l_sdu);

Figure 4.4 Logical link control primitives.

The other data request primitive does not require a connection, which is truly a datagram to the LLC sublayer as shown below:

L_UNITDATA.request(local_address, remote_address, l_sdu);

This request is mapped into an unnumbered information (UI) frame delivered to its MAC sublayer via an MA_DATA.request. After receiving the l_sdu, its peer LLC issues an L_UNITDATA.indication primitive to its upper layer.

Other primitives include L_DISCONNECT and L_RESET.
The bits received by a LLC sublayer constitute the LLC protocol data units as discussed in Section 4.3.2.

4.3.2 LLC Protocol Data Units

The LLC protocol data unit (LPDU) must be precisely defined as proposed standards [IEEE 802.2]. The Control field is either 1 or 2 bytes long depending on the type of frame. Certain frames do not contain sequence numbers, so their Control fields are 1 byte long as shown in Figure 4.5(a). Other frames contain one or two sequence numbers, so their Control fields are 2 byte long as shown in Figure 4.5(b).

The leading byte of a LLC header is the destination service access point (DSAP), which is merely a local reference number of the LLC at the receiving node as shown in Figure 4.6(a). The LSB is an Address flag: 0 implies an

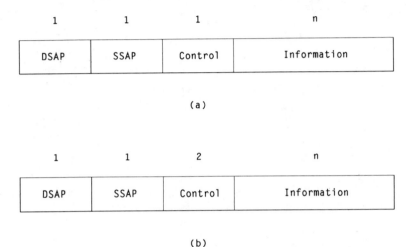

Figure 4.5 LLC protocol data units: (a) Control field with no sequence numbers and (b) Control field with sequence numbers.

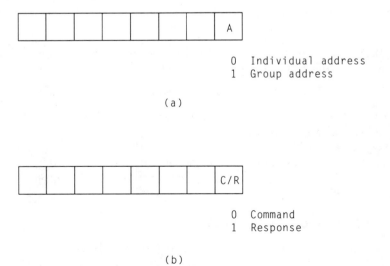

Figure 4.6 (a) Destination and (b) source address points of an LPDU.

individual address and 1 means a group address. DSAP and its hardware address constitute the unique LSAP.

The second byte is the source service access point (SSAP), which is a local reference number of the LLC at the sending node. The LSB of SSAP is the C/R flag: 0 denotes a command and 1 means a response as shown in Figure 4.6(b).

The Control field of an information (I) frame with 7-bit sequence numbers is 2 bytes long with the LSB, 0, in the first byte as shown in Figure 4.7(a). The Control field of a supervisory (S) frame is also 2 bytes long as shown in Figure 4.7(b). The Control field of an unnumbered (U) frame is 1 byte long as shown in Figure 4.7(c). The extended opcode in a U frame is known as the modifier (M) bit. The specifications of the M bit are consistent with the HDLC protocol specified in Chapter 3. The Info field contains data of variable length, from 0 to n bytes.

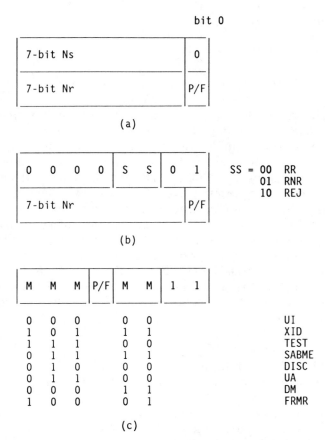

Figure 4.7 Control fields of an LPDU: (a) information frame, (b) supervisory frame, and (c) unnumbered frame.

4.4 ETHERNET

With over 20 million nodes installed worldwide, Ethernet is by far the most popular method of linking computers on a network [1]. The primary reasons are that its performance specifications meet demand and that its cost is low. The wide acceptance of Ethernet led to the development of the technical office protocol (TOP), which is suitable for office use. The characteristics of a standard Ethernet LAN are listed below [ETHERNET]:

- Data rate, 10 Mbps;
- Shielded coaxial cable, full-duplex;
- Maximum distance between stations, 2.5 km;
- Maximum number of stations, 1,024;
- Typical cable length, 500m;
- Characteristic impedance, 50 ohm;
- Baseband, Manchester code transmission;
- Carrier sense multiple access/collision detection (CSMA/CD);
- Clock rate, 20 MHz.

A 5-node Ethernet is shown in Figure 4.8(a), where a circle represents a node or computer. One of the nodes may run the network server software and the rest are clients. At the end of the coax, there is the terminator box that contains the characteristic impedance of the line. The physical layout of a typical Ethernet is depicted in Figure 4.8(b). Right next to the coaxial cable, there is a tap that contains a transceiver (i.e., a transmitter and receiver pair placed in a small metal box). The tap is bolted to the coaxial cable with a pin stuck out in the middle to penetrate the outer layer of coax to make metal contact. Between the tap and the Ethernet communication controller board, there is an interface cable. The controller board resides in the main chassis of a workstation and has its own processor connected to the main CPU via a common I/O bus.

Various Ethernets are developed using unshielded twisted pair (UTP) cables [10BASE-T]. Proposals have been submitted to IEEE to develop a 100 Mbps Ethernet for standardization. Each design differs in its wiring and encoding method. The Fast Ethernet has the following characteristics [100BASE-T]:

- Data rate, 100 Mbps;
- Four UTP cables, full-duplex;
- Maximum distance between stations, 100m;
- Maximum cable length, 250m;
- Baseband, 8B6T ternary code transmission;
- Carrier sense multiple access/collision detection (CSMA/CD);
- Clock Rate, 25 MHz.

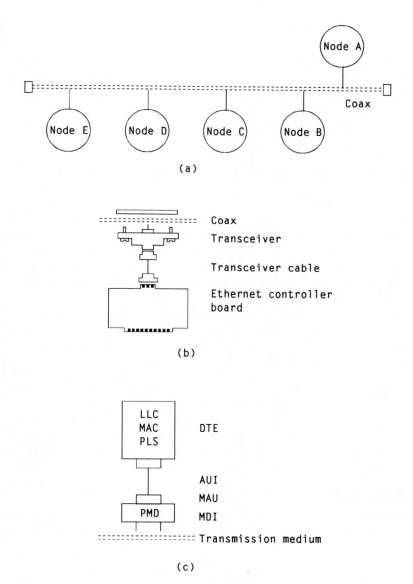

Figure 4.8 Ethernet architecture: (a) 5-node Ethernet, (b) physical layout, and (c) software sublayers.

A speed improvement by an order of magnitude is achieved for the Fast Ethernet due to the following:

1. It uses three UTP cables to transmit data and one for collision detection. Each channel has an effective data rate of 33.33 Mbps or 1/3 of 100 Mbps.
2. It uses 8B6T ternary code to encode 8-bit data into 6 ternary symbols to improve code efficiency.
3. The clock rate is increased to 25 MHz as computed in the following:

$$(1/3) \cdot 100 \text{ Mbps} \cdot (6/8) = 25 \text{ Mbps}$$

Summing up, we have the total increase as shown in Table 4.1.

4.4.1 Ethernet Sublayers

Software layers of Ethernet are shown in Figure 4.8(c). Let us first differentiate hardware units from software units. DTE is the controller board and the tap box is a medium attachment unit (MAU). Between the DTE and the MAU, there is an attachment unit interface (AUI), which is the cable with connectors at both ends. Between the MAU and the coax, there is a medium dependent interface (MDI), which is a metal pin.

The physical interface function of Ethernet is divided into two sublayers: the PLS sublayer and the PMD or physical medium attachment (PMA) sublayer. The data link function is also divided into two sublayers: the LLC sublayer and the MAC sublayer. Altogether, we have four sublayers to perform the physical and data link functions on Ethernet. PLS provides the physical level services to MAC while PMA drives MAU, which mainly contains the transceiver in the tap. LLC, MAC, and PLS all run on DTE, and PMD runs on MAU.

There are also broadband and fiber-optic Ethernets. Needless to say, LAN competition in the field is just too keen. Transmission media for Ethernet are compared in Table 4.2. Note that if data is transmitted at 100 Mbps as in Fast Ethernet, the total length of cable must be reduced.

4.4.2 Ethernet Frames

The MAC sublayer on Ethernet determines all the bits transmitted on the bus that constitute a MAPDU. Both PLS and PMA are mainly responsible for delivering

Table 4.1
Performance Improvement of a Fast Ethernet

Design Description	Factor of Improvement
Three pairs to transmit data (1 · 3)	3
Better encoding method (2 · 8/6)	2.67
Faster clock (25/20)	1.25
Total factor of improvement	10

Table 4.2
Transmission Media for Ethernet

Transmission Medium	Data Rate in Mbps	Range in km	Number of Taps
Unshielded twisted pair	10, or 100 with limitations	2	10
Baseband coaxial cable	10, or 50 with limitations	3	100
Broadband coaxial cable	500 (20/channel)	30	1,000
Fiber-optic cable	45	150	500

and accepting bits on the line. The general format of a MAC frame is shown in Figure 4.9(a). In the frame, there is the MAC header, 0 to n bytes of information, and a 32-bit error-detecting code that is the MAC trailer. If the frame is an LLC data frame, the inner packet may contain protocol information on the upper layers. An Ethernet frame is specified in Figure 4.9(b). Bit 0, or the LSB in a byte, is transmitted first. If a field contains many bytes, the highest order byte is transmitted first, one by one, and the lowest order byte is transmitted last.

The preamble is 7 bytes long with a repeated bit pattern as follows:

'0101010'

so the hardware receiver can synchronize with the timing of an incoming frame.

The second field is a 1-byte start frame delimiter (SFD), which has a different bit pattern:

'10101011'

The next two fields, 2 or 6 bytes each, are the Destination Address (DA) and the Source Address (SA) to conform with other LAN standards as shown in Figure 4.9(c). The leading or sign bit of DA is the individual/group (I/G) bit. A 0 indicates an individual address while a 1 means a group address. However, for SA, the leading bit is always 0. The second bit of a 48-bit address is the universal/local (U/L) bit. A 0 means universally administered and a 1 means locally administered. The U/L bit is not present in a 16-bit address, which always implies universally administered. In practice, an Ethernet address is usually 48 bits long, so the next 46-bit field contains a multidrop address that is unique to Ethernet. That is to say, the hardware address is built-in on the board, and the bits are assigned by the manufacturer. A broadcast address contains 48-bit 1's or 12 F's in hex as shown below:

```
Broadcast Address = FF FF FF FF FF FF
```

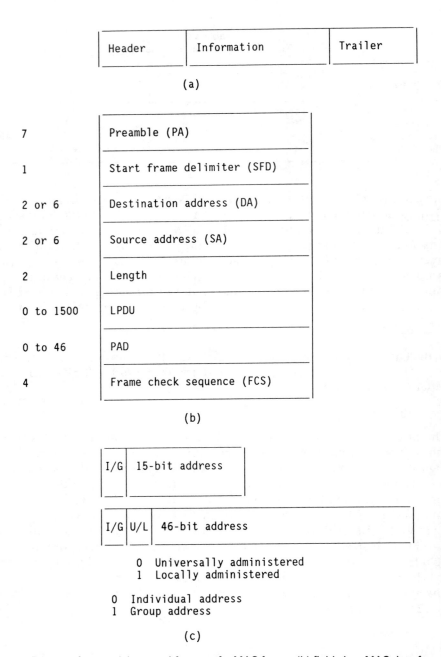

Figure 4.9 Ethernet frames: (a) general format of a MAC frame, (b) fields in a MAC data frame, and (c) Destination Address.

When a broadcast address is used as DA, all the nodes on the bus are supposed to receive the frame. The 2-byte Length field specifies the number of LLC data octets in the frame. The maximum length of an Ethernet frame counting from DA to FCS inclusive is 1,518 bytes. A minimum length is also set because whenever a transceiver detects a collision, it truncates the frame. In order for the receiving node to differentiate a valid frame from a truncated frame, a minimum of 512 bits must be coded in a frame, counting from DA to FCS inclusive. If not, a PAD field is appended after the LLC data to make the total number of bits equal to the minimum length. The Length field plus FCS is 6 bytes long, or 48 bits. The Address field is either 2 or 6 bytes long, the length of PAD in bits is

$$\text{Max}(0, \text{min\_frame\_size} - (8 \cdot n + 2 \cdot \text{address\_size} + 48));$$

where Max is a function to return the maximum of two parameters, 0 or the computed length. Min_frame_size and address_size are in bits, and n is the LLC data length in bytes. The content of the PAD field is unspecified. The last 4 bytes of a MAC frame are the MAC trailer, which contains a 32-bit FCS for error detection.

4.4.3 32-Bit Frame Check Sequence

The 32-bit FCS (FCS-32) is similar to FCS-ITU-T except that it is 32 bits long (the 33-bit polynomial code divisor is given in Chapter 3). The FCS-32 is defined as the complement of the logical sum of the following:

1. The remainder of 32-bit 1's followed by k-bit 0's logically divided by the 33-bit polynomial code where k is the number of bits in the frame;
2. The remainder of the k-bit frame followed by 32-bit 0's logically divided by the same polynomial code.

This FCS-32 can be simulated by software just like the FCS-ITU-T simulation routine. The design of the hardware shift register to generate/detect FCS-32 is similar to the one used in SDLC or HDLC. A fixed 32-bit remainder is always left in the shift register, with the following bit pattern:

$$x^{31} + x^{30} + x^{26} + x^{25} + x^{24} + x^{18} + x^{15} + x^{14} + x^{12} + x^{11} + x^{10} + x^8 + x^6 + x^5 + x^4 + x^3 + x + 1$$

which is c704 dd7b in hex when x equals 2. This pattern is the remainder obtained by dividing the 33-bit polynomial code into a dividend that is the bit string of 32-bit 1's followed by 32-bit 0's.

4.4.4 CSMA/CD Access Method

In Ethernet, carrier sense multiple access/collision detection (CSMA/CD) is used [IEEE 802.3]. *Carrier* really means *signal* because in baseband transmission, there is no carrier at a higher frequency. *Carrier sense* means that before a sending node attempts to transmit, it listens to the line by receiving signals in its hardware buffer. If no one is transmitting, the sending node goes ahead and transmits. *Multiple access* means that each node on the bus can receive the transmitted frame at the same time, including the sending node. *Collision detection* means that there is still a possibility that two or more nodes will transmit at the same time. When that happens, the sending node sends a jam signal (which is a sinusoidal wave at 10 MHz for a duration), shuts down its transmitter, and schedules a retransmission. All collided nodes must back off for a random interval and try again. Before each retry, each node must listen to the line again.

How long each sending node should wait is an internal design issue. If all nodes wait for the same amount of time and then retransmit, collision will occur again. Therefore, we must introduce the random time interval concept in our design.

Random Time Interval

The basic idea is that when more collisions are detected in a row for a particular sending node, that node should wait longer. First, we define a retransmission slot time T as the time required to transmit a frame on the line plus some propagation delays. We then implement an exponential function, 2^n, where n is the number of collisions that a sending node has encountered in a row. The node must wait for a time interval, $(x \cdot T)$ where x is a random integer between 0 and $(2^n - 1)$. Mathematically, we have

$$y = x \cdot T$$

where y is the wait time. This is referred to as the single exponential back-off algorithm as shown in Figure 4.10. Transmission is aborted if 10 collisions are detected in a row.

Optimal Retransmission Slot Time

The retransmission slot time T cannot be too small because when one node has not finished transmitting its frame, another node cannot start its retransmission. The transmission slot time cannot be too big because it would waste bandwidth. The optimal T should be the time required to transmit a frame of minimum size plus the round-trip wave propagation delays. The total length of a minimum frame is computed as

$$512 + (8 \cdot 8) = 576 \text{ bits}$$

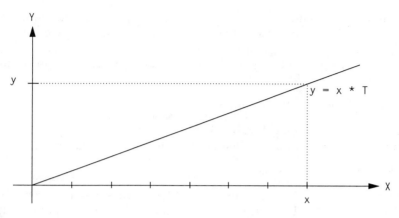

Notes:
1. y is the wait period to retransmit.
2. T is the retransmission slot time.
3. x is between 0 and (2^n - 1) where n is the number of collisions in a row.

Figure 4.10 Single exponential back-off method.

where preamble plus SFD is 8 bytes long. Assuming that the data rate is 10 Mbps and the electromagnetic wave travels in a vacuum, we obtain the optimal T by

$$\frac{576 \text{ b}}{10 \cdot 10^6 \text{ bps}} + \frac{2 \cdot 500 \text{ m}}{3 \cdot 10^8 \text{ mps}} = 60.93 \text{ μs}$$

The retransmission slot time T could be fine-tuned by the system administrator. We conclude that the single exponential back-off method allows very short retransmission delays at the beginning but backs off much longer if the channel is overloaded. For every new frame transmitted, the transmission delay goes back to 0. An Ethernet is overloaded if the amount of time spent on retransmission is over 50%. As a matter of fact, the Ethernet bus should be idle at least 50% of the time.

4.4.5 Other Ethernet Primitives

As far as software is concerned, data primitives are issued between the MAC and the PLS. The MAC may issue a data request as shown below:

   PLS_DATA.request(symbol);

where symbol represents a bit, 1, 0, or a Data Completion flag, which informs the MAC to cease transmission. Note that the primitive has the same meaning as a PH_DATA.request and that the transceiver is a bit I/O device.

After receiving the bit, its peer PLS sends a data indication to its upper layer as shown below:

PLS_DATA.indication(symbol);

where symbol only represents a bit, 1, or 0.

The sending PLS issues a data confirm to the MAC as follows:

PLS_DATA.confirm(status);

where status reports what happened to this data request (delivered or aborted).

Whenever the MAU detects a state change of the transmission medium, it informs the PLS, which in turn issues one of two primitives to its MAC as follows:

PLS_CARRIER.indication(status);

where status indicates carrier, on or off generated as a result of the carrier state change from off to on or on to off, or

PLS_SIGNAL.indication(status);

where status indicates signal_quality_error, on or off generated as a result of the signal quality error signal change from off to on or on to off.

4.5 TOKEN RING

There are over 5 million token ring LANs installed, which is a distant second to Ethernet. Characteristics of a token ring LAN are listed below:

- Data rate, 16 Mbps;
- Shielded twisted pair, simplex;
- Maximum distance between stations, 2.5 km;
- Maximum number of stations, 250;
- Maximum cable length, 625 km;
- Characteristic impedance, 150 Ohms;
- Baseband, differential Manchester code transmissions;
- Token ring access method;
- Clock rate, 32 MHz.

A six-node token ring is depicted in Figure 4.11(a). The same ring is reconfigured with hub-wiring as shown in Figure 4.11(b). It looks like a star, but

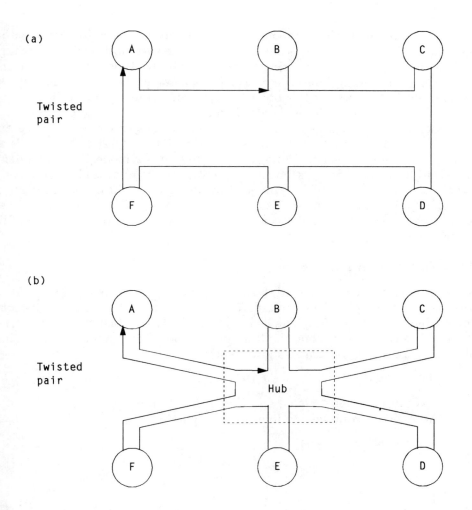

Figure 4.11 A six-node token ring: (a) ring wiring and (b) hub wiring.

it is a ring. Bits flow in one direction on the ring from the sending node, pass other nodes, and return to the same node. It is the responsibility of the sending node to strip the frame off the ring. There are only two types of frames: token frame versus data frame (abbreviated as token vs. frame). The high-order byte is transmitted first before the low-order byte. In a byte, the sign or MSB is transmitted first, which is different from Ethernet.

Each node can operate in one of three modes. In listen mode, the bits pass through the node with 1-bit delay, as shown in Figure 4.12(a). The box is a hardware flip-flop or bistable storage device. In transmit mode, the node intercepts the bit stream, processes the information, and transmits the bits on the line, as shown in Figure 4.12(b). In bypass mode, the node is offline electronically, and therefore introduces no bit delay, as shown in Figure 4.12(c). If any node fails, it can be popped off the ring so the remaining five nodes can be still operational.

4.5.1 Token Ring Frames

A token ring frame consists of all the bits transmitted on the line, which is also a MAPDU. The 3-byte token frame shown in Figure 4.13(a) has a 2-byte header and a 1-byte trailer. The first byte is the starting delimiter (SD), the second byte is for access control (AC), and the third byte is the ending delimiter (ED). The SD uses a special waveform as shown below:

J K 0 J K 0 0 0

where J is the Violation 1 signal and K, the Violation 0.

The AC field contains the following bit pattern:

P P P T M R R R

and

- PPP = priority bits;
- T = token bit;
- M = monitor bit;
- RRR = reservation bits.

PPP is a 3-bit unsigned integer representing the priority of the token or the current ring service. A bit pattern 000 has the lowest priority and 111 the highest. The T bit 0 denotes a token and 1 denotes a frame.

The M bit is used to prevent a token or frame with a nonzero priority from circulating on the ring forever. The M bit should normally be 0. It is the responsibility of the active monitor to set this bit to 1. After circulating on the ring, if the same token or frame with the M bit set to 1 is detected by the monitor, it will be aborted. All other stations shall repeat this bit as received.

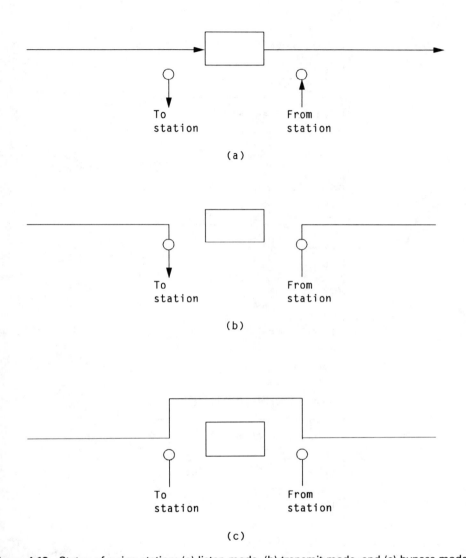

Figure 4.12 Status of a ring station: (a) listen mode, (b) transmit mode, and (c) bypass mode.

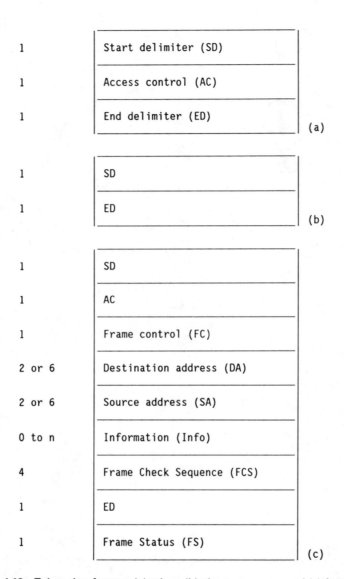

Figure 4.13 Token ring frames: (a) token, (b) abort sequence, and (c) frame.

RRR is a 3-bit unsigned integer representing the reservation priority. If a station has PDUs to transmit, it must make a reservation, namely a priority token request. By doing so, the RRR field in a token or frame may be changed by the requesting node with a reserved priority strictly higher than the current RRR to ensure that the next token issued has this priority. Later when the token circulates back to the requesting node, it can grab the token and transmit its PDU, which has a priority equal to or higher than the token's priority. Then, the token is transformed into a frame, which has a Start-Frame-Sequence (SFS) with the token bit set to 1, an Information-Frame-Sequence (IFS), and an End-Frame-Sequence (EFS).

The ending delimiter (ED) has the following bit pattern:

J K 1 J K 1 I E

where I is the intermediate frame bit and E is the error-detected bit. The I bit is set to 1 to indicate that more frames are to follow. The E bit is set to 1 whenever an error is detected by any node on the ring as the frame passes by it. The initial value of the E bit should be 0 for a token or frame.

There is a 2-byte abort sequence, as shown in Figure 4.13(b). The SD is the first byte and the ED is the second byte. This sequence may occur anywhere in the bit stream and is used to terminate the transmission prematurely.

The format of a frame shown in Figure 4.13(c) has three sequences—the SFS, the IFS, and the EFS.

SFS is comprised of SD and AC with the T bit set to 1. IFS includes a 1-byte frame control (FC), a 2- or 6-byte destination address (DA) and source address (SA), the variable Information (Info) field, and a 32-bit FCS that covers IFS only.

FC contains

F F Z Z Z Z Z Z

where FF denotes a frame type as defined below:

bit 7
↓
00 → MAC frame for control purposes
01 → LLC frame
1x → reserved for future use and x can be 1 or 0

In a MAC frame, ZZZZZZ is the 6-bit opcode of a control function. In a LLC frame, the ZZZZZZ bits are designated as rrrYYY. The rrr bits in the upper 3-bit field are reserved bits set to 0's and the YYY bits denote the priority of the PDU (i.e., Pm).

DA, SA, and FCS are the same as Ethernet. In a MAC control frame, the Info field contains a vector followed by 0, 1, or more subvectors. Info may also contain 0, 1, or more bytes of data that are intended for MAC, network management, or

LLC with no maximum length specified. Inside a LLC frame, the packet header contains protocol information of the upper layers.

The EFS contains a 1-byte ED followed by a 1-byte frame status (FS). FS contains information as defined below:

A C 0 0 A C 0 0

where A is the address recognized bit and C is the copied bit. Both A and C are initialized to 0's by the sending node. Regardless of the E bit, the receiving node sets the A bit if the DA is recognized by its hardware as an individual or group address. It further sets the C bit if the frame is copied into its hardware receive buffer in time. Note that there are two sets of A and C in the FS for error checking. The bit of A and C is valid only when the two sets are consistent. If not, they are treated as 0's and the sending node simply ignores them. All E, A, and C bits are set by the hardware communication controller.

4.5.2 Token Ring MAC Control Frames

Six token ring MAC control frames are designed to communicate among MAC sublayers. The FC field in a MAC control frame has two leading 0's followed by a 6-bit opcode, as shown in Figure 4.14(a). The Info field contains a Vector Length (VL), a Vector Identifier (VI), and a 0, a 1, or more subvectors. VL is 2 bytes long, which denotes the length of Info, and VI is also 2 bytes long, which identifies the function of the vector. Subvectors are position-independent and each subvector has a 1-byte Subvector Length (SVL), a 1-byte Subvector Identifier, and a Subvector Value (SVV) of variable bytes.

The Duplicate Address Test (DAT) is transmitted by each node as part of the initialization process. The DA field contains its own address. If any node sets the A bits in FS and another node on the ring has the same address, then the network management routine is notified.

The Beacon (BCN) is transmitted as a result of serious ring failure such as broken cable and jabbered station. It is transmitted by a node that tries to localize the fault. The Info field contains such items as the immediate upstream neighbor address and a subvector code indicating that its Timer, No Token (TNT) has expired. A timer is reset to 0 to start and expires when its time reaches a limit defined as the TO value.

The claim token (CL_TK) is transmitted by the standby monitor after its 7-sec Timer, Standby Monitor expires. This also implies that the active monitor is no longer in service. The Info field contains its upstream neighbor address, which is the failed active monitor. The DA field contains a broadcast address, so every node knows the source address of the new monitor. After this frame is circulating back, the standby node becomes the new active monitor.

The Purge (PRG) is transmitted by the active monitor after having claimed

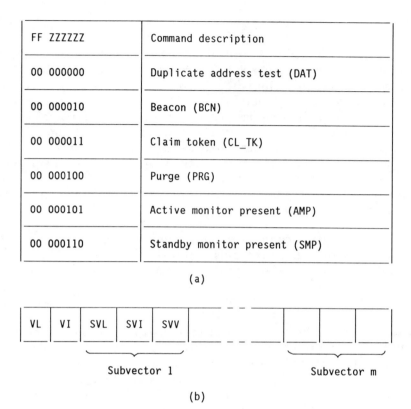

Figure 4.14 (a) FC and (b) information fields in a token ring MAC control frame.

the token or detected the M bit set to 1 in a frame. All spurious bits on the ring will be removed. The Info field contains its upstream neighbor address.

The Active Monitor Present (AMP) is transmitted after its 3-sec Timer of Active Monitor (TAM) expires. The DA field contains a broadcast address, so every node on the ring receives. After receiving an AMP, any station in standby state resets its Timer, Standby Monitor (TSM), and the active monitor resets its TAM. The Info field of this frame contains its upstream neighbor address.

The Standby Monitor, Present (SMP) is transmitted by the standby monitors with the DA set to all 1's. After receiving an AMP or SMP frame whose A and C bits are equal to 0, its Timer, Queue PDU (TQP) is reset. The default time-out value is 10 ms. When this timer expires, an SMP frame is queued for transmission. Via this scheme, every node on the ring knows who its upstream neighbor is.

4.5.3 Token Ring Access Method

The token ring access method is quite interesting [IEEE 802.5]. Since the ring is designed as a circular shift register, it is possible for a node to transmit the latter portion of a frame on a short ring while the receiver on the same node is receiving the beginning of the frame. From the viewpoint of hardware design, each node may operate in one of three modes: listen, transmit, or bypass. It is possible for a node to transmit a *fill* between frames. Fill contains continuous 1's as the quiescent state of the line. In order to be activated back to the ring, the node must operate in transmit mode to receive a token and start from there. Software procedures are discussed as follows.

The token passing is based on assigned priority. We need to define the following terms:

- Pr: Priority register contains the received PPP field;
- Rr: Reservation register contains the received RRR field;
- Pm: Priority of the message or PDU that a node wishes to transmit;
- Sr: Stacked received priority;
- Sx: Stacked transmitted priority.

There is always a token or frame continuously flowing on the ring. Fairness is guaranteed by requiring the same station that jacked up the priority of the ring to return the ring to its original service priority. After the token ring is initialized, a token with both PPP and RRR equal to 0's is flowing on the ring. While running on the ring, any node that wishes to transmit a PDU must request a priority token first by doing the following:

```
CASE of bits received,
    Token:  IF Pr <= Pm,
            THEN set Sr with Pr;
            Set Sx with the greater value of Pm or Rr;
            Transmit the token with PPP set to Sx;
            ELSE
               IF Rr < Pm,
            THEN transmit the token with RRR set to Pm; ENDIF; ENDIF
    Frame:  IF Rr < Pm,
            THEN transmit a frame with RRR set to Pm; ENDIF;
ENDCASE;
```

The first case is when the requesting node has received a token. If Pr is less than or equal to Pm, which is the priority of its PDU, then the requesting node sets Sr to Pr, Sx to the greater value of its Pm or Rr, and PPP in the AC field of the token to Sx. Now, it becomes a stacking node. The word *stack* has nothing to do with the LIFO stack. Only a stacking node can grab any token passing by with less or equal priority and transmit. When that happens, the token is changed to a frame by forming a SFS with PPP set to Pm and the token bit set to 1. IFS and EFS are then appended. All E, A, and C bits are initialized to 0's in the frame.

In a token, if Pr is greater than Pm and Rr is less than Pm, the requesting node can only make a reservation by setting RRR with its Pm. If Rr is greater or equal to its Pm, the node simply repeats the token without taking any action.

The second case is when the requesting node has received a frame with Rr less than its Pm. Therefore, the requesting node makes a reservation by setting RRR in the frame to its Pm. When the sending node finishes its transmission, it puts a token back with PPP set as requested. When the token flows back to the requesting node, it then becomes a stacking node.

Whenever a sending node completes the transmission of its PDU, it strips the frame off the ring and places a token with PPP set to the higher of Sr or Rr. It is the responsibility of the stacking node to restore the ring to its original priority level if there is no reservation requested. In such a case, the RRR field in the token is reset to 0.

The FS provides important information to the sending node with regard to frame transmission. If the two sets of A and C bits in the FS are consistent, the sending node obtains the following information:

1. The destination node is not on the ring, either nonexistent or deactivated.
2. Station exists, but the frame is not copied.
3. Frame is copied.

If a frame is copied correctly with the error bit set to 0, the transmission is done perfectly; otherwise, the sending node must retransmit. Each station keeps a token holding timer (THT), which has a default value of 10 ms. A station may initiate another transmission if such transmission can be completed before its THT expires.

Any intermediate node that is not the destination simply receives the frame, sets the E bit if any errors are detected and retransmits the frame on the ring. Any intermediate node can set RRR in the AC field of a passing frame to signal a priority request; otherwise, it merely acts as a relay station.

The receiving node does the same except for two things. It sets the A bit if the DA is recognized and the C bit if the frame is copied into its receive buffer in time. In the case where any bit is flipped during transmission, the sending node may or may not retransmit depending on the type of data. It is not a serious matter if one bit of voice or video data is flipped. When the sender retransmits, the receiver simply uses the latest frame to replace the old one that has the same sending sequence number. SWP is not implemented on a token ring.

4.5.4 Active Monitor

The active monitor is a special node on the ring running error-recovery routines. It is actually the boss or supervisor of the ring. Conditions, such as *no token on the ring* or *a frame not being removed* are detected and corrected by the active monitor. When a station is inserted into or removed from the ring, it is also the responsibility of the active monitor to smooth things out.

There is only one active monitor on the ring at any point of time. When the monitor fails to perform its duty, clever software is written to ensure continuous operations on the ring. The active monitor function is built-in in all other nodes on the ring in standby mode. Each node takes a position in the command chain depending on its physical position next to the active monitor downstream. A node may become the next active monitor only if no one in the front can take the job. The first node downstream after the active monitor is the immediate successor. A scheme by which each node can identify its upstream neighbor is described in the following.

Neighbor Notification

Each node should know the identity of its upstream neighbor station at any given time. Neighbor notification has its basis built into the address-recognized bit and frame-copied bits in a broadcast frame, which is either an AMP or SMP.

After receiving an AMP frame with A and C bits equal to 0, the node knows itself to be the immediate successor in the command chain. The logic is simple, because the DA field contains a broadcast address that matches the destination address of any node. If there is a node in the front, the A and C bits would have been set by the front node. In the AMP frame, the SA field contains the address of the active monitor, which is fetched as the received upstream neighbors address (RUA) by the immediate receiving node. After 10 ms, the standby node broadcasts an SMP frame with A and C bits reset. As the next receiving node sees the A and C bits equal to 0, it fetches the SA in the frame as its RUA.

With each node knowing its upstream neighbor, the following scheme is developed to pass control from a failed active monitor to a new monitor.

Every 3 sec, the active monitor broadcasts an Active Monitor Present (AMP) message to declare that the boss is in charge. Subsequent nodes will transmit SMP frames, so each node can identify who its upstream neighbor is. If an AMP is not received within 7 sec, the immediate node downstream knows the boss cannot perform its duty and therefore transmits a CL_TK frame attempting to claim the token on the ring. When the CL_TK frame circulates back, the successor becomes the new active monitor.

4.5.5 Other Token Ring Primitives

NMT routines play an important role in token rings. Such a routine can be thought of as a special layer on the side that can transmit data to its peer on the destination node via special MAC data primitives as shown below:

```
MA_NMT_DATA.request( frame_control, DA, SA, m_sdu, service_class);
MA_NMT_DATA.indication( frame_control, DA, SA, m_sdu, status);
MA_NMT_DATA.confirm( status, service_class);
```

where the parameters are self explanatory. The service_class in a data request is the requested priority of its frame while the one in a data confirm is the actual priority provided.

There are also control primitives between NMT and MAC as listed below:

```
MA_INITIALIZE.request( design_parameters, etc);
MA_INITIALIZE.confirm( status);
MA_CONTROL.request( action);
MA_CONTROL.indication( status);
```

Initialize primitives are used to initialize the ring after power on or restart. Design parameters include the specified individual and group addresses, the broadcast address of the particular ring, and timer values. The action parameters of a control primitive include RESET and INSERT.

Between PH and MAC, there are data primitives as listed below:

```
PH_DATA.request( symbol);
PH_DATA.indication( symbol);
PH_DATA.confirm( status);
```

where symbol may represent a bit 0, 1, J, or K. For high-performance communication controllers, the symbol parameter may represent a byte or a block of bytes.

For token ring, a primitive issued by NMT may insert or remove the current node into or from the ring via PH control primitives as listed below:

```
PH_CONTROL.request( action);
PH_CONTROL.indication( status);
```

where the action parameter denotes INSERT or REMOVE, which also implies activated or deactivated. Since token ring LANs use simplex transmission, fiber-optic can be used as the transmission medium to push the data speed over gigabits per second. The design of a token ring LAN is indeed clever.

Slotted Ring

There are other rings using TDM to eliminate the token contention problem. One example is the slotted ring, which has a long frame constantly circulating on the ring. Each node is assigned a time slot in the frame to transmit its own data to other nodes. If there is only one receiver, the frame merely contains data; otherwise, a (DA) must also be coded in the frame. The design has its own merit, but its efficiency is questionable when the total number of nodes on the ring is large.

Fiber-optic rings are also available using the same token-passing concept but speed is much higher, as discussed later in this chapter. Design issues of a token bus are addressed next. Special software must be written to implement the token-passing concept on a physical common bus. How to employ fiber-optics in a token-bus remains a research challenge.

4.6 TOKEN BUS

A token-passing bus or token bus LANs are used by auto companies. Physically, it is a bus but logically it is a ring. A six-node token bus is shown in Figure 4.15. The transmission sequence is A-B-C-D-E-F-A where A is the sending node. There are some differences between a token bus and a token ring. First, a token must also contain the DA of the next receiving node on the bus. Secondly, if a coaxial cable is used, node A must place the entire token frame on the bus with the DA of node B specified. Then, node B receives the token frame, modifies the DA to C, and transmits the token frame to node C. If F is the only node that has data to transmit, a token frame must be transmitted five times on the bus starting from A in a circular fashion before node F can grab it. Thirdly, the physical position of each node on the bus has nothing to do with its logical position to receive the token frame. The physical position is determined by hardware wiring while the logical position is determined by software using (DAs). Physically, the LAN uses a common bus, but software supports token passing. Such a design is known as the token bus. One advantage over token ring is that a data frame can be delivered to any destination node in one hop because every node online receives at the same time.

Token bus is also standardized [IEEE 802.4]. Based on this concept, the auto companies developed the manufacturing automation protocol (MAP) for the manufacturing industry. There are actually three separate entities. Some of the characteristics are listed below.

- Data rate, 1–10 Mbps;
- Shielded coaxial cable, simplex;
- Maximum distance between stations, 2.5 km;
- Maximum number of stations, 30;
- Cable length, 1,280m;
- Characteristic impedance, 75 ohms;
- Broadband using Manchester code modulated by one of the three methods:
    1. Phase-continuous-FSK;
    2. Phase-coherent-FSK;
    3. Duobinary AM/PSK.
- Token-passing bus access method.

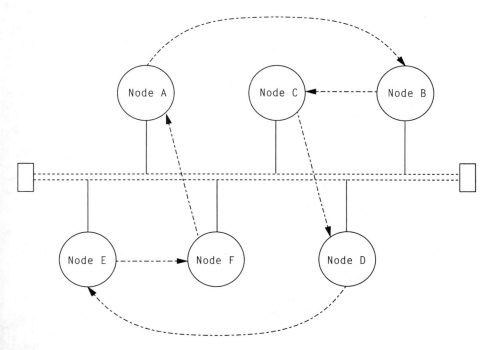

Figure 4.15 A six-node token bus.

If too many nodes are attached to a common bus, the design becomes impractical because of the massive overhead of passing token frames from one node to another.

4.6.1 Token Bus Frames

The general format of a token bus frame is shown in Figure 4.16(a) and an abort sequence is shown in Figure 4.16(b). Even though the basic concepts are similar to token ring, there are some differences. Bit 0, the LSB, is transmitted first. The Info field may contain 0 or more bytes transmitted in ascending order. The Address field has 2 or 6 bytes with the lowest order byte being transmitted first, then one by one in sequence, with the highest order byte transmitted last. Within the Address field, the MSB is transmitted last on the line. FCS is 4 bytes long with x^{31} transmitted first, then bit by bit in sequence, with x^0 transmitted last.

Because of the common bus, a token also needs a DA to designate the next station to receive the token. Hence, there is only one format with the opcode to specify a token or frame. The Preamble contains 1 or more octets of 01 combinations for at least 2 fs regardless of the data rate. The Start Delimiter (SD) is

1 or more	Preamble
1	SD
1	FC
2 or 6	DA
2 or 6	SA
0 to n	Information
4	FCS
1	ED

(a)

1	SD
1	ED

(b)

Figure 4.16 Token bus frames: (a) format of a token or data frame and (b) abort sequence.

shown in Figure 4.17(a). To provide the same logical layout, bit 0 (i.e., the lsb) is placed on the left.

In Manchester code, each bit is divided into two half-bits: a low voltage followed by a high voltage, or vice versa. If one combination is defined as 0, then the other combination must be 1. For instance, a 0 may be denoted by {HL} which means a half-bit of high voltage followed by a half-bit of low voltage. A bit 1 is denoted by {LH}. The symbol N means nondata representation, which is either one full bit of high voltage or one full bit of low voltage. The NN pair, however, has a special meaning, which represents a full bit of low voltage followed by a full bit of high voltage denoted as {LL HH}.

The End Delimiter is shown in Figure 4.17(b). Bit 6 is the Intermediate (I) bit: 1 means more to come and 0 indicates the end of transmission. Bit 7 is the

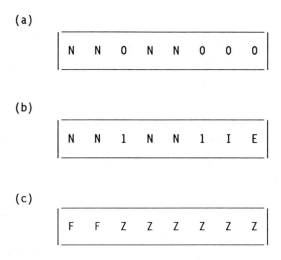

Figure 4.17 (a) SD, (b) ED, and, (c) FC fields in a token bus MAC frame.

Error (E) bit: 1 means error. Because a token is passed from node to node, there is no AC or FS in the frame.

Both DA and SA have the same layout as other LANs with the I/G bit transmitted first. The difference is that the low-order address bit is transmitted first and the msb of the Address field is transmitted last.

In a LLC frame, the bits 3–5 field specifies a MAC action as defined below:

000 ==> request with no response;
001 ==> request with response;
010 ==> response.

The bits 6–7 field specifies a 3-bit unsigned integer, which is the priority of the enclosed PDU. As in token ring, a higher integer means a higher priority with bit 6 as the msb.

4.6.2 Token Bus MAC Control Frames

Token bus MAC control frames are different from those of a token ring because the technology is different. The Frame Control contains an 8-bit opcode specifying a control function as shown in Figure 4.17(c). The FF or bits 0–1 field specifies the frame type as follows:

bit 0
↓
00 ==> MAC control frame;

FF ZZZZZZ	Command description
00 000000	Claim_token
00 000001	Solicit_successor_1
00 000010	Solicit_successor_2
00 000011	Who_follows
00 000100	Resolve_contention
00 001000	Token
00 001100	Set_successor

Figure 4.18 FC field in a token bus MAC control frame.

01 ==> LLC data frame;
10 ==> Network management data frame;
11 ==> Reserved.

The field of bits 2–7 or ZZZZZZ specifies the 6-bit opcode of a MAC control function as shown in Figure 4.18.

There are seven MAC control frames altogether. One of them is the token frame, which is short in length. The remaining six are used for control purposes among the MAC sublayers. Normally, a token is passed from station to station in descending order with regard to the numerical DA of each node. The node with the lowest address then passes the token to the top node, which has the highest address. The address of each node represents the logical sequence on the ring with regard to receiving the token.

Because of the common bus, a request with response frame is designed to pass the token right to the responding node temporarily. In other words, a node may transmit a request with response frame and wait for the destination node to reply. After the destination node transmits its response frame, the token is reverted back to the original sending node and operation continues.

Slot_time is defined to be the maximum time that any station must wait for an immediate response from another station.

A claim_token frame is transmitted by a sending node during the initialization or reinitialization phase. After having successfully completed the transmission of a claim_token frame, the node places a new token on the ring. The frame has a data_unit whose value is arbitrary with a length equal to 0, 2, 4, or 6 multiplied by the slot_time measured in transmitting a number of octets. The data_unit is followed by the FCS and ED.

There are two solicit_successor frames periodically transmitted by any node. A solicit_successor_1 frame is transmitted by any sending node that solicits a deactivated node to enter the ring as its successor. The suffix 1 denotes one response window. Only a node with its address between SA and DA as coded in the solicitor_successor frame can transmit bits in the window to declare itself as the next successor. A solicit_successor_2 frame is designed for the node with the lowest address, and the suffix 2 means two response windows. Those nodes with addresses less than SA enter responses in window 1, and those with addresses greater than SA enter responses in window 2. After placing a solicit_successor frame on the line, if the node hears a valid response message, it will allow the new station to enter the logical ring by recording its address as its new successor and pass the token to it.

A set-successor frame is actually the response message transmitted by any requesting node, after receiving a solicit_successor frame, to be the new successor. In the Data field of this frame, the address of the requesting node is specified to declare itself to be the new successor.

It is possible for many requesting nodes to respond at the same time within either response window (i.e., collisions). Therefore, after having detected garbled bits on the line, the node which has sent a solicit_successor frame then transmits a resolve_contention frame with four response windows. An algorithm is implemented such that each contending node must wait for a random time interval of 0, 1, 2, or 3 slot_times before responding again.

After a sending node detects that its immediate successor has failed, it transmits a who_follows frame to find out who follows its immediate successor. In this frame, the Data field contains the address of its immediate successor with three window time frames reserved for the new successor to respond. Whichever node follows the failed successor responds with a set_successor frame with its address coded in the Data field.

4.6.3 Token Bus Access Method

Stations are connected to the transmission medium in parallel. Token bus software is not much different from token ring, but there are some interesting differences.

First, each node in sequence must receive the entire token frame, change DA to point to the next node, and retransmit the token frame on the bus. It adds system overhead to token passing if the token bus has many stations.

Second, it has some advantages when transmitting data frames. Just because every node on the bus can receive at the same time, software allows the destination node to respond after receiving a frame with response windows.

Third, the token management function is distributed among all the nodes, so there is no active monitor. After transmitting a token frame, each node listens to the line to see if its successor has received the token properly. If not, the predecessor that has just sent a token frame takes action to recover the token by transmitting a who_follows frame to find out who is the next successor, which follows its immediate successor in the logical sequence. After receiving a set_successor frame as the response, the predecessor that has just sent the who_follows frame records the address of the new successor in a table and passes the token to the new successor, and ring operation continues.

It is possible for a node to receive the token and start transmitting data frames. But alas, just when it is ready to transmit the token to the next node, it fails with a token in its hand. The next node in sequence waits with patience. When its Timer-Rotate Token (TRT) expires, the next node knows that the ring is dead. It attempts to reinitialize the ring by transmitting a claim_token frame to notify other nodes on the ring. After a successful completion, it then places a new token on the ring and operation continues.

Any node can also deactivate itself from the ring voluntarily if it is healthy. After receiving the token frame, it transmits a set_successor frame to inform its predecessor by setting the address of its own successor in the Data field as the new successor. It transmits the token frame to its successor and, meanwhile, exits the ring.

So far, three fundamental LANs have been discussed using copper as the transmission medium. In order to achieve a data rate over gigabits per second, fiber-optic LANs were developed. It is also possible to develop a fiber-optic token bus. The research and development effort is huge but not totally insurmountable. Each node may have more than one transmitter and one receiver. The receiving node needs to adjust the position of its receiver, which can accept frames from its predecessor. Different frequencies and emitting angles of the infrared light may be employed by each node. As a consequence, while receiving the latter portion of the frame, a node can also transmit the front end of the same frame, just like a token ring. Difficulties must be overcome when a node is inserted into or removed from the logical ring. A fiber-optic token bus should improve the speed by at least two orders of magnitude.

Fiber-optic token rings are popular in the field with a data rate of 100 Mbps or more. Design issues as well as standards of fiber-optic rings are discussed in Section 4.7.

4.7 FIBER DISTRIBUTED DATA INTERFACE

Fiber Distributed Data Interface (FDDI) is a proposed new standard [2]. There are also FDDIs using twisted pairs as the transmission medium. Some of the FDDI characteristics are listed below:

- Data rate, 100 Mbps;
- Fiber-optic cable, simplex;
- Maximum distance between stations, 2.5 km;
- Maximum number of stations, 500;
- Cable length, 200 km;
- Baseband using 4B/5B encoding scheme;
- Token ring access method;
- Clock rate, 125 MHz;
- Error rate, $4 \cdot 10^{-11}$ Epb.

FDDI rings use multimode fibers. The optical transmitters are LEDs and the receivers are PIN diodes. Its protocol is similar to the IEEE 802.5 standard, with three interesting deviations as described below.

First, software design is somewhat different. As far as architecture is concerned, FDDI uses two rings. One goes clockwise and the other one goes counterclockwise, as shown in Figure 4.19(a). The outer ring is clockwise with sequence A-B-C-D-E-F while the inner ring is counterclockwise with sequence F-E-D-C-B-A. Data frames can be transmitted on either ring.

It has the self-repair capability to provide redundancy. For example, on the clockwise ring, if the fiber-optic cable between node C and D is broken, the outer ring is down but the inner ring is still operational, as shown in Figure 4.19(b). What if both cables between C and D are broken? The two broken rings can be merged into a single ring, as shown in Figure 4.19(c). A frame flows from A to B to C, makes a turn on C, and goes back to B counterclockwise. When the frame gets to node D, it makes another turn and flows back on the clockwise ring again. Software can keep the FDDI ring operational, but hardware repair is on call.

Second, the hardware encoding scheme is different. FDDI uses a 4B/5B code. A group of 4 bits is encoded into a 5-bit pattern called a symbol. A symbol represents 5 bits and has a total of 2^5 or 32 different waveforms. Sixteen of them are data symbols, each representing 4-bit ordinary data; three are used for starting and ending delimiters; two are used for control indicators; and three are used for line-state signaling to be recognized by the hardware controller. The remaining eight symbols are not used.

Using the 4B/5B encoding scheme, 25% of the bandwidth is wasted instead

(a)

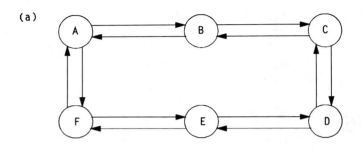

(b)

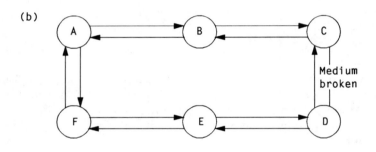

(c)

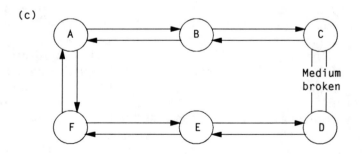

Figure 4.19 A six-node FDDI: (a) dual ring, (b) single ring, and (c) single merged ring.

of 100% as is the case using differential Manchester code. The clock frequency is raised to 125 MHz as computed below:

$$100 \text{ MHz} \cdot (5/4) = 125 \text{ MHz}$$

The duration of each symbol is (5 · 8) or 40 ns and only two symbols are required to encode 8 data bits. The physical layer is divided into two sublayers: PHY and PMD. Both sublayers work as a team to transmit symbols on the line. The transmitter accepts symbols from the MAC, converts each one into a 5-bit code group, and transmits the encoded high-low voltage pattern on the medium. The receiver receives the encoded data, establishes symbol boundaries based on the recognizing of a Start Delimiter, and forwards the decoded symbols to MAC via a PH_DATA.indication.

Finally, the FDDI frame layout is slightly different, as shown in Figure 4.20. The number of symbols instead of bytes is shown on the left-hand side of the field. Three differences are listed below:

1. A Preamble field is added in front of a token or frame in order for the hardware to synchronize with the timing of clock. The preamble is 16-symbol or more, consisting of the quiescent line-state symbols that enable the hardware controller to synchronize with the timing of the clock.
2. There is no Access Control field in either token or frame.
3. There is a FC field added before the ED in the token.

There are other minor differences in design. For example, FDDI provides two classes of service: synchronous versus asynchronous. Each station keeps a Target Token Rotation Time (TTRT), which is the estimated time to receive a token. The synchronous service allows a station to capture a token based on FIFO regardless of the value of its TTRT. The asynchronous service allows a station to capture a token based on assigned priority only when the elapsed time since a token was last received has NOT exceeded TTRT. After TTRT expires, synchronous service is always applied. Like token bus, FDDI also has SMT, which communicates with the bottom four sublayers.

If we break a pair of links in the FDDI dual ring and rewrite the software, we obtain a dual bus architecture as described in Section 4.8.

4.8 DISTRIBUTED QUEUE DUAL BUS

Distributed queue dual bus (DQDB) is another fiber-optic LAN for video and graphics applications. A DQDB architecture is a standard for MANs and pushed by the cable TV industry [IEEE 802.6]. Recall that a MAN is really a large-sized LAN that uses the same hardware and software design. DQDB is different from all the previous architectures in that it has three different features. First, it

(a)

>16 symbols	Preamble (PA)
2	Start delimiter (SD)
2	Frame control (FC)
1 or 2	End delimiter (ED)

(b)

>16	PA
2	SD
2	FC
4 or 12	Destination address (DA)
4 or 12	Source address (SA)
0 to n	Information (Info)
8	Frame check sequence (FCS)
1 or 2	ED
3	Frame status (FS)

Figure 4.20 FDDI frames: (a) token and (b) frame.

maintains a distributed data queue on each bus over the network. Second, it modifies the slotted ring concept in order to eliminate the medium access contention problems. Instead of transmitting frames in the same slot every time, it transmits the frame on an open slot based on FIFO. Third, its frame is 53 bytes long, which is compatible with an asynchronous transfer mode (ATM) cell as discussed in Chapter 6.

4.8.1 DQDB Architecture

Each node is attached to two unidirectional fibers. Bus 1 runs from left to right and bus 2 runs from right to left, as shown in Figure 4.21(a). Because the link between any two nodes is point-to-point, the bus is actually a whip or a broken ring with one link deactivated. Each node should have two sets of transmitters and receivers. On bus 1, a frame is transmitted from node A to B, B to C, C to D, and D to E, so the bus 1 sequence is A-B-C-D-E. Node A is the head, symbolized by a solid circle, and Node E the tail, symbolized by a solid square. The head of the bus always generates a slot on the bus at fixed time intervals. The slot or frame is transmitted from one node to the next node until it reaches the tail, where it is being stripped.

On bus 2, a slot traverses in the opposite direction, from E to D, D to C, C to B, and B to A. Therefore, E is the head and A is the tail. Some of the characteristics of DQDB are listed in Table 4.3.

If the distance between node A and node E is less than 2.5 km, there should be an extra link pair between A and E to provide redundancy. In fact, the dual bus can start anywhere on the ring. From the hardware viewpoint, it is a dual ring, but the software drives a dual bus. If the link between any two nodes is broken (say, between A and B), software can change the ordering of bus 1 from B, to C, D, E and stop at A, as shown in Figure 4.21(b). The new sequence of bus 1 therefore becomes B-C-D-E-A. Bus 2 has the reverse ordering, A-E-D-C-B. In other words, DQDB can do self-repair in the case where the link pair between any two nodes is broken. The physical link pair between node A and node E is shown in Figure 4.21(b) but not in Figure 4.21(a) for the purpose of clarity.

The DQDB frames are similar to the ones used in token bus but it uses 8-byte Address fields to conform with the international telephone number standard as described in Chapter 5.

4.8.2 DQDB Frames

A DQDB frame is the logical group of bits as seen by its upper layer, as shown in Figure 4.22. As usual, a frame consists of a header, a variable Info field of less than 8,192 bytes, and a 4-byte FCS. The header includes a 2-byte Delimiter, a 2-byte Length field for the entire frame, a 2-byte length Check, a 1-byte Control

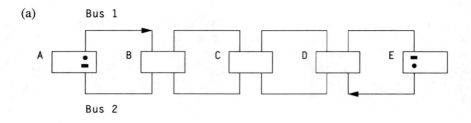

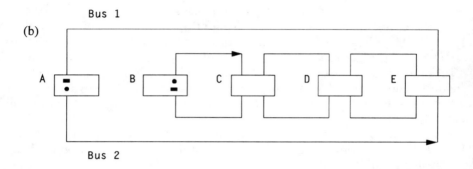

Figure 4.21 A five-node DQDB: (a) Before reconfiguration, bus 1 sequence is A-B-C-D-E, and bus 2 is E-D-C-B-A. (b) After reconfiguration, bus 1 sequence is B-C-D-E-A, and bus 2 is A-E-D-C-B.

Table 4.3
Characteristics of DQDB

Maximum Distance Between Stations	Data Rate
2 km	44.736 Mbps
546m	155.52 Mbps
137m	622.08 Mbps
Two fiber-optic cables, simplex	
Maximum number of stations, 512	
Cable length, 160 km	
Baseband	
DQDB Access Method	
Error rate, $4 \cdot 10^{-11}$ Epb	

Bytes	Field
2	Start delimiter
2	Length
2	Length check
1	Control indicator
8	Destination address
8	Source address
2	Reserved
1	Carrier indicator
2	Carrier select
< 8192	Information
4	FCS

Figure 4.22 DQDB frames.

indicator, an 8-byte DA, an 8-byte SA, a 2-byte Reserved field, a 1-byte Carrier indicator, and a 2-byte Carrier Select.

The Info field may contain up to 8,191 bytes of data, followed by an error-detecting code, FCS-32.

4.8.3 DQDB Slots

The total number of physical bits placed on the bus is 53 bytes long, known as a slot. The slot length is the same as an ATM cell, and DQDB is compatible with the evolving broadband ISDN. Therefore, each frame is segmented into slots. A slot has a 1-byte header followed by a 52-byte segment, as shown in Figure 4.23(a). The slot header for Access Control is specified in Figure 4.23(b).

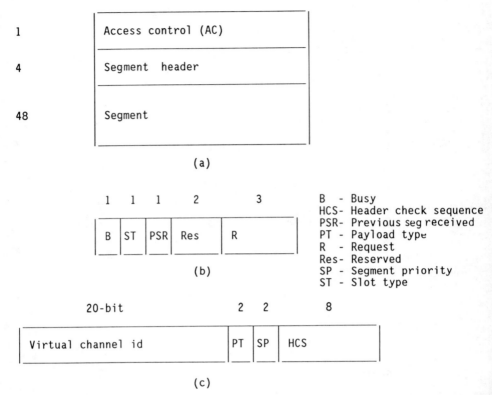

Figure 4.23 DQDB slots: (a) format of a DQDB MAC slot, (b) access control field, and (c) segment header.

Bit 0, the lsb in the first byte, indicates the state of the slot: 0 means free and 1 means occupied or busy. Therefore, it is called the Busy (B) bit. Bit 1 denotes the slot type: 0 means Queue Arbitrated (QA) and 1 means Prearbitrated (PA). Since DQDB supports both circuit- and cell-switching devices, PA slots are provided for synchronous TDM devices whose bit positions are fixed with respect to the beginning of the time frame. Only QA slots can be grabbed by any node on the bus to carry data under certain protocols. Bit 2 indicates the status of Previous Segment Received (PSR). A 1 asks that the previously received segment be cleared and 0 asks otherwise. The next 2-bit field is set to 0, reserved for future expansion. The last 3 bits are designated by R2, R1, and R0. Each one is a Request (R) bit with an assigned priority. In other words, when a node has data to transmit, it sets one of the three R bits, depending on the priority level of its data.

The 52-byte segment has its own header which is 4 bytes long as shown in Figure 4.23(c). The first 20-bit field denotes a virtual channel identifier (VCI). The next 2-bit field denotes the payload type, followed by another 2-bit field that is the assigned priority of the segment. The last 8-bit is the Header Check Sequence (HCS), which uses a polynomial code of degree 8 as shown below:

$$x^8 + x^2 + x + 1$$

4.8.4 DQDB Access Method

On each bus, there is a distributed queue, and each node essentially transmits its slots in a timely order when the data become ready for transmission. Inside a slot, there is a segment that really means a portion or part of a packet. On either bus, only a downstream node can receive. Each node must know the exact transmitting sequence of each bus.

First, let us consider the case where all the slots waiting for transmission have the same priority. The DQDB access method should guarantee fairness using a distributed queue concept. Each bus has its own queue. Since the two buses are symmetrical, we use bus 1 as an example to illustrate the slot transmissions. The head of bus 1 is denoted by Head-1, which is node A. Head-1 is also the tail of bus 2, denoted by Tail-2. Nodes B, C, D, and E are downstream nodes with respect to Head-1. Certain key concepts are listed below:

1. A node on bus 1 can only transmit to a downstream node, which means that the last node, Tail-1, can only receive. Note that Tail-1 must use bus 2 for its slot transmissions.
2. Before a node can transmit a slot on bus 1, the first order of business is to find a frame on bus 2 that has an R bit 0 and then the node sets the R bit to 1, which flows in the other direction. Only Head-1 can avoid this procedure because it is the tail of bus 2. The R bit set to 1 is seen by all the upstream nodes. Next, each node including Head-1 makes a transmission request internally by setting a flag, so to speak. Each node maintains two lists of transmission requests from its downstream nodes. Before a node makes its own request, all requests received are considered the preceding requests. After a node has made its own transmission request, all requests received are the afterward requests.
3. A node may transmit only if all preceding requests from its downstream nodes have been served. Any afterward requests made by the downstream nodes after its own transmission request will not affect its transmission. This guarantees fairness because the distributed queue is truly FIFO.

To implement this algorithm, each node must keep track of the number of preceding requests and afterward requests from its downstream nodes separately. Three variables are used: the Request Counter (RC), the Count Down (CD) register, and the Transmission Request (TR) flag. To understand the basic DQDB operations, we discuss a single FIFO queue on bus 1 only. Since the two buses are symmetrical, bus 2 operations are the same as bus 1.

On bus 2, each node examines the R bit in the slot header. If the R bit is set, which means one of its downstream nodes has made a TR, the current node always increments its RC by 1. The R bit remains unchanged as the node retransmits the slot on bus 2.

On bus 1, if a slot is passing by with a DA matching its own, then the node copies the slot into its receiver buffer. If a free slot is passing by and the node has no data to transmit, it simply passes the same free slot to its downstream. At the same time, it decrements RC by 1 only if its RC is greater than 1. If RC is 0, then it remains unchanged.

The instant when the node has a slot ready to transmit, it must make a TR first. By doing so, it first finds a slot on bus 2 whose R bit is 0, then it sets this bit to make a TR. Meanwhile, it replaces CD with its current RC and resets RC to 0. It also sets its TR flag. Consequently, CD contains the number of preceding requests and RC will contain the number of afterward requests. After having made its own request to transmit, the node decrements CD by 1 instead of RC each time after passing a free slot to its downstream. When the CD reaches 0, which means all preceding requests from downstream nodes have been served, the node can grab the next free slot on bus 1 to transmit its own data or fire. After firing, TR is reset to 0 and RC contains the number of preceding requests again. The whole process must be repeated each time when the node has a slot to transmit.

Head-1 does not listen to bus 1 because it has no upstream nodes. If Head-1 has a slot to transmit, it must also go through the same transmit request procedure, with a minor exception. That is, it does not set an R bit on bus 2 because it has no upstream nodes to notify.

Program design language can be used to describe the distributed queue algorithm, which could be written in software or embedded in the high-speed controller design.

Distributed Queue Algorithm to Transmit Data on Bus 1

```
Listen to bus 2;                    {Listen means to receive a slot
                                     and retransmit it on the line.}
IF the R bit in the slot is set,
THEN increment RC; ENDIF;
IF it has data to transmit,
THEN
Wait until a slot passes by with an R bit 0;
   DO; TR <— 1;                     {Set Transmission Request flag.}
   Set the R bit in the slot on bus 2;
   CD <— RC;
   RC <— 0; ENDDO;
```

```
ENDIF;
Retransmit the slot on bus 2;
Listen to bus 1;
IF Destination Address matches its own,
THEN copy the slot into its receive buffer; ENDIF;
IF a free QA slot passes by,
THEN
   IF the node has its TR flag set,
   THEN
      CASE CD of
      >0 — Leave slot free but decrement CD;
       0 — Place its data in slot;
            Set the Busy bit to 1;
            TR <— 0;
      ENDCASE;
   ELSE
      IF RC > 1, THEN Decrement RC; ENDIF;
   ENDIF;
ENDIF;
Retransmit the slot on bus 1;
End.
```

The design should be modified slightly for Head-1 or Tail-1 because they use only one transmitter and one receiver. The head never receives data and the tail never transmits data. All other nodes on the bus use two transmitters and two receivers.

DQDB Data Flow Example

A data flow example on bus 1 is shown in Figure 4.24(a–d). Nodes B, C, and D reside in the middle of the dual bus. The slot is depicted like a train with the header being the locomotive in the direction of moving. The B bit is the leading bit. The value of each variable changes as the result of an event as explained below:

1. After initialization, each node has its RC, CD, and TR reset to 0.
2. In Figure 4.24(a), node D has a slot ready to transmit. On bus 2, as a slot is passing by with an R bit equal to 0, it makes a TR by setting the R bit in the slot header to 1 and retransmits the same slot on bus 2. Meanwhile, it replaces its CD with RC (which is 0 anyway), resets RC, and sets TR. Since the CD of node D contains 0, it can grab the next available free slot to transmit its data. On bus 2, as the slot with R equal to 1 is passing by C and B, each node increments its RC by 1 respectively. A + in front of the node denotes the increment operation.
3. In Figure 4.24(b), node C has a slot to transmit also, so it makes a TR.

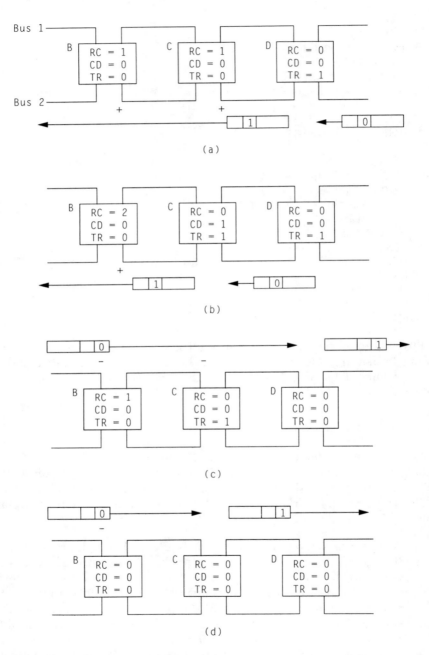

Figure 4.24 Data flow example on DQDB: (a) Node D issues a transmission request; (b) Node C issues a transmission request; (c) Node D transmits a slot; and (d) Node C transmits a slot.

As a result, its CD contains 1, RC is 0, and TR is 1. On node B, its RC has been incremented twice, so it contains 2.
4. As a free slot with the B bit equal to 0 passes by, node B decrements RC by 1 because its RC is greater than 0. Node C sees the same free slot passing by. It cannot use this slot either because its CD is not 0. Therefore, it decrements CD and passes the same slot to downstream. A - in front of the node denotes the decrement operation. Node D sees this free slot. Because its CD is 0 with TR equal to 1, it uses the slot to transmit its data and sets the B bit in the slot header to 1. Furthermore, it resets TR, indicating that it is no longer in TR state.
5. Another free slot passes by. Node B passes it to node C and decrements its RC to 0. This time, node C has its CD equal to 0 with TR equal to 1, so it uses the passing free slot to transmit its data and sets the B bit to 1. After doing that, its resets TR to 0 and bus 1 returns to its initial state.

In theory, each node can transmit a large amount of slots so long as no other node in the downstream wants to transmit. The local FIFO service may not emulate a true global FIFO queue for the entire network, therefore we can place a limit on how many slots a node can transmit per unit time interval in an overload situation.

Bandwidth Balancing

Because a local DQDB may be tied to other DQDBs, to ensure overall fairness, a bandwidth balancing (BWB) mechanism can be considered to prevent any node from hogging the network when it becomes overloaded. The solution is quite simple: We keep a BWB counter for each node [3]. Each time a node transmits a slot, its BWB counter is incremented by 1. When the counter reaches a limit (say, eight) before a fixed time interval expires, the software on the station will stop transmitting. After the time interval expires, its BWB counter is reset, and the overloaded node can transmit again.

We have discussed the DQDB access method of a single bus. The bus 2 operations are symmetrical to bus 1. Therefore, both operations must be compressed into one, so we have two receiver functions interacting with two sender functions. They are all real-time activities. The controller design may contain a large hardware buffer, so the network contains a long shift register. Multiple data streams may also be considered, namely parallel transmission. A special bit pattern must be transmitted periodically to ensure synchronization. In addition, certain control functions can be embedded into the controller chip design. To make things even more complicated, the IEEE 802.6 proposal specifies 3 Request bits in the slot header and each bit represents a specific priority level. This means that a total of three sets of counters are needed to keep track of the three distributed queues on each bus. The DQDB design remains a challenge.

4.9 CONCLUSIONS

So far, we have discussed contemporary LANs. If the transmission medium is not a design factor, there are three major approaches: the common bus, token ring, and token bus. Studies have been performed to determine which one is the best [4]. The truth is, there is no absolute best. Each design has its one merit that meets users requirements just as well, such as speed, reliability, and cost. All LANs will coexist for a long time.

If a LAN is installed in a small business, advanced planning must be carried out in regard to wiring standard. If speed is not a critical factor and the number of nodes is less than 15 confined in a small area, Ethernet seems to be an acceptable solution with the least cost. Nevertheless, it is not appropriate to adapt Ethernet for real-time applications because its transmission is nondeterministic due to collision problems. If speed and distance are of great concern, the fiber-optic token ring is a viable solution. In a university environment, the campus backbone computer network is usually a fiber-optic token ring. On the backbone, each node is known as a router, which is further connected to various LANs. Routers are switching nodes and will be discussed in Chapters 5 and 6.

DQDB architecture uses two buses; one runs from left to right and the other one runs from right to left. If there is an additional pair of links between head and tail, the bus can start anywhere in the ring, thus providing redundancy. Since each node competes for the slot on a FIFO basis, its response time is predictable, which makes it suitable for real-time applications. It is a modern technology pushed by the cable TV industry. Because its covered area is large, DQDB is also referred to as the metropolitan area network.

4.10 SUMMARY POINTS

1. The distance between any two nodes in a LAN is usually less than 2.5 km, with few exceptions.
2. Special transmitter and receiver devices are designed in LANs without using modems.
3. On a LAN, whenever one node transmits, all other nodes receive the frame pretty much at the same time.
4. Access methods on a LAN are different and the main difference lies in the MAC sublayer.
5. From the viewpoint of electronic design, there are two mayor approaches: the common bus and the point-to-point connection.
6. As far as software is concerned, there are four major approaches: one common bus, token ring, token bus, and dual bus.
7. On Ethernet, each node on the bus is allowed to transmit. Collisions occur when two or more nodes try to transmit at the same time.

8. On a token ring, each node is allowed to transmit at one time. A token is flowing on the ring and whoever grabs the token has the right to transmit.
9. On a token bus, hardware is a common bus, but software is a token ring. A Destination Address is always needed in a token frame, which must be transmitted on the bus from node to node.
10. FDDI contains two rings that connect all the nodes through point-to-point links with a data rate of 100 Mbps.
11. DQDB contains two buses using point-to-point links. One bus goes one direction while the other bus goes the opposite direction. It supports real-time applications with a data rate up to 622.08 Mbps.

Problems

Problem 4.1

In a token ring LAN, what is the maximum distance allowed between any two adjacent nodes?

Problem 4.2

Describe the difference between a common bus and a point-to-point link.

Problem 4.3

What are the two sublayers in a LAN that constitute the DL layer in a WAN?

Problem 4.4

What are the sublayers in a LAN that constitute the PH layer in a WAN?

Problem 4.5

Name three LLC primitives.

Problem 4.6

Name three MAC primitives.

Problem 4.7

Name three PLS primitives.

Problem 4.8

Ethernet or token ring LANs use a FCS-32 polynomial code as the divisor, but the modified algorithm is similar to that of SDLC and HDLC. At the receiving end, if there are no transmission errors, the specially designed 32-bit shift register should contain a fixed bit pattern, c704 dd7b in hex. Can you derive this special bit pattern? Verify your answer using a pencil and paper or writing a program in "C" to do the standard 32-bit CRC generation.

Problem 4.9

Describe the CSMA/CD access method.

Problem 4.10

Describe the token management functions performed by an active monitor on a token ring.

Problem 4.11

On a token bus, can we get rid of the active monitor? If so, how can we perform the distributed control function of the token frame on the bus?

Problem 4.12

When a link pair between two nodes on a FDDI is broken, design the appropriate software to merge the two rings into one single ring.

Problem 4.13

Describe the dual bus architecture of a DQDB.

Problem 4.14

If there are 200 nodes on a DQDB and the distance between any two adjacent nodes is 2 km, what is the maximum area in km^2 that the MAN can cover?

Problem 4.15

If a DQDB supports three priority levels, how many distributed queues are there altogether?

References

[1] Bryan, J., "Pumping Up Ethernet," *Byte Journal*, Aug. 1993, pp. 121–126.
[2] Ross, F. E., "FDDI—Fiber, Farther, Faster," *Proc. IEEE INFOCOM*, April 1986, pp. 323–332.
[3] Hahne, E. L., et al., "DQDB Networks With or Without Bandwidth Balancing," *IEEE Trans. on Communications*, Vol. 40, No. 7, 1992, pp. 1192–1204.
[4] Bux, W., "Local-Area Subnetworks, a Performance Comparison," in *Advances in Local Area Networks*, IEEE Press,1987.

Network Layer   5

"Networking" plays an essential part in our success. Bet on it.

The N (network) layer is different from the general Nth layer in the OSI model where N ranges from 1 to 7. The N layer discussed in this chapter is known as the packet layer mainly because packets are the basic transmission units between two peer N layers. Each N layer packet may contain either control or data information. For this reason, the network layer protocol is also referred to as the packet layer protocol (PLP). Each computer on the network is assigned an address unique to the network. The node address is usually an unsigned integer or a group of binary coded decimal (BCD) digits. The node address is global and unique, but the computer at the local site may have an alias or name that is symbolic. There is a subtle difference between naming and addressing. A node name is translated into a node address by a network routine. The global node address identifies the computer on the network, while the local alias merely provides user convenience. That is, the N layer software translates an alias or node name into a global network address before it can be used. The N layer handles the routing of packets in the network plus congestion control, segmentation and reassembly, concatenation and separation of packets, and so forth.

An application task running on node A in San Francisco can communicate with another task running on node D in New York. There are many nodes in the network, but the specific route between node A and node D is shown in Figure 5.1. Node A is said to be the origination node and node D is the destination node. In the middle of the route, there may be node B in Denver and node C in Chicago, referred to as the intermediate nodes. Nodes B and C are merely the switching nodes and may not even have a host.

If the N layer on node A receives a data request from its transport (T) layer, the data packet travels to node D via nodes B and C. At node D, its N layer knows that this is the final destination. If node D has a separate host processor,

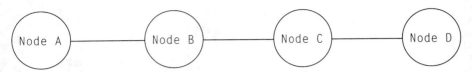

Figure 5.1 Connection between node A and node D in a computer network.

its N layer places a data indication message in the shared memory for its T layer to fetch, interpret, and execute. Various approaches are used in designing the N layer as discussed in the following sections.

5.1 BASIC DESIGN CONCEPTS

Intuitively, the N layer can be thought as an independent task that receives messages from its T layer, NMT routines, or data link (DL) layer. If there is no DL software in the system, the N layer becomes the main driver running on the communication processor, which mainly routes packets to the next node. Whatever the design approach may be, the primary objective of the N layer is to determine the route. Some approaches may be more reliable, while others are simpler. Design decisions should be based upon the network applications. There are two major approaches to designing the N layer: the virtual circuit (VC) model and the datagram model.

5.1.1 Virtual Circuit Model

A VC can be thought as a pipe across the network. At one end, the service user drops a data packet into the pipe and the same data packet pops out from the other end in the same sequence. The programming entity at either end of a VC is referred to as a network service access point (NSAP). A VC can be treated as a resource shared by many service users running on the same host. The layer on top, usually the T layer, drives the VC. The VC models are implemented in many wide area networks (WANs) [1,2][X.25, SNAa].

In a VC model, a connection phase must be performed between two T layers before they can communicate with each other. In other words, a VC must be built first. The origination T layer sends a N layer connect or setup packet, which must find its way to the destination node via many intermediate nodes. The T layer on the origination node initiates the action and the destination node means the computer at the other end of the VC. However, in some datagram models the term *destination node* means the receiving node, which may be either one of the two end nodes.

During the connection phase, all the N layers in the route work as a team to build the forward route as well as the backward route to achieve full-duplex capability between two NSAPs. If a VC connection is successfully completed, the T layer on top can deliver a packet to its peer via a VC between two NSAPs. All the control and data packets must follow the same route afterwards. In the case where a VC failure is detected, the T layer may reassign a different route for error recovery. In other words, packets can still be transmitted without any loss.

Only a VC id, a local reference number, is required in the packet header. A VC may be disconnected after a session, otherwise it is a permanent virtual circuit (PVC). The VC models are used in a network for either telephone or computer communications, but there are some differences. First, for each telephone call a network layer connection/disconnection is required, which also implies a DL layer connection/disconnection between a DTE and a DCE. In computer communications, after a connection is established, the VCs and DLs may stay permanently in the system. Second, if there is only one user at each end of the telephone, the VC connection is usually private. Any node crash in the middle of a VC usually implies termination of the call. In computer communications, there may be multiple users on the same host to share the same VC, so a T layer implementation is necessary to support a multiprogramming environment. Any node crashed in the middle of the route may not cause termination provided that the T layer on top can reassign another VC for error recovery.

5.1.2 Datagram Model

The datagram model is different from the VC model. It is similar to our postal system. Each datagram has a header that contains the receiver's address and the sender's address. Datagram software takes whatever route and delivers the datagram to the destination. Any node crash may not cause failure if the intermediate node knows how to bypass the failed node. Datagram models are implemented in many networks, such as Internet and DNA [3–5]. In some models, each N layer maintains a routing table to ensure that the routing decision is made in the right direction, while others do not even need a routing table. Such systems use the flooding technique as explained below.

Flooding Technique

Flooding means that after a node has received an incoming packet, its N layer sends a copy to all outgoing DLs except the one the packet arrived on. In other words, the N layer software floods all outgoing links with the incoming packet. As a result, no routing table is even required by the N layer. Assume that we have a six-node banking network as shown in Figure 5.2. If node A wants to send a packet to node F, it sends information packet 1 (I1) to node B. Node B floods two

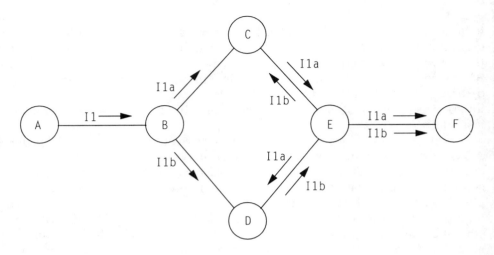

Figure 5.2 Flooding technique used in a six-node network.

copies of I1 to its outgoing links:, copy a of I1 (I1a) to node C and copy b of I1 (I1b) to node D. Node E receives I1a from node C and floods it out to nodes D and F; it also floods the other packet, I1b, received from D to nodes C and F. The destination node F receives two copies of the packet, I1a and I1b, at the end.

The next question is how to avoid infinite loops so the packets will not circulate on the network forever. On the sending node, there is a hop count initialized to 4 in the packet header that is decremented by 1 after each transmission. A hop means transmission of the packet to the next node. When the hop count reaches 0, the packet is discarded regardless.

The flooding technique seems to cause so much overhead because the N layer does not have any routing intelligence. To improve the performance, we may consider the selective flooding scheme, which means that each node maintains a routing table and that each intermediate node only transmits the packet on certain outgoing lines based on the information in the routing table. For example, if the destination is New York, the intermediate node in San Francisco should not route the packet to Hawaii because it is not in the right direction.

If the flooding technique is used, it is possible for packets to arrive out of sequence, and there may also be duplicates. In a pure datagram model, the N layer at the end of the route just delivers whatever packets are received by its T layer on the host, which then sorts packets in sequence, discards duplicates, and requests retransmission of any missing packets.

The key difference between a VC and a datagram is that the VC model keeps strict roadsigns but the datagram model does not. In addition, each datagram header must contain the full destination node address. Also, since the route is not fixed, if a traffic jam is encountered in the middle of the route, a datagram may arrive out of sequence.

Furthermore, a datagram model may not even have a routing table if the flooding technique is chosen. It is interesting to note that during the VC connection phase, the setup packet finds its way from the origination node to the destination node just like a datagram.

If the N layer maintains a routing table with some routing intelligence, the datagram model should be reliable provided that all bugs are cleared in the system.

5.1.3 Virtual Circuit Plus Datagram Model

The third approach is of academic interest only. That is, a VC exists only between the T layer and its adjacent N layers. In other words, the N layer underneath still employs a datagram model. In such a design, the responsibility of sorting packets, discarding duplicates, and requesting retransmission of any missing packets is shifted from the T layer to the N layer on the destination node. This approach has one drawback: The N layer on the destination node is much larger than the N layer on the other nodes. Thus, there are two sets of software to maintain. In contrast, a pure datagram model merely maintains one set of N layer routines.

One major design objective of the N layer is routing. There are many strategies that can be used to route packets in either a VC model or a datagram model, as introduced in Section 5.2.

5.2 ROUTING PHILOSOPHIES

The N layer usually maintains a routing table, which is a data structure containing all the information about the network topology. Routing tables may be updated from time to time by a system administrator. There are many routing philosophies in that a route may be determined by each node in the middle of the route, by the origination node alone, or by a special node whose sole function is to determine the route.

Perhaps, the most popular philosophy is to let each node determine the next hop in the route. Even so, how does each node make its routing decisions? We will provide some clues in the following.

5.2.1 Distributed Routing

Distributed routing means that each node in the middle of the route determines the next hop. Datagram models mostly use distributed routing. If the computer network contains a large number of nodes, VC models should also use distributed routing.

Starting from the origination node, each node determines the next hop in the route. Hierarchical routing may be used to augment distributed routing. In other words, it is possible for the packet layer to examine the bit pattern of a global network address and know exactly what the next hop should be. If distributed routing is used, then the routing table on each node is a local data base that contains information regarding how to route next. Distributed routing is adaptive in the sense that each node updates the entries in its routing table dynamically depending on road conditions. When the computer network has over several million nodes, distributed routing seems to be the only viable solution. That is to say, the N layer on each node determines the next hop regardless of the N layer model (VC or datagram).

5.2.2 Source Routing

Source routing means that the source or origination node determines the entire route. The route may be supplied by the human user or determined by the N layer on the origination node whose routing table contains information about the topology of the entire network.

Source routing has been implemented in both VC and datagram models. In a VC model, before the data transfer phase can begin, the origination node must determine the route first and send a setup or connect packet to the destination node. The special connect packet contains many network node addresses and each one identifies the particular node in the route. While the connect packet travels to the destination, the N layer on each node in the middle of the route also sees the connect packet, knows exactly the next hop, and records this information in the roadsign table. If source routing is used in a datagram model, then the header of each packet must contain all the node addresses in the route and the datagram should become very reliable.

5.2.3 Centralized Routing

Centralized routing means there is a special node whose sole function is to determine the route [6]. The special node is called the routing control center (RCC), on which the supervisory system software not only determines the route but also assigns the I/O buffers for each intermediate node. After receiving the routing information from the RCC, the origination node knows the route just like source routing.

Using centralized routing, each node in the network must have a connection, direct or indirect to the RCC, as shown in Figure 5.3. There two distinct advantages: Only one copy of the global routing table is maintained by the RCC, and the burden of making routing decisions is alleviated from the N layer. One disadvantage is that additional traffic is added to the RCC, which may cause congestion if the number of nodes in the network is too large. In addition,

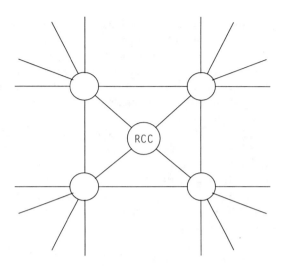

Figure 5.3 Routing control center.

redundancy must be considered in designing the RCC so that any hardware failure will not bring down the entire network.

The centralized routing philosophy is perhaps more important as a concept than as a practice to the system designer. That is to say, the control function of a system can be passed to a specific node, and it doesn't matter what the function is. For example, in a LAN, we may have a central node being the name server whose sole function is to translate a symbolic node name into a numerical network address. Whenever a node in the LAN sees a destination node name whose network address is unknown, it sends a message to the central node to request help. The network system software on the central node receives the request, translates the name into a network address, and returns it to the requesting node. Consequently, a human user need not know the network address of the destination but can use a local alias or name instead in the e-mail address, such as tiger, cougar, bear, or bull.

No matter which routing method is used, source or centralized, before a route can be decided, the node must know the topology of the entire network. In other words, the node should keep a global routing table that specifies the connection of the entire network. Consequently, this table is very large, and its management may become tedious. At any rate, a route should be selected quickly at the lowest possible cost.

Shortest Route Problem

We define the link cost between any two nodes as a function of many variables that may include line length, quality, and queuing delays. If the length of the route mainly represents the cost, the shortest route also means the least cost. Given an origination node, our challenge is to find the shortest route to the destination node. If the number of nodes is large, the computation becomes extensive, and it requires a large memory space. However, all of the routes can be precalculated and placed in a table. When a routing decision needs to be made, the N layer simply uses the destination node address as the key, looks up the table, and selects the route accordingly.

The Dijkstra algorithm finds the shortest route from a particular node to all the destination nodes that are actually implemented in networks, such as TYM-NET and DDN [7,8]. The same computation must be performed for every single node in a network that may become an origination node.

The algorithm uses an iterative approach, which is quite intuitive. After each iteration, the shortest route of one destination node will be determined with the following explanations:

1. First, we define a two-dimensional LinkCost matrix that contains the link cost between any two nodes in the network. In programming, all node ids are numbered from 0 to $n-1$ where n is the total number of nodes (the same as the row dimension or the column dimension). LinkCost[X, Y] denotes the link cost, which is a positive integer between node X and Y. If there is no connection between the two nodes, its link cost is infinity or represented by a very large integer.
2. Each node is associated with three attributes: Cost, PriorHop, and Status. They may be grouped into one structure or separated into three one-dimensional arrays. Each array contains $n-1$ elements. Cost means the minimum total cost to go from the origination node to this node, and PriorHop contains the node id of the previous hop. Status mainly specifies whether the shortest route to this node has been selected. Using any destination node id as the index to poke into the arrays, we can find its cost, previous hop, and status.
3. Define S as the set containing all the nodes whose shortest routes have been selected. Initially, S contains the origination node. S is growing per each iteration when another node is added to it. It takes $n-1$ iterations to find all the routes. There is another set PS of nodes that do not belong to S but have direct links to any one of the nodes in S. In other words, PS contains all the nodes that have the potential to be selected during the iteration. The entries in Cost and PriorHop for all the nodes in S are final (but not yet for PS). In fact, the cost and the prior hop of a node in PS are subject to change until it is selected. Our goal is to find a node in PS after each iteration that has the minimum cost among all. The Status attribute denotes whether a node belongs to S, PS, or neither.
4. Assume that X is the last node selected and added to S. All members that are not in S but that have a direct link to X must be reevaluated because of the

newly added X. Say, node Y is found which may or may not already belong to *PS* as depicted below.

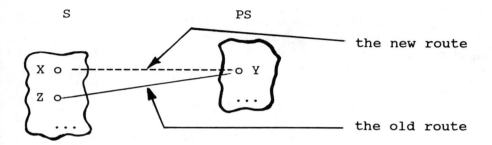

The cost of the new route between the origination node and Y is the cost of X plus the incremental link cost between X and Y. If this new route is cheaper than the old route via Z, then the total Cost and PriorHop entries of Y must be updated to reflect this change. The status of Y, if not yet marked, should be marked as *PS*. Since testing would take more time, we simply mark its Status as *PS* regardless. The iteration process is described by a programming loop repeated $n - 1$ times as follows:

```
REPEAT
                {X: the last node selected to S.
                Y: any node which has a direct connection to X.
                Cost: the minimum total cost array.
                PriorHop: the prior hop array.
                LinkCost: the link cost matrix.}
DO for all the nodes not in S;
IF there is a node Y which is directly connected to X,
THEN
DO;
IF Cost (Y) > (Cost (X) + LinkCost(X, Y)),
THEN Cost (Y) = Cost (X) + LinkCost(X, Y);
PriorHop (Y) = X;
Status (Y) = 'PS';
ENDIF; ENDDO;
ENDIF; ENDDO;
    DO for all the nodes in PS;
    Select node Y which has the minimum cost;
    ENDDO;
                {Mark it as the new member in S.}
Status [Y] = 'S';
X = Y;
UNTIL n-1 times;
```

Let us go through a real example and trace the states of all variables. Given a network containing eight nodes, A, B, C, D, E, F, G, and H, as shown in Figure 5.4, find all the routes from A to other nodes. Note that the positive integer associated with each link denotes its cost.

LinkCost is defined to be an 8 by 8 symmetrical matrix. Each entry of the matrix specifies the link cost between any two nodes. The entry matrix [i,j] is equal to matrix [j,i] and the symbol % denotes infinity or a large number, which means no connection exists between node i and j as shown below:

	A	B	C	D	E	F	G	H
A	0	3	2	%	%	%	5	%
B	3	0	%	2	%	%	%	%
C	2	%	0	4	%	6	%	%
D	%	2	4	0	6	%	4	%
E	%	%	%	6	0	%	4	10
F	%	%	6	%	%	0	3	%
G	5	%	%	4	4	3	0	8
H	%	%	%	%	10	%	8	0

There are seven iterations altogether as listed in Table 5.1.

The S column represents the state before iteration while PS, X, Cost, and PriorHop represent the results after iteration. Before iteration starts, A is assigned to X, the most recently selected node. From A, we need to find only those nodes that are directly connected to A. They are B, C, and G. Therefore, we include B, C, and G in PS and update the entries in cost and prior hop accordingly. After updating, we check that among all the nodes in PS, C has the minimum cost. Consequently, it is brought into S and becomes the newly selected node X for the next iteration.

During the second pass, D and F are included in PS because they are directly connected to C. After their costs and prior hops are updated, comparing all the nodes in PS we include B, which has a minimum cost of 3, in S. The logic is simple. Because the link cost between two nodes is always positive, it is impossible to find another node via to B with a smaller cost.

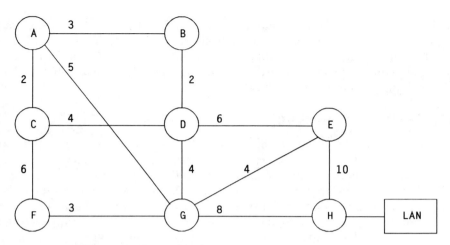

Figure 5.4 An eight-node computer network.

Table 5.1
Variable Values After Each Iteration

	S	PS	X	\multicolumn{7}{c}{Cost of}	\multicolumn{7}{c}{PriorHop of}
				B	C	D	E	F	G	H	B	C	D	E	F	G	H
1	A	C,B,G	C	3	2	%	%	%	5	%	A	A	—	—	—	A	—
2	A,C	B,D,F,G	B	3	2	6	%	8	5	%	A	A	C	—	C	A	—
3	A,B,C	D,F,G	D	3	2	5	%	8	5	%	A	A	B	—	C	A	—
4	A,B,C,D	E,F,G	G	3	2	5	11	8	5	%	A	A	B	D	C	A	—
5	A,B,C,D,G	E,F,H	F	3	2	5	9	8	5	13	A	A	B	G	C	A	G
6	A,B,C,D,F,G	E,H	E	3	2	5	9	8	5	13	A	A	B	G	C	A	G
7	A,B,C,D,E,F,G	H	H	3	2	5	9	8	5	13	A	A	B	G	C	A	G

In pass 3, B is node X, which is connected to D already in *PS*. Note that the sum of Cost B and the link cost between B and D is 5, which is smaller than the old Cost 6. In other words, it is cheaper to go to D via B. Therefore, Cost D is changed from 6 to 5, and its PriorHop should also be changed from C to B. Note that at this point, D or G has the same minimum cost of 5, and either one could be selected into *S*. Because of their ordering, D is selected first. Also in pass 5, after G is included in *S*, the cost of E changes from 11 to 9.

After iterating seven times, the Cost and PriorHop array are finalized specifying both the total cost and the previous hop for all the nodes B, C, ... and H under the assumption that A is the origination node. As an example, from A to H the cost is 13 as denoted by Cost (H). Looking into PriorHop (H), G is obtained as the previous hop. Looking into PriorHop (G), we get A, which is the origination node id, so we stop here. The shortest route is, therefore, A-G-H. To find the route from A to E, we obtain A-G-E and the cost is 9. All the routes are specified in the routing table of A, which may be updated from time to time based on the change of network topology.

5.2.4 Hierarchical Routing

Hierarchical routing is a special technique used to supplement distributed routing. That is, the intermediate node knows exactly what the next hop should be. To achieve this goal, computers are grouped into domains, and there may be one or more links between two domains. A computer in one domain can communicate with another computer in a different domain only via the fixed links. Therefore, it is also known as fixed routing to indicate that certain sections of the route are fixed, and there is no freedom for selection. A typical long-distance telephone number may have many digits as shown below:

    001 1 805 756 2986

The first three digits denote an international access code, which is a local reference number used by the local exchange in Hong Kong to switch to its international routing center. Were the same call placed in Taiwan, the international access code would be changed to 002. Besides the leading digits, the rest represents a unique global telephone address. The first field is the Country id and 1 represents the United States. Other country codes may be between one to three digits. The next three-digit area code denotes a toll office, followed by a three-digit prefix to denote a local exchange. The final four-digit number is the subscriber's id. The international routing center in Hong Kong knows exactly how to route the call to a fixed node in the United States, which is the next hop. Once the call request reaches the United States, the American telephone system knows how to connect the call to the destination, step by step.

    It should be mentioned that in a telephone network, if the traffic between two large cities (say, New York and San Francisco) is heavy, the telephone calls may go through direct trunk lines and bypass the upper hierarchy. Hierarchical routing is also used in a banking network, which has an account id similar to the telephone number. The id consists of a headquarter id, a regional id, a branch id, a local id, and a user id, as shown below:

    Headquarter_id. regional_id. branch_id. local_id. user_id

The transaction records performed at the local office will be forwarded to the branch office first, then to the regional office, and finally to the headquarter. With this layout, it is possible for a customer to withdraw cash from any automatic teller machine and from any bank. A third example is the Internet address, which is a 32-bit unsigned integer broken into two parts: a network id and a host id. The Network id field has a variable length depending on the size of the network. If a network is large, its network id may be shorter and its host id longer so that more computers can be accommodated in the network. If each byte is represented by a decimal number, an IP address may be represented by a dot notation as follows:

    129.65.63.4

The first 2-byte section, 129.65, is the id of a university network, and the next 2-byte section, 63.4, denotes a host id, which specifies a particular computer in the network. In the first 2-byte section, the upper bits may denote a domain id followed by an institution id. If we consider that each domain of computers has its own entry point that knows how to route to other nodes in the network, the network topology is hierarchical. Judging from the upper bits in the network id, the N layer knows exactly how to route the packet. Needless to say, when a network exceeds several million nodes, distributed routing plus hierarchical routing seems to be the only viable solution in determining the route.

Recall that in a VC model, a special connection phase is necessary to establish the route before the data transfer phase can begin. Each intermediate node must know the next hop as determined by one of the routing philosophies. If source or central routing is used, the origination node sends a setup packet to all the intermediate nodes in the route. On the other hand, if distributed routing is used, each node itself in the route must determine the next hop. A route is represented by a data structure in memory that contains roadsigns. Roadsigns are usually placed in a table by which each intermediate node, after receiving an incoming packet, knows where to route next.

5.3 ROADSIGNS

A roadsign table is maintained by the N layer in a VC model. To establish a VC, the origination T layer issues a connect request to its N layer. The N layer on the origination node determines the next hop, builds the roadsign, and sends a connect packet out via a DL_DATA.request. Review Chapter 3 if you are confused. The N layer on the next node receives the connect packet via a DL_DATA.indication. If source routing or central routing is used, then the connect or setup packet contains all the routing information by which each intermediate node simply builds the roadsign. However, if distributed routing is used, the N layer on each intermediate node must consult its local routing table first, determine the route, and then build the roadsign.

A roadsign table is completely different from a routing table. A routing table is a permanent database that specifies the network topology as seen by the intermediate node while a roadsign table contains information about specific routes. A roadsign is torn down after a VC is disconnected, but the routine table stays in the system without modification until the network topology is changed. It should be stressed that the N layer connect packet travels from the origination node, ripples through all the intermediate nodes, and finally gets to the destination node just like a datagram, but only the first time. Once a route is established, the roadsign table specifies the precise route by which all subsequent packets, control or data, must follow.

During the VC connection phase, it is necessary to build a round-trip route between two NSAPs. Since simplex transmission may exist between any two nodes, it is not mandatory to assign the same local VC id to the backward route as to the forward route. However, the VC id between the N layer and its T layer should be the same.

In practice, the sending party always determines the VC id in an outgoing N layer connect packet. Let us go through an example. Assume that we have four nodes, A, B, C, and D, and that node A wants to establish a VC between itself and D as shown in Figure 5.5. The N layer on node A receives a connect request from its T layer, which contains the origination node id, the destination node id, and the VC id (which is 56 as determined by its T layer). The origination N layer on A decides the next hop (because distributed routing is assumed), determines the new VC id, records the roadsign, and sends a N layer connect packet to node B via a DL_DATA.request. However, this time the packet header contains a different VC id (17) as determined by the N layer on A.

Finally, the N layer connect packet arrives on node D. The destination N layer on node D determines the VC id (60), records the roadsign, and sends a connect indication message to its T layer. The destination T layer knows that a VC has been established between A and D and sends a connect response to its N layer using the same VC id (60). If everything goes smoothly, the N layer on D sends out a confirm packet via a DL data request. While the N layer connect confirm packet travels through the N layers of C and B, each one in turn builds the return route.

When the N layer connect confirm packet finally arrives on node A, its N layer records the final roadsign and sends a connect confirm message to its T layer. Note that the N layer on node A uses the same VC id (56) as first determined by its T layer in the confirm message. At this point, the T layer on A also knows that a VC has been established between node A and D.

Roadsigns of this VC between node A and D are shown in Figure 5.6. Each of the four nodes maintains its own roadsigns. The symbol @A means at node A. The arrow → represents an IF-THEN construct. At the tail end of the arrow, we specify an IF clause (i.e., the condition). At the head of the arrow, there is the THEN clause, which specifies the routing decision.

At node A, we have a roadsign that reads

TA | 56 → NB | 17

with the following interpretation:

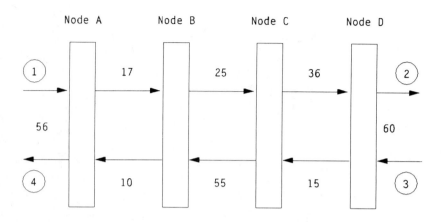

①   N_CONNECT.request(origination_node_id,
　　　　　　　　　　　　destination_node_id,
　　　　　　　　　　　　vc_id, QOS, etc.);

②   N_CONNECT.indication(origination_node_id,
　　　　　　　　　　　　　destination_node_id,
　　　　　　　　　　　　　vc_id, QOS, etc.):

③   N_CONNECT.response(origination_node_id,
　　　　　　　　　　　　　destination_node_id,
　　　　　　　　　　　　　vc_id, QOS, etc.);

④   N_CONNECT.confirm(origination_node_id,
　　　　　　　　　　　　destination_node_id,
　　　　　　　　　　　　vc_id, QOS, etc.);

Figure 5.5 Virtual circuit connection.

IF the N layer receives a packet from its T layer on A with a VC
id, 56, in its header,
THEN transmit the packet to node B with a VC id, 17; ENDIF;

In order to keep the roadsigns physically uniform, we use an arrow pointing in the other direction as shown below:

    TA | 56 ← NB | 10

with interpretation as follows:

IF the N layer receives a packet from node B with a VC id, 10, in
its header,
THEN transmit the packet to its T layer with a VC id, 56; ENDIF;

```
@ node A    TA  |  56    --->     NB  |  17
            Receive 56    then    Send 17
            from    TA            to NB

            TA  |  56    <---     NB  |  10
            Send 56       then    Receive 10
            to TA                 from NB

@ node B    NA  |  17    --->     NC  |  25
            NA  |  10    <---     NC  |  55

@ node C    NB  |  25    --->     ND  |  36
            NB  |  55    <---     ND  |  15

@ node D    NC  |  36    --->     TD  |  60
            NC  |  15    <---     TD  |  60

TA - T layer on node A
NA - N layer on node A
```

Figure 5.6 Roadsigns.

It is interesting to study TYMNET, owned by British Telecom [6]. The N layer on each node uses the same VC id for both directions. It also uses a fixed buffer pair for each of the DL input and output ports. Both the VC id and buffers were assigned by the routing control center. To adopt this buffering convention, we change the roadsigns on node A as shown below:

TA | 56 → NB | 17 using buffer no. 4
TA | 56 ← NB | 17 using buffer no. 5

The first roadsign at node A reads

IF the N layer receives a packet from its T layer on A with a VC id, 56, using buffer 4 as input,
THEN transmit the packet to node B with a VC id, 17, from buffer 4; ENDIF;

The second roadsign says

IF the N layer receives a packet from Node C with a VC id, 17, using buffer 5 as input,
THEN transmit the packet to its T layer with a VC id, 56, from buffer 5; ENDIF;

If we trade pointers to exchange buffers, then there is no data movement in the operation. The next design issue is how to determine roadsigns. We need to explain what a routing table is and what kind of information should be placed in the routing table. Stay tuned.

5.4 ROUTING TABLE

Assume that distributed routing is used in a network as shown in Figure 5.4. Each node determines the next hop strictly based on probability. A particular link is selected often only because its specified probability is high. In other words, given the destination node id, one of many next hops may be selected by the N layer. Recall that the routing table specifies the topology of the network so each entry should contain the information as listed below:

- The destination node id;
- The next hop, which may be its host, an intermediate node, or a gateway to a specific LAN;
- The probability associated with the route.

The routing table at node G is a database used by its N layer to determine the next hop as shown in Table 5.2.

The probability specified in each entry dictates the probable usage of the DL. A 1/2 probability indicates that this node will be selected 50% of the time. At node G, if the destination node is A, there are three ways to select the next hop. Out of 16 times, 12 times we select node A, three times we select F, and one time we select node D. The sum of all probabilities should be one as computed below:

$$(12/16 + 3/16 + 1/16) = 16/16 = 1$$

Table 5.2
Routing Table at Node G

Destination Node	Next Hop	Probability	Remark
A	A	3/4	75%
A	F	3/16	
A	D	1/16	
B	A	1/2	50%
B	D	3/8	
B	F	1/8	
...			
G	TG	1	100% to its T layer on G
ELSE	H	1	Gateway to a LAN

In the N layer design, the routine may read a 4-bit random number in the system. If the number is between 0 and 11 inclusive, node A is selected to be the next hop. If the number is between 12 and 14 inclusive, we select node F. If the number is 15, we select node D.

In the case of hardware failures (say node F is down or the DL to node F is not working), the entries in the routing table must be updated. This job could be done by the system administrator or, better yet, by the N layer itself. After updating, the probability of using node F should be split between node A and D. The probability of using A becomes 14/16 and using D becomes 2/16. The probability of using F should be set to 0, which means that this DL is no longer in service.

It is also possible to set the probability to 1 to indicate a situation of hierarchical routing. Simply put, the next node must be selected as the only route. If the next node is down and redundancy is not provided, then packets cannot be delivered.

Wild Card

In an entry of the routing table, a destination node address may contain a field of 0's, which indicates a wild card. A field of 0's would match any bits in the corresponding field of an actual destination node id. For example, a 129.65.0.0 in the destination node entry would match any destination address whose network id is 129.65, as shown below:

129.65.XXX.XXX

where an X may denote any digit. Note that the Wild Card field is different from a broadcast address. A broadcast address is a special destination node id containing all 1's. For example, a given destination node id, 129.65.255.255, specifies that all users at Cal Poly in San Luis Obispo should receive this packet.

ELSE Entry

At the end of the routing table, if the Destination Node id field is specified as ELSE, which matches any destination node id not found in the table. There may be two or more ELSE entries in the routing table with different probabilities. This provides redundancy in routing. The ELSE entry usually represents the gateway to another network.

If the next hop is to a LAN, the entry indicates that the current node is a gateway and a DL id with a probability set to 1. The DL id in a request message tells its DL layer where to fetch the DL Control Block containing the characteristics of the DL (e.g., UART, USRT, Ethernet, token ring, or token bus). Its DL layer must use the appropriate protocol to transmit frames on the line.

There are other issues related to the N layer design, as introduced in Section 5.5.

5.5 OTHER DESIGN ISSUES

When one computer communicates with another computer, it is possible to have a deadlock. In other words, either computer cannot complete its I/O operations because buffers are not available. Another issue is buffer management. If the system is properly designed, the data movement between I/O buffers can be eliminated. The third design issue is how to provide congestion control in the N layer. Even though most of the N layers have the capability to segment and reassemble large packets, a thorough discussion will be deferred until Chapter 7. Finally, we will discuss the concatenation and separation of small packets.

5.5.1 System Deadlocks

System deadlock is an OS design issue. The deadlock condition occurs when several tasks are running concurrently and each task holds some resources and waits for more from the OS. If there are no more resources available, then no task can proceed and we have a deadlock. The OS simply cannot execute any task that has all the resources locked up. To solve this problem, the OS designers use an "all or none" approach. That is, the OS either assigns all the resources requested by the task or none at all. Thus, at least one task is executable. This is actually a very clever idea to simplify the OS design [IBM 370].

In a computer network, many computers are running in parallel, and each computer has a task in execution. So we can say that multiple tasks are executing simultaneously in a network. If all the I/O tasks on different nodes hold some resources and wait for more, it is possible to have a network system deadlock, and no task can proceed.

The simplest example involves two computers. Each computer uses two buffers for transmitting frames to the other but neither one has buffers for input. Consequently, the two tasks, one on each computer, get stuck, and no one can complete their I/O operation. Another example is where we have three computers. Node A wants to transmit to node B, B wants to transmit to node C, and C wants to transmit to A. If no buffers are available for input on each computer, we have all three computers deadlocked in a loop, as shown in Figure 5.7. The solution is to assign a fixed number of buffers for each port, input, or output, so the DL task always has its own resources [6].

5.5.2 Exchange Buffering

In OS design, when a task requests I/O, it may specify *move* mode or *substitute* mode. Substitute mode implies exchange buffering. The user task must provide

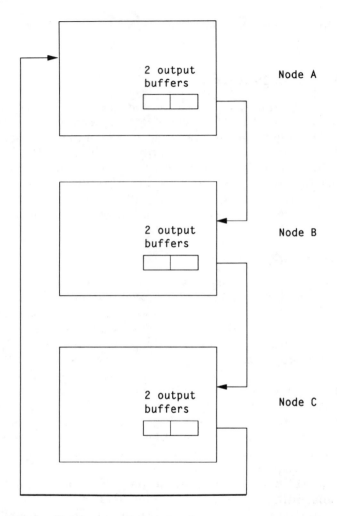

Figure 5.7 System deadlock in a computer network.

a pointer to its buffer. Pointer means memory address. After an I/O system call, the pointer is traded with the one used by the OS, and there is no data movement between the buffer used by the user task and that used by the OS. So, we move pointers instead of actually moving data from one buffer to another.

This exchange buffering technique can be used in the N layer design to eliminate the data movement between buffers, as shown in Figure 5.8. Before a DL sends a DL_DATA.indication to its N layer, each layer has its own transfer vectors and each vector contains a pointer to its buffer, as shown in Figure 5.8(a).

Network Layer 257

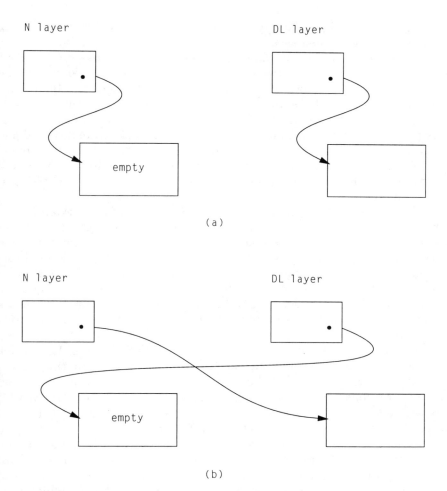

Figure 5.8 Pointer movement to exchange an I/O buffer: (a) before passing a packet to the N layer and (b) after passing a packet to the N layer.

The DL layer has a pointer to its input buffer that contains data. After receiving a DL_DATA.indication, the N layer trades its pointer with the pointer of its DL layer, as shown in Figure 5.8(b). If the N layer is properly designed, it needs only one spare buffer to interchange with an I/O buffer used by its DL layer.

5.5.3 Congestion Control

Congestion means that too many packets are injected into the network so that a particular node has encountered a traffic jam. In other words, there are too many packets waiting in the queue to be delivered to a particular data link. Therefore, special measures must be taken to avoid congestion. Congestion control is different from flow control, though they are closely related. Flow control is a problem between two data links. If the sending DL can pump frames on the line very quickly but the receiving DL cannot dispose all the frames in time, the high-speed DL sender must wait for the receiver on the other side to catch up during transmission. On the other hand, if the N layer has received too many packets from different incoming lines and all packets are destined for the same outgoing line, we have a congestion problem due to the long queuing delays for everyone. If the congestion problem occurs frequently, then we either need to replace the DL with a faster one or add another DL on the side to team up with the old one.

Let us examine the congestion problem. First, we define *workload* to be the number of packets injected into the network. Second, we define *throughput* as the total number of packets delivered to the destination node per unit time as seen by the human user. Figure 5.9(a) depicts the relationship between throughput and workload. When there is no congestion, throughput increases almost linearly with workload. Keep increasing workload to point A, throughput will start to level off. When it gets to point B, throughput then drops drastically to indicate a severe congestion problem, which means that everyone has to wait in the queue.

The same problem can be viewed from a different angle. Let us define *response time* as the wait time for a user to see the action after entering a network command. Figure 5.9(b) shows the relationship of response time versus workload. The response time is low when there is no congestion. As workload increases, response time also increases, but gradually at first and then exponentially to indicate a severe congestion problem.

Network congestion should be avoided by all means. In general, we should put a limit on the total number of packets in the network. Based on the speed of the com port and CPU, it is possible to set a limit on the number of hardware ports supported by the node. Since each port is driven by a DL, which in turn supports many VCs, we can limit the number of VCs on each DL.

Since the T layer injects packets into the network using the sliding window protocol (SWP), it is possible to adjust the sending window size. A sending window size of 0 means that no more packets can be injected into the network by the T layer. Hence, whenever a network begins to show symptoms of congestion, the human user should wait or, better yet, get off the network.

It takes a team effort of the N layer and the T layer to solve the congestion problem. The N layer on the intermediate node must monitor the queue length constantly, and whenever a congestion condition starts to surface, it must convey this information directly or indirectly to the sending T layer, which then reduces its sending rate accordingly. In the following, we will examine the techniques used for congestion control.

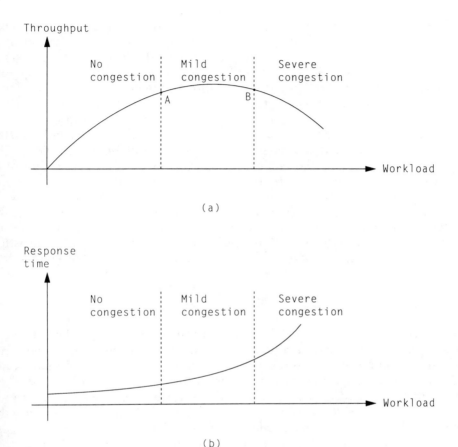

Figure 5.9 Congestion problem: (a) throughput and (b) response time.

Explicit Control

Explicit control means that a congestion is detected and reported to the network system, which in turn takes action to solve the problem. The pacing technique was first introduced by IBM to inform the responsible T layer that a congestion condition has been detected and the T layer will slow down its pace, which means to reduce its sending rate [SNAb]. It is the N layer that has the access to detect a congestion condition. Should the queue length of a particular DL start to increase in the middle of the route, the N layer on the congested node would mark a flag in the packet header to inform the destination T layer. If the backward route becomes congested, the destination T layer is directly responsible, so it will reduce its sending rate. If the forward route becomes congested, the destination T layer will reduce the window size allowed in an Acknowledgment packet, which means the sending T layer should reduce its window size. In other words, the sending window size changes dynamically during packet transmission. It is up to the N layer on the congested node to detect the traffic jam condition and report this piece of information to the destination T layer. Both network and transport layers work as a team to solve the congestion problem.

In a datagram model, a choke packet may be transmitted to the sending node for flow control. In other words, after detecting a congestion condition, the N layer on the congested node sends a message to inform the sending node. The choke packet is designed to request the sending node to reduce traffic. After receiving a choke packet, the routine on the sending node reduces traffic immediately and should ignore the incoming choke packets for awhile to avoid overreaction. This is because when congestion occurs, all jammed nodes in the middle of the route will transmit choke packets simultaneously to the sending node to request for traffic reduction. The basic concept is: whenever congestion occurs, a message should be delivered to the sending node to reduce its sending rate.

Implicit Control

Implicit control means that no flag is marked and the destination T layer reduces its sending rate whenever it finds out that a packet has been dropped. This happens when no SWP is implemented at the DL layer level and there is not enough memory space on the congested node to store the incoming packets. As a consequence, the DL or N layer on a congested node simply drops the incoming packets. This is bad, because whenever a packet is dropped in the route, the sending T layer must retransmit the packet, which means a lot of overhead. On the other hand, it provides an implicit message to the sending T layer that congestion has occurred somewhere in the route and that it should reduce its sending rate for a while.

Even though the T layer normally handles segmentation and reassembly, as discussed in Chapter 7, the ability to segment and reassemble a large packet is also placed into the N layer. Namely, a large packet can be fragmented into pieces that the sending N layer delivers piece by piece and that the receiving N layer reassembles before it delivers the message to its T layer.

5.5.4 Concatenation/Separation

Another issue is how to deal with the small packets. This design concept is derived from the blocking/deblocking capability in the OS. On the current node, if there are many small packets destined for the same destination, it is possible to concatenate them into one big packet and send the big packet to the next hop. This is called packet concatenation. In other words, many small packets are grouped together sharing one packet header. System overhead is reduced because there is fewer I/O operations and less interrupt processing.

At the destination node, packets are separated and delivered to the next node or to its T layer. This is called packet separation. The drawback of this technique is that the N layer must spend time checking the destination node id of many small packets to see if they can be concatenated. If the success rate is too low, the effort may not be justified.

Packet Size

The packet size is variable in most systems. A 128-byte packet size is standard while the maximum size can be 4,096 bytes [X.25]. In the Defense Data Network, the packet size is 1,008 bits. Software designers like big packet size because system overhead is less. However, if the packet size is too big and any bit flips during transmission, the packet must be retransmitted, which results in more overhead or less throughput. Therefore, the optimal packet size is a function of the reliability of the line. In a timesharing system, an input character from the keyboard is transmitted immediately. The valid information in a data packet is therefore one single character.

So far, we have discussed the fundamental issues of network layer design. Next, we will discuss the network layer primitives, NPDUs, data structures, and packet-based network layer software.

5.6 NETWORK LAYER DESIGN

The N layer on each node handles routing, but does not itself perform any I/O. Therefore, it should execute from beginning to end without interruption. Routing decisions must be made within a reasonable time. Even if interrupt is allowed when the N layer executes, control should be passed back to the N layer after processing the interrupt. In other words, the N layer should be logically indivisible for the sake of coding simplicity.

5.6.1 Network Layer Primitives

The N layer primitives are the command messages received from its T layer, DL layer, or the network management routines. The datagram model does not need a connection phase, but a VC model does in that the origination T layer must issue a N layer connect request first to establish a VC before data transfer phase can begin. The four-way N layer connect primitives in a VC model are shown in Figure 5.10.

A VC is very similar to a highway in our state. The origination T layer is the transportation division in a state and the N layer is its engineering department that does the actual building.

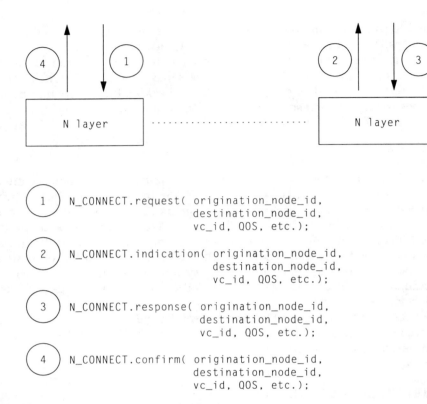

Figure 5.10 Network layer connect primitives.

The transportation division sends a work order to its engineering department to build the highway. In other words, the origination T layer sends a N layer connect request to its N layer to build the VC, as shown below:

N_CONNECT.request(origination_node_id, destination_node_id,
vc_id, QOS, etc);

where the origination_node_id and the destination_node_id represent global computer addresses, vc_id is the VC id determined by its T layer, QOS stands for quality of service, and etc specifies other user-supplied information.

In QOS, we may specify protocol, route determination, and allocation of resources. The speed, transit delay, and reliability of a DL may also be specified for route selection. The etc may include a Delivery Confirm flag, which tells the destination N layer to acknowledge each data packet whenever asked to do so [X.25]. In addition, the SWP may be specified with a default window size of 2. A +ack may also be piggybacked on an outgoing data packet or sent out separately. A -ack must be sent out separately as a Reject packet to inform sender to go back *Nr*, which is the packet sequence number that the receiver is expecting.

After receiving a N_CONNECT.request, the N layer starts building the VC, starting from itself. The origination N layer consults its routing table, determines the VC id, jots down the roadsign, sends the N layer connect packet out via a DL_DATA.request to its DL layer (which adds its own header and trailer to the packet to make a frame), and sends the frame to the next node (since the rules says that the sending party decides the VC id that is placed in the outgoing packet header). So, this time the packet header contains a new VC id. If the new VC id happens to be the same as the old one, it is purely a coincidence. The N layer on the next node receives the N layer connect packet from its DL layer, does the same, and delivers the N layer connect packet with a new VC id to the next hop down the route.

After the N connect packet arrives at the destination node, its N layer jots down the final roadsign of the VC and sends a N layer connection indication to its T layer, as shown below:

N_CONNECT.indication(origination_node_id, destination_node_id,
vc_id, QOS, etc);

The T layer at the destination node records the VC id and sends a N layer connect response to its N layer, as shown below:

N_CONNECT.response(origination_node_id, destination_node_id,
vc_id, QOS, etc);

After receiving this message, the N layer at the destination node sends a N layer connect confirm packet back to the origination node. It may traverse a different route. Each N layer on the intermediate node consults its routing table, jots down the roadsign, and routes the connect confirm packet to the next node until the packet reaches the origination node.

In computer communications, more often than not the return route and forward route are the same in that one VC id is adequate to represent the bidirectional route, as shown below:

@A   TA | 56 ↔ NB | 17

At node A, the right arrow roadsign reads:

IF the N layer receives a VC id, 56, from its T layer,
THEN send a VC id, 17, to node B; ENDIF;

Similarly, the left arrow roadsign says

IF the N layer receives a VC id, 17, from node B,
THEN send a VC id, 56, to its T layer; ENDIF;

That is, between node A and B the forward route is 17 and the return route is also 17.

After receiving the confirm packet, the N layer at the origination node sends a N layer connect confirm to its T layer, as shown below:

N_CONNECT.confirm(origination_node_id, destination_node_id, vc_id, QOS, etc);

At this point, the origination T layer knows that a VC has been built. The VC connection phase is asymmetrical. However, after connection is established, the data transfer phase is symmetrical, which means that the T layer at either side can issue a pipe call to send a data packet to its peer, as shown below:

N_DATA.request(vc_id, n_sdu, status);

where vc_id is the VC id, n_sdu denotes a N layer service data unit, and status tells what happens after the call, such as message queue is full, vc_id is not valid, and so forth. Note that only a vc_id is required in the packet header instead of the full receiving node address. The data packet header specifies packet type, VC id, Status flags, and so forth. The upper T layer keeps track of all the VCs and the end of each VC is known as a network service access point. At the receiving end, the peer T layer receives the packet via an indication as follows:

N_DATA.indication(vc_id, n_sdu, status);

After the data transfer phase is completed, a VC may be disconnected via the N layer disconnect primitives, as shown below:

N_DISCONNECT.request(vc_id, reason);
N_DISCONNECT.indication(vc_id, reason);
N_DISCONNECT.response(vc_id);
N_DISCONNECT.confirm(vc_id);

In some systems, the N layer may deliver the entire N layer packet to its T layer without stripping off the header, which contains useful information at the network layer level. One explanation is that when there is no T layer implemented in the network access methods, the service user above N layer needs to know the VC id in order to identify the route.

The following data primitives are also for data transfers and each one has a different syntax:

N_EXPEDITED_DATA
N_UNITDATA

The N_EXPEDITED_DATA.request primitive is very much like a N_DATA.request except the target N layer bypasses the data packet queue and delivers the packet to its DL layer via a DL_EXPEDITED_DATA.request. After receiving the packet, the peer N layer delivers a N_EXPEDITED_DATA.indication to its T layer. It is not necessary to have a N_EXPEDITED_DATA.response or confirm in the design. The N_UNITDATA.request primitive is equivalent to a datagram call with a long packet header that includes the sending node address, receiving node address, QOS, protocol used by the upper layer, and so forth. The N layer on the receiving node does not acknowledge UnitData packets. After receiving a UnitData packet, the peer N layer just issues a N_UNITDATA.indication to its T layer.

The RESET request primitive is interesting and is used by the service user running above the N layer. This primitive resets a particular VC with two control functions:

1. Notify the N layer at both ends to reset design parameters such as the window size, sequence numbers, and so forth as well as to flush packets in the VC queue, if there is any.
2. Notify all the N layers in the middle of the VC to flush packets in the queue, if there is any.

The reset function needs a round-trip protocol and the four RESET primitives are listed below:

N_RESET.request(vc_id, reason);
N_RESET.indication(vc_id, reason);
N_RESET.response(vc_id);
N_RESET.confirm(vc_id);

Other primitives may be needed for debugging purposes. For example, a N_DIAGNOSTIC.request is issued by the service user to collect information about errors. A N_RESTART.request may be issued by the service user to disconnect all the VCs between two peer N layers, and each VC has two NSAPs.

Needless to say, whenever the N layer receives a request of any kind, it always translates the request into a N layer packet and routes the packet to the next node via a DL data request. The packet ripples to the destination node and its N layer interprets the opcode in the packet header and issues an indication message to its T layer. A packet really means a network protocol data unit (NPDU) as described below.

5.6.2 Network Protocol Data Units

If we treat the T layer as a computer and the N layer as another computer, the N layer primitives could be designed as packets mainly because its packet header is short. As far as the N layer is concerned, it always receives, interprets, and executes packets. It makes no difference where the packet is from. Each packet has a header and a n_sdu, as shown in Figure 5.11(a). A packet is a NPDU, or

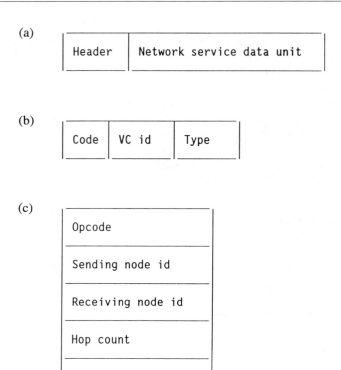

Figure 5.11 Network protocol data units: (a) packet format, (b) packet header of a VC model, and (c) packet header of a datagram model.

simply a network protocol unit, because all packets can be for data or control. The inner portion of the packet is the n_sdu, which is also the TPDU.

In a VC model, the header contains an opcode or code, a VC id to specify the route, and a type as shown in Figure 5.11(b). But in a datagram model, the header contains an opcode, the sending node id, the receiving node id, the hop count, and so forth, as shown in Figure 5.11(c).

It should be stressed that a data packet received from the T or DL layer should have the same format. That is, we have achieved a uniform N layer design: packet in packet out. A T layer places a N layer connect packet in the message queue in shared memory for its N layer to fetch, interpret, and execute. The bits in the packet must be precisely defined, which is the standard for all designers to obey.

The N layer design is uniform in the system in that when the N layer executes, it has its own database that contains pointers to its routing table, roadsigns, empty buffers, and so forth. Besides, certain protocols like X.25 implement SWP between two NASPs. Therefore, its related information must be placed in a memory area known as the network control block (NCB) as described below.

5.6.3 Network Control Block

The NCB mainly contains pointers to various data structures used by the N layer, as shown in Figure 5.12. From the NCB, the N layer can fetch

- The unique network address of the current node;
- The pointer to the routing table;
- The pointer to roadsigns;

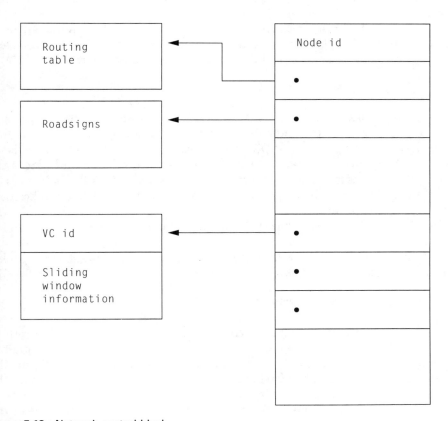

Figure 5.12 Network control block.

- Pointers to various VC control blocks if SWP is implemented between two NASPs.

Each VC is associated with a control block, which is private. A VC control block is very similar to a DL control block, which contains information like window edges, size, status of transmission, and so forth. Note that the N layer in X.25 supports the Delivery Confirmation option, which means SWP.

We are ready to sketch a packet-based N layer design, as discussed in the following.

5.6.4 Network Software Design

If the N layer is designed as an independent task, we use the two system calls to send and receive messages between two tasks. One system call is to send a packet to the N layer task and the other one is for the N layer task to receive a packet.

Let us use the term *message* to represent a string of bits in the OS design. If the OS supports intertask communications via messages, the following system call may be issued to send a message from one task to another:

Send(n_layer_task_id, n_pdu, status);

where n_layer_task_id is the receiver task id, n_pdu denotes the NPDU, and status indicates what happened after the call. This is a regular OS primitive that may be issued by either the T or DL layer in order to send a packet to its N layer task. The OS knows the sending task id from its running TCB and places the packet into the message queue of the receiving task, which is the N layer. The TCB of the N layer task has a pointer to its message queue. The OS takes care of any error exceptions. If the message queue of the N layer task is full, the sending task must wait until there is an opening slot in the queue of the receiving N layer.

By the same token, the N layer must issue a system call to receive a packet from its message queue, as shown below:

Receive(from_task_id, n_pdu, status);

where from_task_id initialized to 0 will contain the sender task id after return, n_pdu is the packet, and status denotes what happens after the call (e.g., time-out error). If there is no packet in the message queue of the N layer, the OS puts the N layer in wait state until later, when a packet arrives and the OS wakes up the N layer, which then processes the packet.

The packet-based N layer design becomes a big loop, as sketched in the following:

N_layer_task:
...
Receive_loop:
...
Receive(from_task_id, n_pdu, status);
    {N layer interprets and executes
     the packet.}
CASE packet of
N_CONNECT.request:
    Determine the VC id, jot down roadsign;
    Change the VC id in the header;
    IF this is the final destination,
    THEN issue a N_CONNECT.indication to its T layer;
    ELSE issue a DL_DATA.request to route the N layer connect
    packet to the next node; ENDIF;
N_CONNECT.response or confirm:
            {Note that the connect response and confirm
             packets have the same format.}
    Determine the VC id, jot down roadsign;
    Change the VC id in the header;
    IF this is the origination node,
    THEN issue a N_CONNECT.confirm to its T layer;
    ELSE issue a DL_DATA.request to route the N layer connect
    confirm packet to the next node; ENDIF;
N_DISCONNECT.request:
            {N_DISCONNECT packets are like the
             N_CONNECT packets except they tear down
             roadsigns of the VC.}
...
N_DATA.request:
    Change the VC id in the header based on roadsigns;
    IF this is the final destination,
    THEN issue a N_DATA.indication to its T layer;
    ELSE issue a DL_DATA.request to route the data packet to the
    next node; ENDIF;
N_RESET.request:
            {N_RESET packets are handled similarly like the
             N connect packet except it resets the VC
             forward and backward.}
...
ENDCASE;
Goto Receive_loop;
Endtask;
End.

Two popular N layer protocols in the field, one using the VC model and the other one using the datagram model, are described in the following.

5.7 X.25 PACKET LAYER PROTOCOL

The X.25 protocol specifies the bottom three layers between a DTE and a DCE in a packet-switching network, as shown in Figure 5.13. The dotted lines between two N or DL layers indicate virtual connections. The connections between two physical layers are real, as shown in solid lines. Between a DCE and the packet-switching network, there is a physical transmission medium. Both the DTE and DCE can be thought of as computers, and each node supports the bottom three layers. Since the N layer on the DTE communicates with its peer N layer on the remote DTE with handshaking capability, the N layer on the DTE is more complicated than the N layer on the DCE.

The X.25 packet layer protocol (PLP) consists of 17 packet types, as shown in Figure 5.14. Some packets have identical formats, but different names. This is because the sending party may be either a DTE or a DCE. For instance, the DTE at the origination node sends a call request packet to its DCE, which in turn sends out the call request packet to the network. At the destination node, the DCE receives the packet, which now becomes an incoming call or call arrived, so it delivers the same packet to its DTE. Of course, the VC id in the packet header is usually different.

The interrupt packet means an expedited data packet that bypasses all the queues in the network. Even though the standard packet size is 128 bytes, a DTE can also handle other packet sizes—16, 32, 64, 256, 512, 1,024, and 4,096 bytes—and reroute the call. Therefore, certain functions, such as segmentation/reassembly, handshaking, and so forth normally performed by the T layer are embedded into the N layer on the DTE. For example, the N layer at the origination DTE may also receive a big piece of user data. It is necessary for the N layer to break up the data message into smaller packets, send out the packets one by one in sequence, and expect an acknowledgment.

Most of the X.25 packet headers are 3 bytes long except those data and flow control packets in extended mode, as shown Figure 5.15(a). Recall that an octet means an 8-bit byte. The lsb in an octet is transmitted first and the first octet is transmitted before the second octet.

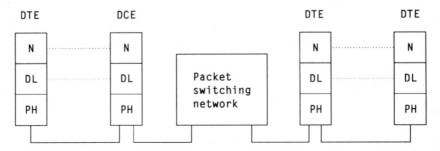

Figure 5.13 X.25 specifies the bottom three layers between a DTE and a DCE in a packet-switching network.

	DTE to DCE	DCE to DTE	3rd Octet in the packet header
1.	Call request	Incoming call	0 0 0 0 1 0 1 1
2.	Call accepted	Call connected	0 0 0 0 1 1 1 1
3.	Clear request	Clear indication	0 0 0 1 0 0 1 1
4.	DTE clear confirm	DCE clear confirm	0 0 0 1 0 1 1 1
5.	DTE data	DCE data	x x x x x x x 0 (mod 8 or 128)
6.	DTE interrupt	DCE interrupt	0 0 1 0 0 0 1 1
7.	DTE interrupt confirm	DCE interrupt confirm	0 0 1 0 0 1 1 1
8.	DTE RR	DCE RR	x x x 0 0 0 0 1 (mod 8) 0 0 0 0 0 0 0 1 (mod 128)
9.	DTE RNR	DCE RNR	x x x 0 0 1 0 1 (mod 8) 0 0 0 0 0 1 0 1 (mod 128)
10.	DTE REJ	DCE REJ	x x x 0 1 0 0 1 (mod 8) 0 0 0 0 1 0 0 1 (mod 128)
11.	Reset request	Reset indication	0 0 0 1 1 0 1 1
12.	DTE reset confirm	DCE reset confirm	0 0 0 1 1 1 1 1
13.	Restart request	Restart indication	1 1 1 1 1 0 1 1
14.	DTE restart confirm	DCE restart confirm	1 1 1 1 1 1 1 1
15.	Diagnostic	Diagnostic	1 1 1 1 0 0 0 1
16.	Registration request		1 1 1 1 0 0 1 1
17.		Registration confirm	1 1 1 1 0 1 1 1

x - a bit '1' or '0'

Figure 5.14 X.25 packet types.

The first octet contains an upper 4-bit general format identifier (GFI) and a lower 4-bit VC group id. The GFI serves as the main opcode, as shown in Figure 5.15(b). The second octet contains an 8-bit VC id. The 4-bit VC group id concatenated with the 8-bit VC id constitute a 12-bit VC id that provides 4,096 combinations. In other words, the total number of VCs supported between a DTE and a DCE is 4,096.

The third octet contains the extended opcode, which may specify the type, sequence numbers, More bit, and so forth depending on the packet. If a packet supports the extended mode operations, a fourth octet is needed to specify mainly, a 7-bit packet receiving sequence number Pr as shown in Figure 5.15(c). It is interesting to examine the X.25 packets in the following.

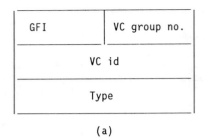

```
Packet type      mod 8         mod 128      Remarks

Call             A D 0 1       A D 1 0      A - Address
Clear            A 0 0 1       A 0 1 0      D - Delivery confirm
Flow control     0 0 0 1       0 0 1 0
Data             Q D 0 1       Q D 1 0      Q - Qualifier
                            (b)


       mod 8                    mod 128


     r r r M s s s 0          s s s s s s s 0
                              r r r r r r r M

M - More
s - a bit in Ps the sending packet sequence no.
r - a bit in Pr the receiving packet sequence no.
                            (c)
```

Figure 5.15 X.25 packet headers: (a) packet header, (b) general format identifier, and (c) type code in a data packet.

Call Request/Accepted

The Call Request/Accepted packet is used to establish a connection between two NSAPs. The msb in GFI (i.e., the sign bit in the first octet) is the Address (A) bit used to denote one out of two address formats.

The seventh bit in the first octet is the Delivery (D) Confirm bit. If the D bit in a call packet is 1, the receiving N layer must acknowledge during the data transfer phase as requested by each individual data packet. That is, if the D bit is set in an individual data packet, an acknowledgment is expected from the N layer on the destination DTE. Most commonly, the D bit in a call request packet is 0, which means that all the sequence numbers and D bits in the data packets to follow must also be 0's (which implies that no SWP is performed).

At the calling end, a 12-bit VC id is assigned by the DTE during the connection phase and must receive the same VC id in any subsequent packet header from its DCE. At the called end, after receiving a call packet, the DCE assigns a VC id and puts it in the incoming call packet header to its DTE. The destination DTE must use this same VC id in any subsequent packet header to its DCE. To avoid conflict, the low end of VC ids is reserved for permanent virtual circuits (PVC), the middle band for the DCE, and the high band for the DTE. The lower and upper limits of each band can be changed via a registration request packet.

The body of a call packet contains the necessary information to complete the desired connection, as shown in Figure 5.16. The address block contains four entries, the address length, and the address itself for each of the DTEs at both ends. The address Length field is 1 byte long, which encodes 2 binary coded decimal (BCD) digits to denote the number of BCD digits in the Address field.

If the A bit in GUI is 0, then a 12-digit address is used; otherwise, a 15-digit address is used. The address is also coded in BCD digits and each digit contains 4 bits. After 1996, ISDN will require that the A bit be set to 1.

The facility length is also in BCDs, which denotes the number of bytes in the Facility field. The Facility field provides design parameters other than the defaults, such as the packet size and window size.

The calling user data is optional and may contain a standard 16-byte field or an extended format for the fast select option with data length up to 128 bytes. Fast select means that the data is piggybacked on the call request packet. A 128-byte reply data can also be piggybacked on the clear confirm packet. In other

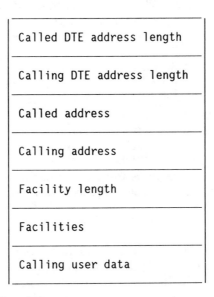

Figure 5.16 Body of a call packet.

words, the fast select packet is essentially a single datagram, handy for credit card verifications, stock market quotations, and so forth. Other user data includes information about reverse charging and call redirection.

Call Accepted/Connected

The call accepted/connected packet is used to confirm the VC connection, which has the same format as the call packet except the user data is supplied from the called side.

Clear Request/Indication/Confirm

The clear request/indication packet is used to disconnect a VC and the clear confirm is to acknowledge the disconnection. They have the same format as the call packet with different opcode and the clear confirm packet does not have a User Data field. The clear request/indication packet has two extra bytes inserted before the address block. The fourth byte denotes the clearing cause and the fifth byte is the diagnostic code, which may be all 0's.

Data Request/Indication

The rightmost 2-bit field in GFI differentiates the operating mode: 01 indicates mod 8 and 10 indicates mod 128. The lsb in the third octet must be a 0 to specify a data packet. The leftmost bit in GFI is the qualifier (Q) bit which, when used, denotes one of two data types. The Q bit is set to 0 if this option is not used. If the D bit in GFI is 1, the N layer on the destination DTE must acknowledge the data packet received. If the D bit is 0, no acknowledgment is required for this data packet.

If the M bit is set to 1, indicating more data to come, the D bit should be 0. If Delivery Confirm is required at the end of the packet sequence, the D bit should be 1 and the M bit should be 0, telling that the destination DTE not only reassembles the data packets into one segment but also acknowledges.

The data packet header contains a packet-sending sequence number Ps and a packet-receiving sequence number Pr, which means that up to Pr - 1 data packets have been correctly received by the N layer on the destination DTE. The sequence number is either 3-bit or 7-bit depending on the operating mode. Just like the DL protocol, a +ack with Pr may be piggybacked on an outgoing data packet.

Flow Control

The flow control packets are optional and include Receive Ready (RR), Receive Not Ready (RNE), and Reject (REJ) in order to support SWP between two peer N layers on the DTE. Each flow control packet contains a Pr, the receiving sequence number (either 3-bit or 7-bit). An RR packet means a +ack, sent as a separate packet when there is no outgoing data packet to be piggybacked on. Since the packet does not contain any error-detecting code, the N layer at the destination DTE can only check missing packets or the data packet header is not interpretable. If so, a REJ packet is returned to inform the sender to Go-Back-N.

Interrupt

The interrupt, or expedited data packet, is sent from the N layer on the origination DTE to its peer N layer on the destination DTE via two DCEs. The interrupt packet contains urgent control information, so it bypasses all the data queues to be transmitted first.

Interrupt Confirm

The N layer on the destination DTE sends an interrupt confirm packet to its DCE and the N layer on the origination DCE delivers the same packet to its DTE. It is an acknowledgment packet containing only a 3-byte packet header.

Reset Request/Confirm

The reset request packet is used to reset all sequence numbers of a particular VC between two end DTEs and flush all packets in the VC if there are any. There are 5 bytes in a reset request packet, the fourth octet contains the reset cause and the fifth octet contains the diagnostic code. The reset confirm packet contains only a 3-byte header for acknowledgment.

Restart Request/Confirm

Five bytes are coded in a restart request packet. The fourth octet contains the restarting cause and the fifth octet contains the diagnostic code. The objective is to clear all existing VCs between two DTEs except the PVC. The restart confirm packet contains only a 3-byte header for acknowledgment.

Registration Request/Confirm

All packet design facilities, such as extended mode, SWP, barring incoming/outgoing calls, and so forth may be changed through a Registration request packet, which contains mainly a registration length followed by a registration block. The registration confirm packet contains mainly of a set of facilities agreed upon by the destination DTE plus a 1-byte cause and a 1-byte diagnostic code, which is 0 upon successful registration. The origination DTE, however, may send another registration request to renegotiate.

Diagnostic

The diagnostic packet is designed for debugging purposes, which may be generated internally in a N layer whenever error conditions occur. Not every network supports this option. The packet contains a header and a 1-byte diagnostic code to specify the cause.

Next, we would like to compare a N layer primitive with a protocol data unit and to see if there is any difference.

5.8 NETWORK LAYER PRIMITIVES VERSUS X.25 PACKETS

Note that the N layer primitives and PDUs are very similar in that they are all messages sent to N layer. The only difference is that a primitive is used to exchange information between a service user and its N layer, which can be thought of as a programming entity. The information delivered to the N layer can be grouped into a NPDU or packet. If we design a message-based N layer, a primitive can be mapped into a packet.

If the DTE at the end of the VC is treated as the T layer, a uniform N layer design can be achieved in that the N layer only deals with packets. In other words, the N layer receives packets, interprets them, and sends them out. The N layer primitives and X.25 packets are compared in Figure 5.17. There is almost

N layer primitive	Packet to DCE	Packet to DTE
N_CONNECT.request	Call request	
N_CONNECT.indication		Incoming call (Call arrived)
N_CONNECT.response	Call accepted	
N_CONNECT.confirm		Call connected
N_DATA.request	DTE data	
N_DATA.indication		DCE data
N_EXPEDITED_DATA.request	DTE interrupt	
N_EXPEDITED_DATA.ind		DCE interrupt
N_EXPEDITED_DATA.response	DTE interrupt confirmed	
N_EXPEDITED_DATA.confirm		DCE interrupt confirmed
N_DISCONNECT.request	Clear request	
N_DISCONNECT.indication		Clear indication
N_DISCONNECT.response	DTE clear confirmed	
N_DISCONNECT.confirm		DCE clear confirmed
N_RESET.request	Reset request	
N_RESET.indication		Reset indication
N_RESET.response	DTE reset confirmed	
N_RESET.confirm		DCE reset confirmed
N_DIAGNOSTIC.request	Diagnostic request	
N_DIAGNOSTIC.indication		Diagnostic indication

Figure 5.17 N layer primitives vs. X.25 packets.

a one-to-one relationship between a primitive and a packet. Since a packet can be sent from a DTE to a DCE, and vice versa, the same packet may represent two primitives. For example, one packet format is used for the request and indication primitives, and likewise for the response and confirm primitives.

In the following, we will discuss the Internet protocol (IP), which is very popular in the academic community. To send an e-mail on the Internet is great, but to handle million-dollar transactions, how many of us are willing to take the risk?

5.9 INTERNET PROTOCOL

The Internet, the oldest network, had a few hundred computers in the early 1980s [9]. In 1994, the well-known Internet consisted of 31,000 networks in 60 nations with one new network added every 10 minutes [10]. Over 20 million people can send e-mail and have access to the information resources via the Internet. The basic transmission unit in IP is referred to as a datagram, which is also in the form of a packet. A datagram has an IP header followed by a PDU of the upper layer. The skeleton of a IP header is supplied by the upper layer, especially when the IP runs on a separate communication processor. Then, the IP fills in the header with more information and during each hop the header is modified as needed.

5.9.1 IP Header

The basic IP header is 20 bytes long with an Option field of variable length, but which must be within a 32-bit boundary, as shown in Figure 5.18 [11,12] [RFC791]. The header mainly contains the information necessary to deliver the datagram. It may also contain information about fragmentation and reassembly of large packets.

In the first word, a 4-bit Vers denotes the version number, the next 4-bit Hlen denotes the header length in 32-bit words, and the right 16-bit half-word denotes the Total length of the datagram header and data in bytes. The right byte in the left half-word is the 8-bit Service type or QOS, as specified below:

Bit 23–22:   Reserved.
Bit 21:   Reliability indication →   1 means high,
                                              0 means normal.
Bit 20:   Throughput indication →   1 means high,
                                              0 means normal.
Bit 19:   Delay indication →   1 means low,
                                              0 means normal.
Bit 18–16:   3-bit priority no.   000, the lowest.

In a large Internet, the host processor may not know the size limitation of the datagram on some other nodes. The IP solves this problem by fragmenting

Vers	Hlen	Service type	Total length

ID	Flags	Fragment offset

Time to live	Protocol id	Header checksum

Source IP address

Destination IP address

Options	Padding

```
Vers                    - Version no.
Hlen                    - Header length in 32-bit word
Service type            - QOS
Total Length            - Total length which is the header length
                          plus the data length in bytes.
ID                      - Datagram id
Flags                   - Flags including the More bit
Fragment offset         - Relative block number in a large datagram
Time to live            - Hop count
Protocol id             - Protocol id of the upper layer
Header checksum         - LRC using odd parity to guard header only
Source IP address       - Sending node address
Destination IP address  - Receiving node address
```

Figure 5.18 Internet protocol header.

the datagram into several smaller pieces. Each piece has its own IP header and the second word is designed for this purpose. The left 16-bit id identifies the datagram and the next 4-bit flag is defined below:

Bit 15:   Reserved.
Bit 14:   Don't (D) bit →   1 means don't fragment,
                                0 means may fragment.
Bit 13:   More (M) bit →   1 means more fragments are to follow,
                                0 means last fragment.
Bit 12:   Reserved.

The D and M bits provide information to the router about the status of fragmentation. The 12-bit Fragment offset denotes a relative block number of the fragment in a large datagram where a block is defined to be 8 bytes. A Fragment offset value of 128 means 1,024 in bytes as computed below:

$$128 \cdot 8 = 1{,}024 \text{ bytes}$$

The destination IP gathers incoming fragments and uses the fragment offset to reassemble the original datagram.

The third word contains an 8-bit Time To Live (TLL), which is the hop count; an 8-bit protocol id to denote the protocol used in the upper layer; and a 16-bit header checksum that is a LRC using odd parity to guard the IP header.

IP Address

Since a datagram model is implemented, the fourth word contains a source IP address and the fifth word contains the destination IP address. An IP address is different from a symbolic name that has the following representation [13]:

> User@domain

'User' represents a user's id and a domain name may have the following format:

> node_id. network_id. type. country

Country ids include US (United States), UK (United Kingdom), CA (Canada), FR (France), and AU (Australia), and the default country is the U.S.

Each country can use its own mnemonics to specify the type. There are five major types as listed below:

- edu: education;
- com: commercial;
- gov: government;
- mil: military;
- org: nonprofit organization.

However, in England, AC (academic) is used for edu and CO (company) is used for com, since a separate name server will translate the symbolic address into a 32-bit IP address.

The class type denotes an institution, corporation, government agency, military branch, or nonprofit organization. They are for administrative purposes only and do not dictate the network domain during routing. In other words, the country id, type, and institution id are used to search for the right IP address by the name server. The symbolic name must be mapped into a 32-bit IP address before it can be used in the packet header. Remember that routing information is in the IP address, not the name.

There are three major network classes plus a special multicast address class, as shown in Figure 5.19.

The class A network has the leftmost bit 0, so the netid (network id) is only 7 bits long to address up to 128 large networks. Each network may have up to 24M nodes (e.g., the Defense Data Network).

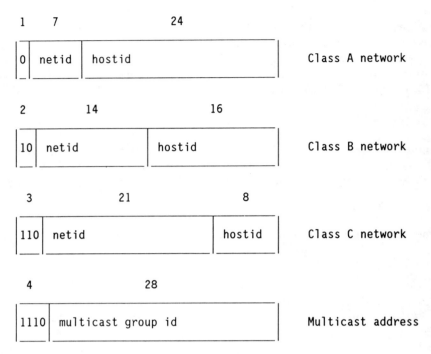

Figure 5.19 Format specifications of an Internet address.

The class B networks have the leftmost two bits 10 and the netid is 14 bits long to address up to 16K medium networks, such as universities. Each campus may have up to 64K nodes. In either a class A or a B network, the hostid may be further decomposed into a subnetwork id followed by a host id.

The class C networks have the leftmost three bits 110, so the netid is 21 bits long to specify up to 2M small networks. Most of the commercial companies are small networks and each company can have up to 256 different local hosts.

The netid in a IP address is unique in that it must be assigned by the network information center (NIC) by either e-mail to hostmaster@nic.ddn.mil or regular mail. The hostid is determined by the local authority associated with each network.

Not all the bits in an IP address are fully utilized. Therefore, more address bits are needed if the current growth rate continues. Logically speaking, the ISDN address format standard should be observed by every party in the business, which has 15 BCD digits reserved but only 13 are used. By the same token, all LAN manufacturers should also observe this unified address format (or perhaps different formats generate more fun if not more jobs).

Sending the same datagram to a group of hosts is called multicast, and IP supports multicasting. If an IP address has the leftmost four bits specified as 1110, then it is a multicast address. There are 2^{28} such combinations. Multicast addressing is one type of multiple delivery, which means that all the nodes in a group will receive the datagram at the same time provided that each node in the group has been assigned the same multicast address. Multicasting is used in many applications. For example, a single message can be sent to a group of hosts to inform a configuration database update or to poll many routers in a group for status information.

A host may belong to one or more multicast groups, but a multicast address can only be used as the destination address. A host may send a datagram to a multicast group without being a member. Members of the same multicast group may be on the same LAN or across network boundaries. Therefore, IP multicasting may be used within a LAN or over the Internet. Special gateways are used to route the multicast datagrams in a LAN.

Most datagrams have no Option field, so their header is 20 bytes long. However, IP allows a variable length Option field that starts at the sixth word containing information for such purposes as testing, debugging, security handling, routing control, and timestamp, as explained below.

IP Options

Each option, in general, has variable length. Some options are 1 byte long as shown below,

```
     7     6     5     4                             0
   |-----|-----------|-------------------------------|
   |  C  |   Class   |        Option Number          |
   |-----|-----------|-------------------------------|
```

The fields consist of a 1-bit Copy flag, a 2-bit Option Class, and the 5-bit Option Number. If the copy bit is set to 1, then the intermediate routers copy the option into all fragments; otherwise, the option is copied into the first fragment. The Option class specifies the general class and the Option number specifies a particular option.

The IP provides optional services of strict source routing, loose source routing, and record route. In addition, other options are supported that include timestamps and security checks.

Strict source routing means that a given route specified in the IP header must be followed strictly and no deviation is allowed at all. Otherwise, its delivery is considered as a failure. This is known as the reliagram (reliable datagram) and the human user must know the network topology well enough to specify the precise route.

Loose source routing, on the other hand provides a set of landmarks that help to find out the way to the destination. However, between two landmarks, deviation is allowed. Source routing information is supplied by the upper layer, so IP knows the exact route. The IP header Option field contains all the intermediate node ids in the route for each datagram to follow. When source routing is specified, datagrams arrive in order without missing or duplicate packets.

A Record Route field may be specified, which provides space to store a list of IP addresses of those routers visited by the datagram. The field length is specified by the sending IP and it is possible for the space to be used up before the datagram reaches the destination. If this happens, the router simply forwards the datagram without adding its address.

Timestamps are used for debugging purposes. The IP provides three different fields for recording timestamps, as indicated below:

- A list of 32-bit timestamps;
- A list of IP addresses and their corresponding timestamp pairs;
- A list of preselected IP addresses provided by the source node where each address has a space reserved for a timestamp. Only the node on the list can record its timestamp when the datagram is passing by.

Security checks are also available in IP. The basic security option parameters consist of a Classification Level flag ranging from confidential to top secret, which assures that the source node is authorized to transmit the datagram. The intermediate nodes may route it and the destination node may receive it. A datagram carrying the basic security option may also include an Extended Security Option field. There are several subformats for this option, depending on the needs of various defense agencies.

The No Operation Option field is used as a filler between options and has a bit pattern of 0000 0001 in binary. For example, it is used to align the next option on a 16- or 32-bit boundary. The End of Option field is used to pad the Option field to a 32-bit boundary, which contains a null byte 0.

When an Internet is connected to a LAN (say, Ethernet), two sets of addresses must be resolved. Each node on the LAN has a 32-bit IP address to identify itself on the Internet. It also has a 48-bit hardware multidrop address to identify itself on Ethernet. Each of the two addresses is unique to its own network. When the server node on Ethernet receives a packet from the Internet, the packet header contains an IP address but the server node needs to know the multidrop address of the destination node on Ethernet. If the server does not have a keyboard for input to establish a matching pair of an IP address and an Ethernet address, it relies upon the address resolution protocol (ARP) to solve the problem [RFC1027]. That is, the server node first broadcasts a message to every node on the bus and asks the destination node to supply its hardware address. After receiving the hardware address of the destination, the server can deliver the packet. The reverse address resolution protocol (RARP), on the other hand, allows a client node on the bus find out its IP address from the server [RFC1903].

5.9.2 Address Resolution Protocol

When the N layer on the server node needs to know the 48-bit Ethernet address of the destination node, it transmits a special ARP frame on the bus to request every node on the bus to pay attention. The ARP frame contains a MAC header, an ARP request message, and a trailer. The destination address (DA) in the MAC header contains all 1's to indicate broadcasting. The ARP message asks each node on the bus: if the enclosed IP address belongs to you, please supply your Ethernet address in a response frame. The format of an ARP or a RARP message is shown in Figure 5.20. The N layer can use any protocol other than IP and the MAC sublayer can be any LAN.

In the message, the first 2 bytes denote the hardware type of LAN (e.g., 0001 in hex means Ethernet). The next 2 bytes specify the protocol type of its service user (e.g., 0800 in hex means IP). The 1-byte Hardware Address Length (HLEN) should be 06 and the 1-byte Protocol Address Length (PLEN), which specifies the length of the IP address, should be 04. The next 2-byte segment is the opcode, defined as follows:

  0001: ARP request
  0002: ARP response
  0003: RARP request
  0004: RARP response

Next is the 6-byte Sender Hardware Address, followed by its 4-byte IP address. The last two fields specify a 6-byte Target Hardware Address and its 4-byte IP Address. In an ARP request message, the Target IP Address is specified, but the Target Hardware Address is left as 0, which denotes a null address or unknown. In a ARP response message, both Sender Hardware and IP addresses will be filled by the target machine that has received the ARP request. The total length of an ARP/RARP message in an IP-Ethernet design is 28 bytes long.

After obtaining the hardware address, the server can deliver the packet as a regular I frame via a L_DATA.request. The LLC sublayer translates it into a MA_DATA.request where the MAC header contains an Ethernet Destination Address and the packet header has an IP address. In addition, the server saves this information in a table so that the second time around, given an IP address as the key, the server simply looks up the table and fetches the corresponding Ethernet address.

Bytes	Field
2	Type of hardware address
2	Type of higher layer protocol
1	Length of hardware address
1	Length of higher layer address
2	Operation code
6	Sender hardware address
4	Sender IP address
6	Target hardware address
4	Target IP address

The operation codes in hex are:

```
0001   ARP    request
0002   ARP    response
0003   RARP   request
0004   RARP   response
```

Figure 5.20 Format of an ARP or RARP frame.

5.9.3 Reverse Address Resolution Protocol

RARP is used when a workstation doesn't have a disk and it asks the server node for its IP address. This is especially true when the workstation boots from its read only memory (ROM) code, which has not incorporated an IP address. Note that the 48-bit multidrop address is built into hardware, which can be read by the operating system. This approach is flexible because all the ROM chips are interchangeable. To request its IP address, the client node sends a RARP request frame on the bus. The frame header contains the Destination Address of the server. Inside the message, the sending node provides its Sender Ethernet Hardware address but its IP Address field is left as 0. After receiving such a request, the server returns a RARP response message to the requesting node. In the RARP response message, both the Target Hardware and IP Address fields are filled with the right information.

Even though both ARP and RARP are designed to solve communication problems between a MAC sublayer on the client node and an upper layer on the server node, they can be classified as specially designed MAC control frames. For Ethernet, the ARP/RARP message follows right after the MAC header with no LLC header in between. For a token ring LAN, the ARP/RARP message follows a MAC header, a LLC header, and a subnetwork access protocol (SNAP) header, in that order. It should be stressed that the ARP/RAPR protocols may be faded away gradually when the server node has an input device and the workstation has a disk.

Debugging the N layer software is quite a challenge because all the activities are real-time. The statistics of message passing between the current node and the next node can be recorded on disk by the network management (NMT) routines as discussed in the following.

5.10 NETWORK MANAGEMENT ROUTINES

The NMT routines can execute as an application task on top of N layer or as part of N layer. One example is the Internet control message protocol (ICMP), as discussed in the following.

5.10.1 Internet Control Message Protocol

The ICMP messages are used to pass control information between the N layer and the network management routines. The format of an ICMP message is shown below:

```
|————————————————|————————————————————|
|  ICMP Header   |     ICMP data      |
|————————————————|————————————————————|
```

After receiving a ICMP message, the N layer adds an IP header to the message to make it a datagram, which is then delivered to the destination.

The ICMP header mainly contains the opcode specifying the following functions [11]:

- Error reporting;
- Reachability testing;
- Congestion control;
- Route change notification;
- Performance measuring;
- Subnet addressing.

If a datagram is corrupted during transmission, the N layer on the destination node simply discards it. However, if the datagram is discarded for other reasons, the destination N layer must issue a destination unreachable error message to the ICMP on the origination node with a reason code given below:

- Destination network is unreachable.
- Destination host is unreachable.
- Specified protocol is not present at destination.
- Fragmentation is needed but the D (Don't) bit is on.
- Communication with the destination network is not allowed for administrative reasons.
- Communication with the destination host is not allowed for administrative reasons.

Other error report messages include that the hop count reaches 0, the packet header is not interpretable, and so forth.

The reachability testing means retry. Usually, an echo request message is sent to the ICMP on the destination node, which in turn sends back an echo reply message to the ICMP on the origination node to confirm the handshaking.

For congestion control, if the N layer on an intermediate node discards a datagram for lack of buffer space, it sends a source quench message to the N layer on the origination node to reduce the sending rate. This is very much like the choke packet.

If multiple gateways are connected to a node, it is possible for one gateway to encounter a traffic jam condition after receiving a datagram. This particular gateway can issue a redirect message to the N layer on the origination node to request a route change.

A timestamp request message can be used to measure the transit delay of a datagram between the origination node and the destination node. In the message, there are three Time fields, as listed below:

- The time when the datagram was sent by the origination node;
- The time when the datagram was received by the destination node;
- The time when the datagram was returned by the destination node.

After receiving the timestamp message, the N layer on the destination node fills the appropriate Time fields and returns the datagram to the origination node.

The N layer on each node uses an address mask to decode the Netid field out of the IP destination address. For example, in a class B network, the address mask used by a subnet server is shown as ff ff ff 00 in hex. Performing a logical and/or mask operation between the IP address and the mask, we obtain both the netid and the subnet id. The ICMP can send an address request message to the N layer on the subnet server, which in turn returns an address reply message containing its address mask. From this address mask, the ICMP knows whether a given IP node is attached to this subnet or not.

There are other network application programs, such as network statistics (netstat), routing table (route), and name server lookup (nslookup), that can be invoked by the user. The netstat command can be entered by any user to examine the statistics of the network. For example, the following command may be entered to display the routing table:

    netstat -r

where -r denotes the routing table display.

The route command can be used to add or delete entries in the routing table by a system administrator. For example, a command may be entered as

    route add default 129.65.17.250 1

where add specifies one of two options (add or delete), default specifies the default entry in the routing table, 129.65.17.250 is the gateway IP address for the next hop, and 1 denotes that the gateway is a remote one.

Another example is

    route add net 129.65.128 129.65.54.100 1

where the keyword net specifies a subnet address. Any IP destination address that matches the given upper 24 bits takes the next hop via the specified gateway.

The nslookup command asks the name server to translate a given symbolic name into an IP numeric address, as shown below:

    nslookup tuba.calpoly.edu

After logging on an Internet computer, the user may obtain the description of any system command by entering the manual (man) command followed by a particular command name, such as netstat or route, as shown below:

    man netstat

Finally, we would like to explore the network devices developed in the field for different purposes.

5.11 NETWORK DEVICES

A network device is a computer that provides the packet-switching function in a computer network. All network devices described in this section are routers (i.e., switching nodes of some kind using different protocols). The network device executes the bottom three layers, and sometimes the N or DL layers may be very simple or even empty.

5.11.1 Packet Assembler/Disassembler

A Packet Assembler/Disassembler (PAD) is a computer that connects many terminals to a packet-switching network, as shown in Figure 5.21(a). It is also a concentrator.

On top of the N layer there is an application layer that reads the characters from various terminals in asynchronous character transmission mode, assembles the characters into a packet, and delivers the packet to its N layer based on X.25. On the X.25 network side, the N layer determines the route and asks its DL to deliver the packet. The DL layer adds its own PCI to the packet and transmits the frame on the line. On the reverse direction of data flow, the application layer receives packets from the X.25 network via the bottom three layers, disassembles the packet into characters, and transmits each character one by one to the destination terminal via the UART port. It should be stressed that on the terminal side, the A layer deals with the PH layer directly and its N and DL layers are essentially hollow.

A PAD has UART chips to communicate with the asynchronous terminals at the character level and USRT chips to communicate with the X.25 network synchronously at the byte block level. Via commands from keyboard, a user may connect to any computer in the network.

5.11.2 Bridge

A bridge is a computer that usually connects two LANs, as shown in Figure 5.21(b). The bridge receives and interprets frames for both LANs, which may be homogeneous or heterogeneous. If the frame received belongs to the LAN on the same side, the bridge takes no action. However, if the frame belongs to the LAN on the other side, then the bridge retransmits the received frame to the other LAN. A bridge is a simple router that has only two ports and mainly executes the bottom two layers. Because a bridge does not require much routing intelligence, both its N and A layers can be combined into one. A special bridge protocol data unit (BPDU) is designed to notify the bridge about the topology change. The service user issues a DL_UNITDATA.request to transmit this BPDU to the bridge.

5.11.3 Router

In a datagram model, a router is the switching node to support many different ports as shown in Figure 5.21 (c). Its DL layer receives frames from one port and passes the inner packet to its N layer to determine the route. From the destination node id in the packet header, the N layer determines the next hop. Usually, if the next node belongs to a LAN, the N layer sends the packet to a particular DL using the same or a different protocol. With N and A layers combined into one single layer, the router contains more lines of code than the bridge. In practice,

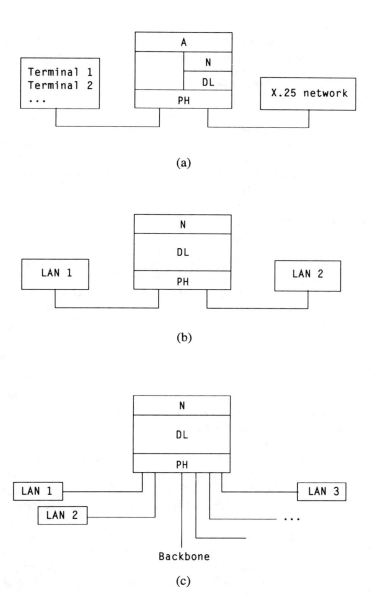

Figure 5.21 Network devices: (a) packet assembler-dissassembler, (b) bridge, and (c) router.

many routers resides in a backbone LAN and each router may further be connected to many different LANs. Any node in one LAN can communicate with a different node in another LAN.

Encapsulation

In the router design, the DL layer strips the protocol control information off the frame and delivers the inner packet to its N layer. After determining the route, the N layer sends down the packet to a DL, which in turn adds the new PCI to the packet and transmits the frame on the line. Encapsulation means that PCI is added to the packet before transmission.

5.11.4 Gateway

A gateway is a switching node that not only provides the routing function, but also converts the protocol format used by upper layers. In other words, a gateway modifies the bits in the inner packet and this particular function can also be combined into the N layer. The gateway function can be embedded into a router or bridge, so we have a sophisticated router design that also handles the format conversion function.

5.12 CONCLUSIONS

We have discussed two N layer designs: the VC model and the datagram model. The VC models are known as connection-oriented protocols while the datagram models are considered as connectionless protocols. In theory, both models should provide reliable services.

If there is only one user on the host, the VC services are adequate for a user to transmit and receive packets between two nodes. This is why X.25 embeds the end-to-end handshaking as well as segmentation/reassembly capabilities into its packet layer design. The X.25 packet layer may use SWP to detect missing packets, but it does not validate the correctness of data. In other words, the packet header does not contain an error-detecting code.

The concept of permanent VCs is interesting in computer network design. As an example, we could have a mesh network backbone just like our interstate highway system. Horizontally, we have Interstate 10, 20, ... to 120 and vertically, 5, 15, ... to 95. Each VC has a global unique id. In the packet header, there should be a VC id, but also the destination address in order to provide the correct exit point. For example, if we take Interstate 70 and decide to exit at Denver, 70 is the unique VC id and Denver is the destination address.

As technology advances, new devices are developed to transmit real-time entertainment data, such as voice or video, where speed is critical but data correctness is not. The primary goal is to transmit/receive data in time. If no handshaking is required at the DL layer level, the N layer becomes the main task running on the communication processor, which interacts with many I/O tasks. Each com port is associated with an I/O task pair: an output task to transmit packet and an input task to receive packets. In other words, the DL layer is merged into the N layer, which may or may not implement the handshaking protocol between two NSAPs. As a result of this, other switching devices such as frame relay and asynchronous transfer mode are developed for future network design. They are also the future protocols proposed for narrowband and broadband ISDNs. Such switching devices are all routers with different names that can be interconnected to make a WAN or LAN backbone. Therefore, we will continue discussing their unique design features and specifications in the next chapter.

5.13 SUMMARY POINTS

1. The N layer mainly transmits/receives packets between two nodes. The basic transmission unit is a packet, therefore the N layer is also known as the packet layer.
2. A packet may contain either control information or data.
3. Each computer on the network is assigned a global node address that is unique to the network. The node address is actually a numerical address represented by a string of bits.
4. The N layer mainly handles the routing function. It also provides congestion control as well as concatenation/separation of smaller packets.
5. If a DL protocol is not enforced, the N layer could be designed as the main driver on the communication processor whose sole function is to deliver packets to the next node.
6. There are two popular models of N layer design: the VC or the datagram.
7. A datagram model is very much like our Postal system. Each datagram has a header that contains the receiver's address as well as the sender's address.
8. The key difference between a VC model and a datagram model is that the former maintains strict roadsigns and the latter does not.
9. When the computer network has a large number of nodes, distributed routing becomes a viable option.
10. Source routing means that the origination node determines the route.
11. The routing table is the local database used by the N layer. The routing table specifies the topology, routing information, and so forth of the network.
12. Congestion means that a node has encountered a traffic jam and the N layer may report this condition to the upper layer or network management routines for remedial action.
13. The N layer does not perform any I/O operation directly, therefore it should execute from beginning to end without interruption. Even if interrupt is allowed when the N layer executes, control should be returned immediately

to the N layer after processing the interrupt. That is to say, the N layer should be logically indivisible.
14. The N layer primitives are the command messages that the N layer receives from its T layer, DL, or NMT routines.
15. If the T layer is a computer and the N layer is another computer, the N layer primitives could be designed as packets because its header is short. As far as the N layer is concerned, it receives a packet, interprets, and executes. Each packet is a NPDU that has a header and a n_sdu.
16. The IP header contains a six-word block that contains the source node address as well as the destination node address.
17. On the communication processor, there are network management routines running as an application program or part of the N layer.
18. A network device is a computer that provides the packet-switching function in a computer network. All network devices are routers (i.e., switching nodes of some kind using different protocols). The network device executes the bottom three layers and sometimes the N or DL layer may be very simple or even empty.
19. Encapsulation means that the protocol control information is added to the packet before transmission.

Problems

Problem 5.1

What is the name of the basic transmission unit between two N layers?

Problem 5.2

What are the major functions performed by the N layer?

Problem 5.3

Describe the two major approaches used in N layer design.

Problem 5.4

What are the key differences between a VC model and a datagram model?

Problem 5.5

Describe the difference between source routing and distributed routing.

Problem 5.6

What is hierarchical routing?

Problem 5.7

What is contained in a routing table?

Problem 5.8

Describe the pacing technique for congestion control.

Problem 5.9

Name five N layer primitives.

Problem 5.10

Name five N layer protocol data units.

Problem 5.11

What is contained in the IP header?

Problem 5.12

Describe the encapsulation concept.

Problem 5.13

What is a router?

The next two problems are proposed as team projects. Suppose that you have three IBM PCs in your lab, namely PC1, PC2, and PC3. Each computer has a com1 port and PC2 in the middle also has a com2 port. PC1's com1 port is connected to PC2's com1 port while PC2's com2 port is connected to PC3's com1 port via null modem cables, as shown below:

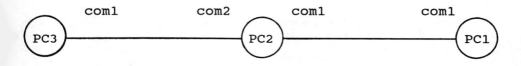

Form a project team of up to three students and select your own leader who should conduct meetings to select the programming language and discuss design, code and debug. A project report should be due at the end of the 10th week.

Problem 5.14

Using the software polling technique, write a talk program on PC1 and PC2 so that the two users can talk via the keyboard in full-duplex mode. This is really a DL layer exercise. The screen should be split into two, one for each user. Study the UART chip first before coding.

Problem 5.15

Using the interrupt driven technique, write a simple character relay program on PC2 that receives characters from one side and transmits it to the other side. This is perhaps the simplest form of a frame relay program you can think of. Running the character relay program on PC2, you can run the same talk program on PC1 and PC3 without modification. In addition, if a TSR (Transient but Stay Resident) system call is used at the end of the relay program to make it resident in memory after execution, a user on PC2 can run any program simultaneously while there is a full-duplex talk session going on between PC1 and PC3. Have fun.

References

[1] Kopf, J., "TYMNET as a Multiplexed Packet Network," *Proc. of the National Computer Conference,* 1977.
[2] Takatsuki, T., et al., "Packet Switched Network in Japan," *Proc. National Computer Conference,* Vol. 46, 1977, pp. 615–621.
[3] Comer, D. E., and D. L. Stevens, *Internetworking with TCP/IP,* Vol. III, Client-Server Programming and Applications, Prentice-Hall, 1993.
[4] Jain, R., et al., Congestion Avoidance in Computer Networks with a Connectionless Network Layer, Technical Report, DEC-TR-506, Digital Equipment Corp., 1987.
[5] Jain, R. and K. Ramakrisshan, "Congestion Avoidance in Computer Networks with a Connectionless Network Layer: Concepts, Goals and Methodology," *Proc. Computer Networking Symposium,* April 1988, pp. 134–143.
[6] Rinde, J. 1977. "Routing and Control in Centrally Directed Network," *Proc. National Computer Conference.*
[7] Dijkstra, E. W., "A Note on Two Problems in Connection with Graphs," *Numer. Math.,* Vol. 1, Oct. 1959, pp. 269–271.
[8] Shay, W. A., *Understanding Data Communications and Networks,* PWS/ITP Publishing Company, 1995.
[9] Hinden, R., et al., "The DARPA Internet: Interconnecting Heterogeneous Computer Networks With Gateways," *Computer,* Sept. 1983.
[10] Leiner, B. M., "Internet Technology - Introduction," *CACM,* Vol 37, No. 8, Aug. 1994, pp. 32–32.
[11] Comer, D. E., *Internetworking with TCP/IP,* Vol. I, Principles, Protocols and Architecture, 3rd ed., Prentice-Hall, 1995.
[12] Halsall, F., *Data Communications, Computer Networks and Open Systems,* 3rd edition, Reading, MA: Addison-Wesley, 1993.
[13] Shoch, J. F., "Inter-Network Naming, Addressing, and Routing," *Proc. IEEE Compcon,* Sept. 1978 pp. 72–79.

High-Speed Wide Area Networks 6

Technology means that in a developed country, you can drink the water; in an underdeveloped country, you can breathe the air.

At the present time, an X.25 packet layer provides adequate digital services to corporate customers. The major applications are long-distance calls and computer communications. In the next decade, all voice and video data will be digitized so they can be blended into one multimedia device that consists of mainly a camera, a computer, and a telephone. With ISDNs under development, digital bit streams are transmitted in real time. Handshaking at the data link (DL) level is not deemed necessary for two reasons. First, the value of real-time entertainment data is not critical. In addition, fiber-optic lines are quite reliable with a low error rate of 10^{-11} Epb. Any error recovery, if needed, can be performed by the upper layer. Consequently, high-speed switching devices are developed to meet the performance requirements of the future. In the following, we will discuss fast routers, such as frame relay (FR) and asynchronous transfer mode (ATM). Other network services, such as switched multimegabit data services (SMDS) and integrated services digital networks (ISDNs) are also introduced.

6.1 FRAME RELAY

A frame relay WAN provides connection-oriented packet data service. In contrast to X.25, the FR protocol bypasses error recovery and flow control altogether. Any error recovery, if needed, can still be performed by its service user. In essence, a FR merely relays frames from one station to another, and its DL layer design is very simple. A frame is the basic transmission unit placed on the line by the hardware transmitter. Figure 6.1 depicts a global WAN backbone using

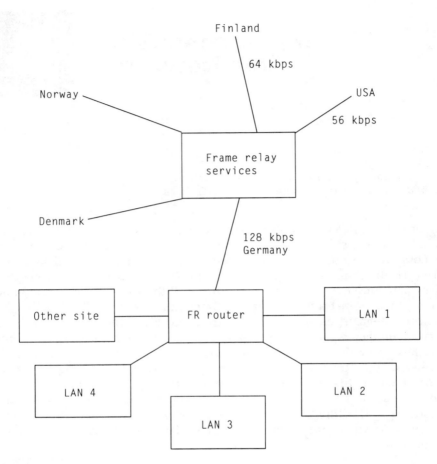

Figure 6.1 Frame relay network.

FRs as routers. The network has connections to many different countries and provides data services of 64 Kbps or 128 Kbps, and up to 2 Mbps to corporate customers. Each terminal site is another router further connected to a LAN [1]. The backbone could be a mesh or hypercube that provides redundancy in routing. As for now, most of the FR WANs still use copper wire as the transmission medium. Because of its low cost and reliability, the FRs are used as international DLs for LAN interconnect.

Because an FR relays frames in a network without performing control functions, its header contains no opcode or sequence numbers. In other words, only unnumbered information (UI) frames are transmitted between two stations without acknowledgment. Consequently, its DL layer design is greatly simplified and its N layer mainly interacts with many I/O tasks, depending on the size of the node. Each com port in the system is driven by two tasks, one to transmit and one to receive. The basic principle of frame switching, however is not different from packet switching.

The FR frames are similar to X.25 with minor modifications as discussed in the following.

6.1.1 FR Frames

Each FR frame has a header, an Information field, and a trailer, as shown in Figure 6.2(a). The header is actually a packet header and a frame header combined. Like X.25, a Frame flag has the bit pattern of 01111110 in binary, which is used to enclose a frame. Frame flags are prepared and stripped by the hardware communication controller, which also handles the bit stuffing problem. The Address field in the header is normally 2 bytes long. If longer addresses are used, the field can be extended to 3 or 4 bytes. The Info field has a variable length in bytes ranging from 64 bytes to over 1,500 bytes. The trailer mainly contains an FCS-ITU-T followed by another Frame flag.

The Address field in the header specifies a logical connection between two network service access points (NSAPs) as shown in Figure 6.2(b). The Data Link Connection Identifier (DLCI) field contains a VC id or local reference number. Bit 0 in each byte is the Extended Address (EA) flag or chaining bit. Using negative logic, an EA 0 means more address bits to follow and a 1 indicates the end of address. With a 2-byte Address field, EA is a 0 in the first byte and a 1 in the second byte. Six bits in the first byte are concatenated with 4 bits in the second byte to constitute a 10-bit DLCI. Bit 7, the high-order bit in the first byte is the most significant bit (msb).

Because of the chaining bit, each additional byte can only supply 7 more bits to the address. A 3-byte Address field provides a 17-bit DLCI as shown in Figure 6.2(c) and a 4-byte address provides a 24-bit DLCI in Figure 6.2(d).

In all three formats, bit 1 in the first byte is the Command/Response (C/R) flag. The network sets the C bit to 1 if the message is a command to the user and to 0 if the message is a response. On the contrary, the user sets the C bit to 0 if the message is a command and to 1 if the message is a response.

Bit 1 in the second byte is the Discard Eligibility (DE) flag. If DE is set, the system software running on the receiving node can discard this frame without reporting to its service user. This usually happens when an error is detected during transmission or the receiving node has encountered a traffic jam condition.

Bits 2 and 3 in the second byte are for congestion control. Bit 2 is the Backward Explicit Congestion Notification (BECN) flag. When BECN is set, it indicates a traffic jam condition encountered in the backward route and the receiver can initiate any congestion avoidance procedures if applicable. Bit 3 is the Forward Explicit Congestion Notification (FECN) flag. When FECN is set, it

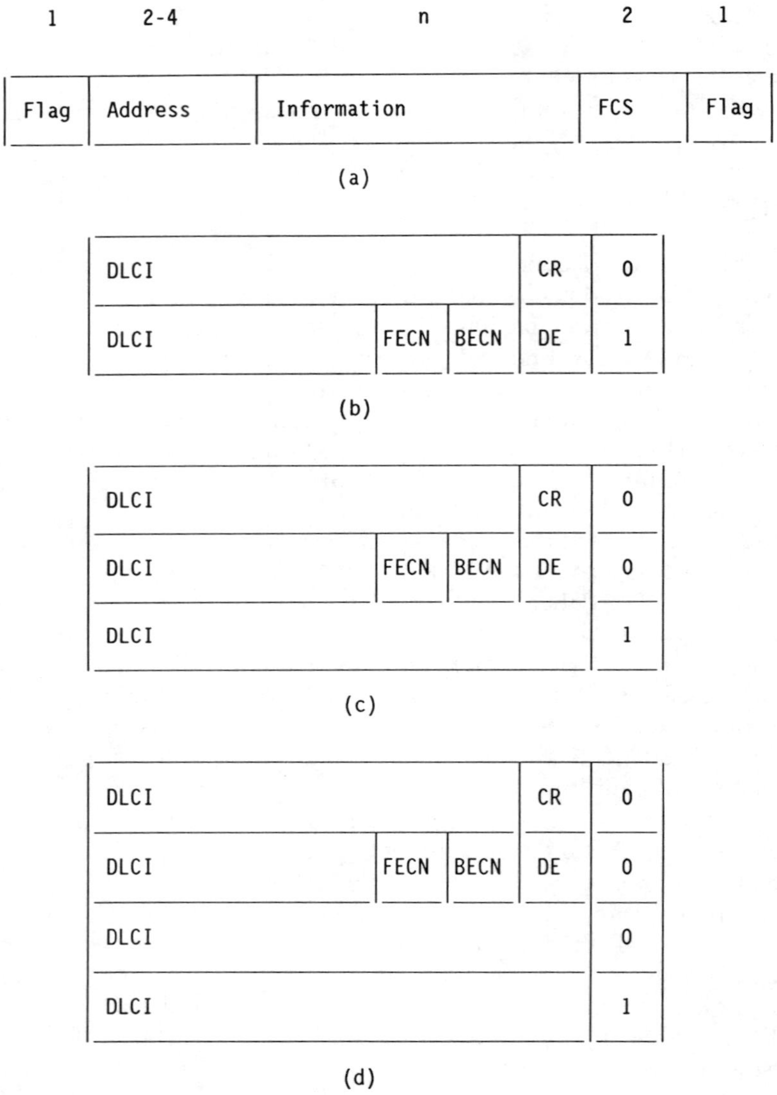

1	2-4	n	2	1
Flag	Address	Information	FCS	Flag

(a)

DLCI				CR	0
DLCI	FECN	BECN	DE	1	

(b)

DLCI				CR	0
DLCI	FECN	BECN	DE	0	
DLCI				1	

(c)

DLCI				CR	0
DLCI	FECN	BECN	DE	0	
DLCI				0	
DLCI				1	

(d)

Figure 6.2 Frame relay frames: (a) general format of an FR frame, (b) 2-byte address, (c) 3-byte address, and (d) 4-byte address.

indicates a traffic jam condition encountered in the forward route. However, the receiver cannot reduce the forward traffic, so it notifies the sender about this condition and the sender will reduce its sending rate accordingly.

Frame Relay is so named because its main function is to relay frames from one station to another. In the following, we will discuss the FR software design from the system point of view.

6.1.2 FR Software Design

FR is noted for its simple DL layer design, which does not require acknowledgment of frames. In other words, neither error control nor flow control is provided by the DL and all data frames are unnumbered. Assuming that each communication controller can transmit or receive a block of bytes. Consequently, the basic primitives at the physical level are Sendframe and Receiveframe as discussed in Chapter 2. The system block diagram of FR software design is shown in Figure 6.3. Each small box represents a task, and the size of the box is not proportional to its code volume or complexity. Since a packet is merged into a frame, there is no difference between them. In other words, the N layer task receives, interprets, and executes frames. The N layer task of a FR is not different from the one discussed in Chapter 5. After receiving a data indication message from its DL, the N layer task soon determines the next hop and, in most cases, sends down the frame to another data link. To be precise, it sends the frame to the transmit task of another DL. To speed up the N layer execution, the roadsign table may be placed in high-speed memory for fast lookup.

The DL software design is similar to the one introduced in Chapter 3, but much simplified. Because a full-duplex com port contains a hardware transmitter/receiver pair, each DL is comprised of two I/O tasks: the transmit task, which transmits frames, and the receive task, which receives frames. Even though the I/O task pair may have its own data base, the code may be shared (including the I/O drivers). After receiving a UI frame from the line, the receive task sends a DL_UNITDATA.indication to its N layer, which determines the next hop and sends the frame with a different VC id to a different transmit task via a DL_UNITDATA.request. The transmit task in turn transmits the UI frame out to the next node. Since the hardware controller also handles the FCS generation and detection, after receiving a spurious frame the receive task must make a decision to either discard the frame or forward it to the N layer regardless.

If the switching system supports 512 lines, we need 512 I/O task pairs, and each pair handles one line. The total number of I/O tasks is 1,024, which is 512×2. Because no handshaking is performed, the receive task rarely communicates with the transmit task on the same link.

The system design concept of FR is fine, but one complaint is about its speed; that is, it is not fast enough. After substantial research is conducted by

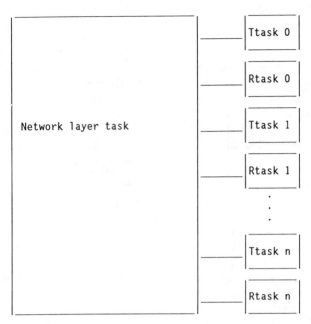

Rtask n - Receive task for data link n.
Ttask n - Transmit task for data link n.

Figure 6.3 System block diagram of frame relay.

different groups, a new technique is explored. Recall that the most widely used T1 carriers employ synchronous TDM and each channel is assigned a time slot in the frame. If there is no data destined for the end user, its time slot is left idle and no one else can use it. Because the timing for each user to receive its data is fixed, this technique is also known as the synchronous transfer mode (STM), which has one potential drawback: wasted bandwidth. In asynchronous transfer mode (ATM), each slot is public and can be used to carry data from one user to another user at any time provided that no one else is using it. Major aspects of ATM are introduced in Section 6.2.

6.2 ASYNCHRONOUS TRANSFER MODE

ATM uses the cell-switching or asynchronous TDM technique to transmit/ receive cells, and each cell is a short packet of 53 bytes. Recall that cell switching is a variant of packet switching. Each cell contains a VC id and therefore may occupy any time slot when it becomes available. The VC id in the cell header is the overhead or price that must be paid to achieve a high-speed transfer rate. A time slot may also be occupied by any user based on an assigned priority basis. In fact, a user may transmit data in burst mode via an ATM.

6.2.1 ATM Network Architecture

No sooner had ITU-T decided to make ATM the core technology for broadband ISDN (BISDN) in the late 1980s than computer manufacturers raced to develop their innovative ATM products to interconnect LANs. Because of their high speed, ATMs may be used as either a WAN or LAN backbone [2]. In other words, ATMs can be standalone to interconnect several LANs. For this reason, commercial ATMs not only provide various types of data link, but also have both UART and USRT ports to support various terminals.

An ATM Network is shown in Figure 6.4. The WAN backbone consists of a nine-node mesh and each node may have many connections to a different city or country. The number nine is just a random number selected to describe the mesh. The local backbone may be a delta ring consisting of three ATMs. Each ATM in the local backbone is connected to a router, which may further be connected to different LANs. We will discuss the design issues and protocols of ATM in the following.

6.2.2 ATM Cells

The basic transmission unit of ATM is a cell. Therefore, ATM is also known as a cell-relay or cell-switching device. How long should the cell be? It really depends on the data type. A longer cell usually implies better throughput. For example, if longer cells are used to transfer a file, the total completion time is less. However, for the telephone or CATV user, a 2-byte cell would be adequate. Consequently, computer manufacturers like a longer cell while telephone or CATV companies like a shorter cell. An ultimate compromise was made that each cell have a 5-byte header followed by a fixed Data field of 48 bytes, as shown Figure 6.5. Needless to say, a cell is always 53 bytes long. Even though it has a different header, the basic design concept between an ATM and FR remains the same; that is, no handshaking between two connection points.

The upper 4 bits in the first byte denote the General Flow Control (GFC) field, which is not used by the network. The next 8-bit field is the virtual path identifier (VPI). After VPI, there is the 16-bit virtual channel identifier (VCI). A virtual path may consist of up to 64K virtual channels. By concatenating the VPI with the VCI, we obtain a 24-bit VC id. However, not that many virtual paths exist, so the upper 4-bit segment in VPI usually is 0. As a consequence, the upper 4-bit segment in VPI is used by some LAN protocols, such as DQDB to contain access control information. The lower 4-bit VPI is concatenated with a 16-bit VCI

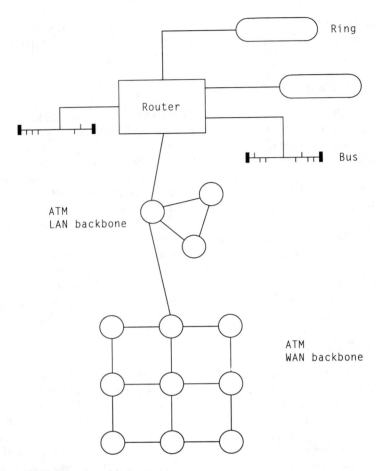

Figure 6.4 ATM network architecture.

to constitute a 20-bit VC id, which is a local reference number between two NSAPs as follows.

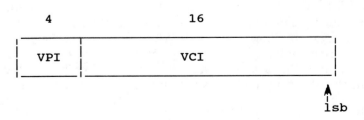

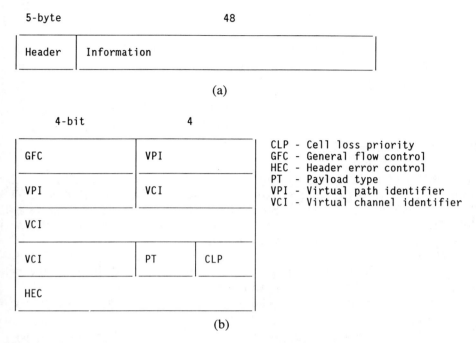

Figure 6.5 (a) General format of an ATM cell and (b) an ATM cell header.

Bits 2 and 3 in the fourth byte denote the Payload Type (PT) field, which specifies the data type of the cell. A 00 indicates the data is from the upper layer. Other values may be assigned to indicate control or network management information. This option provides in-band control in the network as needed.

Bits 0 and 1 in the fourth byte denote the cell loss priority (CLP), which is the priority assigned to the cell. If CLP of a cell is low, the cell may be discarded if the node becomes congested. The fifth byte is the header error control (HEC), the same as the header check sequence adopted by DQDB.

ATM is also connection-oriented in the sense that every cell must travel the same route in a high-speed ATM network. CATV companies push this new technology. To protect their own turf, telephone companies will offer an end user ATM services in the future with a data rate of either 155.52 or 622.08 Mbps. Because the cell length is fixed and short, ATM is not ideal for financial transactions or file transfers. On the other hand, because of its popularity and high speed, ATM will supplement both X.25 and IP.

6.2.3 ATM Protocols

The ATM technology has evolved over a long period of time in research labs around the world. An ATM software model is shown in Figure 6.6. The bottom

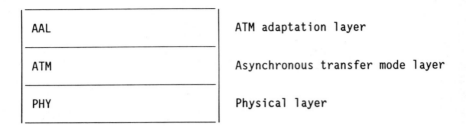

Figure 6.6 ATM layers.

layer is the physical (PHY) or cell layer, which is further divided into the transmission control (TC) sublayer and the physical medium (PM) sublayer. The PM layer handles the bit-level transmission while the TC layer handles cell delineation to identify cells, generate/detect the header check sequence, and insert/remove idle cells, among other functions.

Above the PHY layer is the ATM layer whose design is very similar to the network layer, which determines the next hop, changes VCI/VPI in the cell header at switching points, and performs some flow control.

The top layer is the ATM adaptation layer (AAL), which is actually a special application programming interface (API). There are various types of AALs, and each one is designed to support a special network service, as listed below:

1. AAL1 handles Class A data, constant bit rate (CBR), connection-oriented.
2. AAL2 handles Class B data, variable bit rate (VBR), connection-oriented, with time synchronization.
3. AAL3/4 handle Class C data, VBR, connection-oriented services.
4. AAL5 handles Class D data, VBR, connectionless services.

AALs have some functional overlaps: AAL3/4 means AAL3 and AAL4 combined to provide connection-oriented services with variable bit rate. AAL1 and AAL2 are provided by the CATV and telephone companies while AAL3/4 and AAL5 are provided by LAN manufacturers. AALs also consist of two sublayers: the segmentation and reassembly (SAR) sublayer and the convergence sublayer (CS). Since a PDU or frame may come from any network that usually exceeds 53 bytes, SAR at the sending site segments the PDU and SAR at the receiving site reassembles. The SAR function is normally found in the T layer design, as discussed in the next chapter. With this capability, ATM can be connected to other networks, such as FR, SMDS, BISDN, IP, and LANs, and all you need is to buy an ATM adapter card.

The CS sublayer on the ATM node converts the segmented unit into cells and delivers them to its ATM layer, which in turn asks its PH layer to place the bits on the line.

Two LANs are interconnected via an ATM network, and four ATM nodes are involved in the switching path, as shown in Figure 6.7. A LAN server may send its own medium control protocol data unit (MAPDU) or frame to the ATM network via a datagram call. After receiving the frame through its special DL and PH layers, its AAL5 does the following:

1. Uses the destination address in the frame header as a key and maps it into a VPI/VCI pair;
2. Segments the frame into 44-byte units and adds a 2-byte header and a 2-byte trailer to each unit;
3. Adds a 5-byte cell header in front of each unit to make a cell and then passes the cell to its ATM layer, which does the routing.

The cell ripples through all the intermediate ATM nodes. The ATM layer on each intermediate node only does the routing, and its AAL does not see the cell traffic at all. The peer AAL5 on the destination node receives the cell and performs reassembly. After the entire frame is received, it is delivered to the destination LAN server. The logical link control (LLC) software on each LAN server merely communicates with the AAL on the end ATM.

The crucial information of segmentation is coded inside the unit header and its peer AAL knows how to put the frame back, as shown in Figure 6.8. The frame from any network has its own header, an Information field of variable length, and a trailer. Padding bytes may be needed at the end of each frame to make an integer multiple of 44-byte units. In other words, the frame is segmented into exactly 44-byte units or payloads and each unit is encapsulated with its own 2-byte header and 2-byte trailer.

In the unit header, the leading 2 bits denote the segmented unit type: beginning of a message, continuation of a message, end of a message, or just a single message unsegmented. The term *message* really means the frame accepted from its service user. The next 4-bit field denotes a segment number that is the sequence number of the segmented unit in a message and the last 10 bits denote a message id (MID). In the unit trailer, there is a 6-bit field to denote the length of the unit in bytes, followed by a 10-bit FCS.

At the receiving end, the destination AAL can use the segment number in

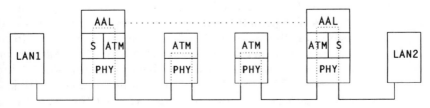

Figure 6.7 ATM end-to-end connection.

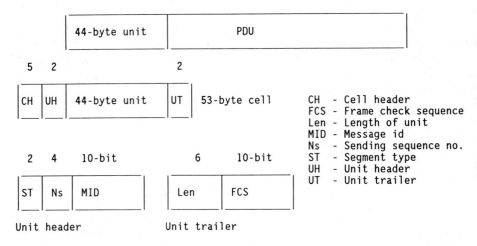

Figure 6.8 Segmentation of cells.

the unit header to put the frame back to its original form, which is then delivered to the LAN server.

Internet Protocol Connection

To connect the IP to ATM is similar. Its AAL5 special software on the end ATM resolves the destination address problem using either table lookup or ARP. The IP address in the packet header must be mapped into a VPI/VCI pair, which specifies the unique NSAP in the ATM network. Then, AAL5 segments the packet and uses the same VPI/VCI pair in the header of every cell to transmit the cell via its bottom two layers. After the initial packet is transmitted, the AAL software caches the connection just established with the understanding that packets with the same address to follow are bound for the same destination.

Switched Multimegabit Data Service

SMDS was intended to provide connectionless or datagram service to various LANs and data terminals interconnected in a wide area network [3]. It was the fruit of research done by Bellcore (Bell Communications Research), a company owned by regional Bells. The primary goal was to transmit a large chunk of data quickly without negotiating the bandwidth, QOS, or assigning priorities to voice and data. Its frame format is compatible with that of DQDB. In the frame header, there are the 8-byte DA and SA fields, each of which may contain a 4-bit Address Type flag followed by a 15-BCD international telephone number [E.164].

SMDS is a service and not a technology offering. SMDS is what the subscriber sees. Just like the IP connection, with the proper software written as a special application interface on two NSAPs, SMDS frames can be fed to an ATM or FR port directly. Therefore, SMDS is also known as a connectionless ATM in that a datagram is delivered via an ATM network.

Because ATMs can be used as switches in both WAN and LAN backbones, this new technology has gathered momentum in the computer industry. An ATM forum was formed by different interest groups to push ATM as the future standard of the next century.

ATM Forum

The over 550-member ATM Forum was intended to meet the following challenges:

1. Unite WAN and LAN technologies on a common platform;
2. Accommodate protocols and applications not designed for ATM;
3. Create new protocols and applications that will take advantage of ATM.

The ability of ATM to bridge both the WAN and LAN worlds will ensure its existence for a long time. Its interoperability among different systems is absolutely necessary and essential. As data flows through the high-speed network, the fewer hardware boxes and algorithms needed to sort information out, the better.

6.3 COMPARISONS OF FRAME RELAY AND ATM

The features of FR and ATM are compared in Table 6.1

FR has several merits, such as large frame size and pacing control, which are attractive for computer communications. ATM, on the other hand, does not need frame delimiters. Due to the fact that cable TV companies also want to share

Table 6.1
Comparison of FR and ATM Features

Function	FR	ATM
1. A variant of packet switching	Yes	Yes
2. DL and N layers merged in one	Yes	Yes
3. Fixed length data	No	Yes
4. Frame delimiters used	Yes	No
5. Large frame size	Yes	No
6. Error recovery between two NSAPs	No	No
7. Congestion control	Yes	No
8. Segmentation and reassembly	No	Yes

this new technology, its fixed frame size makes it ideal to fit into a synchronous TDM slot [4][IEEE 802.6]. In the following, we describe a proposal in order to improve ATM for all-purpose digital communications [5].

An ATM cell should have two sizes, the standard 53-byte size and the extended 159-byte size, three times the standard size. One good reason is that a PDU may be a T layer packet received from a mainframe host or may be a frame from a LAN. If the PDU is 154 bytes long or slightly shorter, it will be segmented into four standard cells by the AAL layer before transmission. However, an extended cell of 159 bytes could be used to store the same frame. Thus, not only is the throughput improved by 25%, it also saves one empty slot, which represents 25% of the signal bandwidth. In such a design, the T layer on the host establishes a VC connection first, knows the VC id, and may transmit an extended cell to ATM, which merely does the routing. The extended cell contains

- A 5-byte cell header;
- A 23-byte unit header, which includes, a 1-byte protocol id, a 1-byte opcode, a 2-byte port id, a 1-byte message id, a 2-byte segment number, a 1-byte window size, and a 15-byte option;
- A 128-byte Info field;
- A 3-byte unit trailer, which includes a 1-byte segment length and a 2-byte FCS.

Remember that the extended cell is a capability added to ATM that allows the T layer to perform the segmentation/reassembly function as elaborated in the next chapter. Other PDUs of variable length can still be segmented by ATM. The cell type may be specified in the leading 4-bit GFC in the cell header.

For network applications, financial transaction processing in particular, we need to add two more capabilities as options. That is, if the extended cell size is used, error control and pacing control should be provided between two NSAPs. Error control is especially desirable when the transmission is not reliable (say, wireless).

While different parties are pushing different products, such as SNA for corporate networks, X.25 for public packet networks, and Internet for e-mail, telephone companies decided to pursue an entirely different technology: narrowband and broadband ISDNs. Narrowband really means that three channels are provided by the basic service and broadband means more channels using fiber optics are provided. Both narrowband and broadband ISDNs are discussed in the following.

6.4 INTEGRATED SERVICES DIGITAL NETWORK

Due to the rapid advances of computer technology, telephone companies decided to go digital all the way, for voice, video, or computer data. As technology matures, we will enjoy the fruits of computer network research in the form of activities such as video games at home, videoconferencing, and interactive TV.

6.4.1 Evolution

Old analog telephone systems sent voice signals on the 4-kHz line. Pure tones of various frequency were also sent on the same line as control signals. This scheme is known as in-band control; data and control signals are blended together. In other words, the user can input control signals via the headset, which may spell trouble.

ISDNs are based on the concepts developed for telephone integrated digital network (IDNs). Control signals are in digital form running at 2.4 Kbps separated from the voice. In other words, the management of analog connections is done on a packet-switching network to which the user has no access. This scheme is known as out-band control, which means that data and control signals are separated on different lines. Using digital technology, separate control channel means overhead and should be avoided, if possible.

Because copper wires are hard assets and can only be phased out over a long period of time, the transition from an existing network to a comprehensive ISDN will take one or more decades. In addition, not everyone needs high-speed data networks. The current ISDN, a collection of many networks and equipment, is depicted in Figure 6.9. In other words, ISDN consists of both circuit-switched and packet-switched networks. In the future, ISDN will be truly integrated, consisting of mainly broadband fiber-optic lines.

6.4.2 Principles

Narrowband ISDN means that there are two circuit-switched B channels and one packet-switched D channel. However, the B channels can also be packet-switched. First, all voice and video signals need to be digitized at the home site before sending. After receiving, voice signals are restored to analog through a digital-to-analog converter. It is interesting to note that the CATV signals can be 100% digital, just like color pixels on a high-performance monitor. The volume of data may be massive, but compression techniques can be used to reduce the volume. In other words, the CATV signals at the home site are pixels and only the audio signals need a digital-to-analog conversion.

Basically, narrowband ISDN is a switched form of TDM at the local loop that mainly provides two circuit-based 64-Kbps B channels and a packet-based 16-Kbps D channel onto a single twisted pair. The total bit rate is 144 Kbps, as computed below:

$$64 \text{ Kbps} + 64 \text{ Kbps} + 16 \text{ Kbps} = 144 \text{ Kbps}$$

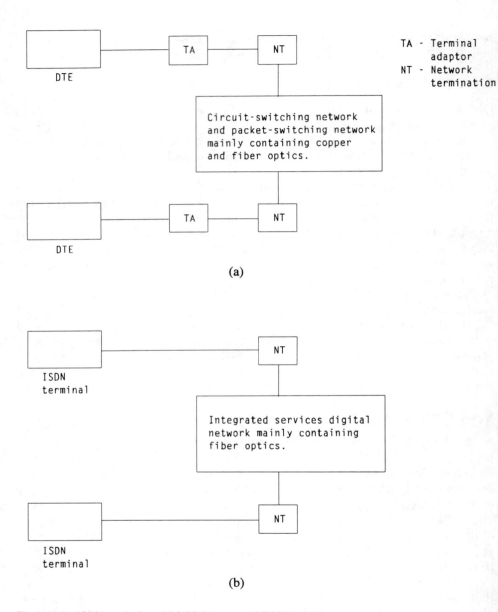

Figure 6.9 ISDN evolution: (a) initial stage and (b) later stage.

However, other bits are needed for framing and synchronization, so the total bit rate of a basic access link is 192 Kbps. Bluntly put, it is an economical version of the T1 services with call setup and handling capabilities.

6.4.3 Services

There are three types of ISDN channels: B, D, and H. For the sake of memorizing, B means basic data, D means destination control, and H means high-speed data. Each channel may provide different data rates as listed below:

- B channel: 64 Kbps;
- D channel: 16 or 64 Kbps;
- H channel: 384, 1536, 1920 Kbps, etc.

B channels are the basic channels to carry user data such as voice, facsimile, telex, or video. It is interesting to note that B channels may be circuit-switched, packet-switched, or semipermanent. A semipermanent connection means that the service supplies a destination address and the network termination (NT) equipment assigns an existing VC without going through the a call setup phase. It is interesting to note that the 64-Kbps data rate provided by a single B channel is adequate for voice.

A D channel is packet-switched, which serves two purposes. It not only carries the signaling information to control the circuit-switched calls on its associated B channels, but also may carry low-speed data like terminal, telex, telemetry, and so forth when there is no signaling information waiting.

H channels are all packet-switched and provide high-speed data services such as fast facsimile, video, data, and so forth. A computer may also use H channels in a high-speed trunk and needs its own TDM scheme for routing.

These channels are grouped together and offered as a package deal to the user. Two popular services are listed below:

1. Basic Service: 192 Kbps with two B channels and one D channel;
2. Primary Service: 2.048 Mbps with 30 B channels and 1 D channel, or 1.544 Mbps with 23 B channels and 1 D channel.

6.4.4 User Interfaces

An objective of ISDN is that a small set of compatible user network interfaces can economically support a wide range of digital services [I.411]. A common interface will be a standard DTE to DCE connection for a telephone, computer, or video terminal. Under ISDN, one or two twisted pairs will be used to provide a full-duplex digital communication link.

Before further discussion, let us explain some terminologies. Terminal equipment (TE) means subscriber equipment, of which there are two types: TE1 and TE2. TE1 is used to support the standard ISDN interface while TE2 encompasses existing non-ISDN equipment with physical interfaces, such as RS232-D or X.21. When a TE2 device is connected to a standard ISDN, a terminal adaptor (TA) is inserted in the middle to make TE2 look like a TE1.

On the network side, an NT equipment is the end point of ISDN as the user sees it. There are many types of NT. NT1 merely provides the basic PH layer interface, such as timing, power transfer, multidrop termination, line maintenance, and monitoring. NT2 is similar to a public branch exchange (PBX), which includes some routing, concentrating, maintenance, and multiplexing functions. That is, an N2 is a full-blown switching node or router that may be connected to another N2 or N1. For example, N2 may include various types of distribution arrangement, such as a star, bus, or ring configuration included within the equipment. A possible combination of NT1, NT2, and TA into one physical entity is being considered by many countries. Such a device supports the bottom three layers and can communicate with any user terminal equipment using a protocol stack as suited.

TEs, NTs, and TAs are interconnected to ISDN as shown in Figure 6.10. Reference points are protocol capabilities used to separate different functional groupings. There are three reference points, as defined below:

- R: Reference point R (rate) between a TE2 and a TA;
- S: Reference point S (system) between a NT and a TE1;
- T: Reference point T (terminal) between two NTs.

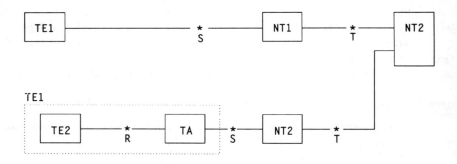

```
*   - Reference point
R   - Rate reference point
S   - System reference point
T   - Terminal reference point
NT  - Network termination
TA  - Terminal adaptor
TE  - Terminal equipment
```

Figure 6.10 ISDN reference points.

6.5 ISDN PROTOCOLS

The ISDN protocol stack is shown in Figure 6.11. Since two channels are involved, B channel is shown on the left and D channel on the right, and each channel has its own protocol stack. Different PH layers are needed for both the basic service [I.430] and the primary service [I.431]. For the basic service, the data streams from both B and D channels are multiplexed over a common physical interface.

B channel is used to transmit data. It uses LAPB for DL control and X.25 Packet protocol to handle routing. However, FR is another option to replace both the DL and N layers.

The D channel is used to transmit control information and its DL protocol is a subset of HDLC with a modified frame header. Routing is based on either I.451 or X.25 as elaborated in the following.

6.5.1 ISDN Frames

For both directions of transmission, a bipolar encoding scheme is used, but instead of alternating ones, it alternates zeros or spaces. It is also known as the pseudo-ternary code in the specifications.

For the basic service, ISDN supplies two 48-bit physical frames at the user interface level. The physical frame from a user to a ISDN terminal is shown in Figure 6.12(a) and from a network terminal to a user is shown in Figure 6.12(b). Note that the two frames are similar but not identical.

It should be pointed out that the physical frame is different from the logical frame as seen by the DL layer. A physical frame is the bit streams received by hardware. Note that the D channel bits are blended with B channel bits and that

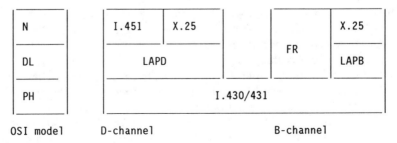

Figure 6.11 ISDN protocol stack.

(a)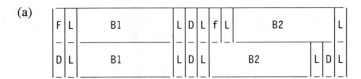

(b)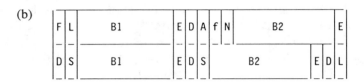

```
A  - Activation
B1 - B1 channel, 8 bits
B2 - B2 channel, 8 bits
D  - D channel, 1 bit
E  - Echo bit of D channel
f  - Auxiliary frame bit (Fa)
F  - Frame bit
L  - DC balance
N  - Complement of Fa
S  - Spare
```

Figure 6.12 Physical frames of ISDN: (a) from user's terminal to network and (b) from network to user's terminal.

each physical frame contains 4-byte B channel data and 4-bit D channel control information plus framing bits. The PH layer software extracts the channel bits, concatenates them, and passes the logical frame to DL.

A is the activation bit. When A is set, it activates the physical device, which may include its power supply. B1 indicates bits of the B1 channel, B2 of the B2 channel, and D is a bit of the D channel. E is the echo bit for the D channel. F is the leading bit or frame bit, which indicates the beginning of the frame. FA is the auxiliary frame bit and the N bit after is its complement. Both FA and N bits are used for synchronization. The L bit is the dc balancing bit, which may be set to a high or low voltage in order to eliminate the direct current. The F bit in each frame can be set to a specific bit pattern to indicate a multiframe. In other words, it is a technique used to group many frames into a bigger one. S is the spare bit reserved for future expansion.

For the primary service, its frame layout is completely different from the basic service. It resembles the T1 carrier as shown in Figure 6.13. The frame contains a total of 193 bits and its period is 125 μs. F is the leading bit, followed

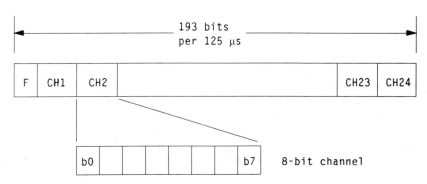

Figure 6.13 Physical frame of ISDN primary service.

by 24 time slots. Each time slot is assigned to a channel, so we can have 24 channels. The total data rate is computed as

$$\frac{193 \text{ bits}}{125 \text{ μs}} = 1.544 \text{ Mbps}$$

which is essentially the DS1 carrier. Each channel contains 8 bits and bit 0 is transmitted first.

The leading F bit is used for framing control and the rest of the 192 bits constitute a payload. Each multiframe contains 24 frames and the F bits as a group provide control information. As an example, the F bit in every fourth frame must have the specific bit pattern 001011. That is to say, the F bit in the fourth frame is a 0, in the 8th frame a 0, in the 12th a 1, ..., and so forth in order to denote a multiframe.

6.5.2 ISDN Channel Protocols

Recall that ISDN supports three types of channel: B, D, and H. For basic service, B channel is used to transmit data while D channel is used to exchange control information. The PH frame contains both the B and D channel bits. The PH layer software extracts and concatenates the B channel bits, and passes the logical B channel frame to the DL. By the same token, PH does the same to D channel. Both B and D channel frames contain packets inside that have variable lengths.

At the DL level, B channel uses link access procedure, balanced (LAPB) and D channel uses link access procedure-D channel (LAPD). Both protocols are pretty much the same (i.e., a subset of HDLC), but LAPD uses a frame header that is slightly modified as described below.

Link Access Procedure-D Channel

LAPD is a protocol that the D channel uses to exchange control information between two DL layers [I.441]. Inside a D channel frame, there is a packet of either I.451 or X.25 type, as depicted by Figure 6.14(a). An LAPD frame contains a different Address field from an LAPB frame, as shown in Figure 6.14(b).

The normal Address field is 2 bytes long. The second byte in the frame header contains a 6-bit service access point identifier (SAPI), followed by a command/response (C/R) bit and an extended address (EA) bit 0. The interpretation of the C/R bit is the same as FR. The assignments of SAPI are specified in Table 6.2

The third byte contains a 7-bit terminal equipment identifier (TEI) followed by an EA bit, which is 1. The TEI assignments are listed in Table 6.3.

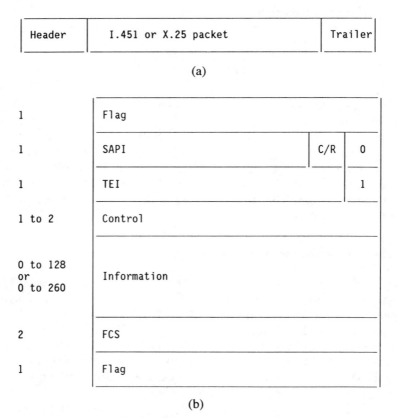

Figure 6.14 (a) General format of a LAP-D frame and (b) LAP-D information frame.

Table 6.2
Service Access Point Identifiers

SAPI Value	Layer 3 or Management Entity
0	Call control procedures
1	Reserved for packet-switching control using I.451 call control procedures
16	Packet-switching control using X.25 packet protocols
32–62	Frame Relay connection
63	DL layer management procedures, which means the message for DL management
Others	Reserved for future expansions

Table 6.3
Terminal Equipment Identifiers

TEI Value	User Type
0–63	Nonautomatic TEI assignment user equipment
64–126	Automatic TEI assignment user equipment
127	Group address

Nonautomatic TEI values are determined by the user, whose system administrator manages their allocations. Automatic TEI values are determined by the network control agency. A group address really means a broadcast address for all the terminal equipment that has the same SAPI.

The combination of a SAPI and a TEI constitutes a local reference number for a DL connection. In the DL protocol, both acknowledged and unacknowledged I frames are supported. An unacknowledged I frame is a UI frame.

At the network layer level, two types of channels are supported. B channel uses the X.25 packet protocol to handle routing. However, as an option, FR can be used to replace both the DL and N layers.

D channel handles virtual circuit connect/disconnect and routing based on either I.451 or X.25. According to the specification, the basic transmission unit at the network layer level is called a message [I.451, Q.931] as elaborated in the following.

6.5.3 ISDN Messages

The general format of an ISDN message is shown in Figure 6.15(a). The term *message* really means *packet* according to the X.25 naming convention. The

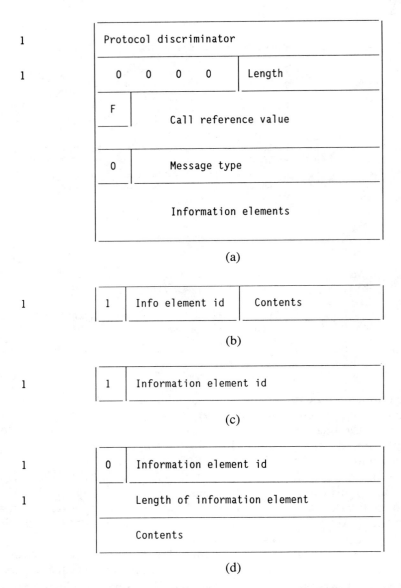

Figure 6.15 I.451 messages: (a) general format, (b) single-octet information element (type 1), (c) single-octet information element (type 2), and (d) variable-length information element.

first byte is the protocol discriminator, which is actually a protocol id to identify where the source message is from (see Table 6.4).

The upper 4 bits of the second byte are 0's and the lower 4-bit field denotes the length of the call reference value in bytes. The leading bit of the third byte is a flag indicating which end of LAPD initiates the call.

The call reference value is a local reference number, just like a VC id, which has a variable length. With only one octet, we can only store a 7-bit unsigned integer. However, the call reference value may occupy multiple bytes in sequence. Just like X.25, the first octet denotes the highest order byte. The order of remaining bytes decreases progressively as the octet number increases. The lowest numbered bit in the highest numbered octet denotes the lsb of the field.

After the call reference value, there is a byte with a leading bit 0 followed by a 7-bit message type that specifies an opcode. The contents of the remainder of the message depend on the message type. Functionally, the I.451 messages are very similar to X.25, but their opcodes are completely different. The four functions to which they are applicable are listed below:

- C: Circuit-switching connection control;
- P: Packet-switching connection control;
- U: User-to-user signaling not associated with circuit-switched calls;
- G: Global call reference.

In Table 6.5, we describe each ISDN message type and its usage at the N layer level. Below the mnemonic, the message type is specified in hex (enclosed in parentheses).

After the message type, there may be one or more information elements that provide the necessary parameters in the message. Just like the X.25, each information element has an id followed by contents, if needed. Two types of 1-byte information elements have been defined with bit 7 equal to 1. Type 1 has a 3-bit id followed by a 4-bit content segment, as shown in Figure 6.15(b) and type 2 has a 7-bit id but the first 3 bits are reserved as 010, as shown in Figure 6.15(c). The variable length information element is shown in Figure 6.15(d), which has

Table 6.4
Protocol Discriminators

Protocol Discriminator	Description
00–07	Not used
08	I.451 user network call control messages
10–3f	X.25 Network, etc.
40–4f	National use
50–ff	Reserved for other network protocols

Table 6.5
Call Establishment and ISDN Message Types

Message	Applicable to	Descriptions
Alerting (01)	C, P, U	Sent by the called user or network to the calling user to signal an alerting condition
Call proceeding (02)	C, P, U	Sent by the called user or network to the calling user to signal that a call is proceeding
Connect (07)	C, P, U	Sent by the called user or network to the calling user to signal the acceptance of a call
Connect acknowledge (0f)	C, P, U	Sent by the network to the called user to acknowledge connection
Progress (03)	C, P	Sent by the user or network that a call is in progress
Setup (05)	C, P, U	Requested by the calling user or network to the called user to establish a call/access connection
Setup acknowledge (0d)	C, U	Sent by the network to the calling or called user to acknowledge the call setup request
Call Information Phase		
Resume (26)	C	Requested by the user to the network to resume a previously suspended call
Resume acknowledge (2e)	C	Sent by the network to the user to signal that a call has been resumed
Resume reject (22)	C	Sent by the network to the user to indicate failure to resume the suspended call
Suspend (25)	C	Requested by the user to ask the network to suspend the call
Suspend acknowledge (2d)	C	Sent by the network to the user to signal that the call has been suspended
Suspend reject (21)	C	Sent by the network to the user to indicate failure to suspend the call
User information (20)	C, U	Sent by one user to another user via the network to transfer information
Call Clearing		
Disconnect (45)	C, P	Requested by the user or network to disconnect the call
Release (4d)	C, P, U	Sent by the user or network that the channel of call reference is to be released
Release complete (5a)	C, P, U	Sent by the user or network to indicate the acceptance of a release message and that the channel and call reference are released
Restart (46)	G	Requested by the user or network to restart the channel or interface (i.e., reset to idle condition)
Restart acknowledge (4e)	G	Sent by the user or network to indicate that restart has been completed
Miscellaneous		
Congestion control (79)	C, U	Sent by the network or user to set or release flow control on user information messages

(*continued*)

Table 6.5 (continued)

Message	Applicable to	Descriptions
Facility (62)	C	Requested by the user or network to negotiate a new set of network parameters
Information (7b)	C, U	Sent by the network or user to provide additional information
Notify (6e)	C	Sent by the user or network to notify of information pertaining to the call
Status (7d)	C, P, U, G	Sent by the user or network to report an error condition or in response to a status enquiry message request
Status enquiry (75)	C, P, U	Sent by the user or network to solicit a status message from its peer

a preceding 0 followed by a 7-bit id, a length of the information element in bytes, and contents of the information element.

One drawback about ISDN is its limited bandwidth, which is not fast enough for certain applications (e.g., real-time videoconferencing). As a result, BISDN was developed using fiber optics to push the data rate to over 600 Mbps.

6.6 BROADBAND ISDN

BISDN is the main trunk of the information superhighway. It was first recommended by ITU-T in 1988, and has been revised every two to four years [I.121]. BISDN has made a quantum jump over ISDN in performance, mainly due to the fiber-optic technologies adopted in this decade.

6.6.1 Functional Architecture

The pace at which BISDN is introduced really depends on the availability of the local fiber subscriber loops. The fact is that telephone companies cannot dismantle their copper wires in one day. In addition, the high-speed applications are still a small portion of the mass market. The functional architecture of a BISDN is shown in Figure 6.16, which comprises narrow ISDN, BISDN, and other interexchange signaling networks. Specially designed for high-speed applications, BISDN supplements other networks. In other words, BISDN provides both narrowband and broadband services. At the network end, there is a local functional capabilities (LFC) device to route traffic to terminal equipment (TE) using fiber interface.

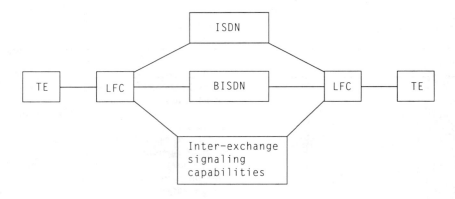

LFC - Local functional capabilities
TE - Terminal equipment

Figure 6.16 BISDN architecture.

Internal to the network, there is an issue about which switching techniques should be used. Because of the wide range of applications, cell switching is selected as its core technology [I.411].

6.6.2 Services

In a broad sense, BISDN is the future network that will provide a wide range of services using a limited set of connection types and multiple user network interfaces. The low end provides the 64-Kbps transmission services, both circuit switching and packet switching. The high end provides the digital data services at 155, 52, and 622.08 Mbps or even higher, full-duplex. Note that the data rate is an integer multiple of 64 Kbps. The traffic on the line may be bursty or continuous, connection-oriented or connectionless.

One general notion is that BISDN provides broadband and other ISDN services. The term BISDN may also be used to emphasize the broadband aspects of ISDN, which essentially means high-speed data transmissions. Two major categories of service have been proposed: interactive services and distribution services. The interactive services are comprised of conversational services, message services, and retrieval services. The distribution services are represented by the classes with or without user control.

6.6.3 User Interfaces

BISDN really means broadband transmission capabilities embedded into an existing ISDN; therefore, the user interfaces remain the same. It supports the same three reference points, except an R reference point may or may not have broadband capabilities. Just like narrowband ISDN, control of BISDN is based on common-channel signaling. The PH layer must provide the necessary electrical and optical interface to support such a high data rate. As the future trend dictates, the user network interface (UNI) of BISDN should be made as simple as possible.

6.7 BROADBAND ISDN PROTOCOLS

Fiber optics are the main hardware technologies used in broadband ISDN. As far as software is concerned, BISDN supports cell switching (i.e., ATM, as discussed earlier in this chapter). ATM is basically a connection-oriented protocol, but can also deliver datagrams. Its header values are assigned to each section of a connection when required, and released when no longer needed. ATM will offer a flexible transfer capability common to all services, including the connectionless or datagram services. In general, BISDN is a superset of ISDN. Therefore, all ISDN protocols coexist with ATM in the network.

6.8 OTHER NETWORKS

ATM is a new software protocol that works on any network. Other high-speed networks include synchronous optical network (Sonet), synchronous digital hierarchy (SDH), and broadband network services (BBNS), to name a few. Sonet offers network services with data rates of 51.84, 155.52, 466.56, 622.08, up to 2,488.32 Mbps and SDH is the European equivalent of Sonet. Just like BISDN, the data rate is an integer multiple of 64 Kbps.

BBNS is a product from IBM and its architecture is shown in Figure 6.17 [6]. The BBNS backbone provides high-speed links at 100 Mbps to LAN routers, FR networks, ATM carrier services, or ATM concentrators. A LAN router may be further connected to many LANs, and an ATM concentrator may be connected to a high-speed file server as well as to many workstations. Each workstation or power PC receives data at 25 Mbps and has a special ATM adaptor card in the chassis.

The crucial software of BBNS is the Nways Broadband Switch Control Program (NBSCP), which manages connections through the ATM network. Since NBSCP handles both ATM cells and variable-length packets, BBNS can accommodate many different frames from other networks, such as token ring, Ethernet, and FR. In addition, NBSCP handles bandwidth management, congestion control, and path switching.

Other fiber networks in the lab that can support data rates up to 10 Gbps will become available in the near future [7].

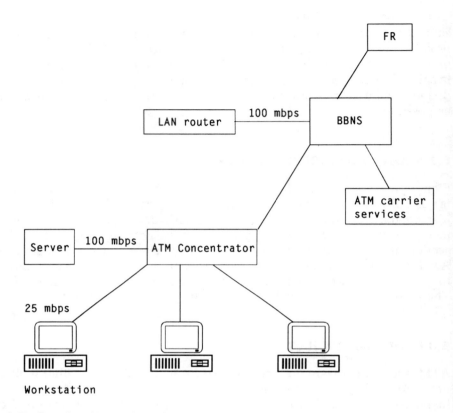

Figure 6.17 Broadband network services.

6.9 CONCLUSIONS

Other ATM devices may have different names, such as direct route (DR), data-switching unit (DSU), connect edge router (CER), high-speed serial interface (HSSI), and so forth. They are all switching nodes to supplement both WAN and LAN technologies. Some new ideas, however are dead before arrival (DBA).

High-speed network services will be phased into our life gradually over the next two decades. With fiber optics to provide data rate over gigabits per second to a person's house, the distinction among LANs, MANs, and WANs will eventually disappear. The reason is not because of a particular protocol, but rather the ultrahigh raw speed provided by the fiber technologies. One day perhaps, most of the families will have video phones and video conferencing will become part of a normal working environment. It is interesting to mention that the interactive TV concept allows us to change the end of a selected movie. While watching a movie, the viewer will see the caption at the bottom of the screen that says: "Press H key for a happy ending." The reviewer has the option to press the H key or not. If the reviewer wishes to cry, then the H key is not pressed. The movie source is able to deliver one out of two different endings to the reviewer's home. Isn't that wonderful?

So far, we have discussed the bottom three layers in a computer network, and they happened to be the most important ones. Remember that technologies come and go, and it pays to review the basic concepts in the early chapters before reading the rest of the book.

6.10 SUMMARY POINTS

1. FR is a packet-switching router that bypasses error recovery and flow control altogether in the DL and N layers based on the X.25 design concept, but with minor modifications.
2. ATM is a cell-switching router used in a LAN or WAN backbone and a cell is a 53-byte packet. ATM doesn't perform the handshaking function either and a user may transmit data in burst mode up to 622.08 Mbps.
3. Both FR and ATM use the asynchronous TDM technique.
4. SMDS is a connectionless ATM that accepts datagrams. In other words, a datagram is mapped into cells first and then transmitted by the cell-switching router.
5. ISDN uses out-band control; data and control signals are separated on different lines.
6. ISDN provides basic services of 192 Kbps with two B channels and one D channel.
7. ISDN protocols include LAPB and LAPD at the DL layer level and X.25 or I.451 at the N layer level, or they combine both layers into a single FR.
8. BISDN means that broadband capabilities are embedded into an existing ISDN using the same user interface.
9. BISDN uses cell-switching and fiber optics.
10. Other high-speed networks include Sonet, SDH, and BBNS.
11. The ultrahigh speed provided by fiber optics will eventually make the distinction among LANs, MANs and WANs disappear.

Problems

Problem 6.1

What is a frame relay?

Problem 6.2

Describe the information in a FR header.

Problem 6.3

What is asynchronous transfer mode?

Problem 6.4

Describe the information in an ATM cell header.

Problem 6.5

Describe the software functions of AAL in an ATM model.

Problem 6.6

Describe the software functions of the ATM layer in a ATM model.

Problem 6.7

What is a SMDS?

Problem 6.8

What are the channel types provided by ISDN?

Problem 6.9

Describe the protocol stack used by ISDN.

Problem 6.10

Name five messages used by the N layer of ISDN as specified in I.451.

Problem 6.11

What is the core technology used by BISDN?

References

[1] Heywood, P., "Global Router Backbone," *Data Communications*, May 1994, pp. 59–72.
[2] Lane. J., "ATM Knits Voice, Data on Any Net," *IEEE Spectrum*, Feb. 1994, pp. 42–45.
[3] Klessig, R.W., and K. Tesink, *SMDS Wide-Area Networking With Switched Multi-Megabit Data Service*, Prentice-Hall, 1995.
[4] Bisdikian, C., et al., "Approaching B-ISDN: An Overview of ATM and DQDB," in *Asynchronous Mode Networks*, edited by Viniotis, Y. and Onvural, R. O., Plenum Press, 1993.

[5] Hsu, J. Y., "Frame Relay vs. Asynchronous Transfer Mode," *Proc. of the IEEE Singapore International Conference on Networks*, July 1995.
[6] Birenbaum, E., "IBM Big Blueprint for ATM," *Data Communications*, Aug. 1994, pp. 31–32.
[7] Ohr, S., "GaAs Finds Home in Wireless & High-speed Data-Communication Applications," *Computer Design*, 1994, pp. 59–68.

Transport Layer 7

When you are in success, be moderate. When you are in adversity, be patient.

The transport layer mainly transmits/receives messages between two transport entities on two different hosts. A transport entity, a programming port, and a transport service access point (TSAP) are all synonymous. A transport connection (TC) between two ports is a system capability implemented by software, and each port is denoted by a port id. Figure 7.1(a) depicts a TC in a VC model while the one in a datagram model is shown in Figure 7.1(b).

A powerful T layer handles segmentation/reassembly of large data messages and error recovery. The transport service user (TS-user), usually the S layer, may drop a very large data message (i.e., t_sdu (transport service data unit)), into a port and the same t_sdu pops up at the other end of the TC. Just as an example, the t_sdu can be 16 MB of any bit pattern. The T layer delivers the entire t_sdu to its peer as follows:

1. The T layer may have its own buffers to store messages, or may share the same buffers used by its service user. In the latter case, the T layer cannot return to its service user until the entire message is transmitted.
2. If the t-sdu message is large, the T layer divides the t-sdu into segments and then data pieces. The T layer adds a header to each data piece to make a TPDU, which is delivered to its peer via a N_DATA.request. Depending on the model, a N_DATA.request can be either a VC call or a datagram call.
3. At the receiving end, the peer T layer fetches information from the packet header, reassembles all the pieces into the original t_sdu, and delivers it to its S layer.

The T layer or transport service provider (TS-provider) also handles multiplexing. In a VC model, the T layer handles both upward and downward multiplexings. Upward multiplexing means that two or more ports on the same host may share one VC to the destination node. Downward multiplexing means

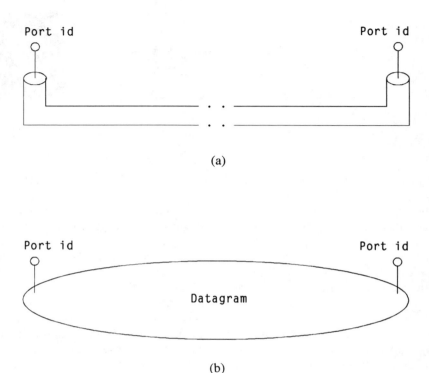

Figure 7.1 Basic concept of a port connection: (a) VC model and (b) datagram model.

that one port employs many VCs. When segmentation is employed, a large t_sdu is divided into segments and then packets. Different groups of segments may take different routes to the same destination node. Finally, a good T layer can also perform error and congestion control during packet transmission. This is important if the layers below do not ensure reliable transmission.

7.1 BASIC DESIGN CONCEPTS

Even though similar to a DL, the T layer requires large memory buffers to implement segmentation/reassembly. The message received from its service user or upper layer is actually limited by its memory size. The T layer knows how to transmit the entire message to its peer on the destination node.

7.1.1 Segmentation and Reassembly

Segmentation/reassembly is a software capability built into the T layer. In network parlance, segmentation also means fragmentation, which means that if the t_sdu is too large, the T layer breaks it up into segments and then packets. A packet contains a small piece of data. As an example, a 1-KB t_sdu is broken into 8 pieces, as shown in Figure 7.2(a). The data pieces are numbered from 0 to 7. The T layer adds a header to each piece to make a TPDU or T layer packet, as shown in Figure 7.2(b). In this particular case, there are a total of 8 TPDUs transmitted to its peer. In the header, the relative packet number in a segment is specified.

At the receiving end, the peer T layer reassembles the original t_sdu and delivers it to its service user as shown in Figure 7.2(c). This process is known as reassembly.

The T layer also handles multiplexing, which is required to support multiprogramming or multitasking.

7.1.2 Upward/Downward Multiplexing

If all the destination ports are on the same host, it is possible to deliver the TPDUs via the same VC, as shown in Figure 7.3(a). In other words, the same VC is shared by many ports on the same host. Upward multiplexing or fan up is used to minimize the connection time.

In contrast, a single port may employ many VCs to transmit the data packets, as shown in Figure 7.3(b). If the data message is too large, it is chopped into segments and then packets. One group of segments takes one route while

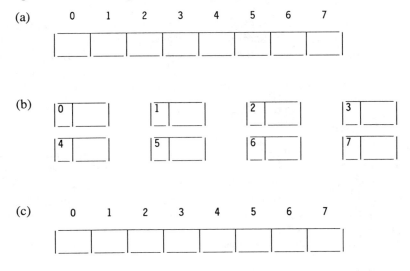

Figure 7.2 Segmentation and reassembly: (a) dividing the original 1-KB t_sdu into eight fragment units, (b) adding a transport header to each unit to make a TPDU, and (c) reassembling the units into the original t_sdu.

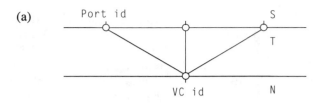

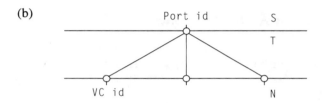

Figure 7.3 (a) Upward and (b) downward multiplexing.

the other group may take a different route, so the time to complete transmission is reduced. The T layer at the receiving end reassembles the data packets into the original t_sdu and delivers it to its upper layer. Downward multiplexing, or fan down, provides the extra bandwidth needed for transmission or to broadcast, which means that all the destination nodes receive the same message from the sending T layer.

7.1.3 Error Control

The sliding window protocol (SWP) can be used to transmit data or info packets between two TSAPs. Each packet has a header, and if the packet is corrupted or missing, the receiver requests sender to retransmit. Piggybacking can also be used in full-duplex transmission when both the sending and receiving T layers have data packets to transmit at the same time. That is, the receiving T layer combines a +ack into an outgoing data packet to its peer. If the window size is greater than 1, we have pipelined transmission as viewed by the T layer.

7.1.4 Flow Control

The receiver can control the speed of transmission by guarding the trailing edge of its window. If a +ack is lost, the sender times out and polls the receiver about what happened. Depending on the reply, the sender takes an appropriate action. If the receiver cannot keep up with the sender's pace, it may drop a data packet. Eventually, the sender times out and polls the receiver. As a consequence, the sender slows down and retransmits the previous packet. In this scenario, the receiver controls the speed of data transmission.

Pipelined transmission means that the T layer can transmit two or more data packets without being acknowledged. In other words, the sending window size is 2 or greater. During the port connection phase, the origination T layer proposes a window size in the connect command. The destination T layer has the final say about the actual window size chosen.

The T layer may have two tasks running in parallel, one to send and one to receive. It is a nontrivial programming effort to attempt recovering errors. The SRJ ARQ discussed in Chapter 3 can be used by the T layer for error recovery. To prove the correctness of the SRJ ARQ algorithm, a finite state machine (FSM) model is proposed in the following.

7.2 FINITE STATE MACHINE MODEL

To simplify our design, we use a 1-bit sequence number in the packet and the maximum window size is two for both sending and receiving windows. Each I (information) packet contains a sending sequence number Ns and the ack packet contains a receiving sequence number Nr, indicating that packets with a sequence number up to $Nr - 1$ have been correctly received.

Even though the window changes continuously, we can define a sending or receiving state based on its window condition. The FSM models for both sender and receiver are discussed in the following.

7.2.1 Transport Sender

The window conditions of a T layer sender are shown graphically in Figure 7.4. Each state is a triple of three characters enclosed in parentheses. The first character is a letter, the second is a digit, and the third is another digit. The initial state is (N 0 0) and the alphabet denotes the class of state:

- N: Normal;
- R: Retransmit;
- T: Time-out (TO).

The second character indicates the number of packets already transmitted but not yet acknowledged. The digit has a value ranging from 0 to 2 as limited by the window size. Inside the pie window, the shaded area indicates that a packet has been transmitted and an X indicates that the packet has been

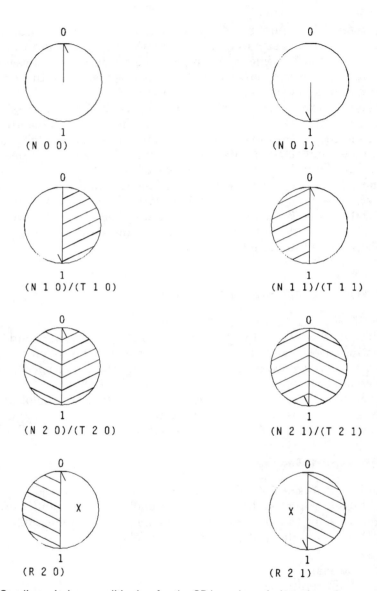

Figure 7.4 Sending window conditioning for the SRJ sender, window size = 2.

retransmitted. If the digit is 2, the sending window is full. In other words, the sender is blocked and must wait for an expected ack before it can transmit again. The third character denotes the trailing edge of the sending window: 0 means packet 0, and 1 means packet 1.

The window condition of state (T 1 0) is the same as (N 1 0), but they represent two different states. Likewise, each of the state pairs (N 1 1)/(T 1 1), (N 2 0)/(T 2 0) or (N 2 1)/(T 2 1) shares the same window condition. (R 1 0) and (R 1 1) are not shown because they can be merged into (N 0 0) and (N 0 1), respectively.

Because the sequence number is 1-bit, only ack0 and ack1 are used to describe the logic flow. The FSM model for a transport sender using SRJ ARQ with window size 2 is shown in Figure 7.5. After a port connection, the sender enters (N 0 0), the initial state. Its sending window is closed. The trailing edge coincides with the leading edge, which lies below 0, and the sender is not supposed to receive any ack packet or have a TO. Each transition is due to an event as explained below:

1. An I packet has been transmitted.
2. A +ack or −ack packet has been received. The symbol "/" in the front means "after receiving."
3. A TO error has occurred.

In (N 0 0), the sender enters state (N 1 0) after transmitting I0. In (N 1 0), many events may happen. After receiving a −ack0, which means I0 is corrupted, the sender goes back to the initial state to retransmit I0. After receiving a +ack1, the sender advances its trailing edge below 1 and goes to (N 0 1). If a TO error occurs, the sender enters state (T 1 0). Then, the sender polls receiver to inquire why. In the case where the response packet gets lost, another TO error occurs and the sender polls again. After polling, if a −ack0 is received, which indicates that the packet I0 is corrupted or missing, the sender needs to retransmit I0. If a +ack1 is received, the sender goes back to normal and enters (N 0 1).

Since pipelined transmission is allowed, the sender in (N 1 0) may transmit I1 to enter state (N 2 0). Now, the leading edge of the sending window coincides with the trailing edge, but the sender knows that its window is full by keeping a separate count variable whose value is 2 instead of 0. The rest of transitions are self-explanatory.

Composite FSM Model of Sender

In programming, we can take advantage of a composite FSM model by keeping track of the conditions of the sending window. The number of states is reduced to 3, as shown in Figure 7.6. In normal state, the sender sends a packet out, receives a +ack and advances its window accordingly. If a −ack Nr is received, the sender enters the retransmit state and retransmits I and Ns where Ns equals

336 Computer Networks: Architecture, Protocols, and Software

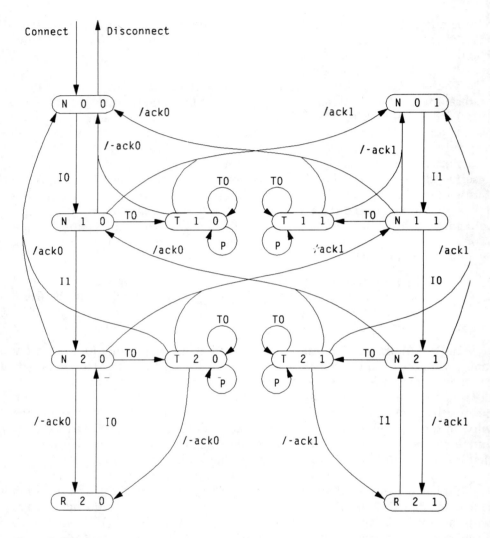

P - Polling
TO - Time-out error

Figure 7.5 FSM model for the SRJ sender, window size = 2.

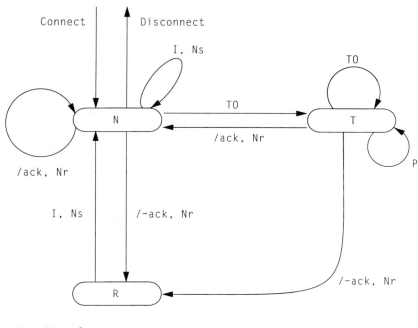

N – Normal state
R – Retransmit state
T – Time-out state

Figure 7.6 Composite FSM model for the SRJ sender, window size = 2.

Nr. If a TO error occurs, the sender enters the TO state and polls receiver. If no response is received, the sender polls again.

In the TO state, after receiving a +ack, *Nr*, the sender goes back to normal. If a −ack *Nr* is received, the sender enters retransmit state to retransmit I, *Ns* where *Ns* equals *Nr*.

7.2.2 Transport Receiver

The receiving window conditions are also complicated, as depicted in Figure 7.7. Each state is represented by three digits. The first digit indicates the number of errors encountered, 0, 1, or 2. The second digit is the number of packets, 0, 1, or 2, waiting for action in the window. In other words, an error has occurred and the receiver cannot advance its window without receiving the expected packet. The third digit is the trailing edge, 0 or 1.

After a port connection is established, the T layer receiver enters the initial state (0 0 0). Since the window size is 2, the leading edge coincides with the

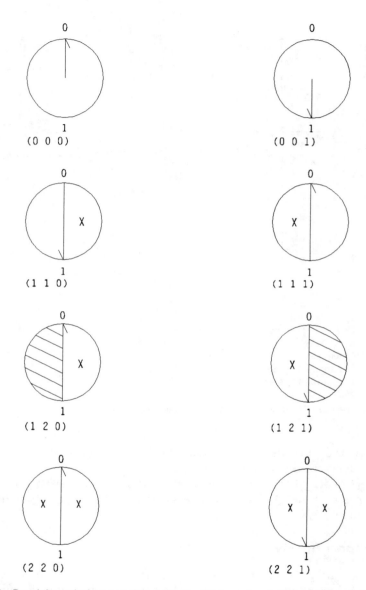

Figure 7.7 Receiving window conditions for the SRJ receiver, window size = 2.

trailing edge of the receiving window with a count variable 0, indicating that no packet has been received in the window. Likewise is state (0 0 1), except that the trailing edge is below 1 instead of 0. State (1 2 0) or (1 2 1) indicates that 2 packets have been received; the first packet is corrupted, but the second one is good. State (2 2 0) or (2 2 1) denotes that 2 packets have been received and both are corrupted.

State (1 1 0) or (1 1 1) indicates that only 1 packet has been received, but corrupted. Therefore, the receiver expects the sender to retransmit the erroneous packet above the trailing edge. State (0 1 0) and (0 1 1) are not necessary because the transport receiver can always transmit another +ack to go back to (0 0 1) or (0 0 0).

The FSM model for a transport receiver using SRJ ARQ with window size 2 is shown in Figure 7.8. The receiver always returns an ack after receiving a

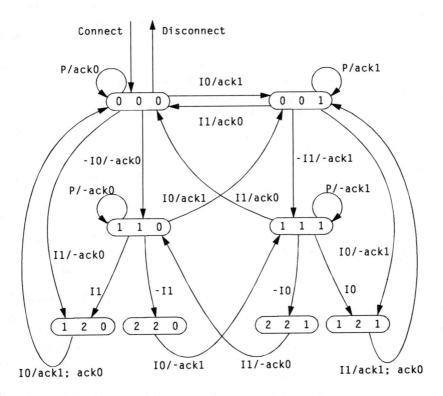

Polling commands and responses are not shown for states (1, 2, 0), (2, 2, 0), (1, 2, 1) and (2, 2, 1).

Figure 7.8 FSM model for the SRJ receiver, window size = 2.

packet as expected. If the received packet is out of sequence, the receiver must save the packet and withhold all of the acks for later processing. There are two types of state transition as explained below:

1. After receiving an I packet, the receiver withholds a response for later processing.
2. After receiving a polling, or I packet, the receiver transmits an ack immediately as indicated by the "/" symbol. As an example, $-$I0/$-$ack0 means that after receiving a corrupted I0, the receiver transmits a $-$ack0 immediately.

In initial state (0 0 0), after receiving a good I0 the receiver transmits a ack1, indicated by the transition I0/ack1 and enters state (0 0 1). After receiving a corrupted I0 ($-$I0), the receiver returns a $-$ack0 and enters state (1 1 0). Note that the receiver must be sure that I0 is corrupted without doubt. Anything else received, such as spurious noise, must be ignored because it is nondeterministic.

In (0 0 1), after receiving a good I1 as expected, the receiver transmits an ack0 and goes back to (0 0 0). After receiving a corrupted I1, the receiver returns a $-$ack1 and enters (1 1 1).

In (1 1 0), after receiving a good I0, the receiver returns a ack1 and goes to (0 0 1). If a good I1 is received because of pipelined transmission, the receiver enters (1 2 0). It is also possible to receive a corrupted I1. Then the receiver enters (2 2 0), indicating that two corrupted data packets have been received in a row.

In (1 2 0), the receiver has received 2 packets; the first one is corrupted, but the second one is good. After receiving an I0, the receiver returns a ack1, then a ack0, and enters (0 0 0).

While in (2 2 0), after receiving a good I0, the receiver responds with a $-$ack1 and goes to (1 1 1).

In (1 1 1), two possible events may happen. After receiving a good I0, the receiver enters (1 2 1); otherwise, (2 2 1).

In (1 2 1), after receiving a good I1 as expected, the receiver returns a ack0, then a ack1, and goes back to (0 0 1). While in (2 2 1), after receiving a good I1, the receiver advances its window and responds with a $-$ack0 because the previous I0 was bad and enters (1 1 0).

If the first digit of the receiver state is 0, which indicates no errors, any polling command will result in a +ack with a sequence number Nr as expected. For example, in (0 0 0), after being polled the receiver returns a ack0 because its trailing edge of the window is 0. On the other hand, when in (0 0 1), the receiver returns a ack1 after being polled.

If the first digit of the state is greater than 0, indicating the number of errors that have occurred, after being polled the receiver returns a $-$ack packet with a sequence number Nr in it, which is the trailing edge or the last digit of the state. In states (1 1 0), (1 2 0), and (2 2 0), after being polled, the receiver returns a $-$ack0 to indicate that I0 has not been correctly received. In states (1 1 1), (1 2 1), and (2 2 1), after being polled the receiver returns a $-$ack1 instead. The receiver must guard the trailing edge of its window carefully. Any polling command received will not change the state of receiver.

Composite FSM Model of Receiver

For the purpose of programming, the composite FSM model for a transport receiver using SRJ ARQ with window size 2 is constructed as in Figure 7.9. The receiver can be in one of four states: (N), (E −), (E − +), and (E − −).

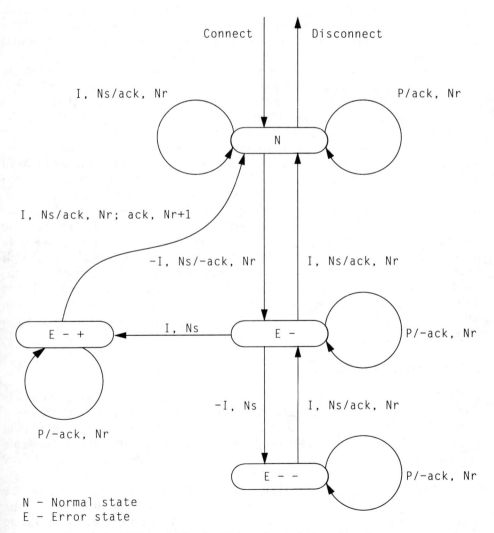

Figure 7.9 Composite FSM model for the SRJ receiver, window size = 2.

In normal state (N), the receiver has not detected any errors. So, after receiving a good data packet as expected, the receiver acknowledges and advances its window. The other three states all start with an E to indicate error. After the letter E, there are three error conditions: $-$, $-\,+$, or $-\,-$. The state (E $-$) means that only one I packet has been received in the window, but is corrupted. (E $-\,+$) means that two I packets have been received; the first packet is corrupted, but the second packet is good. (E $-\,-$) means that two packets in a row have been received and both are corrupted.

In state (N), after receiving a good I, Ns packet as expected, the receiver returns an ack, Nr, which equals $Ns + 1$. After receiving any polling command, the receiver returns an ack with the sequence number Nr in it as expected. If the incoming I packet is corrupted or missing, the receiver enters (E -), as indicated by the transition $-I$, $Ns/-ack$, Nr where Ns equals Nr.

In (E $-$), after receiving a good data packet as expected, the receiver returns an ack, Nr, and goes back to normal state. Due to the fact of pipelined transmission, it is possible for receiver to receive another good packet after the bad one. When this happens, the receiver enters (E $-\,+$) and must hold the ack $Nr + 1$ response until the first data packet is correctly received.

After receiving the next data packet, which is also corrupted, the receiver returns a $-ack$, Nr, and enters (E $-\,-$), indicating that two errors in a row have been received. In state (E $-\,+$), after receiving the expected I packet above the trailing edge, the receiver returns an ack Nr then an ack $Nr + 1$ and goes back to normal. In (E $-\,-$), the receiver must correct errors one by one. After correcting the first error, the receiver enters the (E $-$) state. After correcting the second error, the receiver goes back to normal. Should two successive data packets containing errors be detected by receiver, the protocol would still hold. However, should two successive data packets disappear on the line without being detected, the protocol would fail because the sequence number is only 1 bit long. The receiver does not know that two data packets are lost on the line at the same time. This problem disappears if a longer sequence number is used.

7.2.3 Optimal Window Size

If the TP header contains a 4-bit field as the window size, the maximum size is then 15. Ideally, the initial window size at the T layer level should be the number of hops between the origination node and the destination node so that all data links can be fully utilized in the route. Recall that the window size is the same as the number of buffers allocated. Therefore, the size of the message can be very large, as limited by the memory buffer size set by OS.

When the pacing technique is used to control packet flow, the window size can be reduced whenever a traffic jam condition is detected in the middle of the route. In other words, the window size can be changed dynamically during transmission. It takes a team effort to accomplish this goal. The N layer in the middle of the route detects a traffic jam condition and marks a bit in the packet header. Because this congestion bit is set, the destination T layer places a reduced window size in the ack packet. After receiving this ack packet, the origination T layer reduces its sending window size accordingly to slow things down. Later, when the traffic condition is improved, the destination T layer can request the origination T layer to increase its sending window size via an ack packet. In essence, the optimal window size at the T layer level is determined by road conditions.

7.3 OTHER DESIGN ISSUES

Certain applications require reliable transmission from beginning to end. What if a VC breaks down in the middle of data transmission? A good T layer can do the repair work as discussed in the following.

7.3.1 Virtual Circuit Failure

In a datagram model, if a node or link fails, transmission is likely to continue. But in a VC model, a VC failure in the middle of transmission can be recovered only if the T layer can reassign another VC with the ability to recover. In a telephone network, a VC failure usually means the end of a session. But in a computer network, reliable software can be written for error recovery. That is, the T layer has buffers to save messages for retransmission and can also reassign a new VC when the current VC fails.

After detecting so many TO errors in a row, the T layer knows that the VC is failed. Each port keeps a T layer control block that contains a pointer to the error-recovery routine plus all the information about the packet transmission on the port. When a VC is failed, the T layer fetches the entry address of the error-recovery routine from its control block and passes control to it. Because of the sliding window protocol, the T layer guards the trailing edge of its sending window precisely. After a new VC is established, the T layer continues and retransmits whatever is left in the buffer.

7.3.2 Three-Way Handshake

Recall that the three-way handshake concept is used by LAP in X.25 to establish a connection between a DCE and a DTE operating in normal response mode. It is also possible to use a three-way handshake protocol to establish a port connection, as shown in Figure 7.10(a). The T layer on the origination node sends a T layer Connect Request (CR) packet to its peer, which returns a Connect Confirm (CC) packet to its origination T layer. The origination T layer then sends

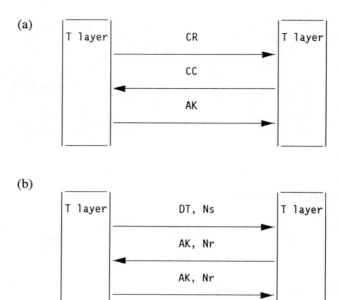

Figure 7.10 Three-way handshake protocols: (a) transport connect and (b) data packet transfer.

an acknowledgment (AK) packet to acknowledge the receipt of the CC. Conceptually, the three-way handshake is fine during the connection phase. However, using a three-way handshake to perform a port connection does not mean that the protocol is superior. It is more likely because its data link layer cannot ensure reliable transmission.

The three-way handshake concept can also be applied to the data packet transmissions as shown in Figure 7.10(b). The origination T layer sends a data packet, DT, Ns, and the destination T layer returns a AK, Nr. The origination T layer sends another AK, Nr to confirm the previous AK, Nr packet.

Granted that the three-way handshake concept has its merit in the connection phase. Whether the concept is truly necessary to transmit data packets remains a debatable issue. This extra handshake causes overhead and confusion. What if the last AK gets lost on the line? As proven by the FSM model, a good SWP is reliable with a two-way handshake. Even though software design is considered as an art, the three-way handshake may cause headaches for pipelined transmissions.

Just like other layers, the T layer provides services to its user and the user issues a message to ask the T layer to perform a service. The messages interpreted by the T layer are collectively known as T layer primitives.

7.4 TRANSPORT LAYER PRIMITIVES

The T layer primitives are messages received from or delivered to its service user, as shown in Figure 7.11. The TS-user is usually the S layer while the T layer is the TS-provider. Suppose that the TS-user wishes to establish a port connection. The user issues a T layer Connect Request to its T layer as shown below,

    T_CONNECT.request(origination_node_id, destination_node_id,
                    port_id, QOS, t_sdu);

where origination_node_id and destination_node_id are node ids to specify two NSAPs; port_id is a local reference number assigned by the S layer; QOS

①   T_CONNECT.request(origination_node_id, destination_node_id,
                      port_id, QOS, t_sdu);

②   T_CONNECT.indication(origination_node_id, destination_node_id,
                       port_id, QOS, t_sdu);

③   T_CONNECT.response(origination_node_id, destination_node_id,
                      port_id, QOS, t_sdu, status);

④   T_CONNECT.confirm(origination_node_id, destination_node_id,
                      port_id, QOS, t_sdu, status);

Figure 7.11 Transport layer connect primitives.

specifies speed, error rate, and probability of failures during transmission; and t_sdu provides user supplied information, such as application task ids. The status parameter is not needed because the origination T layer returns a T_CONNECT.confirm message to report what happened after the call.

A port connection is deemed necessary so long as the host supports a multiprogramming environment regardless of its N layer design, VC ,or datagram. In a VC model, the T layer cannot send a packet without a VC connection. Therefore, the T layer must establish a VC first. In a datagram model, the T layer can always send a packet via a datagram call. We discuss both designs in the following.

In a VC model, using the origination and destination node id pair as the key, the T layer can look up a table to find out whether there is an existing VC. If, fortunately, the T layer finds out that there is an existing VC between two nodes, the N layer connection phase is omitted, as shown in Figure 7.12(a).

On the other hand, a failed search indicates that there is no such existing VC between two given nodes, so the T layer must establish a VC first. As a consequence , the T layer issues a N_CONNECT.request to its N layer, as shown in Figure 7.12(b). It takes time for the N layer to build a VC. When the N layer connection is completed, the T layer receives a N_CONNECT.confirm from its N layer.

At this point, if the N_CONNECT.confirm is positive, the T layer knows there is a VC between two nodes. Now, the T layer sends a CR packet via a N_DATA.request to its peer on the destination node. The destination T layer sends a T_CONNECT.indication to its user. After receiving a T_CONNECT.response, it sends the CC packet to the T layer on the origination node. Finally, the origination T layer sends a T_CONNECT.confirm to its user as shown below:

    T_CONNECT.confirm(origination_node_id, destination_node_id,
              port_id, QOS, t-sdu, status);

where status indicates whether the connection is completed successfully or not and QOS stands for quality of service after negotiation. If the connect is successful, the TS-user at either end knows that there is a port connection between them. The TS-user on top can drop a message of any bit pattern and of any size into the port and its peer will receive the message from the port at the other end.

In a datagram model, the N layer connection phase is not necessary, as shown in Figure 7.13. The T layer simply transmits a CR packet via a N_UNIT-DATA.request or datagram call. The syntax looks different because it is a datagram call. Other T layer primitives are listed below:

T_DATA.request(port id, t_sdu, status);
T_DATA.indication(port id, t_sdu, status);

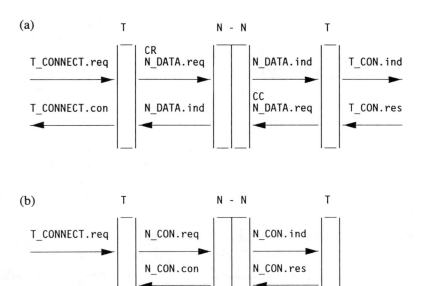

Figure 7.12 Transport connect phase in a VC model: (a) transport connect with an existing VC and (b) transport connect without an existing VC.

T_EXPEDITED_DATA.request(port_id, t_sdu, status);
T_EXPEDITED_DATA.indication(port_id, t_sdu, status);
T_UNITDATA.request(port_id, t-sdu, status);
T_UNITDATA.indication(port_id, t-sdu, status);
T_RESET.request(port_id, reason);
T_RESET.indication(port_id, reason);
T_RESET.response(port_id);
T_RESET.confirm(port_id);
T_DISCONNECT.request(port_id, reason);
T_DISCONNECT.indication(port_id, reason);
T_DISCONNECT.response(port_id);
T_DISCONNECT.confirm(port_id).

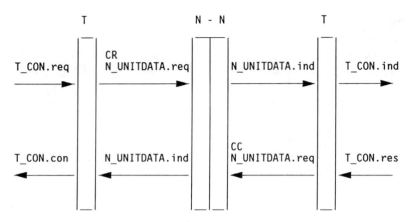

Figure 7.13 Transport connect phase in a datagram model.

A T_DATA.request is issued to transmit a data message via the port, and passing parameters include a port id, the t_sdu, and status, which indicates what happened after the call. The message block delivered to its peer T layer is contained in t_sdu. The T_DATA.request is used to deliver regular data, which implies that the packet must wait in the queue for its turn to be transmitted.

When the t_sdu is very large, the origination T layer segments the message into data packets and the destination T layer reassembles the packets back into message. The data flow of T layer packets is shown in Figure 7.14. Each T layer data packet contains a sending sequence number and each ack packet contains a sequence number expected. The End Of Transmission (EOT) flag is set in the last data packet to indicate the end of the message. After receiving the entire message, the destination T layer sends a T_DATA.indication to its TS-user to inform it of the arrival of the message.

A T_EXPEDITED_DATA.request is designed for transmitting expedited data. In other words, the data packet is delivered immediately without going through the queues. To match the syntax, the destination T layer sends a T_EXPEDITED_DATA.indication to its TS-user indicating the arrival of an expedited data packet.

The T_UNITDATA.request is issued to drop a message in the port in a datagram model while a T_UNITDATA.indication signals the arrival of the message from the port. If the message is very large, the T layer segments the message into data packets and its peer T layer knows how to assemble the packets into a message. In other words, each data packet is a datagram.

The T_RESET primitive resets a port connection, which is a four-way operation.

After the session, a port connection may be disconnected via a T_DISCONNECT, which is again a four-way operation. If a port is not disconnected after session, it is a permanent port or shared resource in the system.

Transport Layer

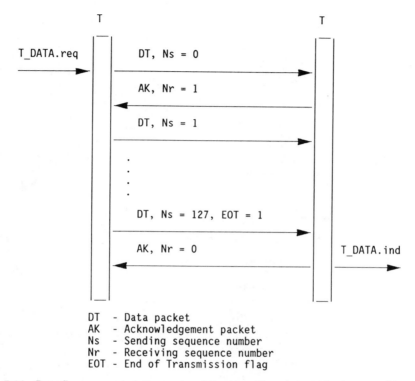

DT - Data packet
AK - Acknowledgement packet
Ns - Sending sequence number
Nr - Receiving sequence number
EOT - End of Transmission flag

Figure 7.14 Data flow example between two T layers with segmentation/reassembly.

7.5 TRANSPORT LAYER PROTOCOL DATA UNITS

A TPDU is essentially a transport packet transmitted between two T layers. The TPDUs are classified into two groups, one for control and one for data. After receiving a T layer primitive from its user, the T layer prepares a TPDU and transmits it to its peer via a N_DATA.request. As a result, the destination T layer receives the TPDU via a N_DATA.indication. That is, the N_DATA.indication primitive contains essentially the same information as the TPDU received.

It is also possible for a T layer to receive a large t_sdu from its user. Under such circumstances, the T layer must segment the t_sdu into data pieces, and each piece has its own header. If the t_sdu is short, the T layer simply adds a header to it to make a TPDU, as shown in Figure 7.15(a).

The T layer header contains opcode, sequence numbers, window size, error-detecting code, and so forth, as shown in Figure 7.15(b). The TPDU is delivered via a VC or datagram call and the N layer adds its header to it to make a NPDU or N layer packet. Therefore, a TPDU is the inner portion of a N layer data packet, as shown in Figure 7.15(c). All the control packets at the N layer level are not delivered to the T layer.

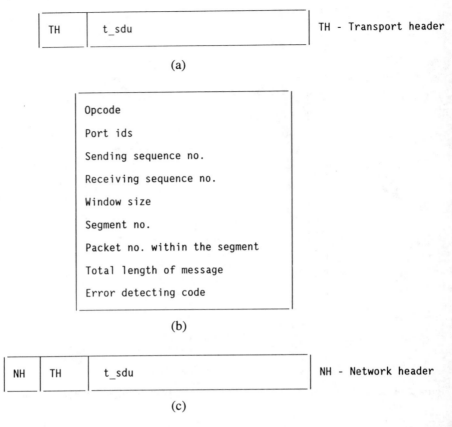

Figure 7.15 (a) Transport protocol data unit, (b) transport header and (c) network layer protocol data unit.

In regard to standards, all TPDUs must be defined precisely and accepted by all the designers. TPDUs are the bits seen by its peer T layer at the other end of a TC.

7.6 TRANSPORT LAYER DESIGN

The basic features of T layer design, such as packet transmission, error/flow control, and segmentation/reassembly, are pretty much the same regardless of its N layer design, a VC or datagram. Each port or TSAP is private to its user, and the T layer mainly manages the traffic between a port and a VC or datagram. Each port has its own database that contains all the information regarding data transfers. The private database of the port is stored in its transport control block (TPCB).

7.6.1 Transport Control Block

The TPCB mainly contains the SWP information pertinent to the port during data transmission, as shown in Figure 7.16. It contains its own sending port id, the receiving port id, and pointers to the error-recovery routines. In addition, it contains information about segmentation and reassembly.

In a transport data request, one of the parameters is the port id from which its associated TPCB can be fetched. The t_sdu contains information about the length and address of the message block. The T layer uses the TPCB to transmit packets and updates the TPCB each time after sending or receiving a data packet.

Sending port id
Receiving port id
Pointers to its t_sdu buffers
Status of packets in its t_sdu
Leading and trailing edges of sending window
Leading and trailing edges of receiving window
Window size
Timers
Pointers to error routines
etc

Figure 7.16 Transport control block.

7.6.2 Software Design of Transport Layer—VC Model

A VC must exist before a port connection can be built on top of it. Intuitively, the T layer can be thought of as an independent task that accepts TPDUs. Therefore, either the S or N layer may place a TPDU in the message queue for the T layer to fetch, interpret, and execute. Assuming that there exists no VC between two nodes, the origination T layer must build a VC first before it can send a CR packet to its peer. A simple sketch of the T layer design is shown below:

>T_layer_task:
>. . .
>Receive_loop:
>. . .
>Receive(from_task_id, message, status);
>>{Control is not passed to the next
>>statement unless there is message.}
>
>CASE message of
>T_CONNECT.request: {Connect, a 4-way operation.}
>>Assign a VC id while the port id was determined by its S layer;
>>Establish a connection between the VC id and port id;
>>IF there exists no VC between two nodes,
>>THEN issue a N_CONNECT.request;
>>>{At this stage, the T layer must wait for the
>>>arrival of N_CONNECT.confirm before it can
>>>send the Connect Request packet via a
>>>N_DATA.request.}
>>
>>ELSE send a Connect Request (CR) TPDU to its peer via a
>>N_DATA.request;
>>ENDIF;
>
>T_CONNECT.response:
>>Send a Connect Confirm (CC) TPDU via a N_DATA.request to the
>>T layer on the origination node;
>
>T_DISCONNECT.request: {Disconnect, a 4-way operation.}
>>Disconnect between the port and the VC;
>>Send a Disconnect Request (DR) TPDU to its peer via a
>>N_DATA.request;
>
>T_DISCONNECT.response:
>>Disconnect between the port and the VC;
>>Send a Disconnect Confirm (DC) TPDU to its peer T layer via
>>a N_DATA.request;
>
>T_RESET.request:
>>{Flush the port which is a 4-way operation.
>>Note that there is no Reset TPDU in the
>>protocol.}
>>Reset the port;

```
    Issue a N_RESET.request to its N layer;
T_RESET.response:
    Issue a N_RESET.response;
T_DATA.request:   {Segment the t_sdu if necessary.}
    IF the t_sdu is large,
    THEN
    REPEAT prepare a segment;
        REPEAT prepare a Data (DT) TPDU;
        Issue a N_DATA.request based on SRJ ARQ;
        IF a VC is broken during packet transmission,
        THEN pass control to an error recovery routine which
        reassigns a new VC and transmission continues; ENDIF;
        UNTIL the entire segment is transmitted;
    UNTIL the entire t_sdu is transmitted;
T_EXPEDITED_DATA.request:
    Prepare an Expedited Data (ED) TPDU;
    Issue a N_EXPEDITED_DATA.request;
            {Expedited data packets bypass all the queues
            in the subsequent layers.}
; ----------------------------------------
; Messages from its N layer.
; ----------------------------------------
N_CONNECT.indication:
    Issue a N_CONNECT.response to its N layer;
N_CONNECT.confirm:
    IF confirm is positive to indicate that a VC connection has
    been established,
    THEN send a Connect Request (CR) TPDU to its peer T layer via
    a N_DATA.request;
    ELSE issue a T_CONNECT.confirm indicating 'VC connection
    failed.' to its S layer; ENDIF;
N_DATA.indication:
    CASE TPDU of
    Connect Request:
        Assign a port id;
        Establish a connection between the VC id and port id;
        Issue a T_CONNECT.indication to its S layer;
    Connect Confirm:
        Issue a T_CONNECT.confirm to its S layer;
    Data:
        Send an Acknowledgment (AK) TPDU via a N_DATA.request
        with a receiving sequence number, Nr;
        IF the data packet is segmented,
        THEN perform reassembly; ENDIF;
        IF the entire t_sdu has been correctly received,
        THEN issue a T_DATA.indication to its S layer; ENDIF;
```

```
        ENDCASE;
    N_EXPEDITED_DATA.indication:
        Send an Expedited Acknowledgment (EA) packet to its peer T
        layer via an N_EXPEDITED_DATA.request;
        Issue a T_EXPEDITED_DATA.indication to its S layer;
    N_RESET.indication:
        Reset the port;
        Issue a T_RESET.indication to its S layer;
    N_RESET.confirm:
        Issue a T_RESET.confirm to its S layer;
    . . .
    ENDCASE;
    . . .
    Goto Receive_loop;
    Endtask;
    End.
```

Note that no Reset packet exists at the T layer level. This is because both the T layer and the N layer can perform the reset operation in one round trip, as shown in Figure 7.17. The sending T layer maps a T_RESET.request into a N_RESET.request. Its N layer sends out a N layer Reset packet via a DL_DATA.request. After receiving a N_RESET.indication, the remote T layer issues a T_RESET.indication. Subsequently, after receiving a T_RESET.response, the remote T layer issues a N_RESET.response to its N layer, which in turn sends a Reset Confirm packet via a DL_DATA.request. After receiving the Reset Confirm, the N layer at the sending side issues a N_RESET.confirm to its T layer, which then maps the message into a T_RESET.confirm.

7.6.3 Software Design of Transport Layer—Datagram Model

The T layer in a datagram model is similar with one exception. That is, no N layer connection is performed at all. Recall that datagram packets may arrive out of sequence and there may also be duplicates. It is the responsibility of the T layer to sort packets, discard duplicates, and request retransmission of any missing packets. The key design features are described below:

```
    CASE message of
    T_UNITDATA.request:
        Send a Unit Data (UD) datagram to its peer T layer via a
        N_UNITDATA.request;
    N_UNITDATA.indication:
        CASE TPDU packet of
        UD:  Throw away duplicates if there are any;
             Sort packets in order;
             Send an Acknowledgment to its peer T layer
             with a receiving sequence number, Nr;
```

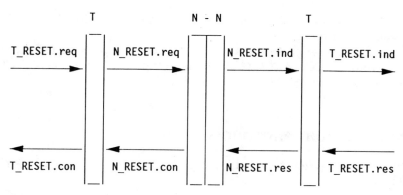

Figure 7.17 The T layer and N layer reset primitives.

```
        IF the Unit Data packet is segmented,
        THEN reassemble; ENDIF;
        IF the entire t_sdu has been correctly received,
        THEN issue a T_UNITDATA.indication to its S layer; ENDIF;
    . . . .
    ENDCASE;
    . . . .
ENDCASE;
    . . . .
END.
```

In general, the datagram service is less reliable unless source routing is selected. In such a design, the header of each datagram specifies the entire route, which may be quite long. If the route cannot be followed strictly as specified, the datagram is not delivered with a return notice.

7.6.4 Permanent Transports

If a transport entity is not disconnected after a session, it becomes a permanent port in the computer network. After connection, ports are symmetrical, which means that either side can allocate a port by specifying the port id. After a session, either side of the T layer should deallocate the port so that other tasks can allocate the port again. Therefore, deallocate means that the port is returned to NOS. Note that Open and Close are synonymous system calls, as discussed in the next chapter.

Permanent ports are resources in a computer network. For example, if there is only one file server running on the remote computer that drives a printer, a client task on the local computer may wish to connect to the file server from time to time. Therefore, any client task can allocate a permanent port customized to its need. After allocation, the client task can send records in ASCII to the port, which also means remote printing.

There are several protocols at the T layer level [1]. We will study the OSI transport protocols [X.214, X224], the transmission control protocol (TCP), and the user datagram protocol (UDP) [2,3].

7.7 OSI TRANSPORT PROTOCOLS

The OSI transport protocol (TP) suite includes five classes, namely TP0 to TP4 as listed below:

1. Class 0: Simple class;
2. Class 1: Basic error-recovery class;
3. Class 2: Multiplexing class;
4. Class 3: Error-recovery and multiplexing class;
5. Class 4: Error-detection, error-recovery, and multiplexing class.

TP0 is the simplest kind and provides the minimum services while TP4 is the most rigorous protocol and provides full error-recovery capabilities. All five classes have the design features to support pipelined transmissions.

7.7.1 General Design Concepts

The capability summaries of TPs are given in Figure 7.18. Each system uses one or more protocol classes to suit its needs and each protocol class is designed for a particular application on the host, as described below.

Classes 0 and 1 specify protocols for a single port in the destination T layer. TP0 provides no error checking at all while TP1 provides limited error recovery, such as detecting missing packets but not validating of the correctness of data packets.

Classes 2, 3 and 4 handle multiple ports in the destination T layer.

TP2 provides no error recovery at all. TP3 provides limited error recovery, such as detecting missing packets but not validating the correctness. TP4 uses a 16-bit Fletcher checksum to detect errors in the header and provides full error recovery. TP1, TP3, and TP4 also can assign an alternate VC for error recovery when an existing VC fails during packet transmission.

7.7.2 Formats of OSI TPDU

The general format of OSI TPDU-normal mode is shown in Figure 7.19(a). Octets are transmitted in sequence and octet number 1 is transmitted first. Each packet

Capability	Class				
	0	1	2	3	4
Single port	X	X			
Multiple ports			X	X	X
No error checking	X		X		
Limited error checking		X		X	
Full-blown error checking					X
Assigning alternate VC		X		X	X
Extended mode			X	X	X

Figure 7.18 Capability summaries of OSI transport protocols.

contains a variable number of octets that include a length indicator (LI), a fixed part, a variable part, and a Data field as specified below:

    octet 1:   LI;
    octet 2 to n: Fixed-part header of the packet;
    octet (n + 1) to p: Variable part;
    octet (p + 1) to the end: Data field.

In the data packet, a sequence number is placed in the fixed header. All five classes may transmit data in normal mode and TP2, TP3, and TP4 can also transmit data in extended mode. Therefore, two types of sequence numbers, normal versus extended, are shown in Figure 7.19(b). A 7-bit sequence number is used in normal mode while in extended mode the sequence number is 31-bit.

Fixed Part Header

The fixed part headers are based on packet types. As an example, the fields in the fixed header of a CR-normal mode are shown in Figure 7.19(c). Octet 1

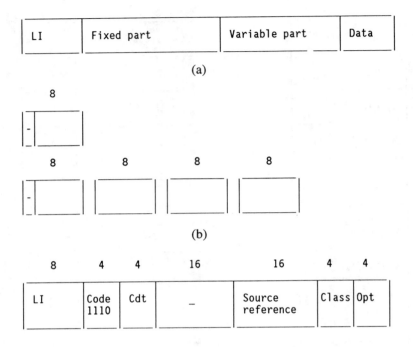

Notes:
1. LI is the length indicator
2. Code 1110 specifies connect request.
3. Cdt (Credit) specifies the proposed window size.
4. Source reference is the sending port no.
5. Class denotes an integer ranging from 0 to 4.
6. Opt (Option) specifies QOS, etc.

(c)

Figure 7.19 (a) General format of an OSI TPDU, (b) sequence number types (normal versus extended), and (c) fixed part headers of CR-normal mode.

contains the LI, which measures the header in bytes, excluding itself. The LI represents an 8-bit unsigned integer with a maximum value of 254 while 255 is reserved for future expansions. Therefore, we have

$$LI = \text{length of the fixed part} + \text{length of the variable part}$$

For example, if the fixed part is 6 bytes long and the variable part is 8 bytes long, LI should be 0000 1110 in binary or 14 in decimal, as computed below:

$$LI = 6 + 8 = 14$$

The total length of header is 15 decimal, including the LI field. The second field is a 4-bit code in octet 2. The code for CR is 1110 in binary. The third field, Credit (CDT), is the lower 4-bit field in octet 2, which is the proposed window size. The receiver can determine an approved credit limit, which may be less than the proposed one. Just like our credit card system, if the credit limit is 5, the sender can send packets out 5 times without receiving an ack. After that, the sender is blocked until it receives a +ack as expected.

The fourth field is a 16-bit 0 known as the Destination-Reference (DST-REF) field or the receiving port id, which is not known yet in a Connect Request.

The fifth field is the 16-bit Source Reference (SRC-REF) field containing the sending port id. The sixth field is the upper 4 bits in octet 7 to denote a class number ranging from 0 to 4. The seventh field is the lower 4 bits in octet 7 to specify options.

Following the fixed part, there is an optional part that has a variable length. The optional part defines less frequently used parameters. If the variable part is present, it shall contain one or more parameters.

Before discussing the details of various TPDUs, let us examine the error-detecting code used in TP4. The last 2 bytes of the variable part of a packet header contain a 16-bit Fletcher checksum code for ARQ.

7.7.3 Fletcher Checksum

Assume that the T layer header has a total of $(L - 2)$ bytes. The idea is to add a 2-byte checksum at the end to make a total of L bytes, as shown in Figure 7.20(a) [4]. Let n denote the position in the packet where X is placed, then the nth or $(L - 1)$ byte is X, and the $(n + 1)$ or Lth byte is Y. We replace $(L - n + 1)$ with 2 as shown below:

$$(L - n + 1) = 2$$

Algorithm of Fletcher Checksum Generation

1. Append 2-byte 0's to a $(L - 2)$-byte long packet header, so the total length in bytes is L. All arithmetic operations are performed mod 255.
2. For each octet sequentially from $i = 1$ to L:
   a. Add the value of the octet to C0;
   b. Add the value of C0 to C1;
3. $X = -C1 + C0$
4. $Y = C1 - 2 \cdot C0$
5. Place X in the $(L - 1)$ byte and Y in the Lth byte as checksum.

It is interesting to see how X and Y are derived. Based on the assumption that

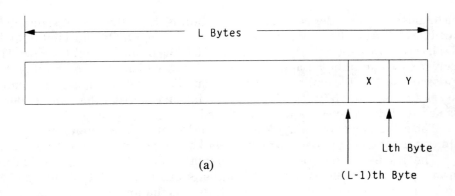

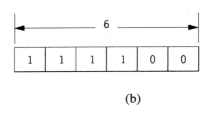

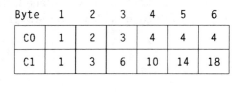

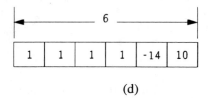

Figure 7.20 (a) L-byte header with Fletcher checksum, (b) header before checksum computation, (c) C0 and C1 after computing each byte, and (d) header with computed checksum.

if the receiver repeats the same arithmetic operations mod 255 for each octet sequentially from $i = 1$ to L by

1. Adding the value of each octet to C0'; and
2. Adding the value of C0' to C1'

and both C0' and C1' should contain 0's, which is a necessary condition to ensure perfect transmission. Therefore, we have

$$C0' = C0 + X + Y = 0$$

$$C1' = C1 + X + (X + Y) = C1 + 2 \cdot X + Y = 0$$

Solving the two equations, we derive X and Y as specified in the algorithm. Note that when the sender computes the original C0 and C1, the entire block length is L with 2 trailing bytes of 0's. Using a length of $(L - 2)$ would be incorrect. Even though the last 2 bytes contain 0's, it would make no difference to compute C0, but it would make a difference to compute C1 because it has cumulative effects depending on the number of iterations.

The implementation of Fletcher checksum is straightforward, especially when the design language allows 8-bit arithmetic. Uppercase letters are used in the design to conform with specifications.

Software Design of Fletcher Checksum

```
; ---------------------------------------------------------------
;    X:          an 8-bit character, the (L - 1)th byte checksum;
;    Y:          an 8-bit character, the Lth byte checksum;
;    XY:         a 16-bit unsigned integer containing the checksum;
;    C0:         an 8-bit character;
;    C1:         an 8-bit character;
;    data_block: array of 8-bit characters whose address is ;
;                passed as a parameter;
;    n:          same as L, the size of data_block passed as a ;
;                parameter;
;    All arithmetic operations are mod 255.
; ---------------------------------------------------------------
Checksum (data_block, n)
Initialize C0, C1, and XY to 0's;
REPEAT
Fetch the next character from the data_block and add it to C0;
Add C0 to C1;
UNTIL L times;
```

X = −C1 + C0;
Y = C1 + 2 · C0;
Add X to XY;
Shift XY 8 bits to the left;
Add Y to XY;
Return XY;

Let us try a simple example as shown in Figure 7.20(b). Assume that the packet header has only 6 bytes and before computation each of the first 4 bytes contains a 1 and the last two bytes contain 0's. In the repeat loop, we compute C0 and C1 step by step as shown in Figure 7.20(c). After the loop, the two checksum bytes in Figure 7.20(d) are computed as

$$X = -C1 + C0 = -14$$
$$Y = C1 - 2 \cdot C0 = 10$$

At the receiving end, we can verify that

$$C0' = \sum_{i=1}^{L} a_i = 1 + 1 + 1 + 1 - 14 + 10 = 0$$

$$C1' = \sum_{i=1}^{L} (L - i - 1) a_i = 0$$

where a_i denotes the value of the ith byte. From the equation of $C1'$, we can also prove that

$$\sum_{i=1}^{L} i \cdot a_i = 1 \cdot 1 + 2 \cdot 1 + 3 \cdot 1 + 4 \cdot 1 + 5 \cdot (-14) + 6 \cdot 10 = 0$$

Note that the mod 255 arithmetic really means 1's complement arithmetic at the byte level. In other words, 1's complement notation is used to represent a negative integer in 1 byte. If the X byte contains −14, it is 1111 0001 in binary (i.e., the 1's complement of 14). To compute the checksum, we treat each byte as an unsigned integer. To program the algorithm in high-level language on a 2's complement processor, two conditions need corrective measures. First, whenever a byte contains all 1's, which represents 255 or −0, it should automatically be changed to 0's. Second, whenever a carry is generated after adding, this end-around-carry must be added to the result one more time to make the result correct. Let us try one more example below. An unsigned integer, 133 in decimal, is represented by 1000 0101 in binary. Adding two such numbers, we should get 11 in decimal or 0000 1011 in binary as shown below:

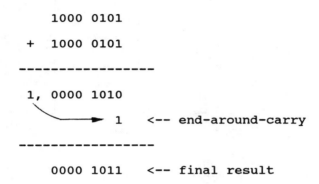

As far as software implementation is concerned, the 16-bit Fletcher checksum has comparable performance in speed and error detection with the FCS-ITU-T using table lookup.

7.7.4 Specifications of OSI TPDU

The fixed-part headers of OSI TPDU-normal mode are specified in Figure 7.21. Each TPDU is also known as a T layer packet. The TPDUs can be grouped into three categories: Connection Control, Data Control, and Flow Control, as discussed in the following.

Connection Control Packets

Four packets are used for connection and disconnection, namely the Connect Request (CR), Connect Confirm (CC), Disconnect Request (DR) and Disconnect Confirm (DC). After a port connection is made, a Protocol Identifier (PI) packet may be sent to the peer T layer to specify a particular protocol.

1. The CR packet is sent to its peer T layer to request a port connection. In the packet, credit, source reference number, class of protocol, and options are specified. The destination reference field is set to 0's because its value is unknown yet. The class codes are listed below:

    - 0000: Class 0;
    - 0001: Class 1;
    - 0010: Class 2;
    - 0011: Class 3;
    - 0100: Class 4.

8	4	4	16	16	4	4
LI	CR 1110	Cdt	—	Source reference	Class	Opt
LI	CC 1101	Cdt	Dest reference	Source reference	Class	Opt
LI	DR 1000	-	Dest reference	Source reference	Reason	
LI	DC 1100	-	Dest reference	Source reference		
LI	DT 1111	-	EOT / Ns	(Class 0, 1)		
LI	DT 1111	-	Dest reference	EOT / Ns	(Class 2, 3, 4)	
LI	ED 0001	-	Dest reference	EOT / ED Ns		
LI	AK 0110	CDT	Dest reference	- / Nr		
LI	EA 0010	-	Dest reference	- / ED Nr		
LI	RJ 0101	CDT	Dest reference	- / Nr		
LI	ER 0111	-	Dest reference	- / Caus		
LI	PI 0000 0001		Others			

Figure 7.21 Fixed-part headers of OSI TPDU-normal mode.

Bits 3–0 denote the option as follows:

- Bit 3: 0 always.
- Bit 2: 0 always.
- Bit 1: 0 → normal mode, for all classes;
    1 → extended mode for Classes 2, 3, 4.
- Bit 0: 0 → explicit flow control for Class 2;
    1 → no explicit flow control for Class 2.

A variable part, octets from $(n + 1)$ to p, is optional. If the variable part is present, it should contain one or more parameters. Each parameter entry consists of three parts: the parameter code, length, and value. An example of the first parameter entry is shown in Figure 7.22. Octet $(n + 1)$ contains the parameter code, octet $(n + 2)$ contains the parameter length m in bytes, and octets $(n + 3)$ to $(n + 2 + m)$ contain the actual parameter value block. The position of the parameter entry is immaterial. Parameters may also be duplicated, and the latter value takes higher precedence.

For TP4, a 16-bit checksum should be present in the CR TPDU and all other TPDUs unless the non-use of checksum option is selected. The checksum parameter entry has the following format:

Parameter code:	1100 0011
Parameter length:	0000 0010
Parameter value:	xxxx xxxx
	yyyy yyyy

Note that the parameter length 2 indicates that the next 2 bytes contain the checksum X and Y, represented by 8-bit x's followed by 8-bit y's. The checksum is placed as the last 2 bytes of the variable part to guard the entire header.

Other parameters in the variable part, mostly not available in Class 0, are specified below:

a. Transport service access point identifiers (TSAP-id)
Parameter code: 1100 0001 for the calling TSAP;
                   1100 0010 for the called TSAP;
Parameter length: n;
Parameter value: identifier of the TSAP.

b. TPDU size
Parameter code: 1100 0000;
Parameter: 1;
Parameter value: 0000 1101 → 2^{13} or 8,192 octets (not allowed in Class 0);
                   0000 1100 → 2^{12} or 4,096 octets (not allowed in Class 0);
                   0000 1011 → 2,048 octets;
                   0000 1010 → 1,024 octets;

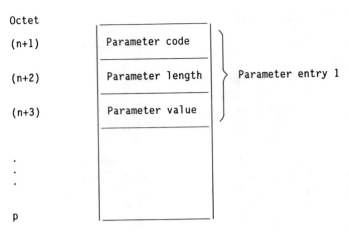

Figure 7.22 Variable-part header of OSI TPDU.

```
                0000 1001 → 512 octets;
                0000 1000 → 256 octets;
                0000 0111 → 128 octets (default).
```

c. Version No.
Parameter code: 1100 0100;
Parameter: 1;
Parameter value: 0000 0001 (default).

d. Protection parameters
Parameter code: 1100 0101;
Parameter length: n;
Parameter value: user defined.

e. Additional option selection
Parameter code: 1100 0110;
Parameter length: 1;
Parameter value:
  Bits 7–4 are 0's;
  Bit 3 = 1 → yes, use expedited network in Class 1;
        0 → no;
  Bit 2 = 1 → yes, use receipt confirmation in Class 1;
        0 → no;
  Bit 1 = 0 → yes, use checksum in Class 4;
        1 → no, as an exception;
  Bit 0 = 1 → yes, use expedited transport service;
        0 → no;
  Bits 3–0, 0001 is the default.

f. Alternate protocol class
Parameter code: 1100 0111;
Parameter length: n;
Parameter value: Each octet is encoded as for octet 7 with bits 3–0 set to 0's.

g. Acknowledgment time
The parameter conveys the maximum acknowledgment time allowed to the destination port, which is not subject to negotiation.
Parameter code: 1000 0101;
Parameter length: 2;
Parameter value: a binary number to denote the maximum acknowledgment time in milliseconds.

h. Throughput
Throughput is defined to be octets per second.
Parameter code: 1000 1001;
Parameter length: 12 or 24;
Parameter value:
  1st 12 octets: maximum throughput;
    1st 3 octets: target value, origination to destination, forward direction;
    2nd 3 octets: minimum acceptable value, forward direction;
    3rd 3 octets: target value, destination to origination, backward direction;
    4th 3 octets: minimum acceptable value, backward direction;
  2nd 12 octets: average throughput;
    1st 3 octets: target value, forward direction;
    2nd 3 octets: minimum acceptable value, forward direction;
    3rd 3 octets: target value, backward direction;
    4th 3 octets: minimum acceptable value, backward direction.

i. Residual error rate
An error rate value denotes the power of 10. For example, a value of 7 means an error occurs per 10^7 bits.
Parameter code: 1000 0110;
Parameter length: 3;
Parameter value: 1st octet → target value;
    2nd octet → minimum acceptable value;
    3rd octet → TSDU size, power of 2 where a value of 7 means 128 bytes.

j. Priority
Parameter code: 1000 0111;
Parameter length: 2;
Parameter value: unsigned integer where 0 is the highest priority.

k. Transit delay
Values are in milliseconds based on a TSDU size of 128 bytes.
Parameter code: 1000 1000;
Parameter length: 8;

Parameter value:
   1st 2 octets: target value, forward direction;
   2nd 2 octets: maximum acceptable value, forward direction;
   3rd 2 octets: target value, backward direction;
   4th 2 octets: maximum acceptable value, backward direction.

l. Reassignment time
This parameter specifies a 16-bit integer in seconds. When a failure cannot be resolved within this time interval, the T layer takes action to reassign a new VC.
Parameter code: 1000 1011;
Parameter length: 2;
Parameter value: an integer value expressed in seconds.

The data field contains the transparent user data, which may not exceed 32 octets. Since the entire packet is a n_sdu to be passed to its Network layer, so the total length of a CR packet shall not exceed 128 octets.

2. The CC packet is returned by the destination T layer, which provides the approved credit, the destination port id, and so forth. The variable part is similar to that of a CR. No user data are permitted in Class 0, but optional in other classes. If user data are permitted, it may not exceed 32 octets.

3. The DR packet is sent to its peer T layer to disconnect the TC. Octet 7 contains a reason as specified below:

      128 + 0   → normal disconnect;
      128 + 1:   → destination transport entity congestion at connect request time;
      128 + 2   → connection negotiation failed;
      128 + 3   → duplicate source reference detected;
      128 + 4   → mismatched references;
      128 + 5   → protocol error;
      128 + 6   → not used;
      128 + 7   → reference overflow;
      128 + 8   → CR refused on the network connection;
      128 + 9   → not used;
      128 + 10 → header or parameter length invalid;
      0   → Reason not specified;
      1   → congestion at TSAP;
      2   → Session entity not attached to TSAP;
      3   → Address unknown.

The variable part may contain:

a. Additional information related to the clearing of the connection;
Parameter code: 1110 0000
Parameter length: n;
Parameter value: Additional information that is user defined.

b. Checksum

No user data are permitted in Class 0, and are optional in other classes. In the case that user data are permitted, it may not exceed 64 octets and the successful transfer of this data is not guaranteed by the transport protocol.

4. The DC packet is returned by its peer T layer to confirm the disconnection. The variable part and user data field are similar to that of a DR packet.
5. The PI packet is sent to the destination T layer to specify a particular transport protocol that is not negotiable. Mechanisms are under study to support such negotiation in the future.

Octet 3 contains the Protocol id as specified below:

```
0000 0000:            reserved;
0000 0001:            OSI TP1, which is the default;
0000 0010 to 0111 1111:   other OSI protocols;
1000 0000 to 1111 1111:   reserved for private use.
```

Octet 4 is the SHARE field to specify the sharing information of a network connection, as shown below:

```
0000 0000:            no sharing;
0000 0001:            sharing is allowed;
0000 0010 to 1111 1111:   reserved.
```

When the sharing field has the value of 0000 0001, the variable part starting with octet 5 may contain one optional parameter as shown below:

```
Parameter code:     1101 1111;
Parameter length:   n;
Parameter value:    a list of n protocol ids, one per octet.
```

The parameter provides information about different transport protocols currently implemented on the shared VC. There is no user data field coded in this packet.

Data Packets

Two types of packets are used to transmit data, the data (DT) and expedited data (ED). A data or information packet is used to transfer regular data while the expedited data packet is used to transfer control information, which does not wait in the queues of the bottom layers.

6. The DT packet is sent by the T layer at either end to its peer. For Class 2, 3, and 4 protocols, each data packet contains the destination port id, and the Class 4 packet also contains the checksum. For Classes 0 and 1, a DT packet does not contain the destination port reference number; therefore, it is two octets shorter.

In normal mode, octet 3 for Classes 0 and 1, or octet 5 for Classes 2, 3, and 4 contains two fields as specified below:

Bit 7: The End Of Transmission (EOT) flag to denote that the current DT TPDU is the last data unit of a complete message block (i.e., the entire t_sdu. EOT is the opposite of a More bit).

Bits 6–0: The 7-bit packet sending sequence number Ns where bit 0 is the lsb.

The fixed part headers of OSI TPDU-extended mode are shown in Figure 7.23. In an extended DT packet, octets 5 to 8 for Classes 2, 3, and 4 contain the following:

Bit 7 of octet 5: EOT flag;
Bits 6–0 of octet 5, concatenated with octets 6, 7 and 8: the 31-bit packet sending sequence number Ns where bit 0 in octet 8 is the lsb.

The variable part contains the checksum code for class 4 protocol if so selected, and the user data field has a length that is the difference between the TPDU size and the length of the header including LI.

Octet 1	2	3, 4	5, 6, 7, 8	9, 10
LI	DT 1110 0000	Dest reference	EOT / Ns	
LI	ED 0001 0000	Dest reference	EOT / ED Ns	
LI	AK 0110 0000	Dest reference	- / Nr	CDT
LI	RJ 0101 0000	Dest reference	- / Nr	CDT
LI	EA 0010 0000	Dest reference	- / ED Nr	

Figure 7.23 Fixed-part headers of OSI TPDU-extended mode.

The sending T layer keeps a Local Retransmission Timer (TL) for each packet sent out as indicated by the following equation:

$$TL = ELR + ERL + AR + X$$

where ELR is the expected maximum transit delay from local to remote, ERL is the expected maximum transit delay from remote to local, AR is the remote acknowledgment time, and X is the local processing time. When the TL expires without receiving an ack, it triggers a TO error.

7. The ED packet contains urgent data that is usually a control message from the service user. The ED TPDU cannot be used in the following:

a. In Class 0;
b. In Class 2 when the "no explicit flow control" option is selected during the connection phase;
c. In all classes when the expedited data transfer option is not selected during the connection phase.

Normal mode is allowed for Classes 1, 2, 3, and 4. Extended mode is allowed for Classes 2, 3 and 4. Both formats are very similar to those of the DT packets except that they maintain their own set of sequence numbers. In addition, the EOT flag in the header is always on. The User Data field contains an expedited t_sdu ranging from 1 to 16 octets.

Flow Control Packets

There are three flow control packets: the Acknowledgment (AK), Reject (RJ), and Protocol Error (ER). Those packets are used to implement sliding window protocols.

8. The AK packet contains a packet-receiving sequence number Nr, which is either 7 bits or 31 bits long. The CDT field is 4 bits long in normal mode, or 8 bits long in extended mode. It is interesting to note that the CDT field in an AK may contain 0's. This indicates that the sending T layer has 0 credit, so it must temporarily halt its transmission of new packets until another AK with a nonzero credit is received.

Its variable part contains the following information:

a. Subsequence number is optional in Class 4. If this parameter is absent, its default value is 0:

Parameter code: 1000 1010;
Parameter length: 2;
Parameter value: 16-bit subsequence number.

b. Flow control confirmation is optional in Class 4. This provision is used to implement a three-way handshake as shown below.

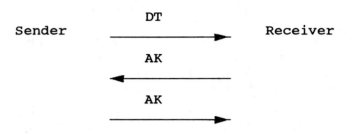

The sender sends a DT TPDU, the receiver returns an AK TPDU, and finally the sender returns an AK TPDU. The AK packet contains the flow control information as specified below:

    Parameter code: 1000 1100;
    Parameter length: 8;
    Parameter value: 32-bit trailing edge of the sending window with sign bit set to 0; (For normal mode, the upper 3-byte field contains 0's.)
                            16-bit sub-sequence number;
                            16-bit CDT.

c. Checksum as the last two bytes in the variable part.

9. The EA packet is similar to AK except that it has its own set of sequence numbers to manage. The variable part may contain a checksum for a Class 4 protocol.

10. The RJ packet indicates a negative acknowledgment also containing a 7-bit or 31-bit receiving sequence number Nr, which implies that data packets with a sequence number up to $Nr-1$ have been correctly received. Selective-Reject ARQ should be used to recover errors of any kind in the T layer.

11. The ER packet indicates that a protocol error is encountered during packet transmission. The fixed part in the header contains the opcode, destination reference number, and a cause in octet 5 as specified below:

    0000 0000: reason not specified;
    0000 0001: invalid parameter code;
    0000 0010: invalid TPDU type;
    0000 0011: invalid parameter value.

The variable part may contain the following parameters:

a. Invalid TPDU

    Parameter code: 1100 0001;

Parameter length: n;
Parameter value: The n-byte TPDU rejected.

b. Checksum

Author's Comments

There are 11 different packets proposed by the OSI Model. In general, the packets are quite elegant. The sequence number is long enough to solve many SWP problems. For example, whenever an error occurs, the receiving T layer can always set the CDT field in an RJ packet to 0, so the sending T layer cannot send any new packets until all old packets are retransmitted correctly.

A Polling packet could be added in order to ease the implementation of SRJ ARQ. After being polled, if the receiving T layer has encountered an error condition of any kind, it transmits a $-$ack with the expected sequence number Nr and the sending T layer needs to retransmit only the packets that contain errors.

Explicit Congestion Control flags should be considered. The N layer in the middle of the route could set this flag to reflect the status of a traffic jam condition. Finally, a 16-bit checksum should be considered to guard not only the T layer header, but also the entire TPDU.

7.8 TRANSMISSION CONTROL PROTOCOL

TCP is a transport protocol used on the Internet. TCP ensures that packets are delivered reliably in sequence to its service user. In other words, TCP handles missing or duplicate packets. The basic transmission unit of TCP is called a segment, with or without data. Each segment has a TCP header that contains six 32-bit words, as shown in Figure 7.24. In each word, bit 31 is the msb and bit 0 is the lsb.

7.8.1 TCP Header Design

In the first word, a 16-bit source port on the left is the sending port id and the right is a 16-bit destination port id. A Full Socket address is defined to be the port id concatenated with an IP address. The second word contains a 32-bit segment sending sequence number Ns. The third word contains a 32-bit segment receiving sequence number Nr of a +ack piggybacked on the outgoing data segment. The sequence numbers are byte addresses initially selected from a random 32-bit clock and agreed upon during the connection phase. After having successfully transmitted a segment, the TCP sender and receiver increment each of their respective sequence numbers by the segment size.

The fourth word is divided into three fields. The 4-bit Hlen (Header Length)

```
 31        27        21        15        7        0
┌──────────────────────────┬──────────────────────────┐
│ Source port              │ Destination port         │
├──────────────────────────┴──────────────────────────┤
│ Sequence number                                     │
├─────────────────────────────────────────────────────┤
│ Acknowledgement number                              │
├──────┬──────────┬────────┬──────────────────────────┤
│ Hlen │ Reserved │  Code  │ Window                   │
├──────┴──────────┴────────┼──────────────────────────┤
│ Checksum                 │ Urgent pointer           │
├──────────────────────────┴──────────────┬───────────┤
│ Options                                 │ Padding   │
├─────────────────────────────────────────┴───────────┤
│ Data                                                │
│                                                     │
└─────────────────────────────────────────────────────┘
```

Notes:

1. Source port is the sending port no.
2. Destination port is the receiving port no.
3. Sequence number is the packet sending sequence no.
4. Acknowledgment number is the packet receiving no. of +ack piggybacked on an outgoing data packet.
5. Hlen is the header length in 32-bit words.
6. Code is 6-bit to specify an operation.
7. Window is the window size.
8. Checksum is the LRC using odd parity.
9. Urgent pointer points to the urgent data in the data field.

Figure 7.24 Transmission control protocol header and data.

on the left denotes a length in units of a 32-bit word, which is also an offset pointing to data, if there is any. The next 6-bit segment is reserved for future expansions and it is followed by another 6-bit segment that defines the opcode. Each bit in the code has a special meaning as defined below:

- Bit 21: URG → the urgent pointer is valid;
- Bit 20: ACK → the acknowledgment field is valid;
- Bit 19: PSH → this segment requests a push, which means immediate delivery;
- Bit 18: RST → to reset the connection;
- Bit 17: SYN → to synchronize the sequence numbers;
- Bit 16: FIN → to finish transmission.

The URG (Urgent) bit tells the T layer that the Urgent field contains a pointer to the last byte of urgent data. Urgent data are used to provide control information such as the "Break" or CTRL-c character, which does not belong to the regular data stream. If the URG bit is set, the T layer bypasses all the queues of regular data and takes immediate actions to deliver this urgent packet either down to its IP layer or up to its service user.

The ACK (Acknowledgment) bit indicates that a +ack is piggybacked on this data segment. The PSH (Push) bit is set to indicate that the current segment needs a push to speed up its delivery. This also means that the data in the buffer is going to be transmitted right away even if it is not quite full. As an example, after having established a connection via a remote login, the human user enters commands ended with a <return> character. The application task reads in keyboard input and issues a TCP service call. The TCP realizes it is a push and therefore passes the data segment to IP.

The RST (Reset) bit is used to reset a port connection or reject to a connect request.

The SYN (Synchronize) bit is set in the first segment with the ACK bit reset to 0. This is equivalent to a Connect Request to ask the receiving T layer to synchronize its sequence numbers. After receiving a SYN request packet, the destination T layer may return a segment with the SYN bit set to accept or the RST bit set to reject.

The FIN (Finish) bit is the End Of Transmission flag of the current transmission block.

The right 16-bit field in the fourth word denotes the window size in bytes. The maximum window size is 64 KB. If the receiving T layer cannot empty its buffer in time, it may send a window size equal to the unfilled portion in its buffer. A window size 0 tells the sending T layer to hold transmission of new packets temporarily.

Recall that the Longitudinal Redundancy Check (LRC) in an IP header guards only the IP header. In the TCP header, the left 16-bit segment in the fifth word is a checksum and the right 16-bit segment is an urgent pointer. The checksum uses even-parity LRC to guard not only the entire TCP segment but also a pseudo IP header on top containing the extracted information from its real IP header, as shown in Figure 7.25. The pseudo header contains three 32-bit words. The first word contains the source IP address; the second word contains the destination IP address; and the third word contains 1 byte of 0's, a TCP protocol id 06 in hex, and a 2-byte total length computed as the sum of the length of the TCP header and the length of its data segment. One advantage of using LRC is its simplicity. Another advantage is that LRC is position-independent and can be placed anywhere in the segment. Because the LRC in the T layer header also guards the N layer control information, this particular design feature is against the basic principle of layering and encapsulation as stressed in the OSI reference model.

The urgent pointer becomes meaningful only when the URG bit is set in the TCP header. When this happens, it means that urgent data is included in the segment and the urgent pointer points to the last octet of the urgent data block.

In the sixth word, bits 31–0 specify the options with possible padding, which is only used during a connection setup. In other words, the SYN bit is set in the TCP segment. At the present time, the only option is MSS (Maximum Segment Size) in bytes. A data segment is variable in size and the MSS usually implies the buffer size of the receiving T layer, which is negotiable. If this option is chosen, the left 2-byte field is a selector and the right 2-byte field specifies a

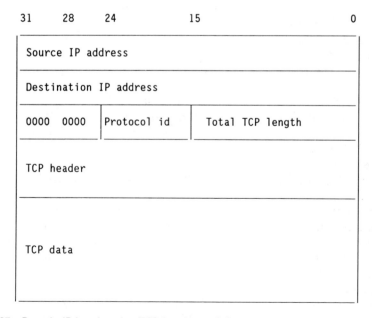

Figure 7.25 Pseudo IP header plus TCP header and data.

MSS up to 64 KB. Normally, a TCP data segment has a Hlen of 5 words or 20 bytes. The IP header is also 20 bytes long. Therefore, in the case that no MSS option is specified, the default maximum segment size in bytes is 536 (576 − 20 − 20), which means a total of 576 bytes are allowed in a transmission unit and the length of the TCP header or IP header is 20 bytes each. TCP also keeps a private database that is very similar to the Transport Control Block. Each control block is associated with a port connection and the basic information is supplied by the application programmer.

Transmission Control Block

There are over 50 parameters in a Transmission Control Block, which is the private data structure used by TCP. To get a flavor, some of the important items are listed below:

- Local IP address;
- Local port id;
- Protocol id, such as TCP and UDP;
- Remote IP address;
- Remote port id;
- Send buffer size;
- Receive buffer size;
- Current TCP state;
- Round-trip normal time;
- Time-out value;
- Number of retransmissions that have been tried;
- Window size;
- Leading and trailing edges of the sending window;
- Maximum sending segment size;
- Leading and trailing edges of the receiving window;
- Maximum receiving segment size;
- Enable/Disable Tracing flag.

7.8.2 User Datagram Protocol

In the TCP/IP suite, there is also the user datagram protocol (UDP) at the transport layer level. UDP provides the basic services by passing datagrams directly to the IP for delivery. In contrast to TCP, UDP does not handle error recovery (neither does IP). As a result of this, packets may get lost in the network for two possible reasons: the memory buffer space is limited, or lightning has taken place during transmission. Needless to say, reliable delivery service is not guaranteed by UDP.

The UDP header is simpler, as shown in Figure 7.26. The left 16-bit segment in the first word is the optional source port id. When this field is used, it provides

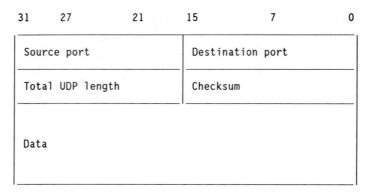

Figure 7.26 Unit datagram protocol header and data.

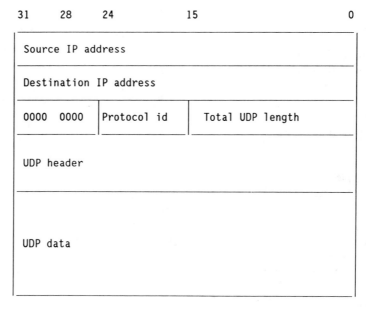

Figure 7.27 Pseudo IP header plus UDP header and data.

the return address for any reply message from the system or destination. The right 16-bit segment denotes a destination port id. In the second word, the left 16-bit segment is the total length of UDP in octets, which includes both the Header and Data fields. The right 16-bit segment is an optional checksum, using odd parity LRC. If no checksum is used, this field contains 0.

When computing the UDP checksum, the T layer assumes that the datagram is preceded by a pseudo IP header as shown in Figure 7.27. Just like TCP, the pseudo header contains information fetched from the real IP header. The UDP checksum guards the pseudo header, the UDP header, and the datagram. In the pseudo header, the first word contains the source IP address and the second word is the destination IP address. The third word contains 1 byte of 0's, a UDP protocol id 11 in hex, and the total UDP length, the same as the one coded in the UDP header.

7.9 CONCLUSIONS

The T layer design is similar to DL in that the T layer drives a VC or datagram just like a DL drives a physical link. The same sliding window protocol concept can be applied. Each computer is represented by a node id—a combination of a Network id, a Region id, a Branch id, and a CPU id. Node ids are used to establish a connection between two end nodes or NSAPs. A transport connection is built on top of a VC or datagram.

The connection phase at either the transport or network level is asymmetrical. However, after the connection is established, it becomes symmetrical. Either service user above the T layer can transmit and receive data packets via a port call while the T layer issues a VC or datagram call to deliver the packets.

In a computer network, permanent ports, VCs, and DLs are valuable resources of the system. They may be shared by different service users. To make a port connection, the T layer service user at either end may allocate or open a permanent port. To disconnect, either side may issue a deallocate or close.

7.10 SUMMARY POINTS

1. The T layer handles transport connection, segmentation/reassembly, upward/downward multiplexing, and error/flow control.
2. The T layer uses SWP to drive a VC or datagram.
3. The finite state machine model can be used to construct a transport sender or receiver.
4. The optimal window size of the T layer is the number of hops between the origination node and the destination node.
5. Using pacing technique, the window size can be reduced or increased during packet transmission.
6. The T layer primitives are used to send messages between a T layer and its service user.
7. The transport protocol data units are the packets sent from one T layer to its peer.
8. The Transport Control Block is a private database used by the T layer for each individual port.

9. In a VC model, the T layer must establish a VC connection first before it can establish a port connection on top of the VC between two T layers.
10. A good T layer can reassign an alternate VC if the current VC fails.
11. In a datagram model, the T layer also needs to establish a port connection on top of the datagram in a multiprogramming environment.
12. Permanent ports are classified as system resources.
13. The OSI transport protocol suite supports five classes; TP0 is the simplest one while TP4 is the most rigorous one.
14. Fletcher checksum is the error-detecting code used in the OSI TP4 header.
15. On Internet, TCP provides reliable services while UDP provides unreliable services.
16. The T layer design is very similar to DL layer design.
17. The T layer must be reliable if the bottom layers are not.

Problems

Problem 7.1

What are the major functions performed by the T layer?

Problem.7 2

Using pipelined transmission, what is the ideal window size if memory space is not a problem?

Problem 7.3

If the VC below a port fails, does that mean that computer communications must terminate? If not, how can the T layer recover errors?

Problem 7.4

Name five T layer primitives?

Problem 7.5

What is the difference between a T layer primitive and a transport protocol data unit? Can you name one primitive that is not mapped into a protocol data unit?

Problem 7.6

What is contained in a Transport Control Block?

Problem 7.7

Describe why permanent ports are valuable resources in the system.

Problem 7.8

Describe the CDT (Credit) field in an OSI TPDU header.

Problem 7.9

Given a 7-byte header that contains 5 integers followed by two bytes of 0's as shown below

```
|---------|
|    1    |
|---------|
|    2    |
|---------|
|    3    |
|---------|
|    4    |
|---------|
|    5    |
|---------|
|    0    |
|---------|
|    0    |
|---------|
```

compute the Fletcher checksum to replace the last two 0's in the header. What is the checksum code in binary? Verify your answer using mod 255 arithmetic.

Problem 7.10

Give your critique about the Fletcher checksum used in the OSI TP4 header.

Problem 7.11

Describe the 6-bit opcode in a TCP header.

Problem 7.12

Describe the main difference between TCP and UDP.

References

[1] Doeringer, W., et al., "A Survey of Light-Weight Transport Protocols for High-Speed Networks," *IEEE Trans. on Communications*, Nov. 1990, pp. 2025–2039.

[2] Comer, D. E., and D. L. Stevens, *Internetworking with TCP/IP*, Vol. II, Design, Implementation and Internals, Prentice-Hall, 1991.

[3] Feit, S., *TCP-IP, Architecture. Protocols, and Implementation*, McGraw-Hill, Inc., 1993.

[4] Fletcher, J. G., "An Arithmetic Checksum for Serial Transmissions," *IEEE Trans. on Communications*, Vol. 30, No.1, Jan. 1982, pp. 247–251.

Session Layer   8

The purpose of life is to improve the life of others.

The T layer services are not easy to comprehend. Therefore, it is necessary to design a programming interface between the application task and the T layer. For this reason, the S layer should be as simple as possible. The primary goal is to achieve programming convenience and avoid complexity. The S layer has its own SPDUs and may be designed as a system interface for the T layer.

The term "session" was coined by IBM and if a port is permanent, it is called a half-session [SNAa]. Each user or application task allocates a half-session, and two half-sessions make a full session as shown in Figure 8.1. Since a user task only deals with the session interface, a lot of details of the lower layers can be hidden. The two tasks communicate with each other via system calls. That is, the two user tasks may establish a session, transmit/receive data, and then disconnect. In that regard, a session also implies all of the activities between two application programs. Examples are file transfers, transaction processing, e-mail, remote login, talk, and so forth. Any two programs may start a session after a Connect Request is successfully completed. Then, either task can transmit data to the remote task. The S layer also handles synchronization in that both tasks must agree on the current progress point before proceeding to the next one.

8.1 BASIC DESIGN CONCEPTS

We will discuss the general concepts of session primitives in the following, which can be applied to any system design.

8.1.1 Connection/Disconnection

Session connection means that an application task wants to establish a session with another task on a remote node. The origination task must issue a Connect

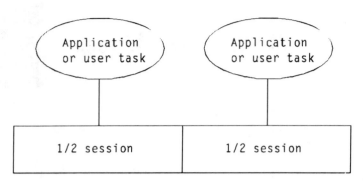

Figure 8.1 Session interface.

Call, which is translated into a transport Connect Request to its T layer. One program may have several sessions at the same time. In other words, the main task may receive many Connect Requests, spin off many descendant tasks as required, and let each descendant task manage its own session. For example, a file transfer server may establish many port connections, and each port is connected to a particular client that can transfer files between two computers. Therefore, it is possible for a file server to support several file transfers at the same time.

After the session, a Disconnect Request is in order so the two tasks may terminate their executions.

8.1.2 Data Transfer Phase

Session connect implies a port connect that is asymmetrical. However, after a session is established between two tasks, the data transfer phase is symmetrical, which means either side can send and receive messages. Most programming applications are half-duplex in nature; namely, the origination task sends out a message and the destination task receives it. Then, the destination task sends out a message and the origination task receives it. The role to send and receive messages alternates until the program ends. The term *message* has a general meaning that could be a Request command, a Confirm, or just data.

It is also possible for a sender to send a message out and wait for an immediate reply. In such a case, the Send and Receive calls are combined into one, but inside there are still two system calls.

8.1.3 Synchronization

The S layer provides two types of synchronization: implicit and explicit. Implicit synchronization means that after a task executes to a certain point, it must wait for the remote task to reach a certain point. As an example, the origination task issues a session Connect Request and the destination task on a remote node issues a Receive Connect. The rendezvous should be performed in the Receive Connect routine on the destination node. In other words, the Connect routine cannot proceed without receiving the T_CONNECT.confirm and the Receive Connect routine cannot proceed without receiving a T_CONNECT.indication.

Another implicit synchronization example is when one task issues a Receive but the data have not arrived yet. What should the task do? Two options are available. The commonly used option is Receive_and_Wait, which means that the task cannot proceed until its data have arrived or timed-out. The second option is Receive_and_Immediate, which means that the task returns immediately with the Status flag indicating what has happened, and the user is responsible for checking whether the data have been received.

A third implicit synchronization example is after issuing a Send Data request, should the user task wait? In real-time systems, the sender need not wait as long as the NOS can empty its buffer.

Explicit synchronization means that any user task can issue a Synchronization point (Syncpt) under programming control. Both tasks may exchange information about the status of progress. If everything runs smoothly, then both sides proceed. Otherwise, both sides should roll back to a previous Syncpt, that means to Resync (Resynchronize). The S layer prepares the Syncpt and Resync messages, but the user tasks must take actions to ensure that all the protected resources are kept intact.

8.2 SESSION PRIMITIVES

The session primitives are used by application programmers. They are usually system calls. Each call is mapped into a T layer request primitive because the session interface interacts with the T layer. The logical flow in a session includes connect, data transfer, and disconnect, as shown in Figure 8.2. The tail end of the arrow identifies the task that has issued this primitive independent of the direction of data flow.

The session connect primitives are similar to the T layer connect primitives except the number is cut to half because the session connect on the origination node not only issues a T_CONNECT.request but also waits for a T_CONNECT.confirm. By the same token, the receive session connect on the destination node handles both T_CONNECT.indication and T_CONNECT.response. The session Connect Request is issued by the origination task as specified below:

```
Connect( task_id@destination_node_id, port_id,
         QOS, status, etc);
         ↑
         DL protocol;
         Priority/performance;
```

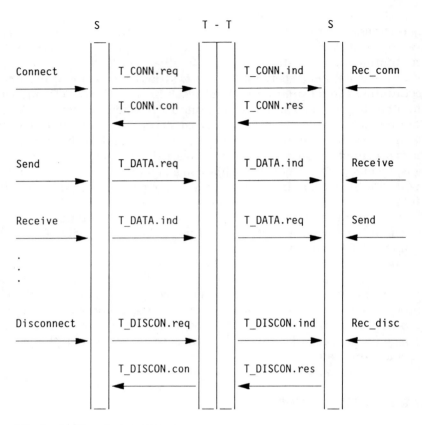

Figure 8.2 Logical flow in a session.

        Encryption/decryption;
        Compression/decompression;
        Data conversion.

where task_id is the destination program name; port_id will be determined by the S layer after connection is made; QOS specifies the quality of services; and status indicates what happened after the call. In some systems, QOS may include parameters such as DL protocol type, data rate, priority, reliability, security, and other performance specifications. A password may be entered by the user or the console operator.

    The destination task issues a Receive Connect as follows:

    Rec_connect(task_id@origination_node_id, port_id,
            QOS, status, etc);

where task_id is the origination program name plus its user_id, port_id is a loca reference number, status indicates what happened after the call, and etc denotes other parameters. Since both sides may exchange information during the negotiation phase, QOS indicates the returned agreement, which is final. Note that a wildcard 0 may be used for the task_id and the origination_node_id in that any task on any node can make a Connect Request. After the connection, task_id will contain the requesting task id and the origination_node_id will contain its node address.

The primitives for data transfer are intuitive. One side issues a Send while the remote side issues a Receive. If acknowledgment is desired, the Confirm message or subcommand is treated as data that is also transmitted via a Send and the receiving end must issue a Receive primitive to match. Needless to say, all messages must be sent via Send primitives. If both sides issue a Receive at the same time without a time-out (TO) escape, then we have a deadlock. Send and Receive primitives are listed below.

Send(port_id, message, status);
Receive(port_id, message, status);

where port_id denotes the programming port, message represents the address of a message buffer, and status indicates what happened after the call. Assume that the message has a header from which the size of message can be fetched. The Data field of the message may be a structure of any bit pattern, any size.

Occasionally, it is necessary to send an escape sequence or control code from one task to another. This is considered as the out-band data. Therefore, a special data service should be provided as shown below:

Express(port_id, message, status);

This is very much like sending mail through Federal Express and the T layer maps this call into a T_EXPEDITED_DATA primitive. Note that during a session, both tasks may transmit and receive data messages at the same time. In the end, both tasks should disconnect before the session ends. In other words, one task issues a Disconnect and the other side issues a Rec_disconnect to quit session. Disconnect and Rec_disconnect primitives are listed below:

Disconnect(port_id, status);
Rec_disconnect(port_id, status);

If permanent ports are supported by the system, each task may issue an Allocate command before a session starts. After the session, each side issues a Deallocate to release or free the port. The Allocate and Deallocate primitives are shown below:

Allocate(port_id, status);
Deallocate(port_id, status);

If the Allocate routine simply allocates port, then the two sides are symmetrical. If the two sides also exchange negotiation messages back and forth during Allocate, then the origination side issues Allocate and the destination side should issue Rec_allocate (Receive Allocate). The Allocate routine transmits a negotiation message to its peer via a T_DATA.request. Then, the Rec_allocate routine in the destination S layer transmits a reply message to its peer, also via a T_DATA.request. A negotiation phase takes place between two sides. In some systems, Open/Close are used in lieu of Allocate/Deallocate.

In order to achieve synchronization explicitly, the two user tasks need to exchange information about the program status from time to time. This could just be application subcommands. If the S layer provides the primitives for explicit synchronization, the readability of program listing would be improved.

Minor Syncpt Versus Major Syncpt

There are two types of Syncpt: minor and major. A major Syncpt is a system checkpoint that contains the running environment of the user task. Taking and restarting from a major Syncpt are the capabilities of a mainframe operating system. A minor Syncpt is just a save point that contains the log of data messages on a reliable disk. If the Syncpt option is specified during the connection phase, the S layer starts to save the transaction log. Later, if anything goes wrong, either task may request to Resync from a previous minor Syncpt. The user program must contain routines to undo all the transactions and restore itself to a previous Syncpt. We will confine our discussion to using minor Syncpt only. Both Syncpt and Resync are similar to send and the remote side issues a Rec_Syncpt (receive Syncpt) to match. Their formats are proposed in the following:

Syncpt(port_id, serial_number, status);
Resync(port_id, serial_number, status);
Rec_Syncpt(port_id, message, status).

The serial_number parameter is used to identify a Syncpt and the status parameter indicates what has happened after the call. Note that Rec_Syncpt may receive a message, either Syncpt or Resync. Both tasks must synchronize at the same Syncpt before they can proceed. If everything runs smoothly, the client task takes a Syncpt to commit work and its peer takes a Syncpt to commit transaction. If there is an error, both sides must exchange a Resync message and agree to a previous Syncpt. That is, both user tasks must undo whatever necessary in the transaction log.

Let us try one example. Assume that a client makes a deposit into his account. At the local bank, the client task transmits all the transaction parameters to its central bank. There is a server task running on the remote computer that updates all the customer accounts online. Each side performs its own activities. After the client has transmitted a transaction request, received a reply and performed its local update, it initiates a Syncpt request. Now, two cases may happen. The first case is that if the remote server has no errors, it sends a Syncpt confirm as shown in Figure 8.3(a). After that, both sides proceed beyond the current Syncpt. The second case is that if the server has encountered an error due to a temporary problem of disk or printer, the server issues a Resync request instead of a Syncpt confirm, as shown in Figure 8.3(b). After receiving the Resync request, the client returns a Resync confirm so that both sides will attempt to restart from a previous Syncpt on disk.

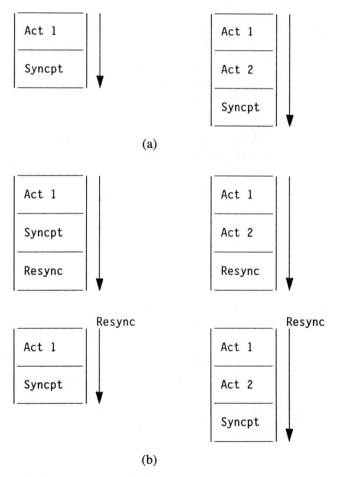

Figure 8.3 Syncpt and Resync: (a) Syncpt agreed and (b) Syncpt disagreed and Resync.

8.3 SESSION SOFTWARE DESIGN

The S layer comprises many system calls. Each session routine performs a particular function. Each routine is executed on behalf of the issuing task, therefore it does not have its own task control block (TCB). Each routine may have its private addressing space for storing the T layer messages.

8.3.1 Connect and Rec_connect

After the origination task issues a Connect, the logic flow is shown below:

>   DO;
>   Assign a port_id for the origination task based on the rule that the sending party always determines the local reference number;
>   Issue a T_CONNECT.request while the origination task_id is coded in t_sdu;
>   Wait for the arrival of a T_CONNECT.confirm or time-out;
>   　　　{The origination task is now blocked. After being woken up,
>   　　　processing continues.
>   　　　}
>   Set status to OK, not OK, or time-out
>   　　　{If no T_CONNECT.confirm is received within a
>   　　　specified time interval, then time-out.
>   　　　}
>   　IF status is OK,
>   　THEN bind the origination port_id with its task_id;
>   　　　{No other user task can use this port_id.
>   　　　}
>   　ENDIF;
>   Exit;
>   ENDDO;

The destination task must issue a Rec_connect in order to perform the rendezvous as described below:

>   DO;
>   Wait for the arrival of a T_CONNECT.indication or time-out;
>   　　　{If there is no T_CONNECT.indication message in the
>   　　　queue,
>   　　　then the issuing task is blocked until the arrival of
>   　　　a T_CONNECT.indication or time-out;
>   　　　else processing continues.
>   　　　}
>   Set status to OK, not OK, or time-out;
>   Issue a T_CONNECT.response with the negotiated QOS;

```
        IF status is OK,
        THEN bind the destination port_id and its task_id;
                {If status is OK, we have accomplished a successful
                rendezvous and no other user task can use this port_id.
                }
    ENDIF;
Exit;
ENDDO;
```

8.3.2 Send and Receive

After a session is established, the two sides become symmetrical and either side may issue a Send primitive as described below:

```
DO;
Issue a T_DATA.request;
Set status;
Exit;
ENDDO;
```

If the expedited data service is provided by the system, we may implement an Express call, which will be translated into a T_EXPEDITED_DATA.request. Or, we can introduce a special flag in the Send call to indicate that it is expedited data. To avoid any abuse of using the EXPEDITED_DATA call, its message size should be limited to a few characters or a hefty cost is imposed on the user.

After one task issues a Send or Express, the remote task must issue a Receive. Receive really means Receive_and_Wait, as described in the following:

```
DO;
Wait for the arrival of a T_DATA.indication or time-out;
         {If there is no T_DATA.indication in the message queue,
         then the issuing task is blocked until the arrival of
         a T_DATA.indication or time-out;
         else processing continues without waiting.
         }
Set status;
Exit;
ENDDO;
```

Any good session must come to an end. How do the two tasks know it is time to quit? The answer is simple. The origination task sends a message to indicate "quit." After receiving the message, the receiving task interprets and knows it is time to quit.

8.3.3 Disconnect And Rec_disconnect

At the end of data transfer, the origination task sends a quit message to its peer task to signal termination. Both tasks then take appropriate actions to terminate the session. The origination task issues the Disconnect primitive as described below:

>   DO;
>   Issue a T_DISCONNECT.request.
>   Wait for the arrival of a T_DISCONNECT.confirm or time-out.
>   {The issuing task is blocked until the arrival of a
>   T_DISCONNECT.confirm or time-out, then the issuing task
>   is woken up, and processing continues.
>   }
>   Free the memory space allocated to the task;
>   Set status;
>   Exit;
>   ENDDO;

The destination task should issue a Rec_disconnect as follows:

>   DO;
>   Wait for a T_DISCONNECT.indication or time-out;
>   {If there is no T_DISCONNECT.indication in the message
>   queue of the session,
>   then the issuing task is blocked until the arrival of
>   a T_DISCONNECT.indication or time-out;
>   else processing continues without waiting.
>   }
>   Issue a T_DISCONNECT.response;
>   Free the memory space allocated to the task;
>   Set status;
>   Exit;
>   ENDDO;

In some systems, if the origination task does not care about receiving a T_DISCONNECT.confirm, then the destination task may also issue a Disconnect. In other words, no handshaking is performed to disconnect a session.

8.3.4 Allocate And Deallocate

When permanent ports are supported by the system, Allocate and Deallocate are used in lieu of session Connect/Rec_connect and Disconnect/Rec_disconnect. Because negotiation may or may not be required between two S layers, the two

Allocate routines on two nodes may be different. The Deallocate routines are pretty much the same regardless of the design.

Without Negotiation

If no negotiation is required, the Allocate routines in each side of the two S layers are identical. In other words, there is no information exchange between the two S layers and the routine simply assign a port to the service user and no other task in the system can use this port. After Allocate, either service user can transmit a message to its peer via a port call. In the end, either side issues a Deallocate to free the port and terminate the session.

With Negotiation

If a negotiation phase is required by the S layer, the Allocate routine in the origination S layer is different from the one in the destination S layer. This distinction has already been recorded in the TCB after port connection. The origination Allocate sends a negotiation message and the destination Allocate receives the message. Then, it returns a reply to negotiate with its peer. Note that both sides transmit the message via a T_DATA.request (i.e., port call). The negotiation messages are received, interpreted, and executed by the Allocate routines. The code section to perform handshaking is different in that one side sends and the other side receives. Both user tasks must issue an Allocate before the session starts. After the session, both tasks issue a Deallocate to free the port.

During the negotiation phase, if the Syncpt option is specified, then the S layer starts to take the first Syncpt or force transaction logging.

8.3.5 Syncpt And Resync

A minor Syncpt represents a copy of the transaction log stored on a reliable disk. In some applications, a user task may wish to recover from any system failures from a previous Syncpt provided that the disk containing the Syncpt is not crashed. After a service user issues a Syncpt or Resync, its peer must issue a Rec_Syncpt to match. To Syncpt or Resync really depends on the processing status of each task, and an error at either side should trigger a Resync. We will discuss the design of a client task using minor Syncpts in the following:

```
DO;
   IF everything OK,
   THEN issue Syncpt request;
   ELSE issue Resync request; ENDIF;
   Rec_Syncpt;     {Wait for the arrival of a message.}
```

```
CASE message of,
Syncpt confirm: Continue;
Resync request:  Issue Resync confirm;
                 Undo everything to the previous Syncpt and restart;
ENDCASE;
ENDDO;
```

The server task has the following logic:

```
DO;
Rec_Syncpt;
  CASE message of
  Syncpt request:
    CASE processing_status of
    No error:  Issue Syncpt confirm;
    Error:  Issue Resync request;
            Issue Rec_Syncpt;
            CASE message of
            Resync confirm:
                Undo everything to the previous Syncpt
                and restart;ENDCASE;
    ENDCASE;
  Resync request:
      Issue Resync confirm;
      Undo everything to the previous Syncpt and restart;
  ENDCASE;
ENDDO;
```

Note that the above design implements a two-way protocol. If the two tasks cannot agree on the Syncpt number, then program execution should be aborted. Figure 8.4 depicts the logic flow of a program that has three Syncpts—1, 2, and 3—during the entire transaction processing. Each Syncpt pair verifies a progress point. After the origination task sends a Syncpt 3 request, the destination task has encountered an error so it returns a Resync request and expects a Resync confirm. Then, both tasks undo things to Syncpt 2 and restart. After that, things run smoothly beyond Syncpt 3 to the end and the program terminates.

Each Syncpt or Resync message is a SPDU, transmitted via a T_DATA.request and received via a T_DATA.indication. The Syncpt and Resync messages have different opcodes in the session header but a request or confirm of the same type should have an identical opcode. Note that a Resync need not be sent at all provided that all of the problems can be resolved locally.

Session Layer 395

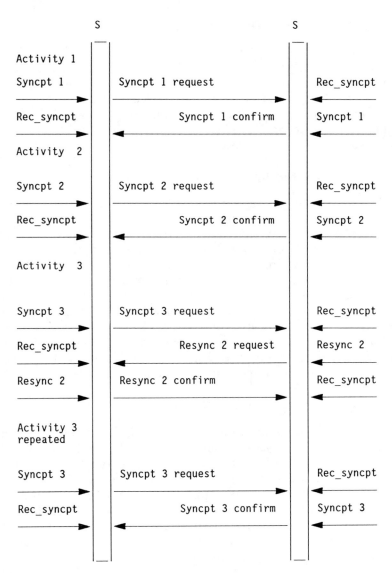

Figure 8.4 Logical flow using Syncpt and Resync.

8.4 NETWORK APPLICATION SOFTWARE DESIGN

Session primitives are used to write network applications. Due to the fact that the session connection phase is asymmetrical, one user task issues a request and its peer must receive the incoming request. This resembles shopping in our daily life. A client must go to the counter first and ask a clerk about the merchandise. The clerk or server is always waiting for an incoming request. This client-server paradigm is used in network programming. Every time the client task initiates a Connect Request, the server task listens and receives the incoming request.

8.4.1 Client-Server Model

In network programming, the client and server are two user tasks running on two different computers. They are application programs for providing special network services. Assume that a PC wants to communicate with another PC. First, a hardware connection must exist between the two computers. If the distance is far, modems are needed to drive the phone line. Secondly, network I/O system software must be in place to provide the necessary tools. Between two computers connected with a direct phone line and assuming each computer supports only one user, a data link layer should be adequate for writing simple network applications such as a two-party games, chat, file transfer, and so forth.

If the server interacts with many clients on different computers, not only do we need to implement the network and transport layers, but also require the OS on the server node to support multitasking.

8.4.2 File Transfer Server With Multiclients

In theory, one server task may communicate with one client. There are cases where the server task may want to communicate with several clients at the same time. For example, a file server may wish to transfer one file to one client and another file to another client at the same time. In other words, after receiving a Connect Request, the file server may spin off a descendant task. Assume that the system is case-insensitive. The server is named FtServer (file transfer server) and the client is named Ft. Both FtServer and Ft are program or task ids and they are also network application commands. A user may enter a command via the keyboard to execute the Ft client program as follows:

    Ft node_id

Any subcommands entered via the keyboard, such as get, put, quit, and so forth are interpreted by the client task, Ft, which is designed as follows:

    Ft: {The Ft client task.}
    . . .
    Connect('FtServer'@node_id, port_id, , status);

```
CASE status of
OK - display message 'Connection completed!';
Not OK or time-out - display error message;
ENDCASE;
Display the Ft prompt on screen to request a subcommand from the user;
Read subcommand;
CASE subcommand of
Get - Send( port_id, header,);
            {'Header' contains information, such as opcode,
            filename, attributes, etc.
            }
    Open filename;
ReceiveLoop:
        Receive( port_id, record,);
        Write record into file;
        IF record is not End-Of-File marker,
        THEN Goto ReceiveLoop;
        ELSE close filename; ENDIF;
Put - . . .
. . .
Quit - Disconnect( port_id);
ENDCASE;
Detach;
Endtask;
End.
```

The FtServer task executes on the remote computer, which listens to the line all the time. After receiving an incoming request, it spins off a descendant task that communicates with the particular client. The logic flow is described in the following:

```
FtServer:
    . . .
    REPEAT
            {The FtServer main task is an infinite loop
            which listens to the incoming request all the
            time. Only a <ctl>-c command from the console
            can terminate this program.
            }
    Rec_connect(task_id@node_id, port_id, , status);
    . . . {Listen to the line.}
      IF status is OK,
      THEN
      Attach( task_id, Ft_task, address_space, port_id,);
            {Spin off the descendant task.}
      ENDIF;
```

```
        UNTIL forever;
        Endtask;

        Ft_task:    {This is the descendent task which is
                    reentrant.}
        . . .
        REPEAT
        Receive( port_id, header, status);
        CASE header of
        Get - Open filename;
            REPEAT
            Read record;
            Send( port_id, record,);
                    {Assume that no handshaking is performed
                    at the application layer level, otherwise
                    a Receive call is in order.
                    }
            UNTIL record contains the End-Of-File marker;
            Close filename;
        Put - . . .
        . . .
        Quit - Rec_disconnect( port id, status);
                Detach; {Terminate this descendant task.
                }
            ENDCASE;
        UNTIL forever;
        Endtask;
        End.
```

If the file server runs on a multiprogramming system as a system task, it may have a name like sys.FtServer, where the prefix indicates that it belongs to the system. Every client task must know this task id before it can make a session connection.

8.4.3 Group Talk Program

In computer communications, several PC users may want to hold a group talk (Gtalk) session on the network. Each user can talk and listen to other users at the same time. A virtual star model is proposed in Figure 8.5. The Gtalk program consists of a server and several clients running on a virtual star. That is, the server runs on the virtual central node, which can communicate with each client through a direct or indirect connection. The server mainly receives data messages from clients and dispatches each message to all of the clients.

To simplify the design, assume that four users are ready to enter the Gtalk command at the console. As a result, the client program executes, makes a connection to the central server, and then spins off two descendant tasks: one to read the line and the other one to write the line. After that, the main client

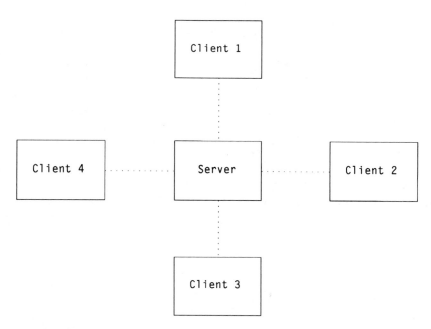

Figure 8.5 Virtual star model.

task enters a loop to read the keyboard. Each time after reading a message from the keyboard, it passes the string to the write task, which in turn transmits the message to the server. On the other hand, after receiving a message from the server, the read task displays it on the screen. Therefore, the client task is comprised of three tasks: one to read the keyboard, the second to read the line, and the third to write the line that refers to the server on the central node.

The server design is more complicated. After receiving a session Connect Request, it spins off a read task to receive messages from this particular client. After all of the clients are connected, the server task enters the transmit loop to wait for a message from any of its read tasks. Each time after receiving a message from its read task, the server transmits it to all of the clients, including the incoming one. This design is feasible, because the Send primitive does not wait for reply and the server can send the message to all of the clients, one by one, sequentially. The details are left as an exercise.

8.5 TCP/IP SESSION

TCP/IP provides three types of network services, as shown in Figure 8.6. They are known as the socket programming interfaces [1–3]. A socket means a port.

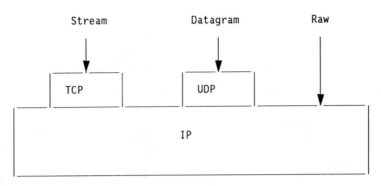

Figure 8.6 Socket programming interface.

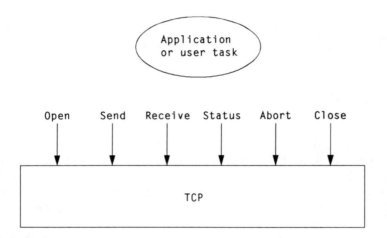

Figure 8.7 TCP session services.

TCP handles streamed data communications, UDP provides datagram services that are not reliable, and IP handles raw datagrams directly. TCP, UDP, and IP are service providers while the application program on top is the service user. TCP requires a session connection phase while UDP does not. The raw data services are primitive but still datagram-oriented; they are designed for those who are interested in developing new protocols.

Before getting into the details of socket programming, let us examine the basic services specified as the TCP standard in Figure 8.7. In TCP, a session connection must be established before data transfer can begin.

8.5.1 TCP Session Services

We first address the TCP services from a functional point of view. Only six services are proposed. Each service is a session command that executes as a function, and a return code is obtained after the call.

Open and Close

Three types of Open commands are available to the user. One type is the Active Open, which is used by a client to initiate a Connect Request. The other two are passive Opens that enable a server to receive incoming Connect Requests. What is the difference between the two passive ones? One of them allows a server to receive an incoming request from any client; it is known as Unspecified Passive Open. The other allows a server only to receive from one particular client; it is known as Specified Open. As in any one of the three Open calls, the system returns a local connection id or socket descriptor. The socket descriptor is a small integer from which the TCB of the port can be accessed.

The Close command is the counterpart of an Open command, which closes a session and releases its data structures.

Send and Receive

The Send command moves data from the application task to the TCP and the Receive command does the same in the opposite direction. To denote an expedited data transfer, an Urgent flag can be coded in the Send command. A Push flag also can be coded to indicate that data needs to be transmitted right away.

Status and Abort

The Status command gets the information about a session connection as listed below:

- Local and remote socket addresses;
- Local connection id;
- Receiving window;
- Sending window;
- Connection state;
- Number of buffers awaiting acknowledgment;
- Number of buffers pending receipt;
- Security information;
- Time-out information.

The Abort command discards all data currently in the sending and receiving buffers and aborts the ongoing session immediately.

All TCP commands are high level and the logical flow is shown in Figure 8.8. Note its similarity to Figure 8.2. The dotted line indicates a return code or actual data flow. Each command actually consists of one or more UNIX system calls. The routine name starts with a lowercase letter and parameters are enclosed in parentheses during the call.

8.5.2 UNIX Network System Calls

For network applications, a server listens to the line and will try to make a connection whenever an incoming Connect Request arrives. In most of the cases, the server task creates a descendant task whose function is to communicate with a particular client. Since the incoming requests may arrive faster than the server can handle them, a queue is formed in the server session. Clients who cannot be served immediately must wait in the queue for their turn. If the queue is full and another client request arrives, then the new client request must be discarded. We need to understand all the system calls that perform the network I/O operations. In addition, we need to know how to create a descendant task.

A socket call is issued to allocate a private database for the socket, as shown below:

   socket(domain, type, protocol);

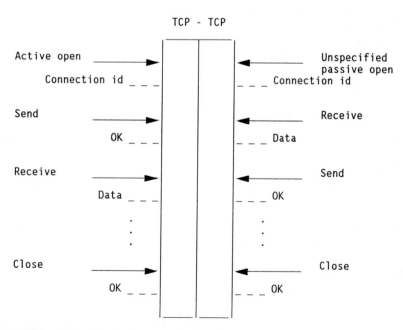

Figure 8.8 TCP session flow between a client and a server.

where domain is an integer of 1 or 2, which specifies local UNIX or Internet, respectively; type is an integer of 1, 2, or 3 that specifies TCP, UDP, or raw IP socket, respectively; and protocol is an integer to identify any particular protocol. If the Protocol field is 0, which means unspecified, then system will select an appropriate protocol in the domain that supports the requested socket type. Some well-known protocol ids are listed below:

ICMP:	1	{Internet control message protocol}
TCP:	6	{Transmission control protocol}
UDP:	17	{User datagram protocol}

There is a special header file, sys/socket.h, that defines the absolute symbols or constants as follows:

```
/*domains*/
#define       AF_UNIX           1       /*UNIX domain, within the local
                                          host */
#define       AF_INET           2       /*Internet domain */
/*Standard socket types */
#define       SOCK_DGRAM        1       /*datagram */
#define       SOCK_STREAM       2       /*stream */
#define       SOCK_RAW          3       /*raw */
```

Absolute symbols can be used in a call to improve the readability of the program. Both the server and client must issue a socket call to establish the skeleton of a TCB, which is the private database associated with a sock or port connection, as discussed in Chapter 7. The call returns a small integer known as the socket descriptor (sd) or connection id from which the private database of the socket can be accessed. Subsequent calls are necessary to fill up all the Information fields in the TCB. As an example, a socket address is the combination of an IP address and a port number as shown below:

```
Socket address = IP address + Port number
```

A TCP connection really means a session or socket connection that is uniquely defined by a pair of socket addresses between two TSAPs. Therefore, a server must reveal its own socket address before any client can make a connection to it. A bind call mainly binds the IP address, an assigned port number, to the socket as shown below:

   bind(sd, &addr, addrlen);

where sd is the socket descriptor; &addr is a pointer to an address structure containing the IP address of the host, the assigned port number; and addrlen specifies the length of the entire address structure in bytes. The netinet/in.h header file declares the sock address structures as shown below:

```
struct sockaddr_in {
    short     sin_family;        /*domain */
    u_short   sin_port;          /*port number */
    struct    in_addr sin_addr;  /*Internet address of host */
    char      sin_zero[8];       /*unused */
```

where sin means socket for input, u_short sin_port declares an unsigned 16-bit port number of the server, the in_addr is another structure contained in this structure that specifies a local IP address, and sin_zero is a character array containing an 8-bit 0. If no port number is specified or the requested port number is not available, then the system will assign a new port number that is free at the time of binding. In some systems, the assigned port number is 1,024 or above [LINUX].

Note that in_addr is the name of another structure, defined below:

```
struct in_addr {
    u_long   s_addr;           /* 32-bit netid/hostid */
                               /* network byte ordered */
};
```

There is only one element in in_addr—a 32-bit unsigned integer named s_addr. The server may have been assigned two IP addresses, one for X.25 and the other one for Ethernet. The server may specify one IP address for the destination node or 0 to indicate that it can be connected through any Internet interface. The address of a 32-bit 0 is denoted by the special symbol, INADDR_ANY.

In practice, the server task must bind its IP address and a port number to the socket. In addition, the port number must be made known to all the clients; otherwise, no one can find the server. The bind call is for this purpose, which means assigning a port number and placing more information in the TCB of the socket. Some well-known port numbers are listed below:

```
FTP      21/tcp      {TCP uses port number 21 for FTP.}
rlogin   513/tcp     {TCP uses port number 513 for rlogin.}
mail     25/tcp      {TCP uses port number 25 for mail.}
```

Note that the client task need not issue a bind call because assigning a port number in advance has no meaning at all. After bind, the server issues a listen call that simply assigns a length to the message queue of the socket as shown below:

listen(sd, n);

where sd is the socket descriptor and *n* is the integer length or number of elements in the queue. It is interesting to note that the system does not wait in the listen routine, so an immediate return is expected just like socket and bind. Instead, waiting is placed in the accept routine below.

    accept(sd, &addr, addrlen);

where &addr points to an address structure specified for the client and addrlen denotes its length. Usually, both &addr and addrlen are specified as 0's, which means that it will accept a connection from any client. After Return, the parameters will contain the value-resulted information about the client's address. After Listen, the server must issue an Accept call to make a TCP connection. If there is no incoming Connect Request from a client, the server task is blocked by default, which means that it is put in wait state. However, if a nonblocking attribute is specified in the socket, Accept will return an error code instead of blocking. The Accept call mainly creates a new TCB for the client, puts the client's socket address and other information into the TCB, and returns a new socket descriptor. It must be stressed that the new descriptor can only be used by the server or its descendant task for communications and it cannot be used to accept another call.

It is clear now that a passive Open is constituted by executing the four system calls mentioned above. After having made a TCP connection, the server task may communicate with the client task directly or spin off a descendant task whose sole function is to communicate with the client. In such a design, the server task goes back to accepting another call.

The client task also needs a socket call to allocate the private database for its socket connection. Then, it puts the destination socket address in the socket and issues a Connect Request as follows:

    connect(sd, &addr, addrlen);

Two things happen after the call. First, the TCP at the client side issues an active Connect Request and waits for a Confirm. If the server task is waiting in the Accept routine, it wakes up and processing continues. After a connection is made, the TCP enters the server's socket address plus other control information into the client's socket. In other words, both the server and client sockets are defined in conjunction with the TCP connection. Even though it makes no sense at all, the client does have an option to issue a bind call before connect so a particular port number may be requested. If the requested port is available, the TCP will assign it to the requester. However, if no bind call is issued, the TCP will assign an unused port number to the client during the connection phase. After the Connect Request is successfully completed, the client's port number will be placed in the TCBs of the socket at both sides.

It is clear that an active Open is mapped into a socket call followed by a connect. After a socket or session connection is established, either side may issue a Send call to transmit a message as shown below:

    send(sd, message, sizeof(message), opt);

where sd is the socket descriptor, message is the address of the buffer, sizeof is a function that returns the length of the message, and opt specifies the option. Mostly, the opt field is 0, which means regular data. If opt is specified as SOF_OOB, which means out-of-band or expedited data, it will be delivered with the URG (Urgent) flag on. The receiving task must issue a recv call to match the remote Send as shown below:

    recv(sd, message, sizeof(message), opt);

where opt may be 0 or SOF_PREVIEW, which means that the message data is not removed from its buffer after the call. In other words, a later recv will return the same data previously previewed. Note that recv returns an integer that is the length of the message received.

In the case where the session is over or the socket is no longer in use, a Close call is issued with the socket descriptor passed as the lone parameter:

    close(sd);

Using sockets to communicate between two tasks is know as socket programming. The best way to understand the basic concept is to go through a programming example.

8.5.3 Socket Programming

The socket programming interface is provided by TCP, UDP, or IP. Therefore, one can write network applications using the set of tools or system calls [BSD4.3, SYSTEM V]. The TCP protocol requires a socket connection phase. On the other hand, UDP only provides unreliable datagram services, known as connectionless protocol; therefore, no socket connection is needed. In other words, the server need not issue Listen and Accept messages, and the client need not issue Connect messages. Raw IP services are even simpler and no bind call is necessary as used by other protocols. Understanding the TCP socket programming interface makes network programming easy. To alleviate the difficulty of coding, a set of header files are provided by the system [2, 4]. The files contain source code that may be included in any C program via the following statements:

```
#include <sys/types.h>
#include <sys/socket.h>
#include <stdio.h>
#include <netinet/in.h>
```

    #include <netdb.h>
    #include <errno.h>

Sys/types.h contains the data type definitions for a set of symbols that are used in the program to improve its readability. Sys/socket.h contains the definition of absolute symbols used as constants in the code. Stdio.h contains the definition of a file descriptor and must be included in any source program that uses any of the I/O routines in the standard library. Netinet/in.h contains various structure definitions of a network address, such as sockaddr_in, in_addr, and so forth. The netdb.h file contains various structure definitions used by the routines in the network library.

The logic flow of instructions between a server and a client is shown in Figure 8.9. The tail side of the arrow indicates which task issues the call and the dotted line indicates either a code is returned or the flow of actual data. To start with, both server and client issue a socket call to construct their own database. The server task needs to issue a bind call in order to acquire a port number, which is then made known to the client. The client task must issue a Connect Request while the server issues a Listen followed by an Accept. If connection is successful, the session begins and either side can transfer data messages to the other side. After the session, either side should issue a Close call to terminate the session.

If a server can spin off descendant tasks as deemed necessary and each descendant or child can communicate with a particular client, then we have a multitasking server, elaborated on in the next section.

8.5.4 Multitasking Server/Client Software Design

Multitasking is a capability of the OS running on the computer. In the UNIX environment, a process means a task. A system call that has no parameters is shown below:

    fork();

This can be executed in any program to create a descendant process running in parallel. The two tasks are shown in the following:

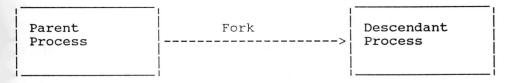

After fork, there will be two processes running asynchronously. The fork call

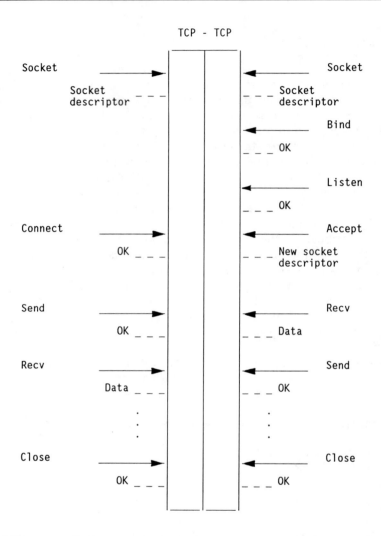

Figure 8.9 TCP system calls between a server and a client.

informs the OS that a descendant process needs to be created. Consequently, the system should do the following:

1. Duplicate the code section and data structure of the current program or process in the user's partition (i.e., memory).
2. Construct a process control block (PCB) for the newly created process, which is the descendant.
3. Copy the parent PCB into the descendant PCB.

4. Upon exit, system returns a special code for each of the two processes. The return code for the descendant process is always 0 and for the parent usually a positive integer that represents the process id of the child. A process id, -1, may be returned to indicate an error condition during task creation.

The important notion is that fork provides two returns (i.e., two exits to be precise). After fork, the return code is usually assigned to an integer variable. Testing the value of this integer, we know which process we are in. If the code is greater than 0, it is in the parent process, which also indicates that a descendant process has been successfully created, so the parent process proceeds. If the return code is 0, it is in the descendant process that usually calls a subroutine to do the work. However, if the return code is -1 in the parent process, then the parent should terminate because an error has occurred during task creation.

After receiving a TCP connection, the server task then issues a fork call. After that, the parent server goes back to accepting another incoming connect request while the descendant task calls a subroutine to handle the communications between itself and the client. One of the parameters is the new socket descriptor. Note that the same port number, 4040, is used by all of the descendants, as depicted in Figure 8.10. Clients 1 and 2 have already been connected and therefore client 1 has been assigned a local port number, 1200, and client 2, 1240. Client 3 is waiting in the queue to be connected next. The reasons why the same port number can be used by all of the descendants without confusion are given below:

1. The TCP header contains both the port numbers of the origination and destination tasks and the IP header contains both the IP addresses of the origination and destination nodes.
2. The destination task uses the same port number with the same IP address, but the socket address of each client is different. It is the combination of the IP addresses and port numbers of both sides that defines a unique socket connection.

It should help a great deal to understand the TCP/IP session interface if we go through the coding example of a multitasking server as shown in Figure 8.11. The C language is chosen for its popularity. The bzero routine fills 0's into the socket address of the server. The first parameter points to a structure while the second parameter is the sizeof function call, which returns the length of the structure. The htonl (Host to network long) routine converts an unsigned long integer from the host convention to the network long convention. If the host also stores the most significant byte in memory first as the leading byte, then there is nothing for htonl to do. However, in some computers, the least significant byte is the leading byte stored in memory first, so htonl will reverse the ordering of bytes in the address so as to conform with the network standard.

The client program with comments is shown in Figure 8.12. If there exist

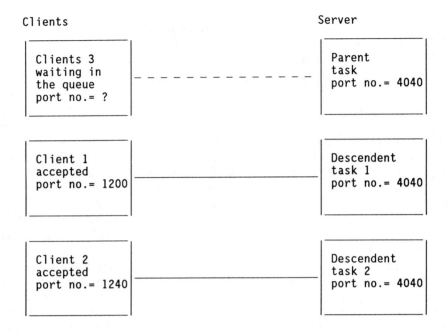

Figure 8.10 A multitasking server communicates with three clients.

Notes:
1. A dotted line indicates connection to be made.
2. A solid line indicates connection already made.
3. The symbol ? means not known yet.

several clients, all of them may execute an identical copy of the program on a different computer. In the program, the bcopy routine copies the IP address denoted by hp → h_addr into the socket address structure to identify the server. The third parameter specifies the length of the structure. The structure has a template name, hostent (host entry) as shown below:

```
struct hostent{
    char      *h_name;          /*official name of host */
    char      **h_aliases;      /*alias list */
    int       h_addrtype;       /*host address type: AF_UNIX or
                                  AF_INET */
    int       h_length:         /*length of address */
    char      *h_addr           /*address */
};
```

```
/* -----------------------------------------------------------
    Name:         John Y. Hsu
    Date:         1995-8-25
    Version:      1.0
    Description:

    This server.c program supports multitasking. After compiling
    and linking, we obtain the executable file named server. To
    run this program, type the following command followed by <cr>:

    server

    The server task makes a connection first, spins off a
    descendent task to receive messages from any client and
    echos on screen. If the message is q<cr>, the descendent
    task then terminates.
   ----------------------------------------------------------- */

#include <sys/types.h>
#include <sys/socket.h>
#include <stdio.h>
#include <netinet/in.h>
#include <netdb.h>
#include <errno.h>

main ()
            /* ----------------------------------------------
                sd:       socket descriptor for the server;
                nsd:      new socket descriptor for the
                          descendent task;
                length:   length of the structure;
                childpid: process id for the child task.
               ---------------------------------------------- */

{
int sd, nsd, length, childpid, do_the_work();
struct sockaddr_in servAddr;
            /* ----------------------------------------------
                (1)  Create a socket for the server task.
                (2)  Zero out the entire socket address structure.
                (3)  Specify the Internet family.
                (4)  Specify the IP address in the s_addr field
                     of the nested in_addr structure as from any
                     IP interface. The htonl routine converts
                     the address format from host to network
                     long and INADDR_ANY is defined in
                     sys/socket.h as 32-bit 0's.
                (5)  The port number requested is 4040.
               ---------------------------------------------- */

    if ( (sd = socket( AF_INET, SOCK_STREAM, 0) ) < 0)
    { perror(" Server socket can not open.");
      exit( 1);
```

Figure 8.11 A multitasking server program in C code.

```
            }
    bzero ( (char *) &servAddr, sizeof( servAddr) );
    servAddr.sin_family = AF_INET;
    servAddr.sin_addr.s_addr = htonl( INADDR_ANY);
    servAddr.sin_port = 4040;

              /* -----------------------------------------------
                   (6)   Bind the socket with a port number.
                   (7)   Find the length of the sock address stucture.
                         Use the getsockname Function to copy the port
                         number into servAddr.sin_port.
                   (8)   Print out the port number assigned.
                  ---------------------------------------------- */
    if ( bind( sd, &servAddr, sizeof( servAddr) ) )
    { perror( "Socket binding failed." );
       exit( 1);
    }

    length = sizeof( servAddr);
    if ( getsockname( sd, &servAddr, &length) )
    {  perror( "getsockname call failed.");
       exit( 1);
    }

    printf( "Port number of the server task is: %d\n ",
             ntohs( servAddr.sin_port) );

              /* -----------------------------------------------
                   (9)   Specify the number of elements in the
                         the queue as 4.
                   (10)  Enter the infinite for loop to accept the
                         incoming call.  You may press ctrl-c to
                         kill the program execution.
                  ---------------------------------------------- */
    listen( sd, 4);

      for ( ; ; )
      {
        if ( ( nsd = accept( sd, 0, 0) ) < 0)
        {  perror( " Clients socket is bad.");
           exit( 1);
        }

        if ( ( childpid = fork() ) < 0 )
        {  perror( "Fork failed.");
           exit( 1);
        }
        else
          if ( childpid == 0)

                   /* -----------------------------------------------
                       This branch is for the descendent task to follow.
                       First, close the duplicate socket of the parent.
                       Then, call the do_the_work routine which uses the
```

Figure 8.11 (continued)

```
                        /* new socket descriptor to communicate with the
                           client. After receiving a q<cr> command, the
                           descendent task closes the new sd and exits.
                                                                         */
        { close( sd );
          do_the_work( nsd );
          printf( "Descendent task terminated with socket id: %d\n",
                  nsd );
          close( nsd );
          exit( 0 );
        }
                /* ----------------------------------------------
                   The parent task follows this branch. It closes
                   the new socket and goes back to accept again.
                   ----------------------------------------------  */
    close( nsd );
    }
                /* ----------------------------------------------
                   The do_the_work routine is mainly an infinite
                   for loop which receives a message from the client
                   and displays it on the screen. If the received
                   message is q<cr>, then return.
                   ----------------------------------------------  */
}
int do_the_work( nsd )
int nsd;

{
int msglength;
char buf[81];

    for ( ; ; )
    {
    bzero( buf, 81 );

    if ( ( msglength = recv ( nsd, buf, 81, 0) ) < 0 )
    {  perror( "Receive failed.");
       return( 1 );
    }

    printf( "Socket id to communicate with this client is: %d\n", nsd );
    printf( "Message length is: %d\n", msglength );
    printf( "Message says: %s\n\n", buf );

    if ( ( msglength == 1) & ( buf[0] == 'q' ) )
        return( 0 );
    }
}
```

Figure 8.11 (continued)

```
/* ------------------------------------------------------------
   ...

   Description:

   This client.c program communicates with the server.
   After compiling and linking, the executable file is named
   client.  To run this program, type the following command
   and press <cr>:

   client  node_id  4040

   The node_id is the alias of a computer on which the server
   program is running.  The port number of the server is
   assumed to be 4040 and must be used in the connect request.
   After the connection, the client enters a loop to read
   the keyborad and send a message to the server.  A message
   of q<cr> indicates quitting, so the client task terminates.
   ------------------------------------------------------------ */

#include <sys/types.h>
#include <sys/socket.h>
#include <stdio.h>
#include <netinet/in.h>
#include <netdb.h>
#include <errno.h>

             /* ---------------------------------------------
                Three arguments are passed to the system as
                follows.
                0:         program name
                1:         server node name
                2:         server port number

                Data structures are listed below:
                sd:        socket descriptor
                buf:       buffer for reading a message from the
                           keyboard
                hostent:   name of a structure template
                --------------------------------------------- */

main ( argc, argv)
int argc;
char *argv[];
{
int sd;
char buf[81];
struct sockaddr_in servAddr;
struct hostent *hp, *gethostbyname();

   if ( argc < 3 )
   {perror( "Enter client node_id 4040.\n");
    exit ( 1);
   }
```

Figure 8.12 A client program in C code.

```
    if ( ( sd = socket( AF_INET, SOCK_STREAM, 0) ) < 0)
    {perror( "Sock creation failed.\n");
     exit ( 1);
    }
            /* -----------------------------------------------
                (1)   Zero out the socket address structure.
                (2)   Specify the socket family.
                (3)   Call the gethostbyname routine to convert
                      the server node name to an IP address into
                      a special structure pointed by hp. The
                      name of the structure template is hostent.
                (4)   Copy the IP address into the socket address
                      structure.
                (5)   Copy the port number into a socket address
                      structure representing the server.
               ----------------------------------------------- */
    bzero( (char *) &servAddr, sizeof( servAddr) );
    servAddr.sin_family = AF_INET;
    hp = gethostbyname( argv[1]);
    bcopy( hp->h_addr, &servAddr.sin_addr, hp->h_length);
    servAddr.sin_port = htons( atoi( argv[2]) );

            /* -----------------------------------------------
                The client task issues a connect request. If
                connection is successful, the client reads a
                string from keyboard containing no space
                characters, e.g. "Client1_says_Hello."
                and sends the message to the server.
               ----------------------------------------------- */

    if ( connect( sd, &servAddr, sizeof( servAddr) ) < 0)
    {  perror( "Connection failed.\n");
       exit( 1);
    }

    for ( ; ; )
    {
    bzero( buf, 81);
    printf( " Please enter a message: ");
    scanf( "%s", buf);
       if ( send( sd, buf, strlen( buf), 0) < 0)
       {  perror( "Send failed.");
          exit( 1);
       }
       if ( (strlen( buf) == 1) & (buf[0] == 'q') )
       {  close( sd);
          printf( "Client task terminates.");
          exit( 0);
       }
    }
}
```

Figure 8.12 (continued)

This structure defines the network address information about a host. A gethostbyname (get host by name) call returns the network address information about the host computer on which the server runs. The next line places the IP address of the server into the client socket address block. The atoi routine converts the server port number from ASCII to integer to be placed in the client socket address. Note that the client has its port number stored in the TCB, which can be accessed via its own socket id. The rest of program is self-explanatory.

The UDP/IP programming examples are much simpler because there is no connection phase. There are other session protocols used in the corporate world, such as SNA, DNA, and so forth. They are implemented for transaction processing systems [5]. We will discuss the SNA session in particular from a system viewpoint.

8.6 SNA SESSION

In SNA, session means activities between two logical units (LUs). LUs are ports through which application programs, terminals, and terminal operators can communicate across the SNA network. A port is a peer entity that is also a private resource. At one end a message is dropped into the port, and another program can retrieve the message from a remote port as long as there is a connection between them. A port has its own character that may be used by a printer, memory, or user program. A user is a person who executes a network application program to communicate with another program. The remote program may not have a human user interactively involved. The talk program has, but the printer program has not.

Therefore, a LU in contrast to a physical unit strictly refers to a software implementation. Through a LU-to-LU session, one end-user program may communicate with another end-user program. Before communication starts, a session connection must be established first. That is, a session is activated when one LU, known as the primary LU or the BIND Sender, sends a BIND SESSION request to another LU, known as the secondary LU or the BIND Receiver. The BIND SESSION request plus the ensuing responses establishes the formal pairing of two LUs in a session. The BIND SESSION request defines the capabilities of the two partners as well as the protocols they can use.

Because each LU represents one of two partners, it is sometimes called a half-session which is really a permanent port. Each half-session can execute a group of functions and, consequently, two formally bound half-sessions make a full session. Many functions are available to the end-user programs, whether it is an application program, a terminal alone, or a terminal and an operator. As a result of this, some LU functions are mandatory while others are optional. The options may be selected by specifying a profile number and by establishing the usage criteria in a BIND SESSION request. In summary, the session services are provided by the LU service manager that is the session layer.

8.6.1 SNA Session Types

Different session types are due to different LUs, and each LU has its own personality. LU Type 1 (LU_T1) sessions are used to manage multiple input and output devices associated with a logical unit such as an operator console. More often than not, during a LU_T1 session diagnostic messages are provided with manmachine interaction. Other Type 1 sessions perform data management services, such as storing data for later retrieval and distribution to multiple destinations. In a LU_T1 session, a half-duplex protocol is adequate for its data transmission.

LU Type 2 (LU_T2) sessions support data communication between an application program and a single display device. The physical device may be dedicated permanently or temporarily to the program during the session. LU Type 3 (LU_T3) sessions support communication between an application program and a single printer. Recall that the display or printer is considered an output device driven by a computer program that contains only one port. If a message is dropped into the port, the message will also be sent to the output device (i.e., displayed or printed). As a result, the transport message header does not even have a port id because the port is unique.

LU Type 4 (LU_T4) sessions are used for data communication between two terminals or between an application program and a terminal. Each terminal, however, may contain a single device or multiple devices. LU_T4 sessions are very similar to Type 1 sessions, particularly for remote data processing applications (e.g., word processing).

8.6.2 LU 6.2 Session

A LU Type 6.2 (LU 6.2) session is used for data communication between two application programs in a transaction processing system (TPS). The TPS functions allow application programmers to write different user programs running on different computers. Therefore, LU 6.2 session services are also known as advanced program to program communication (APPC). Recall that a program turns into a task after being loaded in memory.

The LU 6.2 protocol stack is shown in Figure 8.13. Below the user task, we have the LU 6.2 session layer followed by the path control and data link. The path control layer handles routing just like the network layer in the OSI model. The data link layer of SNA is very sophisticated and broad and contains the physical link plus all the associated software needed for flow/error control. On top, the LU 6.2 session covers both the transport layer and the API. The primitives of the LU 6.2 session protocol are called verbs. A verb is a command to exchange messages. Application programs use these verbs or commands directly to invoke the services they need. Since LU 6.2 supports permanent ports, a session connection is also known as a conversation. Therefore, to allocate a

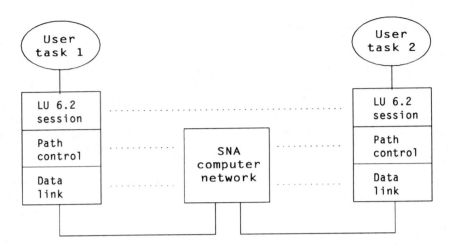

Figure 8.13 LU 6.2 session protocol stack.

conversation, a *half-session* or a *permanent port* mean the same thing. Since permanent ports are available in the system, a conversation can be thought of as an inexpensive session between two end users.

To make a port connection, system initialization routines or the user task must go through the connection phase. This is called to activate a session. The client task must issue an ACTIVATE_SESSION verb to make a Connect Request and the server task issues a passive one to receive this request. By the same token, the client issues a DEACTIVATE_SESSION verb to request Disconnect and the server issues a passive one to dissolve the ports.

The basic set of verbs are listed in Figure 8.14. Note that the verbs may have different syntactic forms under different systems, but the semantics underneath remain the same. Some of the verbs are directly mapped into T layer primitives, but others are not. The commonly used verbs are described below:

1. ALLOCATE is used to request a half-session or conversation with a remote server. The ALLOCATE routines at two sides are not 100% symmetrical. The ALLOCATE routine at the client side sends a request with parameters, such as the destination task id, network id, node id, user id, password, session id, data message, and so forth to the server and waits for a reply. After receiving the request, the remote server authenticates the client, looks up the service and transaction program name in a table, validates the client's authority, assigns an existing port, creates a descendent task to communicate with the client' and sends back a message to reply. After receiving the reply, the ALLOCATE routine at the client side, sets up the half-session and returns a session id to its client, which is used by the client to send/receive subsequent

Allocate
Send_data
Receive_and_wait
Send_error
Deallocate
Get_attribute
Confirm
Confirmed
Request_to_send

Figure 8.14 LU 6.2 session verbs.

messages. At this point, a full session has been established and two user tasks can send messages to each other.
2. SEND_DATA is used to send a data message to the remote task with parameters such as the buffer address and the session id.
3. RECEIVE_AND_WAIT is used to receive a data message from the remote task. If the data message has not arrived, the system puts the issuing task in wait state. After the data message arrives, the system wakes up the issuing task, which becomes dispatchable again. Parameters include the buffer address, session id, and status.
4. SEND_ERROR is used to inform the remote task that an error has occurred during transmission.
5. DEALLOCATE is used to free the port at the end of session. However, the port-to-port connection still exists in the system.
6. GET_ATTRIBUTE is used to gather all the information about the current session.
7. CONFIRM is used to poll the remote program whether it has received data successfully.
8. CONFIRMED is used to issue a +ack to a Confirm request.
9. REQUEST_TO_SEND is used to notify the remote transaction program that it has data to send.

LU 6.2 also provides explicit Syncpt services as session Connect options. A user task can issue SYNCPTs to verify the progress of transaction processing and resynchronize at the application level. Three levels of synchronization services can be specified in an ALLOCATE verb.

Synchronization Services

1. Level 0 (None): When this level is chosen, the LU 6.2 layer provides no synchronization services at all.
2. Level 1 (Confirm): With this level specified, one task issues the CONFIRM request verb to send out a message that requests a confirmation. The remote task returns a CONFIRMED message to indicate that processing has been completed and whether there was an error or not. In the case where there is an error, then recovery becomes the responsibility of the two user tasks. Namely, the CONFIRM and CONFIRMED messages are just application subcommands.
3. Level 2 (Syncpt): With this level specified, certain resources are protected by the LU 6.2 session layer, which has the commitment and responsibility to assure that changes are either made correctly or not made at all. The client task may issue a SYNCPT to request synchronization and ditto the server task. They are designed to implement a two-phase commit protocol at the application level, as described in Chapter 9. If no error occurred during transaction processing, takes_Syncpt to the client means commit work; to the server means commit transaction. If any error occurs, a BACKOUT verb is issued so that the users can undo everything and go back to a previous Syncpt or abort. In other words, the session layers exchange information among themselves on the status of protected resources and allow all the users take the necessary steps to restore the resources to a synchronized state.

8.7 OSI SESSION

The OSI session layer, proposed by the Honeywell group [6], is rich and complex in its context and may be used in conjunction with the presentation and application layers. It provides a variety of services grouped into function units. When two service users wish to establish a session, negotiation parameters may be included in the connection message to use one or more functional units. The minimum service includes session establishment, maintenance, and termination.

A service user may have a number of dialogue units in a session, but only one dialogue can be active at one time. If one session relates to many file transfers, then a dialogue unit may relate to a single file transfer. After receiving a session primitive from its service user, the S layer maps the primitive into a session protocol data unit (SPDU) and transmits it to its peer.

8.7.1 OSI Session Primitives

The S_CONNECT primitive has a four-way protocol, as shown in Figure 8.15(a) [X.215]. In the proposal, a port connection must be established first before a session connection can take place. The origination session service user issues a S_CONNECT.request to its S layer, the service provider. The request is mapped into a Connect SPDU and transmitted via a T_DATA.request to its peer, the destination S layer. In other words, a session connect has its own opcode delivered via a port call. The destination S layer receives this message via a T_DATA.indication, sends a S_CONNECT.indication to its service user, and receives a S_CONNECT.response. At this point, the destination S layer maps the response into an Accept or Reject message and transmits it also via a T_DATA.request. After receiving this message, the origination S layer issues a S_CONNECT.confirm to its service user. If Confirm is positive, a session connection is established between two session service access points. It is quite common that the session connection message contains negotiations parameters. After a session is connected, both service users can send data via a S_DATA.request or a S_EXPEDITED_DATA.request.

There are other OSI session primitives as proposed in Figure 8.15(b). Some of them are designed for a variety of lower layers, such as data links of half-duplex BSC, token ring, and token bus. Each primitive has one or more basic primitives as marked by an x in the column.

S_TOKEN_PLEASE requests the token.
S_TOKEN_GIVE releases one or more specific tokens.
S_CONTROL_GIVE releases all the tokens.
S_TYPED_DATA allows the transmission of data against the normal flow in
    half-duplex mode regardless of the token assignment.
S_CAPABILITY_DATA allows users to exchange data while not in activity.

There are two different Syncpts: a minor one denotes a progress point made in a dialogue and a major one denotes the end of a dialogue unit. In other words, dialogue units are separated by major Syncpts. A serial number is provided in the SPDU so that both S layers know where to restart. Once the program passes a major Syncpt, it cannot request to Resync before that. In other words, Resync can only take place between two major Syncpts. The primitives are described below:

> S_SYNC_MINOR requests a minor Syncpt in the program and may ask for an explicit confirmation from its peer.
> S_SYNC_MAJOR requests a major Syncpt to separate the dialogue units.
> S_RESYNCHRONIZE requests to restore the user task to a previous minor Syncpt after the last major Syncpt. If the data messages need to be retransmitted, it is the responsibility of the user's task to keep all the data structures intact in the code.

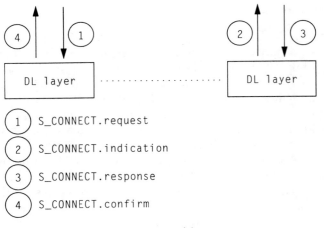

Description	request	indication	response	confirm
S_DATA	X	X		
S_EXPEDITED_DATA	X	X		
S_TYPED_DATA	X	X		
S_CAPABILITY_DATA	X	X	X	X
S_TOKEN_PLEASE	X	X		
S_TOKEN_GIVE	X	X		
S_CONTROL_GIVE	X	X		
S_SYNC_MINOR	X	X	X	X
S_SYNC_MAJOR	X	X	X	X
S_RESYNCHRONIZE	X	X	X	X
S_ACTIVITY_START	X	X		
S_ACTIVITY_RESUME	X	X		
S_ACTIVITY_INTERRUPT	X	X	X	X
S_ACTIVITY_DISCARD	X	X	X	X
S_ACTIVITY_END	X	X		
S_RELEASE	X	X	X	X
S_U_EXCEPTION_REPORT	X	X		
S_P_EXCEPTION_REPORT		X		
S_U_ABORT	X	X		
S_P_ABORT		X		
etc.				

(b)

Figure 8.15 OSI session primitives: (a) S_CONNECT primitives and (b) other session primitives.

An activity means a dialogue unit. An activity may involve transmitting and receiving several data messages in a row between two service users. Some systems may adopt an all or none approach, which means that operations are either done correctly or not done at all. At the onset of an activity, the origination service user may issue an S_ACTIVITY_START.request to begin a sequence of operations. In the end, it sends a S_ACTIVITY_END request. In between, either side can interrupt, resume, and discard the activity. At the destination end, transactions will wait until an S_ACTIVITY_END.indication has been correctly received. The five S_ACTIVITY primitives are listed below:

- S_ACTIVITY_START indicates the beginning of an activity.
- S_ACTIVITY_INTERRUPT interrupts an activity.
- S_ACTIVITY_RESUME resumes an activity.
- S_ACTIVITY_DISCARD discards an activity.
- S_ACTIVITY_END indicates the end of an activity.

During the session, exceptional conditions may be reported and the session may be terminated abnormally or normally, as shown below.

S_U_EXCEPTION_REPORT reports an exceptional condition initiated by the service user.
S_P_EXCEPTION_REPORT does the same except it is initiated by the provider.
S_RELEASE terminates the session in an orderly fashion after session is over.
S_U_ABORT aborts the session without the consent from its peer and this primitive is initiated by the service user. Undelivered SPDUs may be lost.
S_P_ABORT also aborts, except it is initiated by the provider.

Note that most of the OSI session primitives are passed up or down by the S layer without execution. As an example, after receiving a S_Sync_Minor.request via a T_DATA.indication, the S layer informs its service user via a S_Sync_Minor.indication.

8.7.2 OSI Session Protocol Data Units

The format of an OSI SPDU is shown in Figure 8.16(a) [X.225]. The leading byte of the header contains the SPDU Identifier (SI), which specifies 1 out of 21 types. The second field is the Length Indicator (LI), containing the length of the remaining SPDU in bytes; the third field specifies one or more parameters; and the last field is the s_sdu, containing the user supplied data of variable length.

The parameter field can be a parameter identifier PI) unit or a parameter group identifier (PGI) unit. A PI unit has a PI field, a LI and a parameter value PV) as shown in Figure 8.16(b). A PGI unit has its own PGI, a LI field that is the length of the remaining group followed by one or more PI units as shown in

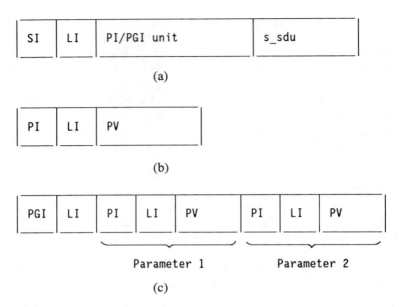

Figure 8.16 OSI SPDU format: (a) general format, (b) parameter identifier format, and (c) parameter group identifier format.

Figure 8.16(c). Note that the Length field of a PI or PGI unit is equal to the length of the unit excluding the header. The structure of session messages conforms with the Abstract Syntax Notation.1 (ASN.1) as introduced in Chapter 9.

8.8 CONCLUSIONS

On top of the T layer, a session interface is needed so as to provide programming convenience to all service users. It has its own SPDUs to support the following functions:

1. Connection management;
2. Data transmission;
3. Synchronization;
4. Resynchronization.

Session Layer 425

Summing up, the S layer provides session services to the application task. Connection management services allow two S layers to establish a connection and exchange negotiation messages. After the session connection, the S layer transmits one or more SPDUs to its peer and handles its own handshaking. In other words, each S layer transmits, receives, interprets, and executes its own SPDUs. Syncpt and Resync are used to improve the readability of the program as well as to achieve reliable computing. On top of session, the two user tasks can use application subcommands to implement the two-phase commit protocol, so operations are either done correctly or not done at all. This important subject will be discussed thoroughly in Chapter 9.

8.9 SUMMARY POINTS

1. The S layer provides the programming interface between a user task and the T layer.
2. The S layer should be simple, elegant, and powerful.
3. A half-session is essentially a permanent port, and two half-sessions make a full session.
4. Connection management at the session level means that a negotiation phase is implemented and the handshaking is handled by two session layers. One side issues Connect and the other side should issue Rec_connect.
5. A session may begin only after a Connect phase is successfully completed. Then, both sides can transmit and receive data messages in full-duplex mode using session data primitives.
6. A regular data message can be transmitted to its peer via a Send while expedited data can be transmitted via an Express call. At the remote end, the peer user task issues a Receive to match.
7. In practice, the Receive routine is blocked if there is no incoming message. However, the Receive_and_Immediate option provides an immediate return with the Status flag indicating whether the data have arrived or not.
8. The Allocate routine allocates a permanent port and the Deallocate routine frees a port.
9. The Syncpt and Resync system calls are used to monitor the progress of program execution.
10. After the session, both sides issue Disconnect to terminate.
11. The client-server model is commonly used in network applications.
12. A file server can support many clients at the same time provided that the OS running on the host supports multitasking.
13. Socket programming means that network applications can be written on top of TCP/IP using sockets.
14. A socket address is the combination of a port number and an IP address.

15. The combination of a client socket address and a server socket address defines a unique socket connection between two TSAPs even though the server may use the same port number to communicate with multiple clients.
16. A fork call informs the system to create a descendent task running in parallel with its parent.
17. LU 6.2 is the session layer of SNA.
18. The OSI session layer is rich and complex, but whether to implement a portion of it or none at all is up to the design team.

Problems

Problem 8.1

Explain why the session connection phase is asymmetrical.

Problem 8.2

Describe the functions of Syncpt and Rec_Syncpt primitives.

Problem 8.3

What is the difference between a server and a client?

Problem 8.4

What is your opinion in regard to designing the session layer as a system interface?

Problem 8.5

Design a Gtalk program on paper that supports up to four clients who can talk amongst each other in full-duplex mode. Create a way to terminate your program. Consider the two-character sequence q<cr> from the keyboard as the quit subcommand.

The following two projects are proposed for transferring files using the client-server model. Form a team of three students and tackle one of the two projects. During file transfers, you have the option to implement sliding window protocols and simulate errors.

Problem 8.6

The first project is to write programs using the socket programming interface to transfer files between two UNIX machines [AIX, LINUX]. Assume that you computing environment supports socket programming and write a file server on the host machine that supports multiple clients. In the server, after accepting an incoming request, a fork call should be issued to spin off a descendant task that communicates with the particular client. To prove a point, run two client programs on two other computers and show that file transfers can be performed at the same time.

Problem 8.7

The second project is to write programs to transfer files between a PC and a UNIX machine. It is more of a challenge in that you have to write your own simple network I/O routines from scratch. Assume that you have a PC connected to a computer system running UNIX and the commercial software Procomm is available to emulate the PC as a terminal. Write a file server on the host machine, then compile and link it into an executable file named server.exe. On the PC, write a client program, then compile and link it into client.exe on drive A. Hopefully, your client program supports three subcommands: get, put, and quit. Then, prepare a simple batch file, tuba.bat, that contains a few MS-DOS commands and where tuba is the name of your host computer. Prepare a Procomm command file named tuba.cmd that contains a sequence of commands to communicate with tuba. Follow the steps below to transfer files between your PC and the host machine:

1. Type **tuba** on your PC to make a connection to the host, and you see the system prompt on the screen.
2. Type **server.exe** to run the file transfer server on the remote node.
3. Type <ALT> <F4> to exit Procomm and return to MS-DOS on your local machine.
4. Change directory to drive A, if necessary.
5. Type **client.exe** to run the client program on your PC.
6. Transfer a file in either direction and quit.
7. Type **exit** to get out of MS-DOS and return to UNIX on the host.
8. Logout.

Hints: Since your PC is treated as a standard I/O device to the server, printf/scanf in C can be used to send/receive messages. On the PC side, character I/O drivers are adequate to drive the RS232 com port. Have fun.

References

[1] Feit, S., *TCP-IP, Architecture. Protocols, and Implementation*, McGraw-Hill, Inc., 1993.
[2] Stevens, W. R., *UNIX Network Programming*, Prentice-Hall, 1990.
[3] Wang, P., *An Introduction To Berkeley UNIX*, Wadsworth Publishing Co., 1988.

[4] Wright, G. R. and W. R. Stevens, *TCP/IP Illustrated*, Vol. 2: The Implementation, Reading, MA: Addison-Wesley, 1995.
[5] Gray, J.N. and A. Reuter, *Transaction Processing: Concepts and Techniques*, Morgan Kaufmann Publishers, 1993.
[6] Bachman, C., et al., The Session Control Layer of an Open System Interconnection, International Organization for Standardization, OSIC/TG6/79–10, 1979.

Presentation and Application Services 9

*Life cannot be recycled;
why not walk through it once with a splash.*

In this chapter, we will discuss both the presentation and application services in a computer network. Ideally, the presentation routines should provide services to any layer to manipulate data. As proposed in the OSI reference model, the P layer belongs to its protocol stack. The P layer is different from the presentation manager running on a PC, which mainly interprets the mouse commands and manages the screen.

9.1 BASIC DESIGN CONCEPTS

The network application programs usually employ the client-server model as discussed in Chapter 8. Both the client and server are user programs running on different computers. However, if a client or server task is divided into two parts, one is written by the user and the other by the system collectively known as the application service elements (ASEs).

There are also many issues regarding the form of data transmitted from one computer to another. If the data block is very large in size and contains many duplicates, it should be compressed to speed up transmission. At the receiving end, proper routines must be executed to restore the data to its original form. Modern modems can even handle the data compression/decompression functions at the bottom level. Nonetheless, the application task should compress data to reduce traffic between layers and improve performance. The second issue is security. For financial transactions, a customer is allowed to withdraw from his or her own account. After the withdrawal, proofs should be available to validate that the transaction has indeed taken place. The third issue is code conversion, because computers use different codes for information interchange and have different internal representations in memory. Consequently, the presentation routines are needed to perform the proper data conversion between two different computers.

9.2 PRESENTATION SERVICES

In the following sections, we will introduce the presentation routines designed as utilities to perform such functions as data compression, decompression, encryption, decryption, and conversion.

9.2.1 Data Compression and Decompression

Transmission speed is of great concern to most users. When a user transfers a large file from one computer to another, he or she only cares about the reliability and speed of data transfer. If the data block contains massive data and there are many duplicates in the code, such as 0's, a compression technique should be applied to shorten the message and thus to improve the speed. The special message of duplicate code contains three fields: the Value, the opcode, and the Count. The Value field specifies the bit pattern; the opcode denotes a duplicate, and the Count field specifies the size of the block in bytes.

Let us go through an example. Assume that the sending user needs to transmit 64 KB of 0's to the remote site as shown in Figure 9.1(a). If a special opcode is reserved to denote duplicate (dup), only a 4-byte message needs to be transmitted on the line, as shown in Figure 9.1(b). The first byte contains 0's, the second byte specifies a dup opcode and the last field, 2 bytes long, specifies the count. It is the responsibility of the receiving user task to decompress the message and obtain 64 KB of 0's. All layers below merely deliver the bit string and do not even know that the data have been compressed.

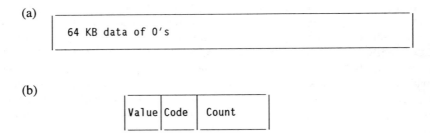

Figure 9.1 Data compression and decompression: (a) before data compression and (b) after data compression.

9.2.2 Encryption and Decryption

If a message is sensitive for security reasons, the sending user task may cipher the message before transmitting to its lower layers. In the case where the encrypted message is intercepted, no one should figure out the meaning of the bits. There are many ways to scramble the bits in a message. One simple method is to shuffle the bits in a special way. The transformation process may also be based on a security key as shown in Figure 9.2. Suppose that task A transmits messages to task B. On the sending side, each message needs to be encrypted through a transformation process so that the encrypted message is Ek(M) where M is the original message and Ek denotes the encryption function using k as the security key. M is known as the plaintext and Ek(M) the ciphertext.

At the receiving end, task B decrypts the message through another transformation process using the same key as shown below:

$$M = Dk(Ek(M))$$

where Dk represents the decryption function using the same security key k. Needless to say, the transformation function and the key should be kept confidential. Since Ek and Dk only represent functions, they may be the same (e.g., EXCLUSIVE OR). If such operations using the same key are performed twice, the original message is restored as proven below:

$$M = M + k + k$$

where k is the security key and + denotes EOR.

Authentication

Authentication is an issue during the negotiation phase of a session connection. The server wants to make sure that the client is truly authentic. One common approach is to use a password. The headache of using a password is that the authenticating computer must keep an internal file of passwords, which itself may present a security problem. Regardless of its drawback, this method is used for most applications. Two measures can be taken to guard the password. First, a password must be entered via the keyboard by the user or the console operator. Second, the password is not echoed on the screen, and better yet, it should not

Figure 9.2 Encryption and decryption using the same security key.

be transmitted on the line. Two issues should be addressed. The first one is how to guard the password and the second one is how to keep the overhead low. Several approaches are presented below.

Password Encryption

The simplest solution is to request the client transmit its user id and the password or personal identification number (PIN) in an encrypted message during negotiation. After receiving the message, the server task at the remote site needs to decrypt the message and find out the password. The server task validates the request and grants admission only if the message is authentic. No one except the receiver should know the decryption function and the password.

Since the length and bit pattern of both the message and the password are secret, this scheme is quite safe and requires two-way handshaking.

Challenge-Response

Challenge-response is a refinement of the previous approach but requires three-way handshaking as depicted in Figure 9.3 [SNAa]. First, the client sends its user id to the server. Next, the server fetches the user's secret password from a database, generates a random number M, encrypts it using the password, and transmits this message to the client as a challenge. Then, the client task deciphers the received message with its own password. The message being authentic, the user should be able to convert it to M and return it as response. In fact, we have implemented

$$M = Dk(Ek(M))$$

where Ek is an encryption function using the clients password as the security key and Dk is a decryption function using the same key. This approach is obviously better, but with more overhead.

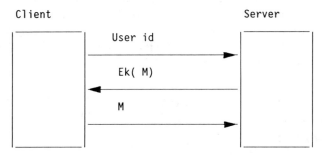

Figure 9.3 Challenge-response.

Digital Signature Using Public Key

The fourth approach is using cryptography to authenticate a particular user [1,2]. In such schemes, each user task is assigned a key pair: one is secret and the other one is public. Based on the number theory, the two keys present a property such that if a message is encrypted using the first key, it can be decrypted using the second key. Before transmission, the sending task must encrypt the message using its own private key or signature.

As an example, a message M is sent from task A to B as shown in Figure 9.4. Each task goes through two steps. Task A first encrypts the message with its secret key and then encrypts the derived message with the public key of B. Therefore, we obtain

$$X = Epb(Esa(M))$$

where X is the transmitted message; Esa is an encryption function using the secret key of A; and Epb is an encryption function using the public key of B. At the receiving end, task B first decrypts the received message with its own secret key and decrypts again with the public key of A to get M,

$$Dpa(Dsb(X)) = Dpa(Dsb(Epb(Esa(M)))) = Dpa(Esa(M)) = M$$

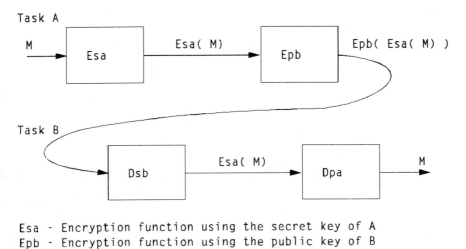

Esa - Encryption function using the secret key of A
Epb - Encryption function using the public key of B
Dsb - Decryption function using the secret key of B
Dpa - Decryption function using the public key of A

Figure 9.4 Digital signature using public key.

where Dsb is a decryption function using B's secret key and Dpa is a decryption function using A's public key. This scheme has achieved better security but requires tedious computation.

9.2.3 Code Conversion

Different computers store the data differently in memory. The data may be different in length, negative integer representations, and memory byte ordering. The external code for information exchange may also be different. For example, IBM mainframes use EBCDIC while others use ASCII. To exchange e-mail between the two classes of computers, either the sending task or the receiving task needs to convert the code from one type to the other.

The big endian computers store the high-order byte first in memory while the little endian computers store the low-order byte first. Figure 9.5(a) defines a structure in C that contains 8 ASCII characters and a 32-bit integer. The two different representations are shown in Figure 9.5(b). Note that the character is

(a)

(b)
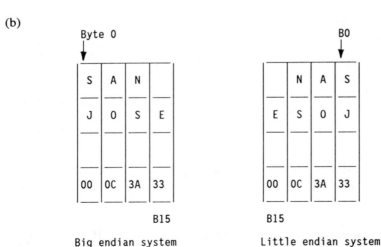

Figure 9.5 Byte addressing in different computers: (a) definition and assignment of cityRecord in C and (b) different representations in memory.

shown in print and the integer is in hex. The character string is stored in ascending order on both computers but the ordering of bytes of an integer is different. If the network address is a 32-bit unsigned integer, it is the responsibility of the sending task to prepare the correct bit pattern, which must conform with the network standard. To pass such a data structure between a big endian computer and a little endian computer, we have a problem. Two approaches can be used. We either convert at one side or have a presentation standard on the line. In the latter approach, both sides need to obey a transmission standard as proposed by the OSI model.

9.3 PRESENTATION LAYER—OSI MODEL

The OSI model has a separate presentation layer on top of the session layer. Just like other layers, the P layer has its own primitives and PDUs. The main function of the P layer is to manipulate data. The data associated with each application task can be collected into groups, called data contexts. Therefore, the presentation PDU (PPDU) contains an identifier followed by a length and a list of data contexts. The identifier serves as the opcode and the data contexts can be thought of as application messages encoded under special rules.

Data structures must be specified in such a way that both sides know exactly how to format, encode, transmit, and decode the data. To solve the problem, the Abstract Syntax Notation 1 (ASN.1) was proposed to specify the syntax of data structures. Note that ASN.1 itself is a language that can be defined by a metalanguage (e.g., Backus Normal Form (BNF) grammar) [X.208].

9.3.1 Abstract Syntax Notation 1

In theory, if two computers are homogeneous, one computer may send data to the other without going through conversions. The pitfall to enforcing a network transmission standard is that one side converts the data to standard and the other side converts it back. If a standard is enforced, ASN.1 is used to define abstract data types and to assign values to data structures. It is a tool to define data structures and to improve the readability of the description. The constructs in ASN.1 are similar to declaration statements in a high-level programming language with strong type checking. ASN.1 also has macro facilities to define new types. Thus, we conclude the following:

1. PDUs at the session, presentation, or application layer level can be specified by ASN.1.
2. An ASN.1 compiler can generate the bit string and English description of PDUs that the layer service provider wishes to exchange with its peer.
3. The syntactic rules for governing the data transmitted on the line are collectively known as the transfer syntax.

In the following, we will discuss the basic concepts, lexical conventions, syntactic notations, and basic encoding rules along with some coding examples.

Basic Concepts

1. Each data object has an identifier that is similar to the variable name used in a declaration block of any high-level language.
2. Each data object is associated with a type that describes the structure of data or can be considered as the attribute of data.
3. Type reference, type name, and type are all synonymous. A type may be externally defined or built-in. All defined types must show up on the left-hand side (LHS) of a type definition equation but not the built-in ones.
4. All type definition equations are grouped into a module, which also has a name or reference.

Lexical Conventions

1. Spaces are suppressed in the notation.
2. A comment is preceded by two leading hyphens (—) in a line.
3. An identifier begins with a lowercase letter that is part of a syntactic definition on the right-hand side (RHS).
4. A type or module reference begins with an uppercase letter and a defined type name shows up on the LHS of a definition equation.
5. A built-in type or keyword usually consists of all uppercase letters.

Syntactic Module Definition

All data type definitions are grouped in a module that has a name, and its general form is shown below:

```
<ModuleReference> DEFINITIONS ::=
IMPORTS <TypeReference>, <TypeReference>, . . .
        FROM <ModuleReference>
EXPORTS <TypeReference>, <TypeReference>, . . .
    BEGIN
        <TypeDefinitionEquation>
        <TypeDefinitionEquation>
        . . .
    END
```

where <ModuleReference> represents a module name; DEFINITIONS, IMPORTS, FROM, EXPORTS, BEGIN, END are keywords; and <TypeDefinitionEquation> is a type definition equation. The IMPORTS statement specifies all the type names defined in a different module but referenced in this module. The EXPORTS statement specifies all the type names defined in this module, but may be referenced in other modules. Each type definition equation has the form:

<TypeReference> ::= <TypeDefinition>

where <TypeReference> is a type and <TypeDefinition> defines the type. In the type definition, there may be another defined type or a built-in type. If the type on the RHS means a collection of objects, then multiple entries are separated by commas and enclosed in braces. Each entry may be a type or an identifier/type pair, followed by an optional set of values or range of values that may be actually assigned to the data.

The ASN.1 compiler translates the syntactic definitions into some intermediate language. Later, a data assignment statement can place bits in the data structure based on a set of basic encoding rules (BER) [X.209]. The bits transmitted on the line are important because they help engineers understand both the syntactic and encoding rules of ASN.1.

Basic Encoding Rules

Based on ASN.1 definitions, each data context is later translated into a string of octets composed of triples, as shown in Figure 9.6(a). Each triple has three fields: the Identifier, the Length, and the Contents. The Identifier field may occupy one or more octets as shown in Figure 9.6(b), the Length field denotes the length of data, and the Contents field contains the bit pattern.

The Identifier field is different from the identifier used in ASN.1 even though they are somewhat related. The two leading bits of the Identifier field denote the class id of a piece of data or data group. Any abstract data type must belong to one of four classes as listed below:

1. Universal: They are the general purpose, application-independent data types, such as integer, Boolean, real, octet string, bit string, and so forth. Universal class is also known as the base encoding class.
2. Application: They are relevant to a particular application and may be defined in other standards.
3. Context-specific: They are not only relevant to a particular application, but only applicable to a local context.
4. Private: They are the data types defined by users, not covered by other standards.

After the class id, there follows a 1-bit Type flag or subclass id, primitive or constructed. "Primitive" means that the data cannot be decomposed further into other data types while "constructed" means a structure that can be decomposed. After the Type flag, a tag id may be specified. Each tag may occupy 5 bits or more, representing a subsubclass. To encode a tag id less than 31, one octet is adequate that consists of a 2-bit class id, a 1-bit Type flag, and a 5-bit tag id or number. If a Tag field contains 31 (i.e., 11111 in binary), one or more octets must follow to construct a larger tag number. The leading bit of each subsequent octet serves as the chaining bit; 1 means more to follow and 0 means end of chaining. Single octet identifiers are adequate for most applications. If no

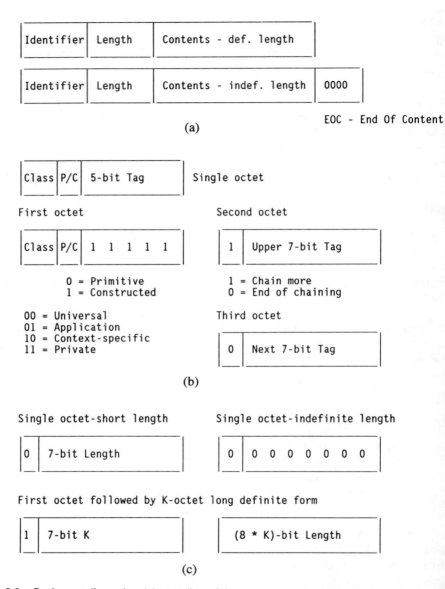

Figure 9.6 Basic encoding rules: (a) encoding of data context, (b) identifier field, and (c) length field.

class or tag ids are specified in a type definition, the default class is UNIVERSAL and its Type flag is derived from the syntax followed. For atomic data, it is primitive; otherwise, it is constructed. The tag id denotes the built-in type in uppercase letters, such as BOOLEAN, INTEGER, BitString, OctetString, VisibleString, SET, SEQUENCE, and so forth as shown in Table 9.1. A user can explicitly specify a class id and a tag id in a square bracket.

The Length field in Figure 9.6(c) indicates that the Contents field may have a definite or indefinite length. If the single octet contains all 0's, then the data have an indefinite length and a special delimiter end of content (EOC) of 16-bit 0's must be appended at the end of data. If the length octet does not contain all 0's, it may specify a short field or a long field depending on the leading bit. If the leading bit is 0, it specifies a short definite length. One octet is adequate and

Table 9.1
ASN.1 Universal Tags

Tag	Built-Type	Description
1	BOOLEAN	TRUE or FALSE → a bye of 1's or 0's.
2	INTEGER	2's complement notation with the minimum number of octets needed for representation
3	BitString	String of bits
4	OctetString	String of octets
5	NULL	Relates to a date item that has no value assigned
6	ObjectIdentifier	The value field is used to identify an object
7	ObjectDescriptor	The value field has readable text to describe an information object
8	EXTERNAL	A type defined in some external document but referenced in this module
9	REAL	Floating point number representation
10	ENUMERATED	An explicit list of integers that a data type may take
11–15	Reserved	
16	SEQUENCE or SEQUENCE OF	A SEQUENCE type has a constructed type flag and represents an ordered set of data of different types. A SEQUENCE OF is similar, but all data have the same type
17	SET or SET OF	A SET type is also constructed, but it represents an unordered set of data of different types. A SET OF is similar, but all data in the set have the same type
23	UTC	The universal time coordinated type specifies time: a 2-digit year, 2-digit month, 2-digit day, followed by hour, minute and second, as YY MM DD hh mm ss
24	Generalized time	Similar to UTC but with a 4-digit year
18–22 & 25–27		Subset of OctetString
28 & up		Unspecified

the remaining 7-bit segment denotes a short length up to 127 octets. If the leading bit is 1, it specifies a long definite length and more octets are needed to represent the total length. Therefore, the 7-bit K in the first octet denotes the number of octets to follow as part of the Length field and the complete Length field has a total of (8 · K) bits.

The Contents or Value field in the triple contains the actual bit pattern of data as described by the following example:

— The CityFile type contains a set of CityRecord.
CityFile ::= [APPLICATION 0] IMPLICIT SET OF
{ CityRecord }

— The CityRecord type has two data items.
CityRecord ::= [0] IMPLICIT SEQUENCE
{ cityName VisibleString,
population INTEGER }

— A cityFile of California may have the encoded values as follows:
{{ cityName "San Jose",
population 801331 }
. . .
}

The CityFile type is an IMPLICIT SET OF CityRecord, which has an APPLICATION class id and tag 0. The SET OF type is built-in, which represents a set of unordered elements of the same type. Note that if the keyword APPLICATION is omitted in the square bracket, the default is Context-specific and [0] really means the Context-specific class with a tag id 0. The first data item in CityRecord is a VisibleString and the second one is an INTEGER. During the encoding phase, the minimum number of octets required will be used to represent the integer. Both cityName and population are identifiers and each one is associated with a type, which happens to be VisibleString, and INTEGER, respectively. After the abstract data types are defined, values can be encoded into the cityFile as a bit string. During the encoding phase, the ASN.1 compiler enforces strong type checking.

An encoding example of the cityRecord of San Jose is shown in Figure 9.7(a) and an encoding description of the cityFile of California is in Figure 9.7(b). Assume that there are 16 similar records in the cityFile and each record has a length of 17 (2 + 2 + 8 + 2 + 3). The total parameter length in the header should be 272 (17 · 16), or 0110 in hex. Each record indicates a parameter group that has its own identifier and length.

The keyword IMPLICIT really means that the defined type shares one header with an existing old type on the RHS of the type definition equation, but it is placed with new attributes as specified. As an example, if the defined type happens to be Application, Context-specific, or Private, and the header of an

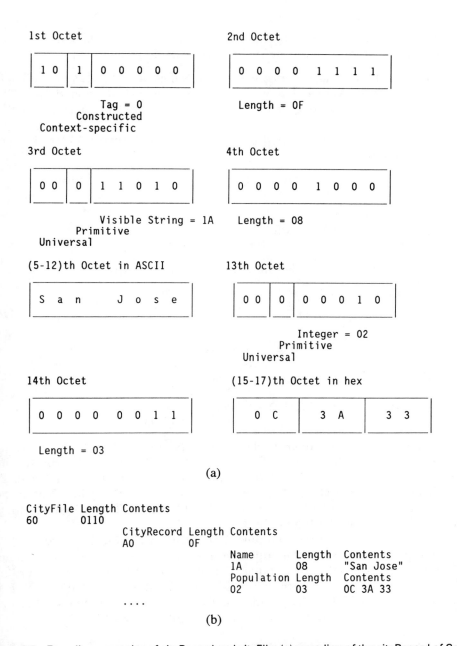

Figure 9.7 Encoding examples of cityRecord and cityFile: (a) encoding of the cityRecord of San Jose and (b) encoding description of the cityFile of California.

existing old type happens to be Universal built-in, then the class and tag ids in the header must be replaced by the new ones as described below:
1. If a different class is specified, the new class and tag ids specified in the square bracket shall be used in the new header. The encoding shall be constructed so long as the old one is constructed; otherwise, it shall be primitive.
2. The Contents octet shall be the same as the Contents octet of the old encoding.

Let us try some examples with the following ASN.1 definitions:

Type1 ::= VisibleString
Type2 ::= [3] Type1
Type3 ::= [3] IMPLICIT Type1
Type4 ::= [APPLICATION 2] IMPLICIT Type3

A value of "Jones" is encoded in hexadecimal as follows:

For Type1:	VisibleString		Length	Contents	
	1A		05	4A6F6E6573	
For Type2:	[3]		Length	Contents	
	A3		07		
			VisibleString	Length	Contents
			1A	05	4A6F6E6573
For Type3:	[3]	Length		Contents	
	83	05		4A6F6E6573	
For Type4:	[APPLICATION 2]		Length	Contents	
	42		05	4A6F6E6573	

Type1 belongs to the Universal class with a tag id 1A. Type2 and Type3 are Context-specific with a tag id 3. Type1, Type3, and Type4 are all primitive and each of them has one header. Type2 is constructed so it has two headers. The first header A3 means Context-specific, Constructed with a tag id 3. The second header 1A means Universal, primitive VisibleString. Type4 belongs to the APPLICATION class with a tag id 2.

Table 9.2 shows more examples of UNIVERSAL, primitive encoding. The NULL type means that the data item has a header but no contents so its Length field is 0. Two special built-in types, CHOICE and ANY, do not have headers. The ANY type is a wildcard, therefore SEQUENCE OF ANY and SEQUENCE are synonymous. The CHOICE type indicates that any known type given in the brace {. . .} may be selected and is useful in defining PDUs [X.227].

9.3.2 Presentation Layer Primitives

Most of the P layer primitives are directly mapped into S layer primitives [X.216]. The P layer acts like a middle man to relay messages between the S layer

Table 9.2
Other Universal Primitive Encoding Examples of ASN.1

ASN.1 type	Value	Encoding
BOOLEAN	TRUE	01 01 FF
BOOLEAN	FALSE	01 01 00
INTEGER	−129	02 02 FF 7F
REAL	0	09 00 (special case)
OctetString	01 23 45 67 in hex	04 04 04 01 23 45 67
VisibleString	Jones in ASCII	1A 05 4A 6F 6E 65 73

Identifier	Length	Data context

Figure 9.8 Presentation protocol data unit.

and its service user. The P layer handles its own connection management. To connect between two presentation service access points (PSAPs), its service user must issue a P_CONNECT.request. The P layer issues a S_CONNECT.request to its S layer to establish session first. After that, the P layer sends a connect presentation (CP) PPDU via a S_DATA.request to its peer and waits for an ack, either accepted or rejected. If accepted, the service user at either end can issue a P_DATA.request to transfer data to its peer.

9.3.3 Presentation Protocol Data Units

To conform with the ASN.1 standard, a PPDU always starts with an identifier followed by a length and data context, as shown in Figure 9.8. The identifier is usually one octet long containing an opcode to specify PPDUs, such as connection request, connection acknowledgment, data transfer, and so forth. The Data Context field has its own header that includes an identifier followed by a length and data. The inner identifier may be thought of as an subcommand code of an application protocol data unit.

9.4 NETWORK APPLICATIONS

A network application is an executable file that can be invoked by entering a keyboard command. Some network commands in an office are listed below:

    rlogin node_id   {Remote login to a particular computer.}
    copy filename, filename@node_id

file.c   crystalCave

Figure 9.9   File transfer using a mouse and an icon.

```
                        {Copy from the first file to the second file.
                         To change the direction of transfer, we simply
                         swap the two parameters. A special alias, e.g.,crystal
                         Cave can be used as the node_id.}
mail user_id@node_id <filename
                        {Copy a file into the user's mailbox.}
users node_id           {Request all user ids on the node, and a wild
                         card * denotes all nodes.}
chess user_id@node_id
                        {Play chess with a user on the node.}
talk user_id@node_id[, user_id@node_id, . . .]
                        {Talk to one or more users on the network.}
```

In a window environment, icons and a mouse can be used to invoke a network command, as shown in Figure 9.9. To copy file1.c to crystalCave on a remote node, a user does the following:

1. Select and open file1.c.
2. Select and open crystalCave.
3. Drag file1.c icon to crystalCave and release.

9.5 APPLICATION SERVICES—TCP/IP

Various network services are available on the Net. In the following, FTP, e-mail, world wide web (www), and remote procedure call (rpc) are discussed.

9.5.1 File Transfer Protocol

File transfer protocol (FTP) is popular on the Net, but requires the human user to have an account on the remote machine [RFC959]. The application task is the client that reads a subcommand from the user, interprets it, and executes it as follows:

```
CASE subcommand of
get   —   Transfer a file from the remote machine;
put   —   Transfer a file to the remote machine;.
```

```
ls    —   List the remote directory;
pwd   —   Print the remote working directory's path name.
cd    —   Change the remote directory;
lcd   —   Change the local directory;
          {lcd . is a trick to print the local working dir.}
...
quit  —   Quit FTP;
ENDCASE;
```

Anonymous FTP

If files are created on the Net for public access, it is not necessary for users to have an account on the remote machine. This leads to the anonymous FTP concept. As an example, the network information center (NIC) allows public access to its Request For Comments (RFCs) and a user steps through the following:

1. Enter the network command,
   ftp nic.ddn.mil   {Connect to a FTP server on the remote node named nic.ddn.mil.}
2. After seeing the ftp> prompt, enter user id,
   anonymous
3. Enter guest as password.
4. Change directory to rfc,
   cd rfc
5. List remote directory,
   ls
6. Get the file rfc1180.txt, a TCP/IP tutorial,
   get rfc1180.txt
7. Exit FTP, we enter,
   quit

All updated RFCs are briefly described in a very useful file, rfc-index.txt in the directory netinfo. To obtain this index file, we change directory first and issue a get as shown below:

   cd ../netinfo
   get rfc-index.txt

9.5.2 E-mail

E-mail is similar to anonymous FTP except the sending user is not required to log in at all and the destination file is the "mailbox" under the remote user's account. While sending an e-mail, the user can do limited line editing, such as backspace. In order to edit the entire page or block, a user may invoke the visual editor (VI) via the command ~vi. After editing, the user types the exit command, ZZ, to go back to the mailer. E-mail is perhaps the most popular network application on the Net in the academic community and the message is usually a string of ASCII characters.

9.5.3 World Wide Web

The World Wide Web (WWW) is also similar to anonymous FTP and has become an influential design on the Net. Loosely speaking, WWW is a global distributed database. Every user on the Internet can have access to WWW without login. Each company has a home page full of new product releases and/or job-seeking information for the new graduates. Because of the massive scale of data, directories are emerging everywhere to guide a user through the proper search. New searching tools, called search engines, are developed to allow users to explore the directory for specific topics. As a simple example, a user may enter a network command as follows:

    mosaic http://www.xyz.com

where mosaic is the client browser running on the local computer and the parameter passed to mosaic is known as the web site's universal resource locator (URL). The URL identifies a server program running on the remote node. In this particular example, the remote server name is http (hypertext transfer protocol) and www.xyz.com represents an alias or node id of the remote computer. Mosaic handles the Connection request and data transfers between the human user and the remote server. After receiving the home page, a user can click the mouse button on any blue word in the document to request further information from the server using the hypertext transfer protocol.

From a commercial viewpoint, the whole Internet catalog offers articles and information on a variety of topics including travel, personal finance, and sports. The catalog contains a collection of more than 1,000 resources divided by subject area. Each Web site provides information in the form of text, sound, graphics, and multimedia. As an example, travel agencies can bring you to different cities via virtual reality. Each corporation pays a fee to sponsor its home page in the catalog. Through mouse and icon, a user can navigate through what he or she wants in a couple of minutes.

9.5.4 Remote Procedure Call

The rpc implementation allows a user to execute a remote program by having a rpc statement in the program with passing parameters [RFC1057]. The design also employs a client-server model and the call has the following format:

    rpc(task_id, node_id, parameter, . . . , reply, status);

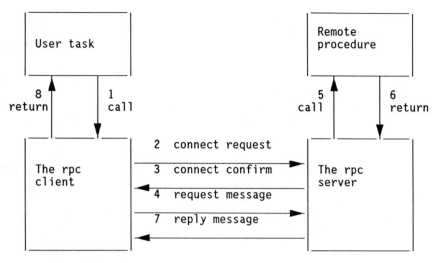

Figure 9.10 Control flow of a remote procedure call.

Remote procedure call is the client program on the local computer that asks its peer, the server on the remote computer, to perform a computation. The remote procedure may retrieve a database or compute extensively in integer or floating point arithmetic. After rpc, the client goes through a stack of network protocols. The user task that issues rpc cannot proceed until the call is returned or time-out. To ease the parameter passing problem, all information can be converted to an external code, such as ASCII. Therefore, the data messages between the client and the server contain a string of characters.

The design of rpc is quite complicated, yet it is easy to use. The control flow at the application level is shown in Figure 9.10. Step 1 shows the rpc call. In step 2, the client makes a port connection first. The remote server confirms the request after verifying the authentication of the user. In step 4, the client sends a formatted message, such as procedure name, transaction id, parameters, and so forth to the server and waits for a reply. The remote server receives the message, interprets it, and calls the remote procedure. In step 6, after return, the server packs the results in a formatted message with the transaction id in it and sends it back to the client as a reply. Finally, the client returns the reply to its user's. Both the request and reply messages are specially designed to suit a particular application.

9.6 APPLICATION LAYER—OSI MODEL

A network application program can be divided into two parts. The part written by the system programmer belongs to the application layer that provides services to the user or user task. The part written by the user is called the user agent (UA). A UA directly communicates with its application layer. Just like other layers, the application layer has its own service primitives and PDUs, as introduced below.

9.6.1 Application Layer Primitives

Each user sends an application request to the application entity (AE) or layer and receives via an indication from its AE. The two AEs communicates with each other via APDUs. Each AE consists of a UA and certain application service elements (ASEs). The ASEs may be general or specific. Each specific application has its own set of primitives for file transfer, message handling, and directory services. However, among all the applications, a common set of primitives is used by almost every application. Therefore, the basic ones are classified into groups and the primitives of each group always start with the same uppercase id followed by an underscore.

Association Control Service Element (ACSE)

The ACSE primitives are for application association, release, and abort, as shown in Table 9.3. Association means to perform a connection between two AEs, release means disconnection, and abort means disconnection involuntarily under exceptional circumstances. Note that there are two abort primitives, one initiated by the user and the other one by the provider. The ACSE usually teams with other ASEs to provide the services as required. The ASCE uses the P layer primitives, P_CONNECT, P_RELEASE, P_U_ABORT, and P_P_ABORT.

Reliable Transfer Service Element (RTSE)

The RTSE primitives are used in conjunction with ACSE to provide reliable transfer services at the application layer level as shown in Table 9.4. Figure 9.11 depicts a model of two AEs using RTES primitives. The user element or agent communicates with the RTSE, which may need to call ACSE for application

Table 9.3
ACSE Primitives

Primitive	Description
1. A_ASSOCIATE	Connect between two AEs
2. A_RELEASE	Disconnect
3. A_ABORT	User-initiated abort
4. A_P_ABORT	Provider-initiated abort

Table 9.4
RTSE Primitives

Primitive	Description
1. RT_OPEN	Open connection between two AEs
2. RT_CLOSE	Close the connection
3. RT_TRANSFER	Transfer data reliably from one AE to its peer
4. RT_TURN_PLEASE	Request token please
5. RT_TURN_GIVE	Give or release token
6. RT_P_ABORT	Abort initiated by the provider
7. RT_U_ABORT	Abort initiated by the user

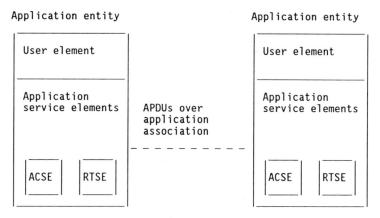

Figure 9.11 Application model using RTSE.

association, release, or abort. Note that RT_OPEN, CLOSE, and ABORT are mapped directly into A_ASSOCIATE, RELEASE and ABORT. The RTSE is intended to be used with other ASEs to perform specific information processing functions. The RTSE uses the P layer primitives, P_ACTIVITY_START, P_ACTIVITY_INTERRUPT, P_ACTIVITY_RESUME, P_ACTIVITY_END, P_ACTIVITY_DISCARD, P_MINOR_SYNCHRONIZE, P_U_EXCEPTION_REPORT, P_P_EXCEPTION_REPORT, P_TOKEN_PLEASE, P_CONTROL_GIVE, and P_DATA.

Commitment, Concurrency, and Recovery (CCR)

The CCR primitives are similar to the LU 6.2 two-phase commit protocol for distributed database applications, as shown in Table 9.5 [3][SNAa]. Figure 9.12

Table 9.5
CCR Primitives

Primitive	Description
1. C_BEGIN	Begin an atomic operation. The origination task will save work in reliable storage as a savept and the destination task saves transaction log likewise
2. C_PREPARE	Prepare to commit; end of phase 1
3. C_READY	Ready or prepared to perform the operation
4. C_REFUSE	Refuse to perform the operation
5. C_COMMIT	Commit work or operation; end of phase 2
6. C_ROLLBACK	Rollback to the previous savept. Undo operations if necessary
7. C_RESTART	Restart from the beginning. Undo all operations if necessary

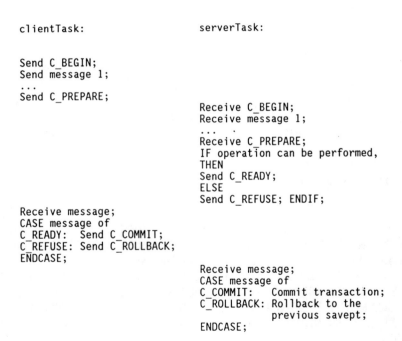

```
clientTask:                          serverTask:


Send C_BEGIN;
Send message 1;
...
Send C_PREPARE;
                                     Receive C_BEGIN;
                                     Receive message 1;
                                     ...
                                     Receive C_PREPARE;
                                     IF operation can be performed,
                                     THEN
                                       Send C_READY;
                                     ELSE
                                       Send C_REFUSE; ENDIF;

Receive message;
CASE message of
C_READY:  Send C_COMMIT;
C_REFUSE: Send C_ROLLBACK;
ENDCASE;
                                     Receive message;
                                     CASE message of
                                     C_COMMIT:   Commit transaction;
                                     C_ROLLBACK: Rollback to the
                                                 previous savept;
                                     ENDCASE;
```

Figure 9.12 Logic flow example of the two-phase commit protocol.

depicts a two-phase commit protocol example for financial transactions. Assume money is transferred from a local bank computer to the headquarter computer. The client on the local node and the server on the remote node want to make sure that the transaction is either done correctly or not done at all. That is, the transaction must be an atomic operation.

At the beginning, the client sends a C_BEGIN message to inform its peer, the server, to force transaction logging on a reliable disk as a save point (savept). Next, the client sends one or more messages that supply parameters for the transaction. The client then sends a C_PREPARE message indicating prepare_to_commit_work. As far as the client is concerned, this is the end of the first phase. The server checks to see if it indeed can commit. If yes, it sends a C_READY message to its client; otherwise, it sends a C_REFUSE. The client checks the received message. If it is a C_READY, then it sends a C_COMMIT message telling the server to go ahead and commit transaction; otherwise, it issues a C_ROLLBACK telling the server to rollback to the previous savept. If the server receives a C_COMMIT, it will perform the transaction; otherwise, it will rollback to the previous savept and end the second phase.

Remote Operation Service Element (ROSE)

The ROSE requires the existence of ACSE to perform application association, release, and abort. Table 9.6 describes the ROSE primitives to support remote operations for interactive processing functions.

9.6.2 Application Protocol Data Units

Just like other layers, different primitives can be mapped into different APDUs. An APDU has its own format, as shown in Figure 9.13. It conforms with the ASN.1 standard in that it has an identifier, a Length field, and a Value field of variable length. The Value field may contain more nested triples. The identifier specifies the APDU, which may be a piece of data or an application

Table 9.6
ROSE Primitives

Primitive	Description
1. RO_INVOKE	Invoke an operation performed by the destination AE
2. RO_RESULT	Returns a result to the origination AE
3. RO_ERROR	Returns a reply to indicate that the requested operation cannot be performed
4. RO_REJECT_U	The destination ROSE user rejects an invoke request
5. RO_REJECT_P	The ROSE provider rejects an invoke request

Figure 9.13 Format of an application protocol data unit.

subcommand. Each subcommand is sent from one application entity to its peer, which then receives, interprets, and executes it. Because there are too many network applications and each one has its own unique specifications, the total volume can be piled up easily to 3-ft high. A few interesting ones under research and development will be addressed in the following.

9.6.3 File Transfer, Access, and Management

The file transfer, access, and management (FTAM) system is a very complex network program using the virtual file store concept [ISO8571]. That is, the origination task converts its file to the virtual file standard and transmits data records one by one to its peer, which then converts the virtual file back to its own format. The word *virtual* means that the file format transmitted on the line doesn't really exist. The FTAM standard is organized into three parts:

- Virtual file definition;
- File service definition;
- File protocol specification.

Figure 9.14 depicts a virtual file store that contains attributes and data units (DUs). Each DU can be thought of as a virtual data record or item to which operations can be performed. The file definition specifies the attributes of a file, divided into two categories: the file attributes and the activity attributes. Each category is further divided into three groups: kernel, storage, and security. The file attributes include file name, structure, size, access control, encryption key, date of creation, owners id, date last modified, and so forth. The activity attributes include current access request, location, application entity, account, password, and legal status.

Figure 9.14 A virtual filestore.

The file service definition defines the operations allowed on the entire file or its DUs. Actions allowed on the complete file includes create, open, close, change attributes, and so forth. Actions allowed on the DUs include locate, read, insert, replace, erase, and so forth.

The file protocol specification describes the services provided by FTAM. Each primitive is preceded by an uppercase letter F. Some of the primitives are for control purposes while others are for data transfers. It takes several steps to build an operational context and the time period is called a regime, which determines the state of the FTAM provider. Depending on the regime, only certain services are allowed at a given period of time.

The FTAM primitives are also application subcommands and most of them can be translated into P layer primitives directly, as introduced below.

FTAM Regime Control

F_INITIALIZE establishes a connection between two AEs. After F_INITIALIZE, other primitives can be issued.
F_TERMINATE terminates the connection.
F_U_ABORT aborts the connection initiated by the user.
F_P_ABORT does the same, but initiated by the provider.

File Management

F_CREATE creates a new file.
F_SELECT selects a file, existing or new, to which subsequent operations will apply. The select subcommand establishes a relationship between the requester and the file.
F_DESELECT deselects a previously selected file.
F_DELETE deletes the selected file.
F_OPEN opens a selected file, which means that all its attributes are fetched into memory. After open, actions for file access are allowed.
F_READ_ATTRIBUTE reads the attribute.
F_CHANGE_ATTRIBUTE changes the attribute.
F_LOCATE locates a data unit.
F_ERASE deletes a data unit.
F_CLOSE closes the file.

Grouping Control

F_BEGIN_GROUP indicates the beginning of a group of operations.
F_END_GROUP indicates the end of a group of operations.

Checkpoint and Restart

F_CHECK inserts a checkpoint mark in the program, which also informs its peer to take a system checkpoint. It is up to the user task to issue a system call in order to take a checkpoint.

F_RESTART informs its peer to restart from a previous checkpoint.

Data Transfer

F_READ transfers the remote file to the local computer.
F_WRITE transfers the local file to the remote computer.
F_DATA transfers a data message to the peer user task. Any user task can issue the primitive to transmit a piece of data. As a matter of fact, each F_WRITE will be decomposed into a sequence of F_DATA requests to transmit individual DUs.
F_DATA_END transfer the last data message with EOT flag turned on.
F_CANCEL cancels the previous data message
F_TRANSFER_END signals the end of transfer.

9.6.4 Message Handling System

A substantial amount of research has been done in designing the message handling system (MHS), which consists of many software components [4] [X.400]. A user is either a person or a task that communicates with another user via MHS. Through MHS, e-mails, telegrams, and faxes can be delivered from one end user to another.

Message Transfer Agent

Figure 9.15 depicts a simple MHS that consists of two message transfer agents (MTAs) and two user agents (UAs). The MTA can send and receive formatted messages to and from another MTA on a different computer. Several MTAs can be interconnected to constitute a message transfer system (MTS). In other words, the MTS is a subset of MHS and MTA is a subset of MTS. A MTA is the basic software routine for delivering messages in MHS.

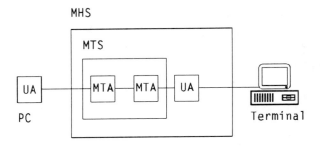

Figure 9.15 Functional model of a message handling system.

User Agent (UA)

A UA resides between a user and MTA. In Figure 9.15, the UA on the left runs on a PC and communicates with a MTA on a different node. The right side is a terminal that has a UA running on the same node with its MTA. The two UAs are different: one is collocated and the other one is remote. To communicate between a remote UA and its MTA, software must be written to support APDUs.

Message Store (MS)

The message store (MS) is a capability added to MHS in 1988 to provide a mailbox facility on the same node with the MTA. The MS provides the MTA with a front-end interface to make it look more like an electronic mail service, as shown in Figure 9.16. The primary function of the MS is to store and permit retrieval of delivered messages. Because UAs can be implemented on a variety of equipment, the MS can complement a UA on a PC by providing a more secure, continuously available storage mechanism. As far as the MTA is concerned, after delivering a message to the MS, its job is completed. The MS may alert a UA when its message arrives. Similarly, the MS accepts and delivers messages on behalf of a UA. To simplify the design, each MS represents one user, and it cannot be shared.

Access Unit (AU)

An AU provides the gateway function between the MHS and an external telecommunication service such as telex. Its main job is to convert the header format from one protocol to the other. Therefore, with an AU, a MHS user can communicate with other message-based systems. The rules for coded information conversion are defined in X.400 so that a standard of message format and content can be established between two dissimilar systems.

Physical Delivery Access Unit (PDAU)

A PDAU is a physical delivery system, just like the postal system or UPS. The unit produces a hard copy of the e-mail together with an envelope that contains

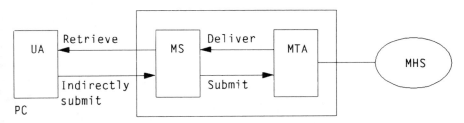

Figure 9.16 Message store in a message handling system.

both the origination and destination users' ids and addresses, supplied by the message header.

MHS Protocols

Within MHS, there are different protocols between two software components and each protocol has its own header, as described below:

> P1 is the protocol is for relaying messages and performing other interactions among various MTAs. It is the backbone protocol in the system.
> P2 is the protocol is for a UA to submit messages to the MTA and to retrieve messages from the MTA.
> P7 is the protocol that enables a UA to interact with a MS, which in fact provides a mailbox facility.

Structure Of Messages

Figure 9.17 depicts the basic structure of a message handled by the MTS. Each message consists of two parts: an envelope and a content. The envelope carries the header information used by the MTS when transferring the message within the MTS. The content is the P2 message or piece of information that the origination UA wishes to deliver to one or more destination UAs. Figure 9.18 depicts the message formation process. The human user supplies the content body to the UA, which composes the P2 message by adding a header to the body and then delivering the message to the MTA. The MTA then adds an envelope to the content and relays the P1 message to the destination MTA. Neither the MTA nor the UA modifies the content body except for necessary conversion. After receiving the fully formatted message, the destination MTA strips the envelope. When the P2 message gets to the destination UA, the header is stripped and only the body content is delivered to the user.

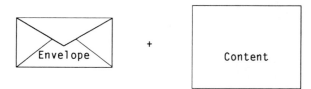

Figure 9.17   Structure of a message.

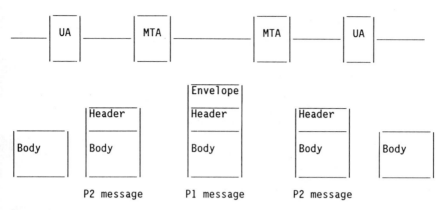

Figure 9.18 Message flow in a MHS

Notes:

1. The P2 header contains IPM (InterPersonal Message) id, origination user name/address, destination user name/address, copy recipients, time stamps, importance, sensitivity, etc.

2. The P1 envelope essentially contains the same P2 header plus trace information, such as MTS message id, distribution list expansion history, redirection history, time of redirection, reason for redirection, etc.

9.6.5 Directory System

The directory system (DS) is a collection of open systems that cooperate and hold a global-distributed database [5][X.500]. The DS provides services to users, who can access or even modify the information or a part of it if permission is allowed. Figure 9.19 depicts the functional model of a DS. The primary function is to search an object with supplied attributes. Different DSs are designed for different applications, such as the following:

1. Given a person's name, city and country, find his or her address, telephone number and e-mail address.
2. Given an e-mail address that is symbolic, find its network address in binary.
3. Given the description of a document, find its anonymous FTP or WWW address.

In a DS, information is arranged as an object or class of objects located at a different computer. A directory system agent (DSA) running on the remote computer manages its database and interacts with its directory user agent (DUA), which executes on behalf of a user or user task. In addition, a DSA communicates with other DSAs in the system regarding data requests. Each DUA gets into the DS via an access point. Two DSAs also communicate with each other via an

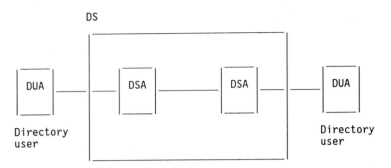

Figure 9.19 Functional model of a directory system.

access point. During the connection, the user and the DSAs optionally verify each other's identity. The directory viewed by a DUA consists of several DSAs interconnected and their associated information database.

Directory Information Tree

The DS has a unified single name space. The physical level representation of the directory information for many applications is referred to as the directory information base (DIB) and its logical level representation is called the directory information tree (DIT). The information database is logically intact but physically distributed. The DIT has a hierarchical tree structure as depicted in Figure 9.20. In the tree, each level represents a class. At the top, the root node contains information about the Country (C) id of the class. In other words, all the objects of the subtree have the same Country id. The second level may specify an Organization (O), such as commercial, education, government, and so forth. The third level may be an Organization Unit (OU), such as university name or company name. The next level may be a common attribute, such as Common Name (CN), Department (DEPT), Location (L), and so forth. The leaf node is an entry that contains the remaining attributes of an object. Each attribute has a type followed by one or more values. To search for an object, some attribute information is specified to invoke the search, as shown below:

{C=US, O=com, OU=IBM, DEPT=Marketing, L=San Jose, CN=John Doe}

The DS enforces a set of rules to ensure that the DIB remains well-formed in the face of modification over time. These rules, known as directory schema, prevent entries having the wrong attributes or data.

Directory Services

The directory services are provided in response to requests from DUAs. Some of the requests are designed for interrogation and modification of the DS. The

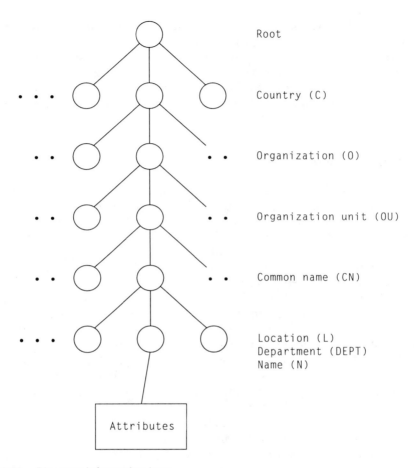

Figure 9.20 Directory information base.

DS always reports the outcome of a request. Sometimes the outcome is abnormal due to error conditions. A number of controls can be imposed to the query, such as the amount of time, the size of results, the scope of search, the priority, and so forth.

Some of the requests may even carry with them a filter expressing that one or more conditions must be satisfied before processing can continue. This allows the set of values returned to be reduced to those that are relevant.

Directory Protocols

Two directory protocols are as follows:

- The directory access protocol (DAP) defines the exchange of requests and outcomes between a DUA and a DSA.

- The directory system protocol (DSP) defines the exchange of requests and outcomes between two DSAs.

Each protocol is defined by an application context and contains a set of protocol elements. For example, the DAP contains elements designed for interrogating and modifying the directory. Since each application context is made of application service elements, the ROSE [X.219] is intended for supporting their interactions.

9.7 CONCLUSIONS

We have discussed some of the network applications in the field, such as file transfer, e-mail, directory service, and so forth. The OSI model has seven layers in its protocol stack. The upper three layers—session, presentation, and application—are connection-oriented, which requires overhead. The S and P layers usually act like relay stations that merely pass a message up or down to its adjacent layer. The ASN.1 is a useful tool to specify PDUs and APDUs in particular. Interesting examples can be found in the final chapter.

On the other hand, the TCP/IP has three layers—physical, network, and transport—plus a programming interface for the T layer. However, an end user is usually connected to a LAN that has its own link layer and medium access control sublayer to handle the transmission of its frames. The newly developed www is loosely a global information database, but its impact far exceeds everyone's expectations. Because of the services provided by the Internet, more organizations including foreign countries would like to join the Net. Since its IP address is only 32 bits long, a change of its addressing structure is imminent in order to meet the explosive demand in the future.

The primary objective of a computer network is to deliver messages from one user to another. Regarding the important design issues, connectivity is one and programming convenience is another. The message transmitted between two end users may contain ASCII characters, memory dumps, or graphical pixels, but regardless of its nature, the message is just a string of bits. If a special file or database is ported from one system to the other, then special utility routines should be written at both ends. That is, one side sends the file, attributes, and data, and the other side rebuilds the file from the information received. A capability should not drag down the entire system. The performance goal of a computer network is to transmit bits to the other end quickly and reliably. This topic is covered in the final chapter.

9.8 SUMMARY POINTS

1. Presentation services include data compression/decompression, encryption/decryption, and conversion.

2. Authentication requires that the end user provide id to prove himself or herself. The id is usually a social security number and password.
3. ASN.1 defines data structures and can be used to describe PDUs.
4. BERs are used to translate ASN.1 into a bit string.
5. In the TCP/IP model, services like FTP, e-mail, WWW, and rpc are available on the Net.
6. In the OSI model, the ACSE is used for association control and RTSE is used for reliable transfer services at the application level.
7. The CCR primitives are used for a two-phase commit protocol in distributed database applications.
8. In an MHS, there are message transfer agents interconnected that provide services to user agents.
9. In a DS, there are directory service agents interconnected that provide services to directory user agents.
10. In the OSI model, the upper three layers can be combined into one interface, and APDUs are merely application subcommands.

Problems

Problem 9.1

Describe the presentation service routines.

Problem 9.2

Design a simple challenge-response authentication system. The user client has a social security number as user id and a PIN as its secret key. The client sends its user id to the server. The server generates a random number M, encrypts it with the corresponding PIN fetched from a confidential database, and sends the encrypted message to the client as a challenge. Then, the client decrypts the message to M using its PIN and sends to the server as response. The following mathematical function should hold:

$$M = D_k(E_k(M))$$

where D_k and E_k represent the transformation functions using the same key. If key = 7, M = 100 and $E_k(M)$ has a simple form of (14, 2), what is the D_k function? Hint: The answer is very easy.

Problem 9.3

Show the representations of a 4-byte decimal integer 4,096 in memory of a big endian computer and a little endian computer. What is the difference in byte ordering?

Problem 9.4

Given the ASN.1 definitions shown below:

    Name ::= [APPLICATION 1] IMPLICIT SEQUENCE
    { givenName VisibleString, initial VisibleString, familyName VisibleString}

show the encoding bit pattern of the following value:

    {givenName "Dunt", initial "NV", familyName "Me"}

Problem 9.5

Describe the seven primitives for Commitment, Concurrency, and Recovery as proposed in the OSI model.

Problem 9.6

What is a virtual file store as proposed in FTAM?

Problem 9.7

Describe the functional model of a MHS.

Problem 9.8

Describe the function model of a DS.

Problem 9.9

What information is placed in the envelope header of a P1 message in MHS.

Problem 9.10

What is your opinion in regard to the design the upper three layers in the OSI model?

References

[1] Anderson, D. P., et al., "A Protocol for Secure Communication and its Performance," *Proc. of the 7th International Conference on Distributed Computer Systems*, IEEE, 1987, pp. 473–480.
[2] Halsall, F., *Data Communications, Computer Networks and Open Systems*, 3rd edition, Reading, MA: Addison-Wesley, 1993.
[3] Gray, J. N. and A. Reuter, *Transaction Processing: Concepts and Techniques*, Morgan Kaufmann Publishers, 1993.
[4] Betanov, C., *Introduction to X.400*, Norwood, MA: Artech House, 1993.
[5] Radicati, S., *X.500 Directory Services: Technology and Deployment*, Van Nostrand Reinhold, 1994.

Network Management   10

Who says, "Time flies."
Time stays, we fly.

This is the final chapter, addressing network management issues that have been lagging behind other design issues in a network design. In theory, a large computer network should operate reliably on a continuous basis. Administration and management of such a network demand intensive labor of highly skilled workers. To ease the burden of network management, software routines are written to assist the network administrators, as introduced in the following.

10.1 NETWORK PERFORMANCE ANALYSIS

The performance of a network really depends on the satisfaction of its users. For large file transfers, users care more about the speed because they cannot log out until the transfer is completed. On the other hand, for financial transactions the user cares about the correctness of each transaction. Whether it takes 4 sec or 5 sec to complete the transaction is of less concern. The manager of a network cares more about whether the network can meet the growing demand for the next five years. If not, can the network be expanded? More importantly, should the network ever crash for unknown reasons, could the engineers identify the failure quickly and take prompt action to solve the problem. Different criteria to achieve high performance of a network are discussed in the following.

10.1.1 Line Speed

Computer throughput is defined to be the number of computations performed per unit time. Network throughput can be defined to be the useful packets or number of bytes transmitted from one computer to another. Intuitively, throughput is linearly proportional to the raw speed of network communication controller. In other words, it is a necessary condition to have fast hardware components to achieve high throughput. But fast communication hardware alone cannot accomplish the job. That is, fast com ports must be supported by fast processing unit, memory, and so forth. In addition, good software must be written to shine the system. As an example, the received packets may contain errors or they may be dropped due to limited buffering space. As a result, the erroneous packets must be retransmitted in certain applications. Retransmission means waste of work and should be avoided by all means. Thus, clever software must be written to avoid packet retransmissions.

A good piece of software usually implies good protocol. Even with the same protocol, different software products may result in different performances. Any network should be well-balanced, which means that all the hardware components should be fully operational without bottlenecks.

Because the main function of a network is to transmit data between two nodes, the transmission speed of data links (DLs) becomes essential. For home users, network applications rarely require massive data transmission, and a fast modem of 28.8 Kbps supported by a fast controller is more than adequate. On the other hand, if the data volume is massive, then high-speed DLs (over Gigabits per second) are required. In such systems, special transducers must be designed to convert energy between light and electric and vice versa.

10.1.2 Response Time

From a different angle, the throughput of a network can be viewed as the response time of an event. When a customer shops for a computer network, he or she usually wants to see a demonstration. One marketing gimmick is to show a fast response time. Response time is defined to be the elapsed time of an event from beginning to end and can be measured by a stopwatch. In other words, response time is used to tell how fast the network actually is. As an example, we can actually measure the time to perform a file transfer between two nodes. Start the watch when a file is transferred from the local node to the remote node. Get the file back and stop the watch when the transfer is completed. The elapsed time tells how fast the network is.

Using the response time approach is simple and convincing. Yet, the above demonstration only deals with a light load condition. Under heavy load, the response time may be pretty bad and the network may even collapse. Testing the performance of a network under heavy load is not easy. One common technique is to go through extensive simulations to determine the upper limit of the heavy load. When the limit is reached, which means that the network is operating at its full capacity, no more new traffic should be injected into the network.

Mathematically, queuing analysis can be applied to predict the length of the queue and the average wait time of each packet. With given parameters, the network response time can be computed as discussed in the following sections.

10.1.3 Queuing Delays

Queuing delay happens in the network when most of the data packets are destined for the same location. The length of the queue for a particular DL increases, so every packet must wait in the queue for its turn, as shown in Figure 10.1. Queuing models are developed to analyze the queuing behavior of computer networks. Generally, a queue is characterized by the following parameters:

- The queue length;
- The number of servers;
- The queuing discipline;
- The interarrival time probability density function;
- The service time probability density function.

In the case where there is not enough buffering space, the incoming packet must be dropped. In a simplified model, we assume that there is infinite memory space to store the queue. The number of servers means the number of DLs between two nodes. To make the computation simple, only one DL for output is assumed so that the number of servers is 1. Queuing discipline defines how the packets are selected by the server. It is a common design that all packets have the same priority, so the queue is a FIFO list.

Next, we assume that packets arrive randomly and independently at time $T1, T2, T3, \ldots$ and so forth. It is correct to say that the interarrival times between two adjacent packets, represented by $T1 - 0, T2 - T1, T3 - T2, \ldots$ are identically distributed with an exponential probability density as shown below:

$$P\{Tn - Tn-1 >= t\} = e^{(-\lambda t)} \text{ where } t >= 0$$

where P is the probability density function and λ is the mean arrival rate. From the equation, P is 1 if t is 0, which means the next request will arrive for sure after $t = 0$. Note that P is 0 if t is infinity. The interpretation is that the probability is 0 for the next request to arrive after an infinite period of time.

The service time implies the transmission time of each packet on the line.

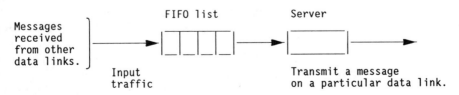

Figure 10.1 Elements of a queuing system.

In order to simplify the model, we assume that the service times are also exponentially distributed with a mean service rate μ. After mathematical derivations, we obtain

$$P\{Sn > t\} = e\char`\^(-\mu t) \text{ where } t >= 0$$

where Sn denotes the nth service time. Such a queue is classified as an M/M/1 queue. The first letter denotes the probability density function of the arrival, the second letter denotes the probability density function of the service time, and the digit denotes the number of servers. The letter M stands for Markov exponential probability density. This is similar to a supermarket that has only one checkout counter. Customers must line up so the clerk can process one cart load at a time. The average queue length and wait time depend on the mean arrival rate and the mean service rate. If the arrival rate surpasses the service rate, the queue builds up over time without bound. If a long queue builds up constantly, then we need to open up a new counter. In a computer network, that means we need to add another data link.

On the other hand, if $\lambda < \mu$, then the queue reaches a statistical equilibrium. With given parameters the average values of queue length and wait time can be computed mathematically. If xt denotes the number of packets that are either in the queue or being transmitted at time $t > 0$, we obtain

$$L = E\{xt\} = \sum_{n=0}^{\infty} n\, P\{xt = n\} = \lambda / (\mu - \lambda)$$

$$T = 1 / (\mu - \lambda)$$

where E denotes the expected value, L is the average queue length, and T is the average wait time in the queue. The results are simple because the queuing model is assumed to be M/M/1. In practice, it can be questionable that the probability density function of the service time is truly exponential. As an example, in an X.25 network, the frames have two types: control and data. The control frames are short and the processing time of each frame is pretty much fixed. The data frames may have variable sizes, but for file transfers the data frame also has the same size, which implies the same processing time. In an ATM network, all cells are 53 bytes long, so the processing time of each cell is about the same.

Our next question is how to determine λ and μ. Before designing a network, we can run simulations. After the network is developed, we can use monitoring devices to take actual measurements of λ and μ. In addition, network management routines can be written to take statistics of network performance.

10.1.4 Error Rate

No matter how reliable the network is, errors do occur from time to time. Some errors are temporary while others are permanent. Temporary errors usually mean that the bits flip during transmission. Permanent errors imply hardware failures. All the links in a network should have a low error rate; the lower the better. There are two groups of hardware failures in the system. One group includes I/O device failures and the second group includes failures of memory and CPU.

The first group mainly imply line failures, which are due to bad pin connections, a bad controller chip, and other component failures on the communication board. Other I/O devices, such as printers and disks, may also fail and demand immediate repair. A good operating system can vary the I/O device offline and request instant repair. Most likely, the maintenance technician pulls out the old board and plugs in a new one that works. If the card-pulling technique fails, then the field engineer will be called in to solve the problem. Under such circumstances, the system will usually be shut down.

The technical personnel always attempt to repair the hardware without shutting the system down. After the repair, a warm boot is adequate because the OS still remains intact in memory. Other times, when the CPU or memory is down (which means a node crash), power must be shut down to call for system repair. After the repair, the system must go through a cold boot and restart. All lost files must be rebuilt from previous backups. If spare hardware components are available, the card-pulling technique can shorten the repair time. After the system becomes operational, the technician has plenty of time to do the repair. The goal is to improve the availability of the system as explained below.

10.1.5 Reliability

Reliability is a critical issue in network design, and any system should be reliable. Once a network breaks down, it should take a short time to restore the system to its fully operational condition. That is, the availability of a network is more meaningful than just good reliability. Ideally, a network should operate 7 days a week and 52 weeks a year except for preventive maintenance. Even during maintenance, only a small portion of the network needs to be shut down and the rest of the network should still be operational.

Reliability is measured by mean time between failures (MTBF), which defines how often the hardware breaks. During the design cycle, all components on the board should go through a sift analysis so that the circuit can stand the worst case of electronic specification tolerances. As to how fast the network can be restored to operational condition, that depends on the mean time to repair (MTTR). The availability of a network is

$$\text{Availability} = \frac{\text{MTBF}}{\text{MTBF} + \text{MTTR}}$$

Consider the following scenario: if the hardware fails every 40 days and the MTTR is 4 hours, we have a very impressive availability as computed below:

$$40 \cdot 24 / (40 \cdot 24 + 4) = 99.59 \%$$

However, if it takes a week to solve the problem, the availability becomes

$$40 \cdot 24 / (40 \cdot 24 + 7 \cdot 24) = 85.11 \%$$

which is not that good. Repairing a large and heterogeneous network is not an easy job. If a network is down over several days, everybody from the network department panics. In order to shorten the MTTR, tools are developed to gather statistical data on disk. The database has a universal platform for all systems. After reading these data, network administrators can have a pretty good idea about what is wrong with the network. Data collection can be achieved by means of hardware monitor devices or network management software routines, as discussed in the following.

10.2 NETWORK MONITORING

To design a network that involves hardware and software, we need to locate the bugs in hardware and software during the development cycle. To assist debugging, various network monitoring devices are used. They are designed for testing at different levels. Each monitor or protocol analyzer has a computer inside equipped with software to support its own printer, disk, keyboard, and display. After development, loop tests can be performed to detect the bottlenecks and fine-tune the network.

10.2.1 Protocol Analyzers

When the hardware is first built, to test whether data are emitted on the line an oscilloscope is adequate to plot the waveform. After the basic hardware is debugged, we can write simple software to transmit and receive a block of characters on the line. To check the correctness of data transmission, it is necessary to display the message transmitted and the response received. As an example, a frame protocol analyzer is available on the market to suit such a need [HP4951]. The protocol analyzer can be used to intercept all the bits on the line and display the data in ASCII or hex. From the display, the designers can diagnose the problems if there is any. This is referred to as passive monitoring because the analyzer never interacts with the station being monitored.

At the next level, packet protocol analyzers are designed to monitor the Internet traffic on an Ethernet bus [HP4972]. The packet protocol analyzer is bigger in size and has been assigned a 48-bit Ethernet address of its own. Not only does the analyzer intercept and display the traffic, it also can gather the statistical data, such as login requests on the bus. From the measurements, the mean arrival time of login requests can be computed. The analyzer interacts very little with other stations except occasionally broadcasting its messages.

At the third level, not only can the analyzer capture and interpret the messages on the line, it also contains agent software to interact with a manager running on a different node. In other words, the manager may exchange network management information with the agent. Generally speaking, the analyzer observes the traffic on the network to which it is attached and displays the statistics gathered in the current session. The capabilities of such an analyzer are listed below [SNIFFER]:

- Monitor up to 1,024 stations;
- Generate visible and audible alarms for the entire network or for individual stations;
- Keep a historical alarm log;
- Keep track of the traffic and historical information of each station as well as the entire network;
- Sort statistics out and only show those items that interest the network administrator;
- Create customized management reports;
- Print the selected information at set time intervals.

In addition, the analyzer can monitor continuously for up to 49 days. After 49 days, the analyzer automatically resets. The communication protocol between the agent and the manager is the simple network management protocol (SNMP). In conclusion, protocol analyzers are useful either to find the development bugs or to locate failures after the network becomes operational.

Before discussing SNMP, we would like to introduce some techniques for debugging the hardware and software. One common approach is to connect the output port to an input port on the same system and perform a loop test, as explained in the following.

10.2.2 Loop Tests

There are many ways to perform a loop test, which can test the hardware, the software, or both. The simplest one to test the logic of a single software module is to transmit bits out on the DTE port and receive bits from the same port. A specially designed terminator needs to be plugged into the connector as shown in Figure 10.2(a). In the terminator, there is a connection between the Transmit data pin and the Receive data pin. If both the hardware and software of the system work properly, the same bits received should be the same as the ones

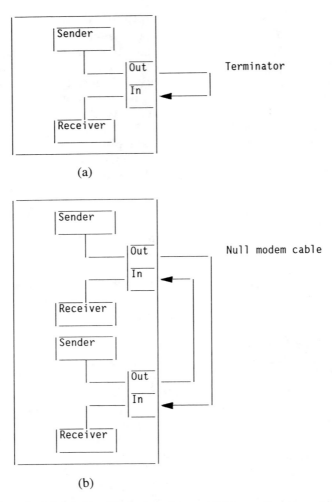

Figure 10.2 Loop test: (a) single software module and (b) two software modules.

transmitted. If the bits don't match, something is wrong in either the hardware, the software, or both.

In Figure 10.2(b), we can test two different software modules on the same machine. A special null modem cable is required to connect two DTEs, and each one has its own data link. Each module has a transmitter/receiver pair denoted by the Out/In box. One module transmits the data while the other module receives. Full-duplex transmission can be simulated as discussed in Chapter 3.

The loop test idea can also be applied to an ATM switch. Figure 10.3(a) shows the stress test of an ATM switch using only two ports [1]. Port 1 is

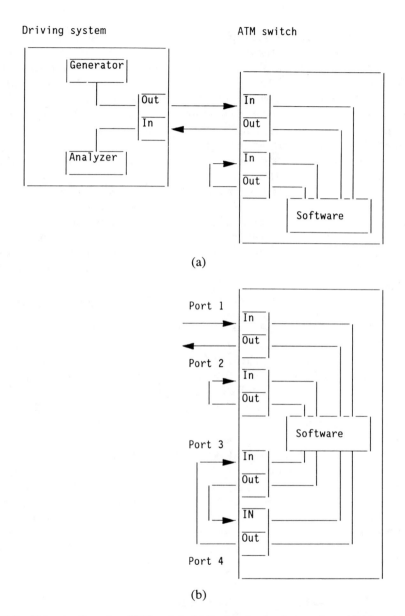

Figure 10.3 Stress testing of an ATM switch: (a) loop test using two ports and (b) loop test using four ports.

connected to the driving system, which has a generator and an analyzer. Generator means sender, analyzer means receiver, and both are software routines. The second port has a terminator plugged in. The bits flow from the generator to the ATM switch via the first port. The software in ATM routes data to the second port. Through the terminator, the data bits reenter ATM. The data are routed again inside the switch and transmitted out on port 1. Finally, the driving system receives the data bits, which are then analyzed. The test should sustain a constant bit rate (CBR) up to 155 Mbps.

There are two goals in performing the test on the ATM switch. One goal is to measure the latency time, which is the delay time of those bits staying in ATM. The latency time varies from system to system and can be measured. To do so, we start the timer when the bits flow into the ATM switch and stop the timer when the bits exit the system. The latency time is related to the length of the serial buffer in the switch and therefore decreases as the bit rate increases. It is necessary in the design to give ATM enough time to route data. The second goal of the test is to check the load balancing of the system, as shown in Figure 10.3(b).

A total of four ports are involved in the test. The latency time is measured and the load balancing condition is also checked to see if the switch can indeed sustain the high bit rate. After entering the switch via port 1, the bits are routed to port 4. Via the loop cable, the bits arrive on port 3 and are routed to port 2, which has a terminator plugged in. Then, the same data bits flow out on port 3, in on port 4, and are finally transmitted out on port 1. Any discrepancies of data flow can be detected by the analyzer on the driving system.

Using monitors or loop tests to debug a single system is quite effective. What if the network has several heterogeneous computers and each one has its own operating system? How can we locate failures when the network is down? Of course, a good network should not be crashed easily. Even when crashes occur, the damages should be confined within a few nodes. The debugging job becomes nontrivial if a generalized network consists of a large number of nodes and each one runs its own protocol under a different operating system. In order to communicate among different systems, the collection of network management data under a common platform becomes a necessary condition in network design. Based on this notion, some network management routines are discussed in the following.

10.3 SIMPLE NETWORK MANAGEMENT PROTOCOL

Network management tools have always been a slow start because there is no hurry unless the network is having problems. However, they are important once the network becomes operational. During the period of time when the OSI network management standards were developed, there was no prospect for translating their drafting documents into software products that would fit into the management needs of TCP/IP. In the late 1980s, the Internet Architecture Board (IAB) felt that it should form a group to develop tools, protocols, and a common database for general network management. As a result of this, simple network management protocol (SNMP) was born for TCP/IP, with considerations based on the framework of the OSI model [RFC1157]. The consequences have exceeded everybody's expectations. Nowadays, the SNMP specifications and source code are available on the Net (Internet) and are further incorporated into many products running on either mainframes or communication processors.

10.3.1 SNMP Architecture

There were three goals in designing the protocol. The first goal was simplicity, which eliminates ambiguity and reduce cost. The second goal was extensibility so that the protocol and the database could be expanded in the future. The third goal was design independence, which means that the protocol should work for any host or gateway regardless of its architecture.

Three basic concepts—the manager, the agent, and the management information base (MIB)—were incorporated into SNMP, which was originally intended to manage TCP/IP networks and Ethernet LANs. The application protocol is, however, independent of TCP/IP. SNMP has its own monitor and control functions using datagram transport services to move information between the management station and the station being managed. A typical SNMP architecture is shown in Figure 10.4.

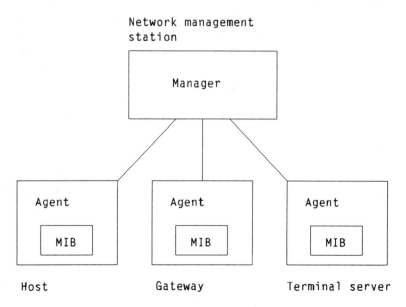

Figure 10.4 SNMP architecture.

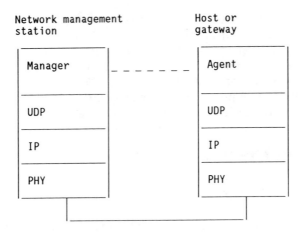

Figure 10.5 SNMP protocol stack.

As far as programming is concerned, the manager is a client running on the management station and the agent is a server running on a network element. Both of them belong to the application layer, as shown in Figure 10.5. In other words, the agent is a network application program whose job is to collect data and interact with the manager and NOS. The network element can be a host, a gateway, a terminal server, and so on. Recall that a gateway is a router that does protocol conversion. The manager is another network application program whose job is to supervise and communicate with its agent. An agent may communicate with another agent on a different host. The manager may be invoked by a human administrator at the console, and SNMP is the communication protocol used between a manager and an agent. The manager and agent use UDP services on the network to exchange messages. The database created on the network element is known as a view of the MIB, which contains objects arranged in a tree structure [RFC1156].

Proxy Agent

A proxy agent is a special network application program running on the host that communicates with the manager. It is designed to perform the two functions listed below:

1. An SNMP management station can control or monitor an I/O device that does not support SNMP. The proxy agent retrieves status information from the device and maps it into the MIB format and communicates with the manager on behalf of the device.
2. A proxy may be used to relay the network management information

from TCP/IP because in some cases the information cannot be directly accessed for security reasons.

10.3.2 SNMP Messages

A manager can ask its agent to report status and performance data from its MIB, which mainly contains information about its physical network interfaces, traffic counts, routing table, and so forth. The information is coded in an SNMP message or string of bits. The manager also provides a user interface to interact with a human administrator who can extract information, analyze data, review the status of components, and make network management decisions. The SNMP message has its own format defined in ASN.1 and each message is a special application subcommand transmitted via a UDP port. The peer at the receiving end interprets and executes the message.

Request messages are sent by the manager. In general, the SNMP request messages are either to set the value of some parameters or to retrieve such a value. A protocol entity is defined as the software routine in the protocol stack. After receiving a request, the agent will ask for authentication services from the system. Only with approval will the request be granted, and the agent on the network element then interacts with a protocol entity on the same node to get or set such variables. In order to reduce the number of message types, certain actions are data-driven. For example, there is no explicit message to ask the agent to reboot. Instead, the manager can set a parameter value in the database indicating the number of seconds until system reboot. Using this notion, there are only five messages types:

1. Get request;
2. Get Next request;
3. Set request;
4. Get response;
5. Trap.

A Get request is sent by the manager routine that wants to read information from a MIB, so the message contains a variable or variable list as passing parameter. A variable is known as a managed object in the database.

The Get Next request is a follow-up message sent by the manager after receiving a response from a previous request or Get request. This message requests the value of the next object in sequence with respect to the current object whose address is given in this request. Based on the address of the current object, the agent traverses the conceptual table within the MIB and returns the value of the next object in sequence along with its address. If the current object happens to be the last entry in a table, then the next object really implies the first object in the table and its value will be returned in a wraparound fashion.

The Set request is also sent by the manager to ask the agent to set the value of one or more variables in the MIB. All the messages of request type are sent by the manager to the agent, which then fulfills the request if access right is permitted.

The Get response message is sent from the agent to the manager as a reply to a Get request, Get Next request or Set request message. All the request and response messages are transmitted or received via UDP calls using port 161.

The fifth message, Trap is unsolicited, which means that after a special event has occurred on the station being managed, the agent sends a Trap message to its manager to report the incident. This feature can be enabled under programming control so that when Trap is desired, a message is transmitted or received via a UDP call using port 162. Special Trap events reported include cold boot, warm boot, link down, link up, and authentication failure.

SNMP Message Format

An SNMP message consists of three basic elements as follows:

- Version number;
- Community name;
- Data.

Each SNMP message is composed of a message header and a PDU, which really implies the inner portion of an application PDU (APDU) (i.e., the entire message). The message header mainly contains a version number and a community name. The SNMP messages are specified in ASN.1 as shown in Figure 10.6. The IMPORTS clause specifies those abstract data types defined in a different module. In this case, ObjectName, ObjectSyntax, . . . , can be found in the structure for management information (SMI) [RFC1155]. The SNMP message always starts with a SEQUENCE header followed by a version number and a community name. The variable version-1 has a value of 0 and the community name is an octet string of any length that indicates a network profile defining the access right of the manager. The third field contains data, which is called the PDU. The data type PDUs indicates that any bit pattern from a CHOICE of five is acceptable. Note that CHOICE doesn't create its own header, so only the PDU header exists in the message.

Each PDU must be defined individually, as shown in Figure 10.7. There is a 1-byte opcode in the header that further differentiates the type of PDUs. However, the semantics of a particular field in a PDU may have different meanings for different messages. As an example, the Error-Status field in a request message always contains a 0. But in a response message, it may contain a number ranging from 1 to 5 as the error code during processing.

Except for Trap, the other four messages share the same format. Each of the messages is specified as an implicit PDU that has the generic attributes common

```
SNMP DEFINITIONS ::= BEGIN
        IMPORTS
                ObjectName, ObjectSyntax, ...
        FROM SMI;

-- top-level message

        Message ::= SEQUENCE {
                        version     INTEGER {
                                        version-1(0)
                                    },
                        community   OctetString,
                        data        PDUs
                    }

-- protocol data units

        PDUs ::=    CHOICE {
                        get-request
                            GetRequest-PDU,
                        get-next-request
                            GetNextRequest-PDU,
                        get-response
                            GetResponse-PDU,
                        set-request
                            SetRequest-PDU,
                        trap
                            Trap-PDU
                    ...

        END
```

Figure 10.6 SNMP messages specified in ASN.1.

to all four. The Request-id field is usually a 3-byte or 4-byte integer and the corresponding response message must contain the same Request-id, which identifies the request. The Error-Status field, a 1-byte integer, specifies an error code that is only relevant in a response message, and mostly this byte contains a 0, meaning no error. A nonzero indicates that an exception has occurred while processing the request. There are a total of five error codes and each one has a value enclosed in parenthesis. We have

tooBig	→ the message exceeds the local limitation.
noSuchName	→ the object in the Variable-Binding field is not found.
badValue	→ the message itself has errors.
readOnly	→ the object has an access right of read-only.
genErr	→ the value of the object cannot be retrieved.

Since a request type of message may contain a list of objects, the agent may encounter errors when processing an object in the list. Therefore, the Error-Index field, if not 0 in a getResponse message, specifies the position of the object in

```
-- Individual PDU is defined as follows.
        GetRequest-PDU        ::= [0] IMPLICIT PDU
        GetNextRequest-PDU    ::= [1] IMPLICIT PDU
        GetResponse-PDU       ::= [2] IMPLICIT PDU
        SetRequest-PDU        ::= [3] IMPLICIT PDU

        PDU ::= SEQUENCE {
                   request-id
                        INTEGER,
                   error-status           -- sometimes ignored
                        INTEGER {
                              noError(0),
                              tooBig(1),
                              noSuchName(2),
                              badValue(3),
                              readOnly(4),
                              genErr(5)
                        },
                   error-index            -- sometimes ignored
                        INTEGER,
                   variable-bindings      -- sometimes ignored
                        VarBindList
                }

        VarBind ::= SEQUENCE {
                   name
                        ObjectName,
                   value
                        ObjectSyntax
                }
        VarBindList ::= SEQUENCE OF VarBind

-- Trap-PDU has a different format not shown here.

    . . .
```

Figure 10.7 SNMP PDUs specified in ASN.1.

a list contained in the received message. This helps debugging because the object that has caused the exception is identified. Intuitively, an index 0 means no errors and 1 points to the first object in the list.

The Variable-Bindings field contains an object list, even though in most messages there is only one object in the list. The object list has a type VarBindList (variable bind list) that describes how the list is constructed. Each list element has a type VarBind, defined to be a pair of two records. The first record specifies the name of the object, which has a type ObjectName. The second record specifies the value of the object, which has a type ObjectSyntax. Recall that both name and value are identifiers or variable names in ASN.1. Before explaining the definitions of ObjectName and ObjectSyntax, let us explore the meaning of an object. The object mentioned so far represents a piece of network management information on disk that is characterized by the following:

1. Object description: A textual name used to describe the object along with the numeric address of the object in the MIB.
2. Syntax: The syntactic description of the object in ASN.1.
3. Definition: A textual description of the semantics of the object type. All objects should have consistent meaning across all machines.
4. Access: Either read-only, read-write, write-only, or not accessible.
5. Status: Either mandatory, optional, or obsolete.

In order to find the object on disk, a unique path name is required, which is encoded into a sequence of integers preceded by a header and a length. The path name in machine code is used by the operating system to traverse a tree structure on disk and locate the object.

The ObjectName type is used to describe the data structure of the path name, which is defined as an OBJECT IDENTIFIER belonging to the Universal class with a tag id 6. Each object in the tree contains a Value field that contains information in the form of integers, strings, and so forth. The Value field is the attribute of the object. In a Set request message, the Value field is NULL, but in a Set response message, the Value field contains the value of an object as requested. The construction of an object name depends on the data structure in which information is stored, as described in the next section.

10.3.3 Management Information Base

The structure of a management information specification provides the framework within which the MIB can be defined and constructed [RFC1156]. Both documents are compatible with the framework of the OSI network management model. The MIB on each network element merely provides a view of the global database. All the Data fields in the MIB are defined in ASN.1 with a definite length, which means no ending delimiters are used at all.

Figure 10.8 shows the hierarchical tree structure of a global database, which is an independent standard. Each circle in the tree is referred to as a tree node, which represents an information entity or object. The root node resides on top of the tree and has a fixed location on disk, so it doesn't need a name. Below the root, there are three subtrees: itu, iso, and joint-iso-itu. In each node, there is a one- or two-digit number below the symbolic name. As an example, iso has been assigned 1. This number is part of a path name to access the node iso. Each node or object contains pointers to its subtrees as well as a Value field containing attributes to describe the object. Below iso, org is assigned 3, dod is 6, and Internet is 1.

An object is associated with a name or path name. If the name is represented by a block of binary numbers, it is said to be in machine-readable form. For a human user, a path name is specified in symbolic form; that is, several ASCII strings separated by periods. Of course, a symbolic name is much longer

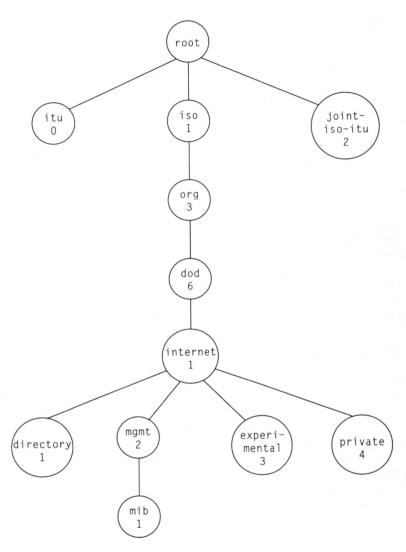

Figure 10.8 A global information tree.

than the machine-readable form. Even though there is a one-to-one relationship between the two, a translation process is required to convert a symbolic name to its machine-readable form. There is another intermediate form that sits right in the middle. That is, we replace the symbolic name of each node with a numeric number in the dot notation. To get to the Internet node in the MIB, a path name has the form of:

1. iso.org.dod.internet
2. 1.3.6.1
3. 2B 06 01 (24-bit in hex)

Note that the first two digits in the path name are encoded into one byte. The SNMP computes the numeric value of the first two digits, x.y as $(x \cdot 40)+y$. For 1.3 in our example, we have $(1 \cdot 40)+3$, which is 43 or 2B in hex.

The MIB is a subtree under mgmt as shown in Figure 10.9. There are eight object groups under the MIB that jointly constitute the network management information database. Each group collects information arranged in a subtree as listed below:

1. System: System (sys) description of the network element, a host or router.
2. Interfaces: The network interfaces (if) on the node.
3. Address Translation: The address translation (at) table of IP addresses and physical addresses.
4. IP: IP software.
5. ICMP: Internet control message protocol software

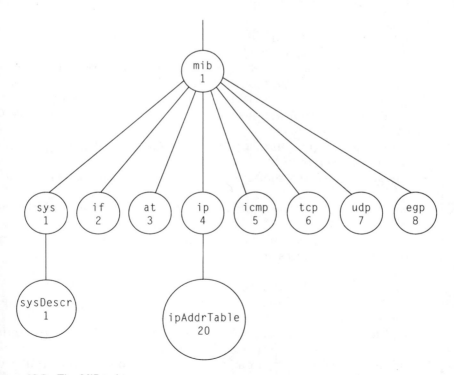

Figure 10.9 The MIB subtree.

6. TCP: Transmission control protocol software.
7. UDP: User datagram protocol software.
8. EGP: Exterior gateway protocol software.

The number below the subtree name is a local address or index, so system has a node address 1 and EGP has 8. Under system, there is an object named sysDescr (system Description) that contains the textual description of the system, and its node address is also 1. A string of node addresses is used to locate the object in the MIB and each object has a Value field that contains a piece of network management information.

Examples Of MIB Objects

Each object can be thought of as a variable or information entity. In fact, an object is a general term used to contain a piece of information such as integer, string, record, and array of records. A record is a structure containing elements of different types. All the objects defined in the MIB have a prefix in lowercase letters identifying the group. Some of the interesting ones are listed below:

1. icmpInMsgs (ICMP input messages): the number of ICMP messages received.
2. ifMtu (interface maximum transfer unit): the maximum size of the datagram in octets allowed on this interface.
3. ifNumber (interface number): the number of network interfaces, regardless of their current state, on which this system can send/receives datagrams.
4. ipInHdrErrors (ip input header errors): the number of datagrams discarded due to errors.
5. ipInDiscards (ip input discards): the number of datagrams discarded due to the lack of buffer space.
6. ipReasmOKs (ip reassembly OKs): the number of times that reassembly is successful.
7. ipReasmFails (ip reassembly fails): the number of times that reassembly has failed.
8. ipAddrTable (ip address table): an array of records where each record contains the addressing information for one of this entity's IP addresses.
9. ipRoutingTable (ip routing table): an array of records where each record contains routing information such as destination IP address, routing metric, next hop, route type, and route age.
10. tcpRtoMin (tcp retransmission time-out minimum value): the minimum value of time-out period in milliseconds.
11. udpInDatagrams (udp input datagrams): the number of input datagrams received.

12. egpInMsgs (egp input messages): the number of egp messages received without error.
13. sysDescr (system description): describes the name and version of the hardware system, operating system, and network software.
14. sysUpTime (system up time): specifies the time in hundreds of a second since the network management system was last reinitialized.

To fetch the value of sysDescr, an object name should be

iso.org.dod.internet.mgmt.mib.system.sysDescr
(1.3.6.1.2.1.1.1.0)

where the suffix 0 is added to indicate that the managed object is a single variable. Let us try something more complicated. Under ip, there is an object named ipAddrTable (ip address table) that is described as follows:

Object: ipAddrTable { ip 20 }
Syntax: SEQUENCE OF IpAddrEntry
Access: read-only
Status: mandatory

The name of this object is ipAddrTable, which has a node address 20 under ip. This object has a data type that describes how the object is built; that is, a sequence of records. Each record in the table has a type, IpAddrEntry (IP address entry). The access right of the table is read-only and its status is mandatory, which implies that every system should implement this table. Since the network element may have several IP addresses assigned to it, each IP address has its own record in the table. Each record is not a tree node, but contains four entries as defined below:

```
IpAddrEntry ::= SEQUENCE {
    ipAdEntAddr
        IpAddress,
    ipAdEntIfIndex
        INTEGER,
    ipAdEntNetMask
        IpAddress,
    ipAdEntBcastAddr
        INTEGER
}
```

The four entries are described in the following:

ipAdEntAddr: The ip Address Entry - Address is the IP address for which this record is prepared.

ipAdEntIfIndex: The ip Address Entry - Interface Index denotes the Interface Index.

ipAdEntNetMask: The ip Address Entry - Network Mask is used to get to the server for this IP address.

ipAdEntBcastAddr: The ip Address Entry - Broadcast Address is used to get to this IP address.

In order to fetch any entry from any record in the table, we need to append a pair of indices after the object name. The first index points to the record and the second index points to the entry. The agent interprets and executes the message received, and the object name sometimes may provide semantic meaning, too. For example, in a getNextRequest message, an object name of

iso.org.dod.internet.mgmt.mib.ip.ipAddrTable.1.ipAdEntNetmask (1.3.6.1.2.1.4.20.1.3)

tells the agent to return the value of an object that is the third entry in the first record even though the message is getNextRequest. However, the returned object name in the getResponse message has a qualifier appended at the end. The qualifier is an IP address fetched from the first entry in the first record. If the returned object name is used again in a subsequent getNextRequest message, the value of the next object in sequence will be returned. Therefore, the object name

iso.org.dod.internet.mgmt.mib.ip.ipAddrTable.1.ipAdEntNetmask
.129.65.82.251
(1.3.6.1.2.1.4.20.1.3.129.65.82.251)

tells the agent to return the value of the next object in sequence that is ipAdEntBcastAddr. The qualifier 129.65.82.251 appended at the end has made a difference.

In the following, we describe the protocol between a series of getNextRequest and getResponse messages. Each message contains two object list elements as shown below:

— The getNextRequest has no qualifiers after object names.
Command = Get next request
Request ID = 620141
Object = {1.3.6.1.2.1.4.20.1.1} (ipAdEntAddr)
Value = NULL
Object = {1.3.6.1.2.1.4.20.1.3} (ipAdEntNetMask)
Value = NULL

— The getResponse returns objects with qualifiers.
Command = Get response
Request ID = 620141
Object = {1.3.6.1.2.1.4.20.1.1.129.65.82.251}
(ipAdEntAddr.129.65.82.251)
Value = [129.65.82.251]
Object = {1.3.6.1.2.1.4.20.1.3.129.65.82.251}
(ipAdEntNetMask.129.65.82.251)

Value = [255.255.255.0]

— The getNextRequest has qualifiers after object names.
Command = Get next request
Request ID = 620142
Object = {1.3.6.1.2.1.4.20.1.1.129.65.82.251} (ipAdEntAddr.129.65.82.251)
Value = NULL
Object = {1.3.6.1.2.1.4.20.1.3.129.65.82.251}
(ipAdEntNetMask.129.65.82.251)
Value = NULL

— The getResponse returns next objects in sequence.
Command = Get response
Request ID = 620142
Object = {1.3.6.1.2.1.4.20.1.2.129.65.82.251} (ipAdEntIfIndex.129.65.82.251)
Value = 0
Object = {1.3.6.1.2.1.4.20.1.4.129.65.82.251}
(ipAdEntBcastAddr.129.65.82.251)
Value = 1

It should also be mentioned that the internal structure of an object in the MIB is different from the data structure of such information used in the network access methods. For example, the address table in the network layer does not need an identifier or length. The MIB standard is strictly designed for universal information retrieval and software development. The necessary software change to accommodate the new additions of objects in the database is greatly reduced.

10.3.4 Encoding of SNMP Messages

To complete our discussion on SNMP and MIB, we should examine the encoding of SNMP messages for the sake of curiosity. All SNMP message are of a definite length and whenever possible and nonconstructed type is used instead of constructed. On a local area network, a SNIFFER analyzer is used to monitor the traffic on the network. The manager runs on another node, which sends a getRequest message to the SNIFFER, which in turn returns a getResponse. Because SNIFFER can intercept and capture messages online, the messages later can be read and displayed.

Figure 10.10(a) shows the encoding of a getRequest message in hex format. Each other line below the code was added for the purpose of interpretation. The message header is a SEQUENCE identifier with a Length field of 40. After counting the 2-byte header, the entire message is 42 bytes long. The version number is 0 and the community name is "public." The opcode is A0, which means context-specific, constructed with a tag id 0. This particular message has a 3-byte request-id 620139. Because the object is a single variable, sysDescr, a 0 suffix is appended to the end of its path name or address. Since more than one

```
30          28          02              01          00
SEQUENCE    len=40      INTEGER         len=1       version-1

04          06          70 75 62 6C 69 63
OCT STR     len=6       p  u  b  l  i  c

A0          1B          02              03          09 76 6B
getReq      len=27      INTEGER         len=3       request-id= 620139

02          01          00              02          01          00
INTEGER     len=1       err-status      INTEGER     len=1       err-index

30          0E          30              0C
SEQUENCE    len=14      SEQUENCE        len=12

06          08          2B      06  01  02  01  01  01  00
OBJ ID      len=8       1.3.    6.  1.  2.  1.  1.  1.  0

05          00
NULL        len=0
```

(a)

```
30          46          02              01          00
SEQUENCE    len=70      INTEGER         len=1       version-1

04          06          70 75 62 6C 69 63
OCT STR     len=6       p  u  b  l  i  c

A2          39          02              03          09 76 6B
getRes      len=57      INTEGER         len=3       request-id= 620139

02          01          00              02          01          00
INTEGER     len=1       err-status      INTEGER     len=1       err-index

30          2C          30              2A
SEQUENCE    len=44      SEQUENCE        len=42

06          08          2B      06  01  02  01  01  01  00
OBJ ID      len=8       1.3.    6.  1.  2.  1.  1.  1.  0

04          1E          4E 65 74 77 6F 72 6B 20 47 65 6E
OCT STR     len=30      N  e  t  w  o  r  k     G  e  n

65 72       61    6C    20 53 6E 69 66 66 65 72 20 53 65 72
e  r        a     l        S  n  i  f  f  e  r     S  e  r

76 65       72
v  e        r
```

(b)

Figure 10.10 Encoding of a getRequest message: (a) getRequest sysDescr and (b) getResponse SysDescr.

object can be listed in the message, the outer SEQUENCE header is needed to specify the type and length of the object list.

After receiving the getRequest, the agent server on SNIFFER returns a getRespopnse message as shown in Figure 10.10(b). Note that this message shares the same request-id, but its opcode is A2 instead. The name of the returned object is also the same, but its value is changed to a textual string, "Network General Sniffer Server," which is 30 bytes long.

We have so far introduced the fundamental concepts of SNMP and its management information base. Regardless of the popularity of this product, a new version was proposed as SNMPv2 (SNMP version 2). It has a different message header that defines both authentication and authorization policies. The PDUs are expanded by adding a few new functions, but it is not upward compatible. The specifications of PDUs can be found in [RFC1448] and its MIB is specified in [RFC1450]. In general, SNMPv2 has a more enhanced security facility that is in line with the OSI network management model as introduced next.

10.4 OSI NETWORK MANAGEMENT MODEL

ITU-T has its long-term commitment to setting standards for OSI networks and has its own network management standards. A monitor communicates with a host using thte common management information protocol CMIP) [ISO9595]. The specifications of network management using CMIP as the protocol are known as common management information services CMIS) [ISO9596]. Inside CMIS, the association control service element (ACSE) and the remote operation service element (ROSE) are called.

10.4.1 Common Network Management Services

Network management services can be performed between two management application entities. The service routines are grouped into CMIS Element (CMISE), a software package that is supposed to work with any OSI-compliant systems. Each service primitive or system call in CMISE starts with an uppercase letter M followed by a underscore as introduced below:

1. The M_INITIALIZE service is issued by a service user, the manager, in order to establish an association with its peer, the agent.
2. M_GET is used to request management information from the managed station.
3. M_EVENT_REPORT is used to report an event associated with management information to the manager. It is a response from the agent due to the receipt of an M_GET.
4. M_SET is used to modify certain variables in the management information base.

5. M_ACTION is used to perform an action on a managed object.
6. M_CREATE is used to create a representation of a new managed object instance, complete with its identification and its associated management information, and register its identification.
7. M_DELETE is used to delete a representation of a managed object instance and delete its registration.
8. M_TERMINATE normally terminates an association between two service users.
9. M_ABORT abnormally terminates an association.
10. M_CANCEL_GET cancels the operation of a previous M_GET. It enables the agent to terminate an I/O operation if the returned message is long.

10.4.2 Distributed Management Environment

The Open Software Foundation (OSF) is a consortium of computer vendors whose goal is to develop software products that enable systems and applications to communicate across local and wide area networks [OSF]. Since SNMP resembles the OSI model in many ways, it is necessary to compromise and OSF intends to combine OSI and SNMP protocols with object-oriented packages as standards. In addition, OSF will release its source code to universities and research organizations. Unfortunately, TCP/IP doesn't have ACSE, ROSE, and ASN.1 services. Therefore, a special software interface must be written between CMIS and TCP/IP. As a result, CMOT (CMIS Over TCP/IP) was developed, so CMIS can be built on the Net using TCP/IP system calls. The CMIS and protocols for the Internet (CMOT and CMIP) can be found in [RFC1189].

As envisioned in the near future, as part of the distributed computing environment, there will be a distributed management environment (DME) over a global network sharing the same database, as shown in Figure 10.11. Different

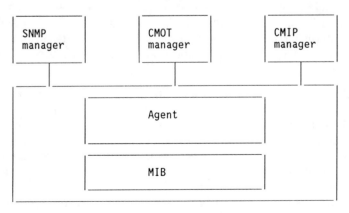

Figure 10.11 Addressing MIB using different protocols.

systems running different protocols can access the global MIB and interchange network information under certain access rules. That is, the MIB format is the de facto standard observed by designers so different systems may exchange network information sharing a common format. Some may use SNMP while others use CMIS or CMOT.

10.5 OTHER NETWORK MANAGEMENT SYSTEMS

There are other commercial systems on network management. Each computer manufacturer has its own product. For example, IBM has NetView, DEC has EMA (Enterprise Management Architecture), HP has OpenView, AT&T has UNMA (Unified Network Management Architecture), and UNISYS has UNMS (Unisys Network Management System) [2]. Each system uses the facilities of its native OS, which is proprietary, and one manufacturer may support two or more operating systems. If the operating system is UNIX or its derivative, then the products are usually SNMP-based. An example is OpenView, which offers a solution for managing both local and wide area networks. Others may be OSI-based or proprietary. UNMA and UNMS are examples of OSI-based systems that also tend to cover a variety of networks, voice and data, public and private, local area and wide area, and so forth.

IBM has developed its own NetView software for network management. There are two versions of NetView: one for AIX, a derivative of UNIX; and the other one for SNA. The AIX version is SNMP-based and usually runs on a dedicated node in an Ethernet or token ring. The SNA version, on the other hand, is designed for mainframes [3][NetView]. Since SNA is a popular commercial network, the main features of its NetView are introduced in the next section.

10.5.1 NetView

The SNA NetView system is very rich and complex and works under a mainframe operating system such as Multiple Virtual Storage (MVS). It has its own virtual telecommunications access method (VTAM) and the network system software of IBM is generally known as SNA. The network management model of SNA is shown in Figure 10.12 [4]. There are three basic components in it: the focal point, entry point, and service point. A point really means a collection of software routines. The three points communicate among each other using a proprietary protocol. A focal point runs on a host (i.e., a mainframe), which provides centralized network management services for a network administrator sitting behind a console. A group of focal points that collect, analyze, and store network management data in SNA constitutes the backbone of NetView.

An entry point runs on an SNA device that is not a mainframe but is capable of performing network management services for itself and other devices attached

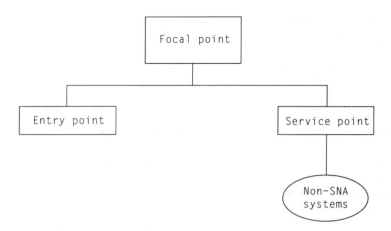

Figure 10.12 Network management model of SNA.

to it. Most of the SNA devices are capable of functioning as entry points. A service point provides measurement support for itself, its attached devices, and other network nodes that do not belong to SNA. A service point is capable of interpreting the network management information and reformatting the information, if necessary, between a focal point in SNA and a focal point outside SNA. The service point is thus a network management gateway between two systems. The ultimate goal is to let other networks communicate with the nodes in SNA.

We have introduced various products on network management. From an economical point of view, the trend is shifting from proprietary services to open services using the same database. A call is for designing the same network interface that interacts with an open operating system running on different hosts [5]. At the present time, CMIP and SNMP are the two major open protocols in the field. SNMP is such a solution to a problem, and market acceptance has driven the standard, rather than standard committees. CMIP, on the other hand, is slightly richer in functionality, but because of the lack of a supporting environment, it costs more money to turn the specification into a product. The two standards however, share the common database concept and each has its own industrial base. Therefore, the two may be merged into one, or more likely coexist, in the future for a long time to come.

10.6 CONCLUSIONS

The number of global computer networks is expanding and the number of nodes in a network is growing at an explosive rate. As a result of this, corporate networks have become mission-critical, and network management tools must therefore ensure that networks operate efficiently all the time. Since the components in a network, such as hardware, operating systems, network system software, and applications have become so complicated, it is a difficult job for a network administrator to locate failures in a network when the reason for the crash is unknown. Fortunately, with the assistance of monitoring devices, network management routines, and a common database to store network information, it is possible to identify failures when the network is down.

As far as corporate management is concerned, there are usually two considerations when purchasing a computer network: performance and cost. The performance of a network mainly depends on its capability and throughput. Since cost is a factor in making decisions, the management wants to make sure that a network can be expanded in the future at a minimal cost. Even though the raw speed of hardware dictates the throughput, the availability of a network should also be considered. That is, the MTBF of a network should be long and its MTTR should be short.

Epilog

I salute you for reading the entire book with perseverance. Any comment to improve this book will be greatly appreciated. My e-mail address is jyhsu@calpoly.edu and best wishes.

10.7 SUMMARY POINTS

1. The network management routines allow a network administrator to monitor and control the network node being managed, such as a host, gateway, or terminal server.
2. The NMT routines in an UNIX system are written as application programs using TCP/IP services. The routines running on the monitoring station are collectively called the manager while the routines running on the host or gateway are known as the agent.
3. The manager communicates with its agent using datagram services, and SNMP defines the meaning of messages.
4. The agent interacts with the protocol entity on the host or gateway in order to collect the network performance data that are being stored in a common database known as MIB.
5. The MIB is distributed on the station being managed and has a hierarchical name space to ensure that each object has a unique path name.
6. Both SNMP messages and the MIB are specified in ASN.1, but only a subset is used.
7. There are only five types of SNMP messages that are designed to set or to

retrieve parameters in the MIB. Control actions are triggered by the parameter and timer settings in the MIB.

8. In the future, there will be a distributed management environment in the network, and different protocols running on different hosts can access and exchange network information among one another.

Problems

Problem 10.1

Name the three basic components in a SNMP software product.

Problem 10.2

What are the three goals in the design of SNMP?

Problem 10.3

What is the difference between a manager and an agent?

Problem 10.4

Explain the Get Next request message in SNMP.

Problem 10.5

Briefly describe the structure of the management information base.

Problem 10.6

What is the reason to have MIB designed as a separate standard?

Problem 10.7

Given an object name in its symbolic form as specified below:

 iso.org.dod.internet.mgmt.mib.system.sysDescr

1. Translate it into the numeric form in dot notation.
2. Encode the name into a bit string and explain why the first byte is 2B in hex.

Problem 10.8

Examine any SNMP message and find out the 1-byte Identifier field for the built-in types: OBJECT IDENTIFIER and NULL.

Problem 10.9

What is the advantage of performing a loop test?

Problem 10.10

If a system has a 30-day MTBF and its MTTR is only 1 hr, what is the availability of the system?

References

[1] Mandeville, R., "The Stress Test: Which Switch Survived?," *Data Communications*, March 1995, pp. 69–77.
[2] Terplan, K., *Communication Networks Management*, 2nd edition, Prentice Hall, 1992.
[3] Johnson, R., *MVS Concepts and Facilities*, McGraw-Hill, 1989.
[4] Herman, J., NetView: IBM's Enterprise-Wide Manager, Northeast Consulting Resources, Inc., April 1989.
[5] Lias, J. L., Jr., "The Economics of Proprietary vs. Open Network Management Solutions," *Proc. IEEE Singapore International Conference on Networks*, July 1995.

Appendix A
Operating System Essentials

An OS consists of a set of control programs running side by side with the user programs. When a user program is loaded into the memory with all the resources allocated, it becomes a task. Therefore, a task is the basic programming entity in a computer. If a task belongs to the OS, it is a system task; otherwise, it is a user task. The execution of all tasks are the same to the OS. To fully understand the processing inside a computer, we introduce the interrupt mechanisms, asynchronous processing, intertask communications, and so on in the following.

A.1 INTERRUPT MECHANISMS

The main purpose of having interrupts in a computer is to improve throughput. Another reason is to protect the system from crashes, which in turn enhances system throughput.

When an interrupt occurs, the currently running program is forced to relinquish control to the OS. This is accomplished by so-called 'context switching' in two steps. First, the CPU hardware saves the old environment onto a stack. Next, the CPU loads a new running environment, usually from low memory at an address specified by the hardware. The running environment includes the program address register and the status register (SR). After this, the interrupt handler (IH) receives control and saves all other hardware registers onto the stack. In the middle of saving the environment, the CPU hardware disables any further interrupts to avoid confusion. The IH routine determines the cause of interrupt, then passes control to a particular interrupt service routine (ISR).

In the newly loaded SR, there is a particular bit whose setting indicates that the machine is in supervisor state. It is only in the supervisor state that a special set of instructions, known as the privileged instructions, can be executed [1] [INTEL486, MC68040]. These privileged instructions are not accessible to the application programmers. They are specifically designed for the OS developers. Privileged instructions mainly perform the system control functions. Examples are to modify the status register, interrupt an I/O processor, return from interrupt, and so forth. If a computer system utilizes I/O processors to run the OS, then all instructions running on the I/O processor are privileged because they are only accessible to the system developers.

There are many types of interrupt. The first type of interrupt is program check, designed to protect the machine from any damage caused by the user due to a programming error. For example, the user tries to divide an integer by zero or execute an instruction that is not valid. The second type of interrupt is system call. Whenever a user wants the OS to perform a system function on his or her behalf, he or she issues a system call. The execution of a system call instruction triggers the hardware interrupt mechanism, which passes control to the OS. System call is also known as supervisor call, trap call, or simply interrupt. After the call is completed, most of the time control will eventually be returned to the instruction after the call.

The third popular type is I/O completion. When an I/O operation is completed, the I/O controller chip may interrupt the main CPU to process this I/O completion event. An I/O controller can be thought of as a simple channel. Thus, it is possible for the main CPU to do some computations at the same time the I/O controller is performing its own I/O operations. It is this great concept that makes asynchronous processing possible. Other types of interrupt include timer, external, and machine check [1][IBM370]. Only with interrupts, it is possible to run many tasks concurrently during a time interval as described in Section A.2.

A.2 ASYNCHRONOUS PROCESSING

An I/O controller chip may perform its I/O operation independently while the main CPU is doing something else. When an I/O operation is completed, the I/O controller interrupts the CPU, which then processes this I/O completion event. Based on its assigned priority, the OS may decide to place the current program being interrupted in the ready queue and execute the program whose I/O has just been completed. That is to say, the current program is being preempted. The OS coordinates the execution of different programs in a computer from beginning to end, which means that all programs take turns to execute on the CPU. Since the I/O completion event is asynchronous and unpredictable, two tasks running in parallel is known as asynchronous processing.

A.3 TASK MANAGEMENT ROUTINES

A job is defined to be one or more job steps. A job step is a single program written by an application or system programmer. When a job step is loaded into memory with all its resources allocated, it becomes a task. There is a subtle difference between a program and a task, even though people use the terms interchangeably. The most frequent job consists of only one job step: load the program into memory and execute the program. The user may enter a command via the keyboard and the OS reads in the command, interprets, allocates resources, creates a task control block (TCB), and places the task in ready queue. Now, the task is ready to execute on the CPU whenever its turn comes. Normally, the command entered by the user is the name of a system command, an executable file, or some batch file containing many job steps in it. With graphical interface, you may click a mouse button on an icon to pass the same information to the OS. The basic concept, however, remains the same. In the following, we define what a task is.

A.3.1 Task Definition

A task is defined to be the basic unit of computation in a computer, with all the resources allocated by the OS. The main resources include the central memory, I/O devices, and CPU. A task may also be referred to as a process or a thread. A task is said to be in running state if it is currently executing on the CPU. With one main CPU, it is possible to have only one running task at a time. A task in ready state has all the resources available except the CPU. Ready means that the task is only waiting for its turn to execute on the CPU. A task in wait state needs some other resource besides the CPU. Other resources usually means a piece of I/O data that is not available until the I/O operation is completed. A task in wait state is said to be blocked and cannot proceed unless the resource it is waiting for becomes available.

A task is CPU bound, or compute-intensive, if it requires a substantial amount of CPU time to finish its computation. As an example, a task to verify whether any 10,000-digit integer is a prime or not is compute-bound. On the other hand, an I/O bound task spends most of its time waiting for its I/O completions. Data processing in a bank requires heavy I/O operations and therefore is I/O bound. It is the OS that tracks the status of the task, changes its state, and coordinates its execution. All tasks inside a computer take turns to execute, and wait from inception to completion. Some of the key concepts are described below.

A.3.2 Task Control Block

Each task is associated with a TCB that contains its running environment, as shown in Figure A.1. A TCB represents a task in memory and is itself a private resource. A TCB is allocated and initialized by the OS after a task creation call. The user and task ids collectively identify the unique task for intertask communications as well as for debugging purposes. The priority number is assigned

```
┌─────────────────────────────────────────────────┐
│ User id                                         │
├─────────────────────────────────────────────────┤
│ Task id                                         │
├─────────────────────────────────────────────────┤
│ Priority no.                                    │
├─────────────────────────────────────────────────┤
│ Status flag                                     │
├─────────────────────────────────────────────────┤
│ Addressing space information -                  │
│     Register save area,                         │
│     Program address register,                   │
│     Status register,                            │
│     Stack pointer, etc.                         │
├─────────────────────────────────────────────────┤
│ Pointer to its message queue                    │
├─────────────────────────────────────────────────┤
│ Pointers to other TCBs                          │
├─────────────────────────────────────────────────┤
│ Pointers to other control blocks associated     │
│ with various I/O devices                        │
├─────────────────────────────────────────────────┤
│ Security, etc.                                  │
└─────────────────────────────────────────────────┘
```

Figure A.1 Task control block.

by the OS and used by the dispatcher to determine which task should execute next if there is more than one task in the ready queue. The Status flag indicates the status of a task in memory: running, ready, wait, Non-Exist, and so forth. With large memory, all TCBs can be statically allocated with the Non-Exist flag set to indicate free status. The register save area in TCB is used to store all the hardware registers and one of them is the stack pointer (SP) to the top of the user's stack. Other information includes the security key, access right, and so forth.

A.3.3 I/O Interrupt Service Routines

After an I/O interrupt, which indicates that an I/O operation has just been completed, the I/O interrupt handler receives control. The IH disables further interrupts, saves the entire register set on the systems stack, and passes control to an I/O ISR to process the interrupt. After processing an I/O completion interrupt, the task becomes ready again but control is passed to the dispatcher, which determines the next task to run. In the case where the task just awakened has a higher priority, it will execute next.

A.3.4 Task Creation/Termination

Two primitives are required to create and terminate a task via system calls: Attach and Detach. After a program is loaded in memory, the OS issues an Attach system call to create a task as shown below:

    Attach(task_id, entry_point, address_space, etc);

where task_id denotes a character string, entry_point is the start address of the task, address_space points to a private addressing space or stack, and the etc parameter may include a port id, a data link id, and a priority number associated with the task. During task creation, the OS allocates a TCB, initialize its contents (i.e., running environment), and marks it ready to be executable. The newly created task is a descendent task of the parent task that issues the Attach system call.

    A Detach system call may be issued to terminate the task as shown below:

    Detach(task_id, status);

where status indicates what happened after the call. The OS simply deallocates the resources owned by the task and marks its TCB as Non-Exist. Every task termination call should find a match of a task creation call in the code. Usually, in a real-time OS, when a parent task terminates, all its descendent tasks are also terminated.

    There are many tasks running in the computer, and each task takes turns to execute and wait until the entire task is completed. The dispatcher is the routine in OS that coordinates the executions of all tasks as described below.

A.3.5 Dispatcher

The dispatcher (i.e., task scheduler) determines which task, if executable, should execute next. When the dispatcher cannot find any task to execute, it puts the CPU into hardware wait state. Any interrupt will wake up the CPU, which then resumes its fetch/interpret/execute cycle. One reason to have this design feature is because the CPU does not want to compete for memory cycles with the I/O controllers, thus improving throughput. The dispatcher examines the ready queue and moves a task to running state by passing control to it. Before passing control to the task, the dispatcher always restores its running environment first.

    The dispatcher is one of the most crucial routines in the OS and receives control from other system routines such as initialization, task creation/termination, an I/O request system call, or after processing an I/O completion. The dispatcher may be interrupted, but control must be returned to it immediately after processing the interrupt. Therefore, the dispatcher routine is logically indivisible and does not need a TCB while it is running. This consideration makes the OS design clean and elegant. While there are many tasks running in the computer, the status of each task is monitored by the task management routines. A task is switched from one state to another by the system and no error can be tolerated.

A.3.6 State Transition Diagram

There are three basic states of a task: RUnning, WAit and REady. We add a fourth state Non-Exist to indicate that a task does not exist. The two upper case letters may be coded as the Status flag in the TCB. The Non-Exist status flag really denotes a TCB that is free to be used.

To understand the basic concept of task executions, a basic state transition diagram is shown in Figure A.2. A task is moved to the ready queue by the initiator, which is the job scheduler. A job scheduler is different from a task

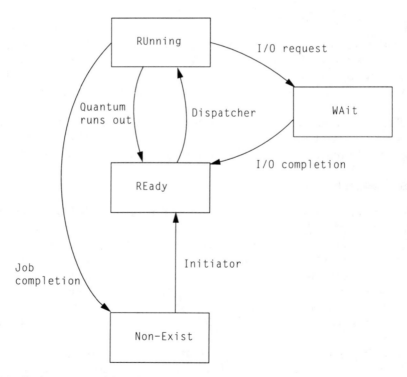

Figure A.2 Basic state transition diagram.

scheduler. A job scheduler schedules jobs and makes sure everything is ready before a task can be placed in ready queue. From there, a task scheduler dispatches a task in the ready queue to running state.

There are three ways to move a task out of the running state. First, when the execution is completed, normally or abnormally, the task is terminated and its TCB is marked Non-Exist. Second, when the allocated time slice, quantum runs out via a timer interrupt, this task is moved back to ready queue waiting for its next turn to execute on the CPU. Third, when the task issues an I/O request system call, it is placed in wait queue, waiting for its I/O completion. When its I/O is completed, the I/O ISR wakes up this task by changing its state from wait to ready. In other words, it becomes dispatchable again. If a task is in wait state, it is said to be blocked.

Task management routines work as a team to assure the smooth running of a task from its inception to completion.

A.4 REENTRANT TASK

A reentrant task is a system design concept to share code. It is possible to have one piece of code in memory but executed by two or more tasks concurrently during a time interval. That is, each task takes a turn executing the same piece of code. This is referred to as code sharing. The purposes are to save memory space, loading time, and hence increase throughput. Since the OS supports asynchronous processing, it is possible for one task to execute the middle section of the code while another task executes the beginning section of the code. They are executing the same piece of code during a time interval. We have one copy of code in memory, but there are multiple executions during the same time interval. The task executing the shared code is said to be reentrant.

The only requirement of writing shared or reentrant code is not to write data into the global addressing space. In other words, to read or execute the global addressing space is fine, but not writing data. Then, where should the data be written? The answer is to write into the private addressing space of the task. The register set is private, so is its stack. It is important to know that memory buffers for I/O should have their own allocated space or be placed on the stack of the task.

When a reentrant task is attached, the OS merely prepares a copy of the TCB and assigns its own addressing space. Figure A.3 depicts one copy of reentrant code in memory, executed by two tasks. Each task has its own TCB and addressing space. Its TCB and addressing space are private to the task and must be allocated by the OS. The ISRs, dispatcher, and so on usually reside in low memory. A system task in the OS may be reentrant and so are compilers and editors in a time-sharing system.

How can two tasks communicate on the same processor? Sometimes a real-time OS employs a message-based design as introduced below.

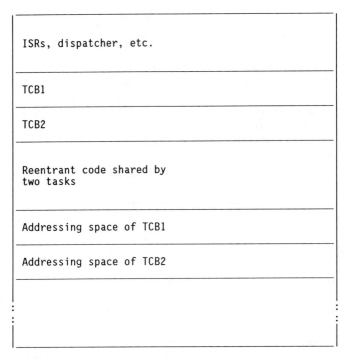

Figure A.3 Reentrant tasks in memory.

A.5 INTERTASK COMMUNICATIONS

One task can send a message to another task running on the same computer. One task issues a Send and the other task must issue a Receive to be in sync. The Send system call is proposed in the following:

   Send(to_task_id, message, status);

where to_task_id is the receiving task id, message may be a descriptor that provides the length and address of the message buffer and Status indicates what happens after the call. The sending task is not blocked so long as the OS can place the message in the message queue of the receiving task. The OS also wakes up the receiving task if it is in wait state.

The receiving task must issue a Receive system call as shown below:

   Receive(from_task_id, message, status);

where from_task_id may specify the specific task from which message is received, message is the same as in Send, and status indicates what happens after the call. The receiving task cannot proceed unless there is a message in its message queue. However, after waiting for a fixed time interval, control may be passed to the next instruction as the result of a time-out escape, and status is set accordingly to reflect this condition.

It is interesting to note that if the from_task_id parameter is set to a specific task id, the system will only accept messages from that particular task. However, the from_task_id may be initialized to all 0's as a wildcard to indicate that messages from any sending task will be accepted. After fetching the message, the from_task_id is set to be the id of the sending task.

It should be mentioned that when two or more tasks are executing at the same time, and if any task wants to modify a shared database in memory, the update operation must be atomic or indivisible. If two or more tasks execute on a single CPU, one easy solution is to disable the interrupts while a task is updating the shared memory block. However, if two or more tasks execute on different CPUs at the same time, we must implement a semaphore mechanism to ensure that the update operation is indivisible, as explained in the following.

A.6 SEMAPHORE

Using shared memory to communicate among different CPUs, a binary semaphore mechanism should be implemented to ensure that only one task on one processor can write a block in shared memory at one time. We need to guard this block, so to speak. In concept, a binary semaphore is very much like a token in a plate. Whoever gets the token first has the right to write the memory block. After writing the block, the owning processor must put the token back to the plate. Thus, only one processor is allowed to write the memory block at one time. The block in shared memory usually contains a message queue that facilities communications between two system routines running on two processors.

A binary semaphore can be a memory word containing mainly a binary 1 or 0. Using positive logic, a 1 means that the token is available while a 0 means that the token is gone. The remaining problem is how to protect the semaphore so no two processors can see an available token at the same time. We need hardware support. Reading the semaphore, testing its value, and setting it to a new value must be performed in one memory bus cycle so it is indivisible.

In other words, a read-modify-write hardware memory cycle must be implemented to ensure that no other CPU can break into the middle of the cycle when the first CPU is testing and setting the semaphore. A memory system handles its cycles as atomic operations, one at a time to one processor. In the 1970s, core memories were popular. Each tiny core stores one bit. Reading the core, we switch its magnetic flux to one direction. After reading, we need to restore its original magnetic flux by switching it to the other direction so we always have a read-write full cycle. Read-modify-write means that the cycle between read and write is prolonged so that the processor has more time to

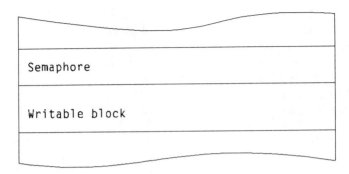

(a) A writable memory block with its binary semaphore.

```
try_later:   lock dec     semaphore
             jz           got_it
             lock inc     semaphore
             jmp          try_later
got_it:      ...

             {Update the shared
              memory block}
             ...

             lock inc     semaphore
```

(b) Assembly language coding.

Figure A.4 Writable block with its binary semaphore.

modify the memory operand. If two or more CPUs want the token at the same time, only one CPU can grab the token, based on its priority on the bus.

In the 1980s, the IBM PC used half-cycles to either read or write the semiconductor memory [IBM PC]. A special 1-byte opcode known as the 'lock' prefix must be placed in front of an instruction to lock the memory bus, if desired. Locking the bus means that no other processor can access the memory at the same time. The 'lock' prefix is a special opcode that tells the CPU hardware to lock the memory bus when the next instruction executes.

The basic concept of a semaphore should be quite clear now. A writable memory block with its associated binary semaphore is shown in Figure A.4(a). It is interesting to examine why the proposed scheme works using the lock prefix on the PC. The assembly language coding is given in Figure A.4(b).

Any CPU must first execute the code at the front before it can write into the block in shared memory. A binary semaphore is initialized to 1, which means available. Decrement (dec) the semaphore by 1 and set the condition code in the status register based on the result. There may be two possible outcomes. If the result is 0, control is passed to got_it, which means the CPU can proceed and update the shared memory block. The jz instruction means jump if result is zero. The other possibility is that the result becomes a negative number, which means another CPU has already grabbed the token. The current CPU hence increments the semaphore immediately to restore its original value and tries later. The jmp instruction means unconditional jump. At the end of updating, the CPU must increment (inc) the semaphore by 1 to put the token back. It is a challenge to understand that all inc and dec instructions must have a lock prefix, and this scheme works for two or more CPUs.

On the PC, there is an XCHG (Exchange) instruction that exchanges the contents of a register and a memory word that is the binary semaphore so we can get rid of the inc and dec instructions. Try to complete the assembly language code as shown below:

```
   . . .
   mov      ax,    0         ;move 0 into ax register.
   lock xchg   ax, semaphore   ;swap ax register with the
                              ;binary semaphore.
   ???
```

Reference

[1] Case, R. P., and A. Padegs, "Architecture of the IBM System/370," CACM, Vol. 21, No. 1, Jan. 1978, pp. 73–96.

Appendix B
Acronyms and Abbreviations

A	application
AAL	ATM adaptation layer
ack	acknowledgement
ACM	Association of Computing Machinery
ACSE	Association Control Service Element
AE	application entity
AIX	advanced UNIX
AM	access method; amplitude modulation
ANSI	American National Standards Institute
API	application Programming Interface
APPC	advanced program to program communication
ARP	address resolution protocol
ARQ	automatic repeat request
ASCII	American Standard Code for Information Interchange
ASE	application service element
ASK	amplitude shift key
ASN.1	Abstract Syntax Notation 1
ATDM	asynchronous time division multiplexing
ATM	asynchronous transfer mode; automatic teller machine
AWG	American Wire Gauge
b	bit, i.e., binary digit
B	byte
BCD	binary coded decimal
BECN	backward explicit congestion control
BISDN	broad integrated services digital network
bit	binary digit
bps	bits per second
Bps	bytes per second

BSC	binary synchronous communications
CACM	Communications of the ACM
CATV	community antenna television or cable TV
CCITT	Comite Consultatif International de Telegraphique et Telephonique, which was renamed to ITU-T
CCR	commitment, concurrency, and recovery
CLP	cell loss priority
CMIP	common management information protocol
CMIS	common management information services
CMOT	CMIS over TCP/IP
com	commercial
CPU	central processing unit
CRC	cyclic redundancy check
CSMA/CD	carrier sense multiple access/collision detection
DA	destination address; directory agent
DARPA	Defense Advanced Research Project Agency
dB	decibel (decimal bel)
DBA	dead before arrival
DCE	data circuit-terminating equipment; distributed computing environment
DDN	Defense Data Network
DE	discard eligibility
DIB	directory information base
DL	data link
DLCB	data link control block
DLPDU	DL protocol data unit
DMA	direct memory access
DME	distributed management environment
DNA	digital network architecture
DOD	Department Of Defense
DPSK	differential phase shift key
DQDB	distributed queue, dual bus
DS	directory system
DTE	data terminal equipment
DUA	directory user agent
EBCDIC	extended binary coded decimal for information interchange
edu	education
Epb	errors per bit
e-mail	electronic-mail
EOR	exclusive OR
fc	cut-off frequency
FCS	frame check sequence
FDDI	Fiber Distributed Data Interface

FDM	frequency division multiplexing
FECN	forward explicit congestion notification
FEP	front end processor
FM	frequency modulation
FR	frame relay
FSK	frequency shift key
FTAM	file transfer, access and management
FTP	file transfer protocol
g or G	giga = 10^9; to measure memory size in bytes it means 2^{30}
Gbps	gigabits per second
GBN	Go-Back-N
GHz	gigahertz
gov	government
HCS	header check sequence
HDLC	high-level data link control
HEC	header error control
hex	hexadecimal
Hz	hertz
I	information
IAB	Internet Architecture Board
ICMP	Internet control message protocol
id	identifier
IEEE	Institute of Electrical and Electronics Engineers
Info	information
IH	interrupt handler
IMP	interface message processor
Internet	Inter-networking
I/O	input/output
IP	Internet protocol
ISDN	integrated services digital network
ISO	International Standards Organization
ISR	interrupt service routine
ITU-T	International Telecommunication Union - Telecommunication Standardization Sector
k or K	kilo = 1,000; to measure memory size it means 2^{10} or 1,024
km	kilometer
LAN	local area network
LAP	link access procedure
LAPB	link access procedure, balanced
LAPD	link access protocol - D channel
LLC	logical link control
LRC	longitudinal redundancy check
lsb	least significant bit

LU	logical unit
m or M	mega = 10^6; to measure memory size it means 2^20 or 1,048,576; meter; More
MAC	medium access control
MAN	metropolitan area network
MAP	manufacturing automation protocol
MAPDU	MAC protocol data unit
Mbps	megabits per second
MB	mega Bytes
mBps	megabytes per second
MHS	message handling system
MIB	management Information Base
mil	military
MTA	message transfer agent
MTS	message transfer system
ms	millisecond = 10^−3 sec
msb	most significant bit
MVS	multiple virtual storage
μs	microsecond = 10^−6 sec
N	network
NAK	negative acknowledgement
NAM	network access method
NBS	National Bureau of Standards
NCB	network control block
Net	Internet
NIC	Network Information Center of TCP/IP
NIST	National Institute of Standards and Technology
NMT	network management
NPDU	network protocol data unit
NRZ	nonrturn to zero
NRZ-I	NRZ-Inverted
NOS	network operating system
ns	nanosecond = 10^−9 sec
NSAP	network service access point
org	organization
OS	operating system
OSF	Open Software Foundation
OSI	open systems interconnection
P	presentation
PAD	packet assembler/disassembler
PAM	phase plus amplitude modulation
PBX	private branch exchange
PC	personal computer

PCM	pulse code modulation
PCI	protocol control information
PDN	public data network
PDU	protocol data unit
PH	physical
PHY	physical
PM	phase modulation
Proc	proceedings
ps	picosecond = 10^{-12} sec
PSK	phase dhift key
PT	payload type
PU	physical unit
QOS	quality of service
QPSK	quadrature phase shift key
RARP	reverse address resolution protocol
RCC	routing control center
RFC	request for comments
RNR	receiver not ready
ROM	read only memory
ROSE	remote operation service element
rpc	remote procedure call
RQE	request queue element
RR	receiver ready
RS	recommended standard
RTSE	reliable transfer service element
RZ	return to zero
S	session
SA	source address
SAPI	service access point identifier
SAW	Stop-And-Wait
SDLC	synchronous data link control
SDM	space division multiplexing
sdu	service data unit
SMDS	switched multimegabit data services
SNA	system network architecture
SNMP	simple network management protocol
SRJ	Selective-Reject
std	standard
STM	synchronous transfer mode
SWP	sliding window protocol
SYN	synchronous
T	transport
TCB	task control block

TCP	transmission control protocol
TDM	time division multiplexing
TLCB	transport layer control Block
TO	time-out
TOP	technical office protocol
TPDU	transport protocol data unit
Trans	transactions
TSAP	transport service access point
UA	user Agent; unnumbered acknowledgement
UART	universal asynchronous receiver/transmitter
UCB	unit control block
UDP	user datagram protocol
UI	unnumbered information frame
UK	United Kingdom
UNIX	UNICS (universal information and computing service)
URL	universal resource locator
USRT	universal synchronous receiver/transmitter
V	volt
VC	virtual circuit
VCI	virtual channel identifier
VPI	virtual path identifier
VRC	vertical redundancy check
VT	virtual terminal
VTAM	virtual telecommunications access method
WAN	wide area network
WWW	World Wide Web

Appendix C
Products and Standards

10BASE-T, Twisted-Pair Medium Attachment Unit (MAU) and Baseband Medium, Type 10BASE-T (Section 14), Supplement to ISO 8802.3.
100BASE-T, Physical Layer Specification for UTP Category 3/4/5 Wiring, Fast Ethernet Alliance.
AIX, AIX Operating System for the PS2 and System/370, Programming Tools and Interface, SC23–2029–1, IBM Corp.
APPCa, APPC Application Development: Authorized Callable Services, GC28–1112–03, IBM Corp.
APPCb, APPC/MVS Handbook for the OS/2 System Administrator, GC28–1133–01, IBM Corp.
ASN.1, Abstract Syntax Notation 1 is specified in X.208–209, Fascicle VIII.5, ITU-T, CH-1211 Geneva 20, Switzerland.
BSC, Binary Synchronous Communications, General Information, GA27–3004, IBM Corp., 1994.
BSD4.3, Berkeley Software Distribution, Version 4.3, University of California at Berkeley, 1986.
Call 370, Call 370 Executive Operating System, Control Data Corporation.
CDC 6600, System Reference Manual, No. 601000000, Control Data Corporation.
Common Source, Global Engineering Documents, 2805 McGraw Ave., Irvine, CA 92714, Tel: (800) 854–7179; Fax: (714) 261–7892, 1994.
E.100–E.333, Telephone Network and ISDN - Operation, numbering, routing and mobile service, Fascicle II.2, ITU-T.
Equinox, EQUINOX Data PBX Installation and Technical Reference Manual, No. 560000, Equinox Systems Inc. Miami, FL, 33168.
Ethernet, The Ethernet, A Local Area Network - Data Link Layer and Physical Layer Specifications, Intel Corp., Santa Clara, CA, 95051.
HDLC, Data Communication - High Level Data Link Control (HDLC)- Frame Structure, International Organization for Standardization, ISO 3309.
HP 4951, Line Protocol Analyzer, Operating Manual, No. 04951-90741, Hewlett Packard Co., Telecommunications Division, 5070 Centennial Blvd., Colorado Spring, CO 80933.
HP 4972, LAN Protocol Analyzer Reference Manual, No. 04972-99910, Hewlett Packard Company.
I.110–I.257, INTEGRATED SERVICES DIGITAL NETWORK (ISDN) GENERAL STRUCTURE AND SERVICE CAPABILITIES, Fascicle III.7, ITU-T.

I.310–I.470, INTEGRATED SERVICES DIGITAL NETWORK (ISDN) OVERALL NETWORK ASPECTS AND FUNCTIONS, ISDN USER-NETWORK INTERFACES, Fascicle III.8, ITU-T.

IBM 370, Principles of Operation, GA22–6821, IBM Corp.

IBM PC, Technical Reference Manual, Personal Computer, IBM Corp., Boca Raton, FL 33432.

IEEE 802.1, Local Area Networks, Overview and Architecture, The IEEE, Inc., 345 E. 47th St., New York, NY, 10017.

IEEE 802.2, Local Area Networks, Logical Link Control.

IEEE 802.3, Local Area Networks, Carrier Sense Multiple Access with Collision Detection Access Method and Physical Layer Specifications.

IEEE 802.4, Local Area Networks, Token-Passing Bus Access Method and Physical Layer Specifications.

IEEE 802.5, Local Area Networks, Token Ring Access Method and Physical Layer Specifications.

IEEE 802.6, Local Area Networks, Distributed Queue Dual Bus Access Method Subnetwork for a Metropolitan Area Network.

Intel 486, Microprocessor, No. 240440–001, Intel Corp.

Intel 8273, Programmable HDLC/SDLC Protocol Controller Reference Manual, Intel Corp.

ISO, International Organization for Standardization (International Standards Organization), CH-1211 Geneva Switzerland, Tel. 22 749 0111.

ISO 8571, File Transfer, Access and Management, 1987.

ISO 9595, Information Processing Systems - Common Management Information Protocol Specification (CMIP), May 1990.

ISO 9596, Information Processing Systems - Common Management Information Service Definition (CMIS), May 1990.

ITU-T, International Telecommunication Union - Telecommunication standard Sector, CH-1211 Geneva 20, Switzerland.

LAP, Link Access Procedure is described in X.25.

LAPB, Link Access Procedure, Balanced is described in X.25.

LINUX, Operating System Manual, Open Software Foundation, Inc., Cambridge, MA, e-mail address: corpcom@osf.org.

LU 6.2, System Network Architecture - Session Between Logical Units, IBM Corp., GC20–1968.

MC68040, Programmers Reference Manual, Motorola, Inc., 1994.

MVS/ESA, Multiple Virtual Storage/Enterprise System Architecture, General Information, GC28–1600, IBM Corp.

nCUBE. 6400 Processor Manual, NCUBE Co., Beaverton, OR 97006.

NetView, NetView Operation, SC31–6019; User's Guide, SC31–7067, IBM Corp.

OSF, Open Software Foundation, Inc., Cambridge, MA, e-mail: corpcom@osf.org.

OSI, *Stable Implementation Agreement for Open Systems Interconnection Protocols*, Version 4, Edition 1, Borland, F. E., IEEE Computer Society Press.

Procomm, Reference Manual, Datastorm Technologies, Inc., Columbia, MO, 65205, 1994.

Q.920–Q.921, Digital Subscriber Signalling System No. 1 (DSS 1), Data Link Layer, Fascicle VI.10, ITU-T.

Q.930–Q.940, Network Layer, User-Network Management, Fascicle VI.11, ITU-T.

RFC791, Internet Protocol, Postel, J., Sept. 1981.

RFC959, File Transfer Protocol, Postel, J. B. and J. K. Reynolds, Oct. 1985.

RFC1027, Using ARP to implement transparent subnet gateways, Carl-Mitchell, S., et al., Oct. 1987.

RFC1057, Remote Procedure Call Protocol Specification, Version 2, Sun Microsystems, Inc., Jun. 1988.

RFC1155, Structure and Identification of Management Information for TCP/IP-based Internets, Rose, M. T. and K. McCloghrie, May 1990.

RFC1156, Management Information Base for network management of TCP/IP-based Internets, McCloghrie, K. and M. T. Rose, May 1990.
RFC1157, Simple Network Management Protocol (SNMP), Case, J. D., et al., May 1990.
RFC1189, Common Management Information Services and Protocols for the Internet (CMOT and CMIP), Warrier, U., et al., Oct. 1990.
RFC1448, Protocol Operations for Version 2 of the Simple Network Management Protocol (SNMPv2), Case, J., et al., April 1993.
RFC1450, Management Information Base for Version 2 of the Simple Network Management Protocol (SNMPv2), Case, J., et al, April 1993.
RFC1903, Reverse Address Resolution Protocol, Finlayson, R., et al., June 1984.
RS-232, RS-232-D Interface Between Data Terminal Equipment and Data Communication Equipment Employing Serial Binary Data Interchange, Electronic Industries Associates.
SDLC, Synchronous Data Link Control Concepts, GA27-3093-04, IBM Corp.
SNAa, Systems Network Architecture, Concepts and Products, GC-3003072-0, IBM Corp.
SNAb, Systems Network Architecture, Format and Protocol Reference Manual; Architecture Logic, SC30-3112-2, IBM Corp.
SNIFFER, Sniffer Network Analyzer Reference Manual, Network General Corp., Menlo Park, CA, 94025.
System V, AT & T and Sun Microsystems, a BSD 4.X derivative released in 1989.
TCP/IP, A tutorial (RFC1180) is available from the Net (Read anonymous ftp in Chapter 9).
T.0-T.63, TERMINAL EQUIPMENT AND PROTOCOLS FOR TELEMATIC SERVICES, Fascicle VII.3, ITU-T.
Token-Ring, Token-Ring Network PC Products Description and Installation, GG24-1739-00, IBM Corp.
V.1-V.42, DATA COMMUNICATION OVER THE TELEPHONE NETWORKS: Series V Recommendations, Fascicle VIII.1, ITU-T.
Wright, G. R. and W. R. Stevens, *TCP/IP Illustrated*, Vol. 2: The Implementation, Addison Wesley, 1995.
X.1-X.32, DATA COMMUNICATION NETWORKS: Services and Facilities, Interfaces, Fascicle VIII.2, ITU-T.
X.40-X.181, DATA COMMUNICATION NETWORKS: Transmission, Signalling and Switching, Network Aspects, Maintenance and Administrative Arrangements, Fascicle VIII.3, ITU-T.
X.200-X.219, DATA COMMUNICATION NETWORKS: Open Systems Interconnection (OSI) - Model and Notation, Service Definition, Fascicle VIII.4, ITU-T.
X.220-X.290, DATA COMMUNICATION NETWORKS: Open Systems Interconnection (OSI) - Protocol Specifications, Conformance Testing, Fascicle VIII.5, ITU-T.
X.400-X.420, DATA COMMUNICATION NETWORKS: Message Handling Systems, Fascicle VIII.7, ITU-T.
X.500-X.521, DATA COMMUNICATION NETWORKS: Directory, Fascicle VIII.8, ITU-T.

Selected Bibliography

Gaughan, P. T., and S. Yalamanchili, "Adaptive Routing Protocols for Hypercube Interconnection Networks," *IEEE Computer*, May 1993, pp. 11–23.

Green, P. E., "The Future of Fiber-Optic Computer Networks," *IEEE Computer*, Sept. 1991, pp. 78–87.

Hsu, J. Y., Implementation of a Pedagogical Operating System on the MC68000, Tech. Report CPSLO-CSC-92–03, Dept. of Computer Science, Cal Poly, San Luis Obispo, CA 93407, Jan. 1992.

Kelly, P. T., "Public Packet switched Data Network International Plans and Standards," *Proc. IEEE*, Vol. 66, No. 11, Nov. 1987, pp. 1539–1549.

Kessler, G. C., and D. A. Train, *Metropolitan Area Networks - Concepts, Standards, and Services*, McGraw-Hill, 1992.

Kim, B. G. and P. Wang, "ATM Network: Goals and Challenges," *CACM*, Vol. 38, No. 2, Feb. 1995, pp. 39–44.

Padmanubhan, K., "Cube Structures for Multiprocessors," *CACM*, Vol. 33, No. 1, Jan. 1990, pp. 43–52.

Patterson D. A., and J. J. Hennessy, *Computer Organization & Design, The Hardware/Software*

Rinde, J. 1979. "Virtual Circuits in Tymnet II," *Proc. National Electronic Conference*.

Spragins, J., et al., *Telecommunications Protocol and Design*, Reading, MA: Addison-Wesley, 1993.

Stallings, W., *Data and Computer Communications*, 4th edition, Macmillan, 1994.

Stevens, W. R., *UNIX Network Programming*, Prentice-Hall, 1990.

Stevens, W. R. *TCP/IP Illustrated*, Vol. 1: The Protocols, Addison Wesley, 1993.

Stout, Q. F., "Mesh Connected Computers with Broadcasting," *IEEE Trans. on Computers*, Vol. 32, 1983, pp. 826–830.

Sugiyama, Y., et al., "Development of Full Automatic Fusion Splicer," *Proc. of 41st International Wire and Cable Symposium*, Reno, NV, Vol. 16, No. 19, Nov. 1992, pp. 132–139.

Tillman, M. A., and D. Yen, "Three Strategies for Interconnection," *CACM*, Vol. 33, No. 2, Feb. 1990, pp. 214–223.

Vetter, R. J., "ATM Concepts, Architecture, and Protocols," *CACM*, Vol. 38, No. 2, Feb. 1995, pp. 30–38.

Weber, J. C., Webmaster's Starter Kit, *Proc. 2nd Web Conference*, Chicago, Oct. 1994.

Wittie, L. D., "Computer Networks and Distributed Systems," *IEEE Computer*, Sept. 1991, pp. 67–76.

About the Author

John Y. Hsu received his B.S.E.E from National Taiwan University (1955–59) and his M.S.E.E. (1963–64) and his Ph.D. (1967–69) from the University of California, Berkeley, specializing in computer system hardware and software. He is currently a professor of computer engineering at California Polytechnic State University in San Luis Obispo. He has held many industrial job titles, such as project engineer, computer architect, and senior software specialist. In addition, he has done over 10,000 hours of consulting work for companies including Federal Electric/ITT, ILLIAC IV, III in Taiwan, CDC, and IBM. Dr. Hsu is a member of IEEE and ACM.

Index

5-layer model, 34
7-layer model. See OSI reference model
10BASE-T, 192
100BASE-T, 192–94
Abstract Syntax Notation.1 (ASN.1), 424
   compiler, 435
   concepts, 436
   defined, 435
   encoding examples, 441, 443
   encoding rules, 437–40
   lexical conventions, 436
   macro facilities, 435
   SNMP messages specified in, 477
   syntactic module definition, 436–37
   universal tags, 439
   See also Presentation (P) layer
Access methods (AMs)
   CSMA/CD, 197–99
   defined, 1
   DQDB, 227–31
   network (NAMs), 1, 20–21
   queued (QAMs), 35
   token bus, 217–18
   token ring, 208–9
   virtual telecommunications (VTAMs), 489
Access unit (AU), 455
Active monitor, 209–10
   defined, 209
   failure, 210
   neighbor notification, 210
   See also Token ring
Active ports, 182–83
Address resolution protocol (ARP), 283–84
   frame, 283

   reverse (RARP), 284–85
   See also Internet protocol (IP)
Advanced Research Project Agency Network (ARPANET), 10
American National Standards Institute (ANSI), 22
Amplitude shift key (ASK) modulation, 72
Analog to digital (A-D) converter
   defined, 78
   illustrated, 79
   See also Digital to analog (D-A) converter
Anonymous FTP, 445
Application (A) layer, 26–27, 447–60
   application entities (AEs), 448
   defined, 26–27, 447–48
   directory system, 457–60
   FTAM system, 452–54
   message handling system (MHS), 454–57
   PDU (APDU), 451–52
   primitives, 448–51
      ACSE, 448
      CCR, 449–51
      ROSE, 451
      RTSE, 448–49
   problems, 461–62
   See also OSI reference model; User agent (UA)
Applications. *See* Application services; Network applications
Application service elements (ASEs), 429
Application services, 444–47
   e-mail, 445–46
   file transfer protocol (FTP), 444–45
   remote procedure call (RPC), 446–47
   World Wide Web (WWW), 446
ASCII characters, 434

Asynchronous processing, 496
  defined, 496
  simulations, 157–58
Asynchronous TDM, 80
Asynchronous transfer mode
        (ATM), 88, 300–308
  adaptation layer (AAL), 304
  ATM Forum, 307
  ATM layer, 305–6
  cells, 301–3
    cell loss priority (CLP), 303
    defined, 301
    extended, 308
    format, 303
    header, 303
    segmentation of, 306
    sizes of, 308
  cell-switching, 300
  end-to-end connection, 305
  frame relay vs., 307–8
  IP connection, 306
  layers, 304
  network architecture, 301, 302
  PHY layer, 304
  protocols, 303–7
  SMDS, 306–7
  software model, 303–4
  See also Wide area networks (WANs)
Asynchronous transmission, 60–61
Atmosphere, 49–50
Attachment unit interface (AUI), 194
Authentication, 431
Avalanche photodiodes (APDs), 52

Bandwidth balancing (BWB), DQDB, 231
Baseband transmission, 83–85
  defined, 83
  See also Broadband transmission
Baud, 72
Binary coded decimal (BCD) digits, 273
Binary semaphore, 503, 504
Binary synchronous communications (BSC)
        protocol, 159–62
  characteristics, 159–60
  defined, 159
  pipelined transmission and, 162
  primary vs. secondary station, 160–62
  SAW ARQ in, 161
Bipolar codes, 55
Bit-stuffing problem, 142
Bridges
  bridge protocol data unit (BPDU), 288

  defined, 288
  illustrated, 289
  See also Network devices
Broadband ISDN (BISDN), 321–23
  defined, 321
  functional architecture, 321–22
  protocols, 323
  services, 322
  user interfaces, 322–23
  user network interface (UNI), 323
  See also ISDN
Broadband network services (BBNS), 323–24
  defined, 323
  illustrated, 324
  software, 323
Broadband transmission, 83–85
  defined, 83
  design of, 84
  illustrated, 85
  with three channels, 83–84
  See also Baseband transmission
Buffer management, 38

Carrier sense multiple access/collision
        detection. *See* CSMA/CD
Cell loss priority (CLP), 303
Cells, 301–3
  CLP, 303
  defined, 301
  extended, 308
  format, 303
  header, 306
  segmentation of, 306
  sizes, 308
  switching, 88
  See also Asynchronous transfer mode (ATM)
Centralized routing, 242–48
  philosophy, 243
  RCC, 242–43
  shortest route problem, 243–48
  See also Routing
Central processing unit (CPU), 2, 5
Challenge-response, 432
Channel-to-channel I/O, 5
Character-stuffing problem, 141–42
Circuit switching, 87
Client-server model, 396
CMIS Element (CMISE), 487
Coaxial cable, 47–49
Code conversion, 429–30, 434–35
  approaches, 435
  byte addressing and, 434

Coding complexity, 11
Common bus, 182, 183, 184
  defined, 183
  with special software, 184
  See also Local area networks (LANs)
Common management information protocol (CMIP), 487
Communication controllers, 89–92
  UART chip, 91–92
  USRT chip, 92
Communication processors, 34–35
Compression, 430
Computer network architecture, 5–8
  defined, 1
  multiprocessing systems, 6–7
Computer networks
  applications for, 18–20
  classifications of, 8–11
  computers on, 7
  defined, 1
  design criteria, 38–39
  features of, 8
  global, 19
  host processors in, 6
  multiprocessing system as, 7
  objectives of, 7–8, 460
  in OSI reference model, 23
  problems, 40–42
  two-node, 2
  See also Computer network architecture
Computers
  on computer network, 7
  defined, 2
  See also Computer networks
Congestion control, 257–60
  defined, 257–58
  explicit, 259–60
  flow control vs., 258
  ICMP, 286
  implicit, 260
  problem, 258–59
  response time, 258
Connection control packets, 363–69
  CC, 368
  CR, 363–68
  DC, 369
  DR, 368–69
  PI, 369
  See also Transport protocols (TP)
CSMA/CD, 197–99
  defined, 197–98

  optimal retransmission slot time, 198–99
  random time interval, 198
Cyclic redundancy check (CRC), 118–30
  CRC-4, 124, 125
  CRC-12, 129
  CRC-32 generation/detection, 129
  defined, 118
  evaluations of, 129–30
  generation algorithm, 120–21
  hardware design, 123–25
  ITU-T generation/detection, 126–27
  ITU-T generation with table lookup, 127–29
  mathematical proof of, 122
  software design, 125–29
  theorem of, 123
  See also Redundancy check

Data circuit-terminating equipment (DCE), 45
Data compression/decompression, 430
Data flow
  DL layer example, 149
  DQDB, 229–31
  point-to-point links, 184
  transport layer, 349
Datagram models, 25, 239–41
  choke packet, 260
  defined, 239
  destination node, 238
  flooding technique, 239–41
  transport layer software design, 354–55
  VC model plus, 241
  VC model vs., 240–41
  See also Virtual circuit (VC)
Data link (DL) layer, 24–25, 113–79
  bit-stuffing problem, 142
  BSC, 159
  character-stuffing problem, 141–42
  data flow example, 149
  design, 143–54
  design concepts, 113–15
  error-detecting codes, 115–30
  functions, 25
  in LANs, 184
  LLC sublayer, 184, 187–91
  MAC sublayer, 184, 185–87
  piggybacking and, 141
  primitives, 143–47
  problems, 175–79
  SDLC, 162–71
  sliding window protocols, 130–41
  XMODEM protocol and, 158–59
  See also OSI reference model

Data link control
    high-level (HDLC), 172–74
    synchronous (SDLC), 162–71
Data link control block (DLCB), 148–50
    contents, 148–50
    defined, 148
    Receive_task routine, 153–54
    Transmit_task routine, 152–53
Data link escape (DLE) character, 142
Data link protocol data unit
            (DLPDU), 32, 147–48
    defined, 147
    mapping, 148
    See also Data link (DL) layer; Data links (DLs)
Data links (DLs), 113
    concurrent tasks and, 143
    connection, 145
    frame exchange, 174
    full-duplex transmission between, 151
    permanent, 145–47
    primitives, 144
    primitives implementation, 147
    protocols, 158
    protocol support, 114–15
    simulations, 154–58
    software design, 150–54
    in telephone network, 143
    temporary, 143–45
    transmission speed, 464
    transmission unit, 113
    See also Data link (DL) layer
Data packets, 369–71
    DT, 369–71
    ED, 371
    See also Packets; Transport protocols (TP)
Data terminal equipment (DTE), 45
Data transmissions, 47–62
    broadband vs. baseband, 83–85
    digital waveforms, 54–60
    media for, 47–54
    pipelined, 135, 156–58, 333
    transmission media, 47–54
    transmission modes, 60–62
Decompression, 430
Decryption. *See* Encryption/decryption
Demultiplexer
    defined, 78
    illustrated, 79
    See also Multiplexer
Destination service access point
            (DSAP), 190–91

Differential Manchester code, 58–60
    defined, 58
    illustrated, 59
    See also Digital waveforms; Manchester code
Differential phase shift key (DPSK)
            modulation
    defined, 74–75
    illustrated, 74
    See also Modulation
Digital signal 1 (DS1), 82
Digital signals, 55–56
    harmonics, 67
    voltage levels, 55
    waveforms, 56
Digital signatures, 433–34
Digital to analog (D-A) converter
    defined, 78
    illustrated, 79
    See also Analog to digital (A-D) converter
Digital waveforms, 54–60
    differential Manchester code (DMC), 58–60
    digital signals, 55–56
    Manchester code, 56–58
Dijkstra algorithm, 244
Direct memory access (DMA) chips, 4, 5
Directory access protocol (DAP), 459
Directory information base (DIB), 458, 459
Directory information tree (DIT), 458
Directory system (DS), 457–60
    applications, 457
    defined, 457
    DIB, 458, 459
    directory protocols, 459–60
    directory services, 458–59
    DIT, 458
    functional model of, 458
    See also Application (A) layer
Directory system protocol (DSP), 460
Dispatcher, 499–500
    defined, 499
    interrupted, 500
    See also OS
Distributed hardware, 11
Distributed management
            environment, 488–89
Distributed queue dual bus (DQDB), 221–31
    access method, 227–31
    architecture, 223
    bandwidth balancing, 231
    buses, 232
    characteristics, 224

Index   525

data flow example, 229–31
defined, 221–23
distributed queue algorithm, 228–29
frames, 223–25
illustrated, 224
slots, 225–27
  defined, 225
  illustrated, 226
  length, 225
See also Local area networks (LANs)
Distributed routing, 241–42
Distributed system model, 10–11

EBCDIC characters, 434
E-mail, 445–46
Encryption/decryption, 431–32
  authentication, 431–32
  challenge-response, 432
  digital signature, 433–34
  password, 432
  using same security key, 431
See also Presentation services
End system (ES), 35
Enterprise Management Architecture
  (EMA), 489
Error control
  defined, 38
  performance and, 38
  transport layer, 332
See also Error rate; Errors
Error-detecting codes, 115–30
  CRC evaluations, 129–30
  CRC hardware design, 123–25
  CRC software design, 125–29
  cyclic redundancy check, 118–23
  defined, 115
  FCS, 168
  generating, 115
  longitudinal redundancy check, 116–18
  vertical redundancy check, 115–16
Error rate, 154, 467
  with given probability, 154
  reliability and, 467–68
See also Network management
Errors
  permanent, 467
  recovery of, 295
  temporary, 467
See also Error control
Ethernet, 192–200
  32-bit FCS, 197
  attachment unit interface (AUI), 194

characteristics, 192
CSMA/CD access method, 197–99
defined, 192
Fast, 192–94
frames, 194–97
  illustrated, 196
  MAC, 196, 197
  maximum length, 197
illustrated architecture, 193
MAC sublayer, 194
medium attachment unit (MAU), 194
medium dependent interface (MDI), 194
physical medium attachment (PMA), 194
primitives, 199–200
sublayers, 194
transmission media, 195
See also Local area networks (LANs)
Exchange buffering, 255–57
  defined, 255–56
  illustrated, 257
  uses, 256–57
See also Network (N) layer
Exclusive OR (EOR), 115–16, 118–19
  16-bit operation, 125
  defined, 115–16
Explicit synchronization, 385
  primitives, 388
See also Synchronization

Fast Ethernet, 192–94
  characteristics, 192
  speed improvement, 194
See also Ethernet
Fiber Distributed Data Interface
  (FDDI), 219–21
  characteristics, 219
  defined, 219
  frame layout, 221
  frames, 222
  hardware encoding scheme, 219
  illustrated, 220
  rings, 219
  self-repair capability, 219
See also Local area networks (LANs)
File transfer, access, management
  (FTAM), 452–54
  checkpoint and restart, 453–54
  data transfer, 454
  defined, 452
  file management, 453
  grouping control, 453
  primitives, 453–54

FTAM (continued)
  regime control, 453
  standard, 452
  virtual filestore, 452
  See also Application (A) layer
File transfer protocol (FTP), 444–45
  anonymous, 445
  defined, 444
  execution, 445
  See also Application services
File transfer server, 396–98
Finite state machine pool model, 333–43
  composite model for receiver, 341–42
  composite model of sender, 335–37
  optimal window size, 342–43
  receiving window conditions, 338
  sending window conditions, 334
  for SRJ receiver, 339
  transport receiver, 337–42
  transport sender, 333–37
  See also Transport (T) layer
Fixed routing. *See* Hierarchical routing
Fletcher checksum, 359–63
  generation algorithm, 359–61
  implementation, 361
  L-byte header with, 360
  software design, 361–63
  See also Transport protocols (TP)
Flooding technique, 239–41
  defined, 239
  illustrated, 240
  overhead, 240
  packet sequence and, 240
  See also Datagram models
Flow control, 38
  congestion control vs., 258
  packets, 371–73
  transport layer, 332–33
  X.25, 274–75
Fourier theorem, 62–71
  analysis conclusions, 71
  analysis examples, 66–71
  generalized equations, 65–66
Frame check sequence (FCS), 124, 168–71
  16-bit shift register, 169
  32-bit, 197
  error detecting code, 168
  ITU-T hardware design, 168–70
  ITU-T software design, 170–71
  special case, 171

See also Synchronous data link
  control (SDLC)
Frame relay, 295–300
  ATM vs., 307–8
  error recovery and, 295
  frame, 297–99
  illustrated network, 296
  as routers, 295–96
  software design, 299–300
  system block diagram, 300
  See also Wide area networks (WANs)
Frames, 113
  defined, 113
  DQDB, 223–25
  Ethernet, 194–97
  FDDI, 221, 222
  frame relay, 297–99
  header, 114
  ISDN, 313–15
  SDLC
    control fields, 164
    format, 163
    information, 165
    supervisory, 165–66
    types of, 163
    unnumbered, 166–68
  SMDS, 307
  token bus, 213–17
  token ring, 202–6
Frequency division multiplexing (FDM), 82
  defined, 82
  See also Multiplexing
Frequency shift key (FSK) modulation, 72–73
Front-end processors (FEPs), 34
Full-duplex transmission, 62
  SRJ ARQ, 139
  between two data links, 151
  See also Transmission modes
Fully interconnected topology
  defined, 14–15
  illustrated, 13
  See also Network topologies

Gateways, 290
Global information tree, 480
Go-Back-N (GBN) ARQ, 135–36
  data link design with, 150
  defined, 135
  receiver error recovery, 136
  sender error recovery, 135–36
  window edge movements, 136, 137
  See also Sliding window protocols (SWPs)

Index 527

Group talk program, 398–99
Half-duplex transmission, 61–62
 SRJ ARQ, 139
 See also Transmission modes
Harmonics, 67
 12th and above, 71
 amplitude of, 68
 first, 69, 70
 phase angle, 68
 waveforms received, 69
Hierarchical routing, 248–49
 defined, 248
 example, 248–49
 See also Routing
High-level data link control (HDLC), 172–74
 defined, 172
 features, 172
 frame control fields, 172, 173
 link access procedure (LAP), 172–73
 link access procedure, balanced
   (LAPB), 173–74
Hypercube topology, 16–18
 advantages of, 18
 defined, 16
 degree 2, 16, 17
 degree 3, 16, 17
 illustrated, 17
 See also Network topologies

Implicit synchronization, 384–85
Institute of Electrical and Electronics
   Engineers (IEEE), 22
Integrated services digital network. *See* ISDN
Interface message processors (IMPs), 34
Intermediate systems (ISs), 34
International Alphabet set No. 5 (IA5), 89–91
 for control, 91
 defined, 89
 specifications, 90
International Organization for
   Standardization (ISO), 22
International Telecommunications Union-
   Telecommunication Standardization
   Sector (ITU-T), 21–22
 FCS, 168–71
 polynomial, 120–21
Internet, 10
 IP layer, 34
 OSI model vs., 34
 TCP layer, 34

Internet control message protocol
   (ICMP), 285–87
 congestion control, 286
 header, 285
 messages, 285
 reachability testing, 286
Internet protocol (IP), 34, 277–85
 address, 279–81
  bits, 280
  format specifications, 280
  network classes, 279–80
  types, 279
 ARP, 283–84
 ATM connection, 306
 datagram, 277
 header, 277–79
  illustrated, 278
  size of, 277
  skeleton, 277
 options, 281–83
 RARP, 284–85
 security checks, 282
 source routing, 282
 timestamps, 282
 See also TCP/IP; Transmission control
   protocol (TCP)
Interprocessor communications, 3–5
 channel-to-channel I/O, 5
 hardware schemes, 3
 interrupt, 4–5
 shared memory, 4
Interrupt, 4–5
 handler (IH), 495
 I/O service routines (ISR), 96, 498–99
 mechanisms, 495–96
Intertask communications, 502–3
I/O
 buffers, 95
 channel-to-channel, 5
 controller, 496
 drivers, 27, 95, 97
 interrupt service routines (ISRs), 96, 498–99
 network routines, 34–37
 operations, 496
 request queue, 94
 system, 1
I/O processors, 2, 496
 in network architecture, 5
 in parallel, 8
ISDN, 10, 308–21
 bandwidth limitations, 321

ISDN (continued)
  broadband (BISDN), 321–23
  channel types, 311
  evolution, 309, 310
  frames, 313–15
    physical frames, 314
    primary service, 315
  messages, 317–21
  narrowband, 309
  principles, 309–11
  protocols, 313–21
    channel, 315–17
    discriminators, 319
    LAPD, 316–17
  protocol stack, 313
  reference points, 312
  services, 311
  terminal adaptor (TA), 312
  user interfaces, 311–13
  See also Wide area networks (WANs)
Job scheduler, 501

Least significant bit (LSB), 88–89
Light emitting diode (LED), 52
Line speed, 463–64
Link access procedure (LAP), 172–73
Link access procedure, balanced
  (LAPB), 173–74
Link access procedure-D (LAPD), 315, 316–17
LinkCost matrix, 244, 246
Local area networks (LANs), 7, 181–234
  active ports and, 182–83
  characteristics, 9
  common bus approach, 182, 183, 184
  defined, 9, 181
  design approaches, 181–82
  design concepts, 181–85
  DL layer, 184
  DQDB, 221–31
  Ethernet, 192–200
  FDDI, 219–21
  illustrated, 182
  innovative technologies, 183–84
  instructions executed, 11
  OSI model vs., 185
  passive ports and, 182–83
  PH layer, 184
  point-to-point links, 182, 183–84
  problems, 233–34
  protocol conversions, 9
  station management (SMT) routines, 184
  sublayers, 184–85

  token bus, 212–18
  token ring, 14, 200–212
  See also Metropolitan area networks (MANs);
    Wide area networks (WANs)
Logical link control (LLC), 184, 187–91
  control fields, 191
  destination service access point
    (DSAP), 190–91
  header, 190
  PDU (LPDU), 187, 189–91
  primitives, 188–89
  service types, 188
  source service access point (SSAP), 191
  See also Sublayers
Logical units (LUs), 416–20
  defined, 416
  LU 1, 417
  LU 2, 417
  LU 3, 417
  LU 4, 417
  LU 6.2, 417–20
Longitudinal redundancy check (LRC), 116–18
  defined, 115
  even-parity, 116, 118
  odd-parity, 116–17
  See also Vertical redundancy check (VRC)
Loop tests, 469–72
  ATM switch, 471
  illustrated, 470
  methods for, 469–70
  ports in, 472
  for system debugging, 472
  See also Network management

Management information base (MIB), 479–85
  addressing in different protocols, 488–89
  defined, 479
  global information tree, 480
  Internet node in, 480–81
  object examples, 482–85
  subtree, 481–82
  See also SNMP
Manchester code, 56–58
  bit division, 214
  defined, 56
  differential (DMC), 58–60
  illustrated, 57
  polarity-dependent, 58
  See also Digital waveforms
Medium access control (MAC), 184, 185–87
  control primitives, 186
  Ethernet frames, 196, 197

Index 529

PDUs, 187
sublayer, 184
sublayer primitives, 186–87
token bus control frames, 215–17
token ring control frames, 205, 206–7
See also Sublayers
Medium attachment unit (MAU), 194
Medium dependent interface, 194
Memory, shared, 4
Mesh topology, 15–16
  defined, 15
  illustrated, 15
  node identification (ID), 15
  two-dimensional, 16
  See also Network topologies
Message handling system (MHS), 454–57
  access unit (AU), 455
  defined, 454
  functional model of, 454
  message flow, 457
  message store (MS), 455
  message structure, 456–57
  message transfer agent (MTA), 454
  physical delivery access unit (PDAU), 455–56
  protocols, 456
  user agent (UA), 455
  See also Application (A) layer
Messages, ISDN, 317–21
  cell reference value, 319
  format, 318
  illustrated, 318
  types of, 320–21
  See also ISDN
Messages, SNMP, 475–79
  encoding, 485–87
  format, 475, 476–79
  header, 476
  request, 475–76
  specified in ASN.1, 477
  See also SNMP
Message store (MS), 455
Message transfer agent (MTA), 454
Metropolitan area networks (MANs), 8
  defined, 9
  LANs vs., 10
  See also Local area networks (LANs);
    Wide area networks (WANs)
Modulation, 71–79
  amplitude, 72
  baud and, 72
  frequency, 72–73

phase, 73–76
phase plus amplitude, 76–77
pulse code, 77–79
techniques, 72
Most significant bit (MSB), 88–89
Multidrop connections, 113, 114
Multiple Virtual Storage (MVS), 489
Multiplexer
  defined, 78
  illustrated, 79
  See also Demultiplexer
Multiplexing, 79–85
  baseband vs. broadband transmission
    and, 83–85
  frequency division, 82
  space division, 83
  time division, 80–82
  upward/downward, 331–32
Multiprocessing systems, 6–7
  as computer network, 7
  defined, 6
  instructions executed, 11
Multitasking
  defined, 407
  server/client software design, 407–16
  server communications, 410
  server program in C code, 411–15

NetView, 489–90
Network (N) layer, 25, 237–94
  concatenation/separation, 260–61
  congestion control, 257–60
  datagram model, 239–41
  defined, 237–38
  design, 261–69
    approaches, 25
    concepts, 238
    packet-based, 268–69
  exchange buffering, 255–57
  Internet protocol (IP), 277–85
  NCB, 267–68
  network devices, 287–90
  NMT routines, 285–87
  packet layer protocol (PLP), 237
  packet size, 251
  PDUs, 265–67
  primitives, 261–65
    connect, 262
    data, 264
    for debugging, 265
    request, 265
    X.25 packets vs., 276–77

Network (N) layer (continued)
  problems, 292–94
  routing philosophies, 241–49
  software design, 268–69
  system deadlocks, 255
  virtual circuit model, 238–39
  virtual circuit plus datagram model, 241
  X.25 protocol, 270–77
  See also OSI reference model
Network access methods (NAMs), 20
  contents of, 21
  defined, 1, 20
  designs and, 20
  development of, 21
  NOS and, 21
Network applications, 18–20, 443–44
  defined, 443
  invocation commands, 443–44
  See also Application services
Network application software design, 396–99
  client-server model, 396
  file transfer server with multiclients, 396–98
  group talk program, 398–99
  See also Session(s); Session (S) layer
Network control block (NCB), 267–68
  defined, 267
  illustrated, 267
Network devices, 287–90
  bridges, 288
  gateways, 290
  Packet Assembler/Disassembler (PAD), 288
  routers, 288–90
Network management, 463–93
  monitoring, 468–72
  NetView and, 489–90
  OSI model and, 487–89
  performance analysis, 463–68
  problems, 492–93
  routines, 285–87
  SNA model, 490
  SNMP and, 472–87
Network monitoring, 468–72
  loop tests, 469–72
  protocol analyzers, 468–69
  See also Network management
Network operating system (NOS), 20–21
  defined, 1
  NAMs and, 20
  See also OS
Network performance. See Performance

Network protocol data units
    (NPDUs), 32, 265–67
  defined, 265–66
  illustrated, 266
  See also Network (N) layer
Network service access point
    (NSAP), 238, 291
Network topologies, 12–18
  fully interconnected network, 14–15
  hypercube, 16–18
  mesh, 15–16
  partially interconnected network, 15
  ring, 14
  star, 12–13
  whip, 12
Nonreturn to zero (NRZ), 54
NRZ-inverted (NRZ-I), 56, 105
Null modem cable, 101–2
  construction, 102
  defined, 101
  illustrated, 103
Nways Broadband Switch Control Program
    (NBSCP), 323
Nyquist theorem, 85–86
  channel capacity and, 86
  defined, 85

Open Software Foundation (OSF), 488
Open systems interconnection. See OSI
    reference model
OpenView, 489
Optical fiber, 50–54
  multistrand, 53
  receiver, 53
  single-mode, 50, 51
  token rings, 218
  transmitter, 53
  two-mode, 51
  See also Data transmissions;
    Transmission media
OS, 495–505
  access methods (AMs), 1
  asynchronous processing, 496
  interrupt mechanisms, 495–96
  intertask communications, 502–3
  on master processor, 6
  reentrant task, 501–2
  semaphore, 503–5
  task management routines, 496–501
  See also Network operating system (NOS)
OSI reference model, 2, 21–34
  A layer, 26–27, 447–60

computer networks in, 23
defined, 22
DL layer, 24–25, 113–79
Internet vs., 34
LAN model vs., 185
layer id, 28
layer primitives, 27–31
    basic, 29–31
    confirm, 29–30
    indication, 29
    request, 30
    response, 29
    See also Primitives
layer specifications, 22–27
layer-to-layer connections, 24
N layer, 25, 237–94
PDUs, 31–33
PH layer, 23–24, 45–112
P layer, 26, 435–43
S layer, 26, 383–427
SNA vs., 33
T layer, 26, 329–81
transport protocol (TP), 356–73
OSI session, 420–24
    defined, 420
    primitives, 421–23
    SPDU, 423–24

Packet Assemblers/Disassemblers (PADs)
    defined, 288
    illustrated, 289
    UART chips, 288
    See also Network devices
Packet layer protocol (PLP), 237
Packets
    concatenation, 260–61
    connection control, 363–69
    data, 369–71
    flow control, 371–73
    separation, 261
    size of, 261
    switching, 87–88
    X.25 types, 270, 271
Parallel computation, 8
Parallel transmission, 60
Partially interconnected topology
    defined, 15
    illustrated, 13
    See also Network topologies
Passive ports, 182–83
Passwords, encryption, 432
Performance, 38–39

analysis, 38–39, 463–68
error rate, 467
hardware design and, 38
line speed, 463–64
monitoring, 39
queuing delays, 465–66
reliability, 467–68
response time, 464
Permanent virtual circuits (PVCs), 37, 239, 273
    in computer network design, 290
    See also Virtual circuit (VC)
Phase plus amplitude modulation
    (PAM), 76–77
Phase shift key (PSK) modulation, 73–76
    differential (DPSK), 73, 74
    quadrature (QPSK), 74, 76
    See also Modulation
Photodiodes (PDs), 52
Physical (PH) layer, 23–24, 45–112
    character set, 89
    communication controllers, 89–92
    data transmissions and, 47–62
    defined, 23
    design, 88–98
    electrical specifications, 46
    functional specifications, 46–47
    I/O drivers in, 27
    in LANs, 184
    mechanical specifications, 46
    physical medium dependent, 184
    physical signal, 184
    primitives, 92–94
    problems, 107–12
    procedure specifications, 47
    software, 45
    software design, 95–98
        of Receiveframe, 97–98
        of Sendframe, 96–97
    UCB, 94–95
    See also OSI reference model
Physical delivery access unit (PDAU), 455–56
Physical interfaces, 98–105
    null modem cable, 101–2
    RS-232 specifications, 98–101
    X.21 specifications, 102–5
Physical medium attachment (PMA), 194
Piggybacking, 141
PIN diodes, 52
Pipelined transmission, 135
    BSC and, 162
    simulation of, 156–58

Pipelined transmission (continued)
  transport layer, 333
  XMODEM and, 162
  See also Data transmissions
Point-to-point connections, 113, 114
Point-to-point links, 182, 183–84
  data flows, 184
  defined, 183–84
  See also Local area networks (LANs)
Presentation (P) layer, 26, 435–43
  ASN.1, 435–42
  contents of, 26
  defined, 435
  PDU (PPDU), 435, 443
  primitives, 442–43
  problems, 461–62
  See also OSI reference model
Presentation services, 430–35
  code conversion, 434–35
  data compression/decompression, 430
  encryption/decryption, 431–34
Primitives
  application layer, 448–51
  data link layer, 143–47
  Ethernet, 199–200
  FTAM, 453–54
  LLC sublayer, 188–89
  MAC sublayer, 186–87
  network layer, 261–65
  OSI model, 27–31
  OSI session, 421–23
  physical layer, 92–94
  presentation layer, 442–43
  session layer, 385–89
  token ring, 210–12
  transport layer, 345–49
Problems
  application layer, 461–62
  computer network introduction, 40–42
  data link layer, 175–79
  LAN, 233–34
  network layer, 292–94
  network management, 492–93
  physical layer, 107–12
  presentation layer, 461–62
  session layer, 426–27
  transport layer, 380–81
  WAN, 325–26
Processors
  communication, 34–35
  defined, 2

front-end (FEPs), 34
host, 6
interface message (IMPs), 34
I/O, 2, 5, 8, 496
main, 5
Program design language (PDL), 37
Protocol analyzers, 468–69
  capabilities, 469
  defined, 468
Protocol control information (PCI), 31
Protocol data units (PDUs), 31–33
  application (APDU), 451–52
  bridge (BPDU), 288
  data link (DLPDU), 32, 147–48
  defined, 31
  LLC (LPDU), 187, 189–91
  MAC (MAPDU), 187
  network (NPDU), 32, 265–67
  presentation (PPDU), 435, 443
  session (SPDU), 420
  SNMP, 478
  transport (TPDU), 349–50
Protocols
  anonymous FTP, 445
  ATM, 303–7
  BISDN, 323
  BSC, 159–62
  defined, 32–33
  directory, 459–60
  DL, 158
  FTP, 444–45
  IP, 34, 277–85
  MHS, 456
  sliding window, 130–41
  TCP, 356, 373–79
  three-way handshake, 344
  TP, 356–73
  two-phase commit, 450
  UDP, 356, 377–79
  X.21, 104–6
  XMODEM, 158–59
  YMODEM, 159
  ZMODEM, 159
Protocol stack
  defined, 33
  ISDN, 313
  LU 6.2, 417, 418
  SNMP, 474
Protocol suite, 33
Proxy agent, 474–75
Pulse code modulation (PCM), 77–79

Index   533

defined, 77
illustrated, 78
See also Modulation
Quadrature phase shift key
    (QPSK) modulation
    defined, 76
    illustrated, 74
    See also Modulation
Quality of service (QOS), 262
Queued access methods (QAMs), 35
Queuing delays, 465–66
Queuing system, 465

Random time interval, 198
Receive_task routine, 153–54
Redundancy, 8
Redundancy check
    cyclic, 118–30
    longitudinal, 116–18
    vertical, 115–16
Reentrant tasks, 501–2
    attached, 501
    defined, 501
    illustrated, 502
    See also OS
Reliability, 467–68
Remote procedure calls (RPCs), 18, 446–47
    control flow of, 447
    design, 447
    format, 446
    implementation, 446
    See also Application services
Request queue element (RQE)
    defined, 94
    pointer relationships, 95
Resource sharing, 7
Response time, 464
Resync, 388–89
    logical flow using, 395
    message, 394
    See also Session(s); Session (S) layer; Syncpt
Retransmission slot time, 198–99
Return to zero (RZ), 54
Reverse address resolution protocol
    (RARP), 284–85
    defined, 284
    frame format, 284
    See also Internet protocol (IP)
Ring topology
    defined, 14
    illustrated, 13

multi-layer, 13
star combined with, 14
See also Network topologies
Roadsigns, 249–53
    illustrated, 252
    table, 249
    of VC, 250–51
    See also Routing
Routers, 288–90
    defined, 288
    encapsulation, 290
    frame relay as, 295–96
    illustrated, 289
    See also Network devices
Routing, 241–49
    centralized, 242–48
    distributed, 241–42
    hierarchical, 248–49
    source, 242
    See also Roadsigns
Routing control center (RCC), 242–43
Routing tables, 253–55
    defined, 253
    ELSE entry, 254
    hardware failures and, 254
    illustrated, 253
    wild card, 254
    See also Routing
RS-232-C interface, 98–101
    illustrated, 100
    signal lines, 99–101
    signals of, 99
RS-232-D interface, 101
    added features, 102
    defined, 101

Segmentation/reassembly, 330–31
Selective-reject (SRJ) ARQ, 136–39
    full-duplex, 139
    half-duplex, 139
    receiver error recovery, 138–39
    sender error recovery, 138
    window edge movements, 138, 140
    See also Sliding window protocols (SWPs)
Semaphore, 503–5
    binary, 503, 504
    incrementing, 505
    reading/testing, 503
    writable block with, 504
    See also OS
Serial transmission, 60

Service access point identifier
  (SAPI), 316, 317
Service data units (SDUs), 30
Session(s), 383
  allocating, 392–93
    with negotiation, 393
    without negotiation, 393
  connection, 383
  data transfer phase, 384
  deallocating, 392–93
  disconnecting, 392
  disconnection, 384
  group talk, 398–99
  half-session, 383
  interface, 384
  logical flow in, 386
  minor vs. major Syncpt, 388–89
  OSI, 420–24
  primitives, 385–89
    Allocate, 392–93
    Connect, 385
    data transfer, 387
    Deallocate, 392–93
    Disconnect, 387, 392
    explicit synchronization, 388
    Receive, 391
    Send, 391
  Resync, 388–89, 393–95
  SNA, 416–20
  software design, 390–95
  Syncpt, 388–89, 393–95
  TCP/IP, 399–416
Session (S) layer, 26, 383–427
  Connect routine, 390
  defined, 383
  design concepts, 383–85
  functions, 26
  network application software design, 396–99
  problems, 426–27
  Rec_connect routine, 390–91
  synchronization, 384–85
  See also OSI reference model; Session(s)
Session PDU (SPDU), 420, 423–24
  illustrated, 424
  length of, 423
  OSI format, 424
  serial number, 421
  See also Session (S) layer
Shannon theorem, 86–87
  defined, 86
  definitions, 86

Shared memory, 4
Signal space diagram, 77
Simple network management protocol.
  See SNMP
Simplex transmission, 61
Simulations, DL, 154–58
  asynchronous processing, 157–58
  of pipelined transmission, 156–58
  of SAW ARQ, 154–56
  See also Data links (DLs)
Single exponential back-off
  algorithm, 198, 199
Sinusoidal waveforms, 62
  illustrated, 63
  in vector space, 64
Sliding window protocols (SWPs), 130–41
  definitions, 130–31
  error recovery and, 132
  GBN ARQ, 135–36
  optimal window size, 139–41
  receiver functions, 132
  SAW ARQ, 132–35
  selective-reject, 136–39
  sender functions, 131
  window diagrams, 131
  window edge movements, 133, 137,140
Slots, 225–26
  defined, 225
  illustrated, 226
  length, 225
  See also Distributed queue dual bus (DQDB)
SNA
  LUs, 416
  NetView, 489–90
  network management model of, 490
  networks, 416
  OSI model vs., 33
SNA session, 415–20
  defined, 415
  LU 1, 417
  LU 2, 417
  LU 3, 417
  LU 4, 417
  LU 6.2, 417–20
    explicit Syncpt services, 420
    protocol stack, 417, 418
    session layer, 417
    verbs, 418–19
  synchronization services, 420
  types, 417
  See also Session(s); SNA

Index   535

SNMP, 472–87
    architecture, 473–75
    defined, 473
    messages, 475–79
        encoding, 485–87
        format, 475, 476–79
        header, 476
        request, 475–76
        specified in ASN.1, 477
    MIB, 479–85
    PDUs, 478
    protocol stack, 474
    proxy agent, 474–75
    See also Network management
Socket programming interfaces, 406–7
    defined, 399
    illustrated, 400
    logic flow and, 407
Software design
    Fletcher checksum, 361–63
    frame relay, 299–300
    multitasking server/client, 407–16
    network, 268–69
    physical layer, 95–98
        of Receiveframe, 97–98
        of Sendframe, 96–97
    session, 390–95
    session network application, 396–99
    transport layer
        datagram model, 354–55
        VC model, 352–54
Source routing, 242
    defined, 242
    IP, 281–82
    loose, 282
    strict, 281–82
    See also Routing
Source service access point (SSAP), 191
Space division multiplexing (SDM), 83
    defined, 83
    See also Multiplexing
Star topology
    defined, 12
    illustrated, 13
    ring combined with, 14
    See also Network topologies
State transition diagram, 500–501
    illustrated, 500
    job scheduler and, 501
    See also Task management routines
Stop-and-Wait (SAW) ARQ, 132–35

    in BSC, 161
    pipelined transmission, 135
    receiver error recovery, 134
    receiver software design, 134–35
    sender error recovery, 132
    sender software design, 134
    simulation of, 154–56
    See also Sliding window protocols (SWPs)
Sublayers, 184–85
    attachment unit interface (AUI), 194
    Ethernet, 194
    local link control (LLC), 184, 187–91
    medium access control (MAC), 184, 185–87
    medium attachment unit (MAU), 194
    medium dependent interface (MDI), 194
    physical medium attachment (PMA), 194
    physical medium dependent (PMD), 184
    physical signal (PLS), 184
    See also Local area networks (LANs)
Switched multimegabit data service (SMDS), 306–7
    defined, 306
    frames, 307
    See also Asynchronous transfer mode (ATM)
Switching, 87–88
    cell, 88
    circuit, 87
    packet, 87–88
Synchronization, 384–85
    explicit, 385, 388
    implicit, 384–85
Synchronous data link control (SDLC), 162–71
    command and response, 165
    defined, 162
    features, 162–63
    frame check sequence (FCS), 168–71
    frames
        control fields, 164
        format, 163
        information, 165
        supervisory, 165–66
        types of, 163
        unnumbered, 166–68
    See also Data link (DL) layer
Synchronous digital hierarchy (SDH), 323
Synchronous optical network (Sonet), 323
Synchronous TDM, 80, 87
Synchronous transmission, 61
Syncpt, 388–89
    logical flow with, 395
    LU 6.2 services, 420

Syncpt (continued)
    message, 394
    minor, 393
    number, 394
    See also Resync; Session(s); Session (S) layer
System calls, 385
System deadlocks
    defined, 255
    example, 255
    illustrated, 256

T1 carrier, 80–82
    defined, 80–81
    renaming of, 82
    transmission rate, 81
Table lookups, 127–29
Task control block (TCB), 94, 497–98
    defined, 94, 497
    illustrated, 498
    pointer relationships, 95
Task management routines, 496–501
    dispatcher, 499–500
    I/O interrupt service routines, 498–99
    state transition diagram, 500–501
    task control block, 497–98
    task creation/termination, 499
    task definition, 497
TCP/IP, 34
    application services, 444–47
    layers, 460
    network services, 399–400
    See also Internet protocol (IP); Transmission control protocol (TCP)
TCP/IP session, 399–416
    Abort command, 401
    Close command, 401
    connection, 400
    flow between client and server, 402
    interface, 409
    Open command, 401, 405
    Receive command, 401
    Send command, 401
    services, 401–2
    Status command, 401
    UNIX system calls, 402–6
    See also Session(s); TCP/IP
Theorems
    of CRC, 123
    Fourier, 62–71
    Nyquist, 85–86
    Shannon, 86–87
Three-way handshake, 343–45

to data packet transmissions, 344
defined, 343
protocols, 344
Time division multiplexing, 79–82
    asynchronous, 80
    defined, 80
    synchronous, 80, 87
    T1 carrier, 80–82
    See also Multiplexing
Timestamps, 282
    recording, 282
    request message, 286
Token bus, 212–18
    access method, 217–18
    characteristics, 212
    fiber-optic, 218
    frames, 213–15
        format, 214
        MAC control, 215–17
    illustrated, 213
    standard, 212
    token management function, 218
    See also Local area networks (LANs)
Token ring, 200–212
    access method, 208–9
    active monitor, 209–10
    characteristics, 200
    frames, 202–6
        contents of, 202
        illustrated, 204
        MAC, 205
        MAC control, 206–7
    illustrated, 201
    primitives, 210–12
    slotted ring, 211–12
    station, 203
    token holding timer (THT), 209
    See also Local area networks (LANs)
Transmission control protocol (TCP), 356, 373–79
    connection, 405
    defined, 373
    header
        design, 373–77
        illustrated, 374
        pseudo IP header and, 376
    session flow, 402
    system calls between server and client, 408
    transmission control block, 377
    user datagram protocol (UDP), 377–79

Index   537

See also Internet protocol (IP); TCP/IP;
         Transport (T) layer
Transmission media, 47–54
    atmosphere, 49–50
    coaxial cable, 47–49
    comparison of, 54
    optical fiber, 50–54
    satellite, 50
    twisted pair, 47
    See also Data transmissions
Transmission modes, 60–62
    asynchronous, 60–61
    full-duplex, 62
    half-duplex, 61–62
    parallel, 60
    serial, 60
    simplex, 61
    synchronous, 61
    See also Data transmissions
Transmit_task routine, 152–53
Transport (T) layer, 26, 329–81
    connect phase in datagram model, 348
    connect phase in VC model, 347
    data flow, 349
    design, 350–56
    design concepts, 330–33
    error control, 332
    finite state machine model, 333–43
    flow control, 332–33
    OSI protocols, 356–73
    PDUs, 349–50
    permanent transports, 355–56
    pipelined transmission, 333
    primitives, 345–49
    problems, 380–81
    segmentation and reassembly, 330–31
    software design
        datagram model, 354–55
        VC model, 352–54
    TCP, 373–79
    three-way handshake, 343–45
    TPCB, 351
    transport protocols (TP), 356–73
    TS-provider, 329
    upward/downward multiplexing, 331–32
    VC failure, 343
    See also OSI reference model
Transport control block (TCB), 351
Transport protocols (TP), 356–73
    capability summaries, 357
    connection control packets, 363–69

    data packets, 369–71
    design concepts, 356
    fixed part header, 357–59
    Fletcher checksum, 359–63
    flow control packets, 371–73
    formats, 356–59
    TPDU
        fixed-part headers, 364, 370
        general format, 358
        specifications, 363–73
        variable part header, 366
Transport service access point (TSAP), 329
Twisted pair, 47

UDP/IP programming, 416
Unified Network Management Architecture
         (UNMA), 489
Unisys Network Management System
         (UNMA), 489
Unit control block (UCB), 94–95
    defined, 94
    global, 94
    pointer relationships, 95
Universal asynchronous receiver/transmitter
         (UART) chip, 61
    characteristics, 91–92
    for data transfer, 124
    I/O driver, 97
    PAD, 288
    receive data register, 92
    uses, 95
Universal synchronous receiver/transmitter
         (USRT) chip, 91, 92
    characteristics, 92
    defined, 92
    uses, 95
Unshielded twisted pair (UTP) cables, 192
Upward/downward multiplexing, 331–32
User agent (UA), 455
    defined, 448
    in functional model, 455
    See also Application (A) layer
User datagram protocol (UDP), 356, 377–79
    defined, 377
    header, 377–78
    pseudo IP header and, 378
    See also Internet protocol (IP);
         Transmission control protocol (TCP)

Vertical redundancy check (VRC), 115–16
    defined, 115
    even-parity, 116, 118

VRC (continued)
    odd-parity, 116–17
    See also Longitudinal redundancy
        check (LRC)
Virtual channel identifier (VCI), 227
Virtual circuit (VC)
    connections, 239
    datagram model plus, 241
    datagram model vs., 240–41
    defined, 238
    failure, 343
    id, 239, 290
    model, 25, 238–39
    permanent, 37, 239, 273, 290
    roadsigns, 250–51
    services, 290
    transport layer software design, 352–54
    See also Datagram model
Virtual telecommunications access method
        (VTAM), 489

Waveforms
    defined, 54
    digital, 54–60
    harmonics and, 69
    sinusoidal, 62–64
Whip topology
    defined, 12
    illustrated, 13
    See also Network topologies
Wide area networks (WANs), 8, 295–326
    ATM, 300–308
    broadband ISDN, 321–23
    defined, 10
    frame relay, 295–300
    instructions executed, 11
    ISDN, 308–21
    problems, 325–26
    terminal sites, 181

well-known, 10
See also Local area networks (LANs);
    Metropolitan area networks (MANs)
Wireless communication, 49–50
World Wide Web (WWW), 446

X.21 specifications, 102–5
    characteristics, 102
    control lines, 104
    protocol example, 104–5
    protocol illustration, 106
    signals, 102, 103
X.25 protocol, 270–76
    call accepted/connected packet, 274
    call request/accepted packet, 272–74
    clear request/indication/confirm packet, 274
    data request/indication packet, 274
    defined, 270
    diagnostic packet, 276
    flow control packets, 274–75
    interrupt confirm packet, 275
    interrupt packet, 270, 275
    network layer primitives vs. packets, 276–77
    networks, 104
    packet body, 273
    packet headers, 270–72
    packet types, 270
    registration request/confirm packet, 275
    reset request/confirm packet, 275
    restart request/confirm packet, 275
XMODEM protocol, 158–59
    defined, 158
    features, 158
    pipelined transmission and, 162
    protective measures, 159

YMODEM protocol, 159

ZMODEM protocol, 159

The Artech House Telecommunications Library

Vinton G. Cerf, Series Editor

Advanced Technology for Road Transport: IVHS and ATT, Ian Catling, editor

Advances in Computer Communications and Networking, Wesley W. Chu, editor

Advances in Computer Systems Security, Rein Turn, editor

Advances in Telecommunications Networks, William S. Lee and Derrick C. Brown

Analysis and Synthesis of Logic Systems, Daniel Mange

An Introduction to International Telecommunications Law, Charles H. Kennedy and M. Veronica Pastor

An Introduction to U.S. Telecommunications Law, Charles H. Kennedy

Asynchronous Transfer Mode Networks: Performance Issues, Raif O. Onvural

ATM Switching Systems, Thomas M. Chen and Stephen S. Liu

A Bibliography of Telecommunications and Socio-Economic Development, Heather E. Hudson

Broadband: Business Services, Technologies, and Strategic Impact, David Wright

Broadband Network Analysis and Design, Daniel Minoli

Broadband Telecommunications Technology, Byeong Lee, Minho Kang, and Jonghee Lee

Cellular Radio: Analog and Digital Systems, Asha Mehrotra

Cellular Radio Systems, D. M. Balston and R. C. V. Macario, editors

Client/Server Computing: Architecture, Applications, and Distributed Systems Management, Bruce Elbert and Bobby Martyna

Codes for Error Control and Synchronization, Djimitri Wiggert

Communications Directory, Manus Egan, editor

The Complete Guide to Buying a Telephone System, Paul Daubitz

Computer Networks: Architecture, Protocols, and Software, John Y. Hsu

Computer Telephone Integration, Rob Walters

The Corporate Cabling Guide, Mark W. McElroy

Corporate Networks: The Strategic Use of Telecommunications, Thomas Valovic

Current Advances in LANs, MANs, and ISDN, B. G. Kim, editor

Digital Cellular Radio, George Calhoun

Digital Hardware Testing: Transistor-Level Fault Modeling and Testing, Rochit Rajsuman, editor

Digital Signal Processing, Murat Kunt

Digital Switching Control Architectures, Giuseppe Fantauzzi

Distributed Multimedia Through Broadband Communications Services, Daniel Minoli and Robert Keinath

Disaster Recovery Planning for Telecommunications, Leo A. Wrobel

Distance Learning Technology and Applications, Daniel Minoli

Document Imaging Systems: Technology and Applications, Nathan J. Muller

EDI Security, Control, and Audit, Albert J. Marcella and Sally Chen

Electronic Mail, Jacob Palme

Enterprise Networking: Fractional T1 to SONET, Frame Relay to BISDN, Daniel Minoli

Expert Systems Applications in Integrated Network Management, E. C. Ericson, L. T. Ericson, and D. Minoli, editors

FAX: Digital Facsimile Technology and Applications, Second Edition, Dennis Bodson, Kenneth McConnell, and Richard Schaphorst

FDDI and FDDI-II: Architecture, Protocols, and Performance, Bernhard Albert and Anura P. Jayasumana

Fiber Network Service Survivability, Tsong-Ho Wu

Fiber Optics and CATV Business Strategy, Robert K. Yates et al.

A Guide to Fractional T1, J. E. Trulove

A Guide to the TCP/IP Protocol Suite, Floyd Wilder

Implementing EDI, Mike Hendry

Implementing X.400 and X.500: The PP and QUIPU Systems, Steve Kille

Inbound Call Centers: Design, Implementation, and Management, Robert A. Gable

Information Superhighways: The Economics of Advanced Public Communication Networks, Bruce Egan

Integrated Broadband Networks, Amit Bhargava

Intelcom '94: The Outlook for Mediterranean Communications, Stephen McClelland, editor

International Telecommunications Management, Bruce R. Elbert

International Telecommunication Standards Organizations, Andrew Macpherson

Internetworking LANs: Operation, Design, and Management, Robert Davidson and Nathan Muller

Introduction to Document Image Processing Techniques, Ronald G. Matteson

Introduction to Error-Correcting Codes, Michael Purser

Introduction to Satellite Communication, Bruce R. Elbert

Introduction to T1/T3 Networking, Regis J. (Bud) Bates

Introduction to Telecommunication Electronics, Second Edition, A. Michael Noll

Introduction to Telephones and Telephone Systems, Second Edition, A. Michael Noll

Introduction to X.400, Cemil Betanov

Land-Mobile Radio System Engineering, Garry C. Hess

LAN/WAN Optimization Techniques, Harrell Van Norman

LANs to WANs: Network Management in the 1990s, Nathan J. Muller and Robert P. Davidson

Long Distance Services: A Buyer's Guide, Daniel D. Briere

Measurement of Optical Fibers and Devices, G. Cancellieri and U. Ravaioli

Meteor Burst Communication, Jacob Z. Schanker

Minimum Risk Strategy for Acquiring Communications Equipment and Services, Nathan J. Muller

Mobile Communications in the U.S. and Europe: Regulation, Technology, and Markets, Michael Paetsch

Mobile Information Systems, John Walker

Narrowband Land-Mobile Radio Networks, Jean-Paul Linnartz

Networking Strategies for Information Technology, Bruce Elbert

Numerical Analysis of Linear Networks and Systems, Hermann Kremer *et al.*

Optimization of Digital Transmission Systems, K. Trondle and Gunter Soder

Packet Switching Evolution from Narrowband to Broadband ISDN, M. Smouts

Packet Video: Modeling and Signal Processing, Naohisa Ohta

Personal Communication Systems and Technologies, John Gardiner and Barry West, editors

The PP and QUIPU Implementation of X.400 and X.500, Stephen Kille

Practical Computer Network Security, Mike Hendry

Principles of Secure Communication Systems, Second Edition, Don J. Torrieri

Principles of Signaling for Cell Relay and Frame Relay, Daniel Minoli and George Dobrowski
Principles of Signals and Systems: Deterministic Signals, B. Picinbono
Private Telecommunication Networks, Bruce Elbert
Radio-Relay Systems, Anton A. Huurdeman
Radiodetermination Satellite Services and Standards, Martin Rothblatt
Residential Fiber Optic Networks: An Engineering and Economic Analysis, David Reed
Secure Data Networking, Michael Purser
Service Management in Computing and Telecommunications, Richard Hallows
Setting Global Telecommunication Standards: The Stakes, The Players, and The Process, Gerd Wallenstein
Smart Cards, José Manuel Otón and José Luis Zoreda
Super-High-Definition Images: Beyond HDTV, Naohisa Ohta, Sadayasu Ono, and Tomonori Aoyama
Television Technology: Fundamentals and Future Prospects, A. Michael Noll
Telecommunications Technology Handbook, Daniel Minoli
Telecommuting, Osman Eldib and Daniel Minoli
Telemetry Systems Design, Frank Carden
Telephone Company and Cable Television Competition, Stuart N. Brotman
Teletraffic Technologies in ATM Networks, Hiroshi Saito
Terrestrial Digital Microwave Communications, Ferdo Ivanek, editor
Toll-Free Services: A Complete Guide to Design, Implementation, and Management, Robert A. Gable
Transmission Networking: SONET and the SDH, Mike Sexton and Andy Reid
Transmission Performance of Evolving Telecommunications Networks, John Gruber and Godfrey Williams
Troposcatter Radio Links, G. Roda
Understanding Emerging Network Services, Pricing, and Regulation, Leo A. Wrobel and Eddie M. Pope
UNIX Internetworking, Uday O. Pabrai
Virtual Networks: A Buyer's Guide, Daniel D. Briere
Voice Processing, Second Edition, Walt Tetschner
Voice Teletraffic System Engineering, James R. Boucher
Wireless Access and the Local Telephone Network, George Calhoun
Wireless Data Networking, Nathan J. Muller
Wireless LAN Systems, A. Santamaría and F. J. López-Hernández

Wireless: The Revolution in Personal Telecommunications, Ira Brodsky

Writing Disaster Recovery Plans for Telecommunications Networks and LANs, Leo A. Wrobel

X Window System User's Guide, Uday O. Pabrai

For further information on these and other Artech House titles, contact:

Artech House
685 Canton Street
Norwood, MA 02062
617-769-9750
Fax: 617-769-6334
Telex: 951-659
e-mail: artech@artech-house.com

Artech House
Portland House, Stag Place
London SW1E 5XA England
+44 (0) 171-973-8077
Fax: +44 (0) 171-630-0166
Telex: 951-659
e-mail: artech-uk@artech-house.com